EXAMPLES & EXPLANATIONS

Constitutional Law

Individual Rights

EDITORIAL ADVISORS

EXAMPLES & EXPLANATIONS

Constitutional Law

Individual Rights

Tenth Edition

Allan Ides
Christopher N. May Professor of Law
Loyola Law School, Los Angeles

Christopher N. May
Professor Emeritus of Law
Loyola Law School, Los Angeles

Simona Grossi
Professor of Law & Theodore A. Bruinsma Fellow
Loyola Law School, Los Angeles

ASPEN PUBLISHING

To contact Customer Service, e-mail customer.service@aspenpublishing.com, call 1-800-950-5259, or mail correspondence to:

Aspen Publishing
Attn: Order Department
1 Wall Street
Burlington, MA 01803

Printed in the United States of America.

1 2 3 4 5 6 7 8 9 0

ISBN 979-8-8941-0185-9

Library of Congress Cataloging-in-Publication Data

Names: Ides, Allan, 1949- author. | May, Christopher N., 1943- author. | Grossi, Simona, author.
Title: Constitutional law: individual rights / Allan Ides, Christopher N. May Professor of Law, Loyola Law School, Los Angeles; Christopher N. May, Professor Emeritus of Law, Loyola Law School, Los Angeles; Simona Grossi, Professor of Law & Theodore A. Bruinsma Fellow, Loyola Law School, Los Angeles.
Description: Tenth edition. | Burlington: Aspen Publishing, [2025] | Series: Examples & explanations | Includes index.
Identifiers: LCCN 2021048497 | ISBN 9798894101859 (paperback) | ISBN 9798894101866 (ebook)
Subjects: LCSH: Civil rights— United States. | LCGFT: Textbooks.
Classification: LCC KF4749.I34 2022 | DDC 342.7308/5— dc23/eng/20211006
LC record available at https://lccn.loc.gov/2021048497

About Aspen Publishing

Aspen Publishing is a leading provider of educational content and digital learning solutions to law schools in the U.S. and around the world. Aspen provides best-in-class solutions for legal education through authoritative textbooks, written by renowned authors, and breakthrough products such as Connected eBooks, Connected Quizzing, and PracticePerfect.

The Aspen Casebook Series (famously known among law faculty and students as the "red and black" casebooks) encompasses hundreds of highly regarded textbooks in more than eighty disciplines, from large enrollment courses, such as Torts and Contracts to emerging electives such as Sustainability and the Law of Policing. Study aids such as the *Examples & Explanations* and the *Emanuel Law Outlines* series, both highly popular collections, help law students master complex subject matter.

Major products, programs, and initiatives include:

- **Connected eBooks** are enhanced digital textbooks and study aids that come with a suite of online content and learning tools designed to maximize student success. Designed in collaboration with hundreds of faculty and students, the Connected eBook is a significant leap forward in the legal education learning tools available to students.

- **Connected Quizzing** is an easy-to-use formative assessment tool that tests law students' understanding and provides timely feedback to improve learning outcomes. Delivered through CasebookConnect.com, the learning platform already used by students to access their Aspen casebooks, Connected Quizzing is simple to implement and integrates seamlessly with law school course curricula.

- **PracticePerfect** is a visually engaging, interactive study aid to explain commonly encountered legal doctrines through easy-to-understand animated videos, illustrative examples, and numerous practice questions. Developed by a team of experts, PracticePerfect is the ideal study companion for today's law students.

- The **Aspen Learning Library** enables law schools to provide their students with access to the most popular study aids on the market across all of their courses. Available through an annual subscription, the online library consists of study aids in e-book, audio, and video formats with full text search, note-taking, and highlighting capabilities.

- Aspen's **Digital Bookshelf** is an institutional-level online education bookshelf, consolidating everything students and professors need to ensure success. This program ensures that every student has access to affordable course materials from day one.

- **Leading Edge** is a community centered on thinking differently about legal education and putting those thoughts into actionable strategies. At the core of the program is the Leading Edge Conference, an annual gathering of legal education thought leaders looking to pool ideas and identify promising directions of exploration.

For Cindi, Barbara, and Aaron

Summary of Contents

Contents		*xi*
Preface		*xxi*
Acknowledgments		*xxiii*
Chapter 1	Introduction to Individual Rights	1
Chapter 2	Substantive Due Process	63
Chapter 3	The Takings Clause	143
Chapter 4	The Contracts Clause	175
Chapter 5	Procedural Due Process and Irrebuttable Presumptions	195
Chapter 6	Equal Protection: Ordinary, "Suspect," and "Quasi-Suspect" Classifications	225
Chapter 7	Equal Protection: Fundamental Rights	313
Chapter 8	The First Amendment: Freedom of Speech and of the Press	371
Chapter 9	The First Amendment: Freedom of Religion	519
Chapter 10	The Right to Keep and Bear Arms	577
Table of Cases		*591*
Index		*607*

Contents

Preface xxi
Acknowledgments xxiii

Chapter 1 Introduction to Individual Rights 1

§ 1.1 Introduction and Overview 1
§ 1.2 The Fourteenth Amendment: An Introductory Overview 4
The Text of § 1 of the Fourteenth Amendment 4
A Brief Historical Survey 6
Early Judicial Trends in Construing the Fourteenth Amendment 8
§ 1.3 The Incorporation Doctrine 10
§ 1.4 The State Action Doctrine 14
§ 1.4.1 The Categorical Approach 17
Private Performance of a Public Function 18
Judicial Enforcement of Private Agreements 23
Joint Activity Between a State and a Private Party 25
State Endorsement of Private Conduct 31
§ 1.4.2 The Two-Part Approach 32
A State Actor Anomaly 42
§ 1.5 Congressional Enforcement of the Civil War Amendments 42
§ 1.5.1 Enforcement of the Thirteenth Amendment 43
§ 1.5.2 Enforcement of the Fourteenth Amendment 47
Parallel Enforcement 48
Nonparallel Enforcement 50
Congressional Interpretation 58
§ 1.5.3 Enforcement of the Fifteenth Amendment 59

Chapter 2 Substantive Due Process 63

§ 2.1 Introduction and Overview 63
The Origins of the Due Process Clause 63
Procedural versus Substantive Due Process 64
Executive Abuse of Power 65
Standards of Review 66
Economic versus Noneconomic Due Process 67

§ 2.2 The Rise and Fall of Economic Due Process 67
§ 2.2.1 Economic Due Process in the *Lochner* Era 67
Liberty to Contract 68
The Decision in *Lochner v. New York* 69
§ 2.2.2 The Demise of *Lochner* 71
§ 2.2.3 Property and Economic Liberty Today 73
Punitive Damages 76
§ 2.3 Noneconomic Liberty from *Lochner* to *Carolene Products* 82
§ 2.3.1 The *Lochner* Era and Noneconomic Liberties 82
§ 2.3.2 *Carolene Products*' Footnote Four 83
§ 2.4 *Griswold* and the Reemergence of Unenumerated Liberties 85
§ 2.4.1 Penumbras and Emanations 85
§ 2.4.2 Alternative Approaches: Liberty and the Ninth Amendment 87
§ 2.4.3 The Risks in Protecting Unenumerated Rights 88
§ 2.4.4 The Fundamental Rights Model with Variations 90
The Basic Fundamental Rights Model 90
The Concept of Impingement 91
Variations on the Basic Strict Scrutiny Model 92
§ 2.5 The Right of Privacy and Personal Autonomy 94
§ 2.5.1 Abortion Before and After *Dobbs v. Jackson* 95
Roe v. Wade and the Trimester Framework 95
Planned Parenthood v. Casey and the End of the Trimester Approach 98
The Undue Burden Test 99
Dobbs v. Jackson Women's Health Organization 100
§ 2.5.2 Marriage 103
§ 2.5.3 Family Integrity 107
Family Living Arrangements 107
The Parent-Child Relationship 110
Nonparental Visitation Statutes 111
§ 2.5.4 Intimate Association 114
§ 2.5.5 Sexual Intimacy 117
§ 2.5.6 Medical Treatment 118
A Right to Choose Certain Medical Treatment? 118
The Right to Reject Unwanted Medical Treatment 121
§ 2.5.7 The Right to Refuse Lifesaving Hydration and Nutrition 122
§ 2.5.8 Suicide and Physician-Assisted Suicide 125
§ 2.6 Other Protected Liberty Interests 128
§ 2.6.1 Freedom of Movement 128
Freedom from Physical Restraint 128

Freedom to Move About and the Right to Remain 130
§ 2.6.2 The Rights to Protection and Care 132
§ 2.6.3 Access to Courts 135
§ 2.6.4 Informational Privacy 136
§ 2.7 What Happened to Life? 137
Abortion 137
Subsistence Benefits 138
The Death Penalty 139
Death Caused by Government Officials 140

Chapter 3 The Takings Clause 143

§ 3.1 Introduction and Overview 143
§ 3.2 Condemnation and Inverse Condemnation 143
§ 3.3 The Requirement of Public Use 146
§ 3.4 An Approach to Analyzing Inverse Condemnation Problems 149
§ 3.5 The Difference Between Physical Occupation and Regulation 150
§ 3.6 Physical Occupations and Invasions 151
§ 3.7 Regulatory Takings 155
§ 3.7.1 Destroying All Use or Value 156
Real Property 156
Personal Property 158
Measuring Loss in Value: The Denominator Problem 158
§ 3.7.2 Partial Deprivations 162
§ 3.7.3 The Nuisance Exception 165
§ 3.7.4 Remedies for Temporary Regulatory Takings 167
§ 3.8 Conditions Attached to Building Permits 168
§ 3.8.1 Only Certain Types of Conditions Qualify 169
§ 3.8.2 The Essential Nexus Requirement 171
§ 3.8.3 The Rough Proportionality Requirement 172
The Nature of the Condition 172
The Extent of the Condition 173

Chapter 4 The Contracts Clause 175

§ 4.1 Introduction and Overview 175
§ 4.2 The Preliminary Questions 177
§ 4.2.1 Is There a Contractual Obligation? 177
Implied Contractual Obligations 178
State Contract Law as an Implied Contractual Obligation 178

§4.2.2 Does a Change in State Law Impair a Contractual Obligation? 180
§4.2.3 Is the Impairment Substantial? 181
§4.3 The Balancing Test and the Reserved Powers Doctrine 184
§4.4 The Special Problems of Contracts to Which a State Is a Party 191

Chapter 5 Procedural Due Process and Irrebuttable Presumptions 195

§ 5.1 Introduction and Overview 195
§ 5.2 A Protected Liberty or Property Interest? 197
§ 5.2.1 What Constitutes Liberty? 197
§ 5.2.2 What Constitutes Property? 200
§ 5.2.3 The Relevance of Custom and Practice 205
§ 5.3 What Constitutes a Deprivation? 206
§ 5.4 The Content of Notice 207
§ 5.5 What Kind of Hearing Must Be Afforded? 209
§ 5.5.1 The "Bitter with the Sweet" Approach 209
§ 5.5.2 The *Mathews v. Eldridge* Test 210
§ 5.5.3 The Requirement of a Prior Hearing 212
§ 5.5.4 Exceptions to the Prior Hearing Requirement 214
§ 5.5.5 The Formality of the Prior Hearing 218
§ 5.6 Possible Post-Deprivation Remedies Where No Liberty or Property Interest Exists 220
§ 5.7 The Irrebuttable Presumption Doctrine 221
§ 5.7.1 Rebuttable and Irrebuttable Presumptions 221
§ 5.7.2 The Doctrine in Its Prime 222
§ 5.7.3 The Doctrine Today 223

Chapter 6 Equal Protection: Ordinary, "Suspect," and "Quasi-Suspect" Classifications 225

§ 6.1 Introduction and Overview 225
§ 6.2 Equal Protection: General Principles 228
§ 6.2.1 Detecting Discrimination: Facial, Design, and Applied 228
Facial Discrimination 228
Discrimination by Design 229
Discriminatory Application 229
§ 6.2.2 The Prima Facie Case 230
Disproportionate Impact 231
Discriminatory Purpose 232

	Legislative History	234
	The Manner of Adoption	234
	Inferring Purpose from Impact and Other Circumstantial Evidence	236
	Inferring Purpose from Application	237
	The *Keyes* Presumption	238
	Difficulties with the Purpose Element	239
§ 6.2.3	Rebutting the Prima Facie Case	241
§ 6.3	The Rational Basis Equal Protection Test	243
§ 6.4	Classifications on the Basis of Race or National Origin	249
§ 6.4.1	Race as a Suspect Classification	249
	The Court's Early Treatment of Race	249
	The Rationale for Strict Scrutiny	252
§ 6.4.2	Scrutiny as a Measure of Constitutionality	253
	Compelling Interest	254
	Narrowly Tailored	255
§ 6.4.3	Racial Segregation of Public Schools	257
	Brown v. Board of Education	257
	Implementing *Brown*	259
§ 6.4.4	Interdistrict Remedies	260
	Proving an Interdistrict Violation	261
	Responding to White Flight	263
§ 6.4.5	Remedying Segregation at the College Level	265
§ 6.4.6	Other Limitations on Desegregation Orders	267
	Minimizing the Degree of Federal Interference	267
	Duration of Federal Desegregation Orders	268
§ 6.4.7	Affirmative Action	271
	Strict Scrutiny for Affirmative Action	271
	Compelling Interests	274
	Narrowly Tailored	279
§ 6.5	Classification on the Basis of Alienage	288
§ 6.5.1	The Standard for State and Local Laws	288
	The Reason for Strict Scrutiny	288
	Governmental or Political Functions	289
	Undocumented Aliens	291
§ 6.5.2	The Standard for Federal Laws	292
§ 6.6	Classification on the Basis of Gender or Legitimacy	293
§ 6.6.1	Gender as a Quasi-Suspect Classification	293
§ 6.6.2	Mid-Level Scrutiny as a Measure of Constitutionality	295
	Important and Legitimate Objectives	295
	Proof of Actual Purpose	296
	Means Substantially Related to Goal	297

Comparing the Tests for Gender and Race Discrimination 303
§ 6.6.3 Legitimacy 304
§ 6.7 Other Possibly Disfavored Bases of Classification 306
§ 6.7.1 The Rejection of New "Suspect" and "Quasi-Suspect" Classes 306
§ 6.7.2 Discrimination Against Out-of-Staters 307
§ 6.7.3 Discrimination Against the Mentally Retarded 308
§ 6.7.4 Discrimination on the Basis of Sexual Orientation 309

Chapter 7 Equal Protection: Fundamental Rights 313

§ 7.1 Introduction and Overview 313
§ 7.2 Equal Protection and Fundamental Rights 313
§ 7.3 The Right to Vote 316
§ 7.3.1 The Absolute versus the Equal Right to Vote 316
§ 7.3.2 Selective Denial of the Franchise 318
§ 7.3.3 Individual Vote Dilution: "One Person, One Vote" 323
The Problem: Unequal Weighting of Votes 323
"One Person, One Vote" 325
At-Large Election Schemes 327
Reapportionment 327
§ 7.3.4 Group Vote Dilution 330
Minimizing Group Voting Strength 330
Dilution Through At-Large Elections 331
Dilution Through Gerrymandering 332
Dilution Through Use of Multimember Districts 333
Vote Dilution and Nonracial Groups: Partisan Political Gerrymandering 334
§ 7.3.5 Nondilutional Race-Based Districting 337
§ 7.3.6 Access to the Ballot 346
§ 7.3.7 Unequal Vote Count 348
§ 7.4 The Right to Travel 349
§ 7.4.1 Durational Residency Requirements 350
§ 7.4.2 Fixed-Point and Fixed-Date Residency Requirements 353
§ 7.4.3 The Equal Protection Alternative to Strict Scrutiny 355
§ 7.4.4 Bona Fide Residency Requirements 357
§ 7.5 Access to the Courts 358
§ 7.6 Welfare and Subsistence 361
§ 7.7 Access to a Basic Education 363

§ 7.8 A Sliding-Scale Approach to Equal Protection 367
§ 7.8.1 Problems with the Three-Tier Model 367
§ 7.8.2 Marshall's Sliding-Scale Approach 367
§ 7.8.3 *Plyler v. Doe* 368

Chapter 8 The First Amendment: Freedom of Speech and of the Press 371

§ 8.1 Introduction and Overview 371
§ 8.2 Introductory Themes 372
§ 8.2.1 Defining Terms: Speech and Press 372
§ 8.2.2 Protected and Unprotected Speech 378
§ 8.2.3 The Distinction Between Matters of Public and Private Concern 378
§ 8.2.4 The Special Problem of Prior Restraints 380
§ 8.2.5 The Overbreadth and Vagueness Doctrines 385
§ 8.3 Content-Based Restrictions on Speech 391
§ 8.3.1 What Constitutes a Content-Based Restriction? 391
§ 8.3.2 Advocacy of Unlawful Conduct: The Clear and Present Danger Test 396
§ 8.3.3 Fighting Words, True Threats, and Hate Speech 404
§ 8.3.4 Free Speech Limitations on Defamation (and Other Torts) 407
The Burdens Imposed by the Actual Malice Standard 408
The Contexts in Which the Actual Malice Standard Applies 410
The Standards for Private-Plaintiff Lawsuits 412
The First Amendment and Speech-Premised Torts Generally 412
§ 8.3.5 Campaign Financing, Campaign Advocacy, and Restrictions on the Initiative Process 414
Campaign Financing and Campaign Advocacy 414
Restrictions on Judicial Elections 419
Restrictions on the Initiative Process 419
§ 8.3.6 Commercial Speech 420
The Definition of Commercial Speech 421
The Rationale for Protecting Commercial Speech 424
The *Central Hudson* Test 425
Mandatory Disclosure Requirements 432
§ 8.3.7 Sexually Explicit Speech—Obscenity and Pornography 434
A Definition of Obscenity 434

	Nonobscene Sexually Explicit Speech — Pornography	438
	Indecent or Vulgar Speech	441
	Indecent Speech and the Internet	442
§ 8.3.8	Speech that Depicts Actual Violence or Cruelty	446
§ 8.3.9	Content Discrimination Within Categories of Unprotected Speech	447
§ 8.3.10	Compelled Speech	449
§ 8.3.11	Ad Hoc Balancing	452
§ 8.3.12	Free Speech Rights of Public Employees and Other Voluntary Participants in Government Programs	455
§ 8.3.13	Government Coercion of Private Parties to Violate the Free Speech Rights of Others	459
§ 8.4	Content-Neutral Restrictions on Speech: The Time, Place, and Manner Test	460
§ 8.4.1	Content Neutrality	460
§ 8.4.2	Narrowly Tailored to Advance a Significant Governmental Interest	463
§ 8.4.3	Alternate Channels for Communication	467
§ 8.4.4	Prior Restraints	468
§ 8.4.5	Injunctions	469
§ 8.4.6	The Special Problem of Copyrights	470
§ 8.5	The Nature of the Public Forum	471
§ 8.5.1	Traditional Public Forum	473
§ 8.5.2	Designated Public Forum	475
§ 8.5.3	Nonpublic Forum	479
§ 8.5.4	Student Speech in Public Schools	482
§ 8.6	Government Speech	487
§ 8.7	The First Amendment Right of Association	491
	The Right of Association and State Regulation of Elections	501
§ 8.8	Special Problems of the Media	505
§ 8.8.1	Access to Information	505
§ 8.8.2	Access to Criminal Proceedings	506
§ 8.8.3	Gag Orders in Criminal Proceedings	506
§ 8.8.4	The Publication of Truthful, Lawfully Obtained Information	507
§ 8.8.5	The Protection of Confidential Sources	509
§ 8.8.6	Forced Access to the Press: Print Media	510

§ 8.8.7 The First Amendment and Modern Technologies 511
The Broadcast Media 511
Developing Technologies — Cable Operators 513
Developing Technologies — Social Media 515

Chapter 9 The First Amendment: Freedom of Religion 519

§ 9.1 Introduction and Overview 519
§ 9.2 The Establishment Clause: Themes, Theories, and Tests 520
§ 9.2.1 Separationist Theory 520
§ 9.2.2 Nonpreferentialist Theory 521
§ 9.2.3 Three Compromise Approaches 522
§ 9.2.4 The *Lemon* Test 523
Secular Purpose 523
Primary Effect That Does Not Advance, Endorse or Inhibit Religion 523
Not Foster Excessive Entanglement with Religion 524
§ 9.2.5 The Establishment Clause Today 525
§ 9.3 The Establishment Clause Applied: Discrimination Between Religions 526
§ 9.3.1 The Ban on Officially "Established" Religions 526
§ 9.3.2 The Limitation on Conferring a Preferred Status 527
§ 9.3.3 The Limitation on Imposing a Disfavored Status 528
§ 9.4 The Establishment Clause Applied: The Discriminatory Promotion of Religion 530
§ 9.4.1 Public Aid to Parochial Schools 532
§ 9.4.2 Prayer in Public Schools 536
§ 9.4.3 Other Contexts 543
§ 9.5 The Free Exercise Clause 545
§ 9.5.1 The Distinction Between Belief and Conduct 545
§ 9.5.2 The Protection of Religious Belief 547
The Right to Profess Religious Beliefs 548
Ecclesiastical Disputes 551
§ 9.5.3 The Protection of Religiously Motivated Conduct 553
The Purposeful Suppression or Selective Nonfunding of Religiously Motivated Conduct 553
The Nonpurposeful Regulation of Religiously Motivated Conduct 563
The Incidental Burdening of Religiously Motivated Conduct 570
§ 9.6 The Accommodation of Religion 573

Chapter 10 The Right to Keep and Bear Arms 577

§ 10.1 Introduction and Overview 577
§ 10.2 *District of Columbia v. Heller* 578
§ 10.2.1 Interpreting the Second Amendment 578
§ 10.2.2 Applying the Second Amendment 581
§ 10.3 Developments Since *Heller* 582
§ 10.3.1 The Range of Protected Arms 582
§ 10.3.2 The Spatial Aspect of the Right to Bear Arms 584
§ 10.4 The *Bruen* Standard of Review 586
§ 10.5 The *Bruen* Standard Applied 587

Table of Cases *591*
Index *607*

Preface

Most of us arrive at law school with at least a minimal awareness of our constitutional system of government. We know generally that the national government is divided into three branches and that the Bill of Rights protects our fundamental freedoms. That awareness probably began with elementary-school Thanksgiving Day pageants, developed substance through various American history and government classes in high school, and finally, for some of us, is topped by an undergraduate course in constitutional law. Outside the educational setting, constitutional law issues ripple through the popular media, with frequent references to abortion, free speech, religion, racial and gender discrimination, gay rights, and so forth.

As law students, however, we learn very quickly that the study of constitutional law is anything but a meditation on the commonplace. And therein lies the treachery. The familiar quickly blends with the arcane, and we are forced to grapple with a tumult of doctrines, distinctions, and qualifications. Indeed, the familiar may soon disappear as we trek through justiciability, the commerce power, state action, and various other subjects that never seem to make the headlines. Even those topics that strike a common chord are presented with a treatment that is most uncommon. Add to this a bevy of wavering doctrines, concurring or opposing opinions, and the changing personnel of the Supreme Court, and the complexity can become overwhelming.

We're here to help. We have written two volumes designed to give you a foundation in the doctrines and methods of constitutional law and constitutional argument. The first, *National Power and Federalism*, covers the powers of the federal courts, Congress, and the president; the doctrines of separation of powers and federalism; and some of the limitations that the Constitution imposes on state power. The second, *Individual Rights*, covers the provisions of the Constitution that protect us against the government, including the Takings and Contracts Clauses; the Due Process and Equal Protection Clauses; the Speech, Press, and Religion Clauses of the First Amendment; and the Second Amendment right to bear arms.

These books try to provoke you into thinking about the larger issues of constitutional law with some depth and perception. They are not outlines. Nor are they research treatises on all the nuances of constitutional law. Rather, they present a problem-oriented guide through the principal doctrines of constitutional law— those covered in typical constitutional law courses— with an emphasis on how one might think about issues that arise within the various contexts in which these doctrines operate. Lawyers, after all, are problem solvers. These books are tools for constitutional law problem solvers (and students confronted with the reality of final exams).

We must include the usual caveat. Our books are not a substitute for your constitutional law class or for a basic casebook. Nor are they a substitute for reading those cases. We hope, however, that they will make the classroom experience richer and more accessible. In fact, our experience is that students who have read these materials along with traditional cases have found the cases more understandable and more easily digested. They have also found that class participation is less threatening and more fruitful. We are confident that you will have the same experience.

The approach that we suggest is quite simple. As you begin a new topic in your constitutional law course, read the related chapter in either *National Power and Federalism* or *Individual Rights*. This will give you an overview of the area and a preliminary sense of how doctrines are applied within the area. In reading the chapters, however, don't just *read* the problems—*do them*! In other words, consider the problem and try to anticipate how it will be solved before you read the accompanying explanation. This will develop your analytical skills. Next, as you read your cases, refer back to the related chapters and chapter sections and assess how each case fits into the overall framework developed by the Court. See if the case comports with the problems and explanations. Be critical. Finally, when you complete the coverage of a topic, review the chapter again. This will give you confidence that you know the material. Students have also found these materials useful as study aids when preparing for their final exams. After all, finals are simply problems to be solved. In any event, don't just read these books; use them to develop your understanding and your skills.

Good luck in your studies and in your careers as problem-solving students of the Constitution.

Allan Ides
Christopher N. May
Simona Grossi

December 2024

Acknowledgments

We would like to express our appreciation to our student research assistants who assisted us in the preparation of the various editions of this book: Lilly Kim (LLS '98), Lauren Raskin (LLS '98), Eric Enson (LLS '99), James V. DeRossitt IV (W&L '96), Ashley DeMoss (W&L '97), Lawrence Striley (W&L '95), Kristen Strain (LLS '01), Kasha Arianne Harshaw (LLS '02), Jessica Levinson (LLS '05), Megan Moore (LLS '07), Gillian Studwell (LLS '07), Daniel Costa (UCLA '11), Mario Grimm (LLS '11), Mashashi Kawaguchi (LLS '11), Vanda Long (UNC '11), Jacquelyn Mohr (LLS '11), Brian Casillas (LLS '14), Lara Kuyumjian (LLS '14), Jason Meyer (LLS '14), Pushkal Mishra (LLS '14), and Ashkahn Mohamadi (LLS '14). Many thanks also to our secretaries, Ruth Busch, Liz Luk, and Diane Cochran.

CHAPTER 1

Introduction to Individual Rights

§1.1 INTRODUCTION AND OVERVIEW

In one sense, the entire body of the Constitution is designed to protect individual rights. In fact, many of the Framers believed that the political structure created by the Constitution was the primary and essential vehicle through which to protect the liberty of the people. Such structural devices as the separation of powers, checks and balances, bicameralism, enumeration of powers, and federalism, among others, were thought to provide a substantial bulwark against governmental tyranny. Alexander Hamilton went further and argued that a detailed bill of rights would be affirmatively dangerous in that it "would contain various exceptions to powers which are not granted; and, on this very account, would afford a colorable pretext to claim more than were granted." *The Federalist No.* 84, at 513 (Clinton Rossiter ed., 1961).

The text of the original Constitution reflects this structural bias by including only a few specific protections for what we now commonly consider individual rights. See, e.g., Art. I, § 9, cls. 2 & 3 (privilege of the writ of habeas corpus, proscription against bills of attainder and ex post facto laws); Art. III, § 2, cl. 3 (right to trial by jury in criminal cases). Yet Hamilton's confidence in political structure was not universally shared. Some thought that the absence of a bill of rights was a major flaw in the proposed Constitution, and a number of states premised their ratification of it on a recommendation that the Constitution be amended to include such a statement of rights. See, e.g., 3 Jonathan Elliot, *The Debates in the Several State Conventions on the Adoption of the Federal Constitution as Recommended by the General Convention in Philadelphia in 1787*, at 657-661 (1836) (proposed amendments by Virginia). Two states, North Carolina and Rhode Island, did not ratify the Constitution until a proposed Bill of Rights had been approved by Congress and submitted to the states for ratification.

In response to these concerns and others, James Madison introduced a series of proposed amendments to the Constitution during the first session of Congress. The Bill of Rights, which was approved by Congress in 1789 and ratified by the states in 1791, was a direct product of Madison's proposals. It includes ten amendments to the Constitution, nine of which address individual rights; the tenth reiterates the limited nature of the government created by the Constitution. In practical effect, the Bill of Rights limits the power of the federal government to transgress the rights described therein. In other words, the rights enumerated in the Bill of Rights act as a trump on the exercise of federal power.

The Supreme Court held early on that the Bill of Rights limited only the authority of the national government and not that of the states. *Barron v. Mayor & City Council of Baltimore*, 32 U.S. (7 Pet.) 243 (1833). Thus, although the body of the Constitution contains a few specific individual rights limitations on state authority—e.g., the Privileges and Immunities Clause of Article IV, § 2, and the Contracts Clause of Article I, § 10—by and large the protection of individual rights against state encroachment was to be found, if at all, in the respective constitutions of the several states. At least, that was the case throughout much of the nineteenth century.

The adoption of the Fourteenth Amendment in 1868, however, radically changed both the Constitution's and the national government's role in the protection of civil rights against state interference, essentially establishing federal supremacy within this realm of civil rights. As we will see below, through a process of incorporation the Fourteenth Amendment became the constitutional vehicle through which courts now apply most provisions of the Bill of Rights to the states. In addition, the Equal Protection Clause of the Fourteenth Amendment eventually came to operate as a powerful and judicially enforceable principle of equality. Finally, the Fourteenth Amendment vested Congress with a broad authority to enforce civil rights against state encroachment. Thus, with the adoption of the Fourteenth Amendment, accompanied by subsequent judicial and congressional interpretations, the Constitution now provides substantial protection against both federal and state encroachments on individual liberty.

Before we examine some of the individual rights protected by the U.S. Constitution, it is important to note the scope of their application, for these rights do not belong to everyone. As to U.S. citizens, the Constitution protects them against actions of the federal government, whether taken within the United States or abroad. As to foreign citizens, "while in the United States they may enjoy certain constitutional rights. . . ." *Agency for International Development v. Alliance for Open Society*, 591 U.S. 430, 434 (2020) (emphasis in original). See *United States v. Verdugo-Urquidez*, 494 U.S. 259, 270-271 (1990) (listing some of these rights). Though the Court once suggested that such rights may be limited to "lawful permanent residents," *Kwong Hai Chew v. Colding*, 344 U.S. 590, 598-597 (1953), it has since repudiated that view. *Plyler v. Doe*, 457 U.S. 202, 212 (1982) ("all persons within the territory of the United States, including aliens unlawfully present, may invoke the Fifth and Sixth Amendments to challenge actions of the Federal Government"). In *Department of Homeland Security v. Thuraissigiam*, 591 U.S. 103 (2020), however, the Court qualified this rule to hold that a Sri Lankan who had crossed into the United States and was immediately apprehended 25 yards from the border did not thereby acquire any rights against the federal government under the Due Process Clause. Such rights, said the Court, only attach to "aliens who have established connections in this country. . . ." Id. at 107. It remains to be seen what it takes for a noncitizen to have "established connections" in the United States, and whether it would also exclude foreign tourists or students visiting from abroad. In terms of the Constitution's scope, in contrast to U.S. citizens abroad, "the Court has not allowed foreign citizens outside the United States or its territories or such U.S. Territories to assert rights under the U.S. Constitution." *Agency for International Development*, supra, 591 U.S. at 434.

With respect to action taken by the states, the Constitution protects everyone who is present within a state, "[w]hatever [their] status under the immigration laws. . . ." *Plyler v. Doe*, supra, 457 U.S. at 210. This flows from the fact that "[t]he provisions of the Fourteenth Amendment," which guaranty rights against the states, "'are universal in their application, to *all persons within the territorial jurisdiction* [of the United States].'" *Verdugo-Urquidez*, supra, 494 U.S. at 271 (quoting *Yick Wo v. Hopkins*, 118 U.S. 356, 369 (1886)) (emphasis in original). Under this principle, aliens who are "unlawfully present" within the United States thus enjoy constitutional rights against the states, though the level of protection may in some cases be less than would otherwise apply. See *Plyler v. Doe*, supra (Texas law allowing public schools to deny admission to undocumented alien children violates Equal Protection Clause even under a relaxed level of scrutiny).

In the chapters that follow, we will examine the substantive and procedural reach of a number of the more important and frequently litigated individual rights limitations on governmental authority. This chapter, however, addresses several preliminary matters. It begins with a brief historical and descriptive perspective on the Fourteenth Amendment. This is designed to provide a foundation for the multitude of doctrines that are built on and around that amendment. Although the provisions of the Bill of Rights merit their own individual consideration, the Fourteenth Amendment stands alone in its radical transformation of our system of government. Next, the chapter examines three preliminary doctrinal matters directly related to the protection of individual rights—namely, the incorporation doctrine, the state action doctrine, and the scope of congressional enforcement powers under the Thirteenth, Fourteenth, and Fifteenth Amendments, otherwise known as the Civil War Amendments.

§1.2 THE FOURTEENTH AMENDMENT: AN INTRODUCTORY OVERVIEW

The Text of § 1 of the Fourteenth Amendment

Section 1 of the Fourteenth Amendment consists of two sentences. The first sentence provides: "All persons born or naturalized in the United States and subject to the jurisdiction thereof, are citizens of the United States and of the State wherein they reside." This sentence accomplishes two things: First, it creates a definition of U.S. citizenship ("All persons born or naturalized"); second, it provides a definition of state citizenship ("reside"). Neither point is controversial today, and there is general agreement that the language of this sentence means exactly what it appears to say. The phrase "subject to the jurisdiction thereof" requires further investigation. That investigation would reveal that the phrase was designed to exclude two classes of persons—children of alien enemies in hostile occupation and children of diplomatic representatives of foreign states. We could also quibble about the word "reside," but without too great an effort, a workable and relatively noncontroversial meaning would be discovered, namely, domicile or place of permanent residence. In short, the first sentence defines citizenship at both the federal and the state levels in relatively clear terms and with only a minimal need to look beyond the specific language used.

Despite the relative clarity of the first sentence, some reference to history is beneficial. Prior to the Civil War, the U.S. Supreme Court had held that an African American sold as a slave was not a citizen of the United States. *Dred Scott v. Sandford*, 60 U.S. (19 How.) 393 (1857). The *Dred Scott* decision, which denied the status of citizenship to slaves, former slaves, and their descendants, was viewed by Republicans as a precipitating and an infamous cause of the Civil War, and the first sentence of § 1 was designed to repeal that decision. This specific purpose would have been clear to contemporary observers, though it is a bit obscure to the modern reader. Even given that purpose, however, the language of the Amendment is much broader than would have been necessary to simply overrule *Dred Scott*. It covers *all* persons born or naturalized in the United States, not just former slaves. In other words, it creates a general definition of citizenship, and we need not look beyond the actual words to discover that definition.

The second sentence of § 1 is both more complicated and less clear. It is divided into three parts. The first part provides, "No State shall make or enforce any law which shall abridge the privileges or immunities of citizens of the United States. . . ." The text does not define the "privileges or immunities of citizens of the United States." One immediately thinks of the Privileges and Immunities Clause of Article IV, which protects the "Privileges and Immunities of Citizens in the several States." See Christopher N. May, Allan Ides & Simona Grossi, *Constitutional Law: National Power and Federalism*, ch. 9 (10th ed. 2025) [hereinafter *National Power & Federalism*]. At the time the Fourteenth Amendment was adopted, judicial decisions had given some content to the "fundamental rights" protected by Article IV. See *Corfield v. Coryell*, 6 F. Cas. 546, 552 (C.C.E.D. Pa. 1823). Do both clauses refer to the same fundamental rights, or is there a distinction between the "privileges or immunities" held by citizens of the United States and the "privileges and immunities" held by citizens in the several states? In other words, has a new category of fundamental rights been created to coincide with the newly created definition of U.S. citizenship? And if so, what are those rights? The text, standing alone, does not provide an answer to these questions.

The next part of the second sentence provides, "[N]or shall any State deprive any person of life, liberty, or property, without due process of law. . . ." This sounds a little easier. Before a state can take away a person's life, liberty, or property, it must provide something called due process of law. Implicitly, the rights to life, liberty, and property are not absolute. A deprivation of these rights is permissible if due process is satisfied. The word "process" suggests procedures; the word "due" suggests appropriate, proper, or reasonable. A person, therefore, is entitled to appropriate procedures before being deprived of life, liberty, or property. Presumably reference to accepted practices will provide guidance as to what procedures will be deemed to satisfy due process. Note also that the category "person" appears to be broader than the category "citizen." All citizens are persons; all persons are not necessarily citizens. The Due Process Clause protects the more inclusive category.

Finally, § 1 provides, "[N]or [shall any State] deny to any person within its jurisdiction the equal protection of the laws." The phrase "equal protection of the laws" suggests at the very least that otherwise neutral laws must be enforced in an evenhanded manner for the benefit of all who fall within the letter of their protection. But does it mean, in addition, that state laws may not discriminate or classify? In other words, does it require that the law itself be evenhanded? Assuming that this is the case and keeping in mind that all laws classify in some manner, is this potential ban on classifications limited to certain types of discrimination? If so, what types of discrimination are banned? Again, the text does not answer these questions.

This cursory examination of the text of § 1 should make at least one thing clear: A reading of a constitutional text begins but rarely resolves, an inquiry into meaning. The language must be placed in a context that includes the surrounding historical events, as well as the specific matters that led to the enactment. Certainly, this is borne out by the obscure language of the second sentence of § 1. These observations are also true even with respect to language that appears clear. The clarity may be an illusion caused by our lack of appreciation for the historical context. For example, we may think we know what equal protection of the laws means, but the authors of the text may have been writing from a very different understanding of the phrase. In short, the text cannot be read in a historical vacuum. A deeper understanding of the text requires at a minimum a passing familiarity with the historical milieu in which the Fourteenth Amendment was adopted.

A Brief Historical Survey

The context surrounding the adoption of the Fourteenth Amendment can be succinctly described as slavery, the abolition movement, the Civil War, and the Reconstruction response to events in the post-Civil War South, including the adoption of the Black Codes. The authors of the Fourteenth Amendment and those who supported it, both in Congress and in state conventions, were immersed in these events. They lived them and were responding to them.

The Thirteenth Amendment, which abolished slavery, had been ratified in 1865, but it was evident (and believed to be evident) that the institution of slavery was being replaced by a system that was designed to keep the former slaves in a condition of virtual servitude. The Black Codes, enacted by most of the southern states, severely restricted the civil rights of former slaves, including the rights to enter into contracts, to purchase property, and to sit on juries. In addition, there was evidence that former slaves were not being given full and impartial protection of otherwise neutral laws. Both formally and informally the former slaves were being treated as noncitizens.

In response to these conditions, Congress passed the Civil Rights Act of 1866, 14 Stat. 27, which provided in pertinent part:

> That all persons born in the United States and not subject to any foreign power . . . are hereby declared to be citizens of the United States; and such citizens, of every race and color, without regard to any previous condition of slavery or involuntary servitude, . . . shall have the same right, in every State and Territory in the United States, to make and enforce contracts, to sue, be parties, and give evidence, to inherit, purchase, lease, sell, hold and convey real and personal property, and to full and equal benefit of all laws and proceedings for the security of person and property, as is enjoyed by white citizens, and shall be subject to like punishment, pains, and penalties, and to none other. . . .

President Andrew Johnson had vetoed the Civil Rights bill on the ground that it was unconstitutional, and though Congress overrode the veto, several Republicans who supported the measure were concerned that the act exceeded the enumerated powers of Congress. This concern provided the initial impetus for the Fourteenth Amendment. One of the primary purposes of that Amendment was to ensure that Congress possessed the power to enact legislation such as the Civil Rights Act of 1866. Section 5 of the Fourteenth Amendment does precisely that. It grants Congress the power to enforce the provisions of the Fourteenth Amendment, including the so-called substantive provisions of § 1 described above. See § 1.5.

Proponents of the Fourteenth Amendment, therefore, probably understood § 1's Privileges or Immunities Clause as encompassing the "civil rights or immunities" described in the Civil Rights Act of 1866. Those rights are remarkably like the fundamental rights associated with Article IV's Privileges and Immunities Clause, and like that clause, the Civil Rights Act prohibited discriminatory treatment of citizens exercising those rights. If this interpretation is correct, one purpose of the Fourteenth Amendment's Privileges or Immunities Clause was to prevent states from denying U.S. citizens, as defined in the first sentence of § 1, the equal exercise of those civil rights and immunities described in the Civil Rights Act.

The legislative history of the Fourteenth Amendment supports this interpretation. That history is replete with cross-references to the Civil Rights Act, suggesting a close affinity between the act and the proposed Amendment. This interpretation also comports with the notion that Congress, through the Fourteenth Amendment, was attempting to construct a constitutional provision that would validate the prior enactment. In fact, immediately after the adoption of the Fourteenth Amendment, the Civil Rights Act of 1866 was reenacted as an enforcement of § 1 rights.

A second strand of history suggests that the Privileges or Immunities Clause may have been intended to have an even wider application. The Court, in *Barron v. Mayor & City Council of Baltimore*, 32 U.S. (7 Pet.) 243 (1833), had held that the Bill of Rights limits only the power of the federal government and not the power of the states. Prior to the Civil War, abolitionists rejected the soundness of *Barron*. For a variety of reasons, they believed that the first eight amendments to the Constitution either were, or should, be fully applicable against the states. This view was shared by several Republicans, many of them former abolitionists, who participated in the drafting and passage of the Fourteenth Amendment. Moreover, even those Republicans who did not expressly subscribe to the complete incorporation theory probably thought that the Privileges or Immunities Clause protected at least some additional fundamental rights beyond those listed in the Civil Rights Act of 1866. For example, the freedoms of press and speech were widely accepted as being fundamental rights held by all U.S. citizens. One cannot say definitively, however, that the purpose of the Privileges or Immunities Clause was to incorporate all or part of the first eight amendments. The surrounding history is certainly consistent with that possibility, but the available information is far from dispositive. See Raoul Berger, *Government by Judiciary: The Transformation of the Fourteenth Amendment* (1977) (arguing that the first eight amendments of the Bill of Rights were not incorporated against the states via the Privileges or Immunities Clause); Michael Kent Curtis, *No State Shall Abridge: The Fourteenth Amendment and the Bill of Rights* (1986) (arguing precisely the opposite). Here, we are left with an ambiguous record and an indeterminate meaning.

If the Privileges or Immunities Clause was in fact designed to prevent the denial of certain fundamental rights, what purpose can be assigned to the Due Process and Equal Protection Clauses? The independent significance of the Due Process Clause is not difficult to envision. It provides procedural protection against the taking of life, liberty, or property. Again, the Republicans were convinced, with some justification, that certain individuals—in particular, former slaves and Union sympathizers—were being deprived of basic civil rights without proper procedures. The Due Process Clause specifically addressed that concern.

Similarly, the independent purpose of the Equal Protection Clause appears to have been to ensure that all laws would be applied to individuals in an evenhanded manner. Consider again the language of the 1866 Civil Rights Act: "[C]itizens, of every race and color, . . . shall have the same right . . . to full and equal benefit of all laws and proceedings for the security of person and property, as is enjoyed by white citizens, and shall be subject to like punishment . . . and to none other. . . ." The Equal Protection Clause speaks directly to this concern—equal *protection* of the laws. It may be, therefore, that the Equal Protection Clause was not seen as an independent limitation on discriminatory laws. The Privileges or Immunities Clause, on the other hand, did provide protection against racial discrimination in the context of the rights protected by the clause.

Taking the foregoing together, what can be said of § 1 of the Fourteenth Amendment? First, the Privileges or Immunities Clause was seemingly intended to prevent state discrimination with respect to fundamental civil rights, such as those protected by Article IV's Privileges and Immunities Clause. Second, the Privileges or Immunities Clause probably was thought to include certain other fundamental rights found in the Bill of Rights, such as freedom of the press and freedom of speech. Third, the Privileges or Immunities Clause may have been designed to incorporate all the provisions of the first eight amendments to the Constitution. Fourth, the Due Process Clause required states to provide fair or reasonable procedures prior to the deprivation of life, liberty, or property. Fifth, the Equal Protection Clause was likely designed to remedy a state's unequal enforcement of the laws.

Early Judicial Trends in Construing the Fourteenth Amendment

Four years after the ratification of the Fourteenth Amendment, the Supreme Court decided the *Slaughter-House Cases*, 83 U.S. (16 Wall.) 36 (1872). At issue was a Louisiana statute that granted a monopoly over the butchering trade in three parishes in Louisiana. The butchers who challenged the statute claimed, among other things, that the monopoly violated the Privileges or Immunities Clause of the Fourteenth Amendment. The premise of the butchers' argument was that § 1 of the Fourteenth Amendment had incorporated the substantive privileges and immunities previously protected by Article IV's Privileges and Immunities Clause, among which was the right to engage in a common calling.

The Court majority rejected this argument, reasoning that since the Fourteenth Amendment draws a distinction between citizens of the United States and citizens of a state, the content of the Fourteenth Amendment Privileges or Immunities Clause, which specifically protects the privileges or immunities of U.S. citizens, must differ from the content of the Article IV Privileges and Immunities Clause, which protects the rights of the citizens of one state while visiting in another state. The federal privileges or immunities would not, therefore, replicate the basic liberty and property rights protected by Article IV. Instead, the federal privileges or immunities would be those that pertained to the Union as a whole, such as the right to petition the federal government. The Court's conclusion here was contrary to the original understanding of those who wrote § 1 of the Fourteenth Amendment. The net effect of this interpretation was to severely limit the utility of the Fourteenth Amendment Privileges or Immunities Clause. For a discussion of a potential resurrection of the Privileges or Immunities Clause, see *National Power & Federalism*, supra, § 9.4.1; and in this volume, § 7.4.

The decision in the *Slaughter-House Cases* had several significant effects on subsequent judicial interpretation of the Fourteenth Amendment. First, beginning in the late nineteenth century, the Court began using the Due Process Clause as a vehicle for incorporating various provisions of the Bill of Rights against the states. In this manner, due process came to signify something more than just a protection for procedural rights. The "selective incorporation" of the Bill of Rights continued throughout the twentieth century such that most of the Bill of Rights has now been incorporated into the Fourteenth Amendment. See § 1.3. In this manner, the Due Process Clause has functioned as a partial surrogate for the moribund Privileges or Immunities Clause.

At about the same time, the Court also began interpreting the Due Process Clause as providing protection for substantive rights not necessarily found in the Bill of Rights. The liberty of contract, for example, was deemed a fundamental right that could not be invaded by the states without sufficient justification. *Allgeyer v. Louisiana*, 165 U.S. 578, 589 (1897). Again, this "substantive" approach to due process operated as a substitute for the judicially eviscerated Privileges or Immunities Clause.

Finally, in the late nineteenth century, the Court began to apply the Equal Protection Clause as something more than a provision for equal enforcement of the law. In *Strauder v. West Virginia*, 100 U.S. (10 Otto) 303 (1880), for example, the Supreme Court struck down a statute that prohibited African Americans from serving on juries. This interpretation of the

Equal Protection Clause filled another gap created by the questionable decision in the *Slaughter-House Cases* by putting teeth into the concept of equality in the context of basic civil rights. In addition, the Court interpreted the Equal Protection Clause as applicable to all races, *Yick Wo v. Hopkins*, 118 U.S. 356 (1886), despite what one could characterize as the narrower focus of the specific concerns that led to the adoption of the Amendment. The scope of this antidiscrimination thrust was, however, limited by the separate-but-equal doctrine announced in *Plessy v. Ferguson*, 163 U.S. 537 (1896). See § 6.4.1.

In short, by the end of the nineteenth century, the foundation for the modern law of the Fourteenth Amendment was established. That foundation consists of a combination of the amendment's text, the pre- and post-ratification history, the legislative intent, and a developing jurisprudence of interpretation and application. The foundation includes a commitment to the judicial protection of both substantive and procedural rights, as well as to an emerging concept of equality under the law.

§1.3 THE INCORPORATION DOCTRINE

As was noted above, the Bill of Rights by its own force applies only to action by the federal government. However, most of the provisions of the Bill of Rights are now fully enforceable against state or local government action by virtue of the incorporation doctrine, a doctrine through which specific provisions of the Bill of Rights have been absorbed into the Due Process Clause of the Fourteenth Amendment. Thus, if public school students claim a violation of their rights of free speech, the First Amendment, as incorporated by the Due Process Clause of the Fourteenth Amendment, will provide the students with a constitutional basis for their claims. This is so because the First Amendment in effect now operates as a limitation on state and local power by virtue of the Fourteenth Amendment.

The process of absorption began in the late nineteenth century, when the Court held that the taking of private property for public use without just compensation violates "the due process of law required by the Fourteenth Amendment." *Chicago, Burlington & Quincy Railroad Co. v. Chicago*, 166 U.S. 226, 241 (1897). The *Chicago, Burlington* Court did not, however, describe the Takings Clause as having been "incorporated" by the Fourteenth Amendment; rather, it concluded that the principle of just compensation was "fundamental" to our system of civil liberties and that the Due Process Clause of the Fourteenth Amendment embraced all such fundamental principles. The question in any case, therefore, was not whether in some technical sense a provision of the Bill of Rights had literally become part of the Fourteenth Amendment, but whether the claimed right was fundamental to our system of justice. Under this approach, not all provisions of the Bill of Rights have qualified for inclusion as part of due process. See, e.g., *Hurtado v. California*, 110 U.S. 516 (1884) (Fifth Amendment requirement of a grand jury indictment not included in Fourteenth Amendment right of due process).

The fundamental rights approach to due process was reaffirmed in *Twining v. New Jersey*, 211 U.S. 78, 98 (1908), where the Court declined to consider whether the Bill of Rights, in its entirety, had been incorporated by the Fourteenth Amendment. The Court deemed the "weighty arguments" in favor of total incorporation to have been foreclosed by prior decisions applying the fundamental rights model. According to the *Twining* Court, a right is protected by the Due Process Clause "not because [it is] enumerated in the first eight Amendments, but because [it is] of such a nature that [it is] included in the conception of due process of law." Id. at 99.

One of the most articulate and often-quoted descriptions of the fundamental rights approach to due process incorporation is found in Justice Benjamin Cardozo's opinion for the Court in *Palko v. Connecticut*, 302 U.S. 319 (1937). By the time of that decision, the Court had already recognized that several provisions of the Bill of Rights were enforceable against the states via the Fourteenth Amendment, including the freedoms of speech and religion, the right of assembly, and, to some extent, the right to counsel. At issue in *Palko* was whether the Double Jeopardy Clause of the Fifth Amendment should likewise be included within this panoply of fundamental rights. In particular, the defendant argued that, consistent with due process, a state could not appeal an acquittal after a jury trial. In rejecting this contention, the Court attempted to draw a principled distinction between those rights included and those rights excluded from due process protection.

> The right to trial by jury and the immunity from prosecution except as the result of an indictment [both of which were excluded from due process at the time *Palko* was decided] may have value and importance. Even so, they are not of the very essence of a scheme of ordered liberty. To abolish them is not to violate a "principle of justice so rooted in the traditions and conscience of our people as to be ranked as fundamental." Few would be so narrow or provincial as to maintain that a fair and enlightened system of justice would be impossible without them. What is true of jury trials and indictments is true also, as the cases show, of the immunity from compulsory self-incrimination. This too might be lost, and justice still be done. . . .
>
> We reach a different plane of social and moral values when we pass to the privileges and immunities that have been taken over from the earlier articles of the Federal Bill of Rights and brought within the Fourteenth Amendment by a process of absorption. . . . If the Fourteenth Amendment has absorbed them, the process of absorption has had its source in the belief that neither liberty nor justice would exist if they were sacrificed. This is true, for illustration, of freedom of thought and speech. Of that freedom one may say that it is the matrix, the indispensable condition, of nearly every other form of freedom.

Id. at 325-327 (internal citations omitted). Applying these principles, the Court concluded that, at least insofar as double jeopardy was implicated by the facts before it, no fundamental principle of justice had been violated. "The state is not attempting to wear the accused out by a multitude of cases with accumulated trials. It asks no more than this, that the case against him shall go on until there shall be a trial free from the corrosion of substantial legal error." Id. at 328.

Justice Cardozo's principled approach to due process does not lead to bright-line conclusions. Quite obviously some degree of subjective judgment must be exercised in determining whether any particular right is essential to an ordered system of liberty. And later decisions by the Supreme Court have disagreed with Cardozo's conclusion that the right to a jury trial and the privilege against compulsory self-incrimination were not fundamental. As the application of the fundamental rights principle in *Palko* indicates, however, the initial tendency of the Court was to be somewhat chary of finding an "absorption" into the Fourteenth Amendment.

Justice Hugo Black endorsed a very different approach to incorporation. In his famous dissent in *Adamson v. California*, 332 U.S. 46, 68 (1947), Black argued that the authors of the Fourteenth Amendment intentionally designed § 1 of that Amendment to make all provisions of the first eight amendments to the Constitution applicable to the states; in other words, one purpose of § 1 was, according to Black, to overturn *Barron v. Mayor & City Council of Baltimore* and make the entire Bill of Rights fully enforceable against the states. Black backed his argument with detailed references to the legislative history of the Fourteenth Amendment that tended to support his total-incorporation view. See 332 U.S. at 92-123 (Appendix to Black, J., dissenting). He also challenged the constitutional legitimacy of the fundamental or "natural" rights model of incorporation, seeing that approach as vesting the judiciary with an unwarranted authority to pick and choose rights according to the fashion of the day. Id. at 86-89. The net result of the Court's approach, according to Black, was that the judiciary was free to ignore vital provisions of the Bill of Rights and at the same time create new rights that had no constitutional warrant. Both practices were, in Black's view, contrary to the principles of limited government and to the very idea of a written Constitution.

During the Warren Court era, Justice John Marshall Harlan became the chief proponent of a variant of the fundamental rights model described in *Palko*. See *Duncan v. Louisiana*, 391 U.S. 145, 171-193 (1968) (Harlan, J., dissenting). In his view, Fourteenth Amendment due process embodied an evolving constitutional standard dependent only on concepts of fundamental fairness and ordered liberty, neither of which was defined or restricted by the provisions of the Bill of Rights. For Harlan, any overlap between the Bill of Rights and due process was "accidental." Id. at 177. Even if the Fourteenth Amendment's Due Process Clause were found to protect some of the same rights protected by the Bill of Rights, the comparable Bill of Rights provision would not be deemed literally "incorporated" into the Fourteenth Amendment. Instead, the two sets of rights would still exist separately, perhaps closely resembling each other, but still separate and distinct. In addition, Harlan's model of due process included the possibility of embracing rights nowhere mentioned in the Constitution. See *Poe v. Ullman*, 367 U.S. 497, 522, 539-555 (1961) (Harlan, J., dissenting) (right of privacy).

Since the early 1960s, the Court has followed a process of incorporation that has increasingly focused on the specific provisions of the Bill of Rights as providing at least a minimal definition of what is fundamental within the American system of liberty and justice. See, e.g., *Benton v. Maryland*, 395 U.S. 784, 793-796 (1969) (overruling *Palko* and holding that protection against double jeopardy is fundamental for purposes of due process). In *Duncan v. Louisiana*, 391 U.S. 145, 149 (1968), the Court described the inquiry as one focused not on a theoretical system of ordered liberty, but on whether the claimed right was "fundamental to the American scheme of justice." In this way, the fundamental rights model and the total incorporation model began to converge. As a result, most provisions of the Bill of Rights, particularly those in the context of criminal procedure, have been incorporated into the Fourteenth Amendment through what has been described as a process of selective incorporation. Essentially, the Court concluded, on a case-by-case basis, that each of the incorporated provisions is fundamental within the American system of justice and liberty.

As matters currently stand, the following provisions of the Bill of Rights have been incorporated into the Fourteenth Amendment Due Process Clause:

- The First Amendment in its entirety;
- The Second Amendment in its entirety;
- The Fourth Amendment in its entirety;
- The Fifth Amendment, except for the requirement of a grand jury indictment for criminal prosecutions;
- The Sixth Amendment in its entirety; and
- The Eighth Amendment in its entirety.

One of the most recent additions to the above list is the Second Amendment right to bear arms. While the Court had previously held that the Second Amendment was not part of the liberty protected by the Fourteenth Amendment, in *McDonald v. City of Chicago*, 561 U.S. 742 (2010), the Court revisited that question and concluded, by a five to four majority, that the right to bear arms was fundamental to our system of ordered liberty and, therefore, incorporated by the Fourteenth Amendment. The decision is slightly ambiguous because Justice Clarence Thomas, one member of the five-person majority, would have premised the incorporation on the Privileges or Immunities Clause rather than on the Due Process Clause, as the other four members of the majority had done. Id. at 805 (Thomas, J., concurring in part, and concurring in the judgment). But the holding is clear: The Second Amendment, as incorporated by the Fourteenth Amendment, constrains state action in contravention of the underlying right. Similarly, in *Timbs v. Indiana*, 586 U.S. 146 (2019), while the Court agreed that the Fourteenth Amendment incorporates the Eighth Amendment's prohibition on excessive fines, the justices divided as to the vehicle for incorporation. While the majority invoked the Due Process Clause (id. at 149-150), Justices Thomas and Gorsuch, in separate concurrences, relied on the Privileges or Immunities Clause. Id. at 157-158.

The Court has held that the neither the Fifth Amendment right to a grand jury indictment in criminal proceedings nor the Seventh Amendment right to a jury trial in civil cases is incorporated by the Fourteenth Amendment. See *Hurtado v. California*, 110 U.S. 516 (1884) (grand jury indictment); *Walker v. Sauvinet*, 92 U.S. 90 (1876) (right to a jury trial in civil cases); *Gasperini v. Center for Humanities, Inc.*, 518 U.S. 415, 432 & n.14 (1996) (right to jury trial in civil cases). The Court has not ruled on the incorporation of the Third Amendment's proscription against the quartering of soldiers.

Although the Court has not been completely consistent on this issue, the standards for measuring the constitutionality of state action potentially inconsistent with an incorporated provision of the Bill of Rights are essentially identical to the standards applied when invoking that same provision as a direct limitation on federal power.[1] See *Benton v. Maryland*, 395 U.S. 784, 795 (1969); *Malloy v. Hogan*, 378 U.S. 1, 10-11 (1964). Justice Harlan, among others, objected to this "jot-for-jot" importation of federal doctrine into the Fourteenth Amendment, see *Duncan v. Louisiana*, supra, 391 U.S. at 181; however, Justice Harlan's call that a more flexible standard of due process be applied against state action has not been followed.

§1.4 THE STATE ACTION DOCTRINE

The Fourteenth Amendment expressly limits the power of a "State" to transgress the substantive and procedural rights created by § 1 of the Amendment. In other words, the Fourteenth Amendment operates as a limit on "state action"—i.e., activity undertaken by a state or local government. Its Due Process and Equal Protection Clauses do not, however, impose any constitutional restraints on purely private activities. Thus, while the term

1. There is one clear exception to this uniformity principle. While the Sixth Amendment requires juror unanimity in federal criminal proceedings, it does not impose that requirement in state criminal proceedings. This is so despite the otherwise full incorporation of the Sixth Amendment. See *McDonald v. City of Chicago*, 561 U.S. 742, 766 n. 14 (2010).

state is defined broadly to include all aspects of state and local government, that definition stops short of including activity that is more properly characterized as private in nature. For example, while a public school may not discriminate based on race by virtue of the Equal Protection Clause, there is no such *constitutional* limitation on the activities of a purely private school. The reason is simple: A private school is not the state. (Of course, state and federal civil rights statutes may make discrimination by private schools unlawful.)

The state action requirement of the Fourteenth Amendment is not unique. It follows the pattern of most constitutional limitations. The Bill of Rights, for example, limits the authority of the federal government; it does not impose limitations on private parties. Similarly, limitations on federal and state government power found in the text of the Constitution impose no impediments to private activity. See Art. I, § 9 & § 10 (describing various limits on federal and state power). The one notable exception to this pattern is found in the Thirteenth Amendment, which abolishes slavery in both the public and the private spheres. The Fourteenth Amendment, however, follows the general rule and not the exception. In short, the state action requirement of the Fourteenth Amendment mandates that the generally recognized constitutional distinction between government and private activity be followed in all cases applying the restraints imposed by the Fourteenth Amendment, including those incorporated by the Due Process Clause.

Because our focus here is on the application of the Fourteenth Amendment, the problem that we confront is one of "state action." However, you should bear in mind that a similar type of "state action" problem may arise with respect to application of the constitutional provisions that apply to the federal government. Technically, such problems pertain to "government action," but the essential principles in this context are the same as those applicable to "state action."

The principle of state action is easily satisfied when the state or any of its subdivisions, such as a state agency or a city or county, either directly or through an officer or employee, is the perpetrator of the challenged activity. In most such cases, the state action doctrine merits at most a passing reference. Activity undertaken by the state, directly or indirectly, is quite simply state action for purposes of the Fourteenth Amendment. Suppose, for example, that a city police officer, while on duty, engages in what is arguably an unreasonable search. In a Fourteenth Amendment challenge to that activity, the state action requirement is easily satisfied, since the activity at issue was undertaken by an agent of the state under the authority of state law. Moreover, the state action requirement remains satisfied even if the officer acted in violation of state law when conducting the search. *Adickes v. Kress & Co.*, 398 U.S. 144, 152 (1970). If the officer acts in an official capacity, the state action requirement is satisfied. (There is one narrow exception to the general rule described in this paragraph, which will be addressed at the end of § 1.4.2.)

The state action doctrine is not, however, as simple as the foregoing example may suggest. Although the Fourteenth Amendment does not directly limit private activity, the distinction between state activity and private activity is sometimes quite elusive, and problems of state action tend to arise in situations in which that distinction may be critical. For example, although a private school is not generally considered a state actor, that conclusion might be altered if the state were intimately involved in the day-to-day operations of the school. In such circumstances, the question becomes whether the state is sufficiently implicated in the private activity to transform the latter into state action. Similarly, if a state delegates its governmental powers to a private entity or a private person, that entity or person may, depending on the scope and nature of the delegation, become a state actor for purposes of the Fourteenth Amendment.

The state action doctrine is designed to determine when ostensibly private conduct will be subject to constitutional restraint—i.e., when private action will be deemed state action, or, less often, when ostensibly state action will be deemed private in nature and, hence, free from constitutional restraint. The tools created by the Court for making these judgments are not wholly determinate. In other words, there is no mathematical formula for finding state action. As the Court has phrased it, what constitutes state action

> is a matter of normative judgment, and the criteria lack rigid simplicity. From the range of circumstances that could point toward the State behind an individual face, no one fact can function as a necessary condition across the board for finding state action; nor is any set of circumstances absolutely sufficient, for there may be some countervailing reason against attributing activity to the government.

Brentwood Academy v. Tennessee Secondary School Athletic Ass'n, 531 U.S. 288, 295-296 (2001). As a general matter, the state action inquiry is fact-specific and policy-bound.

This doctrinal indeterminacy is further exacerbated by what might be described as a philosophical clash between the Warren Court and the later Burger, Rehnquist, and Roberts Courts over the proper scope of the state action doctrine. To oversimplify somewhat, the Warren Court took a relatively generous view of state action that expanded the circumstances under which the constitutional protections of the Fourteenth Amendment would apply, and particularly so in the context of race and equal protection. More recently, the Court has been somewhat more reluctant to find state action. That reluctance, however, has not led to a rejection of the Warren Court precedents. Rather, the more recent state action jurisprudence has developed around those previous decisions, either distinguishing them or reinterpreting them. The net result is a body of law within which there is some doctrinal tension and also some room for interpretive flexibility.

But one need not despair! The underlying question in any state action case is relatively simple: Is the state sufficiently implicated in the challenged activity to warrant an application of the Fourteenth Amendment? Moreover, significant landmark decisions provide some guidance in the resolution of that question, at least in the contexts to which those decisions may apply. Do not, however, expect complete consistency or mathematical certainty. As the Court has often observed, the state action inquiry is largely fact and policy-bound, and therefore each case can be expected to present unique considerations.

One effective way to develop a facility for applying the state action doctrine is to begin by examining four patterns of state action problems that emerged from the Court's efforts to grapple with the underlying doctrine during the post-New Deal and Warren Court eras. Each pattern or category focuses on a particular type of state action problem and at the same time provides insight into the larger state action inquiry. Having considered these somewhat distinct categories and their evolution, the next step is to examine the more generalized approach the modern Court sometimes employs to determine whether the requisites of state action have been satisfied. This latter approach also operates as an overlay on the categorical approach by rationalizing the four patterns into a somewhat unified model that focuses on the responsibility of the state for the challenged action. The discussion that follows is organized around these principles.

A final preliminary point: Many state action cases involve a construction of 42 U.S.C. § 1983, the federal civil rights statute that provides a private remedy for action taken "under color of state law." The phrases "state action" and "under color of state law" have been treated as being synonymous. *American Manufacturers Mutual Ins. Co. v. Sullivan*, 526 U.S. 40, 50 n. 8 (1999); *Lugar v. Edmondson Oil Co.*, 457 U.S. 922, 928-929 (1982). We will do the same.

§1.4.1 The Categorical Approach

The categorical approach to state action focuses on four contexts in which state action has been found. Each category presents a particular type of state action problem, and within each category, special doctrinal rules have developed to help shape the scope of the category. The categories are not, however, completely distinct from one another. They share a common thread of seeking to determine the relationship between the state and the underlying challenged activity. In addition, cases arising in the real world often involve elements of more than one category. Indeed, you may find it useful to view potential state action problems from the perspective of several categories.

Private Performance of a Public Function

The private performance of a public or governmental function may under some circumstances qualify as state action. Stated somewhat differently, if a state permits a private party to exercise what is clearly governmental power, then the activity of the private party will be treated as state action for purposes of the Fourteenth Amendment. This principle is variously referred to as the public function doctrine, the governmental function doctrine, or the sovereign function doctrine. As we will see from the cases, while in theory the scope of this doctrine may appear quite expansive, in practice the actual scope is relatively modest.

One of the leading public function cases is *Marsh v. Alabama*, 326 U.S. 501 (1946). In that case, a Jehovah's Witness claimed a First and Fourteenth Amendment right to distribute literature on the streets and sidewalks of a town that was completely owned and governed by a private company. As described by the Court, "[T]he town and its shopping district are accessible to and freely used by the public in general and there is nothing to distinguish them from any other town and shopping center except the fact that the title to the property [including title to the streets and sidewalks] belongs to a private corporation." Id. at 503. Despite the private ownership and private governance of the town, the Court agreed that the First and Fourteenth Amendments were fully applicable under the circumstances presented. Essentially, by monopolizing all governmental functions within the town, the company had taken on the character of a governmental actor and was, therefore, subject to the same First Amendment restraints applicable to state and local governments. As the Court later described *Marsh*, "[T]he owner of the company town was performing the full spectrum of municipal powers and stood in the shoes of the State." *Lloyd Corp. v. Tanner*, 407 U.S. 551, 569 (1972).

The public function doctrine was also applied successfully in *Smith v. Allwright*, 321 U.S. 649 (1944), a case in which African American voters from Texas challenged their exclusion from participation in primary elections conducted by the Democratic Party. The Party conducted the primary elections under state statutory authority. Moreover, the results of the primary dictated who could appear on the state's general election ballot. Thus, the primary was an integral part of the general election machinery. Given these facts, the Court concluded that the Democratic Party was performing a governmental function as an agent of the state. The racial discrimination practiced by the Democratic Party was, therefore, state action. See also *Terry v. Adams*, 345 U.S. 461 (1953) (similar conclusion with respect to a privately conducted "pre-primary" that, as a practical matter, controlled access to state ballots).

The Court appeared poised to expand the public function doctrine further in the late 1960s, when it held that a privately owned shopping mall is subject to the constraints of the First and Fourteenth Amendments. *Amalgamated Food Employees Union v. Logan Valley Plaza*, 391 U.S. 308 (1968). The Court reasoned that the mall was the "functional equivalent of the business district" at issue in *Marsh v. Alabama*. Id. at 318. The requirement of state action was, therefore, satisfied. The decision in *Logan Valley* was, however, short-lived. Four years later in *Lloyd Corp. v. Tanner*, 407 U.S. 551 (1972), the Court distinguished *Logan Valley* in a manner that cast serious doubt on the continuing legitimacy of the earlier decision. In refusing to find state action on roughly similar facts, the *Lloyd* Court emphasized the unique nature of the facts in *Marsh*, particularly the pervasive scope of the company's authority in that case, suggesting a narrow ambit for the public function doctrine. Finally, in *Hudgens v. NLRB*, 424 U.S. 507 (1976), the Court expressly overruled the decision in *Logan Valley* and again underscored the limited reach of the decision in *Marsh* and of the public function doctrine in general. Id. at 518.

The Court also declined to apply the public function doctrine in *Jackson v. Metropolitan Edison Co.*, 419 U.S. 345 (1974). There, the plaintiff sought to invoke the protections of the Fourteenth Amendment against Metropolitan Edison, a privately owned utility company that had terminated her services. She argued, among other things, that since Metropolitan provided an "essential public service," it performed a public function subjecting its activities to scrutiny under the Fourteenth Amendment. Id. at 352. The Court disagreed: "We have, of course, found state action present in the exercise by a private entity of powers *traditionally exclusively* reserved to the State." Id. (emphasis supplied). The italicized language was meant to and did effectively limit the scope of the public function doctrine. While many municipalities provided public utility services, and while even the private provision of such services is marked with a strong public interest, the provision of utility services was not, in the Court's view, "traditionally exclusively" reserved to the states, but was associated with both the public and the private spheres. By way of contrast, the Court noted that "[i]f we were dealing with the exercise by Metropolitan of some power delegated to it by the State which is traditionally associated with sovereignty, such as eminent domain, our case would be quite a different one." Id. at 352-353. See also *American Manufacturers Mutual Ins. Co. v. Sullivan*, 526 U.S. 40, 54-57 (1999) (private insurer's decision to withhold payment of claim for medical services pending review of claim's validity not traditionally an exclusively public function); *Flagg Bros. v. Brooks*, 436 U.S. 149, 160 (1978) (private sale of stored goods under state law permitting such a sale is not state action, since the resolution of disputes in the commercial world is not the "exclusive prerogative of the sovereign"). The message of *Jackson* was clear: The concept of "public function" is not to be read broadly.

In addition, the fact that the government has funded a private operation for public purposes or public benefit will not necessarily establish that the private operation performs a public function. From the perspective of the modern public function doctrine, the question is not simply whether the government has funded the private activity, but whether that private activity can be fairly characterized as being traditionally and exclusively the prerogative of the state. Thus, in *Rendell-Baker v. Kohn*, 457 U.S. 830 (1982), the Court held that although a privately owned school for maladjusted high school students received 90 percent of its operating budget from the state to educate children who had been removed from public school, it was not performing a public function. The provision of special educational opportunities for such students is not a traditional and an exclusive function of the state. Id. at 842. See *Blum v. Yaretsky*, 457 U.S. 991, 1011-1012 (1982) (privately owned nursing facility that receives state funding does not perform a public function).

Example 1-A

State X requires all persons under the age of 16 residing within the state to attend an accredited elementary or secondary school. The state itself provides an extensive system of public education operated through taxpayer-funded local school districts. In addition, numerous private groups, both sectarian and nonsectarian, provide private education that meets the state's accreditation standards. Mary, who is 15 years old, attends Good Values Prep, a private school accredited by the state. Mary claims that Good Values violated her First and Fourteenth Amendment rights when it punished her for wearing an armband protesting the expulsion of a fellow student. Does Good Values perform a public function by providing students with a state-accredited education?

Explanation

One could certainly argue that schools such as Good Values perform a public function by acting as a surrogate for public schools and by providing a service through which one may comply with the state's mandatory education requirement. Yet given the current status of the public function doctrine, a court is not likely to find that Good Values performs a public function under the given circumstances. While the provision of education through the private sector can be fairly characterized as a public service, perhaps even as an essential public service, education itself has not been *traditionally and exclusively* reserved to the states. Indeed, the "tradition" of public education is a relatively recent phenomenon. In addition, applying the cases, private education seems more like the private utility at issue in *Jackson* than it does the privately run primary election in *Smith v. Allwright*. Education and utility services have long been provided by the private sector. Primary elections, on the other hand, represent a quintessential governmental function as part of the very process of governing. Moreover, the authority exercised by a private school is certainly not as extensive as the quasi-governmental authority exercised by the company-owned town in *Marsh*. Rather, a private school is more like a private shopping mall, both of which exercise authority over a limited private domain. In short, given the Court's relatively strict application of the public function doctrine, Good Values Prep does not perform a public function.

EXAMPLE

Example 1-B

Jails R Us, Inc. (JRU) is a private corporation that owns and operates jails on behalf of municipal governments that wish to privatize their jail operations. The JRU facility accepts prisoners from these municipalities on a contractual basis for a set per diem fee. When an inmate is housed in a JRU facility, he or she is subject to all JRU regulations and to the JRU disciplinary system. Geoffrey, a convicted shoplifter who was transferred to JRU by the City of Metrolex, claims that JRU's disciplinary procedures violate the Fourteenth Amendment. Do the activities of JRU qualify as state action under the public function doctrine?

EXPLANATION

Explanation

By entering a contract with JRU to house Geoffrey, Metrolex delegated its governmental authority to JRU, and as a consequence, the corporation operates as an agent for the municipality—i.e., the state. Moreover, since the punishment for crimes has been *traditionally and exclusively* reserved to the states, the housing of prisoners on behalf of a municipality is a public function within the meaning of the public function doctrine. Indeed, operating a prison is akin to conducting primary elections or governing a company-owned town in the sense that all three represent quintessential governmental operations. See *Rosborough v. Management & Training Corp.*, 350 F.3d 459, 461 (5th Cir. 2003) (employees of a private correctional facility perform a "fundamentally governmental function"); *Street v. Corrections Corp. of America*, 102 F.3d 810, 814 (6th Cir. 1996) (private prison under contract with state held to be a state actor performing a public function); *Ancata v. Prison Health Servs., Inc.*, 769 F.2d 700, 703 (11th Cir. 1985) (employees of private health corporation are state actors when performing the public function of providing required medical services to prison inmates); but see *Holly v. Scott*, 434 F.3d 287, 293-294 (4th Cir.), *cert. denied*, 547 U.S. 1168 (2006) (operation of jails not a function traditionally and exclusively reserved to the states).

Example 1-C

MNN is a private nonprofit corporation that operates New York City's public access cable television channels on Time Warner's cable system. After the City granted Time Warner a cable franchise, the City was in return given several public access channels, as required by state law. The City could have operated these channels itself but instead chose to hire MNN for this purpose. In this capacity, MNN is heavily regulated by the state. After MNN suspended a cable TV producer from the City's channels due to the content of one of its films—content that involved criticism of MNN—the producer sued MNN under § 1983 for violation of its First Amendment rights, claiming that MNN was a state actor. Did MNN's operation of the City's public access channels convert it into a state actor subject to the First and Fourteenth Amendments?

Explanation

First, plaintiff may argue that operating public access channels involves a traditional and exclusive public function. However, history reveals that since their inception, such channels have been operated by both private and public entities. Secondly, plaintiff might try to widen the lens by defining the function here not as the operation of public access channels on a cable system, but rather as the operation of a public forum for speech. Yet this still does not satisfy the "traditional and exclusive test" since private parties sometimes open their property to speech by others, as in the case of shopping centers, grocery store bulletin boards, and company towns. Thus, for state action purposes, hosting speech by members of the public is not a traditional and exclusive governmental function. Had the City chosen to operate the public access channels itself, as some cities have done, the case would have been different and state action would clearly have been present. See *Manhattan Community Access Corp. v. Halleck*, 587 U.S. 802, 809 (2019) (holding that MNN was not performing a public function and noting that "'very few' functions fall into that category").

The dissenters in *Halleck* viewed MNN as in effect a government employee hired by the City to administer its public access channels. Since government employees who act within the scope of their official duties automatically qualify as state actors, there was no need for any further state action analysis. In their view, when MNN "stepped into the City's shoes" to serve as its agent, "the Constitution followed." Id. at 819, 835 (Sotomayor, J., et al., dissenting).

Judicial Enforcement of Private Agreements

The second category involves the judicial enforcement of private action, which may, under relatively limited circumstances, satisfy the state action requirement. The leading case is *Shelley v. Kraemer*, 334 U.S. 1 (1948). There, the Court considered a Fourteenth Amendment challenge to the judicial enforcement of a covenant that restricted the sale of real property to members of the Caucasian race. The Court recognized that the private agreement to discriminate did not violate the Fourteenth Amendment, since the agreement was between private parties. Id. at 13. The enforcement of the covenant by a judicial officer, however, brought the power of the state into the transaction, and the Court concluded that this state involvement was sufficient to establish the presence of state action. Id. at 19-20. In other words, the judicial enforcement of the private agreement transformed that agreement into state action.

If, as one might assume, the critical element in *Shelley* was the act of judicial enforcement, then presumably whenever a judge enforces a private agreement, the private agreement will be attributed to the state. Thus, in any case in which a party seeks to enforce the provisions of a private contract, the party against whom the contract is being enforced can demand that the enforced contractual provisions comply with the Fourteenth Amendment. The private contract is, by virtue of the judicial involvement, transformed into an act of the state. Similarly, under this theory, a private decision to eject a trespasser may well become the action of the state if the property owner resorts to the judicial process. Consequently, a decision to eject solely on the basis of the religious beliefs of the trespasser would be unenforceable as contrary to the First and Fourteenth Amendments.

Shelley has not, however, developed along these lines. See *Bell v. Maryland*, 378 U.S. 226, 326-335 (1964) (Black, J., dissenting) (describing *Shelley* as limited to circumstances in which the judiciary intervenes to prevent a property owner from exercising rights guaranteed by the Fourteenth Amendment). The judicial enforcement of a private agreement or private decision does not automatically transform the underlying private activity into state action. To hold otherwise would be to constitutionalize an almost infinite array of private affairs—from contracts, to wills, to the testamentary disposition of property. In fact, the critical element in *Shelley* was not simply the judicial enforcement of a private agreement in the abstract, but also the judicial enforcement of a particular type of private agreement, namely, a racially restrictive covenant that limited a willing seller's right to convey his or her property to a willing purchaser. The interposition of the judiciary between these parties, essentially forcing the seller to discriminate based on race, provided the critical factor in the finding of state action. By forcing the seller to discriminate, the court—i.e., the state—became complicit in the otherwise private act of discrimination.

Example 1-D

In 1911, General Wallstone bequeathed in trust a large tract of land for use as an all-male military school. Under the terms of the trust, if the school were ever to admit women, the property would revert to General Wallstone's heirs. The trustees have concluded that the all-male admissions policy can no longer be sustained, and they have voted to admit women in the upcoming term. Would a state court order enjoining the trustees from violating the terms of the trust satisfy the state action doctrine as applied in *Shelley v. Kraemer?*

Explanation

Yes. Like the court order in *Shelley*, the order here interposes the judiciary between parties who wish to enter a legal relationship, and it requires one of the parties to discriminate in a manner that would violate the Fourteenth Amendment if it were engaged in by the state. Applying *Shelley*, such a judicial order to discriminate satisfies the state action doctrine.

Suppose, however, that the court in Example 1-D applied neutral principles of state law that required it to enforce the reverter clause in General Wallstone's will, thereby returning the property to the general's heirs. Would state action be satisfied under such circumstances? Unquestionably the court's order is state action. The court, after all, is an official representative of the state. But the court's order is itself neutral; it does not discriminate, and it does not require anyone else to do so. Thus, although state action is satisfied with respect to the court's order, there is no violation of the Equal Protection Clause. The more precise question is whether the court's order will transform General Wallstone's private discriminatory intent into state action. The answer is no. If the court itself does not discriminate or require discrimination, the enforcement of the terms of General Wallstone's bequest, under otherwise neutral principles of law, will not transform that private activity into state action. See *Evans v. Abney*, 396 U.S. 435, 445-446 (1970). The distinction between this hypothetical and the circumstances presented in *Shelley* is that only in the latter case would the court participate in the act of discrimination.

The principle of *Shelley* seems also to have been applied in the context of the First Amendment freedoms of speech and press, although not explicitly so. For example, in *Cohen v. Cowles Media Co.*, 501 U.S. 663 (1991), the Court found that state action is satisfied in a case in which a private party sues a newspaper for breach of a promise of confidentiality. The newspaper raised a First Amendment defense. In a brief discussion of state action, the Court explained, "Our cases teach that the application of state rules of law in state courts in a manner alleged to restrict First Amendment freedoms constitutes 'state action' under the Fourteenth Amendment." Id. at 668. As in *Shelley*, a court order restricting First Amendment freedoms would itself violate the asserted constitutional right.

EXAMPLE

Example 1-E

The *National Snooper* published an article in which it described the police chief of a "northeastern metropolis" as heavily involved in organized crime activities. The allegation was apparently made in reference to Chief Kanner of New York City. Kanner sued the *Snooper* for libel. At trial, Kanner did not submit any evidence that the allegations were false. Nevertheless, the court awarded Kanner $500,000 in damages, holding that under state law, given the egregious nature of the allegations made by the *Snooper*, falsity would be presumed. Would a judicial decree enforcing this judgment satisfy the state action requirement?

EXPLANATION

Explanation

Yes. Application of state rules of law in state courts in a manner alleged to restrict First Amendment freedoms constitutes state action under the Fourteenth Amendment. Under *New York Times v. Sullivan*, 376 U.S. 254 (1964), the award of damages in "*Kanner v. The National Snooper*" violates the "actual malice" standard required by the First Amendment in cases involving the defamation of public figures. See § 8.3.4. Therefore, enforcement of the judgment would constitute state action.

Joint Activity Between a State and a Private Party

If a private party and a state engage in joint activity that results in the deprivation of another's constitutional rights, the activity of the private party may be deemed state action, thus subjecting the otherwise private actor to the same restrictions and remedies under the Fourteenth Amendment as are applicable against the state. See *Dennis v. Sparks*, 449 U.S. 24, 27-28 (1980); *Adickes v. Kress & Co.*, 398 U.S. 144, 152 (1970). The determining factors are the nature and the scope of the relationship between the private party and the state. There are two general patterns under which such joint activity has been deemed sufficient to impute state action to otherwise private activity. The first involves concerted or conspiratorial activity between a state actor and a private actor directed toward depriving another individual of his or her constitutional rights. The second involves the creation of a mutually beneficial relationship between a state and a private actor in which the private actor takes action that would violate the Fourteenth Amendment if undertaken by the state. In both cases, the private activity is treated as state action. We will consider each form in turn.

The first form is relatively easy to spot and apply. If a state actor and a private actor undertake concerted activity that operates to deprive another person of his or her constitutional rights, the activity of the private actor will be treated as state action. The presence of the state actor triggers the state action doctrine, while the "joint" nature of the activity brings any accompanying action undertaken by the private actor within the scope of the doctrine. Thus, in *Adickes v. Kress & Co.*, the Court held that allegations that a Kress employee had conspired with a police officer to deprive a schoolteacher of her Fourteenth Amendment rights were sufficient to assert a cause of action against Kress, a private company, for violation of those rights.

Example 1-F

Harrison is a reporter for a syndicated "police reality" show. As part of his job, he engages in "ride alongs" with city police officers while the latter are performing their official duties. During one of these ride alongs, Harrison convinced Officer Lucas to break into the hut of Jabba, a suspected gang leader. During the break in, Harrison films Lucas rummaging through Jabba's hut in search of incriminating evidence. Jabba has now filed suit against Harrison and the officer, claiming that the two engaged in an unlawful search of his hut in violation of his Fourth and Fourteenth Amendment rights. Is the state action requirement satisfied with respect to Harrison?

Explanation

Yes. As a city police officer, Officer Lucas is a state actor, and any activity undertaken by him in his official capacity qualifies as state action. Under the given facts, Lucas's break-in and search of Jabba's hut is, therefore, state action. Moreover, although Harrison is a private citizen, his participation in the break-in and search will also be deemed state action, since Harrison acted in concert with a state actor.

Example 1-G

Dr. Livesay sued Captain Flint to prevent the latter from removing certain valuable artifacts discovered on property over which Livesay claimed an ownership interest. Flint, however, bribed the presiding judge, the Honorable L.J. Silver, to dismiss the suit with prejudice. After the dismissal, Flint absconded with the goods. Livesay has now sued both Silver and Flint, claiming that the two conspired to deprive him of his property without due process of law. Is the state action requirement satisfied with respect to Flint?

Explanation

Yes. Judge Silver is a state actor acting in an official capacity. His dismissal of Livesay's suit is, therefore, state action. Flint's bribery of Silver makes Flint complicit in that state action, thereby subjecting Flint to the restraints of the Fourteenth Amendment. See *Dennis v. Sparks*, 449 U.S. 24 (1980) (holding that a private party under similar facts remained subject to the Fourteenth Amendment even though the judge who had accepted the bribe was absolutely immune from civil liability).

Private action may also be treated as state action if a state and a private party enter a mutually beneficial or "symbiotic relationship" within which the private party takes action that would violate the Fourteenth Amendment if undertaken by the state. The classic example of this form is found in *Burton v. Wilmington Parking Authority*, 365 U.S. 715 (1961). There, the Supreme Court found a symbiotic relationship between a city that owned and operated a parking structure and its lessee, a restaurant located within the parking structure that discriminated on the basis of race. Critical to the finding of state action was the fact that the restaurant "constituted a physically and financially integral and, indeed, indispensable part of the State's plan to operate its project as a self-sustaining unit." Id. at 723-724. Furthermore, in the words of the Court,

> [i]t cannot be doubted that the peculiar relationship of the restaurant to the parking facility in which it is located confers on each an incidental variety of mutual benefits. Guests of the restaurant are afforded a convenient place to park their automobiles. . . . Similarly, its convenience for diners may well provide additional demand for the [state's] parking facilities.

Id. at 724. In short, the interdependent and mutually beneficial relationship between the state and the restaurant was sufficient to identify the racially discriminatory practices of the privately owned and operated restaurant as state action. In essence, the state was deemed a "joint participant" in the otherwise private acts of discrimination. Id. at 725.

Not all relationships between a state and a private party will transform the activities of the private party into state action. The critical element is the interdependence of the state and the private actor. In *Moose Lodge v. Irvis*, 407 U.S. 163 (1972), for example, the plaintiff challenged certain racially discriminatory practices of a private club as being in violation of the Equal Protection Clause. He argued that the private club's state-issued liquor license created a sufficient relationship between the state and the private club to warrant treating the activities of the club as state action. The Court disagreed and, in so doing, distinguished its decision in *Burton:*

> Here there is nothing approaching the symbiotic relationship between lessor and lessee that was present in *Burton*, where the private lessee obtained the benefit of locating in a building owned by the state-created parking authority, and the parking authority was enabled to carry out its primary public purpose of furnishing parking space by advantageously leasing portions of the building constructed for that purpose to commercial lessees such as the owner of the [private restaurant].

Id. at 175. Although in *Moose Lodge* both the state and the club derived some mutual benefit from the state's licensing and regulatory scheme, that alone was insufficient to establish the requisite interdependence needed to satisfy the state action doctrine.

The *Moose Lodge* Court further emphasized that the mere presence of state regulation or a state licensing scheme will not, standing alone, suffice to transform private action into state action. Id. at 175-176. Only if the state regulation mandates the specific activity being challenged will the otherwise private activity be treated as state action. Id. at 178-179; accord *American Manufacturers Mutual Ins. Co. v. Sullivan*, 526 U.S. 40, 52 (1999). Thus, in *Moose Lodge*, the Court found state action to be present because state law required the club to adhere to its bylaws, which were racially discriminatory; once that law was enjoined, however, the club's discriminatory practices were no longer mandated by the state and, therefore, no longer constituted state action. The plaintiff in *Moose Lodge* sought only prospective injunctive relief. Had he also sought damages for the club's past discrimination against him, the state action requirement would have been met since, at the time of that discrimination, the state law mandating adherence to the club's bylaws was still in effect.

EXAMPLE

Example 1-H

Example 1-A considered whether a private secondary school performed a public function by providing a private school option for satisfying the state's mandatory education requirement. In that example, Mary argued that the school violated her First and Fourteenth Amendment rights when it punished her for wearing an armband. We concluded that the public function doctrine for finding state action was not satisfied. Considering the same facts, however, is the relationship between such a private school and the state sufficient to establish state action under the theory applied in *Burton v. Wilmington Parking Authority?* In other words, is the relationship between the state and the private school mutually beneficial to the extent that the activities of the private school can be imputed to the state?

Explanation

One can certainly argue that the state and the private school mutually benefit one another. The state's mandatory education law creates a potential market for the private schools, and the private schools reduce the overall expense of public education incurred by the state by taking students out of the public system. Thus, the case in favor of finding a symbiotic relationship is stronger than that present in the licensing scheme at issue in *Moose Lodge*, where the state merely licensed and regulated the private actor. On the other hand, the relationship here is not nearly as interdependent as the mutually beneficial economic relationship at issue in *Burton*. In that case, the private restaurant operated as an "indispensable part of the State's plan to operate its project as a self-sustaining unit." 365 U.S. at 723-724. Absent such an interdependent relationship, a court is unlikely to find state action. As a consequence, the more abstract mutual benefit enjoyed by the state and the private school will not be adequate to treat the activities of the school as state action.

Moreover, since the state did not require the school to regulate the wearing of armbands for expressive purposes, state action could not be found on this ground either.

The potential reach of *Burton* in the context of governmental funding of private activity has also been somewhat limited. The mere fact that the government pays for or subsidizes private activity will not establish a symbiotic relationship between the government and the private actor. In *Rendell-Baker v. Kohn*, 457 U.S. 830 (1982), for example, the Court rejected a symbiotic relationship argument in the context of a private school for maladjusted high school students that received 90 percent of its funding from the state. Although the state and the school were in a mutually beneficial relationship, there was no showing that the state derived any benefit from the precise activity being challenged, namely, the school's personnel policies. In distinguishing *Burton*, the Court emphasized that the state in that case "profited from the restaurant's discriminatory conduct." Id. at 843. In *Rendell-Baker*, although the state benefited from its relationship with the school, the state derived no particular benefit from the challenged personnel policies.

The *Rendell-Baker* Court's interpretation of *Burton* is somewhat strained, since there was no showing in *Burton* that the state derived any benefit from the discriminatory practices of the restaurant. As we will see, this reinterpretation is consistent with the modern Court's insistence that private activity be imputed to the state only when the state is somehow responsible for the precise activity being challenged. See § 1.4.2. It is also supported by the Court's policy concern that to hold otherwise might subject a vast array of private actions—including that of government contractors and all persons who receive any form of governmental aid—to the constraints of the Constitution.

Example 1-I

In Example 1-C, could plaintiff satisfy the state action requirement on the basis that MNN, by contracting with New York City to oversee the operation of the City's public access channels, thereby entered into a mutually beneficial or symbiotic relationship with the City so as to convert MNN into a state actor?

Explanation

The City and MNN entered into what was clearly a mutually beneficial contractual relationship. The City benefits in terms of having its public access channels operated properly, while MNN benefits from the compensation received for its services. But merely contracting with the government is not enough to satisfy the symbiotic relationship test, for if that is all it took, countless private entities would be converted into state actors subject to constitutional restrictions on their activities. To narrow the reach of this theory of state action, the nexus must probably be much tighter, such that the city and/or the state benefited from the specific conduct in question, here the termination of plaintiff's access to the City's public access channels. From the facts given, such a nexus would appear to be lacking and the symbiotic relationship test not satisfied. The case would have been different had the cable show that led to the cancellation been one that criticized the City or the State of New York, for then the termination could be seen as one clearly benefiting the governmental actors involved. See *Manhattan Community Access Corp. v. Halleck*, 587 U.S. 802, 819 (2019) (finding no state action in this case though symbiotic relationship argument was not made).

Example 1-J

State T's Department of Agriculture entered into an arrangement with Brea University, a private institution, under which the state agreed to fully fund research by the university's agriculture department regarding the effects of certain food additives on pregnant women. The purpose of the research was to provide the Department of Agriculture with information useful to the promotion of agribusiness within the state. The details and method of the research project were left to the discretion of the university. The women subjected to these experiments, although volunteers, were not informed of potential dangers to their health and to the health of the children they were carrying at the time of the experiments. Now, several years later, a number of these women and their children have suffered severe consequences as a result of the experiments. They claim that the university's failure to fully inform them of potential risks violated the Due Process Clause of the Fourteenth Amendment. Did the action of the university constitute state action for purposes of the Fourteenth Amendment?

Explanation

Probably. Unlike the circumstances present in *Rendell-Baker v. Kohn*, the state here directly benefited from the specific program being challenged. Thus, while the state in *Rendell-Baker* had no stake in the personnel policies of the private school, here the state had a strong interest in the actual experiments being undertaken. Indeed, those experiments were undertaken specifically for the benefit of the state. This would seem, therefore, to present a strong example of a symbiotic relationship between the state and a private party. See *Craft v. Vanderbilt Univ.*, 18 F. Supp. 2d 786 (M.D. Tenn. 1998) (so holding under similar facts).

State Endorsement of Private Conduct

The fourth category involves state authorization or encouragement of private conduct that would violate the Fourteenth Amendment if engaged in by the state. The leading case is *Reitman v. Mulkey*, 387 U.S. 369 (1967). At issue in *Reitman* was a provision of the California Constitution that legalized private acts of racial discrimination in the sale or rental of housing. The effect of the provision was not only to repeal then-existing fair housing laws, but also to immunize racial discrimination in housing from all future "legislative, executive, or judicial regulation at any level of the state government." Id. at 377. The question before the Court was whether a private act of discrimination undertaken pursuant to this provision constituted state action. The Court held that it did, relying largely on the California Supreme Court's conclusion that the provision at issue "significantly encourage[d] and involve[d] the State in private discriminations." Id. at 381. Indeed, the history of the provision indicated that its purpose was to authorize and immunize such discriminations.

The key factor in establishing state action in *Reitman* was the finding that the provision at issue affirmatively authorized and encouraged acts of racial discrimination. Id. Had the statute merely repealed existing civil rights legislation, thus leaving the state neutral on the issue of race discrimination in housing, state action would not have been found. Id. at 376. The affirmative endorsement of otherwise private acts of discrimination, however, sufficiently implicated the state in the discriminatory acts to satisfy the state action requirement.

EXAMPLE

Example 1-K

A statute of state Q requires cable television operators within the state to ban "indecent" programming on commercial cable channels—i.e., channels leased to commercial programmers (e.g., HBO, The Movie Channel). CTO owns a cable franchise within state Q, and pursuant to the above statute, CTO has attempted to regulate the "indecent" content on its access channels. Several commercial programmers affected by CTO's actions have filed suit against the company, claiming a violation of their First and Fourteenth Amendment rights. Do the actions of CTO constitute state action?

EXPLANATION

Explanation

Yes. The state here has not only encouraged but required the particular action being challenged. In other words, the state has not taken a neutral stand but has affirmatively commanded cable operators to ban indecent programming. Thus, if the ban violates the First Amendment, the private action enforcing the ban is attributable to the state.

The issue of "state endorsement" may also play a role in the finding of state action in other categories. For example, an underlying concern in both *Shelley v. Kraemer* and *Burton v. Wilmington Parking Authority* was the potential perception of state endorsement of private discriminatory action. In *Shelley*, a state court's enforcement of a racially restrictive covenant might be seen as a judicial approval of such covenants. *Shelley*, supra, 334 U.S. at 20. Similarly, the public nature of the parking structure in *Burton* seemed to lend the authority of the state to the discriminatory policies of the lessee restaurant. *Burton*, supra, 365 U.S. at 720.

§1.4.2 The Two-Part Approach

In *Lugar v. Edmondson Oil Co.*, 457 U.S. 922, 937 (1982), the Court attempted to distill the state action doctrine into its basic elements:

> Our cases have . . . insisted that the conduct allegedly causing the deprivation of a federal right be fairly attributable to the State. These cases reflect a two-part approach to this question of "fair attribution." First, the deprivation must be caused by the exercise of some right or privilege created by the State or by a rule of conduct imposed by the State or by a person for whom the State is responsible . . . . Second, the party charged with the deprivation must be a person who may fairly be said to be a state actor. This may be because he is a

> state official, because he has acted together with or has obtained significant aid from state officials, or because his conduct is otherwise chargeable to the State.

The *Lugar* two-part approach did not create a new test for state action. Rather, the two-part approach was designed to highlight those factors that have been deemed significant in what is essentially a fact-bound and context-driven inquiry, namely, the extent to which any particular action can or should be deemed attributable to the state for purposes of the Fourteenth Amendment. The second part of this two-part approach encompasses the four categories we previously considered, while the first part of the *Lugar* approach was implicit in the cases around which the categories were constructed. The four categories thus describe specific contexts in which the state action requirement has been met. For example, one can analyze *Shelley v. Kraemer* through the lens of *Lugar*. The claimed deprivation in *Shelley* was caused by a right created by state law—i.e., the right to create racially restrictive covenants—and the party charged with the deprivation was a state actor because he obtained significant aid from a state official, namely, the judge to whom the request for an injunction was addressed. In short, *Lugar*'s two-part approach synthesizes the earlier cases and focuses our attention on the specific problem to be resolved in every state action inquiry: Is the state sufficiently implicated in the challenged activity such that the activity may be characterized as state action?

Both parts of the two-part approach are sufficiently malleable to allow a wide latitude for the application of subjective judgment. As a result, one can expect results under *Lugar* to be somewhat variable, depending on a combination of the facts, relevant policy concerns, and judicial philosophy. Of course, this was also true of the more compartmentalized approach under the categories. Do not think of the two-part approach as a complete substitute for the categorical approach. The separate categories inform the elements of the two-part approach, particularly the second element, and courts, including the Supreme Court, continue to incorporate the categorical approach when the facts so warrant. See *American Manufacturers Mutual Ins. Co. v. Sullivan*, 526 U.S. 40 (1999) (integrating categorical approach with two-part approach).

EXAMPLE

Example 1-L

Lowbar was indebted to Edmunson who, seeking to secure the debt, sought prejudgment attachment of certain of Lowbar's property, claiming that Lowbar was disposing of that property to defeat his creditors. A state statute allowed Edmunson to obtain an attachment by merely filing an ex parte petition alleging the facts described above. Acting on Edmunson's petition, a clerk of the state court issued a writ of attachment, which was executed by the county sheriff. Lowbar then filed suit in federal court, claiming that Edmunson had acted jointly with the state to deprive him of his property without due process of law. His claim was premised on two separate theories: Under the first, he challenged the constitutionality of the state's prejudgment attachment scheme itself; under the second, he claimed that Edmunson had abused the judicial process. Is the state action requirement satisfied?

Explanation

Under the *Lugar* approach, we must first determine whether the claimed deprivation was "caused by the exercise of some right or privilege created by the State or by a rule of conduct imposed by the State or by a person for whom the State is responsible." *Lugar v. Edmondson Oil Co.*, supra, 457 U.S. at 937. Lowbar's first claimed deprivation challenges the attachment right created by the state statute. Therefore, the first element of *Lugar* is satisfied with respect to this claim. As to the second claim, however, this element is not satisfied. Edmunson's alleged *abuse* of the state's attachment process was not created by the state, nor was it imposed by the state or by a person for whom the state was responsible. Rather, the abuse of the state-created attachment scheme was the product of Edmunson's own independent action. Since the *Lugar* two-part approach is conjunctive, we can conclude at this point that Lowbar's second claim does not satisfy the state action requirement.

Next, with respect to the first claim, we must determine whether Edmunson "may fairly be said to be a state actor. This may be because he is a state official, because he has acted together with or has obtained significant aid from state officials, or because his conduct is otherwise chargeable to the State." Id. Although Edmunson is not a state official, he did act together with, and did obtain significant aid from, state officials, namely, the clerk of the court and the county sheriff. Notice that this conclusion flows directly from the "joint activity" category discussed under the categorical approach. The second element is, therefore, satisfied. Consequently, Lowbar has established state action with respect to his first claim, the challenge to the constitutionality of the state's prejudgment attachment scheme. See id., 457 U.S. at 939-942 (similar conclusion under similar facts).

Example 1-M

Brooks's goods were stored in Flagg's warehouse. After Brooks refused to pay the storage costs, Flagg informed her that her property would be sold pursuant to a state law that permitted the private sale of stored goods under such circumstances. Brooks filed suit in federal court, claiming that the threatened sale would violate the Due Process and Equal Protection Clauses of the Fourteenth Amendment. Would Flagg's sale of Brooks's property constitute state action?

EXPLANATION

Explanation

First, was the claimed deprivation caused by the exercise of some right or privilege created by the state or by a rule of conduct imposed by the state or by a person for whom the state is responsible? Yes. Flagg's right to sell Brooks's property was created by the state. This element is, therefore, satisfied.

Next, was Flagg a state actor—i.e., was he a state official, did he act together with or obtain significant aid from state officials, or was his conduct otherwise chargeable to the state? No. He was not a state official, and the sale did not require the presence of a state official. Compare Example 1-L, where the attachment required the participation of state officials. Thus, there is no joint activity here. Moreover, the fact that the right exercised was created by the state is not sufficient to hold that the state is chargeable with the conduct. A more affirmative showing of state complicity is required to satisfy this element. See *Reitman v. Mulkey* (state constitutional right to discriminate in housing implicates state in private action). Therefore, the second element being unsatisfied, Flagg's proposed sale does not constitute state action. See *Flagg Bros., Inc. v. Brooks*, 436 U.S. 149 (1978) (so holding on similar facts).

Of course, one could alternatively argue that the power exercised by Flagg was vested in him by the state and that the state should, therefore, assume responsibility for the exercise of that power on the theory that it involved the private performance of a traditional governmental function. This is especially so since the function exercised by Flagg is public in nature and, therefore, attributable to the state. See *Flagg Bros., Inc. v. Brooks*, supra, 436 U.S. at 168-179 (Stevens, J., dissenting). The *Flagg* Court, however, rejected this argument, signaling a more restrictive approach to state action.

A similar two-part test has emerged in the context of social media platforms operated by public officials. If members of the public in general are allowed to post commentary on the site, a potential freedom of speech issue arises if the public official deletes commentary by an individual or blocks a particular individual from posting comments on the site. The key preliminary question is whether the public official's action constitutes state action. To establish state action, the plaintiff must show that "the official (1) possessed actual authority to speak on the State's behalf, and (2) purported to exercise that authority when he spoke on social media." *Lindke v. Freed*, 601 U.S. 187, 198 (2024). Actual authority to speak on behalf of the state (or local government) can be found in statutes, ordinances, regulations, or in longstanding practices that have the force of law. Whether the government actor was, in fact, exercising or purporting to exercise such a vested authority requires a context-specific inquiry into the postings at issue. If the social media platform is the official website of a government agency, the state action question is easily resolved in the affirmative. If, however, the website is the personal website of the government official, a closer examination is required.

Example 1-N

Fred created a private Facebook profile that he initially shared only with "friends." When Fred began nearing the platform's 5,000-friend limit, he converted his profile to a public "page." This meant that anyone could see and comment on his posts. Shortly thereafter, Fred was appointed city manager of Port Huron, Michigan, and he updated his Facebook page to reflect the new job. For his profile picture, Fred chose a photo of himself in a suit with a city lapel pin. In the "About" section, Fred added his title, a link to the city's website, and the city's general email address. He described himself as "Daddy to Lucy, Husband to Jessie and City Manager, Chief Administrative Officer for the citizens of Port Huron, MI." As before his appointment, Fred operated his Facebook page himself. And, as before his appointment, Fred posted prolifically (and primarily) about his personal life. He uploaded hundreds of photos of his family. He also posted information related to his job. He described mundane activities, like visiting local high schools, as well as splashier ones, like starting reconstruction of the city's boat launch. He shared news about the city's efforts to streamline leaf pickup and stabilize water intake from a local river. He highlighted communications from other city officials, like a press release from the fire chief and an annual financial report from the finance department. On occasion, Fred solicited feedback from the public. Fred's readers frequently commented on his posts and Fred often replied to the comments, including by answering inquiries from city residents. After the COVID-19 pandemic began, Fred posted about that. Some posts were personal, others related to Fred's job, like a description of the city's hiring freeze and a screenshot of a press release about a relief package that he helped prepare.

Kevin was unhappy with the city's approach to the pandemic. He visited Fred's Facebook page and posted derogatory comments about the city's policy and Fred's support of it. Fred eventually deleted Kevin's comments and blocked Kevin from posting comments on the page. Kevin sued Fred claiming a violation of his First Amendment rights. Did Fred's act of deleting and blocking Kevin's COVID-19 comments constitute state action?

Explanation

To establish state action, Kevin must show that state or local law authorized Fred to speak on the city's behalf in the specific context of the city's COVID-19 policies. To answer this question, we must look to statutes, ordinances, regulations, and any persistent customs or usages that carry the force of law. No such sources are cited in the problem. Hence, unless Kevin can show a state-based authorization for Fred's COVID-19 postings, the court will be required to dismiss Kevin's claim due to an absence of state action.

Assuming that Kevin satisfies the authorization prong of the state action inquiry, Kevin must also show that Fred's postings purported to be pursuant to that authorization. In assessing this aspect of the state-action inquiry, the court must look to the context, including the general type of social media platform, the overall content of the commentary on the platform, and the specific topic being addressed in that commentary. Taking these considerations together, nothing in the facts suggests that Fred purported to be speaking on the city's behalf. Rather, his postings appear to be designed to provide his constituents with information. In addition, the fact that his Facebook page contains a link to the city's official website suggests that Fred is not speaking on the city's behalf.

In the case on which this problem is based, the Supreme Court remanded to the lower courts to permit a more detailed examination of the facts as they pertain to the above two-part test. *Lindke v. Freed*, 601 U.S. 187 (2024); and see *O'Connor-Ratcliff v. Garnier*, 601 U.S. 205 (2024) (per curiam) (remanding similar case).

Regardless of the approach taken, the Court's state action doctrine contains a built-in flexibility that allows public policy to play a role in deciding whether constitutional restraints should extend to the conduct in question. In *Halleck*, the Court voiced concern that finding state action there could so broaden the reach of the First Amendment as to ultimately result in less rather than more speech, defeating one of the goals of the First Amendment. For that reason, said the Court,

> merely hosting speech by others . . . does not alone transform private entities into state actors subject to First Amendment constraints.
>
> If the rule were otherwise, all private property owners and lessees who open their property for speech would be subject to First Amendment constraints and would lose the ability to exercise what they deem to be appropriate editorial discretion within that open forum. Private property owners and private lessees would face the unappetizing choice of allowing all comers or closing the platform altogether.

Manhattan Community Access Corp. v. Halleck, 587 U.S. 802, 812-813 (2019). The doctrine's flexibility allowed the Court to avoid what it feared might otherwise be a highly undesirable outcome.

Example 1-O

The National Collegiate Athletic Association (NCAA) is a voluntary association of approximately 960 public and private universities. The role of the NCAA is to adopt rules governing member institutions' recruiting, admissions, academic eligibility, and financial aid standards for student athletes. The NCAA's Committee on Infractions is expressly authorized to conduct investigations into alleged infractions of the rules, to make findings, and to impose sanctions. Member institutions agree contractually to abide by the committee's findings and to comply with any sanctions imposed. The committee conducted such an investigation of the men's table-tennis program at Casino University (CU), a state university and a member of the NCAA. The committee found that Jerry Sharkanian, CU's head table-tennis coach, had violated numerous recruiting rules. Consequently, the NCAA imposed sanctions on CU and issued an order to show cause why further sanctions should not issue unless CU removed Sharkanian as head coach. The university decided to remove Sharkanian rather than risk further NCAA sanctions. Sharkanian filed suit against both CU and the NCAA, claiming that the committee's hearing procedures violated the Due Process Clause of the Fourteenth Amendment. Did the NCAA's actions constitute state action?

Explanation

First, we must consider whether the claimed deprivation was caused by the exercise of some right or privilege created by the state, or by a rule of conduct imposed by the state or by a person for whom the state is responsible. Although the procedures challenged by Sharkanian were not created by the state but by the NCAA, the privilege to conduct the investigation was delegated to the NCAA by the state (i.e., by CU, a state university). Thus, in holding the hearings and imposing sanctions on CU, the NCAA was exercising a privilege that could not otherwise have been exercised without the approval of the state. Moreover, CU's delegation of authority over university personnel matters would seem to make the NCAA a "person for whom the state is responsible."

Assuming our first conclusion is correct, we must next consider whether the NCAA was a state actor. The NCAA did act together with state officials. The NCAA held an investigation and imposed sanctions. The university, which was contractually bound to the NCAA, adhered to the committee's findings and removed Sharkanian from his position rather than risk further sanctions. Thus, CU and the NCAA acted jointly to deprive Sharkanian of his job, much like a private litigant who bribes a state judge to rule against an opposing party and thereby deprives that party of his or her property. See *Dennis v. Sparks*, 449 U.S. 24 (1980) (discussed in § 1.4.1, under "Joint Activity Between a State and a Private Party").

It would seem, therefore, that the activity of the NCAA constituted state action. However, on facts similar to those described here, the Court ruled otherwise, finding no state action. *National Collegiate Athletic Assn. v. Tarkanian*, 488 U.S. 179 (1988). The five-person majority reasoned that the state university had not delegated its authority to the NCAA, since the university remained free to withdraw from the NCAA at any time. Moreover, the Court said that the fired coach, Jerry Tarkanian, was dismissed by the university and not by the NCAA. Since the final act was undertaken by the state, the preliminary acts of the NCAA would not be construed as state action, particularly since the state could ignore the NCAA's orders by simply withdrawing from the NCAA. Thus, in the majority's view, there was no joint activity between the state university and the NCAA. Id. at 191-199. In terms of the *Lugar* two-part approach, the claimed deprivation of due process was solely the product of private conduct, namely, the NCAA hearing procedures, and not the result of the exercise of a right or privilege created by the state. Nor was the NCAA a state actor. It did not act together with the state, the state university being free at all times to withdraw from the NCAA.

The four-person dissent challenged the majority's assertions and argued that the factual pattern presented an unremarkable example of joint activity between a state and a private actor. Id. at 199-203 (White, J., dissenting). Indeed, a strong argument can be made that the state university and the NCAA were involved in a mutually beneficial symbiotic relationship. The majority rejected this argument. But see *Cohane v. National Collegiate Athletic Assn.*, 215 Fed. Appx. 13 (2d Cir.), *cert. denied*, 552 U.S. 1022 (2007) (distinguishing *Tarkanian* and finding plaintiff's complaint sufficient to establish state action on NCAA's part).

Example 1-O contains an important lesson. Under the facts given, one could argue both for and against a finding of state action. Neither the *Lugar* two-part approach nor the categorical approach will provide a definitive answer to the inquiry. Nor will reliance on precedent alone. At best, these approaches help focus the discussion and thereby highlight the critical doctrinal differences between opposing views. But those doctrinal differences may belie the policy judgments that are often at the heart of state action decisions. The *Tarkanian* case presents a good example of this phenomenon. Had the Court found state action, a wide array of activities engaged in by the NCAA would have come under constitutional scrutiny, thus creating a new source of constitutional litigation of both uncertain dimensions and equally uncertain consequences. *Tarkanian* foreclosed that possibility on rather thin doctrinal reasoning, leaving one to ponder whether a desire to limit the scope of judicial review did not play a part in the Court's judgment.

The Court's decision in *Tarkanian* is to be contrasted with its subsequent decision in *Brentwood Academy v. Tennessee Secondary School Athletic Assn.*, 531 U.S. 288 (2001). At issue in *Brentwood Academy* was whether activity undertaken by a private organization, the Tennessee Secondary School Athletic Association (TSSAA), charged with overseeing interscholastic athletic competition among both public and private schools within the State of Tennessee, could be deemed state action. A mechanical application of *Tarkanian* would seem to suggest a negative answer because the TSSAA and the NCAA stand in similar positions with respect to their governance of athletic competition among member schools. The Court, however, concluded that the facts of the cases were distinguishable, leading it to reject the "strict holding" of *Tarkanian*. Id. at 297. To begin with, the TSSAA operated within a single state, thus making the relationship between it and the state more clearly defined than the relationship between any single state and the NCAA. In addition, the public schools of Tennessee not only dominated the membership of the TSSAA (84%) but also allowed their employees (superintendents, principals, vice-principals, and teachers) to devote official working time to running the organization, provided a substantial source of funding for the TSSAA by ceding it the power to charge admission at all interscholastic games, and generally vested the TSSAA with the authority to regulate "an integral element of secondary public schooling." Id. at 299. The Court also observed that members of the State Board of Education were assigned ex officio status on the governing bodies of the TSSAA. Taking all these facts together, the Court explained:

> The entwinement down from the State Board is therefore unmistakable, just as the entwinement up from the member public schools is overwhelming. Entwinement will support a conclusion that an ostensibly private organization ought to be charged with a public character and judged by constitutional standards; entwinement to the degree shown here requires it.

Id. at 302. The Court concluded by finding that there were no policy considerations that would lead to a different conclusion. Specifically, the Court rejected as factually unfounded the TSSAA's contention that a finding of state action would lead to an explosion of § 1983 suits against similar organizations, for this had not been the experience in those federal circuits that had treated such interscholastic regulatory organizations as state actors. Id. at 304.

Notice that the Court's decision in *Brentwood Academy* presents an example of the "joint activity" category of state action that falls somewhere between the conspiracy cases and the symbiotic relationship cases, for the Court did not require a showing of either a conspiracy or a mutually beneficial relationship. The degree of the entwinement alone sufficed to establish state action. In this sense, the "entwinement" principle applied by the Court reflects the adaptability of the underlying doctrine as well as the essential nature of the state action inquiry, namely, whether under the facts and circumstances presented the ostensibly private action ought to be subject to constitutional restraint.

Example 1-P

A white criminal defendant who was charged in state court with assaulting an African American attempted to exercise his allotted peremptory challenges to exclude African Americans from his jury. The prosecution objected to the defendant's racially discriminatory use of peremptory challenges on the ground that it violated the equal protection rights of potential jurors. Does the use of peremptory challenges by a criminal defendant constitute state action?

Explanation

First, both the existence and the scope of peremptory challenges are created by state law. Thus, the claimed deprivation of equal protection rights under the given facts was the product of a right or privilege having its source in state authority. The first part of *Lugar* is, therefore, satisfied.

As to the second part of *Lugar*, the defendant's exercise of peremptory challenges constitutes joint activity with the state, since it could not be accomplished without the assistance of the state judge. Indeed, the entire jury selection system is dependent on participation by state officers and the force of state law. Consequently, a criminal defendant exercising peremptory challenges on a racially discriminatory basis will be deemed a state actor, and the state action requirements are, therefore, met. See *Georgia v. McCollum*, 505 U.S. 42, 50-53 (1992) (so holding on similar facts); see also *Edmonson v. Leesville Concrete Co.*, 500 U.S. 614 (1991) (private litigant exercising peremptory challenges is state actor).

Georgia v. McCollum, on which Example 1-P is based, also presents an example of policy playing a role in a finding of state action. As part of its *Lugar* analysis, the *McCollum* Court emphasized the negative consequences of permitting a criminal defendant to employ racially discriminatory peremptory challenges. "Regardless of who precipitated the jurors' removal, the perception and the reality in a criminal trial will be that the court has excused jurors based on race, an outcome that will be attributed to the State." 505 U.S. at 53. This is much the same policy concern that animated the Court in *Shelley v. Kraemer*, where the Court found that a state court's enforcement of a racially restrictive covenant violates the Equal Protection Clause. There, the "perception and the reality" would have been that the court was forcing private parties to discriminate based on race. A similar perception problem may have played a role in *Burton v. Wilmington Parking Authority*, where the restaurant that discriminated based on race was located in a building that bore the city's name and flew the state flag.

A State Actor Anomaly

As should be evident by now, problems in the context of state action focus largely on those circumstances under which the activities of a private party may be said to qualify as state action. When the party being sued is an officer or employee of the state, the difficulty disappears, and as Justice White observed in *Lugar*, the two-part inquiry collapses into a single principle. 457 U.S. at 937. A state officer, when operating in an official capacity, is a state actor whose activities stem from a right or privilege created by state law. Thus, state action is easily satisfied under such circumstances. There is, however, one narrow exception to this rule.

In *Polk County v. Dodson*, 454 U.S. 312 (1981), the Court held that the activities of a county public defender undertaken in the normal course of representing a criminal defendant do not constitute state action. Although the public defender was a public employee, the Court explained that the public defender, as an attorney, was professionally independent from and in fact an adversary of the state in representing her client. In essence, the public defender's actions were a private matter that could not be attributed to the state. Id. at 319-324. Thus, the special nature of the attorney-client relationship altered the almost universally applicable rule that activities by state officers or employees constitute state action.

The Court has not applied *Polk County* beyond the specific context of that case. See *Tower v. Glover*, 467 U.S. 914, 920 (1984) (conspiracy between public defender and other state officials to secure criminal defendant's conviction constitutes state action). In *West v. Atkins*, 487 U.S. 42 (1988), the Court held that the activities of a doctor under contract with a state constitute state action despite the professional status of the doctor. The Court distinguished *Polk County* as involving the unique ethical obligations of a criminal defense attorney who was an adversary to the state. Id. at 50-52. In general, therefore, the activities of professionals employed by or under contract to a state are attributable to the state under *Lugar*. Id. at 52.

§1.5 CONGRESSIONAL ENFORCEMENT OF THE CIVIL WAR AMENDMENTS

The Thirteenth, Fourteenth, and Fifteenth Amendments each include a clause that grants Congress the power to enforce the provisions of the underlying Amendment. Much of this country's civil rights legislation is premised on these enforcement clauses. Their scope, therefore, can be of critical importance. Note, however, that civil rights legislation may also be premised on other granted powers, including those found in Article I, § 8. See *Heart of Atlanta Motel, Inc. v. United States*, 379 U.S. 241 (1964) (affirming use of Commerce Clause to validate the Civil Rights Act of 1964); *Katzenbach v. McClung*, 379 U.S. 294 (1964) (same); *National Power & Federalism*, supra, ch. 5. In the subsections that follow, however, our focus will be solely on the enforcement powers created by the Civil War Amendments. You should, nonetheless, cross-reference these materials with your understanding of the overall scope of congressional powers.

§1.5.1 Enforcement of the Thirteenth Amendment

The Thirteenth Amendment to the U.S. Constitution expressly abolishes slavery within the United States:

> Neither slavery nor involuntary servitude, except as a punishment for crime whereof the party shall have been duly convicted, shall exist within the United States, or any place subject to their jurisdiction.

U.S. Const. amend. 13, § 1. The abolition is self-executing, and unlike the Fourteenth Amendment, its force applies to both state and private action. *Civil Rights Cases*, 109 U.S. 3, 20-23 (1883). Thus, with the adoption of the Thirteenth Amendment, all forms of slavery or involuntary servitude, both public and private, were banned within the United States.

Despite the self-executing quality of the abolition, however, the authors of the Thirteenth Amendment recognized that legislation would be required to enforce the grant of universal freedom. To that end, § 2 of the Thirteenth Amendment provides that "Congress shall have power to enforce this article by appropriate legislation." This grant of power "clothes Congress with power to pass all laws necessary and proper for abolishing all *badges and incidents* of slavery in the United States; . . ." Id. at 20 (emphasis supplied). Given the scope of the Thirteenth Amendment, that power may be addressed to both public and private conduct.

In the *Civil Rights Cases*, the Court provided a partial list of what it considered to be the badges and incidents of slavery:

> Compulsory service of the slave for the benefit of the master, restraint of his movements except by the master's will, disability to hold property, to make contracts, to have a standing in court, to be a witness against a white person, and such like burdens and incapacities were the inseparable incidents of the institution.

Id. at 22. Under § 2 of the Amendment, Congress has the power to pass legislation designed to eradicate all such practices.

The most important modern case interpreting and applying the Thirteenth Amendment is *Jones v. Alfred H. Mayer Co.*, 392 U.S. 409 (1968). The controversy in *Jones* arose out of a private company's refusal to sell a home to an African American couple. The couple brought suit under 42 U.S.C. § 1982, a statute passed pursuant to the Thirteenth Amendment. Section 1982 provides:

> All citizens of the United States shall have the same right, in every State and Territory, as is enjoyed by white citizens thereof to inherit, purchase, lease, sell, hold, and convey real and personal property.

The lower courts dismissed the suit, having concluded that § 1982 applied only to state action. Two questions were presented to the Supreme Court: First, did the statute apply to private action? Second, if it did, was the statute a valid exercise of Congress's power to enforce the Thirteenth Amendment?

The Court first concluded that the plain language of the statute prohibited all racial discrimination, both public and private, in the sale or rental of property. 392 U.S. at 422-436. Next, the Court explained that the authority given to Congress under § 2 of the Thirteenth Amendment included the power to enact laws that directly regulate the activities of private individuals. Id. at 438. This was so because the Thirteenth Amendment itself was directed at all forms of slavery, both public and private. Id. The only question, therefore, was whether Congress had authority to conclude that racial barriers to the acquisition of property were a badge or incident of slavery. In answering this question, the Court adopted a deferential rational basis test:

> Surely Congress has the power under the Thirteenth Amendment rationally to determine what are the badges and the incidents of slavery, and the authority to translate that determination into effective legislation. Nor can we say that the determination Congress has made is an irrational one. For this Court recognized long ago that, whatever else they may have encompassed, the badges and incidents of slavery—its "burdens and disabilities"—included restraints upon "those fundamental rights which are the essence of civil freedom, namely, the same right . . . to inherit, purchase, lease, sell and convey property, as is enjoyed by white citizens."

Id. at 440-441 (quoting *Civil Rights Cases*, supra, 109 U.S. at 22). Later in its opinion, the Court observed, "If Congress cannot say that being a free man means at least this much, then the Thirteenth Amendment made a promise the Nation cannot keep." 392 U.S. at 443.

Under *Jones*, therefore, the scope of Congress's power to enforce the Thirteenth Amendment is measured by the rationality of a congressional determination that the activity being regulated or prohibited is a badge or incident of slavery. This is a deferential standard designed to recognize the broad latitude of the authority vested in Congress by § 2 of the Thirteenth Amendment.

Example I-Q

Title 42 U.S.C. § 1981 provides that "[a]ll persons within the jurisdiction of the United States shall have the same right in every State . . . to make and enforce contracts . . . as is enjoyed by white citizens. . . ." By judicial construction, § 1981 applies to private action. The African-American parents of a child who had been denied admission to a private school because of the child's race brought suit against the school under § 1981. They argued that the school had refused to enter into a contract with them because of their race. The trial court held that § 1981 applied to the facts before it; that the refusal to admit was a refusal to enter into a contract; and that since the refusal was racially motivated, the proscription of § 1981 applied. Given this construction, does § 1981 represent a constitutional exercise of congressional power under the Thirteenth Amendment?

Explanation

Yes. Like the right to purchase property, the right to make or enter into contracts is a basic civil right that was denied to slaves. Consequently, the denial of both rights was recognized in the *Civil Rights Cases* as badges and incidents of slavery. 109 U.S. at 22. Thus, Congress could rationally conclude that a racial barrier to the making of a contract is a badge or incident of slavery. That being the case, § 1981 falls squarely within the enforcement power granted to Congress by § 2 of the Thirteenth Amendment. See *Runyon v. McCrary*, 427 U.S. 160, 179 (1976) (so holding under similar facts). The fact that § 1981 regulates private activity does not alter this conclusion, since the Thirteenth Amendment limits both private and public activity.

Example I-R

John and Julia, both of whom are African American college students, spent their summer vacation working as volunteers in a voter registration program in a large, rural county in Mississippi. One evening while they were driving along a country road, three local white residents stopped them at gunpoint. While two of the locals pointed guns at the couple, the third beat John and Julia severely and threatened to kill them if they did not leave the community. John and Julia have filed suit against their three assailants under 42 U.S.C. § 1985(3), which provides a cause of action against anyone who conspires to deprive "any person or class of persons of the equal protection of the laws, or of the equal privileges and immunities under the laws. . . ." On the correct assumption that § 1985(3) applies under the given facts, does the statute come within Congress's § 2 powers under the Thirteenth Amendment?

Explanation

Yes. John and Julia were engaged in the exercise of a basic civil right, namely, the right to use public highways and thoroughfares without restraint. This is a right that the law secures to all free members of society. Hence, a private conspiracy to deny that right to African Americans can be rationally described as a badge or incident of slavery.

The preceding example was based loosely on the facts of *Griffin v. Breckenridge*, 403 U.S. 88, 105 (1971), where the Court observed:

> [T]he varieties of private conduct that [Congress] may make criminally punishable or civilly remediable extend far beyond the actual imposition of slavery or involuntary servitude. By the Thirteenth Amendment, we committed ourselves as a Nation to the proposition that the former slaves and their descendants should be forever free. . . . We can only conclude that Congress was wholly within its powers under § 2 of the Thirteenth Amendment in creating a statutory cause of action for Negro citizens who have been the victims of conspiratorial, racially discriminatory private action aimed at depriving them of the basic rights that the law secures to all free men.

The concept of a badge or incident of slavery is not, however, completely elastic. In *Memphis v. Greene*, 451 U.S. 100, 124-129 (1981), for example, the Court held that the closing of a street that incidentally set up a barrier between white and African American communities was not a badge or incident of slavery. Yet the Court's conclusion may well have been different had there been evidence establishing that the street closing was purposefully designed to segregate these neighborhoods.

The Court has yet to hold that the Thirteenth Amendment enforcement power may be exercised beyond the context of racial discriminations. See *Bray v. Alexandria Women's Health Clinic*, 506 U.S. 263, 269 (1993) (declining to decide whether animus toward women falls within the proscription of § 1985(3)). The Court has, however, construed statutes enforcing the Thirteenth Amendment as including discriminations against racial groups other than African Americans. See *Shaare Tefila Congregation v. Cobb*, 481 U.S. 615 (1987) (person of Jewish ancestry may state a cause of action under § 1982); *Saint Francis College v. Al-Khazraji*, 481 U.S. 604 (1987) (person of Arab ancestry may state a cause of action under § 1981); *McDonald v. Santa Fe Trail Transp. Co.*, 427 U.S. 273, 285-296 (1976) (white person may state a cause of action under § 1981).

§1.5.2 Enforcement of the Fourteenth Amendment

Section 5 of the Fourteenth Amendment provides, "The Congress shall have power to enforce, by appropriate legislation, the provisions of this article." Pursuant to this grant of authority, Congress may adopt measures it deems necessary and proper to the implementation or enforcement of the provisions of § 1 of that Amendment—specifically, the Privileges or Immunities, Due Process, and Equal Protection Clauses. Given the *Slaughter-House Cases'* relatively limited interpretation of the Fourteenth Amendment's privileges or immunities, the primary, if not exclusive, focus of the Fourteenth Amendment enforcement power has been the enforcement of the due process and equal protection guarantees.

As a general matter, the scope of the Fourteenth Amendment enforcement power is as broad in its context as is the authority vested in Congress by the Necessary and Proper Clause in Article 1, § 8. *Katzenbach v. Morgan*, 384 U.S. 641, 650 (1966). The Court's decision in *McCulloch v. Maryland*, 17 U.S. (4 Wheat.) 316, 421 (1819), therefore, provides the guiding principles:

> Let the end be legitimate, let it be within the scope of the constitution, and all means which are appropriate, which are plainly adapted to that end, which are not prohibited, but consist with the letter and spirit of the constitution, are constitutional.

See *Katzenbach v. Morgan*, supra, 384 U.S. at 650-658 (applying *McCulloch* standards in context of Fourteenth Amendment enforcement power).

The standards of *McCulloch* do not, however, vest Congress with an unreviewable authority to interpret the Fourteenth Amendment. Rather, at least in the Court's view, § 5 vests Congress only with a discretion, albeit quite broad, to select the "means" through which to enforce the underlying constitutional guarantees, the definition of which remains largely a judicial prerogative. In other words, the § 5 enforcement power does not vest Congress with the authority to define the scope of Fourteenth Amendment rights; instead, it grants Congress the power only to enact measures designed to remedy or prevent violations of rights that are ultimately defined in the process of judicial review. Of course, in enforcing constitutional rights, Congress must engage in a process of interpretation, but whatever interpretation Congress may adopt will be subject to judicial review. Therefore, before we can determine whether any particular exercise of the § 5 enforcement power is within constitutional bounds, we must first define the scope of the right to be enforced.

Problems surrounding the application of the § 5 enforcement power can be seen as clustered around three types of remedial measures:

1. Those that require the plaintiff to prove the violation of a judicially recognized Fourteenth Amendment right;
2. Those that do not require the plaintiff to prove a violation of a judicially recognized Fourteenth Amendment right, but which are nonetheless designed to remedy or prevent the violation of a judicially recognized right; and
3. Those that purport to create Fourteenth Amendment rights not recognized by the judiciary.

The first category we will refer to as parallel enforcement, the second as nonparallel enforcement, and the third as congressional interpretation.

Parallel Enforcement

Parallel enforcement occurs when the congressionally created remedy encompasses all elements of the judicially recognized Fourteenth Amendment right. Essentially, the test here is one of rational basis: Could Congress rationally conclude that the adopted enforcement mechanism—e.g., a private action for money damages to remedy the violation of a constitutional right—was an "appropriate" means to redress or prevent violation of that right? Consistent with the jurisprudence of *McCulloch v. Maryland*, a Court is quite unlikely to second-guess congressional judgment on this score. The creation of such "parallel" private rights of action represents a standard and constitutional exercise of the Fourteenth Amendment enforcement power.

Consider the equal protection proscription against racial discrimination. As we will discuss in further detail in Chapter 6, under the Equal Protection Clause, a state, including its agencies and officers, may not intentionally discriminate based on race except under the narrowest of circumstances. To establish a violation of this equal protection principle, a victim of such discrimination must prove both state action and the prima facie elements of purposeful racial classification and disproportionate racial impact. To enforce this right, Congress could create a private civil remedy for money damages and/or equitable relief. If the statutory scheme required the plaintiff to prove all the elements of a constitutional equal protection claim—namely, state action, purposeful racial classification, and disproportionate impact—the congressionally created remedy would easily pass muster as an exercise of the Fourteenth Amendment enforcement power. Such a parallel measure represents a rational method for enforcing the underlying and judicially recognized constitutional right.

Example 1-S

Eugene, a Japanese American, claims that he was dismissed from his position at State University because of his Asian heritage. He has filed a lawsuit against his supervisor, Smith, seeking reinstatement and back pay, claiming that Smith's actions denied him "equal protection of the law." In so doing, Eugene relies on a federal statute, 42 U.S.C. § 1983, first enacted in 1871, that provides a cause of action for legal or equitable relief against any "person" who, while acting "under color of" state law, violates someone's federal constitutional or statutory rights. Those who may be sued as "persons" under this statute include cities, counties, and other political subdivisions of a state, as well as individual state and local governmental officials. However, suit cannot be brought under § 1983 against a state itself or against a state level agency. Does this statute, as applied in this case, represent a constitutional exercise of Congress's Fourteenth Amendment enforcement power?

Explanation

Yes. Eugene is suing a state employee, not the state itself, so his claim falls within § 1983. If we assume that "equal protection of the law" as asserted in his complaint means equal protection as defined by the judicial branch, then Eugene will be required to establish a prima facie equal protection violation to prevail. Moreover, the "color of state law" requirement is, as was noted above, the virtual equivalent of state action. Therefore, the federal statute as applied in this case represents an unremarkable application of the Fourteenth Amendment enforcement power through which Congress has provided a remedy for the violation of a judicially recognized Fourteenth Amendment right. There is nothing to indicate that this remedial scheme is irrational.

The Court has never held a parallel enforcement mechanism to be beyond Congress's § 5 enforcement power. The Court has also made it clear that Congress, in providing for parallel enforcement of federal constitutional rights, can create a cause of action that plaintiffs may elect to bring in either state or federal court. States cannot then close their courthouse doors to such lawsuits simply because the state may be hostile to having such suits brought against their officials, or because they believe their courts are already overcrowded. See *Haywood v. Drown*, 556 U.S. 729 (2009) (invalidating a New York statute that barred plaintiffs from bringing a § 1983 action in state court against state corrections officers). Thus, in Example 1-S, Eugene had the choice of filing his § 1983 suit in either state or federal court, whichever he deemed to be the most convenient and advantageous.

Nonparallel Enforcement

Nonparallel enforcement occurs when Congress designs a remedy for the enforcement of a judicially recognized constitutional right but allows that remedy to be invoked without requiring the plaintiff to establish a violation of the right itself. For example, Congress may not require the plaintiff to prove every element of the constitutional right, or Congress may create a completely new statutory right designed to insulate the constitutional right from violation. To establish the constitutionality of such measures, Congress must show that the nonparallel enforcement mechanism is designed to remedy the violation of a judicially recognized constitutional right and that the remedy is tailored to accomplish that goal. The test is sometimes characterized as one of rational basis, though recently the Court seems to have adopted a somewhat closer level of scrutiny. The reason for this closer scrutiny stems in part from the current Court's concern for state sovereignty.

Example 1-T

Suppose that the statute described in Example 1-S provided that purposeful racial discrimination would be presumed if the plaintiff showed that he had been dismissed from his job, that he was a member of a racial minority, and that the person hired as a replacement was not a member of a racial minority. The state could rebut the presumption only by showing a legitimate, nonracial business necessity for the dismissal. Thus, Eugene could prevail under this statute without proving a necessary element of an equal protection violation, namely, purposeful discrimination. Would such a statute be valid as an exercise of Congress's § 5 enforcement power?

Explanation

The constitutionality of this congressional action depends on whether Congress acted rationally in devising this remedial scheme. In other words, did Congress have reasonable grounds to believe that a presumption of intent under such circumstances was appropriate to the enforcement of a judicially recognized Fourteenth Amendment right? Possibly. Suppose that Congress concluded that proof of racially motivated intent in state employment discrimination cases was particularly problematic because such intent was rarely documented and could be easily hidden behind ostensibly neutral justifications. Moreover, suppose that Congress found that, because of such problems of proof, the full vindication of equal protection rights in the state employment context was threatened. Under such circumstances, a court may well find that Congress had acted within its § 5 enforcement powers. This is particularly so because the statute is narrowly focused on a particular type of problem, namely, racial discrimination in state employment, and because it provides a mechanism under which the state can rebut the presumption of intent. Therefore, the remedy is not likely to be viewed as overly intrusive into state employment policies. See *In re Employment Discrimination Litigation Against the State of Alabama*, 198 F.3d 1305, 1318-1324 (11th Cir. 1999) (reaching a similar conclusion on similar facts under Title VII of 1964 Civil Rights Act).

Another variation of this second category occurs with statutes that create federal rights that are not themselves embodied in the Fourteenth Amendment but that are designed to ensure the full vindication of Fourteenth Amendment rights. This was the type of problem presented to the Court in *Katzenbach v. Morgan*, 384 U.S. 641 (1966). At issue was a section of the Voting Rights Act of 1965 that prohibited states from denying the right to vote to certain Puerto Ricans who could not read or write English. In other words, the Voting Rights Act created a federal right to be free from literacy tests under specified circumstances. The Court had previously held that the Fourteenth Amendment did not itself create any such right. *Lassiter v. Northampton Election Bd.*, 360 U.S. 45 (1959). Nonetheless, the Court upheld this section of the Voting Rights Act as an appropriate exercise of the Fourteenth Amendment enforcement power. In the Court's words,

> It was well within congressional authority to say that this need of the Puerto Rican minority for the vote warranted federal intrusion upon any state interests served by the English literacy requirement. It was for Congress, as the branch that made this judgment, to assess and weigh the various conflicting considerations—*the risk or pervasiveness of the discrimination in governmental services*, the effectiveness of eliminating the state restriction on the right to vote as a means of dealing with the evil, the adequacy or availability of alternative remedies, and the nature and significance of the state interests that would be affected by the nullification of the English literacy requirement. . . . It is not for us to review the congressional resolution of these factors. It is enough that we be able to perceive a basis upon which the Congress might resolve the conflict as it did.

384 U.S. at 653 (emphasis supplied). In short, the Court deferred to the congressional judgment that the literacy test ban was a rational means to prevent violations of the equal protection guarantee against racial discrimination in the provision of governmental services.

Katzenbach was decided during an era in which the Court was highly deferential to exercises of congressional power, and particularly so in the context of civil rights. Although *Katzenbach* continues to be cited authoritatively, the current Court is, as you may be aware, much less solicitous of broad assertions of congressional power, especially when those assertions interfere with what the Court perceives as the traditional prerogatives of the states. See *National Power & Federalism*, supra, § 4.2.8 (restrictions on congressional abrogation of Eleventh Amendment immunity); § 5.3.4 (restrictions on commerce power). This less deferential judicial attitude has led to what may be described as a tightening of the standards under which nonparallel exercises of the § 5 enforcement power are now measured. Under these new standards, if Congress creates a nonparallel statutory right, the exercise of power will be upheld only if the statutory right is both "congruent" with judicially recognized constitutional rights and "proportional" in terms of the remedy it provides. In other words, it must be shown that the statutory right is truly designed to protect a judicially recognized constitutional right and that the remedy is in proportion to the scope of the perceived constitutional violation. The judicial scrutiny of congruence and proportionality is not particularly deferential.

The Court first applied these new principles in *City of Boerne v. Flores*, 521 U.S. 507 (1997). There the Court held that Congress had exceeded its § 5 power in enacting the Religious Freedom Restoration Act (RFRA). RFRA was passed in response to the Court's decision in *Employment Division v. Smith*, 494 U.S. 872 (1990). In *Smith*, the Court had held that the Free Exercise Clause, as incorporated by the Fourteenth Amendment, does not prevent a state from punishing the use of peyote by a practicing member of the Native American Church. This is so even though the ingestion of peyote is an integral part of the church's system of worship. Since the law at issue was neutral from a religious perspective—i.e., it applied to all uses of peyote regardless of the user's religious beliefs or practices—the Court found no violation of the Free Exercise Clause despite the impact of the law on the practices of the Native American Church. According to the *Smith* Court, as long as a law is not purposefully directed at religious practices—i.e., as long as the law is neutral and of general applicability—it can be enforced without violating the proscriptions of the Free Exercise Clause. This remains true even if the law incidentally and substantially interferes with a religious practice. See § 9.5. Under *Smith*, therefore, only laws designed to prohibit a religious practice because of the religious nature of that practice will run afoul of the First and Fourteenth Amendments.

RFRA was enacted to overrule *Smith* and to require the application of a compelling state interest test whenever any law, enacted at any level of government, substantially burdened a religious practice, regardless of the law's perceived neutrality. For example, under RFRA, a neutral law banning the use of peyote could not be applied against a member of the Native American Church in the absence of a compelling state interest and a showing that the ban represented the least restrictive means to advance that interest.

Supporters of RFRA argued that the statute was remedial in nature and, therefore, within the scope of § 5 as interpreted in *Katzenbach v. Morgan*. In their view, RFRA was designed to ferret out ostensibly neutral laws that were enacted for purposes of religious bigotry. Thus, RFRA would in fact operate as a nonparallel remedial or preventive measure designed to enforce the precise free exercise right defined in *Smith*, namely, the proscription of laws purposefully designed to regulate or prohibit religious practices. The Court, however, did not accept this argument.

The Court in *City of Boerne* began with the proposition that "[w]hile preventive rules are sometimes appropriate remedial measures, there must be a congruence between the means used and the ends to be achieved." 521 U.S. at 530. The Court then examined the legislative history of RFRA and found it bereft of examples of "modern instances of generally applicable laws passed because of religious bigotry." Id. Although that legislative history did include modern examples of neutral laws that adversely affected religious practices, there was no showing that those incidental burdens were the product of religious bigotry or bias. As the Court phrased it, "Congress' concern was with the incidental burdens imposed, not the object or purpose of the legislation." Id. at 531. From the perspective of this legislative history, therefore, RFRA seemed to be designed not to vindicate a judicially recognized right, but to create a new right, broader in scope than any free exercise right currently recognized by the judicial branch.

More important than the absence of legislative history, however, was the lack of what the Court described as "proportionality" between the "sweeping coverage" of RFRA—a permanent and undifferentiated proscription that applied to every facet and level of government—and the violation of any perceived Fourteenth Amendment right.

> Sweeping coverage ensures its intrusion at every level of government, displacing laws and prohibiting official actions of almost every description and regardless of subject matter. . . . RFRA has no termination date or termination mechanism. Any law is subject to challenge at any time by any individual who alleges a substantial burden on his or her free exercise of religion.

Id. at 532. The Court further noted that prior exercises of the § 5 power had been carefully designed to address specific and sometimes notorious violations of Fourteenth Amendment rights. Thus, provisions of the Voting Rights Act subjecting states to Department of Justice review were limited in application to those states with a history of intentional racial discrimination in voting and lapsed in seven years. As the Court observed,

> This is not to say, of course, that § 5 legislation requires termination dates, geographic restrictions, or egregious predicates. Where, however, a congressional enactment pervasively prohibits constitutional state action in an effort to remedy or to prevent unconstitutional state action, limitations of this kind tend to ensure Congress' means are proportionate to ends legitimate under § 5.

Id. at 533.

In short, RFRA failed to pass constitutional muster because, in the Court's view, the broad remedy Congress created was substantially more intrusive on state prerogatives than was warranted by the undifferentiated fear that religious bigotry might be imposed through the adoption of ostensibly neutral laws. After *City of Boerne*, therefore, congressional remedies that do not require a party to establish a violation of a Fourteenth Amendment right—i.e., nonparallel remedies—must be congruent and proportionate to the perceived violation of Fourteenth Amendment rights. Factors to consider in this assessment include the identification of the precise constitutional evil Congress seeks to remedy, the breadth of the remedy, the depth and pervasiveness of the problem being addressed, and any factors tending to limit the scope of the actual remedy to the precise problem Congress seeks to remedy. The more generalized the perceived evil and the congressional response to it, and the more intrusive that response is on state prerogatives, the less likely it is that the Court will find congruence and proportionality satisfied.

Example 1-U

EXAMPLE

Christy, a student at State University, was raped by a member of the university's varsity football team. Her assailant later publicly boasted of what he had done. Moreover, at a hearing before a university disciplinary committee, he admitted to having sexual contact with Christy even though she had twice told him "no." He was found guilty of sexual assault and suspended from school for two semesters. On appeal, the university rescinded his punishment as being "too severe." Christy then filed a civil lawsuit against her assailant under a federal statute, the Violence Against Women Act (VAWA), which provides a federal civil remedy for the victims of gender-motivated violence. To establish a claim under VAWA, Christy must show by a preponderance of the evidence that she was the victim of a violent assault by the defendant and that the assault was at least in part motivated by her gender.

Prior to adopting VAWA, Congress held hearings that established a nationwide pattern of bias in state justice systems against the enforcement of gender-based crimes. Among other things, Congress found that this pattern of bias often resulted in insufficient investigation and prosecution of gender-motivated crime and in unacceptably lenient punishments for those who are actually convicted of such crimes. While Congress did not survey every state, the information Congress gathered led it to conclude that the problem was pervasive. VAWA was designed to provide a partial remedy for this apparent pattern of gender discrimination in state law enforcement and judicial systems. Does the civil remedy created by VAWA represent a proper exercise of Congress's § 5 enforcement powers?

Explanation

To evaluate the constitutionality of VAWA's civil remedy, we must determine if the principles of "congruence" and "proportionality" have been satisfied. We begin with congruence and the underlying constitutional right, namely, the right to be free from gender discrimination in the administration of justice by the states. So described, the underlying right Congress seeks to redress appears to be congruent with the Court's standards for protecting against gender classifications under the Equal Protection Clause. See § 6.6. State action is satisfied since the focus is on state criminal justice systems, and the basic elements of a gender discrimination claim seem to be met as well—i.e., purposefulness and impact. Thus, unlike the situation in *City of Boerne v. Flores*, where Congress was seeking to protect a right the Court did not recognize, under VAWA Congress is trying to redress violations of a well-established constitutional right. Next, as to proportionality, the civil action remedy is broad-based and seemingly permanent, but it does not in any manner intrude into the processes of state government as did the remedy at issue in *Boerne*. Moreover, the breadth of the remedy—i.e., its nationwide availability—can be justified as a reasonable response to findings that indicated the presence of gender bias in the justice systems of a substantial number of states. By way of comparison, in *Boerne*, the breadth of the remedy easily exceeded any perceived constitutional violations.

On the other hand, one can also argue that congruence and proportionality are not satisfied. As to congruence, the absence of any state action requirement in the VAWA cause of action suggests that the actual congruence between gender discrimination in state justice systems and VAWA is illusory. For one thing, the remedy is not corrective of the underlying violation, for VAWA lawsuits against private individuals will not alter the patterns of discrimination in state justice systems. Moreover, the VAWA remedy can be imposed even if there is no underlying constitutional violation—i.e., even if the state fully prosecutes and punishes all acts of gender-based violence. In short, there is an apparent disconnect between the underlying right Congress seeks to protect and the remedy it has created. This brings us to proportionality. Since the VAWA remedy is available regardless of any underlying constitutional violation, to demonstrate proportionality one would arguably need to show that the pattern of gender bias is so pervasive that a more carefully circumscribed remedy would be ineffective. Congress made no such findings. It found only that there was a problem of gender bias in the justice systems of a substantial number of states. A more proportional remedy would be one that was directed only at those jurisdictions in which the presence of gender bias had been established, as was the case in *Katzenbach v. Morgan*. From this perspective, the VAWA civil remedy is not constitutional.

In *United States v. Morrison*, 529 U.S. 598 (2000), under similar facts, and adopting reasoning like that in the immediately preceding paragraph, the

Court held that the civil remedy created by VAWA was beyond the § 5 enforcement powers of Congress. Id. at 619-627. The *Morrison* Court also held that VAWA was not a valid exercise of the commerce power. Id. at 608-619. See *National Power & Federalism*, supra, § 5.3.4.

The Court has applied the *City of Boerne* congruence and proportionality test in five cases involving congressional efforts to abrogate the states' Eleventh Amendment immunity. In three of those cases, the Court found that the congressional measure failed the test. In *Florida Prepaid Postsecondary Education Expense Board v. College Savings Bank*, 527 U.S. 627 (1999), a case involving the enforcement of federal patent laws, the Court found a lack of congruence and proportionality between the abrogation of the states' immunity and any underlying constitutional right. Specifically, because there was no showing of a pattern under which states were violating the constitutional rights of patent holders, the § 5 enforcement powers were not an appropriate vehicle for abrogating the states' immunity. Similarly, in *Kimel v. Florida Board of Regents*, 528 U.S. 62 (2000), the Court found no congruence or proportionality between the provisions of the Age Discrimination in Employment Act (ADEA) and any underlying constitutional right to be free from age discrimination by the states. The state could not, therefore, be sued for statutory violations of the ADEA. Finally, in *Board of Trustees of the University of Alabama v. Garrett*, 531 U.S. 356 (2000) the Court held that the intended abrogation of state sovereign immunity in Title I of the Americans with Disabilities Act (ADA) was ineffective because the substantive provisions of the ADA were neither congruent with nor proportional to any established pattern of state violations of the judicially recognized equal protection rights of the disabled. In essence, the ADA created equality rights beyond those mandated by the Fourteenth Amendment; hence, in seeking to abrogate the states' sovereign immunity pursuant to § 5 of that amendment, Congress exceeded its constitutional powers. The flaw in all three cases was the failure of Congress to connect the remedy it was creating with the protection of a judicially recognized constitutional right. See *National Power & Federalism*, supra, § 4.2.8.

In the fourth case, however, the Court upheld a provision of the Family and Medical Leave Act of 1993 (FMLA) that gave state employees a right to spousal or parental leave under specified circumstances. The Court found that the FMLA leave provision and its accompanying right to sue a state employer were congruent and proportional to the judicially recognized right to be free from state-based gender discrimination. Given the history of gender discrimination in employee benefit plans, including state-based discrimination, the Court concluded that the FMLA was properly tailored to prevent further violations of this constitutional right. Hence, the abrogation of state sovereign immunity in this context represented a proper exercise of § 5 enforcement powers. *Nevada Dept. of Human Resources v. Hibbs*, 538 U.S. 721

(2003). The key difference between *Hibbs* and its three predecessor cases was the presence of a judicially recognized Fourteenth Amendment right in *Hibbs*, as well as a sufficient pattern of state violations of that right.

The Court's most recent application of the congruence and proportionality standard came in *Tennessee v. Lane*, 541 U.S. 509 (2004). *Lane*, like *Garrett*, involved a state's challenge to the constitutionality of a section of the ADA. In contrast to *Garrett*, however, the *Lane* Court upheld the section at issue before it. Recall that in *Garrett* the Court found neither congruence nor proportionality between the ADA's antidiscrimination principle (Title I) and the judicially recognized right of the disabled to be free only from irrational discrimination. By contrast, in *Lane*, the plaintiffs sued under Title II of the ADA, which prohibits states from denying the disabled access to certain public services. At issue in *Lane* was an alleged denial of access to state court facilities, a potential violation of the judicially recognized fundamental right of access to the courts. See §§ 2.6.3, 7.5. Hence, the Court concluded that, unlike the situation presented in *Garrett*, the *Lane* plaintiffs' "access to the courts" claim was congruent with a judicially recognized fundamental constitutional right.

As to proportionality, the *Lane* Court held that despite the broad language of Title II which covers access to fundamental public services like the courts and to nonfundamental services like state-owned hockey rinks, the proper judicial inquiry must focus specifically on the remedy that Title II imposes with respect to the courts—leaving for another day other possible applications of the Act. The Court then concluded that as applied in this setting, Title II's remedy was a proportional one, for it required only that states take "reasonable measures" to remove architectural and other barriers to accessibility. As applied in other contexts, said the Court, Title II might be found to have exceeded the scope of Congress's § 5 enforcement powers. Id. at 530-533. See, e.g., *Zied-Campbell v. Richman*, 2007 WL 1031399, at *11 (M.D. Pa., March 30, 2007), *aff'd*, 428 Fed. Appx. 224 (3d Cir. 2011), *cert. dismissed*, 565 U.S. 961(2011) (because "the remedies connected to Title II, to the extent that it regulates Pennsylvania's duty to accommodate disabled individuals in the context of the state welfare system, . . . are not congruent and proportional to the targeted constitutional infirmity," Title II therefore "does not validly abrogate the Eleventh Amendment immunity of the states.").

The decisions in *Hibbs* and *Lane* apply congruence and proportionality with somewhat more deference toward Congress than was apparent in the earlier cases adopting and applying this standard. This slightly more tolerant judicial attitude does not necessarily reflect a rejection of the earlier cases, but it does suggest that the Court continues to struggle with the scope and rigor of the congruence and proportionality standard. A certain amount of subjectivity, therefore, is likely to be reflected in the decisions.

Congressional Interpretation

The third category of Fourteenth Amendment enforcement measures is, in a sense, as simple as the first. May Congress, pursuant to its § 5 power, create independent Fourteenth Amendment rights—i.e., federal rights that are neither judicially recognized nor designed to enforce a judicially recognized right? In other words, may Congress interpret the Fourteenth Amendment to include rights not otherwise recognized by the judicial branch? For example, if the Supreme Court were to hold that women did not have a right to an abortion, could Congress, *relying solely on its § 5 enforcement power*, establish a statutory Fourteenth Amendment right to an abortion? There is a reasonable argument that Congress does possess such a power. After all, the power to enforce the Fourteenth Amendment is vested in Congress, and to exercise that power, Congress must interpret the provisions to be enforced. Yet the post-*Boerne* answer appears to be in the negative. In the words of the *Boerne* Court, "Any suggestion that Congress has a substantive, non-remedial power under the Fourteenth Amendment is not supported by our case law." 521 U.S. at 527. Moreover, the Court explained,

> If Congress could define its own powers by altering the Fourteenth Amendment's meaning, no longer would the Constitution be "superior paramount law, unchangeable by ordinary means." It would be "on a level with ordinary legislative acts, and, like other acts, . . . alterable when the legislature shall please to alter it." *Marbury v. Madison*, 1 Cranch, at 177. Under this approach, it is difficult to conceive of a principle that would limit congressional power. Shifting legislative majorities could change the Constitution and effectively circumvent the difficult and detailed amendment process contained in Article V.

Id. at 529 (internal citation omitted). To underscore these points, the *Boerne* Court gave no further consideration to the argument that RFRA reflected a congressional interpretation of the free exercise guarantee that was more encompassing than the Court's interpretation. Indeed, implicit in the Court's opinion was a conclusion that if that were the case, the creation of such a substantive right would be well beyond the legislative prerogative of Congress.

In short, congressional powers under the Fourteenth Amendment are remedial only. Congress may not use those powers to create rights not recognized by the judiciary. See also *Oregon v. Mitchell*, 400 U.S. 112 (1970) (majority rejects notion that Congress possesses plenary authority to interpret the Fourteenth Amendment without definitively holding that Congress was absolutely without power to create independent Fourteenth Amendment rights).

Finally, just as Congress may not expand Fourteenth Amendment rights, Congress may not use its § 5 power to limit the scope of judicially recognized rights. Thus, in *Mississippi University for Women v. Hogan*, 458 U.S. 718 (1982), the Court rejected an argument that Title IX of the Education

Amendments of 1972 could validly narrow the scope of the judicially recognized equal protection right to be free from gender discrimination. In the Court's words,

> Congress' power under § 5, however, "is limited to adopting measures to enforce the guarantees of the Amendment; § 5 grants Congress no power to restrict, abrogate, or dilute these guarantees." *Katzenbach v. Morgan*, 384 U.S. 641, 651, n.10 (1966). Although we give deference to congressional decisions and classifications, neither Congress nor a State can validate a law that denies the rights guaranteed by the Fourteenth Amendment.

458 U.S. at 732-733. See also *Saenz v. Roe*, 526 U.S. 489, 507 (1999) ("Congress may not authorize the States to violate the Fourteenth Amendment").

§1.5.3 Enforcement of the Fifteenth Amendment

The Fifteenth Amendment was adopted because of concerns that the Fourteenth Amendment was not broad enough to prevent states from disenfranchising the recently freed slaves. The scope of the Fifteenth Amendment is limited to racial restrictions on voting. Section 1 provides:

> The right of citizens of the United States to vote shall not be denied or abridged by the United States or by any State on account of race, color, or previous condition of servitude.

Section 2 of the Amendment provides, "The Congress shall have power to enforce this article by appropriate legislation." This enforcement power has been interpreted in essentially the same fashion and with the same breadth as the Fourteenth Amendment enforcement power.

An individual who claims denial of the right to vote by state officials based on race could bring what would amount to a "parallel" enforcement action under 42 U.S.C. § 1983, which, as we saw earlier, provides a cause of action against those acting under color of state law who deprive someone of his or her federal constitutional rights. Most of the cases construing the scope of the Fifteenth Amendment enforcement power have involved problems arising in the "nonparallel" category described in our discussion of the Fourteenth Amendment enforcement power. The standards for measuring the scope of both powers are identical. See § 1.5.2. Thus, the Court in *City of Rome v. United States*, 446 U.S. 156, 177 (1980), observed that "under § 2 of the Fifteenth Amendment Congress may prohibit practices that in and of themselves do not violate § 1 of the Amendment, so long as the prohibitions attacking racial discrimination in voting are 'appropriate,' as that term is defined in *McCulloch v. Maryland*. . . ." Of course, as this quotation suggests, the context in which the Fifteenth Amendment power can be exercised relates exclusively to racial discrimination in voting.

EXAMPLE

Example I-V

The federal Voting Rights Act was enacted in 1965 as a temporary measure that was to expire in five years. However, Congress has reauthorized the act several times—in 1970 (for five years), in 1975 (for seven years), in 1982 (for 25 years), and in 2006 (for 25 years). The act regulates the electoral laws of specified "covered" states and local communities having a demonstrated history of racial discrimination in voting and requires federal preclearance and approval of all of their election-related laws. The City of Seven Hills, a jurisdiction that falls within the coverage of the act, recently revised its local electoral system on race-neutral grounds but in a manner that would have the effect of diluting minority voting strength. While there is no evidence of purposeful discrimination in this revision, the Voting Rights Act bars implementation of the city's plan because it would have the "effect" of abridging the right to vote based on race within the meaning of the act. The city claims that, as so applied, the act exceeds Congress's power to enforce the Fifteenth Amendment. In support of its claim, the city argues that because § 1 of the Fifteenth Amendment prohibits only purposeful discrimination, Congress may not use its § 2 enforcement power to bar electoral practices merely because of their discriminatory effect. The city also contends that whatever the act's validity at the time it was first enacted, its 2006 extension exceeded the scope of Congress's § 2 power. Assuming § 1 of the Fifteenth Amendment bars only purposeful discrimination, does the Voting Rights Act, as most recently extended, exceed the Fifteenth Amendment enforcement powers of Congress?

EXPLANATION

Explanation

Under the *City of Rome* standard quoted above, the Fifteenth Amendment § 2 enforcement power allows Congress to prohibit practices that do not themselves violate § 1 of the Amendment if the prohibition is reasonably directed toward enforcement of the Amendment's underlying principles. In *City of Rome*, the Court thus upheld a 1975, 7-year reauthorization of the Voting Rights Act, explaining that, since "Congress could rationally have concluded that . . . electoral changes by jurisdictions with a demonstrable history of intentional racial discrimination in voting create the risk of purposeful discrimination, it was proper to prohibit changes that have a discriminatory impact." 446 U.S. at 177. The Court noted that Congress, after giving "careful consideration" to the matter, "found that a 7-year extension of the Act was necessary to preserve the 'limited and fragile' achievements of the Act and to promote further amelioration of voting discrimination."

Id. at 181-182. At issue here, however, is the much later 2006 reauthorization, adopted 41 years after the Voting Rights Act's original passage, extending its life until 2031. To uphold this as being a proper exercise of the Fifteenth Amendment § 2 power of Congress, it might be necessary, even under a deferential standard of review, to show that the evidence available to Congress at the time of the 2006 reauthorization warranted a continuation of the preclearance requirement in covered jurisdictions.

The Court in *Northwest Austin Municipal Utility Dist. No. 1 v. Holder*, 557 U.S. 103 (2009), avoided deciding whether the 2006 extension of the Voting Rights Act was a proper exercise of the Fifteenth Amendment enforcement power, but strongly suggested it was not. In *Shelby County v. Holder*, 570 U.S. 529 (2013), that suggestion became a reality when a majority of the Court struck down the 2006 extension of the act as beyond the power of Congress. In the Court's view, the "extraordinary" nature of the act's intrusion on state sovereignty, including the disparate treatment accorded covered states, could not be justified on the record compiled by Congress in 2006. As the Court explained it,

> Coverage today is based on decades-old data and eradicated practices. The formula captures States by reference to literacy tests and low voter registration and turnout in the 1960s and early 1970s. But such tests have been banned nationwide for over 40 years. And voter registration and turnout numbers in the covered States have risen dramatically in the years since. Racial disparity in those numbers was compelling evidence justifying the preclearance remedy and the coverage formula. There is no longer such a disparity.
>
> In 1965, the States could be divided into two groups: those with a recent history of voting tests and low voter registration and turnout, and those without those characteristics. Congress based its coverage formula on that distinction. Today the Nation is no longer divided along those lines, yet the Voting Rights Act continues to treat it as if it were. . . .
>
> . . . Congress did not use the record it compiled to shape a coverage formula grounded in current conditions. It instead reenacted a formula based on 40-year-old facts having no logical relation to the present day.

Id. at 551, 554 (internal citation omitted). In short, the coverage and preclearance requirements of the Voting Rights Act must be justified "in light of current conditions." Id. at 549. You might think of this "harder look" at the Fifteenth Amendment enforcement power as a version of the Fourteenth Amendment's congruence and proportionality standard.

CHAPTER 2

Substantive Due Process

§2.1 INTRODUCTION AND OVERVIEW

The Origins of the Due Process Clause

There are two Due Process Clauses, one in the Fifth Amendment and one in the Fourteenth Amendment. The former operates as a limit on the power of the national government, while the latter operates against the power of the states. Both clauses guarantee within their respective spheres that no person shall be deprived "of life, liberty, or property, without due process of law." Since both clauses operate in essentially the same fashion, albeit against different governmental bodies, we will refer to them collectively as the Due Process Clause.

The basic notion behind the Due Process Clause derives from Article 39 of Magna Carta, in which the King of England promised in 1215 that "[n]o free man shall be taken, or imprisoned, or disseized, or outlawed, or exiled, or any wise destroyed . . . but by the lawful judgment of his peers or by the law of the land." While this guarantee severely narrowed the King's prerogative—barring him from depriving a person of life, liberty, or property except in accordance with the law—it placed no constraints on what Parliament might enact as "the law of the land." Magna Carta would thus not have been offended if, pursuant to an act of Parliament, the King imprisoned everyone whose mother's first name began with the letter "V."

While some early American state constitutions closely tracked the language of Magna Carta, the fifth article of the federal Bill of Rights replaced the words "by the law of the land" with the more ambiguous phrase "due process of law." It was possible to have read this clause as going no further than the Magna Carta. Under such a reading, a governmental deprivation of life, liberty, or property would automatically satisfy the Due Process Clause if it was consistent with a law duly enacted by the legislature. However, the Supreme Court rejected such a reading of the Due Process Clause in *Murray's Lessee v. Hoboken Land & Improvement Co.*, 59 U.S. (18 How.) 272 (1856). The Court there ruled that the fact that a deprivation may occur "in conformity with an act of Congress" does not necessarily mean that it satisfies the Fifth Amendment Due Process Clause.

> It is manifest that it was not left to the legislative power to enact any process which might be devised. The article is a restraint on the legislative as well as on the executive and judicial powers of the government, and cannot be so construed as to leave congress free to make any process "due process of law," by its mere will.

Id. at 276. The same principle applies to state legislation challenged under the Due Process Clause of the Fourteenth Amendment. *Davidson v. City of New Orleans*, 96 U.S. 97, 102 (1878) (rejecting notion that a state can "make any thing due process of law which, by its own legislation, it chooses to declare such"). In short, the Due Process Clause operates as an independent check on the exercise of governmental power.

Procedural versus Substantive Due Process

The limitations imposed by the Due Process Clause are of two distinct types—procedural and substantive. Procedural due process commands that when the government acts to deprive a person of life, liberty, or property, it must do so under procedures that are deemed to be fair. As we will see in Chapter 5, procedural due process usually requires that a person be given notice and the opportunity to be heard before a deprivation occurs.

The current chapter examines substantive due process. In contrast to procedural due process, which is concerned with the procedures employed in enforcing a law, substantive due process insists that the law itself be fair and reasonable and have an adequate justification regardless of how fair or elaborate the procedures might be for implementing it. Thus, a law that comports with procedural due process because a person is given notice and a full opportunity to be heard might, nonetheless, violate substantive due process if it is substantively unfair or unreasonable. This substantive due process protection is independent of any other textual guarantees found in the Constitution or its Amendments. Thus, substantive due process protects "life, liberty, and property" even if no other textual right has been infringed.

EXAMPLE

Example 2-A

A state law provides that anyone suffering from AIDS shall be incarcerated in a special state facility until he or she is cured of the disease. The law provides that no one shall be incarcerated until after there has first been a full judicial determination that the person is suffering from AIDS. The alleged victim is entitled to a trial-type hearing with appointed counsel, and an adverse determination by the trial court may be appealed as of right to the state supreme court. Does this law deprive an AIDS victim of liberty without due process of law?

EXPLANATION

Explanation

As a matter of procedural due process, the law is constitutional. The measure provides notice and a full opportunity to be heard before any deprivation of liberty occurs. However, as a matter of substantive due process, the measure is probably unconstitutional. A challenger would argue that no matter how fair the procedures for enforcing it, the substance of the law is so unfair and unreasonable as to violate due process. While the state's goal of protecting the public against the spread of AIDS is an important one, there are arguably less drastic ways of achieving this goal that do not involve such severe interference with personal liberty.

Executive Abuse of Power

Most procedural and substantive due process cases involve alleged deprivations of life, liberty, or property that result from legislative action, i.e., action that was specifically authorized by a statute or regulation. In these instances, where we know that the government intended to cause the deprivation, the only issue is whether the deprivation violates the Due Process Clause. Sometimes, however, a deprivation of life, liberty, or property is caused by an executive official in a situation where no legislation approved the specific deprivation in question. For example, suppose a fire truck collides with an automobile and kills the driver, or a prison guard accidentally drops and destroys an inmate's television set. In these instances, though public employees were operating within the scope of their official duties, the deprivations of life and property were not specifically sanctioned by statute or regulation. Instead, they resulted from what may have been ordinary negligence of a governmental official. Should such executive deprivations be actionable under the Due Process Clause? If so, the Due Process Clause would function like a system of tort law, providing a constitutional remedy whenever executive officials cause injury to persons or property.

The Supreme Court has rejected such a reading of the Due Process Clause, whose principal goal is "protection of the individual against arbitrary action of government." *Wolff v. McDonnell*, 418 U.S. 539, 558 (1974). As the Court has explained, "Our cases dealing with abusive executive action have repeatedly emphasized that only the most egregious official conduct can be said to be 'arbitrary in the constitutional sense.' . . ." *County of Sacramento v. Lewis,* 523 U.S. 833, 846 (1998). This distinction between legislative and executive action is necessary "to preserve the constitutional proportions of constitutional claims, lest the Constitution be demoted to what we have called a font of tort law." Id. at 847 n.8. The Court has thus held that "in a due process challenge to executive action, the threshold question is whether the behavior of the governmental officer is so egregious, so outrageous, that it may fairly be said to shock the contemporary conscience." Id. Otherwise, the deprivation is not constitutionally significant and must be redressed through whatever statutory or common law remedies may exist.

Whether or not executive action is sufficiently arbitrary, egregious, or conscience-shocking to state a due process claim depends on the circumstances under which the government official was acting. In no case, however, will an allegation of mere negligence suffice: "the Constitution does not guarantee due care on the part of state officials; liability for negligently inflicted harm is categorically beneath the threshold of constitutional due process." Id. at 849. At the opposite extreme, "conduct intended to injure in some way unjustifiable by any government interest is the sort of official action most likely to rise to the conscience-shocking level." Id. Between these extremes, there may be occasions when "something more than negligence but 'less than intentional conduct, such as recklessness or "gross negligence"'" will suffice, depending on how much opportunity there was for deliberation, reflection, and forethought. Id. at 849, 851. In *County of Sacramento*, the Court held that only an allegation of "purpose to cause" harm would suffice to state a due process claim in a case involving a motorcycle rider who was killed during a high-speed police chase calling for split-second judgments. Id. at 836, 853-854. By contrast, the Court suggested that an allegation of "reckless disregard" or "deliberate indifference" might be enough to support a due process claim in a case concerning the medical treatment of prisoners or pretrial detainees. Id. at 850-852.

Standards of Review

The determination of whether a law violates substantive due process because it is so arbitrary, unfair, or unreasonable as to lack an adequate justification depends almost entirely on what standard a court employs in assessing these criteria. The Court today generally uses one of two basic standards to decide whether a law violates substantive due process. If a *fundamental liberty interest* is infringed, the Court applies strict scrutiny, in which case a law will usually be struck down unless it is shown to be the least burdensome means of achieving a compelling governmental interest. On the other hand, where only property or a nonfundamental liberty interest is involved, the Court applies a rational basis test, under which a law will be upheld if there is any legitimate goal that a rational legislature *might* have thought the measure would further—whether or not this was actually the law's goal or whether the law actually furthers it. The strict scrutiny and rational basis tests constitute the Court's two basic approaches to substantive due process. However, in certain settings, the Court may employ a variation of the normal strict scrutiny test.

Economic versus Noneconomic Due Process

In thinking about substantive due process, it is helpful to distinguish between economic due process and noneconomic due process. Economic due process involves the Court's application of the Due Process Clause to protect real and personal property and to assess potential infringements of economic liberties, such as the liberty to contract and the liberty to pursue a trade or occupation. The standard of review in all economic due process cases is rational basis. Noneconomic due process deals with the clause's application to laws that infringe on civil or personal liberties, such as the freedom to marry and the freedom from physical restraint. If the noneconomic personal liberty at issue is deemed fundamental, then the standard of review is strict scrutiny. Otherwise, a rational basis standard applies.

Though the Court's decisions in these two areas have taken divergent paths, there was initially no hint of a distinction between economic and noneconomic due process. Indeed, in one of the first decisions to recognize a substantive component to the Due Process Clause, the Court suggested that private property was entitled to the same level of due process protection as personal liberty: "[T]he rights of property are united with the rights of person, and placed on the same ground by the fifth amendment. . . ." *Dred Scott v. Sandford*, 60 U.S. (19 How.) 393, 450 (1857). Yet even though the text of the Due Process Clause gives liberty and property equal billing, the Court today does not treat property or economic liberty as fundamental rights. However, for roughly 50 years, from the late 1880s through the late 1930s, the Supreme Court was far more protective of economic interests than it is today, placing them at least on a par with personal liberties. We will briefly examine that period, known as the *Lochner* era, before turning to the Court's current application of substantive due process in property and economic liberty cases.

§2.2 THE RISE AND FALL OF ECONOMIC DUE PROCESS

§2.2.1 Economic Due Process in the *Lochner* Era

The Fourteenth Amendment and its Due Process Clause were ratified in 1868. Shortly thereafter, the Court rejected some substantive due process challenges to state laws that interfered with property or economic liberty. See, e.g., *Munn v. Illinois*, 94 U.S. 113 (1877) (upholding state regulation of grain elevator rates); *Slaughter-House Cases*, 83 U.S. (16 Wall.) 36 (1872) (upholding Louisiana law conferring monopoly on butchering in New Orleans). In *Munn*, the Court declared that, while state economic regulation may sometimes be excessive, "[f]or protection against abuses by legislatures the people must resort to the polls, not to the courts." 94 U.S. at 134.

By 1887, however, the Court's composition and approach had changed significantly. In *Mugler v. Kansas*, 123 U.S. 623 (1887), the Court rejected a substantive due process challenge to an Iowa law that banned the future manufacture or sale of liquor. But in sharp contrast to the hands-off approach of *Munn*, the Court declared that when states exercise their police powers, "[t]he courts are not bound by mere forms, nor are they to be misled by mere pretenses. They are at liberty—indeed under a solemn duty—to look at the substance of things"; and if it appears that a law "has no real or substantial relation to those objects, or is a palpable invasion of rights secured by the fundamental law, it is the duty of the courts to so adjudge, and thereby give effect to the Constitution." Id. at 661. Federal and state courts were soon using substantive due process as a tool for striking down an array of Populist and Progressive reform measures that regulated corporations and businesses in the interest of farmers, consumers, workers, and children. Among the statutes declared unconstitutional were rate and price controls, measures protecting women and children in the workplace, wage and hour standards, and laws that promoted collective bargaining.

Liberty to Contract

While some of the Court's economic due process decisions hinged on a determination that the government had unreasonably interfered with property, many cases found that there had been a deprivation of an economic liberty—i.e., the liberty to contract. This liberty interest was first recognized by the Court in *Allgeyer v. Louisiana*, 165 U.S. 578, 589 (1897), which held that among the liberties protected by the Due Process Clause is the freedom "to enter into all contracts which may be proper, necessary and essential" to pursue a livelihood. The Court later suggested that liberty to contract is also implicit in the Due Process Clause's "right of private property," *Coppage v. Kansas*, 236 U.S. 1, 14 (1915), for the freedom to enter into contracts is essential to acquiring, exploiting, and disposing of property.

The liberty to contract protected by the Due Process Clauses of the Fifth and Fourteenth Amendments involves the freedom to *enter into contracts* on terms and conditions of one's choosing. This liberty interest should not be confused with the Contracts Clause of Article I, § 10, which prohibits a state from "impairing the Obligation of Contracts" by interfering with the terms of preexisting contracts. See Chapter 4.

The Decision in Lochner v. New York

One of the most revealing examples of the Court's approach to economic due process during the *Lochner* era is the case from which the era took its name—*Lochner v. New York*, 198 U.S. 45 (1905). In a 5 to 4 decision, the Court there struck down a New York law that sought to protect the health of bakers by outlawing their employment for more than 10 hours a day or 60 hours a week. The Court held that the law violated the Due Process Clause because it was "an unreasonable, unnecessary and arbitrary interference with the right of the individual to . . . enter into those contracts in relation to labor which may seem to him appropriate or necessary. . . ." Id. at 56. The approach taken by the Court in striking down the New York law embodied three key features that often characterized the Court's economic due process cases during the *Lochner* era.

First, the *Lochner* Court identified a particular aspect of liberty, liberty to contract, not enumerated or mentioned anywhere in the Constitution, and assigned it extraordinary protection. While the Court said that a law interfering with this liberty would be upheld if it was "a fair, reasonable and appropriate exercise of the police power," id., a seemingly deferential standard, the Justices very closely scrutinized the *means-end relationship* between New York's law and its alleged police-power goal. Despite an impressive body of evidence that linked the long hours bakers worked and their generally poor health, the Court ruled that "the limitation of the hours of labor . . . has no such *direct relation* to and no such *substantial effect* upon the health of the employee, as to justify us in regarding [it] as really a health law." Id. at 64 (emphasis supplied). The Court also suggested that the New York statute was unnecessary because there were other ways to protect the health of bakers, even though the state had already implemented them. Id. at 61-62. Thus, according to *Lochner*, a law that interfered with liberty to contract violated the Due Process Clause unless the Court believed that the measure was necessary to directly advance an important governmental purpose. As the Court later explained, under this approach, "freedom of contract is . . . the general rule and restraint the exception; and the exercise of legislative authority to abridge it can be justified only by the existence of exceptional circumstances." *Adkins v. Children's Hosp.*, 261 U.S. 525, 546 (1923) (invalidating minimum wage law for women and children).

Second, in deciding whether New York's interference with liberty to contract was justified by an important governmental interest, the *Lochner* Court was not interested in the actual facts, relying instead on its own assumptions about reality. Despite abundant evidence demonstrating the adverse effect of long hours on the health of bakers, much of which was summarized in Justice Harlan's dissent, the Court declared that "[t]o the common understanding the trade of a baker has never been regarded as an unhealthy one." *Lochner*, supra, 198 U.S. at 59. Several years later in *Muller v. Oregon*, 208 U.S. 412 (1908), the Court upheld a law that set maximum hours for women who worked in factories and laundries. In this case, the future Justice Louis Brandeis, then a prominent Boston lawyer, filed a 116-page brief, 113 pages of which were devoted to factual data showing the harmful effect of long hours of work on women. The difference between the outcomes of *Lochner* and *Muller* is often attributed to "the Brandeis brief." Yet the factual evidence may have been as irrelevant in *Muller* as it was in *Lochner*, as the *Muller* Court suggested that all of Brandeis's data merely confirmed what the Justices already knew—i.e., the "widespread and long continued belief" that "woman has always been dependent upon man." 208 U.S. at 421. However, in *Lochner*, where the facts ran counter to the Justices' intuitive judgment, the Court ignored those facts and invalidated the law as an arbitrary and unreasonable interference with liberty to contract. Though the majority in *Lochner* denied that it was "substituting the judgment of the court for that of the legislature," 198 U.S. at 56-57, this appears to be exactly what the Court did.

Third and finally, *Lochner* rejected the legitimacy of governmental efforts to redress inequalities in wealth or bargaining power. In addition to finding that New York's health justification for regulating bakers' hours was insufficient to pass muster, the Court concluded that the health goal was a sham. "It is impossible for us to shut our eyes to the fact that many of the laws of this character, while passed under what is claimed to be the police power for the purpose of protecting the public health or welfare, are, in reality, passed from other motives." Id. at 64. Instead, said the Court, the measure was "a labor law, pure and simple," id. at 57, for its "real object and purpose were simply to regulate the hours of labor between the master and his employees. . . ." Id. at 64. Thus, the law was invalid.

What was wrong with a labor law? According to the *Lochner* Court, the only legitimate purpose of government is to promote the *public* good. Labor laws seek to redress inequalities between *private* individuals, in effect taking property from one person (the employer) and giving it to another (the worker). Yet "the interest of the public is not in the slightest degree affected by such an act." Id. at 57. Because such laws are beyond the legitimate scope of the state's police power, they lack a valid purpose and, thus, violate the Due Process Clause. The Court in earlier dicta had said that a law that took property from A and gave it to B would be invalid both as a matter of natural law, *Calder v. Bull*, 3 U.S. (3 Dall.) 386, 388 (1798), and as a violation of substantive due process, *Davidson v. New Orleans*, 96 U.S. 97, 102 (1878). The *Lochner* Court viewed labor laws as falling squarely into this prohibited category.

In striking down New York's attempt to redress inequalities between bakers and their employers, *Lochner* adopted the Social Darwinist view that it is both wrong and futile for government to interfere with the process of natural selection, through which the strong will succeed and the weak must perish. New York had tampered with this process by seeking to assist those bakers who might otherwise be incapable of surviving. As the *Lochner* majority candidly declared: "We do not believe in the soundness of the views which uphold this law." 198 U.S. at 61. The Court later expressed itself even more bluntly: "[I]t is from the nature of things impossible to uphold freedom of contract and the right of private property without at the same time recognizing as legitimate those inequalities of fortune that are the necessary result of the exercise of those rights." *Coppage v. Kansas*, 236 U.S. 1, 17 (1915) (striking state ban on yellow dog contracts, in which workers had to agree not to join a labor union).

Dissenting in *Lochner*, Justice Holmes objected to the Court's endorsement of the views of Herbert Spencer, a prominent Social Darwinist. Holmes wrote that "a constitution is not intended to embody a particular economic theory, whether of paternalism and the organic relation of the citizen to the State or of *laissez faire*." 198 U.S. at 75. Instead, except in rare situations, "the word liberty in the Fourteenth Amendment is perverted when it is held to prevent the natural outcome of a dominant opinion. . . ." Id. at 76. In contrast to the *Lochner* majority, Holmes thus advocated a highly deferential standard of judicial review under the Due Process Clause.

§2.2.2 The Demise of *Lochner*

The approach to economic due process exemplified by *Lochner* was applied by the Court well into the 1930s. Some regulations of business were upheld. These included measures that were necessary for health or safety, as well as laws regulating prices charged by monopolies, public utilities, and other businesses deemed to be "affected with a public interest." Yet many other statutes were invalidated because they interfered with the liberty to contract; among them were wage and hour legislation, laws protecting collective bargaining, and price regulations in industries not "affected with a public interest."

The tide began to turn in the mid-1930s during the Great Depression. In *Nebbia v. New York*, 291 U.S. 502 (1934), the Court upheld a New York law that sought to rescue farmers by setting a minimum price for the sale of milk. Writing at the peak of the Depression, the Court rejected its earlier view that there is a "closed class or category of businesses affected with a public interest" whose prices may, therefore, be regulated; instead, price regulation is potentially valid for any business, including the dairy industry. Id. at 531-537. The Court in *Nebbia* also abandoned its practice of strictly scrutinizing laws that interfere with liberty to contract. In a thinly veiled repudiation of *Lochner*, the Court warned:

> With the wisdom of the policy adopted, with the adequacy or practicability of the law enacted to forward it, the courts are both incompetent and unauthorized to deal. . . . [T]hough the court may hold views inconsistent with the wisdom of the law, it may not be annulled unless palpably in excess of legislative power.

Id. at 537-538. In determining whether or not a law violates the Due Process Clause, said the Court, "every possible presumption is in favor of its validity. . . ." Id. at 538.

Three years later in *West Coast Hotel Co. v. Parrish*, 300 U.S. 379 (1937), the Court upheld a state law setting minimum wages for women and children. In doing so, it overruled *Adkins v. Children's Hospital*, 261 U.S. 525 (1923), a *Lochner*-era decision that had invalidated a similar law for the District of Columbia. The Court in *West Coast Hotel* rejected *Lochner*'s treatment of the freedom of contract as a fundamental liberty. While freedom to contract was still a protected aspect of liberty, it did not warrant the special protection afforded to a fundamental liberty. As Chief Justice Hughes wrote for the Court:

> The Constitution does not speak of freedom of contract. It speaks of liberty and prohibits the deprivation of liberty without due process of law. . . . [A] regulation which is reasonable in relation to its subject and is adopted in the interests of the community is due process.
>
> *This essential limitation of liberty in general governs freedom of contract in particular.*

300 U.S. at 391-392 (emphasis supplied). The Court reiterated that in such cases great deference must be shown to the legislature. "Even if the wisdom of the policy be regarded as debatable and its effects uncertain, still the legislature is entitled to its judgment." Id. at 399.

West Coast Hotel also rejected another critical aspect of *Lochner*, namely, its conclusion that laws seeking to redress inequality in bargaining power violate due process because they do not promote the *public* good. Citing the nation's "recent economic experience" in the Great Depression, the Chief Justice explained:

> The exploitation of a class of workers who are in an unequal position with respect to bargaining power and are thus relatively defenceless against the denial of a living wage is not only detrimental to their health and well being but casts a direct burden for their support upon the community. What these workers lose in wages the taxpayers are called upon to pay.

Id. While the Court would still insist that laws advance the public good, the vision of what was in the public interest had expanded greatly since the time of *Lochner*.

West Coast Hotel's enlarged view of the public good was consistent with one of the principles recognized by the *Lochner* Court itself. In this respect, *Lochner* contained the seeds of its own destruction. The *Lochner* doctrine acknowledged that governmental intervention was permissible if it was on behalf of those who, *as a group*, were especially vulnerable and unable to protect themselves in the struggle for existence, as the public as a whole would be harmed if the entire group performing a socially useful function were allowed to perish. During the *Lochner* era, this exception was applied sparingly. It was extended to underground coal miners (*Holden v. Hardy*, 169 U.S. 366 (1898)) and women (*Muller v. Oregon*, 208 U.S. 412 (1908)), but not to bakers, as "[t]here is no contention that *bakers as a class* . . . are not able to assert their rights and care for themselves without the protecting arm of the State. . . . They are in no sense wards of the State." 198 U.S. at 57 (emphasis supplied). Yet within *Lochner*'s framework, if changing economic and social conditions were to render most groups of workers unable to defend themselves in the competitive marketplace, governmental intervention would then be justified on a far more sweeping basis. This is exactly what occurred during the Great Depression.

By 1937, the Supreme Court had rejected all three of the features that characterized its approach to economic due process during the *Lochner* era. First, though the liberty to contract was still protected by the Due Process Clause, it was no longer a fundamental liberty whose infringement would trigger strict scrutiny. Second, since freedom to contract was now just an ordinary liberty, the Court in reviewing a law that impaired this liberty interest would cease to substitute its own judgment for that of the legislature and would instead treat the measure as being presumptively valid. Finally, laws that sought to redress inequalities of wealth or bargaining power on behalf of certain groups would no longer be overturned if they did not further the public good.

The extreme deference to the legislature that the Court displayed in *West Coast Hotel* has continued to the present time. As a result, substantive due process challenges for alleged interference with property or economic liberty are almost certain to fail. The following section addresses the Court's contemporary approach to such economic due process cases.

§2.2.3 Property and Economic Liberty Today

The Court today uses the rational basis test to decide whether a governmental deprivation of property or economic liberty is so arbitrary or unreasonable as to violate substantive due process. The rational basis test was first articulated in *United States v. Carolene Products Co.*, 304 U.S. 144 (1938), where the Court rejected a substantive due process challenge to a federal law excluding nondairy milk products from interstate commerce. The producers of these goods complained that the law impaired the value of their property and interfered with their freedom to contract with buyers in other states. However, the Court rejected their claims, holding that a law "affecting ordinary commercial transactions" is valid as a matter of substantive due process if it "rests upon some rational basis within the knowledge and experience of the legislators." Id. at 152. To satisfy this test, it is unnecessary that the legislature have made findings identifying either the purpose of the law or the basis on which it might further its goal. "Even in the absence of such aids the existence of facts supporting the legislative judgment is to be presumed. . . ." Id. Thus, "where the legislative judgment is drawn in question . . . the issue [is] whether any state of facts either known *or which could reasonably be assumed* affords support for it." Id. at 154 (emphasis supplied).

Under the rational basis test, courts may engage in the purely speculative exercise of hypothesizing a legitimate goal that the challenged law might have been designed to further. Whether this was the law's actual goal and whether the law in fact furthers it are both irrelevant. The only question is whether there is some legitimate end that a rational legislature might have thought the law would further. In *Williamson v. Lee Optical, Inc.*, 348 U.S. 483, 488 (1955), the Court thus upheld an Oklahoma statute that drastically curtailed the ability of opticians to practice their profession: "It is enough that there is an evil at hand for correction, and that it might be thought that the particular legislative measure was a rational way to correct it." Id. The statute's ban on advertising eyeglass frames, for example, was found not to violate substantive due process, on the basis that "[i]f the advertisement of lenses is to be abolished or controlled, the advertising of frames must come under the same restraints; *or so the legislature might think*." Id. at 490 (emphasis supplied).

The rhetoric and the result in *Lee Optical* made clear that the Court's approach to economic due process had returned to the noninterventionist model that prevailed in the late nineteenth century before *Lochner*. With respect to rhetoric, *Lee Optical* chose to "emphasize again" what the Court said in *Munn v. Illinois*, 94 U.S. 113, 134 (1877), one of the leading pre-*Lochner* substantive due process cases: "'For protection against abuses by legislatures the people must resort to the polls, not to the courts.'" 348 U.S. at 488. And in terms of result, *Lee Optical* bore a striking resemblance to another pre-*Lochner* economic due process decision—i.e., the *Slaughter-House Cases*, 83 U.S. (16 Wall.) 36 (1872), upholding Louisiana's butcher monopoly law. In both instances, the Court rejected substantive due process challenges to laws that severely limited the right of individuals to practice their chosen occupation.

The rational basis test employed in economic due process cases today is so deferential as to be virtually toothless. It is always possible to hypothesize a conceivable purpose for a challenged law. In some instances, the Court has not even bothered to go through this ritual. See, e.g., *Ferguson v. Skrupa*,

372 U.S. 726, 731 (1963) (law restricting business of debt adjusting to attorneys did not violate due process because "the Kansas Legislature was free to decide for itself that legislation was needed to deal with the business of debt adjusting"). While other clauses of the Constitution—such as the Takings Clause and the Equal Protection Clause,—or constitutional doctrines—such as the dormant Commerce Clause—may afford meaningful protection against governmental interference with property or economic liberties, challenges based on *substantive* due process are virtually certain to fail. However, property and economic liberties do receive protection as a matter of *procedural* due process. See Chapter 5.

EXAMPLE

Example 2-B

The City of Oakville has an ordinance that makes it illegal for anyone who owns a pet to work as a bus driver. Mary recently received a yellow canary as a birthday present. Shortly after she mentioned this to a co-worker, Mary was fired from her job as a bus driver for the Oakville School District. Mary has challenged her dismissal, claiming that it violated the Fourteenth Amendment Due Process Clause. Is Mary likely to win?

EXPLANATION

Explanation

To the extent that Mary is raising a procedural due process claim, she might succeed if the city failed to give her notice and an opportunity to be heard before it fired her. See Chapter 5. However, Mary is likely to lose a substantive due process challenge. While the ordinance impairs her liberties to pursue an occupation and to contract for employment, all that a defender of the law or the court must do is suggest some hypothetical goal that the city might rationally have thought the law would further. Almost any story will do. The city may have believed that bus drivers who own pets would be tempted to bring their animals to work, interfering with their ability to drive safely. Or the city might have thought that pet owners would get animal hair, bird feathers, or snake scales in their eyes, impairing their ability to see the road clearly. Either scenario would more than likely suffice to sustain the ordinance as a rational safety measure. That the ordinance is both foolish and unnecessary to further these hypothetical safety goals does not matter. In the area of economic due process, the remedy for foolish or oppressive laws is, as the Court declared in *Munn* and *Lee Optical*, to complain to the legislature rather than to the courts.

Some have been critical of the sharp distinction that the Court has drawn in the substantive due process area between property and economic liberties on the one hand and civil and personal liberties on the other. While the former receive only rational basis review, which ordinarily means no protection at all, the latter often trigger strict scrutiny. Yet certain economic freedoms, such as the liberty to pursue one's livelihood, and certain types of property, such as one's home and basic earnings, are as vital to an individual as the most coveted personal liberties. Writing for the Court, Justice Stewart observed:

> [T]he dichotomy between personal liberties and property rights is a false one. Property does not have rights. People have rights. The right to enjoy property without unlawful deprivation, no less than the right to speak or the right to travel, is in truth a "personal" right, whether the "property" in question be a welfare check, a home, or a savings account. In fact, a fundamental interdependence exists between the personal right to liberty and the personal right in property. Neither could have meaning without the other.

Lynch v. Household Finance Corp., 405 U.S. 538, 552 (1972). Moreover, the line between economic liberty and personal liberty is not always an easy one to draw. In *Lochner*, for example, while liberty to contract from the employer's standpoint may have been simply a matter of economics, to the individual baker what was at stake was personal health and survival. Yet the Court has shown no inclination to give heightened scrutiny even to those economic liberties and species of property that are central to a person's existence.

Punitive Damages

The one notable exception to the rule that substantive due process claims are generally unavailing in cases involving deprivations of property or economic liberty concerns the award of punitive damages. In *BMW of North America, Inc. v. Gore*, 517 U.S. 559 (1996), which involved a seller's failure to disclose that a supposedly new car had been partly repainted, the Court held that Alabama had denied defendant BMW substantive due process by awarding $2 million in punitive damages when plaintiff's actual damages amounted to only $4,000—a 500-to-1 ratio. The Court declined to "draw a bright line marking the limits of a constitutionally acceptable punitive damages award," but concluded that "the grossly excessive award imposed in this case transcends the constitutional limit" and, therefore, deprived BMW of property without due process of law. Id. at 585-586. See also *TXO Production Corp. v. Alliance Resources Corp.*, 509 U.S. 443, 458 (1993) (punitive damages award may be "so 'grossly excessive' as to violate the substantive component of the Due Process Clause").

In *Cooper Industries, Inc. v. Leatherman Tool Group, Inc.*, 532 U.S. 424 (2001), the Court held that the determination of whether any award of punitive damages was excessive within the meaning of the Fourteenth Amendment presents a question of law to be examined de novo by the responsible trial or appellate court. Id. at 436-440. Moreover, the Court explained that in "evaluating a punitive damages award's consistency with due process [a court must] consider three criteria—the "*Gore* factors": (1) the degree or reprehensibility of the defendant's misconduct, (2) the disparity between the harm (or potential harm) suffered by the plaintiff and the punitive damages award, and (3) the difference between the punitive damages awarded by the jury and the civil penalties authorized or imposed in comparable cases." Id. at 440 (citing *Gore*, supra, 517 U.S. at 574-575). The purpose of the three-factor test is to limit the potential size of punitive damages to what the Court perceives as a rational and acceptable range that comports with due process.

Reprehensibility, "[t]he most important indicium of the reasonableness of a punitive damages award," is assessed by looking at whether (1) the harm caused was physical as opposed to economic; (2) the conduct evinced an indifference to or a reckless disregard of the health or safety of others; (3) the target of the conduct had financial vulnerability; (4) the conduct involved repeated activities or was an isolated incident; and (5) the harm was the result of intentional malice, trickery, or deceit, or was instead a mere accident. *State Farm Mutual Automobile Ins. Co. v. Campbell*, 538 U.S. 408, 419 (2003). In seeking to establish reprehensibility, while the plaintiff may introduce evidence of similar harms the defendant has caused to others, the defendant cannot then be punished for those distinct harms. Rather, a defendant may be punished only for the harm caused to the plaintiff, though the egregiousness of that harm may be a function of how others were also treated. To separately punish a defendant for its treatment of those not before the court could violate procedural due process, for the defendant might be deprived of any meaningful opportunity to defend against those allegations. *Philip Morris USA v. Williams*, 549 U.S. 346, 353-355 (2007). On procedural due process, see §§ 2.1, 5.1.

Example 2-C

EXAMPLE

Campbell caused an automobile accident in Utah where one person was killed and another seriously injured. His insurer, State Farm, contested liability and declined to settle the ensuing claims for the policy limits, despite contrary advice from its own investigators, who found that Campbell was at fault and that he would probably be found liable at trial. In taking the case to trial, State Farm assured Campbell that he would have no personal liability for the accident, that State Farm would represent his interests, and that he did not need separate counsel. The case went to trial and the jury returned a judgment of $185,000, far exceeding the $50,000 policy limit. State Farm refused to handle Campbell's appeal and initially refused to pay the amount of damages in excess of the policy limit, telling Campbell he had better put his house up for sale. Approximately 18 months later, after Campbell's appeal failed, State Farm finally paid the entire judgment. Campbell then sued State Farm for bad faith, fraud, and intentional infliction of emotional distress. At trial, Campbell introduced evidence of State Farm practices in other states that tended to show a nationwide company policy of capping payouts to meet corporate fiscal goals. The jury awarded Campbell $2.6 million in actual damages, an award later reduced to $1 million. The jury also awarded Campbell $145 million in punitive damages, which was first reduced by the trial court to $25 million and then reinstated to the original amount by the state supreme court. Is this 145-to-1 award of punitive damages so grossly excessive as to violate the Due Process Clause?

Explanation

On similar facts, the U.S. Supreme Court held that the punitive damages award was grossly excessive. *State Farm Mutual Automobile Ins. Co. v. Campbell*, 538 U.S. 408 (2003). As to the first *Gore* factor, reprehensibility, the Court agreed that while State Farm's conduct "merits no praise" and that some type of punitive relief was appropriate, "a more modest punishment for this reprehensible conduct could have satisfied the State's legitimate objectives . . . ." Id. at 419-420. Applying the five reprehensibility considerations described in *Campbell*, we see that, first, while the injury might be viewed as purely economic since State Farm put no one's health or safety in danger, State Farm's treatment of the plaintiff caused him severe emotional distress, including fear he would have to sell his home. Second, State Farm's actions reflected a clear indifference and disregard for the plaintiff's well-being, as seen in its initial assurances that he would face no personal liability, followed by its refusal to appeal the judgment, its failure to pay the plaintiff, and its advice that he sell his home. Third, as to the plaintiff's financial vulnerability, State Farm believed Campbell would have to sell his house to pay the judgment, which suggests that he did not have many other assets. Fourth, the plaintiff offered evidence of similar conduct by State Farm in other states. However, the Supreme Court noted that State Farm's conduct in other states might not have been identical to the challenged conduct and that it might have been legal in the states where it was taken:

> Lawful out-of-state conduct may be probative when it demonstrates the deliberateness and culpability of the defendant's action in the State where it is tortious, but that conduct must have a nexus to the specific harm suffered by the plaintiff. A jury must be instructed, furthermore, that it may not use evidence of out-of-state conduct to punish a defendant for action that was lawful in the jurisdiction where it occurred.

Id. at 422. Here, the out-of-state evidence touching on reprehensibility lacked a demonstrated nexus, and the jury was not instructed that such evidence could not be used to punish State Farm for those distinct wrongs.

Fifth and finally, it would need to be determined whether State Farm's treatment of Campbell was a mere accident or was instead part of an intentional effort to deceive him. If State Farm had an avowed practice of limiting policy payments, this would suggest that its conduct here was that of intentional deceit rather than merely accidental.

As to the second *Gore* factor, the ratio between punitive damages and compensatory damages, the Court attempted to draw a brighter line than it had in *Gore*. While cautioning that "there are no rigid benchmarks that a punitive damages award may not surpass," the Court suggested that, "in practice, few awards exceeding a single-digit ratio between punitive and compensatory damages, to a significant degree, will satisfy due process." Id. at 425. Such "[s]ingle-digit multipliers," said the Court, "are more likely to comport with due process, while still achieving the State's goals of deterrence and retribution, than awards with ratios in [the] range of 500 to 1, or, in this case, of 145 to 1." Id. at 425. In this particular case, the Court noted that a ratio of 4 to 1 "might be close to the line of constitutional impropriety." Id. at 425. Thus, while the 145-to-1 award challenged here was not invalid per se, it was at least presumptively unconstitutional. Id. at 426. Yet the Court also emphasized that the test is a flexible one:

> [R]atios greater than those we have previously upheld may comport with due process where 'a particularly egregious act has resulted in only a small amount of economic damages.' The converse is also true, however. When compensatory damages are substantial, then a lesser ratio, perhaps only equal to compensatory damages, can reach the outermost limit of the due process guarantee.

Id. at 425 (internal citation omitted). In this particular case, the plaintiff had been awarded compensatory damages of $1 million, suggesting that something lower than a 4-to-1 ratio might have been appropriate.

Finally, applying the third *Gore* factor, disparity with other analogous civil penalties, the Court concluded that the award of $145 million punitive damages dwarfed the most relevant civil sanction under state law, namely, a $10,000 penalty for civil fraud. Id. at 428. In conclusion, said the Court, "[a]n application of the *Gore* guideposts to the facts of this case, especially in light of the substantial compensatory damages awarded . . . *likely* would justify a punitive damages award at or near the amount of compensatory damages"—i.e., punitive damages of about $1 million. Id. at 429 (emphasis supplied). However, it stopped short of holding that a 1-to-1 ratio was the constitutionally permissible maximum. Rather, said the Court, "[t]he proper calculation of punitive damages under the principles we have discussed should be resolved, in the first instance, by the Utah courts." Id. at 429.

On remand, the Utah high court read the Supreme Court's 1-to-1 suggestion as being "words of prediction, not direction . . ."; after carefully reviewing the *Gore* factors, the state court held that a 9-to-1 ratio, the highest "single-digit ratio" possible, was proper in this case. *Campbell v. State Farm Mutual Automobile Ins. Co.*, 98 P.3d 409, 412, 417-419 (Utah 2004) (approving a punitive damages award of $9,018,780.75). State Farm again appealed, but the Supreme Court declined further review. 543 U.S. 874 (2004).

Despite the Court's attempt to set numerical guidelines for assessing punitive damages, state and lower federal courts have continued to struggle with the limits that due process imposes in this area. Some courts have read *State Farm*'s discussion of the single-digit cap—the second *Gore* factor—as being applicable only in cases where neither of the other *Gore* factors plays a significant role. Courts have also emphasized *State Farm*'s distinction between cases seeking to redress mere economic harm and those seeking recovery for personal injury or death, the latter perhaps warranting a higher ratio. In *Williams v. Philip Morris, Inc.*, 340 Ore. 35, 63, 127 P.3d 1165, 1181 (Ore. 2006), *cert. dismissed*, 556 U.S. 178 (2009), the Oregon Supreme Court upheld a 97-to-1 punitive damages award in a widow's suit to recover for the smoking-related, lung-cancer death of her husband, explaining, "Single-digit ratios may mark the boundary in ordinary cases, but the absence of bright-line rules necessarily suggests that the other two guideposts—reprehensibility and comparable sanctions—can provide a basis for overriding the concern that may arise from a double-digit ratio."

Where multiple defendants are found jointly and severally liable for compensatory damages, and punitive damages are also awarded against the defendants, courts are divided on how to measure the punitive-to-compensatory ratio. Some courts calculate it on a *per-defendant* basis, while others use a *per-judgment* calculation. If the purpose of limiting punitive damages is to protect the defendant from being subject to excessive punishment, while at the same time allowing a jury to punish reprehensible conduct and deter future wrongdoing, it makes sense to assess the ratio on a per-defendant basis. That there are co-defendants whose conduct was also reprehensible should not by itself automatically lessen the amount for which a particular defendant can be held liable. See *Bert Co. v. Turk*, 298 A.3d 44 (Pa. 2023) (noting judicial split and adopting a per-defendant approach).

EXAMPLE

Example 2-D

Four defendants are found jointly and severally liable for $100,000 in compensatory damages; judgment will accordingly be entered against each of them in that amount, even though plaintiff can only recover a total of $100,000 from the four of them combined. The jury also awarded punitive damages against the defendants in amounts that varied based on the degree of their individual reprehensibility. These punitive damages awards were for $200,000, $400,000, $600,000, and $800,000, or a total of $2 million. Do the punitive damages awards exceed a 9:1 cap?

EXPLANATION

Explanation

The answer hinges on which approach a court uses. Under a *per-defendant* approach, since each defendant is liable for $100,000 in compensatory damages, a 9:1 cap will allow punitive damages up to $900,000 against each of them. The verdict here comports with that, for the ratios vary from a low of 2:1 (200,000 ÷ 100,000) to 8:1 ($800,000 ÷ $200,000). By contrast, under a *per-judgment* approach, we look only at the total amount plaintiff can recover from the four defendants combined, i.e., here $100,000. Viewed from this perspective, the ratio of the judgment's $2 million in punitive damages to its $100,000 in compensatory damages 20:1 ($2 million ÷ $100,000), is far in excess of a 9:1 cap. As the court said in *Bert Co.*, supra, a per-defendant approach allows the jury to find "each defendant's misconduct morally reprehensible but to varying degrees." 298 A.3d at 71 (internal citation omitted). While the per-judgment approach also allows the amounts to vary, they may be capped at a sufficiently lower level that defeats the punitive and deterrent purposes of such awards.

State Farm suggested that higher than single-digit ratios may be warranted where egregious acts result in little or no economic harm, for a plaintiff may otherwise have little incentive to sue and wrongdoers little impetus to correct their ways. On this basis, the court in *Mendez v. County of San Bernardino*, 540 F.3d 1109 (9th Cir. 2008), a civil rights action arising from an illegal arrest and search, held that punitive damages of $5,000 were appropriate even though the jury awarded only $2 in nominal damages—a ratio of 2,500 to 1 (but still far less than the $250,000 in punitive damages the jury originally awarded). Conversely, the Supreme Court has suggested that if a suit is brought as a class action on behalf of a large number of plaintiffs, the incentive-to-sue rationale for allowing higher punitive damages ratios all but vanishes and that "the constitutional outer limit may well be 1:1." *Exxon Shipping Co. v. Baker*, 554 U.S. 471, 514 n.28 (2008).

State and lower federal courts have also struggled with the third *Gore* factor—i.e., consideration of the civil or criminal penalties that may be imposed for similar wrongdoing. Some courts have held that for punitive damages to significantly exceed such comparable penalty levels would violate procedural due process by not affording defendants adequate notice as to the possible economic consequences of their actions. See, e.g., *Clark v. Chrysler Corp.*, 436 F.3d 594, 607-608 (6th Cir. 2006) (reducing punitive damages in wrongful death action to a 2-to-1 ratio with relevant statutory damages); *Bains LLC v. Arco Products Co.*, 405 F.3d 764, 774-777 (9th Cir. 2005) (in civil rights action where compensatory damages were $50,000, reducing $5 million in punitive damages to between $300,000 and $450,000, where the comparable statutory penalty was $300,000, and where a 9-to-1 ratio would allow $450,000); *Lincoln v. Case*, 340 F.3d 283, 294 (5th Cir. 2003) (reducing $100,000 punitive damages award to maximum statutory penalty of $55,000). Other courts have treated comparable statutory penalties as providing guidance rather than a strict limitation on punitive damages awards. See, e.g., *Flax v. DaimlerChrysler Corp.*, 272 S.W.3d 521, 539 (Tenn. 2008), *cert. denied*, 556 U.S. 1257 (2009) (upholding $13 million punitive damages award when third *Gore* factor would have allowed only $125,000, noting that "the Supreme Court has never held that the third guidepost is dispositive" and that the punitive-to-compensatory ratio was only 5.35 to 1); *Willow Inn, Inc. v. Public Service Mutual Ins. Co.*, 399 F.3d 224, 237-238 (3d Cir. 2005) (upholding $150,000 punitive damages award, perhaps 30 times the applicable civil penalty). Treating statutory penalties as offering guidance rather than strict limits is supported by the Supreme Court's decision in *State Farm Mutual Automobile Ins. Co.*, supra, where the Court, after observing that the maximum civil penalty for the petitioner's wrongful conduct was a $10,000 fine, suggested that a punitive damages award of $1 million—100 times the maximum civil penalty—might nonetheless comport with due process. 538 U.S. at 429.

§2.3 NONECONOMIC LIBERTY FROM *LOCHNER TO CAROLENE PRODUCTS*

§2.3.1 The *Lochner* Era and Noneconomic Liberties

When the Court in *Allgeyer v. Louisiana*, 165 U.S. 578 (1897), set out to define the meaning of the word "liberty" in the Due Process Clause, its list included more than just nontextual economic freedoms such as liberty to contract and the freedom to pursue an occupation. In addition, the Court recognized that the clause protects such unenumerated personal liberties as freedom from physical restraint, freedom to enjoy all of one's faculties, and freedom to reside (and work) where one wishes. Id. at 589.

The Court expanded the list of unenumerated personal liberties that are protected by the Due Process Clause in several cases decided at the height of the *Lochner* era. In *Meyer v. Nebraska*, 262 U.S. 390 (1923), the Justices struck down a Nebraska law that criminalized the teaching of German and other foreign languages in the schools. The Court held that the statute arbitrarily and unreasonably interfered with several liberties protected by the Due Process Clause, including the right of parents to have their children learn German. Id. at 399-401. The *Meyer* Court took a broad view of the nontextual personal liberties protected by the Due Process Clause. While it cited *Allgeyer* and *Lochner*, *Meyer* went well beyond those cases, declaring that among the liberties protected by the Fourteenth Amendment are "the right . . . to acquire useful knowledge, to marry, establish a home and bring up children, . . . and generally to enjoy those privileges long recognized at common law as essential to the orderly pursuit of happiness by free men." Id. at 399. Two years later in *Pierce v. Society of Sisters*, 268 U.S. 510 (1925), the Court relied on *Meyer* to overturn an Oregon law that compelled parents to send their children to public rather than private school; the statute violated due process, said the Court, because it "unreasonably interfere[d] with the liberty of parents and guardians to direct the upbringing and education of children under their control." Id. at 534-535.

The process that the Court applied in *Meyer* and *Pierce* with respect to certain personal liberties was indistinguishable from that which it had employed in *Lochner* concerning liberty to contract. In each case, the Court first defined an unenumerated liberty as being protected by the Due Process Clause. It then elevated that nontextual liberty interest to what amounted to "fundamental" status and accorded it a strict level of judicial protection. During the *Lochner* era, the Court thus used substantive due process as a means of invalidating statutes that interfered with judicially created liberties of both an economic and a noneconomic nature.

§2.3.2 *Carolene Products'* Footnote Four

In the late 1930s, when the Supreme Court abandoned its interventionist approach to substantive due process in the economic sphere, it indicated that a similar retreat was called for in other areas as well. In *United States v. Carolene Products Co.*, 304 U.S. 144 (1938), the Court had held that laws impairing liberty to contract were subject merely to rational basis review. But in dicta contained in footnote four, Justice Stone's opinion for the Court suggested that the rational basis standard should govern other unenumerated liberty interests as well. Stone wrote that more rigorous judicial scrutiny is called for only in three exceptional situations: (1) if "legislation appears on its face to be within a *specific prohibition* of the Constitution, such as those of the first ten amendments"; (2) if legislation "restricts those *political processes* which can ordinarily be expected to bring about repeal of undesirable legislation," such as impairments of the right to vote; and (3) if legislation is aimed at "*discrete and insular minorities*" who, because of prejudice against them, are unable to protect themselves through the ordinary political processes. Id. at 152-153 n.4 (emphasis supplied). The first of these exceptions involves the Due Process Clause. The other two primarily concern the Equal Protection Clause and are discussed in Chapters 6 and 7.

According to the first exception of footnote four, if an unenumerated liberty interest is at stake, such as the liberty to contract at issue in *Carolene*

Products, a mere rational basis standard of review should be employed. The only liberties that would trigger more demanding scrutiny are those *specifically enumerated* in the Bill of Rights. For these purposes, if a Bill of Rights provision has been incorporated into the Fourteenth Amendment, it will be deemed to be "equally specific" as to the states even though the text of the Fourteenth Amendment does not mention it. Id. at 152 n.4.

The intended effect of footnote four on the Due Process Clause was to divide the universe of constitutionally protected liberties into two categories: those such as freedom of speech that are mentioned in the Bill of Rights and those such as liberty to contract that are unenumerated but that the Court has nonetheless deemed to be protected. In Justice Stone's view, while the textual liberties of the first category should be entitled to heightened protection, those in the second category should receive only minimal protection under a rational basis test.

Carolene Products thus implicitly rejected the substantive due process approach taken in *Meyer v. Nebraska* and *Pierce v. Society of Sisters*, the two leading *Lochner*-era cases dealing with personal liberties. In both of those cases, the Court had applied a strict standard of review to overturn state laws that infringed on unenumerated liberty interests in acquiring knowledge and raising children. According to footnote four, since only nontextual liberties were involved, the state laws should have received rational basis review under the Due Process Clause. However, the *Carolene Products* Court mentioned *Meyer* and *Pierce* as cases where strict scrutiny may have been justified under the Equal Protection Clause, 304 U.S. at 153 n.4, for both involved statutes that targeted minority groups who at the time were victims of extreme prejudice—i.e., German Americans in *Meyer* and Roman Catholics in *Pierce*. While *Meyer* and *Pierce* were thus perhaps defensible in equal protection terms, as substantive due process cases they had been discredited.

Not surprisingly, in the decades following *Carolene Products*, the Supreme Court very seldom overturned laws that interfered with unenumerated liberty interests. The collapse of substantive due process in the late 1930s affected all nontextual liberties. Liberty interests that were not specifically enumerated in the text of the Constitution, whether they were economic or personal in nature, were thus generally denied any substantive due process protection. There were a few exceptions. In *Aptheker v. Secretary of State*, 378 U.S. 500 (1964), the Court invalidated a federal law barring certain Communist Party members from obtaining passports, ruling that the law violated the Due Process Clause by impairing the nontextual "right to travel abroad." Id. at 505. In *Skinner v. Oklahoma*, 316 U.S. 535, 541-542 (1942), involving a state law that allowed mandatory sterilization of repeat felons, the Court applied strict scrutiny to protect the unenumerated right to procreate, though it did so under the Equal Protection rather than the Due Process Clause.

§2.4 *GRISWOLD* AND THE REEMERGENCE OF UNENUMERATED LIBERTIES

The collapse of substantive due process in the late 1930s has been permanent with respect to property and economic liberty. However, in the area of personal liberty there was a revival that began in the mid-1960s with *Griswold v. Connecticut*, 381 U.S. 479 (1965).

Griswold struck down a Connecticut law that made it illegal to use or counsel others to use contraceptives. The Court held that as applied to advice given to married couples, the statute violated the Due Process Clause by interfering with the "right of privacy" in marriage and by in effect allowing the government to invade "the sacred precincts of marital bedrooms. . . ." Id. at 485-486. The newly recognized right of marital privacy, though nowhere mentioned in the Constitution's text, was found to lie "within the zone of privacy created by several fundamental constitutional guarantees." Id. at 485. The Court applied an extremely strict standard of review and invalidated the statute without any consideration of the state's possible justifications for it.

Griswold made it clear that the rebirth of substantive due process was limited to the sphere of personal liberties. The Court expressly declined to revive *Lochner v. New York* and said that it would not "sit as a super-legislature to determine the wisdom, need, and propriety of laws that touch economic problems, business affairs, or social conditions." Id. at 482. Justice Douglas, speaking for the Court, explained that in contrast to *Lochner*, the statute at issue in *Griswold* "operates directly on an intimate relation of husband and wife and their physician's role in one aspect of that relation." Id. Yet he did not explain the significance of the distinction between economic and personal affairs, or how this critical distinction was to be made. Nor did he explain why, if the *Lochner* Court had acted as a "super-legislature," the *Griswold* Court was not acting so as well.

§2.4.1 Penumbras and Emanations

The *Griswold* Court offered an unusual explanation as to the source of the newly discovered constitutional right of marital privacy. In earlier cases, such as *Allgeyer v. Louisiana* (1897) and *Meyer v. Nebraska* (1923), the Court announced that certain liberties were included in the "liberty" protected by the Due Process Clause. Justice Douglas, writing for the Court in *Griswold*, chose not to follow this route. Instead, he sought to link the right of privacy in marriage to specific guarantees of the Bill of Rights. The First, Third, Fourth, and Fifth Amendments, said Douglas, "have penumbras, formed by emanations from those guarantees that help give them life and substance." 381 U.S. at

484. The right of marital privacy lies within these penumbras, hidden in the shadows of the First Amendment's right of association, the Third and Fourth Amendments' protection of the home, and the Fifth Amendment's guarantee against self-incrimination.

There are several reasons why Justice Douglas may have insisted on tying the right of marital privacy to specific provisions of the Bill of Rights rather than simply declaring it a protected aspect of "liberty" under the Due Process Clause. First, he may have hoped to distinguish his approach from that taken by the Court during the *Lochner* era; rather than inventing a new constitutional right, the Court in *Griswold* was exercising judicial restraint by merely protecting a right that was derivable from the Constitution's text. Yet the penumbras and emanations approach was hardly a means of imposing judicial self-restraint. Douglas's discovery of marital privacy within the penumbras of the Bill of Rights was far from self-evident, requiring at least a small leap of judicial faith. Moreover, the penumbras and emanations approach can justify virtually any liberty interest the Court might wish to create. Indeed, *Lochner* could easily be reinterpreted and justified on this basis, for liberty to contract may be said to lie within the penumbras and emanations of several constitutional provisions—including the Due Process Clause's protection of "property" and the Contracts Clause of Article I, § 10.

Douglas's penumbras and emanations approach may also have been designed to square *Griswold* with the framework of *Carolene Products*. There, as we saw, the Court in footnote four suggested that strict scrutiny should be applied under the Due Process Clause only if a law is contrary to a "specific prohibition" of the Constitution. Though footnote four was only dictum, Douglas agreed with this aspect of it. He also subscribed to Justice Black's position that under § 1 of the Fourteenth Amendment, it is wrong for the Court to use a "natural-law-due-process" approach to create any additional rights against the states beyond those explicitly set forth in the Bill of Rights. *Adamson v. California*, 332 U.S. 46, 68-92 (1947) (Black, J., and Douglas, J., dissenting); see also *Duncan v. Louisiana*, 391 U.S. 145, 162-171 (1968) (Black, J., and Douglas, J., concurring). See § 1.3.

However, use of the penumbras and emanations approach to determine the scope of the Bill of Rights drains the "specific prohibitions" of the Bill of Rights of any coherent meaning, as Justice Black complained in his *Griswold* dissent. This is evident from the fact that the *Griswold* Court used this rationale to rescue and revive two *Lochner*-era personal liberty cases—*Meyer v. Nebraska* (1923) and *Pierce v. Society of Sisters* (1925)—which had seemingly been discredited as due process precedents by *Carolene Products*. The decisions in *Meyer* and *Pierce* were now reinterpreted and reaffirmed as having been justified under the penumbras and emanations principle. According to *Griswold*, the liberty interests in learning German and in directing the education of one's children that were protected by those earlier rulings in fact lay within the shadows of the First Amendment. 381 U.S. at 482.

§2.4.2 Alternative Approaches: Liberty and the Ninth Amendment

The penumbras and emanations theory did not satisfy all members of the *Griswold* majority. Justice Harlan, in a separate concurring opinion, rejected the approach. Instead, he rested the right of marital privacy squarely on the word "liberty" in the Fourteenth Amendment Due Process Clause, without linking it to any provision of the Bill of Rights. Because the right of marital privacy is "implicit in the concept of ordered liberty," it is, therefore, constitutionally protected. 381 U.S. at 500. While this approach gave the Court considerable leeway, Harlan noted that any "judicial 'self-restraint' " imposed by the penumbras and emanations theory "is more hollow than real." Id. at 501. In a separate concurrence, Justice White also declined to endorse the penumbras and emanations theory and, like Harlan, relied simply on the word "liberty" contained in the Due Process Clause.

Three other members of the *Griswold* majority also agreed with Justice Harlan that the right of marital privacy is an aspect of due process "liberty" but buttressed their conclusion with the Ninth Amendment. That Amendment states, "The enumeration in the Constitution of certain rights shall not be construed to deny or disparage *others retained by the people*" (emphasis supplied). While Douglas had referred to the Amendment in passing, Justice Goldberg, joined by Chief Justice Warren and Justice Brennan, relied on it as authority for construing the Fourteenth Amendment Due Process Clause to encompass rights not enumerated elsewhere in the Constitution. Justice Goldberg wrote: "The language and history of the Ninth Amendment reveal that the Framers of the Constitution believed that there are additional fundamental rights, protected from governmental infringement, which exist alongside those fundamental rights specifically mentioned in the first eight constitutional amendments." Id. at 488. While not "an independent source of rights protected from infringement by either the States or the Federal Government," id. at 492, the Ninth Amendment provides a rule of construction for the courts in interpreting other provisions of the Constitution, such as the word "liberty" in the Due Process Clause. On this basis, Justice Goldberg concluded that the unenumerated "right of privacy in the marital relation is . . . a personal right 'retained by the people' within the meaning of the Ninth Amendment" and that it is, therefore, among the "fundamental" personal liberties that are "protected by the Fourteenth Amendment from infringement by the States." Id. at 499.

Justice Goldberg's reliance on the Ninth Amendment drew fire from Justices Stewart and Black, who believed that "[t]he Ninth Amendment, like its companion the Tenth, . . . was . . . adopted by the States simply to make clear that the adoption of the Bill of Rights did not alter the plan that the *Federal* Government was to be a government of express and limited powers, and that all rights and powers not delegated to it were retained by the people and the individual States." Id. at 529-530 (Stewart, J., and Black, J., dissenting) (emphasis in original). It was intended to "protect state powers against federal invasion," not as a basis for recognizing unenumerated rights that may be judicially enforced against the federal or state governments. Id. at 520 (Black, J., and Stewart, J., dissenting). One difficulty with the Stewart-Black reading, however, is that it renders the Ninth Amendment synonymous with the Tenth and thus redundant. The Tenth Amendment does say that those powers not conferred on the federal government are reserved to the states or to the people. The Ninth Amendment says something quite different—that the people have other rights against the government besides those enumerated in the Bill of Rights. If these other rights are not judicially enforceable, if there is no remedy for their violation, then they are not rights but mere norms or platitudes that government officials may ignore with impunity. It is difficult to believe that the Founders would have troubled themselves to include the Ninth Amendment if this is all that it was intended to accomplish.

§2.4.3 The Risks in Protecting Unenumerated Rights

While the seven members of the *Griswold* majority offered a variety of bases for finding a fundamental right of marital privacy, they all agreed that the Court may give protection to liberty interests that are nowhere specifically mentioned in the text of the Constitution. A clear majority, in other words, refused to give the Constitution a strictly literal reading that would protect only those specific liberties—such as the Third Amendment guarantee against having soldiers quartered in one's home during peacetime—that are spelled out in full by the text itself. To construe the document as Justices Black and Stewart proposed in their dissent would have given an extremely narrow reading to the "liberty" protected by the Due Process Clause. Moreover, it would have been contrary to the apparent intent of the Founders, who included the Ninth Amendment to guard against just such a crabbed reading of the Constitution's enumeration of rights.

In the years since *Griswold*, the Court has added to the personal liberties that are protected by the Due Process Clause. In doing so, the Court has disavowed Justice Douglas's penumbras and emanations explanation, *Whalen v. Roe*, 429 U.S. 589, 598 n.23 (1977), and candidly acknowledged that the task requires giving meaning to the "Fourteenth Amendment's concept of personal liberty," *Roe v. Wade*, 410 U.S. 113, 152-153 (1973). Even some of the Court's more conservative members accepted the validity of this judicial undertaking. In *Thornburgh v. American College of Obstetricians & Gynecologists*, 476 U.S. 747, 789 (1986), Justice White, joined by Justice Rehnquist, declared that

> this Court does not subscribe to the simplistic view that constitutional interpretation can possibly be limited to the "plain meaning" of the Constitution's text or to the subjective intention of the Framers. The Constitution is not a deed setting forth the precise metes and bounds of its subject matter; rather, it is a document announcing fundamental principles in value-laden terms that leave ample scope for the exercise of normative judgment by those charged with interpreting and applying it.

Similarly, in *Richmond Newspapers, Inc. v. Virginia*, 448 U.S. 555, 579 (1980), Chief Justice Burger, writing for the majority, noted that "[n]otwithstanding the appropriate caution against reading into the Constitution rights not explicitly defined, the Court has acknowledged that certain unarticulated rights are implicit in enumerated guaranties." More recently, in *Dobbs v. Jackson Women's Health Org.*, 597 U.S. 215, 237 (2022), the Court agreed that "the Due Process Clause protects two categories of substantive rights" — those "guaranteed by the first eight Amendments," and "a select list of fundamental rights that are not mentioned anywhere in the Constitution." Justice Thomas, concurring, argued that the entire substantive due process jurisprudence should be abandoned. Id. at 332-333 (Thomas, J., concurring). No other member of the Court endorsed this position.

The issue that has continued to divide the Justices is not the question of whether the Court should give constitutional protection to unenumerated, nontextual liberty interests, as Thomas would argue, but rather what sources it may look to in doing so and how those sources should be construed. For example, should the Court consider only the Founders' specific intent, or is it permissible to consider the more general concepts the Founders hoped to protect? Are history and tradition legitimate guides, and if so, at what point and at what level of generality are they to be measured? To what extent is the Court confined to past case law? And of what relevance are principles of philosophy, political theory, or sociology? These important questions are explored in Christopher N. May, Allan Ides & Simona Grossi, *Constitutional Law: National Power and Federalism*, ch. 1 (10th ed. 2025) [hereinafter *National Power & Federalism*].

When the Court seeks to define and protect rights that are not specifically enumerated in the text of the Constitution, it takes some institutional risks. One is that the Court may lose credibility if it is perceived by the public as having simply enshrined the personal beliefs and prejudices of individual Justices. Another risk is that by operating without close textual moorings, the Court may seek to protect values that are so out of touch with those of the public that people will refuse to accept the Court's judgment. Both of these dangers materialized during the *Lochner* era, when the Court, in the name of liberty to contract, continued to impose the doctrine of laissez-faire on a nation prostrated by the Depression.

Similar concerns may arise when the Court overrules one of its prior decisions to take away rights that were previously recognized. This was the case in *Dobbs v. Jackson Women's Health Org.*, supra. The Court there overruled its "watershed" decision in *Roe v. Wade*, 410 U.S. 113 (1973), which had recognized a woman's fundamental constitutional right to choose to have an abortion. In response to suggestions that this might reflect negatively on the Court, the majority replied, "we cannot allow our decisions to be affected by any extraneous influences such as concern about the public's reaction to our work. That is true both when we initially decide a constitutional issue *and* when we consider whether to overrule a prior decision." 597 U.S. at 291 (emphasis in original).

As Justice Powell wrote in *Moore v. City of East Cleveland*, 431 U.S. 494, 502 (1977):

> Substantive due process has at times been a treacherous field for this Court. There *are* risks when the judicial branch gives enhanced protection to certain substantive liberties without the guidance of the more specific provisions of the Bill of Rights. As the history of the *Lochner* era demonstrates, there is reason for concern lest the only limits to such judicial intervention become the predilections of those who happen at the time to be Members of this Court. That history counsels caution and restraint. But it does not counsel abandonment . . . .

(Emphasis in original; footnote omitted.)

§2.4.4 The Fundamental Rights Model with Variations

Since *Griswold*, the constitutional right of privacy has expanded well beyond a married couple's freedom to decide to use birth control. This fundamental right has been extended to unmarried individuals and has been held to embrace other personal decisions mostly having to do with marriage, family, and bodily integrity. In analyzing claimed violations of these fundamental liberty interests, the Court has adopted what might be thought of as a basic due process model. In some cases, the Court applies a variation of this model. We will first examine the basic model and then consider a few variations.

The Basic Fundamental Rights Model

In contrast to *Griswold*, where Justice Douglas's opinion for the Court struck down a Connecticut law under what amounted to a per se rule of invalidity, the Court typically employs a more subtle approach in fundamental rights due process cases. That basic approach consists of five steps or inquiries:

1. Does the interest in question qualify as a *protected liberty* under the Due Process Clause?
2. Is the protected liberty one that is deemed *fundamental?*
3. Does the challenged law *impinge on* or *unduly burden* that fundamental liberty interest to a degree sufficient to trigger strict scrutiny?
4. If a fundamental liberty has been impinged on or unduly burdened, does the law substantially further a *compelling governmental interest?*
5. Has the government chosen the *least burdensome means* of achieving its compelling interest?

Step 1 of this basic model is usually noncontroversial, since virtually all forms of individual freedom qualify for at least minimal due process protection. See § 5.2.1; but cf. *Paul v. Davis,* 424 U.S. 693 (1976) (interest in reputation not a liberty interest protected by Due Process Clause). Step 2 of the analysis, however, presents the more difficult question of determining whether any particular liberty interest is entitled to special protection as a fundamental right. Sections 2.5 and 2.6 examine those liberty interests the Court has deemed fundamental (or nonfundamental) and the methods through which the Court has arrived at those conclusions. The various opinions in *Griswold* laid the foundation for that process. Step 3 requires an assessment of the degree to which the liberty interest is burdened, since de minimis infringements will not trigger strict scrutiny. Finally, steps 4 and 5 apply strict scrutiny, under which the challenged law or practice violates the Due Process Clause unless it is shown that the measure is necessary to achieve a compelling governmental interest. The latter two steps are not reached, however, unless we have obtained affirmative answers to inquiries 1, 2, and 3. If any of the first three inquiries is answered in the negative, the court will apply only the rational basis standard of review.

The Concept of Impingement

There are several important points to remember about the impingement or undue burden requirement. First, virtually all the rights we enjoy under the Constitution are negative rather than positive rights. In other words, they operate as protections against governmental interference, not as guarantees of governmental assistance. As the Court has explained:

> The [Due Process] Clause is phrased as a limitation on the State's power to act. . . . It forbids the State itself to deprive individuals of life, liberty, or property without "due process of law," but its language cannot fairly be extended to

> impose an affirmative obligation on the State to ensure that those interests do not come to harm through other means.

DeShaney v. Winnebago County Dept. of Social Servs., 489 U.S. 189, 195 (1989). The government has no affirmative constitutional duty to assure that each of us can exercise, enjoy, or realize the benefits of a particular right. For example, the freedoms to marry and to use contraceptives are fundamental liberties under the Due Process Clause, yet the government is not constitutionally obligated to find one a spouse, pay for the wedding, or purchase contraceptives for someone who cannot otherwise afford it. Nor is there a federal constitutional right to an education, even though education is a necessary predicate to a meaningful exercise of our First Amendment freedoms of speech and the press. All that the Constitution usually requires is that the government not actively interfere—whether through criminal punishment or otherwise—with our ability to exercise our constitutional rights.

This negative rights approach contrasts with some state constitutions which require that the government provide certain benefits. See, e.g., *San Antonio Ind. School Dist. v. Rodriguez*, 411 U.S. 1, 111-112 & n.68 (1973) (Marshall, J., dissenting) (noting that 48 state constitutions guarantee an affirmative right to a basic public education); *Aliessa ex rel. Fayad v. Novello*, 96 N.Y.2d 418, 427-428, 754 N.E.2d 1085 (N.Y. 2001) (under N.Y. Const., Art. XVII, § 1, "care for the needy is not a matter of 'legislative grace', it is a constitutional mandate").

Second, even where the government does interfere with our ability to exercise a protected liberty interest, not all forms of governmental interference are serious enough to count as impairments of constitutional rights. The purpose of the impingement or undue burden requirement is to separate insignificant governmental actions from those substantial enough to trigger strict scrutiny. For example, the application of a general sales tax to the purchase of contraceptives would probably not be deemed to impinge on the freedom to practice birth control, whereas a law that criminalized such sales would impose an undue burden and would be subject to strict scrutiny.

Variations on the Basic Strict Scrutiny Model

The Court does not always follow this basic five-step due process model in analyzing laws that allegedly interfere with a fundamental liberty interest. One variation involves eliminating the last two steps of the analysis and asking only the first three questions. Under this approach, if the law places an "undue burden" on a fundamental liberty interest, it is invalid; if it does not impose an undue burden, it will be upheld under a rational basis standard of review. This variation was once used to assess laws that interfered with a woman's freedom to obtain an abortion but it is no longer in use. See § 2.5.1.

A second variation involves eliminating the last step of the basic analysis and ending with the fourth inquiry. If a law impinges on a fundamental liberty interest (thereby satisfying steps 1, 2, and 3), the only remaining issue is whether the measure furthers a compelling governmental interest; if it does, the law will be upheld whether it was the least burdensome means available to the state. This variation greatly relaxes the standard of review, for the government does not have to show that it was necessary to burden the fundamental liberty in question. This variation was used in *Youngberg v. Romeo*, 457 U.S. 307 (1982), to reject a suit brought against a state hospital by a mentally retarded inmate who claimed that the hospital had violated his liberty interests in safety and freedom from bodily restraint. See § 2.6.1.

A third variation on the basic model involves skipping steps 2 and 3 of the analysis, in effect assuming arguendo that a fundamental liberty interest was impinged on, and then upholding the law on the ground that the government's action was justified. By taking this route, the Court avoids having to decide whether a claimed interest qualifies as a fundamental liberty under the Due Process Clause. The Court used this approach in *Cruzan v. Director, Missouri Department of Health*, 497 U.S. 261 (1990), to sustain a Missouri law that prevented a family from withdrawing artificial feeding equipment from their daughter, who was hospitalized in a persistent vegetative state. The Court refused to decide whether the state had abridged the daughter's claimed fundamental liberty to refuse life-sustaining food and hydration. Instead, it held that even if the state had unduly burdened such a liberty, the state had an adequate basis for doing so. See § 2.5.7.

Finally, the Court may avoid the strict scrutiny model entirely by finding that a challenged law or practice does not pass muster even under a rational basis standard of review, thereby making it unnecessary to decide whether the liberty interest in question is a fundamental one. The Court appears to have taken this route in *Lawrence v. Texas*, 539 U.S. 558 (2003), where it struck down a Texas statute that made it a crime for two adults of the same sex to engage in intimate sexual conduct. In holding that one of the liberties protected by the Due Process Clause is the right of adults to engage in private consensual sexual activity, the Court never addressed the question of whether this newly recognized liberty was a fundamental one. Instead, as the dissent suggested, the Court invalidated the statute under "the rational-basis test. . . ." Id. at 594 (Scalia, J., dissenting). While the majority in that case may have applied a stricter than usual version of the rational basis test, the Court's approach allowed it to avoid having to decide whether the liberty interest in question was a fundamental one.

§2.5 THE RIGHT OF PRIVACY AND PERSONAL AUTONOMY

The right of marital privacy recognized by the Court's path-breaking 1965 decision in *Griswold v. Connecticut* was soon extended to persons who were not married and to conduct that did not occur in the privacy of the home. The Court held that unmarried persons (*Eisenstadt v. Baird*, 405 U.S. 438 (1972)), including minors (*Carey v. Population Servs. Intl.*, 431 U.S. 678 (1977)), have the same fundamental liberty interest in using contraceptives as did the married couples protected by *Griswold*. With this expansion of *Griswold*, it became increasingly difficult to speak of the right in question as being one of privacy, much less of marital privacy. The Court, therefore, reformulated the liberty interest recognized in *Griswold* as one that "protects *individual decisions* in matters of childbearing from unjustified intrusion by the State." *Carey v. Population Servs. Intl.*, supra, 431 U.S. at 687 (emphasis supplied). What had begun as a right of privacy was thus transformed into an interest in "personal dignity and autonomy," the right "to define one's own concept of existence," *Planned Parenthood v. Casey*, 505 U.S. 833, 851 (1992), and "the interest in independence in making certain kinds of important decisions." *Whalen v. Roe*, 429 U.S. 589, 599-600 (1977). While courts continued to speak of a constitutional right of privacy, this phrase was normally used to mean the same thing as a right of personal autonomy.

After a steady 50-year expansion of the right to personal autonomy, the pendulum abruptly swung back with *Dobbs v. Jackson Women's Health Organization*, 597 U.S. 215 (2022). The Court there rejected its earlier right-to-autonomy formulation of "liberty," as it involved too high "a level of generality," one that "could license fundamental rights to illicit drug use, prostitution, and the like." Id. at 257. Under *Dobbs*, when deciding what is a protected liberty, the questions must be "whether the right at issue . . . is rooted in the Nation's history and tradition, *and* whether it is an essential component of what we have described as 'ordered' liberty." Id at 234 (emphasis in original). If it is not, then it must be shown to be "part of a broader entrenched right that is supported by precedent." Id. Absent these showings, only "rational-basis review" applies, "even when the laws at issue concern matters of great social significance and moral substance. Id. at 300-301. On that basis, *Dobbs* overruled *Roe v. Wade*, 410 U.S. 113 (1973) and *Planned Parenthood v. Casey*, supra, which had held that a woman has a due process liberty to terminate her pregnancy.

The *Dobbs* Court sought to allay these concerns: "[T]o ensure that our decision is not misunderstood or mischaracterized, we emphasize that our decision concerns the constitutional right to an abortion and no other right." 597 U.S. at 290. And Justice Kavanaugh, concurring, wrote: "Overruling *Roe* does *not* mean the overruling of those precedents, and does *not* threaten or cast doubt on those precedents." Id. at 345-346 (emphasis in original). Yet these disclaimers are less than convincing in view of Justice Thomas' concurring opinion ("in future cases we should reconsider all of this Court's substantive due process precedents, including *Griswold*, *Lawrence*, and *Obergefell*," id. at 332, and in view of Justices Breyer, Sotomayor, and Kagan's dissent:

> [N]o one should be confident that this majority is done with its work. The right *Roe* and *Casey* recognized does not stand alone. To the contrary, the Court has linked it for decades to other settled freedoms involving bodily integrity, familial relationships, and procreation. . . . So one of two things must be true. Either the majority does not really believe its own reasoning. Or if it does, all rights that have no history stretching back to the mid-19th century are insecure. Either the mass of the majority's opinion is hypocrisy, or additional constitutional rights are under threat. It is one or the other.

Id. at 362-363. Indeed, four Justices in *Dobbs* suggested that the decision in that case could or should result in a reconsideration of *Griswold*, it being unclear whether the right of married couples to use contraceptives would still qualify as a protected liberty under the Court's new test. See id. at 332-333 (Thomas, J., concurring); id. at 383-386 & n.8 (Breyer, J., Sotomayor, J., and Kagan, J., dissenting).

§2.5.1 Abortion Before and After *Dobbs v. Jackson*

Roe v. Wade *and the Trimester Framework*

The Court's first right of privacy decisions involved laws that, by barring the use of contraceptives, had the effect of forcing individuals to have children and create a family against their wishes. In striking down these laws, the Court held that one of the fundamental liberties protected by the Due Process Clause is the "decision whether to bear or beget a child." *Eisenstadt v. Baird*, 405 U.S. 438 (1972). This decision was as much impaired by laws outlawing abortion as by bans on the use of contraceptives. In 1973, the Court recognized this fact, holding that the right of privacy in matters concerning procreation and family "is broad enough to encompass a woman's decision whether or not to terminate her pregnancy." *Roe v. Wade*, 410 U.S. 113, 153 (1973).

Roe involved a Texas statute that made it illegal to have an abortion except where necessary to save the mother's life. By absolutely prohibiting most abortions, the statute impinged on a woman's fundamental liberty to choose an abortion, thus triggering strict scrutiny under the Due Process Clause. Texas therefore had to show that its interference with this right of personal privacy "was necessary to support a compelling state interest. . . ."

Id. at 156. The Court agreed that the state had two compelling interests in regulating the abortion decision: the interest in protecting *maternal health* and the interest in protecting *potential life*. In an opinion written by Justice Blackmun, the Court held that neither of these interests was compelling at the outset of pregnancy. Rather, the interest in protecting the mother's health became compelling only at the end of the *first trimester* (i.e., after about three months of pregnancy); before then, the Court explained, it was as safe for a woman to have an abortion as it was to proceed with childbirth. The state's interest in potential life, on the other hand, did not become compelling until roughly the end of the *second trimester* (i.e., after about six months of pregnancy); only then the fetus was *viable*, that is, capable of surviving outside the mother's womb.

Under this trimester framework, the state's interest in regulating abortion became stronger as the period of pregnancy lengthens. During the first trimester, the state had no compelling reason to regulate abortion, though it might require that abortions be performed by a licensed physician. In the second trimester, the state acquired a compelling interest in protecting maternal health. This interest allowed the state to impose restrictions necessary to ensure that the abortion procedure was safe, but it was not sufficient to justify a total prohibition on abortion. During the last trimester of pregnancy, the state acquired a compelling interest in protecting the fetus. At this point, the state might "regulate, and even proscribe, abortion except where it was necessary, in appropriate medical judgment, for the preservation of the life or health of the mother." Id. at 165. Once the fetus had become viable, the state might restrict or completely outlaw *nontherapeutic abortions*—i.e., those that were not medically necessary to protect the mother's health or life; however, the state might not prevent a woman from choosing to have a *therapeutic abortion*.

While *Roe* invalidated prohibitions on abortion during the first and second trimesters, the decision left room for states to regulate the procedures for obtaining abortions. Such regulations might be upheld under the trimester framework if they did not unduly burden the abortion decision (and thus did not trigger strict scrutiny), if they became applicable after the first trimester and were necessary to protect maternal health, or if they were limited exclusively to the third trimester.

In the years following *Roe*, state and local governments tested the limits of that decision by enacting laws that restricted the ability of women to obtain abortions. These measures were challenged, forcing lower courts and the Supreme Court to apply and clarify the ruling in *Roe*. The Court upheld some first- and second-trimester restrictions on the abortion process, including requirements that women give written consent and that doctors keep certain records (*Planned Parenthood of Central Missouri v. Danforth*, 428 U.S. 52 (1977)); that tissue samples be examined by a pathologist (*Planned Parenthood Ass'n of Kansas City, Mo., Inc. v. Ashcroft*, 462 U.S. 476 (1983)); and that immature minors obtain the consent of a parent, or that they wait 48 hours after notifying both parents (*H.L. v. Matheson*, 450 U.S. 398 (1981)). However, many other pre-viability restrictions were struck down, including so-called informed-consent provisions that required doctors to make specific statements to a woman concerning the fetus, and a 24-hour waiting periods (*City of Akron v. Akron Center for Reproductive Health, Inc.*, 462 U.S. 416 (1983)); laws limiting abortions exclusively to hospitals or licensed clinics (*Doe v. Bolton*, 410 U.S. 179 (1973)); bans on certain inexpensive abortion methods (see, e.g., *Planned Parenthood of Central Missouri v. Danforth*, supra); requirements that all minors, regardless of maturity, obtain the consent of a parent or a judge (*Bellotti v. Baird*, 443 U.S. 622 (1979)); and requirements that doctors report personal information about abortion patients to the state (*Thornburgh v. American College of Obstetricians & Gynecologists*, 476 U.S. 747 (1986)). The Court also struck down a number of third-trimester restrictions that, to protect the fetus, jeopardized maternal health. See, e.g., *Stenberg v. Carhart*, 530 U.S. 914 (2000)).

The Court was sharply divided in many of these cases. The majority typically applied a low threshold for determining whether a restriction unduly burdened or impinged on a woman's fundamental liberty interest and was thus subject to strict scrutiny. As a rule, the Court's majority found the impingement requirement to be satisfied if a regulation had the effect of delaying, discouraging, or increasing the cost of an abortion. The dissenting Justices, on the other hand, employed a higher threshold of impingement, so that regulations that did not constitute an absolute barrier to abortion were tested and upheld under a rational basis standard. See, e.g., *City of Akron v. Akron Center for Reproductive Health, Inc.*, supra, 462 U.S. at 461-475 (O'Connor, J., White, J., and Rehnquist, J., dissenting) (applying rational basis review to a law that imposed a 24-hour waiting period, required second-trimester abortions to be performed only in a hospital, and forced physicians to read a statement to pregnant women concerning the fetus).

By 1989, the split within the Court had reached the point where four Justices—Rehnquist, White, Scalia, and Kennedy—had gone on record urging that *Roe v. Wade* either be overruled or limited to statutes that outlawed abortions; laws that simply regulated the abortion procedure would be reviewed under the rational basis standard. It appeared that only one more vote was needed to overrule *Roe*. When Justices Brennan and Marshall, both staunch supporters of *Roe*, resigned from the Court in the early 1990s, President George H.W. Bush replaced them with David Souter and Clarence Thomas. In light of Bush's campaign promises to appoint anti-abortion judges to the federal bench, it was widely expected that these new Justices would provide the necessary votes to finally overturn *Roe*. The vehicle for the anticipated coup de grace was *Planned Parenthood v. Casey*, 505 U.S. 833 (1992), a case challenging the Pennsylvania Abortion Control Act.

Planned Parenthood v. Casey and the End of the Trimester Approach

In *Planned Parenthood v. Casey,* the Court struck down that part of Pennsylvania's abortion law that required married women, except in certain limited circumstances, to notify their husbands before having an abortion. The Court upheld the rest of the act, including an informed-consent provision that required physicians to give women specific information about the fetus; a 24-hour waiting period; a parental consent requirement for immature minors; and a record-keeping and reporting requirement for facilities performing abortions. To uphold these latter provisions, the Court had to overrule several prior decisions that had declared similar regulations to be unconstitutional. And while *Casey* preserved what it viewed as the "essential holding" of *Roe v. Wade,* it rejected *Roe*'s trimester framework, replacing it with a new "undue burden" test for analyzing the validity of all abortion restrictions.

Casey was the product of a highly splintered Court. Four Justices—Rehnquist, White, Scalia, and Thomas—voted to overrule *Roe* in its entirety and to sustain all the challenged regulations. Justice Blackmun, on the other hand, adhered fully to *Roe* and believed that all the Pennsylvania restrictions were invalid. Justice Stevens also endorsed *Roe* and voted to invalidate most of the state's restrictions. With the Court split four to two, the outcome lay in the hands of Justices O'Connor, Kennedy, and Souter. They issued a joint opinion that staked out a middle position between completely overruling *Roe* and preserving the decision intact.

The authors of the joint opinion, some of whom had been quite critical of *Roe,* explained that the principle of stare decisis prevented them from abandoning *Roe* in its entirety. They declared that "the essential holding of *Roe v. Wade* should be retained and once again reaffirmed." 505 U.S. at 846. This essential holding was that a woman has "the right . . . to choose an abortion before viability and to obtain it without undue interference from the State," and the right to elect an abortion even after viability where it is necessary to protect her health or her life. Id.

However, said the joint authors, "We reject the trimester framework, which we do not consider to be part of the essential holding of *Roe.*" Id. at 873. That framework "undervalues the State's interest in the potential life within the woman." Id. at 875. While *Roe* said that interest becomes compelling only at viability, they believed "there is a substantial state interest in potential life throughout pregnancy." Id. at 876. This upgrading of the interest in potential life gave the state a much stronger ground for regulating abortion during the first and second trimesters. It also eliminated any reason for distinguishing between the first and second trimesters, since the state now had a compelling reason for restricting abortion from the very beginning of pregnancy. On the other hand, the joint authors refused to abandon the "viability line" that divides the second and third trimesters. As they explained, part of "*Roe*'s central holding is that viability marks the earliest point at which the State's interest in fetal life is constitutionally adequate to justify a legislative ban on nontherapeutic abortions." Id. at 860. Thus, under *Casey*, prior to viability a woman still had a fundamental right to choose an abortion—even if it was not necessary to protect her life or her health. After viability, the state might outlaw abortion except where it was necessary to preserve the health or life of the mother.

The Undue Burden Test

Besides abandoning the trimester framework, Justices O'Connor, Kennedy, and Souter refused to apply the same strict scrutiny approach used in other fundamental rights due process cases. Under the standard approach, a law that impinged upon or burdened a fundamental liberty would be upheld only if it was the least burdensome means of achieving a compelling governmental interest; the fact that the government had "unduly" burdened the right was not by itself necessarily fatal. See § 2.4.4. However, under the joint opinion's new undue burden test for judging abortion regulations, a law or practice that unduly burdened a woman's liberty interest in the abortion decision was invalid, without also asking whether or not it was the least burdensome means for achieving the state's interest. As the *Casey* Court said, "an undue burden is an unconstitutional burden." 505 U.S. at 877. At first blush, the undue burden test might appear to increase the protection afforded the abortion decision, for the states seemingly had no opportunity to justify a regulation once it was found to impose an undue burden. In reality, however, the new standard made it much easier for the government to regulate abortion than it was under *Roe*.

According to the undue burden test, a law would be found to impose an undue burden "if its *purpose* or *effect* [wa]s to place a substantial obstacle in the path of a woman seeking an abortion before the fetus attain[ed] viability." Id. at 878 (emphasis supplied). As far as the purpose element was concerned, a law imposed an undue burden if it was "calculated to . . . hinder" a woman's freedom of choice. Id. at 877. This element was not violated if the state's purpose was "to persuade the woman to choose childbirth over abortion." Id. at 878. Since a state could almost always claim that its purpose was "to persuade" rather than "to hinder," it was hard to imagine any law being held to constitute an undue burden because of its purpose.

With respect to the effect element of the test, it was harder to establish that a law unduly burdened the right to choose an abortion than it was under *Roe* and its progeny. According to the joint opinion, the government could adopt measures that interfered with a woman's ability to obtain an abortion, so long as they did not "place a *substantial obstacle*" in a woman's path to obtaining an abortion—i.e., so long as they did not actually prevent or "prohibit [her] from making the ultimate decision to terminate her pregnancy before viability." Id. at 879. Thus, "that a law . . . ha[d] the *incidental* effect of making it more *difficult* or more *expensive* to procure an abortion [would not] be enough to invalidate it." Id. at 874 (emphasis supplied). Previously, regulations that made it more difficult or more costly to obtain an abortion were routinely found to impinge on a woman's freedom of choice and usually struck down. *Casey* overruled earlier decisions that had invalidated waiting-period and informed-consent requirements, for these were not deemed to pose "substantial obstacle[s]."

Though *Casey*'s undue burden test was subscribed to by only three Justices, it represented the holding of the Court in that case. Any doubt as to the status of the undue burden test was eliminated in *Stenberg v. Carhart*, 530 U.S. 914, 930 (2000), where a majority of the Court for the first time endorsed the test to evaluate the constitutionality of laws regulating abortion.

At least at first blush, *Casey* seemed to have left the government with no opportunity to defend a law that posed a substantial obstacle to women seeking an abortion. That changed in *Whole Woman's Health v. Hellerstedt*, 579 U.S. 582, 607-609 (2016). There, the Court for the first time read *Casey* as having set forth a "balancing" test—one which "requires that courts consider the burdens a law imposes on abortion access together with the benefits those laws confer." Id. at 607-608. Under *Hellerstedt*'s balancing approach, the government could defend a law that might otherwise impose an unacceptable burden on abortion access by showing that the measure produced real benefits to the state. Because it was difficult in this setting to compare benefits and burdens (a task akin to comparing the length of a line to the weight of a stone), *Hellerstedt*'s reformulation of *Casey* meant that abortion restrictions would be found to impose an "undue burden" only if they posed a "substantial obstacle" and the government failed to show that they produced any real health benefits. Id. at 624.

Dobbs v. Jackson Women's Health Organization

The undue burden standard formulated in *Casey* and its progeny made it much easier for the government to regulate and restrict abortions, significantly weakening the protections first set forth in *Roe*. In May 2021, the Court granted cert in a case presenting the question: "Whether all pre-viability prohibitions on elective abortions are unconstitutional." *Dobbs v. Jackson Women's Health Org.* (petition for cert., 2020 WL 3317135 (U.S. June 15, 2020) (No. 19-1392)), *cert. granted*, 141 S. Ct. 2619 (2021) (mem.). While the cert petition said that "the questions presented . . . do not require the Court to overturn *Roe* and *Casey*," a footnote invited just that: "If the Court determines that it cannot reconcile *Roe* and *Casey* with other precedents or scientific advancements showing a compelling state interest in fetal life far earlier in pregnancy than those cases contemplate, the Court should not retain erroneous precedent." 2020 WL 3317135, supra, at *5 & n.1.

2. Substantive Due Process

In *Dobbs v. Jackson Women's Health Org.*, 597 U.S. 215 (2022), the Court accepted that invitation and overruled both *Roe* and *Casey*. In doing so, it held that in deciding "whether the Fourteenth Amendment's reference to 'liberty' protects a particular right," it must be shown that: (1) "the right in issue . . . is rooted in our Nation's history and tradition" and "an essential component of . . . 'ordered' liberty"; or that (2) it "is part of a broader entrenched right that is supported by other precedents." Id. at 234. In the Court's view, a woman's right to an abortion satisfied neither of these tests.

As to the first possibility, the Court explained:

> In this country during the 19th century, the vast majority of States enacted statutes criminalizing abortion at all stages of pregnancy. . . . By 1868, the year when the Fourteenth Amendment was ratified, three-quarters of the States, 28 out of 37, had enacted statutes making abortion a crime even if it was performed before quickening. Of the nine States that had not yet criminalized abortion at all stages, all but one did so by 1910.

Id. at 248-249. Nor did this historical landscape begin to change until relatively recently.

> Until the latter part of the 20th century, there was no support in American law for a constitutional right to obtain an abortion. No state constitutional provision had recognized such a right. Until a few years before *Roe*, no federal or state court had recognized such a right. Nor had any scholarly treatise.

Id. at 216-217. "The inescapable conclusion," said the Court, "is that a right to abortion is not deeply rooted in the Nation's history and traditions. On the contrary, an unbroken tradition of prohibiting abortion on pain of criminal punishment persisted from the earliest days of the common law until 1973." Id. at 250.

Nor did the right to seek an abortion qualify as being an integral part of another entrenched right supported by precedent. The claimed "broader right to autonomy and to define one's 'concept of existence' prove too much," said the Court, for "[t]hose criteria, at a high level of generality, could license fundamental rights to illicit drug use, prostitution, and the like." Id. at 257.

Because the Court found no protected liberty interest to be involved, it applied a rational basis test to uphold the Mississippi statute which outlawed abortion after 15 weeks' gestation except in cases of medical emergency or fetal abnormality. The state legislature, said the Court, "could have thought that it would serve legitimate state interests," including respect and preservation of prenatal life, protection of maternal health and safety, and mitigation of fetal pain. Id. at 301. Nothing more was required under the rational basis test.

2. Substantive Due Process

The decision in *Dobbs* addressed the question of whether the Due Process Clause gives women a "liberty" interest in having an abortion. Because it does not, the Court held, states may *prohibit* abortion if they have a rational basis for doing so. However, as the dissenters in *Dobbs* pointed out, *Dobbs* did not answer the question of whether the Due Process Clause required the states to allow abortions when needed to protect a woman's life and health. See 597 U.S. at 393 (Breyer, J., Sotomayor, J., and Kagan, J., dissenting).

In overruling *Roe* and *Wade*, the *Dobbs* Court noted that it was "time to heed the Constitution and return the issue of abortion to the people's elected representatives." Id. at 232. At the time the case was argued, at least 21 states allowed abortion (id. at 339 (Kavanagh, J., concurring)), while 26 states opposed it. Id. at 292. As Justice Kavanaugh suggested, "[a]fter today's decision, all of the States may evaluate the competing interests and decide how to address this consequential issue." Id. at 339 (Kavanaugh, J., concurring). Some state high courts did just that. See, e.g., *Hodes & Nauser, MDs, P.A. v. Kobach*, 551 P.3d 37 (Kan. 2024) (state constitution's fundamental right of personal autonomy protects a pregnant person's right to terminate pregnancy); *Members of Medical Licensing Board of Indiana v. Planned Parenthood Great Northwest*, 211 N.E.3d 957 (Ind. 2023) (state constitution protects woman's right to abortion where necessary to protect her life or protect her from serious health risk); *Wrigley v. Romanik*, 988 N.W.2d 231 (N.D. 2023) (state constitution gives a woman a fundamental right to obtain an abortion to preserve her life or her health); *Oklahoma Call for Reproductive Justice v. Drummond*, 526 P.3d 1123 (Okla. 2023) (state constitution guarantees inherent right to terminate pregnancy where necessary to protect mother's life).

Other post-*Dobbs* state courts went in the opposite direction. See, e.g., *Planned Parenthood Great Northwest v. State*, 522 P.3d 1132 (Idaho 2023) (state law criminalizing abortion after detection of fetal heartbeat is only subject to rational basis review under state constitution); *Planned Parenthood South Atlantic v. State*, 892 S.E.2d 121 (S.C. 2023) (state law barring abortion after detection of fetal heartbeat does not violate state constitution because state has compelling interest in protecting lives of the unborn); *Planned Parenthood of Southwest and Central Florida v. State*, 384 So. 3d 67 (Fla. 2024) ("receding" from prior decision based on *Roe* and holding that state constitution does not guarantee the right to receive an abortion). The Arizona Supreme Court reached the same end but by a different route. Without addressing the constitutional issue, it ruled that an 1864 Arizona law banning abortions "except those necessary to save a woman's life," and that had never been repealed, became operable and prospectively enforceable with the overruling of *Roe*. *Planned Parenthood Arizona, Inc. v. Mayes*, 545 P.3d 892 (Ariz. 2024).

Example 2-E

In 2019, Georgia enacted the Living Infants Fairness and Equality (LIFE) Act. It prohibits abortions after a fetal heartbeat is detected, with certain enumerated exceptions, including where a mother reasonably believed an abortion was necessary to prevent a medical emergency. Anyone who performs or assists in performing an abortion in violation of the act may be imprisoned for up to ten years. Does the LIFE Act violate a pregnant woman's rights under the Due Process Clause?

Explanation

Prior to the Supreme Court's 2022 decision in *Dobbs*, the LIFE Act would have been unconstitutional. Under *Roe* and *Casey*, before the point of viability — about 26 weeks into pregnancy — states could regulate but not prohibit abortions. Because fetal heartbeats are detectable about six or seven weeks into pregnancy, the LIFE Act would have violated a woman's fundamental liberty to elect an abortion before viability. After *Dobbs*, however, the LIFE Act is only subject to rational basis scrutiny since the right to seek an abortion is no longer a fundamental liberty under the Due Process Clause. The Act clearly passes muster under that test for it is a rational way of furthering the state's legitimate interest in respecting "prenatal life at all stages of development." *Dobbs v. Jackson Women's Health Org.*, supra, 597 U.S. at 301. See *SisterSong Women of Color Reproductive Justice Collective v. Governor of Georgia*, 40 F.4th 1320 (11th Cir. 2022) (so holding and reversing district court decision that was issued before *Dobbs* was decided).

§2.5.2 Marriage

One of the fundamental liberties protected by the right of personal autonomy is the right to marry—i.e., the freedom to decide to enter into the marital relationship. In *Loving v. Virginia*, 388 U.S. 1, 12 (1967), the Court described marriage as "one of the 'basic civil rights of man,' fundamental to our very existence and survival." The Court later explained that "the right to marry is part of the fundamental 'right of privacy' implicit in the . . . Due Process Clause." *Zablocki v. Redhail*, 434 U.S. 374, 384 (1978). Laws that impinge on or unduly burden the freedom to marry are subject to strict scrutiny under the Due Process Clause. The Court has suggested, however, that because marriage has traditionally been governed by the states, it may be more difficult than in other fundamental liberty cases to establish that a law has sufficiently burdened the right to marry to trigger strict scrutiny.

In trying to determine when a law that interferes with the marriage decision will receive strict scrutiny under the Due Process Clause, cases decided under the Equal Protection Clause may be instructive. This is because laws that impinge on the freedom to marry on a *discriminatory* basis are also subject to strict scrutiny under the Equal Protection Clause. See § 7.2. Since these impingement requirements are similar, the equal protection cases shed light on what types of restrictions on the right to marry are likely to trigger strict scrutiny under the Due Process Clause.

Laws that directly and seriously interfere with the decision to marry—e.g., by prohibiting a person from exercising this fundamental liberty—impose an "undue burden" on the right to marry and trigger a generally fatal strict scrutiny. See *Zablocki v. Redhail*, supra (law barring marriage by certain parents who have not complied with child support orders violates Equal Protection Clause); *Loving v. Virginia*, 388 U.S. 1 (1967) (ban on marriage between whites and nonwhites violates Due Process and Equal Protection Clauses).

On the other hand, "reasonable regulations that do not significantly interfere with decisions to enter into the marital relationship" will not be "subjected to rigorous scrutiny." *Zablocki*, supra, 434 U.S. at 386. Traditional state requirements that merely delay exercise of this right—e.g., minimum age requirements for marriage and waiting periods for divorce (a legal prerequisite for remarriage)—are unlikely to be tested under strict scrutiny. Cf. *Sosna v. Iowa*, 419 U.S. 393 (1975) (applying less than strict scrutiny to uphold one-year waiting period for divorce under Equal Protection Clause, but without specifically addressing law's impact on right to marry). Even some traditional restrictions that permanently interfere with the marriage decision, such as laws against bigamy and incest, may not be regarded as unduly burdening the right to marry. See *Zablocki*, supra, 434 U.S. at 392 (Stewart, J., concurring); id. at 398-399 (Powell, J., concurring); see also *Reynolds v. United States*, 98 U.S. 145 (1879) (affirming a polygamy conviction and expressly endorsing the Western tradition of monogamy). Yet other traditional restrictions that seriously interfere with the right to marry may be subjected to strict scrutiny despite their lineage. See *Loving v. Virginia*, 388 U.S. 1 (1967) (using strict scrutiny to overturn Virginia's anti-miscegenation laws that dated from seventeenth century and had counterparts in many other states).

Since it is often unclear whether a law will be found to impinge on the right to marry, it is a good idea in cases of doubt to employ a dual analysis, approaching the problem first on the assumption that the law imposes an undue burden and then on the assumption that it does not.

Example 2-F

Alice is 16 years old and was recently married. Shortly after her marriage, the state terminated her $550-per-month welfare grant under a law that allows those who are under 21 to receive welfare benefits only if they are unmarried. Does this law violate Alice's rights under the Fourteenth Amendment Due Process Clause?

Explanation

Alice will argue that the law interferes with her liberty interest in marriage. Since the right to marry is a protected and fundamental liberty interest, the first two steps of the basic due process analysis are satisfied. Alice will have a harder time meeting the undue burden requirement. The state has not directly interfered with the marriage decision by prohibiting her from getting married. On the other hand, it has indirectly punished her for deciding to marry by terminating her subsistence benefits as a result. In *Califano v. Jobst*, 434 U.S. 47 (1977), the Court held that the termination of Social Security benefits to a child who marries does not impinge on the liberty interest in marriage; there, however, the benefits were relatively low and were not intended to meet subsistence needs. Alice will claim that because of the critical nature of the benefits at stake, her case is distinguishable from *Jobst* and that the state has, therefore, impinged on her fundamental liberty to marry.

If the Court agrees, the law will receive strict scrutiny. Under step 4, the state may claim a compelling interest in encouraging children on welfare to work or educate themselves before starting their own families, thus reducing the chances that they will continue to be dependent on welfare. Alice would respond that the mere saving of money is not a compelling interest; if it were, the government could justify curtailing our most basic liberty interests such as freedom of speech and assembly on the ground that their exercise is too costly. Even if the interest in saving money were compelling, Alice will argue under step 5 that the state has less burdensome ways to achieve its goals, such as simply requiring children who are on welfare to work or attend school whether or not they are married. Thus, if the court applies strict scrutiny, the law might well be struck down on the basis that it was not necessary for the state to interfere with Alice's right to marry to achieve its goal of reducing welfare costs. If, on the other hand, the court were to apply the rational basis test, the law would be upheld, since a rational legislature could reasonably conclude that this law was a good way to reduce long-term dependence on welfare.

2. **Substantive Due Process**

In *Obergefell v. Hodges*, 576 U.S. 644 (2015), the Court held that the fundamental right to marry extended to same-sex couples. The Court's decision was premised on what it described as "four principles and traditions," id. at 665, each of which demonstrated that a couple's sexual orientation had no bearing on the scope of the right. First, "the right to personal choice regarding marriage is inherent in the concept of individual autonomy." Id. The exercise of that autonomous choice allows a couple to "find other freedoms, such as expression, intimacy, and spirituality. This is true for all persons, whatever their sexual orientation." Id. at 666. Next, the right to marry is also premised on a right of "intimate association," which, as a matter of precedent, extends fully to same sex couples. Id. at 667 (citing *Lawrence v. Texas*, 539 U.S. 558 (2003)); see § 2.5.5. Third, the right to marry "safeguards children and families and thus draws meaning from related rights of childrearing, procreation, and education." Id. at 667. Concerning this point, the Court observed:

> As all parties agree, many same-sex couples provide loving and nurturing homes to their children, whether biological or adopted. And hundreds of thousands of children are presently being raised by such couples. Most States have allowed gays and lesbians to adopt, either as individuals or as couples, and many adopted and foster children have same-sex parents. This provides powerful confirmation from the law itself that gays and lesbians can create loving, supportive families.

Id. at 668. "Fourth and finally," the Court explained, "this Court's cases and the Nation's traditions make clear that marriage is a keystone of our social order." Id. at 669. Here the Court noted that society offers symbolic and tangible benefits to the married couple by placing marriage "at the center of so many facets of the legal and social order." Id. at 670.

> There is no difference between same- and opposite-sex couples with respect to this principle. Yet by virtue of their exclusion from that institution, same-sex couples are denied the constellation of benefits that the States have linked to marriage. This harm results in more than just material burdens. Same-sex couples are consigned to an instability many opposite-sex couples would deem intolerable in their own lives.

Id. In short, the *Obergefell* Court concluded that the right to marry was inherent in the liberty protected by the Fourteenth Amendment and that this right extended to same- and opposite-sex couples equally. See *United States v. Windsor*, 570 U.S. 744 (2013) (striking down as irrational a federal statute that defined marriage as limited to opposite-sex couples); see also §§ 6.7.4, 7.2.

However, in the wake of *Dobbs v. Jackson Women's Health Org.*, 597 U.S. 215 (2022), the Court might reconsider its holding in *Obergefell*, for a same-sex couple's right to live together might not be deeply rooted in this Nation's history and traditions, implicit in the concept of ordered liberty, or part of a broader entrenched right supported by precedent. See id. at 332 (Thomas, J., concurring) (suggesting reconsideration,); id. at 345-346, 362-363 (Breyer, J., Sotomayor, J., and Kagan, J., dissenting) (recognizing possibility of reconsideration).

§2.5.3 Family Integrity

Family Living Arrangements

The right to marry was held to constitute a fundamental liberty partly because marriage establishes "the relationship that is the foundation of the family in our society." *Zablocki v. Redhail*, supra, 434 U.S. at 386. The family constitutes a sphere of life that lies at the heart of what is private and personal. To shield this sphere from unwarranted governmental intrusion, the Court has held that the interest in maintaining the integrity of the family is a protected aspect of the fundamental right of privacy under the Due Process Clause. This liberty interest usually comes into play in settings where the government has interfered with family living arrangements by making it difficult or impossible for family members to share a common household. See *Moore v. City of East Cleveland*, 431 U.S. 494 (1977) (invalidating ordinance that barred a grandmother, her son, and two grandsons from living together in the same home).

Example 2-G

A city ordinance provides that no household may be occupied by more than two persons under the age of ten. As a result of the ordinance, the Sutro family, which includes three children under the age of ten, is being evicted from the apartment where they have lived for the past 12 years. Can the Sutros avoid being evicted on the ground that the ordinance violates their rights under the Fourteenth Amendment Due Process Clause?

Explanation

The fundamental liberty interest recognized in *Moore* protects the right of persons who are related by blood or marriage to live together in a common household. The city's ordinance directly and substantially interferes with this right by barring the Sutros from preserving the integrity of their family unit. The only way they could avoid being evicted is by sending one of the children to live somewhere else or by giving the child up for adoption. The ordinance clearly impinges on the family's fundamental liberty interest. It is no answer that the Sutros could live together as a family in some other city. This option was available to the family in *Moore* but did not suffice to avoid the application of strict scrutiny there.

Since the first three steps of the due process analysis have been satisfied, the ordinance will be struck down unless the city can show that it furthers a compelling governmental interest and that it is the least burdensome means of doing so. The city may argue that it has an interest in preserving the peace and tranquility of residential areas and that households with many young children often disturb others, particularly senior citizens. It is far from clear that this interest is sufficiently compelling to justify a law that strikes so close to the heart of the family. Small children have always been part of the American landscape, and the noise that they make is an unavoidable fact of life.

Even if a court were to find this interest to be compelling, there are less burdensome ways of achieving the city's goals, such as by enforcing noise control ordinances, allowing landlords to limit the occupancy of certain buildings to senior citizens, or perhaps even zoning parts of the city exclusively for adults.

As is true with the liberty interest in marriage, however, not all laws that burden a family's interest in living together are necessarily subject to strict scrutiny.

Example 2-H

EXAMPLE

A state welfare program provides assistance to needy families with children. The state pays $150 per month for each child living in the home, with a maximum monthly grant of $450 per household. Mary and Joe, who live with their six children, receive a welfare grant of $450 per month. This is not enough to meet their basic needs. If Joe and three of the children were to move to a different apartment, they would be eligible for a separate grant of $450 per month, so that the family would receive $900 per month. Does the state's "maximum grant" rule violate the Due Process Clause by forcing poor families to break up their shared living arrangements?

Explanation

EXPLANATION

Probably not. In contrast to *Moore v. City of East Cleveland*, and to Example 2-G, the state has not made it illegal for family members to maintain a common household. While the structure of the welfare program may give needy families an incentive to split their household, the incentive is probably weak. While the Mary and Joe could double their welfare benefits by breaking up their household, the additional rent and utility costs associated with doing so might more than offset the additional income they would receive. Because the state has probably not impinged on their liberty interest in family integrity, the state's maximum grant rule would be upheld under the rational basis test. See *Lyng v. Castillo*, 477 U.S. 635 (1986) (no impingement on liberty interest in family integrity where government gave reduced food stamps to households with related persons even though family could increase its food stamp allowance by living apart); *Dandridge v. Williams*, 397 U.S. 471 (1970) (upholding state maximum grant in Aid to Families with Dependent Children (AFDC) welfare program). In our hypothetical, strict scrutiny might be triggered if the state instead refused to pay *any* welfare benefits to households with more than three children, for then the incentive for a needy family to split into separate households might be economically irresistible.

In *Department of State v. Muñoz*, 144 S. Ct. 1812 (2024), the Court was asked to recognize that the liberty interest in living with one's spouse protects a citizen's interest in living with their noncitizen spouse in this country. In contrast to *Moore v. City of East Cleveland*, supra, the spouses did not both reside in the United States; instead, while Sandra Muñoz was a U.S. citizen who lived in California, her husband, Ascencio-Cordero, was an El Salvadoran citizen who had been denied an immigrant visa to come to this country, without any explanation as to the reason for the denial. Muñoz's claimed liberty interest was thus factually different from what the Court had recognized in earlier cases. As the *Muñoz* Court wrote:

> We start with a "careful description of the asserted fundamental interest." Muñoz invokes the "fundamental right of marriage," but the State Department does not deny that Muñoz (who is already married) has a fundamental right to marriage. Muñoz claims something distinct: the right to *reside with her noncitizen spouse in the United States*. That involves more than marriage and more than spousal cohabitation—it includes the right to have her noncitizen husband enter (and remain in) the United States.

Id. at 1822 (emphasis in original) (internal citations omitted). The Court then noted that Muñoz "'does not advance a substantive right to immigrate one's spouse'," for there is no such right, but rather only a "procedural due process" right to notice and an opportunity to be heard concerning the reasons for the State Department's denial of "the right to *reside with her noncitizen spouse in the United States*." Id. (emphasis in original). As the Court put it, she thus claimed "a substantive due process right that gets only procedural due process protection." Id. Even if there were such a right "fundamental enough to be implicit in 'liberty," said the Court, it is not "'deeply rooted in this Nation's history and tradition.' On the contrary, the through line of history is recognition of the Government's sovereign authority to set the terms governing the admission and exclusion of noncitizens. And Muñoz points to no subsidiary tradition that curbs this authority in the case of noncitizen spouses." Id. at 1822-1823 (internal citation omitted).

The liberty interest in maintaining the integrity of the family does not protect all groups of people who wish to share a common household. While the Court in *Moore* was willing to extend the constitutional protections of family beyond the traditional nuclear family consisting of parents and their children, the Court has held that there are limits on how far the definition of family can be stretched for due process purposes. In *Village of Belle Terre v. Boraas,* 416 U.S. 1 (1974), the Court thus applied the rational basis test to uphold a zoning ordinance that barred six college students from occupying a house together. The key difference between *Moore* and *Belle Terre* was that in the latter case, the ordinance "affected only *unrelated* individuals. It expressly allowed all who were related by 'blood, adoption, or marriage' to live together. . . ." *Moore,* supra, 431 U.S. at 498 (emphasis in original). However, even if unrelated individuals are not able to invoke the liberty interest in family integrity, they may be able to protect their right to live together through another fundamental liberty interest, namely, the freedom of intimate association. See § 2.5.4.

The Parent-Child Relationship

The liberty interest in preserving the integrity of the family is closely related to the interest of parents in their children. Indeed, the parent-child relationship lies at the heart of our notion of family. When the Court in *Moore v. City of East Cleveland* held that there is a fundamental liberty interest in maintaining family living arrangements, it relied on earlier cases such as *Meyer v. Nebraska* and *Pierce v. Society of Sisters,* which recognized that parents have a liberty interest in raising their children. This same liberty interest is implicated when the state seeks to disrupt the parent-child relationship through such actions as removing a child from the custody of its parents or denying a parent visitation rights.

Yet not all parent-child relationships are protected by the liberty interest in family. While *Moore* seemed to suggest that ties of blood, adoption, or marriage are *necessary* for there to be a "family" that can invoke the liberty interest in preserving family relationships, the existence of these ties will not always be *sufficient* to create a constitutionally protected family unit. In *Michael H. v. Gerald D.*, 491 U.S. 110 (1989), Michael claimed a fundamental liberty in maintaining a parental relationship with his biological daughter, Victoria—a relationship that the state sought to terminate by denying him all visitation rights. Even though earlier cases had recognized that parents, including unwed fathers, have a fundamental liberty interest in the parent-child relationship, the Court rejected Michael's challenge. Justice Scalia, writing for the plurality, emphasized that Michael was an *adulterous* natural father, for the child's mother was married to and living with another man at the time the child was born. Because the relationship between an adulterous natural father and his child has not been traditionally protected by our society, Michael and Victoria were not deemed to be a "protected family unit" for purposes of the Due Process Clause. As a result, neither Michael nor his daughter could claim a constitutional liberty interest in the biological parent-child relationship that existed between them.

Michael H. exemplifies the sharply contrasting approaches individual Justices may take in construing the Constitution. See generally *National Power & Federalism*, supra, § 1.7. While no member of the Court urged that the word "liberty" in the Due Process Clause be limited to those specific interests that the drafters of the Fifth and Fourteenth Amendments had in mind, the Justices disagreed as to what method of interpretation should be employed. Justice Scalia, joined by Chief Justice Rehnquist, asserted that the Due Process Clause protects only those liberties that are "rooted in history and tradition. . . ." 491 U.S. at 123. In determining whether this test was met, Scalia insisted that an asserted liberty interest be described narrowly in terms of "the most specific tradition available. . . ." Id. at 128 n.6. Thus, the relevant inquiry in *Michael H.* focused on "historical traditions *specifically relating to the rights of an adulterous natural father*, rather than inquiring more generally 'whether *parenthood* is an interest that historically has received our attention and protection.'" Id. at 127 n.6 (emphasis supplied). Since there was no tradition protecting adulterous fathers, Scalia and Rehnquist concluded that Michael had no liberty interest whatsoever in preserving his relationship with Victoria.

Other Justices adopted less restrictive methodologies in *Michael H.* Justices O'Connor and Kennedy agreed with Scalia that the Court was obligated to look to history and tradition but rejected his "imposition of a single mode of historical analysis"; instead, they believed that it might sometimes be proper to consider "relevant traditions protecting asserted rights at levels of generality that might not be 'the most specific level' available." Id. at 132 (O'Connor, J., and Kennedy, J., concurring in part). Justices Brennan, Marshall, and Blackmun objected both to Scalia's narrow approach to history and tradition, and to his focus on history and tradition to the exclusion of other possible sources of interpretation. While history and tradition are not irrelevant, said Brennan, the Court should not "[r]equire specific approval from history before protecting anything in the name of liberty." Id. at 141 (Brennan, J., Marshall, J., and Blackmun, J., dissenting). In Brennan's view, the Court may reason from earlier precedents by asking whether a claimed liberty interest is "close enough to the interests that we already have protected to be deemed an aspect of 'liberty' as well." Id. at 142. Justice White appeared to adopt an approach similar to Brennan's.

Nonparental Visitation Statutes

All 50 states have enacted statutes that allow persons who are not a child's parents to obtain a court order granting them visitation rights with the child. These statutes vary widely in terms of who may seek such visitation, the circumstances under which a petition seeking visitation may be filed, and the showing that is required before a court may grant visitation rights. If a child's custodial parents favor visitation by grandparents or other third parties, the matter will usually be handled amicably and informally, without judicial intervention. State nonparental visitation statutes are thus likely to come into play only when a child's parent or parents oppose the visitation sought by a third party. If a court orders visitation under such circumstances, it interferes with parents' fundamental liberty interest in directing the upbringing of their children. On the other hand, to allow parents unilaterally to block visitation by grandparents or others who have developed a close relationship with a child may interfere with the child's liberty interest in preserving familial or family-like bonds and undermine the state's interest in protecting children from harm. Nonparental visitation statutes thus raise complex issues of substantive due process.

A sharply divided Supreme Court addressed these issues for the first time in *Troxel v. Granville*, 530 U.S. 57 (2000). The case involved a Washington statute that allowed "any person" to petition for visitation rights "at any time," and authorized courts to order such visitation over a parent's objection if the judge decided that "visitation may serve the best interest of the child." Under this statute, a state trial court granted visitation rights to the Troxels, who were the paternal grandparents of two children whose father had committed suicide. The rights granted were more extensive than the children's mother, Tommie Granville, was willing to allow. On appeal, the Washington Supreme Court held that the statute was facially invalid because it unconstitutionally infringed on the fundamental right of parents to raise their children. The U.S. Supreme Court affirmed six to three, but none of the six opinions in the case commanded a majority of the Court. Though seven Justices agreed that nonparental visitation statutes may at times violate parents' fundamental liberty interest in directing the upbringing of their children, these Justices were unable to articulate any general principles governing this area. Instead, as Justice O'Connor wrote in a plurality opinion joined by three of her colleagues:

> We do not, and need not, define today the precise scope of the parental due process right in the visitation context. In this respect, we agree with Justice Kennedy that the constitutionality of any standard for awarding visitation turns on the specific manner in which the standard is applied and that the constitutional protections in this area are best "elaborated with care." Because much state-court adjudication in this context occurs on a case-by-case basis, we would be hesitant to hold that specific nonparental visitation statutes violate the Due Process Clause as a *per se* matter.

Id. at 73.

The plurality concluded that the statute was unconstitutional as applied to this case. Rather than employing the Court's basic strict scrutiny model or any of its recognized variations (see § 2.4.4), the plurality declared the law invalid because of "the combination of several factors here" that made it too easy for the state to infringe on Granville's "fundamental right to make decisions concerning the rearing of her two daughters." Id. at 68. First, there was no allegation that the children's mother was an unfit parent. "[S]o long as a parent adequately cares for his or her children (*i.e.*, is fit), there will normally be no reason for the State to inject itself into the private realm of the family to further question the ability of that parent to make the best decisions concerning the rearing of that parent's children." Id. at 68-69. Second, in finding that visitation by the grandparents was in the children's best interest, the Washington trial court—unlike courts in many other states—was not required to give any deference or weight to the mother's opposition to the petition, thereby ignoring the "presumption that fit parents act in the best interests of their children." Id. at 68. Finally, rather than seeking to bar visitation entirely, Granville merely opposed the frequency and length of the visits sought by the grandparents. The plurality thus suggested that if a state accords more deference to a fit parent's wishes than Washington did—e.g., by employing a rebuttable presumption that third-party visitation is not in a child's best interest—a nonparental visitation statute might be valid. The state's interest in intervention would be even more compelling if there were a showing of parental unfitness or if a parent sought to deny all visitation to those with whom the child had developed a close relationship.

Concurring separately, Justice Souter voted to affirm the Washington Supreme Court's ruling that the statute was facially invalid because it allowed the state, at the behest of "'any party' at 'any time'" to impair a parent's relationship with her child "merely because the judge might think himself more enlightened than the child's parent." Id. at 78-79. In contrast to the plurality, Justice Souter did not discuss whether a narrower, more deferential statute might pass constitutional muster.

To the extent that the plurality and Justice Souter focused primarily on the liberty interests of parents, Justices Stevens and Kennedy, in separate opinions, suggested that children may have a countervailing liberty interest in preserving relationships with persons other than their parents. As Justice Stevens wrote, "Cases like this do not present a bipolar struggle between the parents and the State over who has final authority to determine what is in a child's best interests. There is at minimum a third individual, whose interests are implicated in every case to which the statute applies—the child." Id. at 86. Children have "liberty interests in preserving established familial or family-like bonds," which may warrant state protection "against the arbitrary exercise of parental authority that is not in fact motivated by an interest in the welfare of the child." Id. at 88-89. In a similar vein, Justice Kennedy noted that there are cases

> in which a third party, by acting in a caregiving role over a significant period of time, has developed a relationship with a child which is not necessarily subject to absolute parental veto. . . . In the design and elaboration of their visitation laws, States may be entitled to consider that certain relationships are such that to avoid the risk of harm, a best interests standard can be employed by their domestic relations courts in some circumstances.

Id. at 98-99. It seems likely that Justices Stevens and Kennedy, like the plurality, would have upheld a nonparental visitation statute that was less sweeping than the "any person" at "any time" measure enacted by Washington.

Nor is there any doubt that Justice Scalia would have sustained such a law, for he was the only Justice who found no constitutional difficulties with the Washington statute either on its face or as applied. In his view, nonparental visitation statutes do not trigger constitutional concern because the Due Process Clause does not protect the unenumerated right of a parent to raise children. Justice Thomas would probably agree. He concurred in the judgment on the basis that existing case law recognizes a fundamental right of parents to direct the upbringing of their children. However, Thomas pointedly added that since none of the parties had argued that the Court's "substantive due process cases were wrongly decided," he would leave for another day the question of whether "the original understanding of the Due Process Clause precludes judicial enforcement of unenumerated rights under that constitutional provision." Id. at 80.

In sum, while *Troxel* affirmed that parents have a liberty interest that comes into play when a state grants visitation rights to third parties, the parent's right is far from absolute. Instead, it is likely to yield where, under a narrower statute aimed at protecting preexisting relationships, the state requires a stronger showing that nonparental visitation is necessary. How strong that showing must be, however, remains an open question. The Washington Supreme Court held that merely protecting a child's "best interests" is never enough to justify third party visitation; instead, such interference with a parent's liberty to raise her children is permissible, it said, only when necessary to prevent "harm or potential harm" to the child. Though Justices Stevens and Kennedy appear to have endorsed use of a "best interests" standard, the rest of the Court declined to address this critical issue.

§2.5.4 Intimate Association

The fundamental liberty interest in family integrity extends only to relationships that are based on ties of blood, adoption, or marriage. Other group relationships, such as those that existed among the would-be college roommates in *Village of Belle Terre,* are not protected by the liberty interest in family. However, some nonfamily groups may nonetheless enjoy constitutional protection under another aspect of the right of privacy and personal autonomy—i.e., the freedom of intimate association. See also § 8.7 (discussing the First Amendment right of association). Like the interest in family integrity, which it closely resembles, this fundamental liberty affords "certain kinds of highly personal relationships a substantial measure of sanctuary from unjustified interference by the State." *Roberts v. United States Jaycees,* 468 U.S. 609, 618 (1984). Such relationships promote personal autonomy, for they "act as critical buffers between the individual and the power of the State." Id. at 619. Moreover, since "individuals draw much of their emotional enrichment from close ties with others," the freedom of intimate association "safeguards the ability independently to define one's identity that is central to any concept of liberty." Id. When this liberty interest comes into play, it may enable a group to resist governmental actions that might either force the group to disband or compel it to accept unwanted members.

For a group to qualify for protection under the right of intimate association, it must possess some of the attributes that characterize a family, such as "relative smallness, a high degree of selectivity in decisions to begin and maintain the affiliation, and seclusion from others in critical aspects of the relationship." Id. at 620. In addition, the Court will consider the group's purpose and congeniality.

In *Roberts v. United States Jaycees,* the Jaycees argued that a state human rights law that required the Jaycees to admit women violated the group's freedom of intimate association under the Due Process Clause. However, the Court held that the Jaycees could not invoke this right because its local chapters were quite large and its membership policies essentially nonselective. See also *Board of Directors of Rotary Intl. v. Rotary Club of Duarte,* 481 U.S. 537 (1987) (rejecting claim that state-ordered admission of women violated group's right of intimate association).

In the prison setting, while the Court has stopped short of holding that "any right to intimate association is altogether terminated by incarceration or is always irrelevant to claims made by prisoners," this right, like many other liberty interests, is severely curtailed by the fact of imprisonment. *Overton v. Bazzetta,* 539 U.S. 126, 131 (2003). *Overton* thus explained that because "freedom of association is among the rights least compatible with incarceration," restrictions on an inmate's ability to be visited by family and intimate friends need only "bear a rational relation to legitimate penological interests." Id. at 131-132. The Court on this basis reversed a Sixth Circuit decision that had invalidated a Michigan law limiting prisoners' ability to have even noncontact visits, conducted behind a glass panel, with minors (including an inmate's children), relatives, former prisoners, and friends, and that barred inmates who engaged in substance abuse from having any visitors other than attorneys and clergy members for two years or more. The Court did suggest that while some of these restrictions might not have passed muster had they been challenged individually or as applied in specific settings, "[t]hese considerations cannot justify the decision of the Court of Appeals to invalidate the regulation as to *all* noncontact visits." Id. at 136 (emphasis supplied). Yet given the Court's determination to "accord substantial deference to the professional judgment of prison administrators," id. at 132, it is probably unlikely that even a more focused challenge would in the end succeed.

EXAMPLE

Example 2-I

Beverly owns a house with ten bedrooms. She lives there with eight adult boarders who are not related by blood, marriage, or adoption. Over the years, the group has developed strong social, economic, and psychological commitments to each other. They share expenses, rotate chores, and eat evening meals together. In addition, they often attend movies, go bowling, and take vacations together. A city zoning ordinance provides that no household may contain more than five people who are unrelated by blood, marriage, or adoption. The city has sued Beverly for an injunction, claiming that she is in violation of the ordinance. May Beverly oppose enforcement on the ground that the ordinance violates her rights under the Fourteenth Amendment Due Process Clause?

EXPLANATION

Explanation

Beverly cannot invoke the fundamental liberty interest in protecting family living arrangements, since this right applies only to groups that are related by blood, adoption, or marriage. However, she may be able to invoke the privacy-based right of intimate association. In contrast to the students in *Belle Terre,* her household shares many attributes normally associated with a typical family. Beverly can argue that the group is relatively small and congenial, that she is very selective in whom she takes in as boarders, and that the group's purpose transcends mere convenience. She and her tenants have formed bonds that are intimate and enduring, and similar to those developed in traditional family households.

If the court finds that Beverly and her tenants are protected by the right of intimate association, the city's effort to break up her household impinges on this right so as to trigger strict scrutiny. Even if the city has compelling interests in limiting density, controlling noise, and reducing the number of cars in residential areas, there are other ways to achieve these goals without burdening the right of intimate association. See *City of Santa Barbara v. Adamson,* 27 Cal. 3d 123, 610 P.2d 436 (1980) (state constitution barred use of zoning ordinance to force dissolution of household of 12 unrelated persons who shared many attributes of family).

§2.5.5 Sexual Intimacy

The Court's most recent expansion of the substantive liberties protected by the Due Process Clause is the right of consenting adults to engage in intimate sexual behavior, including that with members of the same sex, "in the most private of places, the home." *Lawrence v. Texas*, 539 U.S. 558, 567 (2003). In reaching this decision, the Court overruled *Bowers v. Hardwick*, 478 U.S. 186 (1986), a case that had upheld Georgia's criminal sodomy statute as applied to sexual conduct engaged in by two adult men in the privacy of their home. The *Bowers* Court had framed the issue before it as being "whether the Federal Constitution confers a fundamental right upon homosexuals to engage in sodomy," id. at 190, rather than viewing the case as one involving personal autonomy and the "interest in independence in making certain kinds of important decisions." *Whalen v. Roe*, 429 U.S. 589, 599-600 (1977). As the *Lawrence* Court observed, by framing the issue as it did, *Bowers* "fail[ed] to appreciate the extent of the liberty at stake. To say that the issue . . . was simply the right to engage in certain sexual conduct demeans the claim the individual put forward, just as it would demean a married couple were it to be said marriage is simply about the right to have sexual intercourse." 539 U.S. at 567.

In concluding that adults have a protected liberty interest in their intimate sexual behavior, the Court in *Lawrence* cited a broad array of sources, including the Supreme Court's earlier privacy decisions; the fact that the number of states criminalizing sodomy had fallen dramatically from 50 states in 1960 to only 13 states by 2003; rulings by the European Court of Human Rights and by courts in other countries recognizing such a right as being "an integral part of human freedom"; and, perhaps most surprisingly, the decisions of five state courts refusing to follow *Bowers* in construing their own state constitutions. Id. at 576. The Supreme Court's willingness to overrule *Bowers* was heightened by the fact that the *Bowers* Court was simply incorrect in its belief that "[p]roscriptions against [such] conduct have ancient roots." *Bowers v. Hardwick*, supra, 478 U.S. at 192. As the *Lawrence* Court carefully showed, "there is no longstanding history in this country of laws directed at homosexual conduct as a distinct matter." 539 U.S. at 568. Instead, "American laws targeting same-sex couples did not develop until the last third of the 20th century." Id. at 570. Moreover, the nineteenth-century state laws prohibiting sodomy generally "do not seem to have been enforced against consenting adults acting in private." Id. at 569. Yet the Court in *Lawrence* at the same time downplayed the fact that state laws targeting homosexual sodomy were of relatively modern vintage. For even if there had been a well-established tradition of prohibiting such conduct in the United States, the Court noted that "[h]istory and tradition are the starting point but not in all cases the ending point of the substantive due process inquiry." Id. at 572 (internal quotation marks omitted).

Justice Kennedy's opinion for the Court in *Lawrence* was careful not to address the question of whether this newly protected liberty was one that qualified as being "fundamental" for due process purposes. Instead, it was enough for the Court to conclude that the Texas sodomy statute under which the two male petitioners had been convicted "furthers no legitimate state interest which can justify its intrusion into the personal and private life of the individual." Id. at 578. While Justice Scalia in his dissent repeatedly emphasized that the majority had applied only "rational-basis review," albeit perhaps less deferentially than that standard is sometimes employed, the Court did not need to reach the question of whether this was a fundamental liberty if the state's law could not pass muster even under a rational basis test. It is thus possible that the Court may in some future case hold that the right it so carefully delineated in *Lawrence* is in fact a fundamental one for due process purposes.

The Court's failure to resolve the fundamental-right issue may have reflected a degree of caution and uncertainty on its part as to when and under what circumstances a state might legitimately infringe on this newly created liberty interest. In light of the more recent decision in *Dobbs v. Jackson Women's Health Organization*, 597 U.S. 215 (2022), such caution proved far-sighted. For even though *Lawrence* purported to apply only a rational basis standard of review, a number of Justices in *Dobbs* expressed fear that *Lawrence* might now be reconsidered and overruled (see id. at 362-363, 385 n.8 (Breyer, J., Sotomayor, J., and Kagan, J., dissenting)), while Justice Thomas expressly called for such action. Id. at 332-333 (Thomas, J., concurring).

§2.5.6 Medical Treatment

A Right to Choose Certain Medical Treatment?

The Court has recognized that the privacy right to "independence in making certain kinds of important decisions," *Whalen v. Roe*, 429 U.S. 589, 599-600 (1977), extends to some decisions concerning what medical treatment one wishes to receive. In *Roe v. Wade*, 410 U.S. 113, 164-165 (1973), the Court held that even after a fetus has become viable, a woman retained the right to choose an abortion if this medical procedure is necessary to protect her health or her life. That holding was reaffirmed in *Stenberg v. Carhart*, 530 U.S. 914, 921 (2000). This suggested that the liberty interest recognized in *Roe* was composed of two distinct strands: first, a general right to choose an abortion for whatever reason a woman wishes; and second, the right of a woman to make choices concerning her health, including the decision to have a therapeutic abortion. Under *Roe*'s framework, while the state's interest in protecting the fetus was strong enough after the point of viability to outweigh the first of these liberties, it was not sufficient to outweigh a woman's freedom to choose medical procedures necessary to protect her health or her life.

Under *Roe* and its progeny, courts were divided on the question of how those cases applied to the use of drugs or to medical treatments outside of the abortion context. While some courts acknowledged that a fundamental liberty interest was implicated, they were quick to then find that the government was justified in barring use of the desired drug or treatment. See, e.g., *Abigail Alliance for Better Access to Developmental Drugs v. Eschenbach*, 495 F.3d 695, 711 (D.C. Cir. 2007) (en banc), *cert. denied*, 552 U.S. 1159 (2008) (terminally ill adult patients have no fundamental right protected by Due Process Clause to have access to investigational drugs); *United States v. LeBeau*, 985 F.2d 563 (table), 1993 WL 21970, at *16-*18 (7th Cir. 1993) (rejecting privacy-based claim with respect to unlicensed drugs); *United States v. Burzynksi Cancer Research Inst.*, 819 F.2d 1301, 1313-1314 (5th Cir. 1987), *cert. denied*, 484 U.S. 1065 (1988) (same). Yet a few courts were willing to uphold such a right. See, e.g., *Andrews v. Ballard*, 498 F. Supp. 1038, 1048-1051 (S.D. Tex. 1980) (state law limiting practice of acupuncture to licensed physicians violates patient's fundamental privacy interest in deciding whether to obtain medical care); *Rutherford v. United States*, 438 F. Supp. 1287, 1298-1301 (W.D. Okla. 1977), *aff'd*, 582 F.2d 1234 (10th Cir. 1978), *rev'd on other grounds*, 442 U.S. 544 (1979) (government violated cancer patient's fundamental right of privacy by prohibiting use of Laetrile).

The question is what effect might *Dobbs v. Jackson*, supra, have on this issue? As we saw, the Court there rejected *Roe* and *Casey*'s conclusion that a woman's interest in protecting her health and her life outweighed the state's interest in protecting a fetus. However, *Dobbs* did not address whether people might have such a liberty interest outside of the abortion context. Under the *Dobbs* framework, that determination would likely turn on whether the right to make health or life-saving medical decisions, in settings that do not threaten anyone else's life or health, is deeply rooted in the nation's history and traditions, or part of a broader entrenched right to protect one's life.

EXAMPLE

Example 2-J

A State X law bars healthcare providers from performing certain gender-affirming surgeries or administering hormones and puberty blockers to transgender minors who are experiencing gender dysphoria (i.e., a lack of alignment between their biological sex and their perceived gender). The prohibition applies regardless of whether the minor, their parents, or their physicians are in favor of such treatments. Does the State X law violate a minor's parents' due process right to choose medical care for their children?

EXPLANATION

Explanation

The answer will hinge on how broadly or narrowly the right in question is framed. If it is whether parents have a "fundamental right to direct the medical care of their children," such a right would likely satisfy *Dobbs* as being deeply rooted in this nation's history and tradition. State X's law clearly impinges on this liberty interest, for it totally prohibits the treatments in question. While the state has a compelling interest in protecting the health and well-being of minors, there are probably less burdensome ways of achieving this, such as requiring the procedure to be approved by the minor's parents, guardian, and/or physician.

If, however, the right is more narrowly defined as being whether parents have "a fundamental right to obtain reasonably banned medical treatments for their children," the answer is quite different, for there is no history, tradition, or unbroken practice recognizing such a right, nor is it part of a broader entrenched right. As such, only rational basis review applies and the law clearly passes muster, for the state may reasonably have thought that a total ban was the best way to protect minors against irreversible procedures that they might later come to regret.

In *L.W. ex rel. Williams v. Skrmetti*, 83 F.4th 460 (6th Cir. 2023), the court upheld state laws that prohibited sex-transition treatment for minors who had experienced gender dysphoria. The district court, framing the issue as being whether parents have a "fundamental right to direct the medical care of their children," concluded that *Dobbs* was satisfied because such a right is deeply rooted in this nation's history and tradition. Id. at 469. The court of appeals reversed. In a 2-to-1 decision, it held that the district court had framed the issue at too broad and general a level, i.e., it had "overstate[d] the parental interest by climbing up the ladder of generality to a perch — in which parents control all drug and other medical treatments for children. . .. Level of generality is everything in constitutional law, which is why the Court requires 'a "careful description" of the asserted fundamental liberty interest.'" Id. at 475 (internal citation omitted). Under the Court of Appeals' approach, the issue, properly framed, was whether parents "have a constitutional right to obtain reasonably banned treatments for their children." Id. So narrowed, the answer under *Dobbs* was clear: "This country does not have a 'deeply rooted tradition'" or "custom of permitting parents to obtain banned medical treatments for their children and to override contrary legislative policy judgments in the process." Id. at 473, 475. The court then upheld the laws as being a rational way to further the state's interest in protecting children. The dissent, like the district court, would have applied strict scrutiny and invalidated the laws because they impaired a parent's "fundamental right to control medical choices for their children, a right deeply rooted in this nation's history. . .." Id. at 507. Given the current Court's interest in narrowing the range of protected liberty interests, it would likely agree with the approach taken by the Sixth Circuit majority here.[1]

The Right to Reject Unwanted Medical Treatment

In the abortion cases, the liberty interest in making decisions about one's health involved the right to receive or undergo certain medical procedures. This liberty interest may also come into play in the context of decisions to refuse medical treatment. In *Jacobson v. Massachusetts,* 197 U.S. 11, 24-30 (1905), decided at the height of the *Lochner* era, the Court recognized that there is a liberty interest in rejecting unwanted medical care. The modern Court has reaffirmed this liberty interest. See, e.g., *Washington v. Harper,* 494 U.S. 210 (1990) (prisoner has fundamental liberty interest in avoiding forced administration of antipsychotic drugs); *Vitek v. Jones,* 445 U.S. 480 (1980) (prisoner has liberty interest in avoiding mandatory behavior modification treatment); *Parham v. J.R.*, 442 U.S. 584 (1979) (person has liberty interest in not being confined unnecessarily for medical treatment). This liberty was initially viewed as part of the right of bodily integrity—i.e., the right to be free from state interference with one's physical person. In more recent years, it has been treated as an aspect of the liberty interest in privacy and personal autonomy.

Even in a post-*Dobbs* world, this liberty interest might still qualify as being fundamental, if it is shown to be deeply rooted or part of a broader well-established right. Cf. *L.W. ex rel. Williams v. Skrmetti*, supra, 83 F.4th at 476 ("While our longstanding traditions may give individuals a right to refuse treatment, there is no historical support for an affirmative right to specific treatments. *See Washington [v. Glucksberg*, 521 U.S. 702, 725-726 (1997).]").

Like other liberty interests, the right to refuse unwanted medical treatment is not absolute. The Court in *Jacobson* found that the state's goal of preventing smallpox was sufficient to outweigh an individual's interest in refusing a smallpox vaccination. In *Washington v. Harper,* the Court ruled that in the prison setting, where constitutional rights are of diminished stature, the state did not violate substantive due process by forcibly administering antipsychotic drugs to prisoners diagnosed as suffering from a mental disorder that made them likely to cause harm to themselves or to others. In *Harper,* the state did not need to show that the forced administration of drugs was necessary to achieve its goals; it was enough that the policy was reasonably related to legitimate penological interests. However, the *Harper*

1. Petitions for cert were filed in this case by both the United States, which had intervened in the action, and by the individual plaintiffs. The United States' petition, challenging the law solely under the Equal Protection Clause, was granted. *United States v. Skrmetti*, 144 S. Ct. 2679 (2024). The individual plaintiffs' petition, which invoked both the Due Process and Equal Protection Clauses, remained pending as of this writing. *L.W. ex rel. Williams v. Skrmetti*, supra, *petition for cert. filed*, No. 23-466 (U.S. Nov. 27, 2023).

Court noted that in another setting not involving prisoners, "the State . . . would have been required to satisfy a more rigorous standard of review." 494 U.S. at 223.

Unlike the federal Constitution, where the right to choose or reject medical care is not mentioned in the text, some state constitutions specifically address the issue. Among the "inalienable rights" set forth in the California Constitution, Art. 1, § 1, is "enjoying and defending life" and "pursuing and obtaining safety . . .." This provision "guarantees to the individual the freedom to choose to reject, or refuse to consent to, intrusions of his or her bodily integrity," and embraces "the competent adult's decision to refuse life-sustaining medical treatment . . .." *Conservatorship of Wendland*, 26 Cal. 4th 519, 531-532, 110 Cal. Rptr. 2d 412, 421-422 (2001).

§2.5.7 The Right to Refuse Lifesaving Hydration and Nutrition

The liberty to refuse unwanted medical treatment may sometimes be equivalent to choosing the time and manner of one's death. For example, if a person suffering from a life-threatening disease is told that unless she takes a certain drug she will die, a decision to refuse that drug is in effect a decision to die. The same is true of the more tenuous liberty to choose to receive a particular drug or medical procedure. A decision to take what one knows to be a lethal dose of morphine to relieve excruciating pain has the same *effect* as a decision to die even though one's *intent* may be very different. In our previous discussion of the liberty to receive or reject a particular drug or medical treatment, the individual's choice did not pose a direct threat to life or raise a certainty of death. Does the liberty interest in medical treatment reach far enough to encompass a right to die?

This question was presented in a narrow form in *Cruzan v. Director, Missouri Department of Health*, 497 U.S. 261 (1990). There, the Missouri Supreme Court refused to allow the withdrawal of artificial food and hydration procedures from a patient who was in a persistent vegetative state because there was no "clear and convincing evidence" that the withdrawal accorded with the patient's wishes. The patient's parents challenged the state court's ruling on the ground that it violated their daughter's fundamental liberty to refuse unwanted medical treatment. Their position was supported by decisions from a number of state courts, which had found such a right as a matter of common law, and in some cases as part of the constitutional right of privacy.

In an opinion by Chief Justice Rehnquist, the Supreme Court came close to but stopped short of recognizing such a liberty interest. Rehnquist conceded that "[t]he principle that a competent person has a constitutionally protected liberty interest in refusing unwanted medical treatment may be inferred from our prior decisions." Id. at 278. Moreover, he agreed that "the logic of these cases" would cover a refusal of "the forced administration of life-sustaining medical treatment, and even of artificially-delivered food and water essential to life. . . ." Id. at 279. Yet even then a state might be justified in barring exercise of such a liberty in situations where death would result, for "the dramatic consequences involved in refusal of such treatment would inform the inquiry as to whether the deprivation of that interest is constitutionally permissible." Id. Having toyed with the idea, the Court declined to hold that the liberty to refuse unwanted medical treatment includes a right to refuse life-sustaining treatment. Rather, said the Court, "*for purposes of this case, we assume* that the United States Constitution would grant a competent person a constitutionally protected right to refuse lifesaving hydration and nutrition." Id. (emphasis supplied). While five Justices in *Cruzan* expressed the view that such a right does exist (id. at 287 (O'Connor, J., concurring); id. at 304-314 (Brennan, J., Marshall, J., and Blackmun, J., dissenting); id. at 330-344 (Stevens, J., dissenting)), their views were not necessary to the decision and thus do not constitute a holding of the case. As the Court has subsequently noted, *Cruzan* "assumed, and strongly suggested"—but did not hold—"that the Due Process Clause protects the traditional right to refuse unwanted lifesaving medical treatment." *Washington v. Glucksberg*, 521 U.S. 702, 720 (1997).

Once the *Cruzan* Court assumed that a *competent person* has a fundamental liberty to reject life-sustaining medical treatment and that this will trump any countervailing state interests, the case presented the additional difficulty that the decision to withdraw food and hydration was made not by the patient, but by her parents and guardians. This being so, Missouri claimed an interest in protecting (rather than thwarting) the patient by making sure her surrogates' decision to withdraw life-sustaining treatment in fact reflected her true desires. Though the facts left no doubt that the parents were acting with the purest of motives, the state had a valid interest in assuring that its right-to-die procedures would not be abused by those purporting to act on behalf of an incompetent. The Missouri Supreme Court ruled that withdrawal of life-sustaining treatment from an incompetent person is permitted only if the patient has previously executed a formal "living will" or if there is other "clear and convincing, inherently reliable evidence" that the decision conforms to wishes the patient had expressed while competent. The state court found that neither of these requirements was satisfied in the case before it. 497 U.S. at 268-269.

The U.S. Supreme Court affirmed, ruling that the state's strict procedural requirements did not violate the Due Process Clause. The Court applied a modified strict scrutiny test under which it simply balanced the state's interests against the liberty interests of the patient. See § 2.4.4. The Court found that the state's interests in preserving life and assuring the authenticity of a person's decision to die were sufficient to outweigh any possible frustration of a patient's liberty interest. The dissent objected that less rigorous procedural requirements would protect the state's interests equally well, 497 U.S. at 321-326 (Brennan, J., dissenting), but the Court did not require the state to show that these less burdensome alternatives were for some reason inadequate.

Having found that any state interference with the *patient's* liberty was justified, the *Cruzan* Court rejected the argument that the state had violated the liberty interests of the patient's family. Any liberty to reject life-sustaining medical treatment belongs exclusively to the individual, not to his or her family, friends, or legal guardians. The state is under no obligation "to repose a right of 'substituted judgment'" with others; "we do not think the Due Process Clause requires the State to repose judgment on these matters with anyone but the patient herself." Id. at 286. Accordingly, "the State may choose to defer only to those wishes, rather than confide the decision to close family members." Id. at 286-287. The Court left open the possibility that a state might be required to defer to the decision of a surrogate where a patient had expressed a clear desire that the decision to withdraw life-sustaining treatment be made for her by that individual. Id. at 287 n.12.

Example 2-K

As a result of an automobile accident, James lost use of both legs and must breathe with a respirator. He is 36 years old, is married, and has two young children. This past year James on several occasions removed his respirator, but each time his nurse promptly reconnected it, citing a state law that requires that all reasonable steps be taken to keep a patient alive. James has brought suit, asking that the state law be declared unconstitutional and that he be allowed to disconnect his respirator and die. How should the court rule in his case?

Explanation

Unlike *Cruzan*, there is no doubt here concerning the patient's wishes. James is fully competent and has expressed his desires in unmistakably clear terms. The only issue is one that the *Cruzan* Court did not have to address—i.e., whether the state may thwart a competent individual's decision to reject life-sustaining medical treatment.

Assuming the court recognizes a *fundamental* liberty to refuse lifesaving medical treatment, *Cruzan* suggested that this interest must be balanced against the interests of the state. The state here is likely to assert several interests: preserving life, preventing suicide, and protecting innocent third parties such as family members and loved ones. The Court in *Cruzan* suggested that the strength of these interests may vary, depending on a person's condition and prognosis.

The quality of James's life is certainly impaired by the fact that he is a paraplegic and dependent on a respirator. Yet in contrast with more typical right-to-die cases, he is neither comatose nor suffering from a painful and incurable degenerative disease. Thus, the state's interests in preserving life and preventing suicide would seem to be quite strong. Moreover, since James has a wife and two small children, the state's interest in protecting innocent third parties is more compelling than it would be in a case involving someone who was single and/or elderly.

James will respond that his fundamental liberty to make "choices central to personal dignity and autonomy," *Casey*, supra, 505 U.S. at 851, should allow him, not the state, to decide how long he will be kept alive by artificial means. However, for the reasons noted, there is a good chance the state's interests will be found to outweigh James's liberty to reject life-sustaining medical procedures.

§2.5.8 Suicide and Physician-Assisted Suicide

Closely related to the issue raised in *Cruzan* is whether those who are terminally ill have a constitutional right to obtain medication from their doctors to hasten their deaths. Persons in this situation, rather than seeking to *reject lifesaving* treatment, as was the case in *Cruzan*, wish to *receive life-ending* medication. Yet both cases could be said to involve the same liberty interest—i.e., the "right to die."

Any thought that *Cruzan* had implicitly recognized a constitutional, open-ended "right to die" was put to rest by *Washington v. Glucksberg*, 521 U.S. 702 (1997), and *Vacco v. Quill*, 521 U.S. 793 (1997). *Glucksberg* unanimously rejected a due process challenge to a Washington law that made it a crime for anyone, including physicians, to assist another in committing suicide. *Vacco* held that a similar New York law did not violate the Equal Protection Clause.

The Court in *Glucksberg* noted that "we have required in substantive-due-process cases a 'careful description' of the asserted fundamental liberty interest." 521 U.S. at 721. Because the Washington law prohibited "aid[ing] another person to attempt suicide," the issue was not, as the Ninth Circuit had put it, whether there is an all-embracing "right to die" or "a liberty interest in determining the time and manner of one's death." Id. at 722-723. Instead, said the Court, "the question before us is whether the 'liberty' specially protected by the Due Process Clause includes a *right to commit suicide* which itself includes a right to assistance in doing so." Id. at 723 (emphasis supplied).

Having thus framed the issue, the Court ruled "that the asserted 'right' to assistance in committing suicide is not a fundamental liberty interest protected by the Due Process Clause." Id. at 728. The nation's history and tradition rejected such a right, for assisted suicide had long been banned and continued to be illegal in nearly every state. Nor could such a liberty be distilled from the Court's prior substantive due process cases. While many of those cases, including *Roe* and *Cruzan*, had recognized constitutional liberties that involve "personal autonomy," this did "not warrant the sweeping conclusion that any and all important, intimate, and personal decisions are so protected. . . ." Id. at 727. Those cases had turned on a finding that the specific activities or decisions at stake were "so deeply rooted in our history and traditions, or so fundamental to our concept of constitutionally ordered liberty, that they are protected by the Fourteenth Amendment." Id. The fact that suicide entails an exercise of personal autonomy was, therefore, not enough to elevate this nontraditional interest to fundamental liberty status.

The Supreme Court's reluctance to find a fundamental liberty in *Glucksberg* was heightened by the fact that such a ruling would come in the midst of a vigorous national debate about assisted suicide and related issues concerning the protection of personal dignity and independence at the end of life. For the Court to have stepped in and declared that there is a constitutional right to assistance in committing suicide would have preempted that debate. By contrast, as the Court observed in the concluding paragraph of its opinion, "Our holding permits this debate to continue, as it should in a democratic society." Id. at 735. See also *Kligler v. Attorney General*, 198 N.E.3d 1228, 1253-1259 (Mass. 2022) ("we cannot conclude that physician-assisted suicide ranks among those fundamental rights protected by the Massachusetts Declaration of Rights"); *Morris v. Brandenburg*, 376 P.3d 836, 839, 855 (N.M. 2016) (New Mexico's Constitution should not be read more broadly than the U.S. Constitution so as to recognize "a fundamental or important right to physician aid in dying").

Once the Court in *Glucksberg* held that no fundamental liberty interest was present, it easily sustained Washington's assisted suicide ban under the rational basis test. The ban was found to be reasonably related to a number of legitimate state interests, including saving human life, assuring proper treatment for those suffering from depression or mental illness, preserving trust in the doctor-patient relationship, protecting vulnerable groups (such as the poor, the elderly, and persons with disabilities) from those who might seek to bring about their premature death, and guarding against euthanasia. Id. at 728-735. The Court thus upheld Washington's assisted suicide ban on its face and "'as applied to competent, terminally ill adults who wish to hasten their deaths by obtaining medication prescribed by their doctors.'" Id. at 735.

Glucksberg left open the possibility that future challengers of an assisted suicide ban might be able to claim a fundamental liberty interest, but the Court warned that any such claim would have to be "quite different" from the "asserted liberty interest in ending one's life with a physician's assistance" rejected in that case. Id. at 735 n.24. If there is such a right, the Court did not describe it. However, several Justices suggested they might look favorably on a claim that "a mentally competent person who is experiencing great suffering has a constitutionally cognizable interest in controlling the circumstances of his or her imminent death." Id. at 736 (O'Connor, J., Ginsburg, J., and Breyer, J., concurring); see also id. at 791 (Breyer, J., concurring) (noting that there may be a fundamental liberty interest in the "avoidance of severe physical pain (connected with death)"). Such a liberty interest in avoiding pain was not implicated by these Washington and New York statutes, since both states allowed doctors to provide patients with drugs sufficient to control pain even where this would hasten death. Id. Justice Stevens, though agreeing that there is no "open-ended constitutional right to commit suicide," likewise believed that "there are situations in which an interest in hastening death is legitimate" and "entitled to constitutional protection." Id. at 740-742 (Stevens, J., concurring). It is thus conceivable that a terminally ill individual might be able to establish a protected liberty interest in physician-assisted suicide, but as the Court noted in *Vacco,* he or she "would need to present different and considerably stronger arguments than those advanced" in the Washington and New York cases. 521 U.S. at 809 n.13.

In *Vacco,* the Court found that New York's assisted suicide ban did not violate the Equal Protection Clause. Because no fundamental right and no suspect classification were involved, only a rational basis standard of review was called for. See § 6.3. The plaintiffs argued that New York's law could not meet this test because the state, consistent with *Cruzan,* allowed competent individuals to choose to die by refusing lifesaving medical treatment, but denied competent individuals the right to achieve the same end by taking lethal medication. The Court disagreed, concluding that "the distinction between assisting suicide and withdrawing life-sustaining treatment, a distinction widely recognized and endorsed in the medical profession and in our legal traditions, is both important and logical; it is certainly rational." Id. at 800-801.

The two situations differ, said the Court, in terms of both the cause of death and the actors' intent. When life-sustaining treatment is withdrawn from a terminally ill patient, death is caused by the underlying disease; when an individual is given lethal medication, however, death is caused by the medication. With respect to intent, when life-sustaining treatment is withdrawn, the intent of the patient and her physician is not necessarily to cause death, but perhaps to live without unwanted medical technology, surgery, or drugs. In the case of assisted suicide, on the other hand, the intent of the patient and her physician must at least in part be to cause the patient's death. As the Court observed, "The law has long used actors' intent or purpose to distinguish between two acts that may have the same result." Id. at 802. In addition, the very fact that many other states drew a similar distinction between the withdrawal of life-support systems and physician-assisted suicide itself supported the reasonableness of the New York law.

§2.6 OTHER PROTECTED LIBERTY INTERESTS

§2.6.1 Freedom of Movement

Freedom from Physical Restraint

The liberty protected by the Due Process Clause has been held to include freedom of movement. This fundamental liberty interest may be impaired by government in a number of ways. One involves subjecting someone to "physical restraint of his person." *Allgeyer v. Louisiana,* 165 U.S. 578, 589 (1897). "'Liberty from bodily restraint always has been recognized as the core of the liberty protected by the Due Process Clause from arbitrary governmental action.'" *Youngberg v. Romeo,* 457 U.S. 307, 316 (1982) (quoting *Greenholtz v. Nebraska Penal Inmates,* 442 U.S. 1, 18 (1979) (Powell, J., concurring)). This liberty interest has usually been asserted in institutional settings, such as hospitals or prisons, where inmates allege that the government has placed excessive restrictions on their freedom of physical movement. The Court has not been especially sympathetic to such claims.

In the prison context, the Court has held that a criminal conviction and a sentence of imprisonment extinguish the right to be free from confinement and any constitutional liberty interest in not being transferred within the prison system or subjected to more severe conditions of confinement. See, e.g., *Hewitt v. Helms,* 459 U.S. 460 (1983) (prisoner has no due process liberty interest in avoiding solitary confinement); *Meachum v. Fano,* 427 U.S. 215 (1976) (prisoner has no due process liberty interest in avoiding transfer to maximum security prison with more burdensome conditions). Though no constitutionally based liberty interests were implicated in these situations, prisoners can sometimes invoke other substantive due process liberty interests, such as the right to intimate association (see § 2.5.4), or the right to procedural due process where liberty interests have been created by statute or regulation. See § 5.2.1. Prisoners may also be able to invoke other constitutional provisions, such as the Cruel and Unusual Punishment Clause of the Eighth Amendment, to challenge the conditions of their confinement. And as the Court recognized in *Young v. Harper,* 520 U.S. 143 (1997), inmates who have been conditionally released from prison under parole or other similar programs normally have a statutorily created liberty interest in their continued freedom that will entitle them to procedural due process if their parole is to be revoked or terminated.

The liberty interests of those confined in public mental hospitals have received only slightly greater protection from the Court. In *Youngberg v. Romeo*, 457 U.S. 307, 324 (1982), the Court recognized that, unlike prisoners, those in state mental institutions retain constitutional liberty interests in freedom of bodily movement and in "reasonably nonrestrictive confinement conditions." However, the Court refused to employ its normal strict scrutiny test, which would have required the state to show that any such restrictions are necessary to achieving a compelling interest. Instead, the Court applied a balancing test and concluded that the state's interest in operating such institutions in accord with professional standards outweighs any interest an inmate has in preserving physical liberty. Such restrictions are, therefore, automatically valid as long as "professional judgment deems [them] necessary to assure . . . safety or to provide needed training." Id. See § 2.4.4.

The right to be free from physical restraint takes on a somewhat different cast as it pertains to aliens who are either subject to (or potentially subject to) deportation. In *Zadvydas v. Davis*, 533 U.S. 678 (2001), the question presented was whether an alien who had been found to be unlawfully within the United States could be held in custody indefinitely while the government searched for a country that would accept him. To avoid what the majority deemed a "serious constitutional problem" under the Due Process Clause, the Court narrowly construed a federal statute that arguably allowed indefinite detention under such circumstances. Id. at 690. Hence, the statute at issue was construed as not authorizing detention beyond an initial 90-day period once it became reasonably clear that removal from the United States was not feasible (e.g., because no other nation would accept the detained alien). In such cases, the alien must be released from detention, albeit subject to reasonable conditions and supervision. Id. at 698-700.

The question presented in another case was whether an alien who is a permanent, lawful resident, but who has been found by the federal government to be deportable, could, in the absence of a showing of flight risk, be held without bail pending a removal hearing. *Demore v. Hyung Joon Kim*, 538 U.S. 510 (2003). The Court found no due process violation in this practice. The Court began by observing that "Congress regularly makes rules regarding aliens that would be unacceptable if applied to citizens." Id. at 522 (quoting *Mathews v. Diaz*, 426 U.S. 67, 79-80 (1976)). In essence, the Court found that the government's interest in ensuring the presence of a deportable alien at a removal hearing was sufficient to overcome any constitutional objections to a practice of detention regardless of flight risk. Further, the Court found that the question presented differed from its prior ruling in *Zadvydas* in two ways. First, the detention in *Zadvydas* occurred under circumstances where removal was no longer reasonably feasible. Id. at 527-528. Second, unlike the indefinite detention in *Zadvydas*, the detention pending a removal hearing was of a much shorter, finite duration. Id.

The decision in *Demore* is generally consistent with the Court's institutional reluctance to interfere with matters pertaining to immigration and naturalization. See also § 6.5.2 (rational basis for federal laws that classify based on alien status).

Freedom to Move About and the Right to Remain

The due process liberty of physical movement may also be implicated by governmental interference with a person's freedom to move about. The liberty to move about in the sense of being able to travel freely from one state to another has been linked to a number of constitutional provisions, including the Commerce Clause of Article I, the Privileges and Immunities Clause of Article IV, the First Amendment right to petition government, and both the Equal Protection and Privileges or Immunities Clauses of the Fourteenth Amendment.

The freedom to move about is protected as well by the Due Process Clause. This due process liberty has been invoked to strike down limitations on international travel. *Aptheker v. Secretary of State*, 378 U.S. 500, 505-514 (1964) (statute denying passports to Communists invalid partly because it impaired the Fifth Amendment liberty to travel abroad). It is also implicated by laws that interfere with a person's freedom simply to walk or move about. See *Papachristou v. City of Jacksonville*, 405 U.S. 156, 164 (1972) (invalidating vagrancy ordinance on vagueness grounds, but suggesting that Due Process Clause protects the liberty to wander and stroll around). In *City of Chicago v. Morales*, 527 U.S. 41 (1999), the Court struck down a Chicago anti-gang loitering ordinance on vagueness grounds, but three Justices suggested that "the 'liberty' protected by the Due Process Clause" includes "the freedom to loiter for innocent purposes," the "right to remove from one place to another according to inclination," and "an individual's decision to remain in a public place of his choice. . . ." Id. at 53-54 (Stevens, J., Souter, J., and Ginsburg, J.). See *Betancourt v. Bloomberg*, 448 F.3d 547, 555 n. ** (2d Cir.) (Calabresi, J., dissenting), *cert. denied*, 549 U.S. 1034 (2006) (N.Y. City ordinance making it "unlawful for any person to . . . leave . . . any box . . . or other movable property . . . upon any . . . public street or any public place, or to erect thereon any shed, building or other obstruction," may violate the "right to remain" of a homeless person who slept one night on a city park bench inside a tube made of cardboard boxes).

The Supreme Court has yet to resolve the question of what level of scrutiny is applicable in cases involving restrictions on purely local or intrastate movement. The issue arises in a number of settings, including juvenile curfew ordinances and anti-stalking laws that make it illegal to follow another person around in public. While state and lower federal courts agree that the right to move about is a protected liberty interest, they disagree as to what standard of review to apply in such cases.

Example 2-L

The City of Glenwood adopted a curfew making it illegal for anyone under the age of 18 to be on the streets between the hours of 11 P.M. and 6 A.M. The purpose of the curfew is to protect children from becoming victims or perpetrators of crimes. Does the curfew violate the Fourteenth Amendment Due Process Clause?

Explanation

If a child's freedom to move about is deemed a "fundamental" liberty, strict scrutiny would apply since this law clearly impinges on that right. The city would then have to prove that the curfew is necessary to achieve a compelling governmental interest. While protecting children from becoming victims of crime is a legitimate goal, it may not be compelling enough to justify such a serious impairment of a basic liberty. For if this goal is compelling as to children, it might likewise justify imposing curfews on other groups thought to be particularly vulnerable, such as the elderly, women, and persons with disabilities. Indeed, if valid, a protection rationale might justify imposing a general curfew, since everyone is potentially a victim of street crime. There are similar difficulties with the city's goal of preventing children from becoming perpetrators of crime. If this were deemed sufficient to justify such a severe curtailment of children's freedom of movement, it would seemingly allow a curfew to be imposed on everyone since it is impossible to know who might otherwise perpetrate a crime. Under strict scrutiny, even if these goals are found to be compelling, the city must show that the law is no more restrictive than necessary to achieve its ends. There would appear to be many equally effective alternative approaches that would not so heavily burden the freedom of movement. These would include enhanced policing; better street lighting; increased educational, employment, and recreational opportunities for youths; and requiring minors on the street at night to be accompanied by or have the written permission of a parent. For the ordinance to pass strict scrutiny, the city would have to show that these less intrusive alternatives would not be as effective in achieving its goals.

The city, on the other hand, would urge that the rational basis standard or, at most, an intermediate standard of review, should apply here, both because this involves only local—as opposed to international or interstate—travel, and because its curfew only impairs the rights of children.

The Court has recognized that children may have fewer constitutional rights than adults because of their "peculiar vulnerability," "their inability to make critical decisions in an informed, mature manner," and the need to respect the "parental role in childrearing." *Bellotti v. Baird*, 443 U.S. 622, 633-639 (1979) (plurality opinion). However, arguably none of these reasons for diluting the rights of minors is present here. There is probably no evidence that children are peculiarly vulnerable to street crime. Second, with the exception of very young children, the decision to leave the house at night is not one that a mature adult is likely to make any differently than a child; most people who have someplace to go at night will do so even though they are aware of the potential dangers. Finally, the curfew interferes with rather than respects the parental role in childrearing, for it usurps a parent's right to decide when a child should be allowed out of the house after 11 P.M. Compare *In re A.G.*, 181 Cal. App. 4th 989 (Ct. App. 2010) (applying intermediate scrutiny to invalidate juvenile curfew law as violating juvenile's due process right to local travel), *Anonymous v. City of Rochester*, 13 N.Y.3d 35, 915 N.E.2d 593 (2009) (applying intermediate scrutiny to invalidate juvenile curfew law as violating father's due process right to control son's upbringing, and son's due process right to freedom of movement), *State v. J.P.*, 907 So. 2d 1101 (Fla. 2004) (applying strict scrutiny to invalidate juvenile curfew ordinance as violating juvenile's due process rights to privacy and freedom of movement), and *Nunez v. City of San Diego*, 114 F.3d 935 (9th Cir. 1997) (applying strict scrutiny to invalidate juvenile curfew ordinance as violating juvenile's due process right to freedom of movement and travel), with *State v. Doe*, 148 Idaho 919, 934-936 (2010) (applying strict scrutiny but nevertheless upholding juvenile curfew ordinance as not violating juvenile's freedom of movement), and *Hutchins v. District of Columbia*, 188 F.3d 531 (D.C. Cir. 1999) (en banc) (same).

§2.6.2 The Rights to Protection and Care

As we noted earlier, the liberties guaranteed by the Due Process Clause are *negative* liberties in the sense that they usually confer merely a right to be free from governmental interference with one's ability to exercise certain freedoms. The Due Process Clause normally places the government under no affirmative duty to assure that people are able to enjoy their liberties if for some reason they cannot fully do so on their own. See § 2.4.4.

There is, however, one exception to this rule. If the government assumes or enters into a "special relationship" with an individual that results in "restraining the individual's freedom to act on his own behalf—through incarceration, institutionalization, or other similar restraint of personal liberty"—the government may have "affirmative duties of care and protection" so as to assure that the individual's liberty interests are satisfied.

DeShaney v. Winnebago County Dept. of Social Servs., 489 U.S. 189, 197-200 (1989). The right to protection and care exists only where the government has limited an individual's "freedom to act on his own behalf," thereby rendering the individual "more vulnerable" than he or she would otherwise have been. Id. at 200-201.

In *Youngberg v. Romeo*, 457 U.S. 307 (1982), this principle was invoked to find that the state owed a duty of protection and care toward those involuntarily confined in a state mental hospital. These inmates had both a *negative liberty* interest in being free from state interference with their physical safety and bodily freedom, and an *affirmative liberty* to be provided with "such training as an appropriate professional would consider reasonable to ensure [their] safety and to facilitate [their] ability to function free from bodily restraints." Id. at 324. In addition to affirmative duties of protection and training, the state owed these individuals a general affirmative duty of care. Since the demise of *Lochner*, the interest in acquiring the necessities of life is normally a negative liberty that receives only minimal protection as part of the liberty in earning a livelihood. However, the hospital inmates in *Youngberg* had an affirmative due process right to have their subsistence needs met by the state. Id. As the Court later explained, "[W]hen the State by the affirmative exercise of its power so restrains an individual's liberty that it renders him unable to care for himself, and at the same time fails to provide for his basic human needs—e.g., food, clothing, shelter, medical care, and reasonable safety—it transgresses the substantive limits on state action set by . . . the Due Process Clause." *DeShaney*, supra, 489 U.S. at 200.

In *DeShaney*, the Court distinguished *Youngberg* and held that a state had no affirmative constitutional duty to protect a child from being beaten by its father. Since the child in that case was living at home rather than in the care or custody of the state, the Court found there was no "special relationship" comparable to that which existed in *Youngberg*. And though the state knew of the dangers the child faced living at home with his father, the state still had no affirmative duty to protect the child because the dangers were not of the state's "creation, nor did it do anything to render [the child] any more vulnerable to them." Id. at 201.

Even if it can be shown that a setting is one in which the government has an affirmative constitutional duty to protect and care for an individual's well-being, the government will not be found to have violated this duty on the basis of mere negligence by its employees or agents. For the government to "deprive" a person of life, liberty, or property within the meaning of the Due Process Clause, it must be shown that the impairment was caused either by a deliberate decision on the part of governmental officials—or possibly by recklessness or gross negligence. See *Davidson v. Cannon*, 474 U.S. 344 (1986) (negligence by prison officials that resulted in an inmate being assaulted by another inmate did not implicate the affirmative liberty to protection while in state custody). See also § 2.1.

Example 2-M

Lucy is a freshman at Central State University, where she lives on campus in a school dormitory. She was recently attacked in the middle of the night by an intruder who forced his way into her locked dormitory room. The only lock on the door consists of a push button in the doorknob. As a result, the door may be opened from the outside by sliding a credit card between the latch and the door frame. Several months before the attack, a group of students asked the school to either install better locks or permit the students to do so at their own expense. The school denied both requests on the ground that it did not wish to turn the dormitories into fortresses. Can Lucy sue the state-owned school on the ground that it violated her rights under the Fourteenth Amendment Due Process Clause?

Explanation

Lucy will argue that because she was living in the school's dormitory, a special relationship existed that placed the state under an affirmative constitutional duty to protect her due process liberty interest in bodily safety. The school will reply that Lucy freely chose to attend the university, thus distinguishing her case from *Youngberg*, where the state hospital inmates were involuntarily committed. Lucy will respond that despite the voluntary nature of her decision to attend the university, once there, she was in the state's care and custody; unlike the child in *DeShaney*, she was not living at home with her parents. And as a freshman, she may have been required to live in the dormitory. Moreover, the school restrained Lucy's freedom to protect herself by prohibiting her from installing a better lock on her door and, in doing so, increased her vulnerability to danger.

If the court agrees that the school had an affirmative constitutional duty to protect Lucy's personal safety, the school's refusal to install adequate locks is the kind of deliberate conduct that is sufficient to implicate the Due Process Clause: The school was specifically advised of the problem and consciously chose not to do anything about it. Contrast the situation if Lucy's door had been equipped with a proper lock that, because of the school's negligence, was not in working order; such negligence would not trigger the Due Process Clause unless the school knew of the defect and had refused to repair it. Once Lucy establishes a deprivation of her liberty interest in protection, the school must show that its refusal to install proper locks served a compelling interest, a showing it would be hard-pressed to make. Cf. *Vernonia School Dist. 47J v. Acton*, 515 U.S. 646, 655 (1995) ("we do not, of course, suggest that public schools as a general matter have such a degree of control over children as to give rise to a constitutional 'duty to protect.'"); *Morrow v. Balaski*, 719 F.3d 160, 170 (3d Cir.) (en banc), *cert. denied*, 571 U.S.

1110 (2013) ("[E]very other Circuit Court of Appeals that has considered the issue . . . has rejected the argument that a special relationship generally exists between public schools and their students. . .. [A]s a general matter, [they] do not have a *constitutional* duty to protect students from private actors." (Emphasis in original.)).

§2.6.3 Access to Courts

The Court has recognized a limited due process right of access to courts that may be violated by government action that prevents a party from filing a lawsuit. There are essentially two types of access claims: (1) those in which the government has created an impediment to the present filing of a lawsuit and (2) those in which the government acted in the past to prevent filing a claim that is now foreclosed. The first type of access claim is typically analyzed as a potential violation of equal protection. For example, a filing fee that prevents an indigent from pursuing a legal remedy would fall into this category. For discussion of such equal protection access to courts problems, see § 7.5. The second category involves what is more properly characterized as a substantive due process right. The essence of this category is that government action has caused the loss or diminution of a meritorious claim by preventing an individual from accessing the courts.

To establish a due process right of access claim, the plaintiff must show a preexisting right of action that is no longer available because of the government's action or inaction. The plaintiff must also establish that the remedy she seeks through her right of access claim cannot be achieved through the assertion of any other presently available claims for relief. *Christopher v. Harbury*, 536 U.S. 403, 414-415 (2002). In this sense, the right of access claim is ancillary to and dependent on the claim that has now been foreclosed. It exists only if there was a previously available claim and only if the current remedy sought under the rubric of "right of access" would not otherwise be available. In *Harbury*, the plaintiff asserted that U.S. government secrecy regarding the whereabouts of her husband, a Guatemalan rebel leader who had been captured by Guatemalan armed forces, had foreclosed her ability to file suit in a court of the United States at the time of her husband's capture, when it was still possible to save his life. She failed to allege, however, what her substantive claim would have been had she been given the true facts in a timely fashion. Nor, most importantly, could she explain why the remedy sought under her right of access claim—monetary damages—was not available under currently unforeclosed tort claims. Hence, the Court held that she had failed to allege a cognizable right of access claim.

§2.6.4 Informational Privacy

In two cases decided over 40 years ago, the Supreme Court alluded to a constitutional privacy "interest in avoiding disclosure of personal matters." *Whalen v. Roe*, 429 U.S. 589, 599-600 (1977); see also *Nixon v. Administrator of General Services*, 433 U.S. 425, 457 (1977). Neither case directly implicated any such right, and the Court did not revisit this "informational-privacy" right until its decision in *National Aeronautics and Space Admin. v. Nelson*, 562 U.S. 134 (2011). At issue in that case was a government-ordered background check for all contract employees—i.e., non-civil servant employees, at NASA's Jet Propulsion Laboratory—many of whom had worked at the lab for decades and had never been subjected to a government background investigation. Among the routine questions the employees were required to answer was one pertaining to any recent use of illegal drugs, including any information pertaining to "any treatment or counseling received." Id. at 141. The disclosed information would be subject to the protections afforded by the federal Privacy Act, including the Act's nondisclosure requirements. Id. at 156. Nonetheless, the employees claimed that requiring them to answer the questions violated their constitutional right to informational privacy.

The Court assumed "for present purposes that the Government's challenged inquires implicate a privacy interest of constitutional significance." Id. at 146. But the Court went on to hold that whatever the scope of this informational privacy right, the right was not violated by the "reasonable" questions posed by the Government here. Id. at 152. In the Court's words, "[W]e conclude that the challenged [questions] consist of reasonable, employment-related inquiries that further the Government's interest in managing its internal operations." Id. The reasonableness of the Government's action was further supported by the fact that once collected, the information was "subject to substantial protections against disclosure to the public." Id. at 155. While the Court did not elaborate on the scope of the presumed constitutional right to informational privacy, it is at least clear that the level of scrutiny is something less than strict but at the same time perhaps less deferential than the traditional rational basis standard.

Justices Scalia and Thomas wrote concurring opinions in which they argued that there was no such constitutional right to informational privacy. 562 U.S. at 159 (Scalia, J., concurring) ("A federal constitutional right to 'informational privacy' does not exist."); id. at 168 (Thomas, J., concurring) ("the Constitution does not protect a right to informational privacy").

While the Supreme Court stopped short of recognizing a constitutional right to informational privacy, some lower federal courts have taken that step. In *A.C. ex rel. Park v. Cortez*, 34 F.4th 783, 787 (9th Cir. 2022), the court held that "[f]ederal constitutional law recognizes a 'right to informational privacy' stemming from 'the individual interest in avoiding disclosure of personal matters.'" (Internal citations omitted.) The right extends only to highly personal, highly sensitive information of an "intimate nature." *Doe v. Bonta*, 101 F.4th 633, 637-639 (9th Cir. 2024). Moreover, the right is conditional and may be infringed under a "balancing test" if the government's interest in disclosure is shown to outweigh an individual's privacy concerns. In this balancing, a court will look at the type of information requested; the potential harm from any subsequent non-consensual disclosure; the safeguards against unauthorized release; the strength of the need for disclosure; and whether any statute or other recognized public interest favors access. In *Cortez*, the plaintiff minors had earlier sued the county, alleging that in the course of a child abuse investigation, its social workers had violated their Fourth Amendment rights by interviewing them without a court order or parental consent. In defending that suit, county attorneys reviewed plaintiffs' child-abuse files without a court order. The minors then sued the county for having disclosed this information to their attorneys. The Ninth Circuit, while recognizing plaintiffs' right to informational privacy claim, found that the county's need for the information outweighed any potential harm to plaintiffs, given that it was never used in the underlying lawsuit, that only attorneys had access to it, and that it was critical to defending the underlying lawsuit. Not surprisingly, given that a balancing test involves less than strict scrutiny, most of the cases where courts have recognized a right to informational privacy have likewise concluded that the right was not violated.

§2.7 WHAT HAPPENED TO LIFE?

We have examined the extent to which liberty and property are protected as a matter of substantive due process. Yet the first interest mentioned in the Due Process Clause—ahead of both liberty and property—is life. Strangely enough, there have been almost no cases in which the Court has considered the application of substantive due process to governmental conduct that impairs a person's fundamental interest in life.

Abortion

This issue of life did not play a direct role in the abortion cases because the Court held that a human fetus is not a "person" within the meaning of the Due Process Clause. Thus, state laws allowing abortion did not cause a deprivation of a "life" within the meaning of the Fourteenth Amendment. See *Roe v. Wade*, 410 U.S. 113, 156-158 (1973). However, the interest in life was indirectly involved in *Roe*, for the Court there held that a state could not outlaw therapeutic abortions necessary to preserve a pregnant woman's life. With the overruling of *Roe* in *Dobbs v. Jackson Women's Health Organization*, 597

U.S. 215 (2022), it is no longer clear that a woman's interest in protecting her own life is sufficient to give her a federal constitutional right to have an abortion. See § 2.5.1.

Subsistence Benefits

The interest in life played no role in the cases dealing with federal and state welfare, medical care, housing, and food assistance programs. Governmental decisions denying, terminating, or reducing these benefits do not impinge on (and thus do not trigger) the *constitutional* interest in life, no matter how severe their actual impact on a person's life. The Court has held that "even where such aid may be necessary to secure life, liberty, or property interests of which the government itself may not deprive the individual," the Due Process Clause "generally confer[s] no affirmative right to governmental aid. . . ." *DeShaney v. Winnebago County Dept. of Social Servs.*, supra, 489 U.S. at 196. The government is thus under no more of an obligation to assure the basic necessities of life than it is to assure that people are able to exercise their constitutional liberty interests. See, e.g., *Harris v. McRae*, 448 U.S. 297 (1980) (government has no constitutional duty to provide funds to indigent women who otherwise cannot afford to have abortions); *Lindsey v. Normet*, 405 U.S. 56, 74 (1972) (government has no constitutional duty to provide adequate housing); and see *City of Grants Pass v. Johnson*, 144 S. Ct. 2202 (2024) (city's refusal to allow homeless people to sleep in streets, parks, or other public places does not violate Cruel and Unusual Punishments Clause of the Eighth Amendment). While governmental decisions affecting a person's benefits under these programs may give rise to statutory claims or implicate other constitutional principles—such as equal protection or the procedural due process protection of property—the due process interest in life is simply not implicated. The only exception would be in those cases where there is a special relationship that places the government under an affirmative duty to protect a person's life, liberty, and property. See § 2.6.2.

In contrast to our Constitution, which generally places the government under no affirmative duty to assure the necessities of life, Article 25(1) of the Universal Declaration of Human Rights provides:

> Everyone has the right to a standard of living adequate for the health and well-being of himself and of his family, including food, clothing, housing and medical care and necessary social services, and the right to security in the event of unemployment, sickness, disability, widowhood, old age or other lack of livelihood in circumstances beyond his control.

Similar affirmative rights to the necessities of life are found in the constitutions of many other countries, although as a practical matter, these provisions may often be unenforceable. And see §2.4.4 (The Concept of

Impingement) (noting that New York's state constitution requires the state to care for the needy).

The Death Penalty

One area in which the substantive due process interest in life would be expected to have played a prominent role—but where it has played no independent role—is the death penalty. The function that the Due Process Clause might have served in this area is quite different from that performed by the Eighth Amendment's Cruel and Unusual Punishment Clause. The latter clause has been construed to impose certain substantive and procedural limitations on the use of the death penalty. See, e.g., *Madison v. Alabama*, 586 U.S. 265 (2019) (Eighth Amendment bars execution of prisoner who lost his sanity after sentencing); *Hurst v. Florida*, 577 U.S. 92 (2016) (Sixth Amendment requires a jury to find every fact necessary to impose a death sentence); *Moore v. Texas* 581 U.S. 1 (2017) (Eighth Amendment requires that courts use the most current standards for assessing intellectual disabilities, and that if an individual's IQ score falls within test's standard-error range, courts must consider other evidence of intellectual-functioning deficits); *Brumfield v. Cain*, 576 U.S. 305 (2015) (Eighth Amendment bars execution of those with an intellectual disability even if their IQ is 75); *Kennedy v. Louisiana*, 554 U.S. 407 (2008) (Eighth Amendment bars execution as penalty for rape of a child where crime did not result in, and was not intended to result in, death of the victim); *Panetti v. Quarterman*, 551 U.S. 930 (2007) (Eighth Amendment bars execution of person whose mental illness prevents them from rationally understanding why state seeks to impose death penalty); *Roper v. Simmons*, 543 U.S. 551 (2005) (Eighth Amendment precludes execution of individuals who were under age 18 at time they commit a capital offense); *Atkins v. Virginia*, 536 U.S. 304 (2002) (Eighth Amendment precludes execution of the mentally retarded); *Woodson v. North Carolina*, 428 U.S. 280 (1976) (requiring heightened degree of reliability in jury decision to impose death penalty); *Gregg v. Georgia*, 428 U.S. 153 (1976) (requiring channeling of jury discretion in death penalty cases). A few Justices have suggested that the Eighth Amendment bars use of the death penalty in all cases. See *Hall v. Oklahoma*, 488 U.S. 878 (1988) (Brennan, J., and Marshall, J., dissenting separately); *Tucker v. Louisiana*, 578 U.S. 1018 (2016) (Breyer, J., joined by Ginsburg, J.) (dissenting from denial of cert.).

Even when these Eighth Amendment safeguards have been honored, however, substantive due process would play the much more fundamental role of requiring the government to defend its decision to take a person's life rather than impose a lesser punishment. Life is expressly mentioned in the Due Process Clause. It is surely as fundamental as any conceivable liberty interest, for without life, there can be no liberty. Since the death penalty impinges on the interest in life in the most direct and severe manner possible, the government should seemingly have the burden of proving not only that the death penalty furthers a compelling state interest, but also that no less life-threatening form of punishment would serve its goals equally well. Even if the interests in retribution, general deterrence, and/or incapacitation (specific deterrence) were deemed to be compelling, the government would have the additional burden of showing that the death penalty furthers these goals and does so more effectively than life imprisonment without possibility of parole, or any other form of punishment. Given the highly inconclusive nature of most of the studies and statistics concerning the death penalty, it seems unlikely the government could carry this burden. Yet for reasons that remain unexplained, the Supreme Court has not employed a substantive due process analysis to test the constitutionality of the death penalty. Most state courts that have addressed this question under the due process clauses of their state constitutions have rejected the argument for applying strict scrutiny. See *Commonwealth v. Hairston*, 249 A.3d 1046, 1054, 1058-1059 (Pa. 2021) (death penalty not per se invalid under state constitution's prohibition against "cruel punishments"); State *v. Ramseur*, 524 A.2d 188, 213-216 & n.12 (N.J. 1987) (collecting authorities); *Johnson v. State*, 731 P.2d 993, 1006 (Okla. Ct. Crim. App.), *cert. denied*, 484 U.S. 878 (1987). However, in *State v. Santiago*, 122 A.3d 1, 9 (Conn. 2015), after the state legislature prospectively abolished the death penalty, the state supreme court held that to apply it to offenses committed before the abolition date "would violate the state constitutional prohibition against cruel and unusual punishment" since "this state's death penalty no longer comports with contemporary standards of decency and no longer serves any legitimate penological purposes."

Death Caused by Government Officials

In *County of Sacramento v. Lewis*, 523 U.S. 833 (1998), a police car, while engaged in a high-speed pursuit, ran over and killed Lewis, a passenger on the motorcycle the police were chasing. Lewis's parents filed a § 1983 complaint alleging that their son "was deprived of his right to life in violation of substantive due process. . . ." Id. at 840. The Court disposed of the case on the basis that mere "reckless disregard" of life by executive officials is not in this context sufficiently egregious or conscience-shocking to state a due process claim. See § 2.1. Because the majority treated egregiousness as a "threshold" and "antecedent" issue, it did not address whether there is "a substantive due process right to be free of such executive action. . . ." Id. at 847 n.8. Nor did Justice Stevens, who declared that "the question is both difficult and unresolved. . . ." Id. at 859. Only Justices Kennedy and O'Connor were willing to concede that "an interest protected by the text of the Constitution is implicated: The actions of the State were part of a causal chain resulting in the undoubted loss of life. We have no definitional problem, then, in determining whether there is an interest sufficient to invoke due process." Id. at 856. On the other hand, Justices Scalia and Thomas, citing the lack of textual, historical, and precedential support, rejected the alleged substantive due process "right to be free from 'deliberate or reckless indifference to life in a high-speed automobile chase aimed at apprehending a suspected offender.' " Id. at 862. The fact that only two members of the Court agreed that cases like this potentially raise due process "life" issues reveals just how peripheral this term in the Due Process Clause has become.

CHAPTER 3

The Takings Clause

§3.1 INTRODUCTION AND OVERVIEW

The Takings Clause of the Fifth Amendment, also referred to as the Just Compensation Clause, provides that the federal government may not take private property for public use without paying just compensation. The clause also applies to the states through the Fourteenth Amendment. See § 1.3. This chapter explores the question of when the government will be deemed to have taken a person's property. The separate issue of what constitutes just compensation is not usually part of the basic Constitutional Law course. Suffice it to say that just compensation is ordinarily measured in terms of the fair market value of the property that the owner has lost through the taking.

§3.2 CONDEMNATION AND INVERSE CONDEMNATION

The most obvious setting in which the Takings Clause comes into play is when the government invokes its power of eminent domain to seize or confiscate private property. The power of eminent domain allows the sovereign to take private property for public use. While the state and federal governments may acquire property through purchase, there may be instances where a private owner either is unwilling to sell or demands an exorbitant price. The power of eminent domain permits the government to take property against the owner's wishes. If it does so, however, the Fifth and Fourteenth Amendments command that the owner be paid just compensation, calculated based on the property's fair market value.

The several states possess the power of eminent domain as a complement to their police power to promote the general welfare. The federal government has no enumerated power of eminent domain but may nevertheless exercise this authority to the extent it falls within the Necessary and Proper Clause. Thus, the United States could use the power of eminent domain to acquire land on which to build a post office, this being necessary and proper for the government to establish post offices under Article I, § 8.

If the federal government or a state wishes to exercise the power of eminent domain, it normally brings a condemnation action against the property in question. When the government institutes a condemnation proceeding, it acknowledges that property is being taken; the only issue is usually how much compensation is due. This straightforward exercise of eminent domain is studied in Real Property and Eminent Domain classes and is not a part of the course in Constitutional Law.

There is a second and more subtle way in which property may be taken within the meaning of the Takings Clause. This involves situations where the government, without invoking its power of eminent domain by filing a condemnation action, acts in such a way as to *in effect* take private property, but without admitting that it is doing so or offering to pay just compensation. In these so-called de facto or constructive takings cases, the property owner may be forced to bring an inverse condemnation action, asking a court to order the payment of just compensation on the ground that the government has in fact taken the plaintiff's property. In contrast to eminent domain proceedings, where the government concedes that it is taking the property, the key issue in an inverse condemnation action is whether or not a taking has occurred.

For example, suppose that Tom owns four acres of undeveloped land on the outskirts of Elm City. If the city wishes to use the land as a municipal park, it could attempt to buy the land from Tom at whatever price he is willing to accept. If Tom refuses to sell or demands an unreasonable price, the city can invoke its power of eminent domain by bringing a condemnation action and asking a court to determine what compensation is due. Under either of these scenarios, however, the city will have to pay Tom for the land—i.e., either his asking price or just compensation determined based on the property's fair market value.

What if the city instead passes a zoning ordinance that permits Tom's land to be used only for recreational purposes? Or it adopts a law allowing the public to use the property as a place of recreation on weekends? Or the city bars Tom from erecting any structures on the land? While each of these options may further the city's goal of setting aside land for public recreational use, in none of them has the city sought to exercise its power of eminent domain by condemning the land, nor has the city agreed to pay Tom any compensation. The city has regulated the extent to which Tom or the public may use the land, but without acknowledging that a taking may have occurred. In these circumstances, Tom might bring an inverse condemnation action against the city, requesting the court to find that the city has worked a de facto taking of his land and that just compensation is due.

In *Knick v. Township of Scott*, 588 U.S. 180 (2019), the Court held that those whose property has been subject to a de facto taking by a city, county, or other political subdivision of the state may bring an inverse condemnation action in federal court under 42 U.S.C. § 1983 without having to first seek just compensation under state law in state court. The state-court-exhaustion requirement not only delays a property owner's ability to obtain redress in cases where the state remedies ultimately prove futile, but it also poses a risk that the state court will find no taking to have occurred—a finding to which the federal court would then have to give preclusive effect under 28 U.S.C. § 1738. *Knick* overruled the Court's prior decision in *Williamson County Regional Planning Commission v. Hamilton State Bank of Johnson City*, 473 U.S. 172 (1985), which had imposed such an exhaustion requirement. However, if state administrative avenues are available that could "clarify or change" the challenged state action so that it would no longer constitute a taking, a property owner may need to exhaust those avenues before bringing a § 1983 action, for otherwise it may not be clear that a taking has occurred. But where such avenues do not exist, or where it is clear the state's taking action is final, a § 1983 inverse condemnation claim is ripe for federal adjudication. See *Pakdel v. City and County of San Francisco*, 594 U.S. 474 (2021).

The situation is less clear where it is the state itself, rather than a political subdivision, that effects a taking. In this setting, § 1983 is of no use, for a state or state-level agency is not a "person" who can be sued under that statute. Some courts have held that in such instances, plaintiffs may sue directly under the Takings Clause itself, though the Supreme Court has not expressly endorsed this approach. Other courts have found that such plaintiffs have a Takings Clause remedy under state law in state court, to the extent a state's inverse condemnation laws allow such actions. See *DeVillier v. Texas*, 601 U.S. 285 (2024) (finding that Texas law provided a state court remedy for plaintiffs' inverse condemnation claims against the state, making it unnecessary to address whether the Takings Clause itself affords an inverse condemnation cause of action).

Even though most of the examples in this chapter involve real property, the Takings Clause applies as well to personal property, including both tangible personal property, such as horses and automobiles, and intangible property, such as bank accounts and trade secrets. See *Horne v. Department of Agriculture*, 576 U.S. 350, 358-361 (2015) (Takings Clause clearly applies to government appropriation of personal property). It is also important to note that "a State may not sidestep the Takings Clause by disavowing traditional property interests long recognized under state law." *Phillips v. Washington Legal Foundation*, 524 U.S. 156, 167 (1998) (Texas could not avoid takings issue with respect to the interest earned on lawyers' trust accounts by deeming such interest to no longer be "private property"); *Tyler v. Hennepin County*, 598 U.S. 631 (2023) (Minnesota could not avoid takings issue with respect to the excess value of a homeowner's property that was sold to satisfy a tax debt by passing a law that extinguished an owner's traditional interest in that surplus).

In this chapter, we explore the question of when governmental regulation or treatment of private property will be deemed to constitute a taking so as to require that the government pay just compensation. First, however, we will address a constitutional doctrine that pertains to the government's authority to condemn property through eminent domain, i.e., the public use doctrine.

§3.3 THE REQUIREMENT OF PUBLIC USE

If a person's property is taken through an eminent domain proceeding, the only remedy usually available is payment of just compensation. A property owner ordinarily cannot obtain an injunction to prevent the government from continuing with the challenged action. However, because the Fifth Amendment requires that even a compensated taking be for a public use, if it is demonstrated that a taking is not for a public use or a public purpose, the government's action may be enjoined. The Court has "many times warned that one person's property may not be taken for the benefit of another private person . . . even though compensation be paid." *Thompson v. Consolidated Gas Utilities Corp.*, 300 U.S. 55, 80 (1937).

While the public use requirement would appear to limit the government's ability to take property, as a practical matter it is virtually impossible to defeat a taking on this ground. This is because "the scope of the 'public use' requirement of the Taking Clause is 'coterminous with the scope of a sovereign's police powers.'" *Ruckelshaus v. Monsanto Co.*, 467 U.S. 986, 1014 (1984). The requirement has been found satisfied even when the direct beneficiaries of a taking are other private parties rather than the general public. Such a redistribution of property will be upheld as long as it "is rationally related to a conceivable public purpose. . . ." *Hawaii Housing Auth. v. Midkiff*, 467 U.S. 229, 241 (1984).

Example 3-A

The City of New London has experienced decades of economic decline. To revitalize its economy, and after extensive planning accompanied by public hearings, the city adopted an economic development plan designed to attract more business. In part, the plan was adopted to entice a major pharmaceutical manufacturer to locate a $300 million research facility within the city. The development plan, which focused on an area that would be adjacent to the research facility, included a waterfront conference hotel, a small urban village with private residences, restaurants, shops, and a marina for recreational and commercial uses. To implement the plan, the city was required to purchase or acquire through eminent domain a number of private residences. Eventually, the title to this acquired property would be transferred to new private owners, such as the owners of the hotel, the private residences, the restaurants, etc. Susan's home is located within the redevelopment area. She has, however, refused to sell it. She also claims that the city may not exercise eminent domain over her property since the taking would not be for a public use, but rather for the private benefit of the future owners to whom the city would deed the property. Is she correct?

Explanation

No. The above facts are drawn from the Court's decision in *Kelo v. City of New London, Conn.*, 545 U.S. 469 (2005). There the Court explained that although a sovereign could not take the property of one person "for the sole purpose of transferring it to another private party," a sovereign was empowered to "transfer property from one private party to another if [the] future use" was designed to advance a public purpose. Id. at 477. The Court noted that in construing the term "public purpose," it had long "eschewed rigid formulas and intrusive scrutiny in favor of affording legislatures broad latitude in determining what public needs justify the use of the takings power." Id. at 483. In other words, so long as the exercise of that judgment is rationally related to a conceivable public purpose, it will be upheld. The question presented in this Example, therefore, is whether the comprehensive development plan adopted by the city represents a rational response to the decades of economic decline the city had experienced. It plainly does. A city, confronted with such circumstances could rationally conclude that the comprehensive redevelopment of an economically distressed section of the city would serve the public purpose of improving the city's overall economy. This remains true even though there are countervailing, rational arguments disputing the value or workability of the plan and even if some of the property taken is to be transferred into private hands for private use. In the words of the *Kelo*

Court, the city's "determination that the area was sufficiently distressed to justify a program of economic rejuvenation is entitled to our deference." Id. at 483. Thus, the "plan unquestionably serves a public purpose. . . ." Id. at 484.

The public use doctrine fully applies in the context of eminent domain proceedings—i.e., those proceedings in which the government affirmatively seeks legal title to a person's property—albeit in a rather toothless manner. Whether it also applies to a regulatory action by the government that arguably operates as a taking "in effect"—i.e., so-called inverse condemnations—is unclear. See §§ 3.6, 3.7. However, as a matter of substantive due process, all action by the government must, at the very least, be rationally related to some legitimate end. See § 2.2.3 ("Property and Economic Liberty Today"). This rational-basis due process argument, which is plainly applicable in the context of inverse condemnation proceedings, can be seen as the rough equivalent of the public use argument. Both standards are equally deferential to the legislative judgment, and, consequently, regardless of which one applies in a particular case, the result should be the same. In other words, asking whether a particular government action is rationally related to a conceivable public purpose is virtually the same as asking whether that action is rationally related to some legitimate government end.

At one time, due largely to dicta included in a 1980 Supreme Court opinion, it was thought that in cases of inverse condemnation, the Takings Clause itself required a type of heightened ends/means analysis. See *Agins v. City of Tiburon*, 447 U.S. 255, 260 (1980) (seeming to endorse a substantial relationship test in the context of inverse condemnation). The Supreme Court has since rejected that dictum, explaining that from the perspective of the Takings Clause, the primary question in an inverse condemnation proceeding is whether the government action is "functionally equivalent to the classic taking in which government directly appropriates private property or ousts the owner from his domain." *Lingle v. Chevron U.S.A., Inc.*, 544 U.S. 528, 539 (2005). In other words, the key question in such a case is whether there has been a taking in effect. The focus of the inquiry is on the nature and severity of the burden imposed by the government and not on an ends/means analysis of the government's purpose. Id. Of course, after *Lingle*, a party bringing an inverse condemnation action remains free to challenge the rationality of the government's action as a matter of substantive due process. See id. at 548-549 (Kennedy, J., concurring). Again, that due process argument can be seen as the rough equivalent of the public use doctrine as it has been applied in the context of eminent domain.

§3.4 AN APPROACH TO ANALYZING INVERSE CONDEMNATION PROBLEMS

To determine whether a compensable taking of private property has occurred, it is helpful to approach the problem through a series of inquiries. This approach is unnecessary when the government has chosen to exercise its power of eminent domain, for it has then acknowledged that property is being taken and that compensation must be paid. The inquiries suggested here are designed rather for cases involving de facto takings where the government has not admitted that a taking has occurred or that just compensation is due.

The inquiries are framed so as to recognize the fact that the government may effect a taking in three different ways:

- By physically invading, occupying, or seizing private property;
- By regulating the use of private property; or
- By imposing conditions on the development of property.

The inquiries are as follows:

A. Has the government effected a per se taking by causing an intermittent or continuous physical invasion of private property? If so, did the government's action fall within one of the exceptions to this per se rule because:
   1. The invasion was an isolated temporary event, such as flooding of land caused by the government's release of water from a dam? Or,
   2. The invasion was an isolated temporary event consistent with longstanding background restrictions on property rights, such as entry to abate a nuisance? Or,
   3. The invasion was pursuant to a reasonable right of access ceded to the government as a condition for receiving certain benefits, such as permits or licenses that allow for health and safety inspections? Or,
   4. The invasion was a restriction on an owner's right to exclude certain individuals where the owner had opened the property to the public, such as a law barring the exclusion of those distributing leaflets at a shopping center.

B. Has the government regulated the owner's use of their private property? If so,
   1. Is there a taking because the regulation stripped the property of all use or value? Or,

2. Is there a taking because the regulation substantially diminished the value of the property?
3. If the regulation did cause a taking, does the nuisance exception apply?

C. Has the government attached a condition to a building permit that would have effected a taking had the condition been imposed outright? If so, the condition amounts to a taking unless the following two inquiries are both answered in the affirmative:
1. Does the condition bear an essential nexus to a legitimate government purpose?
2. Are the nature and extent of the condition roughly proportional to the impact of the proposed development?

We discuss each of these steps or inquiries in the balance of this chapter.

§3.5 THE DIFFERENCE BETWEEN PHYSICAL OCCUPATION AND REGULATION

The first step in deciding whether there has been a taking of property is to determine the character of the governmental action. For these purposes, the government may act in either of two distinct capacities. In some cases, it causes a physical occupation or invasion of the property by public officials or third parties. In other instances, the government merely regulates the use to which the property may be put by its owner.

There is an easy way to distinguish a physical occupation or invasion of property from a mere regulation of use. In cases of physical invasion, private property is seized or used by the government or by third parties acting with the government's permission. By contrast, in cases of regulation, an owner is not forced to let others use their property but is instead restricted in the uses to which he or she may put the property.

Example 3-B

State X is considering two alternative means of improving the public's ability to view the ocean while traveling along the coast. The first would involve requiring owners of beachfront property to provide a viewing spot on their land so that travelers may stop and look at the ocean. The second approach would require owners of beachfront land to leave a 15-foot visual corridor on each side of their property in which nothing may be built. How would each of these requirements be characterized for purposes of a takings analysis?

Explanation

The first requirement would involve a physical occupation or invasion, for it authorizes use of private property by third parties—i.e., members of the public. The second requirement would entail a mere regulation of use, for while the owners' use of the property is restricted, neither the government nor any third party has been authorized to invade or occupy the land.

In the context of personal property, the government's seizure or confiscation of property is the equivalent of a physical invasion. Thus, in *Webb's Fabulous Pharmacies, Inc. v. Beckwith*, 449 U.S. 155 (1980), a taking occurred when a county appropriated all interest that accrued on an interpleader fund while it was deposited with the court clerk. Similarly, in *Horne v. Department of Agriculture*, 576 U.S. 350 (2015), the Court held that a government marketing order that required raisin growers to "set aside" a portion of their crop for the government constituted a "physical taking" of that portion.

§3.6 PHYSICAL OCCUPATIONS AND INVASIONS

The Supreme Court has long held that a taking will more readily be found when there has been a physical invasion than when the government is merely regulating an owner's use. This is partly because physical invasions by the government or government-authorized third parties are more likely to interfere with the use and enjoyment of property than are laws that merely restrict the owner's use. In addition, physical invasions are arguably more disruptive of an owner's basic expectations. While we can readily anticipate limitations being placed on how we may use our property, we are less prepared for situations in which "a *stranger* directly invades and occupies [our] property." *Loretto v. Teleprompter Manhattan CATV Corp.*, 458 U.S. 419, 436 (1982) (emphasis in original).

The Court's greater willingness to find a taking when there has been a physical invasion of property was first reflected in its rule that a permanent or indefinite physical occupation constitutes a per se taking. This per se rule applied regardless of the extent of loss inflicted or the importance of the public benefit that might result from the invasion. Such a permanent physical occupation occurs, for example, where the government or a third party acting pursuant to its authority is given a right to use private property on an indefinite and continuous basis. In *Loretto v. Teleprompter Manhattan CATV Corp.*, 458 U.S. 419 (1982), the Court thus found a per se taking when New York required that owners of apartment buildings allow cable television companies to install cables in their buildings. The fact that the cables occupied less than two cubic feet of space and that the harm to the owners was minimal had no bearing on whether a taking had occurred. These factors were relevant only to the amount of just compensation New York would have to pay. Physical invasions subject to the per se rule are not limited just to the placement of fixed structures on land. A permanent invasion would likewise occur if, for example, a state gives the public an easement to cross a private beach at any hour of the day or night, even though there may be times when no one is exercising their right to be there. See *Nollan v. California Coastal Comm'n*, 483 U.S. 825, 831-832 (1987).

Example 3-C

The State of Washington requires that attorneys deposit all client funds in interest-bearing trust accounts. Client funds that cannot earn net interest for the client because the cost of setting up and administering the account would exceed the amount of interest earned must be pooled with the funds of other clients in an Interest on Lawyers Trust Accounts (IOLTA) account. The net interest earned in the IOLTA account is transferred to the Legal Foundation of Washington (LFW), which then uses the earnings for charitable purposes including the provision of legal assistance to indigents. George, a client whose funds were deposited in an IOLTA account, claims that the transfer of his proportionate share of the interest on that account to LFW amounts to a per se taking of his personal property entitling him to just compensation. The facts establish that, had George's funds been placed in a separate account, no net interest would have accrued. In other words, the cost of administering that account would have exceeded the interest earned. The facts also establish, however, that George's funds did generate net interest within the IOLTA account. Is George entitled to just compensation?

Explanation

The Supreme Court has held that interest earned on a client's funds is the property of the client—i.e., the interest belongs to the owner of the principal. *Phillips v. Washington Legal Foundation*, 524 U.S. 156, 172 (1998). A government-enforced transfer of that interest to a third party would, therefore, amount to a per se taking entitling the owner to just compensation. On similar facts, the majority of the Court in *Brown v. Legal Foundation of Washington*, 538 U.S. 216 (2003), assumed that a per se taking had occurred: "As was made clear in *Phillips*, the interest earned in the IOLTA accounts 'is the "private property" of the owner of the principal.' If this is so, the transfer of the interest to the Foundation here seems more akin to the occupation of a small amount of rooftop space in *Loretto*." Id. at 235. Despite this assumed per se taking, however, the Court held that no compensation was due because the client funds were only deposited in IOLTA accounts if no net interest would accrue in an individual account. Hence, the client suffers no net loss by the taking of his proportionate share of the interest earned in the IOLTA account. Id. at 237-240.

The per se rule for physical invasions is equally applicable if the government has given itself or certain members of the public a right of access for only limited periods of time. For purposes of the per se rule, it is the permanency of the *right to invade*, not the permanency of the authorized *invasion itself*, that is critical. If the right to enter is of permanent or indefinite duration, then there has been a per se taking, even if the occupations that are allowed are themselves only intermittent rather than continuous. That the invasions are of limited frequency or duration may affect the amount of just compensation that is due but does not alter the conclusion that a per se taking has occurred. In *Cedar Point Nursery v. Hassid*, 594 U.S. 139 (2021), the Court thus held that there had been a per se physical taking when California allowed union organizers to enter private agricultural land for up to three hours a day but no more than 120 days per year. The state regulation was not transformed from a per se taking into a mere use restriction just because access was granted only to union organizers, for only a narrow purpose, and for only a limited amount of time.

EXAMPLE

Example 3-D

Elm City gives the public a right to use Tom's four acres of land every weekend for recreational purposes. Is this a per se taking?

EXPLANATION

Explanation

While the public does not have the right to use Tom's land at all times, it has been given an indefinite right to use the property on a regular and recurring basis. That the occupation is broken and discontinuous should not defeat the application of the per se rule. Otherwise, the government could avoid the per se rule by giving the public access to private land for 11 months a year or 20 hours a day rather than on a full-time basis. The fact that the public may use Tom's property solely on weekends is relevant to determining what compensation is due but does not alter the conclusion that a per se taking has occurred.

The Supreme Court has recognized that not all state or state-authorized physical invasions trigger application of the per se rule. See *Cedar Point Nursery*, supra, 594 U.S. at 159-162. First, isolated, temporary physical invasions are subject to a more flexible balancing approach that compares the importance of the public benefit with the economic impact on the owner. Such invasions may sometimes be treated as individual torts rather than as appropriations of property. Or a court may evaluate them under an approach like that used in cases involving regulation of use. See *Arkansas Fish and Game Comm'n v. United States*, 568 U.S. 23, 38-40 (2012) (whether temporary flooding of land caused by water releases from federally operated dam constitutes a taking depends on a consideration of multiple factors, including duration, foreseeability, investment-based expectations, and severity). See § 3.7.

Second, government-authorized physical invasions will not constitute a taking if they comport with longstanding background restrictions on property rights, for such actions merely involve the assertion of a preexisting limitation upon the landowner's title. This is true, for example, of government-authorized entry upon private land to abate a nuisance, to avert an imminent public disaster, or to effect an arrest.

Third, the government may require property owners to cede a right of access as a condition for receiving certain benefits, if the grant of access serves the same legitimate police-power purposes as a refusal to grant those benefits in the first place. Thus, a government license to allow the manufacture of pesticides may be conditioned on the government's right to periodically enter and inspect the pesticide plant. And see § 3.8.2.

Finally, where an owner has invited members of the public to use private property for certain purposes, the government may regulate the owner's ability to exclude specific individuals without being deemed to have caused a physical invasion. In these instances, it was the owner—not the government—who opened the property to the public in the first place. States may thus bar landlords from evicting tenants who have complied with their leases, just as civil rights statutes may prohibit owners of hotels, restaurants, and other businesses from ejecting patrons because of their race. While such laws do have the effect of allowing private property to be occupied by individuals whom an owner might prefer to evict, for takings purposes, they are mere regulations of use, not state-mandated physical invasions. See *PruneYard Shopping Center v. Robins*, 447 U.S. 74 (1980) (no per se taking where state barred private shopping center from denying access to those wishing to distribute leaflets on the premises). The owner still retains the right to at any time entirely close the property to the public by dedicating it to another use. See *Yee v. City of Escondido*, 503 U.S. 519 (1992).

EXAMPLE

Example 3-E

Elm City advised Tom that he must allow the public to use his land every summer for camping purposes and that no one may be denied access on account of their race. Does this amount to a taking?

EXPLANATION

Explanation

The city's action constitutes a per se taking, as a permanent physical invasion, for Tom had not invited the public to use his property. But if Tom had decided to use the land as a public campground, the city's requirement that he not discriminate would have amounted to a mere regulation, even though it means that Tom will have to admit some people whom he might prefer to exclude.

Since the Takings Clause does not bar the government from taking private property, but instead merely requires that it pay just compensation for doing so, the state can rescue a law that might otherwise violate the clause by insisting that a landowner be paid for whatever damages the taking may have caused. In many instances, the price of invoking this requirement would be prohibitive, such that the state will abandon the activity in question. However, in cases like *Cedar Point Nursery*, where the cost to a landowner of giving union organizers limited state-mandated access to their property may be so insignificant that the state can avoid a taking by simply requiring that the union pay the landowner a nominal fee for entry. See *Cedar Point Nursery*, supra, 594 U.S. at 179 (Breyer, J., et al., dissenting) (noting this option and suggesting that the lack of any damage to plaintiffs here was perhaps reflected in the fact that their complaint sought only declaratory and injunctive relief).

§3.7 REGULATORY TAKINGS

The other capacity in which the government may act for purposes of Takings Clause analysis is as a regulator. Rather than itself occupying or authorizing others to invade private property, the government imposes restrictions on what a person may do with his or her own property. In some situations, a court may find that the nature or extent of the interference caused by the regulation of use is such as to constitute a regulatory taking for which just compensation must be paid.

The Court is more tolerant of regulatory interference with property than it is of interference caused by physical invasion. This stems from the fact that in an organized society, regulation of private activity for the common good is unavoidable. At the same time, virtually all state and federal regulations have a negative impact on some property interests. If every government-induced reduction in property value were deemed to constitute a taking for which compensation had to be paid, government at all levels would come to a standstill. The Court has refused to read the Takings Clause to produce such an outcome.

While the Court has accepted that government must be able to regulate without being hamstrung by the Takings Clause, it has also emphasized that "if regulation goes too far it will be recognized as a taking." *Pennsylvania Coal Co. v. Mahon,* 260 U.S. 393, 415 (1922). The difficulty is that the Court has "generally eschewed any 'set formula' for determining how far is too far, preferring to 'engage in . . . essentially ad hoc, factual inquiries.'" *Lucas v. South Carolina Coastal Council,* supra, 505 U.S. at 1015.

Despite the lack of a "set formula," a regulation may be found to have worked a taking in two situations: (1) the regulation strips property of virtually all use or value; or (2) the regulation substantially diminishes the value of the property. If either of these tests is met, the regulation will probably be deemed to constitute a prima facie taking. The government may then be able to rebut the conclusion that a taking has occurred by showing that the so-called nuisance exception applies. Otherwise, it will have to pay just compensation. We will address each of these factors and the nuisance exception in the sections that follow.

§3.7.1 Destroying All Use or Value

A court may find a prima facie regulatory taking when a use restriction effectively deprives property of all use or value. The extent of loss that must be inflicted to create such a taking depends on whether the regulation affects real property or personal property.

Real Property

In the case of real property, the Court will automatically find a prima facie taking if a regulation deprives land of all economically beneficial or productive use so that it must be left economically idle. Use restrictions that have this effect are sometimes referred to as "confiscatory regulations" or "total regulatory takings." *Lucas v. South Carolina Coastal Council,* supra, 505 U.S. at 1026, 1029. The Court has said that it will be "extraordinary" and "relatively rare" that a regulation will be deemed to deprive real property of all economically beneficial uses so as to trigger this categorical rule. Id. at 1017, 1018. Thus, the Court has held that a temporary moratorium on land development 32 months in duration and imposed for purposes of creating a comprehensive land use plan did not trigger the categorical rule even if during the moratorium the owner was denied all economically beneficial use of the land. *Tahoe-Sierra Preservation Council, Inc. v. Tahoe Regional Planning Agency,* 535 U.S. 302, 319-343 (1986).

Example 3-F

Tom had planned to build 12 homes on the 4 acres he owns in Elm City. The city recently passed a zoning ordinance that bars Tom from erecting any permanent structures on his land. As a result, his property has declined in value by 80 percent and is now usable only for agricultural purposes. Can Tom establish a prima facie taking?

Explanation

Despite the severe impact of this law, Tom cannot automatically establish a prima facie taking on the basis of loss in value, since his land retains market value. See *Palazzolo v. Rhode Island,* 533 U.S. 606, 631 (2001) ("A regulation permitting a landowner to build a substantial residence on an 18-acre parcel does not leave the property 'economically idle.'"). However, as we will see, even though Tom cannot invoke the categorical rule for total regulatory takings, he may be able to establish a partial taking due to the substantial loss in value that his property has suffered. See § 3.7.2.

If it can be shown that the impact of a use restriction is to deprive real property of virtually all economic value, a prima facie taking is established under the Court's categorical rule even if the property retains some noneconomic use. Thus, in Example 3-F, if Tom had been able to demonstrate that the zoning ordinance stripped his property of virtually all market value, the fact that he could still use the property for his own purposes, such as camping, hunting, or kite flying, would not alter the conclusion that a prima facie taking had occurred.

Moreover, a prima facie taking would still have been established if, after passage of the ordinance that precluded Tom from making any economically viable use of the property, the city had bought the land from him for $50,000. Once a regulation strips property of all economically viable use, the state cannot avoid a finding that it effected a taking simply by buying or offering to buy the property for use as open space. Where the effect of a regulation is to deprive real property of all economically viable use, with the result that its only remaining value is to the state as open space, a taking has occurred. If, as is presumably the case, the price paid by the state was less than the property's fair market value before the confiscatory regulation was adopted, the government must pay the difference as just compensation. Were the rule otherwise, the government could avoid a total regulatory taking by simply buying or offering to buy the property for a nominal or sub-market-value price. See *City of Monterey v. Del Monte Dunes at Monterey, Ltd.*, 526 U.S. 687 (1999) (affirming finding of total regulatory taking where the government, after repeatedly denying permission to develop the land, bought the land from the property owner for $4.5 million).

Personal Property

In the case of personal property, it is more difficult to establish a prima facie taking on the basis of a regulation's impact on use and value. In contrast to real property, it must be shown that the use restriction has stripped personal property of all worth, both *economic and noneconomic*. The mere fact that personal property no longer has any market value is not enough. The Court has justified this disparate treatment on the ground that it is more foreseeable that the regulation of commercial dealings may render personal property economically worthless. In *Andrus v. Allard*, 444 U.S. 51 (1979), the Court thus ruled that there was no taking when a federal statute banning the sale of eagle feathers reduced their market value to zero, for the feathers still had noneconomic value to their owners, who remained free to possess, exhibit, donate, or bequeath them.

The Court's insistence that personal property be stripped of all economic and noneconomic value makes this basis for finding a regulatory taking almost meaningless as far as personal property is concerned. About the only time the test would be met is if the government seized or confiscated the property. If the seizure were permanent, there would probably be a taking on the basis of a physical invasion or occupation, and there would then be no need to establish a taking based on loss of use or value. However, if the confiscation were only temporary, this regulatory taking argument might be of help in establishing a "temporary taking." See § 3.7.4.

Measuring Loss in Value: The Denominator Problem

To decide whether a regulation has deprived real or personal property of all market value, it is necessary to define the scope of the property whose value has been reduced. For example, if a governmental regulation destroys the market value of a 40-acre section of an owner's 160-acre parcel of land, does this represent a 100 percent loss of 40 acres, or only a 25 percent loss of 160 acres? Because this test for a regulatory taking requires courts "to compare the value that has been taken from the property with the value that remains in the property, one of the critical questions is determining how to define the unit of property 'whose value is to furnish the denominator of the fraction.'" *Keystone Bituminous Coal Assn. v. DeBenedictis*, 480 U.S. 470, 497 (1987).

The Court has expressed conflicting views as to how this so-called denominator problem should be resolved. It has sometimes insisted on looking at the parcel as a whole, including those parts of the parcel that may not have been affected by the use restriction in question. On other occasions, however, the Court has suggested that it may be proper to focus solely on that part of the property that is subject to the use restriction. As the Court said in *Lucas v. South Carolina Coastal Council*, supra, 505 U.S. at 1016 n.7, if

> a regulation requires a developer to leave 90 percent of a rural tract in its natural state, it is unclear whether we would analyze the situation as one in which the owner has been deprived of all economically beneficial use of the burdened portion of the tract, or as one in which the owner has suffered a mere diminution in value of the tract as a whole.

The parcel-as-a-whole approach was employed in *Penn Central Transp. Co. v. City of New York*, 438 U.S. 104 (1978), where the Court rejected an argument that New York's historic preservation law would have effected a taking had the measure stripped the airspace above Grand Central Station of all market value.

> "Taking" jurisprudence does not divide a single parcel into discrete segments and attempt to determine whether rights in a particular segment have been entirely abrogated. . . . [T]his Court focuses rather both on the character of the action and on the nature and extent of the interference with rights in the parcel as a whole—here, the city tax block designated as the "landmark site."

Id. at 130-131. Under this approach, if a use restriction deprives 40 acres in a 160-acre parcel of essentially all economic value, the loss will be measured as 25 percent of the whole parcel, not as 100 percent of the 40-acre section.

Example 3-G

Tom sold all rights to the coal beneath his land to the Ajax Mining Company. Ajax would like to remove the entire coal deposit, but state law requires that enough pillars of coal be left in place to prevent the land surface from collapsing. Consequently, Ajax is unable to remove 2 percent of the coal from under Tom's land. Can Ajax establish a prima facie taking on the basis that the coal that must be left in place has been stripped of 100 percent of its market value?

Explanation

Under the *Penn Central* approach, to decide whether Ajax has suffered a total loss of its property, we must determine what value, if any, remains in the parcel as a whole. Since Ajax owns all the coal under Tom's land, the parcel as a whole for these purposes consists of the entire coal deposit; the coal pillars that must be left in the ground do not constitute a separate parcel for takings purposes. Ajax has thus suffered only a 2 percent loss in the market value of its property and, therefore, cannot establish a prima facie taking on this basis. On the other hand, one might argue that the coal that had to be left in place is a "separable property interest" and on this basis conclude that there had been a taking, since the state regulation extinguishes the whole bundle of rights in an identifiable segment of property.

Example 3-G is based on *Keystone Bituminous Coal Assn. v. DeBenedictis,* supra, where the majority, applying the parcel-as-whole approach, found that no taking had occurred. 480 U.S. at 501-502. The dissent, by contrast, rejected the *Penn Central* approach and instead treated the coal that had to be left in place as a "separable property interest"; the dissent on that basis concluded that there had been a taking since the state regulation "extinguishes the whole bundle of rights in an identifiable segment of property. . . ." 480 U.S. at 517-518 (Rehnquist, J., et al., dissenting).

The Court has acknowledged that resolving the denominator problem is not a matter of applying bright-line rules. Rather, it is a task whose "central dynamic . . . is its flexibility," one comprised of "ad hoc, factual inquiries, designed to allow careful examination and weighing of all the relevant circumstances." *Murr v. Wisconsin,* 582 U.S. 383, 393-394 (2017). In addressing this issue, the parcel in question is not to be limited "in an artificial manner to the portion of property targeted by the challenged regulation," nor, for Takings Clause purposes, is it necessarily defined in accord with state property law. Id at 396.

The Court has stressed that "no single consideration can supply the exclusive test for determining the denominator." Id. at 397. Instead, three principal factors must be taken into account: (1) how the land is treated under state and local law in terms of how it is bounded or divided, and the kinds of restrictions that have been historically imposed, especially any that predated its acquisition by the current owner; (2) the property's physical characteristics, including the physical relationship of any distinguishable tracts, and whether it is located in an area likely to be subject to environmental or other regulation; and (3) an assessment of the property's value under the challenged regulation, taking into account factors that may lessen its value as well as any offsetting factors that may enhance its value or the value of other land belonging to the same owner. Id. at 397-399. In making the third determination, lot lines will not necessarily define the relevant parcel, for these may artificially narrow the true scope of a property owner's reasonable expectations. A lot-line focus could also "create the risk of gamesmanship by landowners, who might seek to alter the lines in anticipation of regulation that seems likely to affect only part of their property." Id. at 402. The overall inquiry is an objective one, seeking to "balance[d] the legitimate goals of regulation with the reasonable expectations of landowners." Id.

Example 3-H

Joseph owns two adjacent lots, A and B, situated on the St. Croix River in Wisconsin. The lots were separately conveyed to him by his parents in 1994 and 1995; they had acquired them at different times during the 1960s. The parents built a small cabin on Lot A, while Lot B remained vacant. Each lot has less than an acre of land suitable for development. In 2005, Joseph decided to replace the Lot A cabin with a larger structure. To fund the project, he would sell Lot B. However, a 1976 state law, enacted to protect the wild, scenic, and recreational qualities of the St. Croix River, prospectively barred the use of adjacent lots as separate building sites unless each has at least one acre of land suitable for development. That law also provides that adjacent lots that come under common ownership after 1976 cannot be sold or developed as separate lots unless each meets the minimum size requirement. Since neither of Joseph's lots is large enough to be sold separately, he was advised that he could not sell Lot B alone. However, the lots could still be sold together. If they were, it is estimated that their combined valuation would have been $698,000, even with the ban against building on Lot B. If the lots could have been sold separately as two distinct and fully buildable properties (something state law disallows as to Lot B), their combined value would have been $771,000. Joseph has filed an inverse condemnation action in state court, alleging that the state law effected a regulatory taking by depriving him of "all, or practically all, of the use of Lot B because the lot cannot be sold or developed as a separate lot." How should the court rule on Joseph's inverse condemnation claim?

Explanation

Since nothing has been or can be built on Lot B, and since it cannot be separately sold, the lot has arguably been deprived of all economically beneficial or productive use. If we focus on Lot B alone, there would appear to have been a total or 100% loss. While this approach has been the traditional focus of takings claims, a court need not take such a constricted view. If we instead broaden our focus and use, as the denominator, the value of Lots A and B combined, it is clear there has been nothing close to a total loss of economically beneficial or productive use, for even with the ban against building on Lot B, the remaining value of the combined lots is $698,000, less than 10 percent below their $771,000 combined value had no restrictions been imposed.

To decide whether Joseph's property should be evaluated as a single parcel consisting of Lots A and B, rather than as Lot B standing alone, we must use the multifactor standard set out in *Murr v. Wisconsin*, supra. Here, those factors point strongly in favor of viewing Joseph's lots as a single parcel. First, under state law, the two would be treated as a single parcel for these purposes because they merged in 1995 when they came under Joseph's common ownership. Moreover, the lots were brought under his common ownership well after this state law took effect, creating an objectively reasonable expectation that the property would be treated in this way. Second, the physical characteristics of the properties make it reasonable to treat them as a single parcel, for they are contiguous and are located along a river that has long been regulated by the federal, state, and local governments. Third, the prospective value that Lot B brings to Lot A supports treating the two as one for these purposes. Lot B clearly lost value vis-à-vis what it would have been could it have been built upon and sold separately. However, this loss is significantly offset by the benefits of using Lots A and B as an integrated whole that now has increased privacy and recreational space. Treating Joseph's property as a whole thus makes sense. By treating the lots as a single parcel, they have a combined value of $698,300. This is more than 90 percent of their pre-regulatory value and precludes there having been a regulatory taking under *Lucas*. See *Murr v. Wisconsin*, 582 U.S. 383 (2017) (so holding on similar facts).

Regardless of how one resolves the denominator problem, the smaller a property owner's holdings, the better the chance of establishing a prima facie taking on the basis of total loss in value. Thus, in *Penn Central*, if the owners of Grand Central Station had sold the airspace over the station to a developer who planned to erect a skyscraper there, the developer could allege a prima facie taking on the basis of a total loss in market value if the city's historic preservation law subsequently barred all economic use of the airspace. Even under the parcel-as-a-whole approach, the parcel against which the loss in value is measured would no longer consist of the entire station, but would be the airspace alone, for this is all that the developer owned. Similarly, in our example involving the destruction of a 40-acre section of land, if the rest of the 160-acre parcel were owned by someone else, the owner of the 40-acre section could claim a prima facie taking by having suffered a 100 percent loss in the economic value of his or her land.

§3.7.2 Partial Deprivations

Even if a regulation does not strip real property of all economic value, it is still possible that a court will find that there has been a partial regulatory taking if the loss in value is substantial. A mere diminution in value will not automatically establish a taking—i.e., no categorical rule applies. Instead, courts will examine such partial diminutions on a case-by-case basis. Thus, in *Lucas v. South Carolina Coastal Council*, supra, 505 U.S. at 1019 n.8, the Court agreed that "in at least *some* cases the landowner with

95 percent loss will get nothing, while the landowner with total loss will recover in full." Id. (emphasis in original). However, it was error to assume that simply because an owner who has suffered a less-than-total loss and who therefore could not "claim the benefit of our categorical formulation," was necessarily foreclosed from seeking just compensation. Id. In some instances, "the landowner whose deprivation is one step short of complete" may be entitled to compensation, depending on the circumstances of the case. Id.

There is no "set formula" for determining what constitutes a sufficiently substantial diminution in value to amount to a taking. *Penn Central Transp. Co. v. City of New York*, supra, 438 U.S. at 124. In each case, the inquiry is essentially ad hoc and fact-bound. Id. In making this inquiry courts will examine several factors. "Primary among those factors are 'the economic impact of the regulation on the claimant and, particularly, the extent to which the regulation has interfered with distinct investment-backed expectations.'" *Lingle v. Chevron U.S.A., Inc.*, supra, 544 U.S. at 538-539 (quoting *Penn Central*). Also of relevance is "the 'character of the governmental action'—for instance whether it amounts to a physical invasion or instead merely affects property interests through 'some public program adjusting the benefits and burdens of economic life to promote the common good'. . .. " Id. at 539. The aim of the *Penn Central* inquiry is to

> identify regulatory actions that are functionally equivalent to the classic taking in which government directly appropriates private property or ousts the owner from his domain. . . . [T]he *Penn Central* inquiry turns in large part, albeit not exclusively, upon the magnitude of a regulation's economic impact and the degree to which it interferes with legitimate property interests.

Id. at 539-540.

EXAMPLE

Example 3-1

In 1972, shortly before the enactment of the federal Clean Water Act, Florida Rock purchased a wetlands parcel in order to extract the underlying limestone. At the time, mining in the wetlands was legal. In 1977, the Army Corps of Engineers adopted regulations requiring owners of wetlands parcels to obtain permits under § 404 of the Clean Water Act. Florida Rock, which had previously begun mining operations on the parcel, applied for a permit, but the Corps concluded that the proposed mining would cause irremediable loss of an ecologically valuable wetland parcel and create undesirable water turbidity. The permit application was denied. Consequently, the value of Florida Rock's parcel was reduced by 73 percent. Florida Rock has filed an inverse condemnation claim against the Corps. How should the court rule?

EXPLANATION

Explanation

First, since the Corps' action did not destroy all economic value of the wetlands parcel, the categorical rule of *Lucas v. South Carolina Coastal Council* cannot be applied. Florida Rock may, however, be able to show that under *Penn Central* it has suffered a compensable, partial deprivation of its property. Certainly, a 73 percent reduction in value suggests a significant economic impact on Florida Rock's investment. Moreover, given that the mining of limestone was legal when the property was purchased, Florida Rock can claim that the permit denial has frustrated its legitimate and distinct investment-backed expectations. Finally, although the permit denial appears to be part of a government program to adjust benefits and burdens in the promotion of a common good—i.e., it does not amount to something like a physical invasion—the character of the action can be seen as the functional equivalent of an actual taking since the owners of the wetlands are being asked to shoulder the entire burden. Therefore, under *Penn Central*, Florida Rock has a strong argument that it is entitled to just compensation for a partial deprivation of its property. See *Florida Rock Indus., Inc. v. United States*, 18 F.3d 1560 (Fed. Cir. 1994), *cert. denied*, 513 U.S. 1109 (1995) (remanding under similar facts for an application of *Penn Central*); *Florida Rock Indus., Inc. v. United States*, 45 Fed. Cl. 21 (1999) (on remand applying the *Penn Central* factors and finding a partial deprivation). Cf. *Stop the Beach Renourishment, Inc. v. Florida Dep't of Environmental Protection*, 560 U.S. 702, 731-733 (2010) (state action affecting the boundary between private beachfront property and state-owned "submerged" land does not amount to a taking of private property when the state action is consistent with background principles of state property law).

One context in which this issue may be important is where the government, in stripping a piece of property of all economic value, gives the owner certain "transferable development rights," or TDRs. Since TDRs can be sold to others who may then use them to develop their own property, TDRs have market value. Should the government be able to defeat a finding that there has been a regulatory taking simply by giving the owner some TDRs and then claiming that the land has not been deprived of all market value? Or should the award of TDRs be irrelevant to the question of whether there has been a taking, and instead affect only the additional compensation the owner is entitled to, over and above the value of any TDRs received? To the extent courts allow a regulatory taking to be established by a partial diminution in market value, how TDRs are treated will make no difference; the property owner will in any event receive just compensation for the net loss in market value inflicted by the government. On the other hand, if a total deprivation is necessary to establish a regulatory taking, the use of TDRs could be extremely beneficial to the government. For example, by giving a property owner TDRs worth $1,000, the government might avoid a finding that it has taken a parcel of land worth $250,000. As of 2024, the Supreme Court had yet to resolve this issue of how TDRs should be treated in regulatory takings cases. See *Suitum v. Tahoe Regional Planning Agency*, 520 U.S. 725, 728 (1997); but see id. at 747-750 (Scalia, J., O'Connor, J., and Thomas, J., concurring) (arguing that TDRs should not be put "on the taking rather than the just compensation side of the equation" and are thus irrelevant in deciding whether there was a taking); *Barancik v. County of Marin*, 872 F.2d 834 (9th Cir. 1988), *cert. denied*, 493 U.S. 894 (1989) (relying on TDRs to reject takings claim in agricultural zoning case).

§3.7.3 The Nuisance Exception

If a government regulation is shown to have worked a prima facie taking because it is arbitrary, because it defeats basic expectations, or because it has stripped property of all use and value, the government may nonetheless avoid the conclusion that a taking has occurred by showing that the regulation falls within the nuisance exception.

At one time, the nuisance exception was read broadly to allow the government to prohibit virtually any use of property that it deemed to be "noxious" or "akin to" to a nuisance, whether or not it was a nuisance at common law. In more recent years, the Court has limited the exception to regulations that do no more than make explicit those "restrictions that background principles of the State's law of property and nuisance already place upon land ownership." *Lucas v. South Carolina Coastal Council*, supra, 505 U.S. at 1029. See *Stop the Beach Renourishment, Inc. v. Florida Dep't of Environmental Protection*, supra, 560 U.S. at 731-733 (state action affecting the boundary between private beachfront property and state-owned "submerged" land does not amount to taking when the state action is consistent with background principles of state property law). And see *Palazzolo v. Rhode Island*, supra, 533 U.S. at 629-630 ("[A] regulation that otherwise would be unconstitutional absent compensation is not transformed into a background principle of the State's law by mere virtue of the passage of title.").

The nuisance exception thus does not apply to regulations that outlaw "a productive use that was previously permissible under relevant property and nuisance principles." Id. at 1029-1030. The prohibited use must rather be one that "was *always* unlawful" according to principles of the common law, in which case the forbidden use was not part of the owner's "bundle of rights" to begin with. Id. at 1027, 1030 (emphasis in original). While the government is free to impose new restrictions on the use of property in order to prevent harms that were accepted at common law, the nuisance exception cannot be invoked to avoid the payment of just compensation if such restrictions have the effect of causing a taking.

Example 3-J

Tom received permission from Elm City to build a nuclear power plant on his land. A year after the plant went into operation, the city ordered it shut down when it was discovered that the plant sits on an earthquake fault. Tom claims a prima facie taking because the city's action has stripped his property of all market value and because the city has interfered with Tom's expectations that stemmed from the city's prior assurances that he could build the plant there. May the city invoke the nuisance exception to prevent a court from finding that a compensable taking has occurred?

Explanation

The use that the city has prohibited is one that would qualify as a public nuisance under principles of the common law, since it poses a grave threat to public health and safety. Even though nuclear power plants were unknown to the common law, the threatened harm—the loss of human life—is one that the common law of public nuisance was designed to prevent. The city may, therefore, invoke the nuisance exception to defeat Tom's claim that his property has been taken.

If, after a state outlaws a particular use of property, the state courts rule that no taking occurred because the prohibited use was a common law nuisance, the state's ruling on the nuisance issue is not necessarily controlling for purposes of the Takings Clause. The U.S. Supreme Court may review the state judiciary's determination to make sure that it rests on "an *objectively reasonable application* of relevant precedents. . . ." *Lucas v. South Carolina Coastal Council*, supra, 505 U.S. at 1032 n.18 (emphasis in original). If the Supreme Court concludes that the state has attempted to recast the background principles of the common law, the nuisance exception will not apply, and the state may have to pay just compensation.

Example 3-K

Tom's four acres of land in Elm City consist of undeveloped swamp and marshland. Many surrounding owners of such wetlands previously filled or drained their property to build on it. However, in 1980, the state supreme court held that the filling or draining of wetlands is a common law nuisance. Relying on this decision, the state has passed a law that prohibits any further alteration of local wetlands. As a result, Tom's property has been stripped of all economic value. May the state avoid paying just compensation by invoking the nuisance exception?

Explanation

Though state courts have the last word as to what their common law of nuisance is, the U.S. Supreme Court may decide whether a state-declared nuisance qualifies under the nuisance exception to the Takings Clause. Here, the fact that the prohibited use was long tolerated by the state strongly suggests that it was not "*always* unlawful" under "background principles of the State's law of property and nuisance." As the Court said in *Lucas*, "that a particular use has long been engaged in by similarly situated owners ordinarily imports a lack of any common-law prohibition. . . ." 505 U.S. at 1031. In our example, while the state is free to adapt its law of nuisance to contemporary needs, it may have to pay just compensation for having deprived Tom's land of all economically beneficial use.

§3.7.4 Remedies for Temporary Regulatory Takings

As we have seen, if a regulation goes too far, it will be found to constitute a taking. When the regulation was originally enacted, the government may not have realized that it would be held to work a taking for which just compensation must be paid. Once the true costs of the measure become known, the state may decide to repeal or abandon it. However, the government must still pay just compensation for any temporary taking of property that occurred during the period the regulation was in effect.

Example 3-L

An Elm City zoning ordinance prohibited Tom from erecting any permanent structures on his land. Tom brought an inverse condemnation action against the city, claiming that the ordinance works a taking because it has denied him all economically beneficial use of his land. After three years of litigation, the court found in Tom's favor. The city immediately repealed the ordinance and advised Tom that he may now build on the property. Does the city owe Tom any just compensation?

Explanation

By repealing the ordinance, the city has assured that there will be no further taking of property. However, the temporary taking that occurred between the time the ordinance was first applied to Tom's land and the time it was repealed is compensable under the Takings Clause. The city cannot avoid the just compensation requirement by simply abandoning a regulation the moment a court finds that it has effected a taking. See *Lucas v. South Carolina Coastal Council*, supra, 505 U.S. at 1010-1014; *First English Evangelical Lutheran Church of Glendale v. County of Los Angeles*, 482 U.S. 304 (1987) (county cannot refuse to pay just compensation for period of time before a state court finally determines that a regulation constitutes a taking).

The result would have been the same if, instead of repealing the ordinance, the city later bought the land from Tom at less than its pre-ordinance fair market value. While any taking due to loss of all economically beneficial use of the land was temporary, ending when Tom sold the land to the city, he could still seek just compensation for the period between the adoption of the ordinance and his sale of the property. See *City of Monterey v. Del Monte Dunes at Monterey, Ltd.*, 526 U.S. 687 (1999) (affirming finding of a "temporary regulatory taking," based on city's refusal over a ten-year period to approve any of 19 site development plans, where landowner ultimately sold the property to the state).

§3.8 CONDITIONS ATTACHED TO BUILDING PERMITS

The state may sometimes cause a taking if, as a condition for granting a building or development permit, it insists that the owner dedicate property for public use or submit to certain use restrictions. In contrast to other forms of takings, in these so-called *exactions* or *dedications* cases the government does not absolutely insist that property be opened to public use or that specific uses be prohibited. Instead, it gives the property owner a choice: either agree to the state's condition or forgo the right to develop the land. Since a permit is usually necessary before property can be developed, the state may attempt to employ the permit process as a means of exacting from the owner something for which it would otherwise have to pay just compensation.

EXAMPLE

Example 3-M

Elm City wishes to build a park, but the only suitable land is Tom's four-acre parcel on the edge of town. How might the city seek to achieve this objective?

EXPLANATION

Explanation

The city would normally have to buy Tom's land or use its power of eminent domain and pay him just compensation. However, if by chance Tom needs a building permit because he wants to erect a house on his land, the city might condition the permit on Tom's agreeing to dedicate an acre of his property for a public park. If this scheme were allowed, Elm City could acquire a public park without having to pay for it.

This manipulation of the permit process is invalid because it involves an unconstitutional condition. The government is hinging the receipt of a discretionary benefit (i.e., a building permit) on the recipient's surrender of a constitutional right (i.e., the right to just compensation). If the condition were imposed outright, it would be a per se taking entitling Tom to just compensation, for it works a permanent physical invasion. By instead insisting that Tom give up an acre of his land if he wants a permit, the city is using its control over a governmental benefit to in effect buy up Tom's constitutional right to just compensation.

To prevent the state from using the permit process as a means of evading the just compensation requirement, the Court has created a special test that must be met whenever a building permit condition is such that, *if it were imposed outright,* it would constitute a taking. Under this two-part exactions test,

1. There must be an *essential nexus* between a legitimate state interest and the permit conditions exacted by the state, and
2. The permit conditions must be related in both *nature* and *extent* to the impact of the proposed development.

If either part of this test is not met, the condition or exaction will be found to constitute a taking for which just compensation must be paid. *Dolan v. City of Tigard*, 512 U.S. 374 (1994). These standards apply whether the "government *approves* a permit on the condition that the applicant [complies with the condition] or *denies* a permit because the applicant refuses to do so." *Koontz v. St. Johns River Water Management District*, 570 U.S. 595, 606 (2013) (emphasis in original).

Until recently, courts were divided on the question of whether the unconstitutional conditions doctrine applies when a condition is imposed legislatively rather than administratively, i.e., when it is a state statute or municipal ordinance, rather than an administrative agency, that imposes the condition. The Supreme Court resolved this conflict in *Sheetz v. County of El Dorado*, 601 U.S. 267 (2024), ruling unanimously that "there is no basis for affording property rights less protection in the hands of legislators than administrators. The Takings Clause applies equally to both—which means that it prohibits legislatures and agencies alike from imposing unconstitutional conditions on land-use permits." Id. at 279.

§3.8.1 Only Certain Types of Conditions Qualify

The Court's exactions test does not apply to all types of building permit conditions. It may be used to establish a taking only where the exaction is one that would have amounted to a taking had the state imposed it outright. If the condition would not have caused a taking were it imposed as a flat requirement, there is obviously no danger that the state is using its control over the permit process to avoid paying just compensation, and the two-part exactions test does not come into play. Application of the test is thus typically limited to "land-use decisions conditioning approval of development on the dedication of property to public use." *City of Monterey v. Del Monte Dunes at Monterey, Ltd.*, supra, 526 U.S. at 702.

Example 3-N

Tom applied for a permit to construct a 300,000-square-foot warehouse on his land in Elm City. The city conditioned the permit on Tom's agreeing to plant 45 trees on the property and to limit the building's height to 70 feet. The city has imposed similar conditions on other property owners. The effect of the conditions is to reduce the value of the property, but not to prevent it from being used for warehouse purposes. Will the imposition of these conditions trigger the exactions test?

Explanation

These conditions are not the type that will trigger the Court's exactions test. If they had been imposed as mandatory requirements rather than as conditions on granting a building permit, the exactions would not have worked a taking under our regular takings analysis. None involves a physical invasion by government or the public; none is arbitrary, since similar conditions were imposed on others; there is no indication that Tom relied on assurances that the conditions would not be imposed; and the conditions do not render the property economically worthless. There is thus no risk that the city is using the permit process to evade its obligation to pay just compensation. The exactions test, therefore, does not apply.

By contrast, had the city conditioned Tom's permit on his not developing a vacant lot he owned in the center of town, this might have triggered the exactions test if the result was to strip the lot of all market value, for this limitation would have constituted a prima facie taking had it been imposed outright rather than as a permit condition.

In *Koontz v. St. Johns River Water Management District*, supra, the Court held that the government's imposition of a monetary condition on the granting of a land use permit could trigger the exactions test. The Court made it clear that not all monetary burdens imposed on property owners would fall within this principle. Thus, neither taxes nor reasonable permit fees call for special judicial scrutiny and neither is typically considered a "taking" within the meaning of the Takings Clause. But when a monetary imposition operates as an exaction, it will be treated as such. For example, if a landowner seeking a land use permit is required to choose between granting an easement across her land—a clear exaction—and paying a substantial fee for the improvement of adjoining public property, a court is likely to find that the fee operates as a monetary exaction. *Koontz, supra*, 570 U.S. at 613-615. Moreover, if at the time the government originally acted it did not purport to be exercising its taxing power, a court is unlikely after the fact to treat the exaction as being the equivalent of a tax and hence exempt from the reach of the Takings Clause. Id. at 615-617.

§3.8.2 The Essential Nexus Requirement

If a building permit condition would have amounted to a taking had it been imposed outright, then it will be deemed to constitute a taking unless the Court's exactions test is met. The first part of this test insists that there be an essential nexus between a legitimate governmental interest and the permit condition.

This requirement was not satisfied in *Nollan v. California Coastal Commission*, 483 U.S. 825 (1987), where California exacted a lateral public easement across a beachfront lot in return for permitting the owners to build a larger house on their property. If this condition had been imposed outright, it would have involved a permanent physical invasion and a per se taking. The state said that it imposed the condition because the proposed development would reduce the public's view of the sea from the roadway behind the house. While the Court assumed that the state's goal of protecting visual access to the ocean was legitimate, there was no essential nexus between that goal and the condition that the public be granted an easement to cross the property at the shoreline. Allowing people to walk along the beach in no way furthers the goal of assuring or enhancing visual access from the highway. The Court noted that had the state instead exacted the condition that the owners provide a public viewing spot on their property, this would have met the essential nexus requirement since such a condition would have furthered the goal of improving visual access to the ocean that would otherwise be impaired by the proposed building.

Example 3-O

EXAMPLE

Tom applied for a permit to build a small shopping mall on his property in Elm City. The city conditioned the permit on Tom's building a 1,000-space public garage on his land. Does the exactions test apply here, and if so, is the essential nexus requirement satisfied?

Explanation

The exactions test applies because the condition, had it been imposed outright, would have amounted to a permanent physical invasion and hence a per se taking. The first part of the exactions test, the essential nexus requirement, is met because the city's legitimate goal of assuring adequate parking space is clearly promoted by a condition that Tom build a public parking garage.

§3.8.3 The Rough Proportionality Requirement

If the essential nexus requirement is met, the government must also show that both the *nature* and the *extent* of the permit condition bear a rough proportionality to the projected impact of the development. In other words, if the state is to avoid having to pay just compensation, it must demonstrate that it is not exacting more than is appropriate to compensate for the negative effects caused by the proposed use.

The Nature of the Condition

The conditions attached to a building permit must, by their nature, relate to the anticipated impact of the development in question. Otherwise, even if a condition meets the essential nexus test because it furthers a legitimate state interest, it will constitute a compensable taking.

For example, in the *Nollan* case discussed above, California might have defended its permit condition that the Nollans give the public a lateral easement across their beach, not on the ground that it promoted *visual* access from the highway (which it did not), but on the basis that it enhanced the public's *physical* access to the sea. While this condition would meet the essential nexus requirement, since it advances a legitimate state goal, it would still have failed the second part of the exactions test because there was no evidence that the proposed development would reduce the public's physical access to the sea. There would thus have been no logical relationship between the nature of the condition and any negative impact caused by building a new house.

The same problem was posed in *Dolan v. City of Tigard*, 512 U.S. 374 (1994). There, among the conditions imposed by the city in granting a permit to enlarge a hardware store and its paved parking lot were that the landowner not build on part of the property lying within a floodplain, and that she dedicate this land to the city for recreational purposes. The condition that Dolan not build in the floodplain met the rough proportionality requirement, for this restriction would reduce the danger of flooding created by the enlarged store and lot. However, the additional requirement that she deed this land to the city was not, by its nature, related to any negative impact of the proposed development; it did not tend to mitigate or offset any identifiable burdens that would be caused by the new store. The city was instead using the permit process in an attempt to acquire public recreational land without having to pay for it.

Example 3-P

In Example 3-O above, Elm City conditioned Tom's permit to build a shopping mall on his constructing a public parking garage. This condition is, by its nature, reasonably related to the impact of the proposed development, since the new mall will increase the demand for public parking. Suppose that the city instead, to enhance recreational opportunities for people living in the area, had conditioned the permit on Tom's building a public swimming pool next to the mall. Would the city's action pass muster under the exactions test?

Explanation

This exaction would meet the essential nexus test, for a pool would further the city's recreational goal. However, it would fail the first part of the rough proportionality requirement, since the pool, by its nature, does not relate to or tend to offset any negative impact of the proposed shopping development.

The Extent of the Condition

Even if the *nature* of the condition is such that it relates to public needs created by the proposed use, the *degree or extent* of the condition must also bear a rough proportionality to the anticipated impact of the development. Otherwise, by exacting more than is reasonably necessary to correct problems created by the project, the government is using the permit scheme as a means of taking property without paying just compensation for it.

In *Dolan v. City of Tigard*, supra, this requirement was not met by one of the permit conditions imposed on the landowner—i.e., that to enlarge her hardware store, she must dedicate a 15-foot strip of land to the city for a pedestrian/bicycle pathway. Unlike the condition that she deed land within the floodplain to the city, the *nature* of this exaction was reasonably related to the negative impact of the development, for the pathway would tend to offset some of the traffic created by the new store. However, the city failed to show that the *extent or degree* of the exaction was roughly proportional to the impact of the development, for it did not prove to what extent the estimated 435 additional daily car trips generated by the project would be reduced if customers could reach the store by a pedestrian/bicycle pathway. The Court explained that while "[n]o precise mathematical calculation is required, . . . the city must make some effort to quantify its findings in support of the dedication for the pedestrian/bicycle pathway beyond the conclusory statement that it could offset some of the traffic demand generated." *Dolan*, supra, 512 U.S. at 395-396.

Example 3-Q

In Example 3-O, involving Tom's desire to build a shopping mall, we saw that the condition that he construct a 1,000-space parking garage was reasonably related by its *nature* to the negative impact of the mall. Might the condition, nonetheless, constitute a compensable taking?

Explanation

Yes. The condition will still amount to a compensable taking unless the city proves that the *extent and degree* of the exaction are roughly proportional to the increased parking demand caused by the project. The city will have to estimate the number of new parking spaces likely to be needed as a result of the customers visiting Tom's mall. Unless that number is fairly close to 1,000, the permit condition would fail the rough proportionality requirement.

It is important to remember that the exactions test for finding a taking does not apply to all governmental regulations of land use. Rather, it may be used only with respect to conditions that are attached to a building or development permit, and then only if the conditions would have constituted a taking had they been imposed as mandatory requirements. Thus, in *City of Monterey v. Del Monte Dunes at Monterey, Ltd.*, supra, the Court refused to apply the exactions test in a case in which a city simply denied a development permit without imposing any conditions for its approval. As the Court explained,

> we have not extended the rough-proportionality test of *Dolan* beyond the special context of exactions. . . . The rule applied in *Dolan* considers whether dedications demanded as conditions of development are proportional to the development's anticipated impacts. It was not designed to address, and is not readily applicable to, the much different questions arising where, as here, the landowner's challenge is based not on excessive exactions but on denial of development. We believe, accordingly, that the rough-proportionality test of *Dolan* is inapposite to a case such as this one.

526 U.S. at 702-703.

CHAPTER 4

The Contracts Clause

§4.1 INTRODUCTION AND OVERVIEW

The Contracts Clause limits the power of a state to alter the legal obligations created by preexisting contractual relationships. Specifically, Article I, § 10, of the Constitution provides, "No State shall . . . pass any . . . Law impairing the Obligation of Contracts." The clause sought to keep states from continuing to pass laws abrogating or postponing their citizens' Revolutionary War debts or requiring that creditors accept newly minted paper money as legal tender. It was "intended to establish a great principle, that contracts should be inviolable." *Sturges v. Crowninshield*, 17 U.S. 122, 206 (1819) (Marshall, C.J.). The clause barred any and all state impairments without regard to extent, degree, or type:

> The objection to a law, on the ground of its impairing the obligation of a contract, can never depend upon the extent of the change which the law effects in it. Any deviation from its terms, by postponing, or accelerating, the period of performance which it prescribes, imposing conditions not expressed in the contract, or dispensing with the performance of those which are, however minute, or apparently immaterial, in their effect upon the contract of the parties, impairs its obligation.

Green v. Biddle, 21 U.S. (8 Wheat.) 1, 84 (1823). Over time, this stringent view of the Contracts Clause gave way. But in its prime, "it was perhaps the strongest single constitutional check on state legislation during our early years as a Nation." *Allied Structural Steel Co. v. Spannaus*, 438 U.S. 234, 241 (1978). See *Iten v. County of Los Angeles*, 81 F.4th 979, 986-987 (9th Cir. 2023) (noting origin of Contracts Clause); *Melendez v. City of New York*, 16 F.4th 992, 1016-1026 (2d Cir. 2021) (tracing evolution of Contracts Clause).

The Court gradually retreated from this strict originalist vie to accommodate the "inherent police power of the State 'to safeguard the vital interests of its people.'" *Energy Reserves Group, Inc. v. Kansas Power & Light Co.*, 459 U.S. 400, 410 (1983). Today, the Contracts Clause is subject to the reserved powers of the states to protect the health, safety, and welfare of their citizens under their police powers. Thus, not all state laws that alter contractual obligations—be they private contracts, or public contracts to which the state is a party — are void under the Contracts Clause. In general, the test is one of reasonableness, in which a court examines the expectations of the contracting parties, the severity of the impairment, and the public interest at stake. As we will see, the standard of review in most private contract cases is a quite lenient one, to the point where some have suggested that its limitation on state power is nonexistent. The Court has rejected that charge: "If the Contract Clause is to retain any meaning at all . . . it must be understood to impose *some* limits upon the power of a State to abridge existing contractual relationships, even in the exercise of its otherwise legitimate police power." *Allied Structural Steel Co. v. Spannaus*, supra, 438 U.S. at 242 (emphasis in original). And, in cases where states seek to alter obligations in contracts to which the state is itself a party, the level of judicial scrutiny is more demanding. See § 4.4.

From an analytical perspective, the examination of every Contracts Clause problem begins with three questions, each of which must be answered affirmatively to establish a potential violation of the clause:

- Is there a contractual obligation?
- Does a change in state law impair the contractual obligation?
- Is the impairment substantial?

See *General Motors, Inc. v. Romein*, 503 U.S. 181, 186 (1992). If each of these questions is answered affirmatively, the next step is to determine whether the state has acted reasonably under the circumstances. *Energy Reserves Group*, supra, 459 U.S. at 411-413. Here, the substantiality of the state's interest is measured against the extent of the impairment. The specific elements of this analysis will be examined below.

By its terms, the Contracts Clause does not apply to the federal government. The Due Process Clause of the Fifth Amendment, however, may be triggered by federal legislation that has a substantial, retroactive effect on a preexisting contractual relationship. The test for such retroactive legislation involves a modestly heightened rational basis review. See *United States v. Carlton*, 512 U.S. 26, 30-31 (1994) (upholding the retroactive application of a federal tax law under the rational basis test, but noting that rationality in the context of retroactivity requires a somewhat stronger showing than rationality in the context of prospective applications); and see *Eastern Enterprises v. Apfel*, 524 U.S. 498, 537-538 (1998) (noting that laws with "severely retroactive impact" may be so "arbitrary and irrational" as to "violate[] substantive due process," but voicing "concern [] about using the Due Process Clause to invalidate economic legislation").

Be careful not to confuse the due process concept, liberty of contract, with the interest that is protected by the Contracts Clause. The liberty of contract that comes into play under the Due Process Clause involves the freedom to enter into contracts, see § 2.2.1, while the Contracts Clause protects one's freedom from unreasonable state interference with the terms of a contract previously entered into. In other words, the Contracts Clause in no manner limits the ability of a state to legislate *prospectively* with respect to the substantive terms that may be included in future contracts or with respect to the conditions under which future contracts may be formed. The essence of a Contracts Clause violation is a change in state law that alters obligations established by a preexisting contract.

§4.2 THE PRELIMINARY QUESTIONS

§4.2.1 Is There a Contractual Obligation?

For purposes of the Contracts Clause, the question of whether a contractual obligation exists is ultimately a question of federal law. *General Motors. Inc. v. Romein*, supra, 503 U.S. at 187. Yet despite this often-stated rule, one should not expect to discover a large body of federal contract law elucidating such matters as offer, acceptance, and consideration. The focus of this preliminary inquiry is most often on general principles of contract law, including any state and local variations on those principles. After all, these are the principles relied on by the parties in creating what purports to be a contractual relationship. The term *contract*, therefore, is used in the ordinary sense of the word as connoting an agreement for consideration between two or more persons under which the parties obligate themselves to one another. See *Louisiana v. New Orleans*, 109 U.S. 285, 288 (1883).

The "federal" aspect of this initial question serves more as a potential trump on state law principles that might be used to eviscerate what otherwise seem to be contractual rights. In other words, although state law provides guidance in determining whether a contract exists, state law may not be used to circumvent the protections afforded by the Contracts Clause by *retroactively* defining the law of contracts in a manner that obliterates the legitimate contractual expectations of the parties.

Implied Contractual Obligations

Quite often in a Contracts Clause dispute, it is clear from the express provisions of the contract that a contractual obligation or right exists, and the critical question is whether that obligation has been substantially impaired. At times, however, the issue is whether an unstated obligation or right should be deemed an implied term of the contract. The *Romein* case, for example, involved a Contracts Clause challenge to a 1987 Michigan statute that required General Motors (GM) and the Ford Motor Company (Ford) to pay workers' compensation benefits that they had previously withheld under the terms of a 1981 statute. As construed by the Michigan Supreme Court, the 1981 statute permitted employers to coordinate benefits by paying reduced workers' compensation to workers who received benefits from other sources, including workers who were injured before the effective date of the 1981 statute. In 1987, the state legislature amended the 1981 statute to require that full rather than reduced benefits be paid to workers whose injuries predated the 1981 law. The result was that GM and Ford were ordered to pay an additional $25 million in withheld benefits. The auto makers claimed that the 1987 statute's "retroactive" imposition of this refund violated the Contracts Clause.

The essence of the auto makers' argument was that the existing contracts with their employees included an implied term that gave the employer the right to rely on past disability payment periods as closed and that the 1987 statute impaired this contractual obligation. In ruling against the auto makers, the U.S. Supreme Court explained that while the terms of a contract may be implied, no such implication was proper under these facts:

> Michigan law does not explicitly imply a contractual term allowing an employer to depend on the closure of past disability compensation periods. Moreover, such right does not appear to be so central to the bargained-for exchange between the parties, or to the enforceability of the contract as a whole, that it must be deemed to be a term of the contract.

503 U.S. at 188-189. In arriving at its conclusion, the Court accorded "respectful consideration and great weight to the views" of the Michigan Supreme Court, which had also found that the employment contracts at issue did not contain the implied provision asserted by GM and Ford. Id. at 187. Thus, the Court's resolution of this "federal" question was strongly informed by state law.

State Contract Law as an Implied Contractual Obligation

On occasion, a party asserting a Contracts Clause claim will argue that a repealed provision of state law was an implied term of a contract and that by repealing that law, the state impaired a contractual obligation. Typically, however, state laws are treated as implied contractual terms "only when those laws affect the validity, construction, and enforcement of contracts" or when those laws are part of the bargained-for exchange between the parties. *General Motors, Inc. v. Romein*, supra, 503 U.S. at 189. For example, the remedy of specific performance is a legal device used to enforce certain types of contracts. The right to obtain specific performance would, therefore, be an implied term in those contracts if it was part of a state's law at the time the contract was made. A repeal of the remedy might well run afoul of the Contracts Clause if the repeal made preexisting contracts unenforceable. On the other hand, a provision of state law that allows employers to coordinate benefits for injured employees has no bearing on the validity, construction, or enforceability of a contract. Rather, it provides a substantive right that may or may not have been negotiated between the parties. Therefore, this provision of state law would be an implied term of an employment contract *only if* benefit coordination was part of the bargained-for exchange between the parties.

Example 4-A

On July 1, 1985, Bill and Ted entered into a real estate financing agreement under which Bill lent Ted $100,000 for the purchase of a new home. The loan, which was secured by the purchased property, was amortized over 30 years, during which time Ted was to make monthly payments. At the time the agreement was reached, the state law of foreclosure permitted a defaulting debtor to redeem the secured property within one year of a foreclosure sale, as long as the debtor had not abandoned the property. In the case of abandonment, however, the state law provided no period of redemption, and the purchaser at foreclosure was granted immediate possession. Several years later and while the agreement was still in effect, state law was amended to create a one-year redemption period even for abandoned property. Was the original state law on redemption an implied term of Bill and Ted's agreement?

Explanation

Probably. Because foreclosure is an important remedy for the enforcement of contracts between creditors and debtors, the state's law of foreclosure as it stood on July 1, 1985, might well be an implied term of the contract between Bill and Ted. Under that law, if Ted had defaulted on the loan and abandoned the property, Bill would have had a right of foreclosure and immediate sale, with no obligation to give Ted an opportunity to redeem the property. Under the law as amended, Ted would retain a right to redeem the property within one year of foreclosure, thereby altering the immediate enforceability of Bill's rights under the contract.

§4.2.2 Does a Change in State Law Impair a Contractual Obligation?

Once a contractual obligation has been identified, the next step to consider is whether that obligation has been impaired by a change in state law. This inquiry should create little difficulty. Simply compare the terms of the obligation created by the contract with the provisions of the state law being challenged. If the change in state law *increases, diminishes,* or *extinguishes* an obligation created by the contract, the state law has impaired the obligation. As illustrated by Example 4-A, a change in the state law of foreclosure that created a redemption period for abandoned property diminished Bill's implied right of immediate foreclosure and, therefore, impaired an obligation created in the original agreement. One could also view the change in state law as increasing Ted's rights of redemption. In either case, the contractual obligation has been altered and thus impaired.

EXAMPLE

Example 4-B

Allied operates a factory within the State of Minnesota. Its 30 employees are covered under a company-sponsored pension plan. Under the plan, employees are eligible for a pension at age 65. The amount of the pension is computed by a formula that considers the employee's length of service and their annual compensation. An employee who leaves the company before reaching age 65 loses all pension benefits unless that employee has worked for the company a total of 15 years and is at least 60 years old at the time of departure. Because of a business slowdown, Allied has announced its intention to close its Minnesota plant. Consequently, many of Allied's employees will lose their pension eligibility. In response, the state has adopted legislation that requires Allied and other like-situated businesses that terminate their operations in Minnesota to treat pensions as vested for all employees with ten or more years of seniority. The net result is that Allied must pay a $185,000 pension funding charge to cover these newly vested pensions. Does this legislation impair a contractual obligation between Allied and its employees?

EXPLANATION

Explanation

Yes. By retroactively increasing the pension obligations of the employer, the state has impaired contractual obligations between the parties. Presumably the employer and the employee bargained for a particular benefit package under which the employer was obligated to pay a pension if the employee satisfied certain specified terms. To revise that package retroactively is, in essence, to rewrite the terms of that bargained-for exchange. Under the revised contract, the employer's obligations are increased, while the employees' obligations are diminished. Regardless of the perspective from which one views this impairment, the critical factor is that the state has interfered with the terms of a preexisting contract. Consistent with the Contracts Clause, a state is free to regulate the vesting of pensions prospectively if it does not alter the contractual expectations of the parties by rewriting the terms of the contract that already exists between them. See *Allied Structural Steel Co. v. Spannaus*, 438 U.S. 234 (1978) (finding violation of Contracts Clause on these facts).

§4.2.3 Is the Impairment Substantial?

Only substantial impairments of contractual obligations trigger further Contracts Clause scrutiny. Stated somewhat differently, "minimal alteration of contractual obligations may end the inquiry at its first stage." *Allied Structural Steel*, supra, 438 U.S. at 244-245. As a practical matter, however, courts do not often find a clear impairment of a contractual obligation to be so insubstantial as to warrant no further scrutiny. While this occasionally happens, the tendency is to measure the "substantiality" or "severity" of the impairment and then gear the level of judicial scrutiny to the perceived harm. A truly substantial impairment will generate a closer examination of the state's justification, while a lesser impairment will generate more deferential scrutiny.

Under what circumstances will an impairment be deemed substantial enough to warrant close judicial scrutiny? The answer to this question remains somewhat elusive. We can say with certainty that the substantial-impairment rule does not require a total destruction of contract rights, but that it does require something more than a technical alteration of those rights. The critical issue in determining substantiality is the extent to which the state has upset the *reasonable expectations of the contracting parties.*

In determining the reasonableness of the parties' expectations, the Court looks to at least four factors. One concerns what the parties intended or expected to create through their contractual relationship. *Energy Reserves Group*, supra, 459 U.S. at 411. Second, the more central a particular contractual expectation is to the bargained-for exchange, the more likely an impairment of that expectation will be deemed substantial. Third is the economic consequence of the change in state law. The greater the consequence, the more likely a court is to find a substantial impairment; this is particularly true if the contract was designed to avoid the economic burden imposed by the change in state law. Finally, if the subject of the contract relates to an area the state has heavily regulated in the past, a court is unlikely to find a substantial impairment: a party engaging in an activity that has been subject to regulation cannot *reasonably* expect to rely on contractual rights to avoid or insulate themselves from the consequences of further state regulation.

EXAMPLE

Example 4-C

Returning to the facts of Example 4-B, was the state's imposition of a retroactive pension obligation a substantial impairment of the contractual obligation between the employer and its employees?

EXPLANATION

Explanation

We must try to ascertain the extent to which the state has interfered with the reasonable expectations of the parties. First, there is little doubt that the employer expected or intended that pensions would be funded only in accord with the specific terms of the employment agreement. And it is quite likely that the employer made pension investments based on those expectations. Moreover, nothing in the facts indicates that the employees had any other expectation. Even though the employees may have hoped or assumed that the company would remain in business a sufficient length of time for their pensions to vest, nothing in the contract directly supports that expectation. Second, although the pension plan may not have been the key ingredient in the employment contract, the plan was probably of more than marginal significance to both parties, since it was certainly part of the compensation package. Third, the economic consequences of the change in state law are severe, namely, an unanticipated $185,000 penalty imposed on a relatively small company. Finally, in the absence of information to the contrary, there is no suggestion that the state had previously regulated pensions in a manner that would have alerted the employer to anticipate changes in state law. Considering these factors together, the impairment is likely to be found substantial. See *Allied Structural Steel*, supra, 438 U.S. at 244-247.

EXAMPLE

Example 4-D

To finance its system of public education, the State of Texas sold millions of acres of public land under contracts in which the purchasers were required to make a down payment of 1/40 of the value of the land plus annual payments of interest and principal. The contracts provided for termination of the contract and forfeiture of the land for failure to pay interest. However, the defaulting purchaser was given an open-ended right to reinstate his or her claim at any time by filing a request, accompanied by the payment of delinquent interest, as long as rights of a third party had not intervened. On the other hand, state policy required that any forfeited property be placed for sale immediately, thus increasing the likelihood that third party rights would intervene prior to any request for reinstatement. Thirty years after entering these contracts, Texas adopted legislation that limited the potential reinstatement period to a maximum of five years from the date of forfeiture. Does this measure substantially impair an obligation established in the purchase contracts?

Explanation

Probably not. The possibly impaired obligation is the contractual term that grants purchasers an open-ended right to reinstate ownership upon the payment of delinquent interest. By diminishing that right, the five-year limitation impairs a contractual obligation. Whether this impairment is substantial turns largely on the contractual expectations of the parties. If the purchasers entered into these contracts under the reasonable expectation that they would retain forever an irrevocable right to redeem the forfeited property, then the newly imposed limitation could be seen as a substantial impairment of that expectation. But given the very real possibility that the rights of third parties would intervene because of the state's policy of immediately placing the property for sale, any expectation of permanent redemption rights would seem almost fanciful. Moreover, the purchasers would have a difficult time establishing that the supposed unlimited right of redemption was central to these contracts when first entered. Presumably, the contracts were entered into with an intent to abide by their terms and thereby avoid forfeiture. Yet despite these conclusions of "insubstantiality," a court, rather than ending the analysis there, might still examine the state's justification, albeit under a very deferential standard of review. See *El Paso v. Simmons*, 379 U.S. 497, 509-517 (1965) (finding no impairment of contract on similar facts).

Example 4-E

Mark and Kaye married in 1997. A year later, Mark purchased a life insurance policy naming Kaye as primary beneficiary, and his two children from a prior marriage as contingent beneficiaries. In 2007 the couple divorced; their divorce decree made no mention of the insurance policy. After Mark died in 2011, Kaye and his children made competing claims to the insurance proceeds—Kaye on the basis that she was the named beneficiary, the children based on a 2002 Minnesota "revocation-on-divorce" statute. That statute, which is like laws enacted in many other states, provides that when a couple divorces, if one spouse has designated the other as the beneficiary of a life insurance policy, their divorce automatically revokes the designation, on the theory that the policyholder would want that result. If the policyholder does not agree, they can simply rename the ex-spouse as beneficiary, something Mark never did. Kaye argues that because the Minnesota law would nullify the beneficiary designation in Mark's 1998 insurance contract, it violates the Contracts Clause and she is therefore entitled to the policy benefits. Does Minnesota's law "substantially impair" the terms of Mark's life insurance contract?

EXPLANATION

Explanation

The 1998 life insurance policy is a contract that pre-dated Minnesota's 2002 revocation statute. That law impairs that contract by canceling the designated beneficiary. To decide whether this substantially upsets the parties' reasonable expectations, we look first at what the contracting parties would have intended or expected through their contractual relationship. Here, had Mark thought about it, he might well have expected to change the policy's primary beneficiary should Kaye no longer be his wife. If so, the Minnesota law would further rather than defeat his expectations. Second, while the designation of beneficiary was central to the insurance contract when it was entered, it is less likely that retaining Kaye as the beneficiary after a marital dissolution would have been part of those expectations. Third, while the economic consequences of the automatic cancellation proved significant after the fact, Mark's ability to override that cancellation by mailing a change-of-beneficiary form made it cost-free and easy for him to avoid those consequences had he so desired. Finally, insurance has long been regulated by the states. Before Minnesota did so, many other states had adopted similar revocation-on-divorce laws. It is therefore unlikely a court would find Minnesota's law to have worked a "substantial impairment" of the insurance contract. See *Sveen v. Melin*, 584 U.S. 811 (2018) (so holding on these facts and thus not reaching question of whether Minnesota acted reasonably under the circumstances).

§4.3 THE BALANCING TEST AND THE RESERVED POWERS DOCTRINE

If the impairment is deemed sufficiently substantial to warrant further judicial review, a court will balance the severity of the impairment against the public's interest in abrogating the contractual obligation at issue. However, there is a strong presumption that the states retain their reserved powers to promote and protect the health, safety, and welfare of their citizens. Stated somewhat differently, "One whose rights, such as they are, are subject to state restriction, cannot remove them from the power of the State by making a contract about them." *Hudson Water Co. v. McCarter*, 209 U.S. 349, 357 (1908). As a result of this presumption in favor of the state's right to exercise its police powers, it is difficult, though not impossible, to establish a violation of the Contracts Clause.

The balancing test focuses on the reasonableness of the challenged action. In the Court's words,

> Legislation adjusting the rights and responsibilities of contracting parties must be upon reasonable conditions and of a character appropriate to the public purpose justifying its adoption. As is customary in reviewing economic and social regulation, however, courts properly defer to legislative judgment as to the necessity and reasonableness of a particular measure.

United States Trust Co. v. New Jersey, 431 U.S. 1, 22-23 (1977). This is simply another way of saying that the state's action must be reasonable under the circumstances, a classic and highly deferential due-process-type formula.

Although the general standard is one of reasonableness, the level of judicial scrutiny is somewhat variable. "The severity of the impairment measures the height of the hurdle the state legislation must clear. . . . Severe impairment . . . will push the inquiry to a careful examination of the nature and purpose of the state legislation." *Allied Structural Steel,* supra, 438 U.S. at 245. The opposite is true as well. However, even in cases of substantial impairment, a state law will still be upheld if it "is drawn in an 'appropriate' and 'reasonable' way to advance 'a significant and legitimate public purpose.'" *Sveen v. Melin,* 584 U.S. 811, 819 (2018). In undertaking this inquiry, the Court has "refuse[d] to second-guess" the legislature's identification of "the most appropriate ways of dealing with the problem." *Keystone Bituminous Coal Ass'n v. DeBenedictis,* 480 U.S. 470, 504, 506 (1987). However, as we will see, if a state seeks to lessen its own contractual obligations, the level of scrutiny may be more rigorous. See § 4.4.

Example 4-F

EXAMPLE

During the Great Depression, communities throughout the United States were faced with massive unemployment, a crash in the real estate market, and a virtual epidemic of home foreclosures and evictions. In response to this crisis, the State of Minnesota adopted the Mortgage Moratorium Act (MMA), which granted county courts the authority to extend the period during which a homeowner could redeem their home from foreclosure. The practical effect of the MMA was to prevent banks from effectively exercising their contractual rights of foreclosure during the extension period. The homeowner was, however, required to pay the mortgagee reasonable rental value during any judicially granted extension, and the homeowner also remained liable for any accrued interest or deficiency. The MMA was to remain in effect "only during the continuance of the emergency," but no more than two years in any event. By impairing the contractual rights of foreclosure, did the MMA violate the Contracts Clause? Or, stated in terms of the judicial inquiry, was the adjustment of contract rights effected by the

MMA "upon reasonable conditions and of a character appropriate to the public purpose justifying its adoption"?

Explanation

First, we must consider the severity of the impairment. Unquestionably the MMA alters the contractual rights of the mortgagee, for the mortgagee cannot obtain or convey title during the extension period. In this sense, the rights of the mortgagee are clearly diminished. On the other hand, the MMA does not alter any other obligations under the mortgage contracts, and it provides a compensatory protection to the mortgagee by requiring the homeowner to pay reasonable rental value during the extension period. Thus, in one sense, the impairment is severe in that it clearly alters the contractual expectations of the parties; in another sense, however, the impairment is relatively minor, since it merely extends the period of redemption and during this time the mortgagee's interests are otherwise protected. Yet regardless of which perspective one takes, the degree of impairment is certainly substantial enough to warrant further judicial scrutiny.

Having discovered a sufficiently substantial impairment of contractual rights, the next step is to determine if the impairment is reasonable under the circumstances. A state has a legitimate and even substantial interest in preventing widespread dislocation caused by an epidemic of foreclosures and evictions. Moreover, the means adopted by the state seem appropriate to the public purpose, since they intrude on contractual expectations only to the extent necessary to advance that purpose for the duration of the emergency. Specifically, the impairment is temporary, is geared to addressing the precise crisis confronted by the state, and is designed so as to otherwise protect the economic interests of the mortgagee. Thus, given the deference normally accorded a state in this realm and the relatively limited nature of the impairment, the MMA did not violate the Contracts clause. See *Home Building & Loan Ass'n v. Blaisdell*, 290 U.S. 398, 444-447 (1934) (holding that the MMA did not violate the Contracts Clause).

Example 4-G

In Examples 4-B and 4-C, we considered a state law that retroactively imposed pension obligations on an employer about to close its business within the state. We concluded that the law impaired the employment contract, and that the impairment was substantial, given the expectations of the parties and the significant economic impact of the increased obligations. Assume now that the state's interest in imposing that retroactive pension obligation was to protect employees with "unvested" pensions who are working for companies about to terminate operations within the state. Is this contractual impairment "upon reasonable conditions and of a character appropriate to the public purpose justifying its adoption"?

Explanation

The public purpose asserted by the state, namely, the protection of employees whose pension rights may be foreclosed by businesses that terminate operations within the state, is certainly legitimate and, from the perspective of the affected employees, even quite important. The public interest is not, however, commensurate with the interest at issue in Example 4-F, where the state was confronted with severe economic problems generated by the Depression. Nothing in the facts indicates that Minnesota was faced with an epidemic of such closures. Moreover, the intrusion on the contractual expectations of the parties here is much more severe than was the case with the mortgage moratorium described in Example 4-F. The mortgage moratorium was temporary and was designed to minimize the economic impact on the mortgagee. Here, by contrast, the impact on the employer is immediate, drastic, and permanent. Given the severity of the impairment and the relatively discrete problem being addressed by the state, a court could well find that the state had exceeded the scope of its reserved powers. In other words, the contractual impairment was not "upon reasonable conditions and of a character appropriate to the public purpose justifying its adoption." See *Allied Structural Steel*, supra, 438 U.S. at 244-251 (so holding on these facts).

The discussion in Examples 4-B, 4-C, and 4-G, all involving *Allied Structural Steel*, could lead one to conclude that the Contracts Clause is a potent weapon for challenging the constitutionality of state laws that retroactively impair contractual obligations. However, the 1978 decision in that case was something of an anomaly and did not herald a revival of the Contracts Clause as a means of invalidating state legislation. Thus, five years later, the Court in *Energy Reserves Group*, supra, rejected a Contracts Clause challenge on the basis that any impairment of petitioner's contract was not "substantial" enough to trigger the clause given that the industry in question had long been heavily regulated by the state. 459 U.S. at 413-416. Moreover, said the Court, even if there had been a substantial impairment, the state's action was "reasonable." Id. at 416-419. Then, in *Keystone Bituminous Coal Association v. DeBenedictis*, 480 U.S. 470 (1987), the Court agreed that while a state law had worked "a substantial impairment of a contractual relationship," it went on to conclude that the state had acted reasonably: "We refuse to second-guess the [state's] determinations that these are the most appropriate ways of dealing with the problem." Id. At 504, 506. And, more recently, in *Sveen v. Melin*, supra, (see Example 4-E), the Court again found there to have been no substantial impairment. Indeed, *Allied Structural Steel*, decided more than

45 years ago, was the last time the Supreme Court invalidated a state law under the Contracts Clause.

Example 4-H

After the outbreak of COVID-19 in 2020, the City of Los Angeles enacted an eviction moratorium ordinance to help ensure housing security and promote public health during the pandemic. The ordinance bars most residential evictions during a Local Emergency Period (LEP), as declared by the Mayor. It also delays tenants' rent payment obligations, and bars landlords from evicting tenants for non-payment of rent or charging late fees or interest for up to 12 months after the LEP's expiration. Landlords who violate the ordinance can be sued by a tenant for up to $10,000 in penalties, plus costs and attorney's fees. As the same time, in order to ease the financial burden on landlords, the City has given them some flexibility in meeting their obligations to pay utility bills and property taxes. It also created an Emergency Rental Assistance Program to help tenants make rent payments to their landlords. Plaintiff landlords have sued the City to enjoin the eviction moratorium ordinance, on the ground that it violates the Contracts Clause. How should the court rule on this claim?

Explanation

First, the ordinance clearly impairs landlord-tenant contracts by relieving tenants of their contractual duty to pay rent and by barring landlords from enforcing contractual provisions that would allow them to evict tenants and collect back rent, late fees, and interest. Second, these impairments affect the most central clauses of a lease agreement, i.e., the right to collect rent and the right to evict. Third, the ordinance has immediate and serious economic consequences for landlords. Finally, while the landlord-tenant relationship has long been regulated by the state, the novelty and extent of the burdens imposed would appear to go well beyond a landlord's reasonable expectations as to what government oversight will entail. The impairment here is therefore sufficiently "substantial" to trigger application of the Contracts Clause.

We must then decide whether the ordinance is "reasonable" and "of a character appropriate to the public purpose justifying its adoption." However, in making this inquiry, a court must show considerable deference to the City and its judgment as to what means were appropriate for dealing with the COVID-induced housing emergency. Here, the City has a strong public interest in avoiding housing displacement, preventing additional homelessness, conserving the City's affordable housing stock, and protecting public health from the dangers created by people living in the streets. In contrast to *Blaisdell* (see Example 4-F), however, tenants here are not required to make current rent payments during their period of extended occupancy. As a result, the ordinance's economic burden on landlords is far greater than it was in *Blaisdell*. Yet nothing in *Blaisdell* said such a requirement was necessary to preserve the constitutionality of the eviction moratorium at issue there. And while *Blaisdell* did not require a state to use the least burdensome means at its disposal, Los Angeles has taken steps to alleviate the hardship landlords might otherwise face. While the burden imposed on landlords here is quite substantial, "courts properly defer to legislative judgment as to the necessity and reasonableness of a particular measure." *Energy Reserves Group*, supra, 459 U.S. at 413. It is not for a court "to second-guess" the legislature's identification of "the most appropriate ways of dealing with the problem." *Keystone Bituminous Coal Ass'n*, supra, 480 U.S. at 506. On this basis, the City's eviction moratorium law may well pass muster. See *Apartment Ass'n of Los Angeles County v. City of Los Angeles*, 10 F. 4th 905 (9th Cir. 2021), *cert. denied*, 142 S. Ct. 1699 (2022) (rejecting Contracts Clause challenge to City of Los Angeles eviction moratorium law).

We saw earlier that the Court's reading of the Contracts Clause represents a total departure from the original understanding. In *Sveen v. Melin*, supra, Justice Gorsuch rejected the modern Court's reasonableness test and urged a return to the Founders' view that a state cannot, under any circumstances, retroactively alter contractual rights. As Justice Gorsuch wrote:

> The very section of the Constitution [Art. I, § 10] where the Contracts Clause is found permits states to take otherwise unconstitutional action when "absolutely necessary," if "actually invaded," or wit[h] the Consent of Congress." Cls. 2 and 3. But in the Contracts Clause the framers were absolute. . . .
>
> For much of its history, the Court construed the Contracts Clause in this light. The Court explained that any legislative deviation from a contract's obligations, "however minute, or apparently immaterial," violates the Constitution. . . . But while absolute in its field, the Clause also left significant room for legislatures to address changing social conditions. States could regulate contractual rights prospectively. They could retroactively alter contractual *remedies*, so long as they did so reasonably. And perhaps they could even alter contracts without "impairing" their obligations if they made the parties whole by paying just compensation. But what they could *not* do is destroy substantive contract rights — the "Obligation of Contracts" that the Clause protects.

584 U.S. at 827-829 (emphasis in original) (internal citations omitted). No other members of the Court have as yet endorsed Justice Gorsuch's view.

Some lower federal courts have begun to apply the Contracts Clause—even in the private contract settings—in ways that show less deference to the states than in times past. In *Heights Apartments, LLC v.Walz*, 30 F.4th 720 (8th Cir. 2022), the Eighth Circuit held that landlords could invoke the

Contracts Clause to challenge a series of COVID-related gubernatorial orders that imposed an eviction moratorium of indefinite duration. The court held the impairment to be a substantial one, for it stripped landlords of the right to exclude others and regain possession. And, while the landlord-tenant relationship is one that has been heavily regulated, the reach of these unprecedented orders exceeded the parties' reasonable expectations. The court suggested that the orders likely violated the Contracts Clause as not being reasonably tailored since they barred evictions in cases involving material breaches of the lease that had nothing to do with COVID or with the nonpayment of rent.

Example 4-I

During the COVID-19 pandemic, New York City passed the Guaranty Law ("Law"). It permitted individual guarantors of commercial leases (usually the owners of tenant-businesses) to permanently escape personal liability for rent that their shuttered businesses could not pay during the 16 months of the pandemic. The Law's purpose was to help ensure that small businesses, even if they had to temporarily close, could return and reopen without facing back-rent obligations that might cause them to remain closed forever. Several landlords challenged the Law as violating the Contracts Clause. How should the court rule and why?

Explanation

First, the Law clearly impairs an express contractual obligation—the duty of commercial tenants to pay rent. Second, the substantial impairments requirement is easily met since in any lease agreement, the payment of rent is a tenant's primary obligation and a landlord's central concern. Third, the economic consequences of the Law are severe for it permanently deprives landlords of up to 16 months of rent. Finally, though the landlord-tenant relationship has long been regulated, a factor that would often defeat finding a substantial impairment, the measure here—a permanent cancellation of a tenant's obligation to pay rent—is virtually unheard of. In contrast to *Home Building & Loan Ass'n v. Blaisdell*, supra (see Example 4-F), the tenant here is not required to pay the landlord anything, either during or after the emergency. On this basis, there appears to be a substantial impairment sufficient to trigger the Contracts Clause.

Under the balancing test, the severity of the impairment here calls for a more demanding reasonableness test, even though only a private contract is involved. On the city's side of the balance, the interest in protecting small businesses against pandemic-related closure is certainly a substantial one, both for the businesses and for the larger community. On the landlords' side of the balance, the burden imposed is likewise a heavy one, for the Law could force some to mortgage or sell their property. The harm imposed is also permanent because landlords can never recover rent for the months in question. A more reasonable approach would have been to let tenants delay but not completely forego payment. Moreover, rent relief is afforded here regardless of a tenant's needs or ability to pay. And if the goal of the Law is to keep businesses from shutting down, a more reasonable approach would be to condition rent relief on a business's resuming operation. Finally, the Law places the full cost of saving small businesses on landlords, the City bearing none of the financial burden. On this basis, application of the balancing test might well result in concluding that the city here violated the Contracts Clause. See *Melendez v. City of New York*, 16 F.4th 992 (2d Cir. 2021), *decision on remand*, 668 F. Supp. 3d 184 (S.D.N.Y 2023) (New York City's Guaranty Law violates Contracts Clause), *appeal filed*, Case No. 23-683 (2d Cir. April 27, 2023).

§4.4 THE SPECIAL PROBLEMS OF CONTRACTS TO WHICH A STATE IS A PARTY

Most of the examples we have considered so far have involved state interference with *private contracts*—i.e., contracts entered into between private parties. When a state interferes with a *public contract*—i.e., a contract to which the state itself is a party—the Contracts Clause analysis is different in two respects from that applied in the case of private contracts. First, the reserved powers doctrine may render the clause wholly inapplicable to certain public contracts. Second, if the Contracts Clause does apply, the standard of review will be less deferential than that for private contracts since the state may be acting to further its self-interest rather than that of the public at large.

The reserved powers doctrine takes on a special importance when applied to public contracts. Under this aspect of the reserved powers doctrine, a state will not be bound by any contractual obligation that purports to "surrender an essential attribute of its sovereignty." *United States Trust Co.*, supra, 431 U.S. at 23. Stated somewhat differently, "the legislature cannot bargain away the police power of a State." *Stone v. Mississippi*, 101 U.S. 814, 817 (1880). The net result is that "one legislature cannot abridge the powers of a succeeding legislature" by binding the latter in a manner that limits its authority to protect the health, safety, and welfare of the community. *Fletcher v. Peck*, 10 U.S. (6 Cranch) 87, 135-139 (1810). Thus, a contract under which a state agreed not to regulate safety conditions in the workplace would be void ab initio. A subsequent legislature would, therefore, be free to ignore the provision without further consideration of the Contracts Clause. See also *West River Bridge Co. v. Dix*, 47 U.S. (6 How.) 507, 532-536 (1848) (power of eminent domain may not be contracted away).

The exact contours of this aspect of the reserved powers doctrine have not been fully defined by the Court. The Court has made it clear, however, that the doctrine will not insulate a state's "purely" financial obligations from Contracts Clause review. *United States Trust Co.*, supra, 431 U.S. at 25. A state may, therefore, contractually bind itself to grant a tax exemption or to desist from exercising its power to spend money under certain defined circumstances. And the Contracts Clause will stand as a substantial barrier to any effort by the state to relieve itself of these obligations. This, of course, assumes that the financial obligation does not prevent or prohibit the state from exercising its police powers. If it does, the obligation is invalid and not entitled to Contracts Clause protection. For example, suppose that a state agrees to operate a nuclear reactor for a specified number of years as security for a revenue bond through which the reactor was financed. The agreement is financial in the sense that the pledge functions as a security for the bondholders. But if the state later discovers that the plant is on an active earthquake fault, the contractual obligation, although ostensibly financial, will not prevent the state from shutting down the reactor.

Example 4-J

EXAMPLE

The Port Authority of New Jersey, a state entity, issued bonds under which it agreed that the revenues pledged as security for the bonds would not be used to subsidize mass transit operations. Subsequently, the State of New Jersey passed legislation that retroactively repealed this security provision. The purpose of the repeal was to free up much-needed funds to improve mass transit facilities to encourage private automobile users to shift to public transit. Essentially, the repeal was one step in an effort to alleviate serious problems of traffic congestion. Bondholders sued, challenging the repeal as a violation of the Contracts Clause. Does the reserved powers doctrine insulate the repeal from Contracts Clause analysis?

Explanation

EXPLANATION

Since the state is, in essence, a party to the contract, the first question must be whether this contractual obligation runs afoul of the reserved powers doctrine. In other words, did the contract between the Port Authority and the bondholders contract away the police powers of the state? The promotion of public transportation is well within the police powers of a state. This would be especially true in states, such as New Jersey, where highway congestion is a particularly acute problem. One could argue, therefore, that the bond provision limits the state's authority to exercise its police powers in the context of mass transit. But the bond provision does not *prevent* or *prohibit* the state from improving its mass transit facilities or from promoting public transit; it merely precludes the state from using certain specified revenues to do so. Thus, to accomplish its goals, the state would simply have to dip into some other financial resource. The state has not contracted away its authority to exercise its police powers in the context of mass transit. The obligation, therefore, is purely financial and is not void under the reserved powers doctrine. See *United States Trust Co.*, supra, 431 U.S. at 23-25.

If the reserved powers doctrine does not render a public contract void ab initio, then the Contracts Clause will be applied with greater rigor than it would be if the state had interfered with a private contract. When a state attempts to relieve itself of its own contractual obligations, the Court is understandably more suspicious of the state's motivations. This suspicion does not alter the factors considered by the Court, but it does lead to a significantly less deferential treatment of the state's justifications for its actions. Thus, in *United States Trust Co.*, the Court explained that while the same constitutional standard governs private and public contracts, "[i]n applying this standard [to public contracts], complete deference to a legislative assessment of reasonableness and necessity is not appropriate because the State's self-interest is at stake." 431 U.S. at 25-26. The result is a heightened, although not necessarily fatal, scrutiny. Essentially, the state must prove that its action was both *reasonable* and *necessary* to effect an important public purpose. Id.

Example 4-K

In Example 4-J, we concluded that the contractual provision was not void ab initio under the reserved powers doctrine. Continuing with the same facts, was the state's repeal reasonable so as to pass muster under the Contracts Clause?

Explanation

In assessing the reasonableness of the state's repeal, since the state is a party to the contract the normal deference due the state will not be afforded. Instead, the state must demonstrate that the repeal was both reasonable and necessary to effect some important public purpose. This standard is unlikely to be met unless the state can show that the problem of traffic congestion can be solved by no means short of the repeal. If there are reasonable alternatives, such as the encouragement of carpooling or the use of other resources, then the Contracts Clause will not allow the state to relieve itself of its contractual obligation. See *United States Trust Co.*, supra, 431 U.S. at 25-32 (New Jersey's retroactive repeal of its mass transit bond security provision violated the Contracts Clause).

CHAPTER 5

Procedural Due Process and Irrebuttable Presumptions

§5.1 INTRODUCTION AND OVERVIEW

The Due Process Clauses of the Fifth and the Fourteenth Amendments prohibit the federal government and the states from depriving a person of "life, liberty, or property, without due process of law." A law that impairs a liberty or property interest may be struck down under the Due Process Clause either because of the law's substantive content or because of the process by which it is enforced. The first of these bases for invalidation involves substantive due process, while the second involves procedural due process. A *substantive* due process claim asserts that a law is invalid because the government lacks a sufficient reason or justification to warrant interfering with liberty or property. See Chapter 2. A *procedural* due process argument, on the other hand, assumes that a law is otherwise valid, but asserts that the manner employed in enforcing or applying it is unfair.

Procedural due process usually requires that before the state may impair a person's life, liberty, or property interests, it must give him or her notice and a reasonable opportunity to be heard. By forcing the government to use a "fair process of decisionmaking" when it implements a law, procedural due process seeks "to ensure abstract fair play to the individual" and to minimize "unfair or mistaken deprivations" that may result from the government's having acted based on erroneous information. *Fuentes v. Shevin*, 407 U.S. 67, 80-81 (1972).

The difference between substantive and procedural due process may be seen more clearly through an example.

EXAMPLE

Example 5-A

A state X law prohibits doctors from performing more than one abortion per month; any doctor who violates this statute is barred from the further practice of medicine. State X recently notified Dr. Mary Jones that her medical license has been revoked because she performed two abortions last March. How might Dr. Jones challenge the validity of the state's action?

EXPLANATION

Explanation

Dr. Jones might first argue that the law is substantively invalid because it interferes with her liberty interest in practicing her profession or because it burdens her patients' liberty interest in the abortion decision. If either of these arguments is successful, the law will be struck down as a matter of substantive due process, and Dr. Jones will be allowed to keep her license.

However, if these challenges to the substantive validity of the law fail, Dr. Jones might argue that her procedural due process rights were violated because the state, in applying this otherwise valid law to her, did not use a fair decision-making process. She would assert that state X should not be allowed to revoke her license without first giving her notice and an opportunity to be heard. If Dr. Jones were to prevail on this procedural due process argument, the state could not revoke her license until after it granted her a hearing. This would allow Dr. Jones to show that the state was mistaken in believing she had violated the law or that it was unfair under the circumstances to enforce this law against her.

A lawyer defending Dr. Jones would prefer to win on substantive as opposed to procedural due process grounds. A substantive due process victory would preclude the state from revoking Dr. Jones's license even if she violated the statute. By contrast, a procedural due process argument would only afford Dr. Jones a chance to be heard and show that the state was mistaken concerning her conduct. Nevertheless, a procedural due process challenge would still be of value, for if Dr. Jones were allowed to present her side of the story, she might still be able to persuade the government to change its mind.

Procedural due process is not triggered when the government acts in a legislative capacity—i.e., when it enacts or adopts a particular rule or policy. However, as noted in the previous example, a plaintiff to whom a particular rule or policy is applied may be able to invoke both substantive and procedural due process. See, e.g., *Department of State v. Muñoz*, 144 S. Ct. 1812 (2024) (rejecting plaintiff's arguments asserting a substantive due process right to have her noncitizen husband reside with her in the United States and a procedural due process right to have her husband's visa proceeding reviewed).

Procedural due process comes into play only when the government acts in an adjudicatory capacity—i.e., when it applies that rule or policy to specific individuals. Thus, if a state welfare department issues a regulation providing that no one may receive welfare benefits for more than two years, procedural due process does not give welfare recipients or anyone else a constitutional right to be heard in connection with the *adoption* of the regulation. At this legislative or rulemaking stage, fairness and due process are protected in other ways, such as through the right to vote, the right to petition the government, and the freedoms of speech and press. However, if the state later seeks to *enforce* the two-year rule by terminating those who have been on the rolls for the maximum allowable time, those threatened with termination have a procedural due process right to notice and an opportunity to be heard to prevent unfair or mistaken deprivations of benefits.

There are three major steps in analyzing a procedural due process problem:

1. The right to procedural due process is triggered only if a protected interest in life, liberty, or property is threatened by governmental action.
2. The impairment of the protected interest in life, liberty, or property must be sufficient to trigger the application of procedural due process.
3. If the constraints of procedural due process apply, both the timing and the nature of the required hearing will depend on the circumstances of the particular case.

In the balance of this chapter, we will explore each of these steps of the procedural due process analysis. We will also look at the related doctrine of irrebuttable presumptions. However, this chapter does not focus on the procedural due process protections that attach to life, as this is a subject of criminal procedure.

§5.2 A PROTECTED LIBERTY OR PROPERTY INTEREST?

§5.2.1 What Constitutes Liberty?

Liberty interests that are entitled to procedural due process protection may stem from a variety of sources, including the Constitution, statutes, regulations, and simply official custom and practice. And see *Kerry v. Din*, 576 U.S. 86, 108 (2015) (Breyer, J., dissenting) ("the Due Process Clause entitles [a plaintiff] to such procedural rights as long as . . . she seeks protection for a liberty interest sufficiently important for procedural protection to flow 'implicit[ly]' from the design, object, and nature of the Due Process Clause").

All of the constitutional liberty interests that qualify as liberties for purposes of substantive due process are likewise protected as a matter of procedural due process. See Chapter 2. These include fundamental liberty interests, such as freedom of speech and the right to privacy, as well as "garden variety" liberty interests, such as the liberty to contract and the freedom to pursue a trade. While fundamental liberties and "garden variety" liberties are treated quite differently under substantive due process, they stand on equal footing when it comes to triggering the right to procedural due process. Thus, in Example 5-A above, when the state revoked Dr. Jones's license to practice medicine, this impaired her liberty interest to practice her profession; though this interest receives little meaningful protection as a matter of substantive due process, its impairment is sufficient to trigger Dr. Jones's procedural due process right to notice and an opportunity for a hearing.

For purposes of procedural due process, liberty interests may also derive from nonconstitutional sources, such as federal or state statutes, regulations, and policies. If, through any of these means, the government creates or recognizes certain liberty interests *and provides that they may be impaired only for cause,* these nonconstitutional liberty interests may be entitled to full procedural due process protection. If, on the other hand, the government creates a liberty interest and does not limit the grounds on which it may be withdrawn, the interest can be impaired without triggering any procedural due process protection.

Example 5-B

Smith was convicted of burglary and sentenced to ten years in prison. A state law authorizes mandatory sentence reduction for prisoners' good behavior. Under this law, prisoners may earn good-time credits, which can be revoked only for "flagrant or serious misconduct." Prison officials revoked Smith's good-time credits on the ground that he had smuggled a knife into his cell; the revoked credits would have allowed Smith to leave prison six months early. Did Smith have a procedural due process right to notice and an opportunity to be heard before the state revoked his good-time credits?

Explanation

Smith has no *constitutionally based* liberty interest in receiving credit for good behavior. The Constitution does not compel prison officials to reward good behavior in this manner. Yet Smith may be able to show that he has a *nonconstitutional* liberty interest in a shortened prison sentence, for state law seems to allow good-time credits to be revoked *only* for specified reasons—i.e., for "flagrant or serious misconduct." If Smith can show that these grounds are exclusive in the sense that they constitute a mandatory limitation on the discretion of prison officials, he will have a state-created liberty interest protected by the Due Process Clause. See *Wolff v. McDonnell*, 418 U.S. 539 (1974) (finding protected state-created liberty interest based on similar facts). In that event, Smith's due process rights would have been violated by the state's revocation of his good-time credits without notice and an opportunity to be heard.

The Court has similarly found that a statutorily created liberty interest usually exists when inmates are conditionally released on parole or under a similar early-release program. As long as the state explicitly or implicitly promised that the individual would be reincarcerated only if the conditions of release were violated, a protected liberty interest exists. See *Young v. Harper*, 520 U.S. 143 (1997) (state must afford procedural due process when terminating pre-parole release); *Morrissey v. Brewer*, 408 U.S. 471 (1972) (state must afford procedural due process when revoking parole).

The Court has taken a different and much less hospitable approach to procedural due process complaints by prisoners concerning changes in the circumstances or degree of their confinement. In these cases, the language of the prison regulations is not controlling, for this might create a disincentive for states to promulgate procedures governing prison management. And to the extent that there are regulations, this could overly involve courts in the day-to-day management of prisons. Instead, in the prison setting, a state-created liberty interest will be found to exist (regardless of the language of any applicable regulations) only if the nature of the deprivation is such that it "imposes atypical and significant hardship on the inmate in relation to the ordinary incidents of prison life." *Sandin v. Conner*, 515 U.S. 472, 484 (1995). Changes in an inmate's treatment that do not "present a dramatic departure from the basic conditions" of prison life will not trigger procedural due process protection—even if state law allows those changes to occur only for cause. Id. at 485. See also *Wilkinson v. Austin*, 545 U.S. 209, 221-223 (2005). In *Sandin*, the Court thus held that a prisoner's transfer to solitary confinement for 30 days "did not present the type of atypical, significant deprivation in which a State might conceivably create a liberty interest." Id. at 486. However, the Court emphasized that a significant change in the "duration" of an inmate's confinement—such as that suffered by Smith in Example 5-B—could qualify for procedural due process protection as a state-created liberty interest. Id. at 487.

EXAMPLE

Example 5-C

The Ohio State Penitentiary (OSP) is a maximum-security prison with highly restrictive conditions. It was designed to segregate the most dangerous prisoners from the general prison population. An inmate will be assigned to an OSP only if specific factors have been satisfied. Inmates placed in OSP are denied almost all human contact, even to the point that conversation is not possible from cell to cell; the inmate's cell light may be dimmed, but it remains on for 24 hours; and the inmate may exercise only one hour per day in a small indoor room. Basically, the OSP inmates are deprived of almost all environmental or sensory stimuli and human contact. Moreover, placement in OSP is for an indefinite time, limited only by an inmate's sentence. The inmate's placement in OSP is reviewed once a year. In addition, during placement in OSP, an otherwise eligible inmate is ineligible for parole consideration. Would an inmate incarcerated within the Ohio prison system have a liberty interest in not being transferred to OSP?

EXPLANATION

Explanation

Whether such an inmate would have a protected liberty interest—i.e., one that entitles him to the protection of procedural due process—depends not on the language of the governing prison policy, but rather on whether an OSP placement "imposes atypical and significant hardship on the inmate in relation to the ordinary incidents of prison life." *Sandin v. Conner*, supra, 515 U.S. at 484. In *Sandin*, the Court held that this standard was not satisfied with respect to a 30-day transfer to solitary confinement. By contrast, an OSP assignment, although like the typical solitary confinement in terms of the isolation imposed on an inmate, is for a significantly longer duration and perhaps for an entire life sentence. In addition, those placed in OSP lose their eligibility for parole for that same indefinite time. *Sandin* would therefore appear to be distinguishable. The Supreme Court so held under similar facts in *Wilkinson v. Austin*, supra. In the Court's view, the harsh isolation, the indefinite length of the placement, and the loss of parole eligibility together imposed atypical and significant hardships in relation to the ordinary incidents of prison life. The inmates thus had a protected liberty interest against being placed in OSP.

§5.2.2 What Constitutes Property?

Property interests are not created by the Constitution, but stem from other sources, such as state or, less frequently, federal law. Property within the meaning of the Due Process Clause embraces all the traditional forms of real and personal property. Thus, procedural due process protections apply if the government seeks to enforce a lien against real property, garnish a person's wages, or attach a bank account because all of these are types of property long recognized under state law.

For procedural due process purposes, the term property also embraces many public benefits and statutory entitlements that were once regarded as mere privileges or gratuities not deserving constitutional protection. Welfare benefits, unemployment compensation, tax exemptions, Social Security pensions, public employment, licenses to engage in a trade or profession, and a myriad of other governmental benefits today may all qualify as property for procedural due process purposes. The Court has rejected the "rights/privileges distinction" under which the government was once free to ignore the Constitution in dealing with mere privileges or public benefits.

A governmental benefit qualifies as property for procedural due process purposes if it may be denied or withdrawn only for cause. This test for determining whether public benefits are a protected form of property is the same as that used in deciding whether government-created liberties are entitled to procedural due process protection: That is, has the state agreed that it will not deny or impair the interest except under certain conditions? If the government by statute, regulation, contract, or otherwise has so provided, an individual is normally entitled to notice and an opportunity to be heard in connection with an impairment of that interest.

Example 5-D

In Example 5-A above, if the state seeks to revoke Dr. Jones's medical license, would she be entitled to procedural due process?

Explanation

Yes. The state has threatened to impair both liberty and property interests. We noted earlier that revocation would infringe on Dr. Jones's constitutional liberty interest in pursuing a profession. In addition, because the state grants medical licenses only to those who meet certain eligibility criteria and revokes such licenses only for cause (e.g., performing too many abortions), a medical license is a statutory entitlement that qualifies as a form of property protected by procedural due process.

By contrast, if the government has not tied its hands by limiting the grounds on which it may deny or withdraw a benefit, no *property* interest is involved, and procedural due process will be triggered only if a *liberty* interest happens to be impaired.

EXAMPLE

Example 5-E

Chuck was hired as a summer law clerk in the State Attorney General's Office. He expected to work during June, July, and August, but on July 2, Chuck was fired. When he asked why, his boss told him that he could not divulge the reason. Was Chuck entitled to notice of the reasons for his firing and an opportunity to be heard?

EXPLANATION

Explanation

To establish that he had a property interest in the summer clerkship, Chuck would have to show that there was some basis on which he could legitimately and objectively expect not to be fired without cause. If there was no statute, regulation, written office policy, or formal contract to this effect, Chuck might be able to rely on correspondence or advertisements announcing the position. If, for example, a letter offered him a three-month clerkship with the Attorney General's Office and announced the position as being for three months, a court might find an implicit assurance that the job would not be terminated within that period unless good cause existed. This would be enough to create a property interest in the position.

If Chuck cannot establish a property interest in the position, he is unlikely to trigger procedural due process protection on the basis that a liberty interest was impaired. While he does have a liberty interest in pursuing employment, he remains free to seek other work. Nor was his liberty interest in his good name directly impaired, since no reasons were given for his termination. See *Board of Regents of State Colleges v. Roth*, 408 U.S. 564, 578 (1972) (an at-will college professor has no "property" interest in his job within the meaning of the Fourteenth Amendment so as to require the university to hold a hearing before terminating him).

EXAMPLE

Example 5-F

Jessica's estranged husband took their children from Jessica's home in violation of a judicial restraining order. When notified of the husband's action and of the contents of the restraining order, the city police refused to take any action. Several hours later, after repeated requests by Jessica that the police intervene, the husband murdered the children. Jessica has filed a civil rights suit against the city police department. Among other things, she claims that the department's refusal to enforce the restraining order violated her property interest in that order. In so arguing, she relied on a state statute that provided, "A peace officer shall use every reasonable means to enforce a restraining order [and] shall arrest, or, if an arrest would be impractical under the circumstances, seek a warrant for the arrest of the restrained person when the peace officer has information amounting to probable cause. . . ." Has Jessica adequately alleged a property interest entitled to due process protection?

Explanation

The key question is whether state law has created a right of enforcement such that the police retained no enforcement discretion. If, however, state law permits the officers to exercise discretion in determining whether to enforce a restraining order, then no such entitlement was created. The statutory language quoted above sounds mandatory, but that language must be read against the backdrop of the criminal justice system in which police officers are generally accorded broad enforcement discretion. In other words, what may appear to be mandatory language may well signify nothing more than a strong admonition to exercise one's discretion on the side of enforcement. In a case involving similar facts, the Court, by a 7-to-2 majority, found no enforceable property interest. *Town of Castle Rock, Colo. v. Gonzales*, 548 U.S. 748 (2005). The Court said that the "deep-rooted nature of law-enforcement discretion" required "some stronger indication" of a legislative intent than was evident in the statutory language to rebut the presumption of enforcement discretion. Id. at 761. In so ruling, the Court noted that many criminal statutes include similar "mandatory" language and yet are not thought to have eliminated the enforcement discretion of the police. The Court also expressed skepticism that a "right to enforcement" could ever be treated as a property interest, in part because the interest has no apparent monetary value and in part because the interest is indirect. Id. at 766-768.

Many governmental benefits are provided under statutes or regulations that entitle people to receive those benefits if they meet certain specified eligibility conditions. This is true, for example, of drivers' licenses, welfare benefits, unemployment insurance, homestead exemptions, Social Security, workers' compensation, and medical licenses. These benefits are property for purposes of procedural due process. See *Goldberg v. Kelly*, 397 U.S. 254, 261-262 (1970) ("Such benefits are a matter of statutory entitlement for persons qualified to receive them. . . . The constitutional challenge cannot be answered by an argument that [they] are 'a "privilege" and not a "right."'"). An individual can thus be said to have a property interest in their *claim* to these benefits, in the sense that the government by law cannot deny the claim or application of one who meets the eligibility criteria. And, once a person has been found eligible, the same statutes and regulations that define eligibility now give the recipient a property interest in the *benefits themselves*, thus providing assurance that they will not be withdrawn or terminated except for cause. While the government is generally free to decide whether a particular benefit shall have any specified eligibility conditions and what those conditions shall be, the doctrine of "unconstitutional conditions" may bar it from imposing conditions that require a recipient to surrender a constitutional right or that punish them for having exercised the same. See §§ 5.6, 7.6, 9.5.3 ("The Incidental Burdening of Religiously Motivated Conduct").

If one has only a property interest in a claim — i.e., a legitimate expectation that the claim will not be denied except for cause — the due process right to a hearing simply means that before the claim is *finally denied* and the case closed, the applicant must be given an opportunity to be heard. Yet since a mere *applicant* does not have a property interest in the benefits themselves, the right to a hearing does not mean that the government must pay the applicant benefits pending the hearing. Instead, the right to receive benefits or aid pending the hearing exists only for a *recipient* who, having been found eligible, has a property interest in the benefits themselves.

Example 5-G

Delores was found eligible to receive state workers' compensation benefits based on her having suffered a work-related injury. A state statute provides that those found eligible to receive workers' compensation benefits are also eligible to have their employer or the employer's workers' compensation insurance carrier pay for all of a worker's "reasonable and necessary" medical treatments. If a worker's doctor submits a bill, the insurer may challenge the expense and withhold payment until a "utilization review" hearing is held to determine whether the expense was "reasonable and necessary." Delores has challenged this procedure claiming that by withholding medical payments without a pre-deprivation notice and opportunity to be heard, the state has violated her right to procedural due process. How should the court rule on this constitutional claim?

Explanation

The state has not violated Delores's procedural due process rights. Although she has been found eligible to receive workers' compensation benefits, eligibility for medical payments exists only if a particular expense was "reasonable and necessary." While Delores clearly has a property interest in her *claim* for medical payments since her claim cannot be denied without cause, she does not have a property interest in any *medical payment* until it has first been determined that the treatment in question was reasonable and necessary. Only then does a property interest in the payment attach. Therefore, the right to a hearing before she is deprived of her property does not require that medical payments be paid before a hearing has occurred. See *American Manufacturers Mutual Ins. Co. v. Sullivan*, 526 U.S. 40 (1999).

If, on the other hand, Delores had been found eligible to receive payment for a series of medical treatments that were deemed to be reasonable and necessary, she would probably be entitled to notice and hearing *before* the carrier could withhold further payments for those treatments. In this case, Delores would have a property interest in the payments themselves, not just in her claim for payment. See id. at 63 (Breyer, J., and Souter, J., concurring).

§5.2.3 The Relevance of Custom and Practice

It may be possible to prove the existence of a protected liberty or property interest even if there is no express statute, regulation, or contract provision stating that the interest will not be denied or terminated except for cause. Even without a formal provision establishing a liberty or property interest, the protections of procedural due process may be called into play if it can be shown that there is an "unwritten 'common law'" custom or practice under which a particular privilege or benefit will be withdrawn only for certain reasons. *Perry v. Sindermann*, 408 U.S. 593, 599-603 (1972).

Were custom and practice irrelevant, a state could avoid the strictures of procedural due process by the formalistic device of including in every law dealing with governmental benefits or jobs a clause stating: "The benefits or employment provided for by this law may be terminated at any time, with or without cause." If a program is in fact administered so as to create a legitimate expectation that its benefits will not be denied or withdrawn without cause, procedural due process guarantees attach.

The Court thus relied on custom and practice as a separate basis for finding that Nebraska state prisoners had a protected liberty interest in not being sent to a mental hospital. The Court noted that "in practice prisoners are transferred to a mental hospital only if it is determined that they suffer from a mental disease or defect. . . . This 'objective expectation, firmly fixed in state law and official penal complex practice,'" created a liberty interest and triggered the protections of procedural due process. *Vitek v. Jones*, 445 U.S. 480, 489-490 (1980).

EXAMPLE

Example 5-H

In Example 5-E above, how might Chuck use custom and practice to show that he had a protected property interest in his clerkship position on the basis of custom and practice?

Explanation

Even if there was no explicit statutory, regulatory, or contractual provision limiting the bases on which he could be fired, Chuck might prove that the well-established practice of the Attorney General's Office is to retain summer clerks for the entire three-month summer period unless their work is unsatisfactory. If Chuck makes this showing, procedural due process protects him to the same extent as if state law expressly provided that summer law clerks may be fired during the period of their clerkship only for cause.

§5.3 WHAT CONSTITUTES A DEPRIVATION?

Not every governmental action that impairs a liberty or property interest will necessarily trigger the protections of procedural due process. First, if the deprivation resulted from a mere lack of due care by governmental officials, the Due Process Clause does not come into play. As the Court said in *Daniels v. Williams*, 474 U.S. 327, 328 (1986), "[T]he Due Process Clause is simply not implicated by a *negligent* act of an official causing unintended loss of or injury to life, liberty, or property." (Emphasis in original.) Instead, "an infringement must be intentional, or at least reckless, to come within the reach of the Due Process Clause." *Allen v. Cooper*, 589 U.S. 248, 261 (2020). See also § 2.1. If the conduct does not trigger due process, relief, if any, will depend on the extent to which the government has allowed itself to be sued in tort.

Second, even an intentional act that impairs a liberty or property interest will trigger the protections of procedural due process only if the impairment exceeds a certain threshold; if the impact is one that the Court regards as "de minimis" or "insubstantial," *Goss v. Lopez*, 419 U.S. 565, 576 (1975), the Due Process Clause is not applicable. This is closely analogous to the principle sometimes applied in substantive due process cases—i.e., that a law will not receive strict scrutiny unless it "impinges on" or "unduly burdens" a fundamental liberty. See § 2.4.4.

The Court relied on the notion of a de minimis impairment to avoid triggering procedural due process in *Board of Regents of State Colleges v. Roth*, 408 U.S. 564 (1972). There, the Justices rejected a college professor's argument that the state's refusal to renew his one-year contract impaired his liberty interests in his good name and in securing future employment. While the Court later acknowledged that the state's failure to rehire Roth "might make him somewhat less attractive to other employers . . . it would stretch the concept too far 'to suggest that a person is deprived of "liberty" when he simply is not rehired in one job but remains as free as before to seek another.'" *Bishop v. Wood*, 426 U.S. 341, 348 (1976). In the Court's eyes, the impairment of Roth's liberty interests was too insignificant for procedural due process to come into play.

EXAMPLE

Example 5-I

In Example 5-A involving the state's revocation of Dr. Jones's license to practice medicine, we saw that this action may have impaired Dr. Jones's liberty interest in practicing her profession and her property interest in the license itself. However, suppose that a few weeks after Dr. Jones was notified of the revocation, the state advised her that the action was the result of a clerical error. May Dr. Jones still assert that the state violated her procedural due process rights?

EXPLANATION

Explanation

If the state proves that the revocation was a result of mere negligence, the Due Process Clause would simply not apply. However, if the secretary's conduct rose to the level of gross negligence or reckless disregard for Jones's rights, Dr. Jones might be able to claim a procedural due process violation, since she was given no notice or opportunity to be heard. The state might then argue that any harm to Dr. Jones's liberty and property interests was de minimis if the revocation was in effect for such a brief period that it did not really interfere with Dr. Jones's ability to practice medicine.

§5.4 THE CONTENT OF NOTICE

Once we have cleared the first two hurdles by demonstrating that a threatened governmental action will cause a deprivation of a protected liberty or property interest, procedural due process is triggered. The questions that remain focus on what type of notice and what kind of hearing must be afforded.

The Court discussed the procedural aspects of notice in *Mullane v. Central Hanover Bank and Trust Co.*, 339 U.S. 306, 314-315 (1950):

> An elementary and fundamental requirement of due process in any proceeding which is to be accorded finality is notice reasonably calculated, under all the circumstances, to apprise interested parties of the pendency of the action and afford them an opportunity to present their objections. The notice must be of such nature as reasonably to convey the required information, and it must afford a reasonable time for those interested to make their appearance. But if with due regard for the practicalities and peculiarities of the case these conditions are reasonably met, the constitutional requirements are satisfied.

Procedural law is interested in the *method* of notice an individual is entitled to—e.g., when personal service is required, when service by mail is adequate, when notice by publication may suffice. *Mullane* stated that "[t]he means employed must be such as one desirous of actually informing the absentee might reasonably adopt to accomplish it." Id. at 315. For a more recent application of this principle, see *Dusenberry v. United States,* 534 U.S. 161 (2002) (notice to federal inmate by certified mail with the return receipt signed by a prison official was reasonably calculated to apprise the prisoner of a civil forfeiture proceeding).

The notice given must also have a specific *content* to satisfy due process. Where the government seeks to terminate or withdraw benefits or services, the Court has sometimes required that the notice provide a recipient with specific information concerning the remedies and procedures available for challenging the threatened governmental action so that the individual can fully protect his or her interests. In *Memphis Light, Gas & Water Division v. Craft,* 436 U.S. 1 (1978), the Court held that the Due Process Clause required a municipal utility company to give customers advance notice and an opportunity to be heard before terminating their utility services. The notice, said the Court, must be "'reasonably calculated' to inform them of the availability of 'an opportunity to present their objections' to their bills," and must "advise the customer of the availability of a procedure for protesting a proposed termination of utility service as unjustified." Id. at 14-15.

Memphis Light's requirement that notice must inform an individual of the remedies available for challenging the government's action, and how those remedies may be invoked, is the exception rather than the rule. In *City of West Covina v. Perkins,* 525 U.S. 234 (1999), the Court held that a police department that had seized goods from a home pursuant to a warrant did not have to notify the homeowner—who was absent at the time of the search—as to the legal remedies and procedures available for obtaining a return of the goods. All that was necessary, said the Court, was that the owner be given notice that the property had been taken by the police. In rejecting the argument that procedural due process also required notice of existing legal remedies, the Court distinguished *Memphis Light* on the ground that there,

> the administrative procedures at issue were not described in any publicly available document. . . . While *Memphis Light* demonstrates that notice of the procedures for protecting one's property interests may be required when those procedures are arcane and are not set forth in documents accessible to the public, it does not support a general rule that notice of remedies and procedures is required.

Id. at 242. Instead, where "state-law remedies . . . are established by published, generally available state statutes and case law," it is up to the individual to consult "these public sources to learn about the remedial procedures available to him. The City need not take other steps to inform him of his options." Id. at 241.

An additional "notice" issue arises in criminal proceedings. A criminal statute that fails to give adequate notice of its potential coverage might run afoul of the void-for-vagueness doctrine. See § 8.2.5. See also *Johnson v. United States*, 576 U.S. 591, 597 (2015) (the "vagueness" and "indeterminacy of the wide-ranging inquiry required by the [sentencing provision of the Armed Career Criminal Act] denies fair notice to defendants and invites arbitrary enforcement by judges"); *FCC v. Fox Television Stations, Inc.*, 567 U.S. 239 (2012) (FCC regulations regarding the broadcast of indecent material violated due process in that they failed to provide broadcasters adequate notice of what was proscribed).

§5.5 WHAT KIND OF HEARING MUST BE AFFORDED?

Assuming notice is adequate, the remaining due process question concerns the kind of hearing that is required. This involves two separate considerations. First, as to timing, must an opportunity to be heard be afforded before the deprivation occurs, or will a post-deprivation hearing suffice? Second, how formal or informal may the hearing be? We will briefly consider both questions.

§5.5.1 The "Bitter with the Sweet" Approach

In answering the question of what kind of hearing must be afforded, a few members of the Court have taken the position that if a *government-created* liberty or property interest is involved, the government may decide for itself what procedures, if any, will accompany a decision affecting that interest. As Justice Rehnquist wrote in *Arnett v. Kennedy*, 416 U.S. 134, 153-154 (1974), a case involving the dismissal of a federal employee, "[W]here the grant of a substantive right is inextricably intertwined with the limitations on the procedures which are to be employed in determining that right, a litigant . . . must take the bitter with the sweet."

However, the Court's majority has consistently rejected the "bitter with the sweet" approach, for "[t]he right to due process 'is conferred, not by legislative grace, but by constitutional guarantee. While the legislature may elect not to confer a property [or liberty] interest . . . it may not constitutionally authorize the deprivation of such an interest, once conferred, without appropriate procedural safeguards.'" *Cleveland Board of Educ. v. Loudermill*, 470 U.S. 532, 541 (1985). Thus, regardless of the type of liberty or property interest involved, if procedural due process protections are triggered, the timing and the nature of the required hearing are determined according to constitutional standards and not by reference to federal or state law.

Example 5-J

Helen was hired as a public school teacher by the city of Plainville. According to her contract, Helen could be fired only if the superintendent determined that her dismissal was in the best interests of the city. The contract further provided that if Helen were fired, she would be entitled to prompt post-termination notice of the reasons for her firing and an opportunity to respond in writing. If Helen is fired by the city and is afforded only the procedures specified by her contract, can she claim that the city has violated her rights to procedural due process?

Explanation

The city chose to give Helen a property interest in her job by stating in her contract that she may be fired only for cause; moreover, termination deprives her of this interest. The requirements of procedural due process, therefore, apply here. While the city did not have to give Helen a property interest in her job, having done so, it is the Due Process Clause, not the terms of her contract, that will determine whether the procedures she was given are adequate. Helen is thus free to argue that the city's action was unconstitutional because she was not given notice or an opportunity to be heard prior to her dismissal. We will discuss this prior hearing requirement in § 5.5.3.

§5.5.2 The *Mathews v. Eldridge* Test

In resolving the issues of when a hearing must occur and how elaborate the hearing must be, the Court often uses a balancing test that takes into account three factors: (1) the significance of the private interest that will be affected by the governmental action; (2) the extent to which additional procedural safeguards would reduce the risk of error; and (3) the public interest in resolving the matter quickly and efficiently. This test, which derives from *Mathews v. Eldridge*, 424 U.S. 319, 335 (1976), involves a cost-benefit analysis in which the Court evaluates the need for a particular procedure by balancing the added benefits it might afford an aggrieved individual against the burdens that the procedure might impose on the government and the public. As the Court said in *Mathews*, "At some point the benefit of an additional safeguard to the individual affected by the administrative action and to society in terms of increased assurance that the action is just, may be outweighed by the cost." Id. at 348. The Court has also cautioned that in applying the *Mathews* test, "substantial weight must be given to the good-faith judgments" of those who determined that the challenged procedures were adequate. Id. at 349.

However, even in cases where the procedures employed might not have satisfied the requirements of procedural due process as determined by the *Mathews* factors, the Court may nonetheless conclude "that any due process violation was harmless" if it appears "beyond a reasonable doubt" that use of the correct procedure would have made no difference in the outcome of the case. *Tennessee Secondary School Athletic Assn. v. Brentwood Academy*, 551 U.S. 291, 303-304 (2007).

Example 5-K

For the past five years, Dorothy has received state disability benefits because of a back condition that prevents her from working. The state recently terminated Dorothy's benefits after concluding that the condition no longer prevents her from engaging in employment. Prior to the termination, the state gave Dorothy a statement of the reasons for the proposed termination, an opportunity to review the state's evidence, a chance to respond to the state's case in writing, and the right to submit further evidence. She was also advised that she could later seek a full trial-type hearing before the State Disability Appeals Board, which had the authority to restore her benefits retroactively if it determined that an error had been made. Can Dorothy successfully claim that her procedural due process rights were violated because the state did not give her a trial-type hearing before cutting off her benefits?

Explanation

Since state law presumably provides that disability benefits may be terminated only for cause, Dorothy has a protected property interest in the continued receipt of those benefits, thereby triggering the protections of procedural due process. Whether the procedures afforded her were sufficient must be determined by applying the *Mathews* test.

First, the private interest affected here is important. Disability benefits may represent the principal or sole source of income for those entitled to receive them. However, since there is a right to an elaborate post-termination hearing that could result in benefits being retroactively restored, the individual interest is not as strong as it would be if there were no right to a subsequent hearing.

Second, the court will look to the "fairness and reliability of the existing pre-termination procedures, and the probable value, if any, of additional procedural safeguards." *Mathews*, supra, 424 U.S. at 343. Here, since the termination decision turns largely on standard medical reports from physicians and specialists, the state's existing procedures are likely to pose a low risk of error. A trial-type hearing at which witnesses testify in person and are subject to cross-examination by counsel would no doubt improve the truth-finding process, but probably not by a great deal. By contrast, the added benefit of an evidentiary hearing would be greater if issues of witness credibility and veracity were more directly involved; this would be the case, for example, if benefits were being terminated because a recipient had allegedly concealed outside income that would render him or her ineligible for state assistance.

Finally, *Mathews* requires courts to consider the public interest in avoiding the expense, delay, and other societal costs of affording more elaborate pre-termination procedures. Here, the burden of conducting in-person trial-type hearings is greater than under a scheme that permits only written submissions. Moreover, the delay entailed in holding pre-termination evidentiary hearings would mean that the benefits might be continued for a longer period for those who were ineligible. While the state might seek to recover these payments, the recipients might well be judgment proof.

On balance, and considering the deference courts show toward a government's chosen procedural scheme, Dorothy's procedural due process challenge is likely to fail here. See *Mathews v. Eldridge*, 424 U.S. 319 (1976) (finding no procedural due process violation on similar facts).

§5.5.3 The Requirement of a Prior Hearing

With respect to timing, the Court has "described 'the root requirement' of the Due Process Clause as being 'that an individual be given an opportunity for a hearing *before* he is deprived of any significant [liberty or] property interest.'" *Cleveland Bd. of Educ. v. Loudermill*, supra, 470 U.S. at 542 (emphasis in original). This is the general rule, to which there are exceptions in situations where a prior hearing may be impossible or impracticable. See § 5.5.4. The prior hearing requirement makes good sense given that procedural due process is intended as a safeguard to help minimize the occasions when the government mistakenly impairs liberty or property interests. While post-deprivation remedies in the form of damages or injunctive relief may help compensate for the harms that result from erroneous governmental action, it is preferable, where possible and practicable, that such injuries be avoided in the first place.

But even if a party has been deprived of a protected interest, and a pre-deprivation hearing is feasible, such a hearing is required only if, under the relevant substantive legal principles, there is some ground on which to challenge that deprivation. For example, if the government seeks to condemn A's car on the basis that it was used in a criminal enterprise, and A denies any such use, A must be afforded a hearing to contest the government's factual claim. A, however, would not be entitled to a hearing for the purpose of proving an irrelevant point—e.g., that A was out of town when the crime was committed. This relevancy principle was applied in *Connecticut Dept. of Public Safety v. Doe*, 538 U.S. 1 (2003), where a convicted sex offender contested his inclusion in a sex offender registry, based on his contention that he was entitled, as a matter of procedural due process, to prove that he was not currently dangerous. The Court assumed that his inclusion on the list deprived him of a liberty interest by stigmatizing him as a sex offender but concluded that he was not entitled to a hearing prior to the posting because inclusion on the registry was not dependent on whether he was currently dangerous. In the Court's words,

> even if respondent could prove that he is not likely to be currently dangerous, Connecticut has decided that the registry information of *all* sex offenders—currently dangerous or not—must be publicly disclosed. Unless respondent can show that that *substantive* rule of law is defective (by conflicting with a provision of the Constitution), any hearing on current dangerousness is a bootless exercise.

Id. at 7-8 (emphasis in original). Given that the respondent made no such substantive contention, he was not entitled to a hearing. In short, a hearing is required only if the party's challenge to the government's action is relevant to establishing the illegitimacy of the deprivation.

Example 5-L

EXAMPLE

Ollie was employed as a highway patrol officer by state Z. After the state received an anonymous tip that Ollie had accepted bribes from motorists in exchange for not giving them speeding tickets, the state fired him. Under state Z law, highway patrol officers may be fired only for cause. A fired officer may appeal to the State Civil Service Board, which can order reinstatement with back pay. Did state Z violate Ollie's procedural due process rights by dismissing him without a prior hearing?

Explanation

EXPLANATION

Procedural due process is triggered here. Ollie had a property interest in his job since he could be fired only for cause, and the dismissal deprived him of this property interest. State Z might argue that Ollie had no right to a prior hearing because any benefit he would derive from this is outweighed by the burdens such a requirement would impose on the state. Under the *Mathews v. Eldridge* balancing test, however, Ollie was probably entitled to a prior hearing.

First, the private interest at stake is the vital one of retaining employment and earning a livelihood; that interest was seriously impaired when

Ollie was fired. Second, the risk of the state's erroneously impairing this interest would be greatly reduced by a prior hearing, for the decision turns entirely on issues of fact. Here, the state acted solely on the basis of an anonymous report; unless the decision maker is more fully informed, the chance of error is high. Third, the benefit that Ollie would derive from a prior hearing is probably not outweighed by the burden such a hearing would place on the state. The cost to the state of the hearing itself is low since the hearing need not be elaborate. See § 5.5.5. Nor is this a case where a delay in keeping Ollie on the job would endanger public health or safety, for Ollie's alleged misconduct harms the state only in a financial way. And even if a more serious danger existed, the state could suspend Ollie, with or without pay, rather than summarily firing him. It is thus likely that state Z violated Ollie's procedural due process rights by not affording him a prior hearing. See *Cleveland Bd. of Educ. v. Loudermill*, 470 U.S. 532 (1985).

§5.5.4 Exceptions to the Prior Hearing Requirement

Despite the general principle that an opportunity for a hearing must be afforded *before* there is a deprivation of liberty or property, the Court sometimes allows a hearing to be held only after the deprivation has occurred. These exceptions have involved situations where it would be impossible or impracticable to conduct a prior hearing or where a court believes that any risk of an erroneous, serious deprivation is low.

In rare instances, it is virtually impossible for the government to hold a prior hearing. An example of this was presented in *Hudson v. Palmer*, 468 U.S. 517 (1984), where prison guards intentionally destroyed an inmate's personal property during a search. Since the guards' conduct was "random and unauthorized," there was no way the state could have conducted a hearing before the property was destroyed. The Court held that procedural due process was satisfied by the post-deprivation tort remedy available to the inmate under state law.

Most exceptions to the prior hearing requirement involve situations where it would be *possible* to hold a hearing before the deprivation occurs, but where doing so would for one reason or another be *impracticable*. In considering whether to make an exception on grounds of impracticability, the Court often weighs the benefits that would flow from affording a prior hearing against the burdens that this requirement would place on the government and the public, sometimes expressly invoking the *Mathews v. Eldridge* three-factor balancing test.

The classic case where impracticability may allow the government to dispense with a prior hearing in favor of post-deprivation remedies is an emergency, when swift action is necessary to avert serious public harm. Thus, if the Food and Drug Administration believes that there is a mislabeled drug on the market that could be fatal if consumed, it may order the drug seized without first affording the drug's manufacturer an opportunity to be heard. See *Ewing v. Mytinger & Casselberry, Inc.*, 339 U.S. 594 (1950). While a prior hearing would reduce the risk of a mistaken governmental seizure, the benefit this would afford the company in terms of protecting its profits is outweighed by the harm that could result to the public if a prior hearing had to be conducted. See also *Culley v. Marshall*, 601 U.S. 377 (2024) (where a vehicle is seized under a civil forfeiture law following an arrest for a drug offense, due process requires a timely forfeiture hearing but does not also require a "preliminary hearing" to determine whether police may retain the vehicle pending the full forfeiture hearing, given the risk that the vehicle could be removed, destroyed, or put to illegal use before that hearing occurs).

The Court has also allowed the government to ignore the prior hearing rule in some non-emergency situations. In *Ingraham v. Wright*, 430 U.S. 651 (1977), the Court upheld a Florida statute that authorized the infliction of corporal punishment on schoolchildren without giving them an opportunity to be heard before punishment was imposed. The Court agreed that procedural due process was triggered, for paddling impairs a child's liberty interest in bodily security. But using the *Mathews v. Eldridge* balancing test, the Court found that it would be impracticable to require a prior hearing in this setting. It concluded that the danger of an excessive or erroneous paddling was sufficiently low and any benefit from a prior hearing was outweighed by the burden such a requirement would place on teachers and school officials. Accordingly, the post-deprivation common law remedies available to students under state law were deemed sufficient to satisfy the demands of procedural due process. See also *Kaley v. United States*, 571 U.S. 330, 333-341 (2014) (pre-trial seizure of assets traceable to criminal activity for which a party has been indicted was constitutional under *Mathews*' balancing formula, since there was no "probable value" in revisiting the grand jury's probable cause determination).

EXAMPLE

Example 5-M

When Edwin's car was parked in a no-parking zone, the city towed his car and imposed an impoundment fee. After paying the $134.50 fee, Edwin recovered his car. He then requested a hearing to contest the towing, claiming that a tree had obstructed his view of the no-parking sign. The city granted him a hearing 27 days later. The city would have granted him a hearing within 48 hours had he been unable to pay the impoundment fee, a situation that arises approximately 50 times a year. The city claims, however, that given finite court space and limited officer availability, it needs more administrative flexibility in scheduling hearings for the 1,000 or more cases in which an impoundment is challenged by those who were able to pay the fee. Hearings in cases where the impoundment fee has been paid take place within 30 days of the incident. Did the city's failure to provide Edwin a more timely hearing violate due process?

Explanation

Applying the *Mathews v. Eldridge* balancing test, we first consider the private interest at stake. Edwin has been deprived of money. This is a property interest, but in terms of the harm caused by the deprivation, it is less severe than being deprived of one's livelihood, of one's car or, for someone on the margin of subsistence, of one's welfare benefits. Second, the risk of erroneous deprivation would not seem to depend on the timing of this post-deprivation hearing. Nor is there a significant risk that evidence will disappear or become unusable during the waiting period, for presumably a photograph of the offending tree can be taken. Finally, the city has a legitimate interest in administering its program efficiently. Taking these factors together, it would seem, as the Court held under similar facts, that no violation of due process has occurred. In the Court's words, "the 27-day delay in holding a hearing here reflects no more than a routine delay substantially required by administrative needs." *City of Los Angeles v. David*, 538 U.S. 715, 719 (2003).

Example 5-N

Homer was suspended without pay from his job as a police officer with the state university after the district attorney informed the university that Homer had been arrested and charged with possession of marijuana. The university gave Homer no notice or opportunity to be heard before suspending him. A week after the suspension, the criminal charges were dismissed. Two weeks later Homer was given a hearing by university officials at which it was found that he had possessed marijuana; as a result, he was demoted to a position as groundskeeper. Were Homer's procedural due process rights violated by the timing of the hearing?

Explanation

The university took two actions that may have impaired Homer's procedural due process rights: the suspension, and the demotion three weeks later. Because Homer was given notice and an opportunity to be heard before he was demoted, the timing of the hearing presents no problem as to that action. However, the lack of notice and opportunity to be heard prior to the initial three-week suspension raises a distinct procedural due process issue.

Assuming that under the university's rules Homer could be suspended only for cause, he had a property interest that was infringed by the suspension. Since the suspension was without pay and lasted three weeks, the infringement was not de minimis. The suspension action, therefore, triggered the requirements of procedural due process.

Whether a pre-deprivation hearing was required must be determined by applying the *Mathews* test. First, the private interest at stake, Homer's means of livelihood, is an important one. Yet in contrast to Ollie in Example 5-L, Homer was suspended temporarily rather than fired. While he received no pay in the interim, other job benefits may have continued. Second, the failure to offer a prior hearing carried a much lower risk of error than in Ollie's case. The university acted not on an anonymous tip but on information from the district attorney, an independent outside party with probable cause to believe Homer had committed a crime. Whether or not Homer was actually guilty of that crime, the arrest and charge were themselves objective facts that gave the university valid grounds to suspend an employee. Since the university acted based on reliable information, any added benefit of a prior hearing in terms of preventing an erroneous deprivation was relatively low. Finally, on the state's side of the balance, the university had a strong interest in maintaining public confidence in the integrity of its police by not having accused felons on the force. Under these circumstances, the university was probably justified in dispensing with a pre-suspension hearing. See *Gilbert v. Homar*, 520 U.S. 924 (1997) (upholding summary suspension on similar facts, but remanding case for a determination of whether delaying the post-suspension hearing for 16 days after charges had been dropped violated procedural due process. On remand, the district court held that the "delay does not rise to the level of a procedural due process violation. . . ." *Homar v. Gilbert*, 63 F. Supp. 2d 559, 570 (M.D. Pa. 1999)).

In *Lujan v. G & G Fire Sprinklers, Inc.*, 532 U.S. 189 (2001), the Court addressed an interesting variation on the pre-deprivation hearing theme. In that case, the state, under a contract, withheld payments to G & G, a subcontractor on a public works project, based on the state's allegation that G & G had failed to comply with the prevailing wage requirements of the state labor code. The withholding was not preceded by notice or a hearing. The only recourse available to G & G was to file a civil suit in state court in which it could seek to establish entitlement to the monies withheld. The Court held that this formula did not violate the Due Process Clause. In so ruling, the Court did not refer to the impracticability of holding a pre-deprivation hearing. Rather, the Court concluded that given the contingent nature of the property interest at stake—a yet-to-be-proven claim of entitlement—the post-deprivation civil trial process afforded G & G all the process that was due. In the Court's words, G & G

> has not been denied any present entitlement. G & G has been deprived of payment that it contends it is owed under a contract, based on the

> State's determination that G & G failed to comply with the contract's terms. G & G has only a claim that it did comply with those terms and therefore that it is entitled to be paid in full. Though we assume for purposes of decision here that G & G has a property interest in its claim for payment, it is an interest . . . that can be fully protected by an ordinary breach-of-contract suit.

Id. at 196. The scope of *Lujan* may well be limited to those cases in which the claimed deprivation stems from a contractual relationship with the government entity responsible for the deprivation. Under such circumstances, one's claim of entitlement is always contingent on proof of contractual compliance.

§5.5.5 The Formality of the Prior Hearing

If a prior hearing is required by due process, "[t]he formality and procedural requisites for the hearing can vary, depending upon the importance of the interests involved and the nature of the subsequent proceedings." *Boddie v. Connecticut*, 401 U.S. 371, 378 (1971). The Court has normally not required a full trial-type hearing prior to adverse action taken by an administrative body or agency, as opposed to action taken by a court of law. When administrative action is involved, the Court has tended to uphold relatively informal prior hearing procedures, often justifying them under the *Mathews v. Eldridge* balancing test. It is ordinarily enough that the government gives a person notice of the proposed action and the reasons for it, as well as an opportunity to respond either in person or in writing. These rudimentary procedures are especially likely to suffice if, as is usually true, more elaborate post-deprivation remedies are available in the form of a full administrative hearing, judicial review, or an independent tort action.

Example 5-O

In Example 5-L, suppose that under state Z law, before Ollie can be fired as a highway patrol officer, he must be told the reasons for his dismissal and given a chance to explain why he thinks the action should not be taken. In accord with this procedure, Ollie's boss called Ollie into his office and told him that he was being fired because he had taken bribes. Ollie said that this was not true and that there must have been a mistake. He was then fired. His boss advised Ollie that he could appeal his dismissal to the State Civil Service Board and thereafter, if necessary, obtain judicial review. Were Ollie's procedural due process rights violated?

Explanation

Ollie's rights were probably not violated here. He has a right to procedural due process, since, as noted earlier, state law gives him a property interest in his position and the dismissal deprives him of that interest. This is not a situation where it is either impossible or impracticable to afford a prior hearing. But since post-deprivation administrative and judicial remedies are available, all that Ollie was entitled to prior to his dismissal was notice and an opportunity to tell his side of the story, both of which he was given. See *Cleveland Bd. of Educ. v. Loudermill*, 470 U.S. 532 (1985).

However, if post-deprivation remedies do not exist, or if they would be of little utility because the harm caused by an erroneous deprivation is irreparable, the prior hearing must afford much more complete procedural safeguards. Thus, in *Goldberg v. Kelly*, 397 U.S. 254 (1970), the Court held that before welfare benefits may be terminated, a recipient must be given a trial-type hearing; even though the state provided recipients with full post-deprivation remedies, the injury caused by a mistaken cutoff of subsistence benefits is likely to be grave and irreparable.

Similarly, in *Vitek v. Jones*, 445 U.S. 480 (1980), the Court held that before a prisoner may be transferred to a mental hospital for treatment, due process requires an opportunity for a hearing that includes the right to introduce evidence, the right to present and cross-examine witnesses, the assistance of counsel or other competent help, an independent decision maker, and a written decision. The nature of the harm caused if a prisoner were mistakenly subjected to such treatment, coupled with the fact that the state provided inmates with no post-transfer remedies, made it essential to afford a trial-type hearing before a transfer could occur.

The right to an independent decision-maker, one of the most important due process requirements, does not mean that a judge or administrative hearing officer must have had no prior involvement with the case or with the parties. In *Vitek*, for example, the Court held that the person "conducting [an inmate's] transfer hearing need not come from outside the prison or hospital administration." Id. at 496. Absent proof that a judge is "actually, subjectively biased"—evidence that is hard to come by—the due process "inquiry is an objective one" that asks "whether the average judge in his position is 'likely' to be neutral, or whether there is an unconstitutional 'potential for bias.'" *Caperton v. Massey*, 556 U.S. 868, 881 (2009). In *Caperton*, the Court held that due process was violated when a newly elected state supreme court justice refused to recuse himself even though he had recently received "an extraordinary amount" of campaign contributions through the efforts of the corporate appellant's board chair and principal officer. Id. at 872.

The specific procedures to be afforded in the administrative hearing setting fall under the domain of administrative law.

§5.6 POSSIBLE POST-DEPRIVATION REMEDIES WHERE NO LIBERTY OR PROPERTY INTEREST EXISTS

We saw earlier that the government may create liberty or property interests that are entitled to procedural due process protection even if there was initially no constitutional right to the benefit in question. It is on this basis that there is often a right to a hearing if a state seeks to revoke a prisoner's parole, terminate welfare benefits, dismiss a public employee, or cancel a student's scholarship. The key to whether procedural due process attaches to these non-constitutional interests is whether they may be denied or withdrawn only for cause. If the government has reserved the right to withhold or terminate the interest on any basis it chooses, no liberty or property is involved, and the Due Process Clause does not come into play.

Yet under "the unconstitutional conditions doctrine," the "government 'may not deny a benefit to a person on a basis that infringes his constitutionally protected interests'. . . ." *Sheetz v. County of El Dorado*, 601 U.S. 267, 275 (2024) (internal citation omitted). Thus, if a person can show that a purely discretionary benefit was withheld on a constitutionally forbidden ground, the government may, in a post-deprivation proceeding, be forced to grant or restore the benefit unless it can prove that it had a legitimate reason for its action.

Example 5-P

Frannie was an untenured public-school teacher whose contract was not renewed. She believes that she was not rehired because she had criticized the city mayor during a radio interview. No statutory or contractual provision assures untenured teachers that they will be rehired in the absence of cause, nor is there a custom or practice to this effect. Were any of Frannie's constitutional rights violated by her nonrenewal?

Explanation

Frannie had no procedural due process right to a hearing prior to her dismissal; she lacked a property interest in her job since she could be dismissed for no reason whatsoever. Nor will nonrenewal impair her liberty to seek future employment. See § 5.3. However, if Frannie can show that a motivating factor in her nonrenewal was her exercise of First Amendment rights by speaking on the radio, the city will have to rehire her unless it can prove that Frannie would have been let go even had she not engaged in this constitutionally protected activity. Otherwise, the city will have been permitted to impose an unconstitutional condition on rehiring untenured teachers—i.e., to be rehired, they must surrender their First Amendment rights. See *Mt. Healthy School Dist. Bd. of Educ. v. Doyle*, 429 U.S. 274 (1977).

§5.7 THE IRREBUTTABLE PRESUMPTION DOCTRINE

As we have seen, procedural due process is designed as a safeguard against possibly erroneous deprivations of liberty or property. Persons whose liberty or property interests are threatened by governmental enforcement of a law are entitled to a hearing at which they may show that the government is wrong about the facts and that they therefore do not fall within the purview of the law in question. However, an individual may also seek a hearing not to correct the government's version of the facts, but to rebut an express or implied presumption contained in a law.

§5.7.1 Rebuttable and Irrebuttable Presumptions

Suppose that a city ordinance provides that any police officer whose weight exceeds 300 pounds will be fired unless the officer can prove that he or she is still capable of functioning effectively. This law contains an express *rebuttable* presumption that police officers weighing over 300 pounds cannot perform their duties. If Max is notified by the city that he is being fired from his job as a police officer because he weighs 310 pounds, Max might seek a hearing for two very different purposes. First, as a matter of procedural due process, Max has a property interest in his job, since he can be fired only for cause; he is, therefore, probably entitled to a prior hearing to show that the city is mistaken about his weight and that the ordinance should not apply to him. Second, if Max falls within this law because he weighs more than 300 pounds, he may still seek a hearing to rebut the presumption that he is too heavy to be a police officer.

The city might have instead drafted this ordinance so that it contained an *irrebuttable* presumption. The law might have said: "A police officer who weighs more than 300 pounds is unfit for duty and will be fired." If Max were notified that he was being fired under this law, he again might want a hearing to prove that though he weighs 310 pounds, he is physically fit for duty. However, because the city has not afforded him a chance to be heard on this issue, the presumption is irrebuttable. (While Max would also be entitled to a hearing to contest the city's claim that he weighs more than 300 pounds, this would be of little use to him if the city's information is correct.)

In contrast to the two preceding examples, both of which contained express presumptions, the city might have written the ordinance so that the irrebuttable presumption on which it is based is implicit in the measure but does not appear on its face. Such a law might read: "Any police officer who weighs more than 300 pounds will be fired." We can discern the presumption underlying this law once we identify its purpose. If the city council minutes or the city attorney defending the ordinance indicate that its goal is to assure that police officers are physically fit, the measure rests on the implicit irrebuttable presumption that any officer weighing over 300 pounds is unfit for duty.

If the city were to use such an irrebuttable presumption, whether express or implied, Max might claim that he is entitled to a hearing to challenge the presumption by showing that however true it may be of others, it is not true of him. In other words, he might argue that the city must convert the presumption from an irrebuttable to a rebuttable one, thereby affording him a chance to show that the generalization on which the law is based does not apply to his case—i.e., that despite his weight, he is in fact physically fit.

§5.7.2 The Doctrine in Its Prime

Under the holding in *Vlandis v. Kline*, 412 U.S. 441 (1973), Max's case, described in § 5.7.1 above, would probably prevail on his claim that he was entitled to a hearing. *Vlandis* prohibited the government from using a permanent irrebuttable presumption "when that presumption is not necessarily or universally true in fact, and when the State has reasonable alternative means of making the crucial determination." Id. at 452. Max, on this basis, would be entitled to an opportunity to prove that he can perform a police officer's duties notwithstanding his weight. Not everyone who weighs over 300 pounds is unfit for the position; nor would it be impractical to give him a hearing, for the city no doubt already gives periodic exams to make sure that officers and applicants are qualified for the job.

As a practical matter, however, the effect of allowing Max to challenge this ordinance on the ground that it contains an irrebuttable presumption is to insist that the law not be overinclusive in terms of its goal. Normally an overinclusive classification will be struck down only if it is one that calls for heightened scrutiny under the Equal Protection Clause, either because it burdens a fundamental right or because it involves a suspect or quasi-suspect classification. See Chapters 6 and 7. Neither of these factors is present in Max's case, as there is no fundamental liberty interest in employment and weight is not a suspect or quasi-suspect basis of classification.

From a litigant's standpoint, the irrebuttable presumption doctrine articulated in *Vlandis* was a boon. It allowed successful challenges to be brought against a vast array of statutory classifications even though there was no basis for invoking heightened scrutiny under the Equal Protection Clause. For virtually every law rests on an irrebuttable presumption. If the presumption does not appear on the face of the statute, it is discernible as soon as the purpose of the measure is identified. For example, a speed limit law irrebuttably presumes that anyone going over the speed limit is driving unsafely. A statute requiring that one pass a bar exam to practice law irrebuttably presumes that everyone who cannot pass the exam is unqualified for the profession. A law setting a mandatory retirement age irrebuttably presumes that anyone over that age can no longer perform effectively. And so on. Since all of these measures employ generalizations that are not universally true in fact, and since it is possible to give individualized hearings to those who claim that the underlying presumption does not hold in their case, all of these measures would be vulnerable to challenge under the irrebuttable presumption doctrine as set forth in *Vlandis*.

§5.7.3 The Doctrine Today

Two years after *Vlandis* was decided, the Supreme Court in *Weinberger v. Salfi*, 422 U.S. 749 (1975), drastically narrowed this avenue of attack. *Weinberger* involved a Social Security Act provision that denied survivors' benefits to widows and stepchildren whose relationships to the deceased wage earner had existed for less than nine months before his death. The legislative history revealed that this eligibility provision was adopted to discourage marriages entered into to collect Social Security benefits. The district court held that the act contained an implicit irrebuttable presumption—i.e., that every marriage occurring less than nine months before a wage earner's death was a sham. Since this presumption is not universally true, the trial court held that the applicant was entitled to a hearing to show that the law was overinclusive as to her—i.e., that her marriage was bona fide and that she was, therefore, entitled to widow's benefits.

The Supreme Court reversed. Recognizing that *Vlandis* could be "a virtual engine of destruction for countless legislative judgments which have heretofore been thought wholly consistent with the Fifth and Fourteenth Amendments," 422 U.S. at 772, the *Weinberger* Court limited the irrebuttable presumption doctrine to cases where heightened scrutiny would be called for under the Equal Protection Clause. Otherwise, the government would be free to legislate based on generalizations that involve irrebuttable presumptions. Such presumptions—whether implied or express—are constitutional if the government "can rationally conclude . . . that generalized rules are appropriate to its purposes and concerns. . . ." Id. at 785; see *Usery v. Turner Elkhorn Mining Co.*, 428 U.S. 1 (1976) (Congress did not act arbitrarily in selecting 10- and 15-year time frames as reference points for a rebuttable presumption concerning coal miners' eligibility for certain disability benefits).

The irrebuttable presumption doctrine is still of value in situations where intermediate or strict scrutiny is warranted under the Equal Protection Clause. In these cases, rather than invalidating a law entirely, a court may permit the government to continue using the classification in question but require that it give each individual an opportunity to rebut the presumption on which the classification rests.

EXAMPLE

Example 5-Q

A state X law provides that anyone who has been convicted of spousal abuse is barred from marrying again. On what grounds might the statute be invalidated?

EXPLANATION

Explanation

If the statute were challenged under the Equal Protection Clause, it would receive strict scrutiny, since the measure prohibits a class of persons from exercising the fundamental liberty to marry. See § 7.2. A court could invalidate this law under the Equal Protection Clause by finding that the state's interest in guarding against spousal abuse is not compelling enough to justify a total ban on marriage, or that a less discriminatory way to achieve this goal would be to require that the new spouse be given notice of the prior conviction before the marriage takes place.

However, a court might instead use the irrebuttable presumption doctrine. Under this approach, the state law would be analyzed as containing the implied irrebuttable presumption that all persons convicted of spousal abuse are sufficiently likely to repeat this behavior that they must be barred from remarrying. A court might agree with the state that while such a prior conviction warrants concern, it cannot justify using a blanket prohibition against remarriage. The court could, therefore, insist that if the state wishes to use the presumption, it must be made rebuttable, thereby affording convicted spouse abusers a chance to prove that there is no danger they will again engage in such behavior.

The irrebuttable presumption doctrine thus allows a court to invoke a less intrusive remedy as far as the state is concerned. Rather than barring the state from making any use whatsoever of a particular classificatory scheme, the state may continue to use the classification if it does so in a non-conclusive way. Where the doctrine comes into play, it has the effect of giving a person a right to a hearing that would not otherwise exist.

CHAPTER 6

Equal Protection: Ordinary, "Suspect," and "Quasi-Suspect" Classifications

§6.1 INTRODUCTION AND OVERVIEW

The Constitution prohibits the state and federal governments from denying people the equal protection of the laws. Section 1 of the Fourteenth Amendment provides: "No State shall . . . deny to any person within its jurisdiction the equal protection of the laws." Though nothing in the Constitution's text imposes a similar restriction on the federal government, the Court has construed the Fifth Amendment Due Process Clause as "contain[ing] an equal protection component prohibiting the United States from invidiously discriminating between individuals or groups." *Washington v. Davis*, 426 U.S. 229, 239 (1976). Under most circumstances, the protections afforded by these Amendments are coextensive. But see *Hampton v. Mow Sun Wong*, 426 U.S. 88, 100 (1976) ("there may be overriding national interests which justify selective federal legislation that would be unacceptable for an individual State," such as in the context of discrimination against aliens). In this chapter, the term Equal Protection Clause will be used to include the equal protection guarantees of both the Fifth and the Fourteenth Amendments unless otherwise indicated.

The Equal Protection Clause might seem to bar the government from engaging in any type of discriminatory conduct. Yet if this were literally true, virtually no laws would be constitutional. Every law classifies by imposing burdens or conferring benefits on a selective basis, singling out some people or activities for treatment different from that accorded to others. A police officer who enforces a speed limit law pulls fast drivers out of the stream of traffic and allows other drivers to proceed unimpeded. A law regulating child labor treats employers who hire 10-year-olds differently from those who hire 25-year-olds. Each of these laws would be unconstitutional if the equal protection guarantee prohibited all discrimination on the part of government.

The Equal Protection Clause has never been interpreted as outlawing all forms of discrimination. Instead, the clause prohibits government from engaging in arbitrary or invidious discrimination—i.e., from employing classifications that cannot be justified on the basis of any legitimate governmental interest and that are perhaps adopted merely for the sake of harming a particular group. For the government to treat people differently who are similarly situated, or to treat people the same who are not similarly situated, offends fundamental standards of fairness. Such arbitrary action on the part of government officials suggests that they are either acting capriciously or misusing their authority to reward friends and/or punish enemies. Whichever the case, governmental conduct that draws arbitrary distinctions between people violates the democratic principle that all persons stand equal before the law.

The question that the courts face in seeking to implement the Equal Protection Clause is how to determine whether a classification is unconstitutional. What type of explanation must the defender of a discriminatory law offer to persuade a judge that the classification is relevant to a legitimate governmental interest?

EXAMPLE

Example 6-A

A state law provides that to work as a carpenter, one must have a high school diploma and weigh at least 160 pounds. By classifying based on education and weight, this law discriminates against those who lack a high school education and those who weigh less than 160 pounds. Shortly after the law took effect, Sheila, who is black, was fired from her carpenter's job because she weighs only 125 pounds and never graduated from high school. Can Sheila successfully challenge the law on the ground that it violates the Equal Protection Clause?

EXPLANATION

Explanation

The answer depends on how closely a court will examine the explanation offered by the law's defender. The defender may argue that the weight minimum assures that carpenters are able to carry lumber safely on the job. The high school diploma requirement helps assure that carpenters can read blueprints and make the calculations necessary to build structures that are safe. If a court accepts this explanation, the classifications drawn by the law are not arbitrary or invidious since they further the state's legitimate interests in safety.

However, a judge who is prepared to scrutinize the measure more closely might find this explanation unconvincing. If strength is really a concern, why did the state adopt a weight requirement rather than insisting that carpenters be able to lift a certain number of pounds? And if the ability to read blueprints and make calculations is so critical, why require a high school diploma, which does not necessarily guarantee these abilities when the state could instead give a test to see if a person has these skills? Like a suit of clothes made for someone else, this law fits the alleged safety goal so poorly as to suggest that it was enacted for some other purpose. Suppose a court applies this more exacting standard of review. In that case, it might reject the safety explanation and, in the absence of any other plausible justification, conclude that the measure discriminates arbitrarily in violation of the Equal Protection Clause.

As the above example suggests, whether a law will be invalidated under the Equal Protection Clause depends heavily on how rigorous a standard of review a court will apply. The Supreme Court analyzes most equal protection problems according to a three-tier model, which consists of three possible standards of review. If a law or practice discriminates based on race, alienage, or national origin, or if it selectively burdens the exercise of a fundamental right, the Court will apply strict scrutiny. If the measure discriminates based on gender or legitimacy, it will be examined under somewhat less exacting intermediate scrutiny. Finally, most other classifications—e.g., federal tax and benefits programs, ordinary commercial transactions, disability—are tested under a highly deferential rational basis standard of review. The first two standards of review are sometimes referred to as involving "heightened scrutiny," a term that may refer to either strict or intermediate scrutiny.

The key to approaching an equal protection problem is to first determine what type of discrimination is involved. If the law discriminates on any of the bases that trigger strict or intermediate scrutiny, there is a very good chance it will be found to violate the Equal Protection Clause. On the other hand, if the discrimination is such that it will be reviewed only under the rational basis standard, almost any explanation offered in support of the classification will usually suffice. Thus, in Example 6-A, if Sheila could show that the effect of the high school diploma requirement is to exclude a disproportionate number of racial minorities and that this was the purpose of the law, a court would apply strict scrutiny and almost certainly invalidate the requirement. Similarly, if Sheila could prove that the weight requirement bars most women from carpentry jobs and that this was one of the reasons behind the measure, this aspect of the law would be examined under intermediate scrutiny and would probably be struck down. However, if Sheila is unable to show that the law discriminates on either of these bases, the court would probably apply a mere rational basis standard of review and likely uphold the measure.

To analyze an equal protection problem, it is necessary to answer three basic questions:

1. What type of discrimination is involved?
2. If the type of discrimination is one that calls for heightened scrutiny, has the plaintiff established a prima facie case that the defendant has been unable to rebut?
3. Has the defender of the law justified the discrimination under the applicable standard of review?

The first two questions will be explored in the following section. The remaining sections of this and the next chapter will consider the third question by examining application of the three-tier model to various forms of discrimination. We will see that the Court's approach to equal protection has been somewhat more subtle and varied than the three-tier model might suggest. Even though the Court still formally adheres to this model, it has also incorporated refinements that allow the model to be employed with some degree of flexibility.

§6.2 EQUAL PROTECTION: GENERAL PRINCIPLES

§6.2.1 Detecting Discrimination: Facial, Design, and Applied

To determine the standard of review that will be applied in an equal protection case, we must identify the type of discrimination involved. Is it a type that calls for strict scrutiny or intermediate scrutiny, or is it a type that triggers only a rational basis standard of review? There are several ways to make this determination. First, we can examine the face of the law to see what classifications are drawn by its text (facial discrimination). Second, we can probe behind the law to see what kind of discrimination it may have been designed to accomplish (discrimination by design). Finally, we can look to how the law is enforced or applied (discriminatory application).

Facial Discrimination

The most obvious place to look to determine the bases on which a law classifies is the face of the law itself—i.e., its text. In Example 6-A, the law regulating carpentry facially discriminates against those who lack a high school diploma and against those who weigh less than 160 pounds. A law does not need to use any specific words to discriminate facially based on a particular trait if it is obvious from the text that the law classifies in a particular way. A law that said, "No descendants of slaves may own land" discriminates based on race just as though it had read "No blacks may own land." Moreover, a law will be deemed to discriminate facially against a particular group even if it does not burden every member of that group. A law that states "Aliens may attend the university only after they have lived in this state for ten years" discriminates facially based on alienage. The fact that the law also discriminates within the class of aliens by classifying based on length of residence does not alter the fact that the measure, on its face, singles out aliens for adverse treatment. Thus, in *Rice v. Cayetano*, 528 U.S. 495 (2000), the Court held that a state constitutional provision limiting the right to vote to certain "descendants" of specified "peoples" constituted racial discrimination, even though not all descendants of those peoples were given the right to vote. "Simply because a class defined by ancestry does not include all members of the race does not suffice to make the classification race neutral." Id. at 516-517.

Discrimination by Design

Laws may classify in ways that are not apparent from reading their text. A law that is facially neutral may, nonetheless, have been designed to cause discrimination of a certain type. If a law disproportionately burdens a particular group and it can be shown that such discrimination was part of the law's purpose or design, the law will be deemed to involve discrimination against that group despite its facial neutrality. In Example 6-A, the statute requiring that carpenters weigh at least 160 pounds may have been adopted as a subtle means of excluding most women from the trade of carpentry, just as the high school diploma requirement may have been intended to exclude racial minorities. If Sheila could prove that the law had those effects and that they were part of the law's design, the measure would be tested for equal protection purposes under heightened scrutiny as involving both gender discrimination and racial discrimination.

Discriminatory Application

A law that is facially neutral and that was not adopted for the purpose of discriminating in a particular way may still be discriminatory as applied. As the Court has said, "the purpose of the equal protection clause of the Fourteenth Amendment is to secure every person within the State's jurisdiction against intentional and arbitrary discrimination, whether occasioned by express terms of a statute or by its improper execution through duly constituted agents." *Village of Willowbrook v. Olech*, 528 U.S. 562, 564 (2000) (quoting *Sunday Lake Iron Co. v. Township of Wakefield*, 247 U.S. 350, 352 (1918)). A statute making it illegal to drive over 55 mph does not discriminate on its face or by design against any group of speeding motorists. Yet the law could be challenged under the Equal Protection Clause as involving gender discrimination if it were shown that the police who enforce the measure give tickets only to female drivers. Similarly, in Example 6-A, even if the high school graduation requirement was not designed to discriminate against racial minorities, the statute would be deemed to involve racial discrimination if it were shown that the state routinely waives this requirement for white applicants.

§6.2.2 The Prima Facie Case

A plaintiff mounting an equal protection challenge must establish a prima facie case of discrimination. To establish a prima facie case, the plaintiff must allege and prove two elements, impact and purpose—i.e., the plaintiff must show that (1) the law has a disproportionate or disparate impact on a particular group, and (2) the impact on this particular group is intentional in the sense that it results from a discriminatory purpose or design. Think of these elements as serving to disclose the criterion on which a discriminatory line has been drawn. Thus, a law that disproportionately harms more women than men and that was designed to have this effect is a law that discriminates based on the criterion of gender.

If a plaintiff seeks heightened scrutiny, then the impact and purpose elements must each focus on a criterion that triggers a heightened review. For example, if a plaintiff can show that a law has a disproportionate impact on a racial group and that the law was purposefully designed to have that impact, strict scrutiny will apply. If either one of these elements is missing, however, the classification will probably fall into a "nonsuspect" category to which the rational basis standard applies.

Where a law is facially discriminatory against a particular group, the prima facie case of discrimination against that group is established by the text of the law itself. A law providing that "elementary school teachers must be citizens of the United States" obviously has a disproportionate impact on aliens, since it burdens them and no one else. Nor is there any question as to whether this discrimination was purposeful as to aliens, since aliens are expressly singled out for special treatment by the very text of the statute.

If a law is not facially discriminatory, however, the prima facie case may be far more difficult to establish. The plaintiff must allege and prove both disparate impact and discriminatory purpose by looking beyond the text of the law. And again, to trigger heightened review, both the impact and the purpose must be directed toward a specially protected classification, such as race or gender.

Disproportionate Impact

To establish that a law has a disproportionate impact, the plaintiff must prove that the law's practical effect is to burden one group of persons more heavily than it does others.

Example 6-B

In Example 6-A, Sheila lost her job as a carpenter because she did not meet either the education or the weight requirement set by state law. If she wishes to challenge the law under the Equal Protection Clause, she may be able to have it reviewed under heightened scrutiny by establishing a prima facie case of racial discrimination, gender discrimination, or both. Leaving aside the element of purpose, how might Sheila satisfy the disproportionate impact element of the prima facie case?

Explanation

With respect to the education requirement, Sheila might consult census data showing the educational levels of members of the workforce in her state. If this data shows that a significantly higher percentage of whites than blacks complete high school, she will arguably have made a prima facie showing that the law will have a disparate impact on blacks by disqualifying a larger proportion of blacks than whites.

Similarly, Sheila could satisfy the impact element for a prima facie case of gender discrimination if she can show that the percentage of working-age men weighing more than 160 pounds is substantially higher than the percentage of working-age women who exceed this weight.

While most equal protection cases involve discrimination against a group or class of persons, of which the plaintiff is a member, equal protection claims may be brought "by a 'class of one,' where the plaintiff alleges that she has been intentionally treated differently from others similarly situated and that there is no rational basis for the difference in treatment." *Village of Willowbrook v. Olech*, supra, 528 U.S. at 564. In other words, the only trait on which a class-of-one equal protection claim is premised is the trait of being the plaintiff. You might think of this as the it's-all-about-me classification. In *Olech*, the Court held that the plaintiff had stated a claim for relief under the Equal Protection Clause by alleging that the village demanded a 33-foot easement to connect her property to the municipal water supply while requiring only 15-foot easements from other property owners. Plaintiff asserted that she was intentionally singled out for this "irrational and wholly arbitrary" treatment because she had previously brought an unrelated, successful lawsuit against the village. The Court held that "the number of individuals in a class is immaterial for equal protection analysis." Id. at 564 n.*.

In *Engquist v. Oregon Department of Agriculture*, 553 U.S. 591, 607 (2008), the Supreme Court held that "the class-of-one theory of equal protection has no application in the public employment context. . . ." The Court reasoned that since the government has "significantly greater leeway in its dealings with citizen employees than it does when it brings its sovereign power to bear on citizens at large," extending the class-of-one theory into the workplace setting would transform "a vast array of subjective, individualized assessments" into constitutional claims, in effect constitutionalizing public employee grievances. Id. at 599, 603. The *Engquist* Court thus held that a discharged public employee could not bring a class-of-one equal protection claim against her superiors, based on allegations she was singled out for adverse treatment because of their animosity toward her.

Discriminatory Purpose

The second element of the prima facie case is discriminatory purpose. This element was first explicitly recognized in *Washington v. Davis*, 426 U.S. 229 (1976), a case in which it was alleged that the District of Columbia police department was discriminating on the basis of race in recruiting new officers. The Court held that even if the disproportionate impact element of the plaintiffs' prima facie case was established, the plaintiffs failed to prove discriminatory purpose on the part of the defendant police department. It is a "basic equal protection principle," said the Court, "that the invidious quality of a law claimed to be racially discriminatory must ultimately be traced to a racially discriminatory purpose." Id. at 240. The same principle applies with respect to other types of discrimination. See *Johnson v. California*, 545 U.S. 162 (2005) (defendant must prove discriminatory purpose when challenging government's use of "race-based" peremptory strikes in jury selection). Stated somewhat differently, heightened scrutiny will be triggered under the Equal Protection Clause only if there is de jure, as opposed to de facto, discrimination. As the Court has stressed, the critical "differentiating factor" between the two is that the former requires a showing of "*purpose* or *intent*" to discriminate while the latter does not. *Keyes v. School Dist. No. 1*, 413 U.S. 189, 208 (1973) (emphasis in original).

Proving that a challenged law or practice was motivated by a discriminatory purpose is automatic where a statute or policy is discriminatory on its face, for there is then no doubt as to the presence of a discriminatory intent. If the measure is facially neutral, however, satisfying the purpose element may pose a major stumbling block. It is not enough to show merely that those who adopted the law or practice did so with the knowledge that it would have foreseeable discriminatory effects. "'Discriminatory purpose' . . . implies more than intent as volition or intent as awareness of consequences." *Personnel Administrator of Mass. v. Feeney*, 442 U.S. 256, 279 (1979). The plaintiff must allege and prove that the measure was adopted "at least in part 'because of,' not merely 'in spite of,' its adverse effects upon an identifiable group." Id.

To satisfy the purpose requirement of the prima facie case, a plaintiff need not allege or prove "that the challenged action rested solely on . . . discriminatory purposes. Rarely can it be said that a legislature or administrative body operating under a broad mandate made a decision motivated solely by a single concern, or even that a particular purpose was the 'dominant' or 'primary' one"; instead, it is normally enough "that a discriminatory purpose has been *a motivating factor* in the decision. . . ." *Village of Arlington Heights v. Metropolitan Housing Dev. Corp.*, 429 U.S. 252, 265-266 (1977) (emphasis supplied).

The only exception to this requirement involves race-based electoral districting, where the prima facie case requires proof "that race was *the predominant factor* motivating the legislature's decision. . . ." *Miller v. Johnson*, 515 U.S. 900, 916 (1995) (emphasis supplied). See § 7.3.5. This is a heavy burden on the plaintiff, often requiring "direct evidence" to supplement circumstantial evidence, and "alternative maps" to overcome the presumption of legislative good faith. *Alexander v. South Carolina State Conference of the NAACP*, 144 S. Ct. 1221, 1234-1235 (2024). The Court explained that "direct evidence often comes in the form of a relevant state actor's express acknowledgment that race played a role in the drawing of district lines," id. at 1234. Moreover, "the plaintiff[] fail[s] to meet the high bar for a racial-gerrymandering claim [when] failing to produce, among other things, an alternative map showing that a rational legislature sincerely driven by its professed partisan goals would have drawn a different map with greater racial balance." Id. at 1235. If the plaintiff does not meet this burden, a court will draw adverse inferences against it and in favor of the legislature. Id. at 1235-1236, 1249. However, if the plaintiff proves that race was the predominant factor motivating the legislature's decision, then the state bears the burden of showing that the design of that district withstands strict scrutiny. See *Wisconsin Legislature v. Wisconsin Election Commission*, 595 U.S. 398, 401 (2022); and, for vote dilution claims brought under the Voting Rights Act of 1965, the state can meet this burden by showing that "its race-based sorting of voters is narrowly tailored to comply with the [Act]." Id.

Example 6-C

In Example 6-B, suppose that after establishing the discriminatory impact element of her prima facie case for racial and gender discrimination, Sheila showed that when the law was pending before the state legislature, a number of groups testifying against the measure pointed out that it would negatively impact racial minorities and women. Would this suffice to establish discriminatory purpose?

Explanation

This evidence is not by itself enough to satisfy the element of purpose, for while it certainly suggests a possibility that legislators were animated by a discriminatory intent, it is equally possible they adopted the law in spite of, not because of, its adverse effects on these groups. Sheila will need to come up with other evidence of discriminatory purpose, evidence that would show that it is more likely than not that the measure was adopted for a discriminatory purpose.

While the mere awareness of "foreseeable and anticipated disparate impact" will not by itself support a finding of discriminatory purpose, the Court has held that "foreseeable consequences" may be "utilized as one of the several kinds of proofs" from which an inference of discriminatory purpose may be drawn. *Columbus Bd. of Educ. v. Penick*, 443 U.S. 449, 464-465 (1979).

Legislative History

There are several ways in which a plaintiff may be able to prove the element of purpose where a law is facially neutral. It is possible that the legislative history pertaining to the measure's adoption will reveal a discriminatory intent. This is uncommon, since those who are motivated by an invidious purpose rarely leave a public record to document their wrongdoing. Nevertheless, such evidence is sometimes available. In *Hunter v. Underwood*, 471 U.S. 222 (1985), the Court invalidated a 1901 Alabama constitutional provision that disenfranchised anyone convicted of a crime involving moral turpitude, after finding that the provision was racially discriminatory. The impact element of the plaintiffs' prima facie case was established by showing that the provision had disenfranchised ten times as many blacks as whites. The purpose element was satisfied by historical materials showing that a "zeal for white supremacy ran rampant" in the constitutional convention that had adopted the provision. Id. at 229.

The Manner of Adoption

Discriminatory purpose may sometimes be inferred from the way in which the challenged measure was adopted. If the process that led to its adoption did not follow the normal procedures or if it involved a departure from the substantive criteria that normally govern such matters, the irregularity may suggest the presence of a discriminatory intent.

Example 6-D

In Example 6-A, suppose that the state adopted the law requiring that carpenters have a high school diploma and weigh at least 160 pounds as an emergency measure two days after a local newspaper reported that 150 women and minorities were about to graduate from a federally funded training program for carpenters. The bill was drafted by the Brotherhood of Carpenters and was not reviewed by any of the state legislative committees that normally have jurisdiction over such matters. Would this evidence establish the element of discriminatory purpose?

Explanation

The unusual timing and procedure that led to the enactment of this law might allow the inference that it was motivated by a desire to exclude minorities and women from the carpentry trade.

Example 6-E

In 2012, the federal Department of Homeland Security (DHS) inaugurated the Deferred Action for Childhood Arrivals (DACA) program. This allowed undocumented youths brought into this country as children to have deportation actions against them deferred and work authorizations granted for years. In September 2017, eight months after President Trump took office, DHS rescinded DACA. As a result, no new DACA applications were accepted, and current recipients would become subject to deportation. The decision to end the program was made while its validity was still being litigated in federal court. Plaintiffs, who are current DACA recipients, have sued to challenge DHS's rescission decision as being racially discriminatory in violation of the Fifth Amendment. Plaintiffs allege: (1) that President Trump, whose Attorney General ordered the program terminated eight months after Trump took office, had made numerous pre- and post-election comments disparaging Latinos and their migration from Mexico, and describing Mexican immigrants as "people that have lots of problems," "the bad ones," "criminals, drug dealers, and rapists," and "animals" responsible for the "the drugs, the gangs, the cartels, the crisis of smuggling and trafficking, and MS13"; (2) that the rescission decision's history suggested something unusual was at work since three months earlier DHS had said it remained committed to DACA; and (3) that the program's termination had a heavily disproportionate impact on Latinos from Mexico, who comprised 78 percent of DACA recipients. Have plaintiffs made out a prima facie case of racially discriminatory intent with respect to the decision to terminate DACA?

Explanation

At this stage of the litigation, to make out a prima facie case, plaintiffs must allege that discriminatory purpose was "a motivating factor" in the challenged decision. Here, they have arguably done that. But the question is how strong the cited evidence must be to give rise to a plausible inference that such intent was at work. First, there is no direct evidence that President Trump, who made repeated racist statements about Latinos, was the one responsible for the decision to terminate DACA. Nor is there evidence of any racially discriminatory intent on the part of the Attorney General, the person who made the termination decision. Yet it is plausible to assume that the Attorney General was acting in accord with the President's wishes, particularly on an issue the President cared so much about. Second, while the decision's history suggests something unusual was at work, the government may claim it was simply taking signals from the courts which had questioned DACA's legality. Third, the disproportionate impact on Latinos is not by itself proof of discriminatory intent, for as a program specifically aimed at helping Latinos, any negative decision affecting DACA would have a singular impact on them. Yet combined with other evidence of discriminatory intent, that impact may carry some weight. While no one of these factors by itself is sufficient to establish the intent element of plaintiffs' prima facie case, together they may give rise to a reasonable inference at this pleading stage of the case. Of course, plaintiffs would have to later support these allegations with evidence sufficient to carry their burden of proof at trial.

The Supreme Court disposed of this case by ruling that DACA's termination violated the Administrative Procedure Act. *Department of Homeland Security v. Regents of the University of California*, 591 U.S. 1 (2020). However, five justices addressed the constitutional question. Four of them, for the reasons suggested above, believed that none of the plaintiffs' allegations, "either singly or in concert," gave rise to a "plausible inference" that recission was motivated by racial animus. Id. at 34-35 (Roberts, C.J., et al.). Writing separately, Justice Sotomayor believed a prima facie case of racially discriminatory intent had been made, a view shared by the three lower federal courts that had addressed this issue below. She would therefore have allowed the case to proceed on remand so that plaintiffs, through discovery, might be able to provide additional support for their claim of racial animus.

Inferring Purpose from Impact and Other Circumstantial Evidence

Although a disproportionate impact alone will not suffice to establish a discriminatory purpose, proof of impact along with other circumstantial evidence may satisfy the plaintiff's burden. Even if there is no direct evidence revealing the subjective state of mind of those who adopted the challenged measure, "an invidious discriminatory purpose may often be inferred from the totality of the relevant facts. . . ." *Washington v. Davis*, 426 U.S. 229, 242 (1976)

In *Rogers v. Lodge*, 458 U.S. 613 (1982), the Court dealt with an equal protection challenge to an "at-large" county election system under which a five-member board of commissioners was selected. The county was not divided into districts; instead, every registered voter in the county could vote for all five seats on the board. The net effect of this system was that blacks, who comprised a minority of the registered voters countywide, were never elected to office. This disparate impact on the black community did not establish purposeful discrimination. However, coupling this impact with other evidence, the Supreme Court affirmed a lower court's ruling that the at-large system was being maintained for discriminatory purposes. That evidence was all circumstantial—e.g., blacks comprised a substantial majority of the population but made up a distinct minority of the registered voters; there was also overwhelming evidence of racial bloc voting, a history of past racial discrimination in voter registration and in education, continuing segregation in the public schools, various examples of discrimination in the political process, a failure of the political process to address the needs of the black community, and discriminatory use of public monies. Viewed as a whole, these facts provided a sufficient basis for the district court to conclude that the county's at-large system was being maintained for racially discriminatory purposes. More recently, though, in *Alexander v. South Carolina State Conference of the NACCP*, 144 S. Ct. 1221 (2024), a case involving a gerrymandering claim, the Court noted how proving intent with circumstantial evidence alone might be more difficult, especially "when the State raises a partisan-gerrymandering defense . . . because partisan and racial gerrymanders 'are capable of yielding similar oddities in a district's boundaries' when there is a high correlation between race and partisan preference." Id. at 1234-1235.

In Example 6-B, Sheila might not meet the discriminatory purpose element merely by showing that the law had a heavily disproportionate impact on racial minorities and women who wished to become carpenters. To fall within *Rogers*, Sheila would have to present additional circumstantial evidence sufficient to convince a court that the law was adopted or maintained for purposes of racial or gender discrimination. But if the court were to follow an approach similar to the one in *Alexander v. South Carolina State Conference of the NACCP*, the bar might be set higher.

Inferring Purpose from Application

Proof that a facially neutral statute is being applied in a discriminatory fashion will also satisfy the purpose element of the plaintiff's burden. For example, in *Yick Wo v. Hopkins*, 118 U.S. 356 (1886), the Court struck down a San Francisco city ordinance that required a permit to operate a laundry in a wooden building. This ordinance, though facially neutral, was enforced in such a way that applications from all 201 Chinese applicants were denied, while virtually every non-Chinese application was approved. The disproportionate impact was so extreme as to allow an inference "that no reason for it exists except hostility to the race and nationality to which the petitioners belong. . . ." Id. at 374. To fall within *Yick Wo*, a plaintiff must prove that the law is being administered in a discriminatory manner. This would be the case in Example 6-B if Sheila could show that the state followed a practice of regularly waiving the education and weight requirements for whites and for males, while strictly enforcing them against minority and female applicants.

The Keyes *Presumption*

Discriminatory purpose may also be established if the actor whose conduct is in question has been guilty of the same type of intentional discrimination in another, but closely related, area. Under these circumstances, the *Keyes* presumption may allow a court to infer that the actor's currently challenged conduct was motivated by the same evil intent. The presumption takes its name from *Keyes v. School District No. 1*, 413 U.S. 189 (1973), a school desegregation case in which the plaintiffs were able to prove that the defendant school board had intentionally segregated schools in one part of the district but could not prove a similar purpose with respect to other segregated schools in the same district. The Court held that the plaintiffs could satisfy the purpose element of their prima facie case as to the latter schools by in effect transferring the board's invidious intent from one part of the district to another. "[A] finding of intentionally segregative school board actions in a meaningful portion of a school system, as in this case, creates a presumption that other segregated schooling within the system is not adventitious. It establishes, in other words, a prima facie case of unlawful segregative design on the part of school authorities. . . ." Id. at 208.

In *Keyes*, the presumption of discriminatory intent was applied with respect to actions taken at roughly the same time, though in different parts of the city. The *Keyes* presumption has also been employed in a historical or temporal sense to transfer the element of intent from one time to another. Where a school board has been guilty of purposeful discrimination at some point in the past, this may allow a presumption that the actor's "subsequent" or "current" conduct was similarly motivated. Id. at 210-211 & n.17. And see *Dayton Bd. of Educ. v. Brinkman*, 443 U.S. 526, 535-538 (1979) (employing *Keyes* presumption to supply element of intent where school board had purposefully segregated schools several decades earlier).

Though the Court has applied the *Keyes* presumption in an expansive manner in school segregation cases, the Court does not appear to have employed the presumption either in other types of race discrimination cases or in cases involving discrimination on grounds other than race, such as alienage and gender. Thus, it is not clear that the *Keyes* presumption has any role to play outside the school desegregation context.

EXAMPLE

Example 6-F

In Example 6-B, suppose that Sheila challenged the carpenter qualifications law partly on the ground that it was being enforced in a racially discriminatory manner by the State Licensing Board. According to Sheila, all whites who apply are granted a license regardless of their weight or level of education, whereas racial minorities who do not meet these requirements are rejected. Assuming that the element of disparate impact can be proved by statistics from the board's files, how might Sheila prove the element of racially discriminatory purpose?

EXPLANATION

Explanation

In addition to perhaps asking the court to infer intent from discriminatory application as in *Yick Wo*, Sheila might determine whether the board was ever found by a court to have engaged in purposeful racial discrimination in the past. If such a finding exists, Sheila could ask the court to invoke the *Keyes* presumption, in effect transferring the element of evil intent from that prior incident to the present case. However, since this is not a school desegregation case, it is possible, but unlikely, that the court would allow the use of *Keyes*.

If courts were to permit broad use of the *Keyes* presumption, the distinction between de jure and de facto discrimination would all but collapse. There are probably few governmental entities that have not, at some time in their history, been guilty of purposeful racial discrimination. If *Keyes* could be used routinely to challenge current laws and practices that have a racially disparate impact, plaintiffs could almost always satisfy their prima facie case by borrowing the element of intent from the past. It is perhaps for this reason that the Court has employed the *Keyes* presumption only in the context of school desegregation cases. Even in that setting, the Court is likely to limit the presumption to actions that are very similar in nature. Thus, for example, the mere fact that a school board may have been guilty of past racial discrimination in hiring teachers would probably not permit use of the *Keyes* presumption in a later case charging the board with racial discrimination in assigning pupils to schools.

Difficulties with the Purpose Element

Even though a plaintiff might in theory meet the purpose element of the prima facie case in a number of different ways, this element is frequently hard to satisfy in the context of suspect or quasi-suspect criteria, such as race or gender. As a result, the plaintiff's equal protection challenge is often reviewed and rejected under a rational basis standard of review. In essence, the failure to establish discriminatory purpose alters the nature of the classification. Thus, a job test that disproportionately disqualifies more blacks than whites is not racially discriminatory within the meaning of the Equal Protection Clause unless the purpose of using that test is to discriminate based on race. Without proof of a racially discriminatory purpose, the classification—those who pass the test and those who fail—is nonsuspect and subject only to rational basis review.

Yet forcing plaintiffs to prove the existence of invidious intent means that governmental actions that were undertaken with a discriminatory purpose will be upheld by courts applying the rational basis standard of review whenever plaintiffs lack the resources or the ability to uncover proof of the defendants' improper motivation. This is especially troubling in the area of racial discrimination, for as Justice Powell observed, "[I]f one goes back far enough, it is probable that all racial segregation, wherever occurring and whether or not confined to the schools, has at some time been supported or maintained by government action." *Keyes v. School Dist. No. 1*, supra, 413 U.S. at 228 n.12 (Powell, J., concurring and dissenting). For this reason, Justices Powell and Douglas urged the Court to abandon the de jure/de facto distinction, at least in the context of school desegregation cases. Id. at 219-236.

It has also been objected that to demand proof of conscious or deliberate intent to discriminate is often to demand the impossible—not because the challenged action was free of discriminatory bias, but because that bias was unconscious. To focus, as the Supreme Court has, on proof of discriminatory purpose is to create "an imaginary world where," in a constitutional sense, "discrimination does not exist unless it was consciously intended." Charles Lawrence, "The Id, the Ego, and Equal Protection: Reckoning with Unconscious Racism," 39 *Stan. L. Rev.* 317, 325 (1987).

The Court has, nevertheless, adhered to the requirement that to trigger heightened scrutiny under the Equal Protection Clause, a plaintiff must prove discriminatory purpose as part of the prima facie case. The Court has defended this approach by noting that if disproportionate impact alone were enough to elevate the standard of judicial review, this "would raise serious questions about, and perhaps invalidate, a whole range of tax, welfare, public service, regulatory, and licensing statutes that may be more burdensome to the poor and to the average black than to the more affluent white." *Washington v. Davis*, supra, 426 U.S. at 248 & n.14. In addition, judges would be transformed into a set of racial bookkeepers, forced to measure the gains and losses of each racial and ethnic group affected by a challenged law. Finally, a disparate impact approach would destroy our ideal of a colorblind society, for to avoid a potential violation of the Equal Protection Clause, governmental entities would be compelled to evaluate every proposed action in terms of its likely racial impact—a troubling, if not impossible, task.

§6.2.3 Rebutting the Prima Facie Case

Once the plaintiff has established a prima facie case, whether it is of racial discrimination, gender discrimination, or some other type of discrimination that triggers heightened scrutiny, the court will give the defendant an opportunity to rebut the prima facie case. If the defendant can do so, then the court will evaluate the statute under the rational basis standard of review rather than under either strict or intermediate scrutiny. On the other hand, if the defendant is unable to rebut, the court will proceed to apply the appropriate level of heightened scrutiny.

A defendant can attempt to rebut the plaintiff's prima facie case of discrimination in three possible ways: (1) by disproving the element of impact; (2) by disproving the element of purpose; or (3) by showing that the discriminatory impact was not caused by the defendant's purposefully discriminatory acts.

The first way a defendant can rebut the prima facie case is by showing that those allegedly discriminated against by the challenged law or practice have not in fact been harmed or burdened any more heavily than others. This typically involves proving that the data on which the plaintiff relied to show disparate impact is outdated, was obtained by faulty methods, or is for some other reason inaccurate.

Example 6-G

In Example 6-B, Sheila established a prima facie case of racial and gender discrimination with statistics showing that a smaller percentage of blacks than whites graduate from high school and that a lower percentage of women than men weigh over 160 pounds. How might the defendant rebut this element of the prima facie case?

Explanation

The defendant could rebut the showing of disparate impact by proving that despite Sheila's statistics concerning the working-age population in general, this law's education and weight requirements have not resulted in the exclusion of blacks or women at higher rates than whites or males. For example, the defendant's figures might show that under the high school graduation requirement, 23 percent of white applicants were rejected, as compared with 20 percent of black applicants, and that the weight restriction led to the rejection of 9 percent of males, but only 5 percent of females. If the defendant could make these showings, the law would not be discriminatory against racial minorities or women. Instead, the measure would be one that discriminates on the bases of education and weight, classifications that are subject only to a rational basis equal protection review.

The second means of rebutting the prima facie case is to show that those responsible for the challenged action were not moved by a discriminatory purpose. In a case where this element of the plaintiff's prima facie case was satisfied through use of the *Keyes* presumption, the defendant may be able to prove that despite its discriminatory intent in other situations, the actions at issue in this case were not so motivated. To rebut this element of the prima facie case, however, a defendant must show that its actions were not "to any degree motivated" by a discriminatory purpose—i.e., that such a purpose "was not among the factors that motivated their actions." *Keyes v. School Dist. No. 1*, supra, 413 U.S. at 210. In *Hunter v. Underwood*, 471 U.S. 222, 230 (1985), for example, the state sought to rebut the prima facie case of race discrimination by arguing that "the real purpose" behind its disenfranchisement of those convicted of crimes involving moral turpitude "was to disenfranchise poor whites as well as blacks." This argument failed, said the Court, for it "concedes . . . that discrimination against blacks . . . was a motivating factor for the provision. . . ." Id. at 231.

Finally, a defendant may rebut the prima facie case by showing that there is no link between the discriminatory purpose and the disproportionate impact complained of. In other words, the defendant can seek to demonstrate that its deliberate efforts to discriminate were gratuitous and unnecessary because the same results would have occurred anyway because of other factors.

EXAMPLE

Example 6-H

The Village of Avondale denied a request from Metro, Inc., to rezone a parcel of land on which Metro wished to build a ten-story low-income housing project. Metro sued the village, alleging that its refusal to rezone was racially discriminatory. Metro established a prima facie case by proving that the village's decision would have a racially disparate impact, since most tenants in the proposed project would be racial minorities, and by showing that the refusal was prompted by a desire to keep minorities from moving into the village. How might the village rebut Metro's prima facie case of racial discrimination?

EXPLANATION

Explanation

Even if the village cannot disprove the elements of impact or purpose, it can rebut Metro's prima facie case by showing that for other reasons the project never would have been built. The village might, for example, prove that even in the absence of any racially discriminatory purpose, the rezoning request would have been denied under a uniformly applied ordinance that limits buildings to six stories in height. Or the village might show that if the rezoning request had been approved, the project would still not have been built because Metro lacked the necessary funding. In either of these ways, the village would have shown that the injury complained of is not attributable to the village's improper discriminatory purpose. The village's action would then be evaluated under a mere rational basis standard of review. See *Village of Arlington Heights v. Metropolitan Housing Dev. Corp.*, 429 U.S. 252, 270 n.21 (1977).

In some instances, a defendant may be able to rebut only a portion of the plaintiff's prima facie case, in which event the court would apply heightened scrutiny to those aspects of the plaintiff's case that have not been rebutted. Thus, in a school desegregation case where the plaintiff made a prima facie showing that the school board had purposefully segregated the elementary and secondary schools in the district, the defendant might be able to show that the secondary schools would have become segregated in any event because of factors for which the board was not responsible, with the result that no prima facie case of race discrimination would exist as to the secondary schools.

In this chapter, we will examine the Court's application of the equal protection guarantees of the Fifth and Fourteenth Amendments, first under the rational basis standard of review and then where the plaintiff has established a prima facie case that triggers heightened scrutiny based on a suspect or quasi-suspect classification. In Chapter 7, we will consider the application of strict scrutiny where there has been discrimination with respect to a fundamental right.

§6.3 THE RATIONAL BASIS EQUAL PROTECTION TEST

If a law does not involve a suspect or quasi-suspect classification and does not discriminate with respect to a fundamental right, the courts will apply a rational basis test to decide whether the law violates the equal protection provisions of the Fifth or the Fourteenth Amendment. *Armour v. City of Indianapolis*, 566 U.S. 673, 680-681 (2012). Over the years, the rational basis equal protection standard has been applied with varying degrees of rigor. From the late 1890s until the late 1930s, the Court often used the test to invalidate state and local laws on the ground that they discriminated arbitrarily. Yet during the same period, the Court also applied the test leniently to uphold challenged classifications. This oscillation between strict and relaxed applications of the rational basis test came to an end in the 1940s. Since then, in applying what is now sometimes referred to as the traditional rational basis test, the Court evaluates most classifications with such extraordinary deference that the test has frequently been described as "toothless."

The traditional rational basis standard of review requires only that there be some *conceivable* reason for the challenged classification, whether or not this was the actual purpose that motivated the legislature. A classification subject to mere rational basis review comes before a court "bearing a strong presumption of validity," and its challengers "have the burden 'to negate every conceivable basis which might support it.'" *FCC v. Beach Communications, Inc.*, 508 U.S. 307, 314-315 (1993). The asserted rationale may rest entirely on "rational speculation unsupported by evidence or empirical data." Id. at 315. The classification need not fit its supposed end "with mathematical nicety. . . ." *Dandridge v. Williams*, 397 U.S. 471, 485 (1970). It can be overinclusive, underinclusive, illogical, and unscientific, *Metropolis Theatre Co. v. Chicago*, 228 U.S. 61, 69-70 (1913), and may involve approaching an issue incrementally, "one step at a time, addressing itself to the phase of the problem which seems most acute to the legislative mind," *Williamson v. Lee Optical, Inc.*, 348 U.S. 483, 489 (1955). And if, as is often the case, the classification involves "a process of line-drawing," the fact that the legislature had to draw the line somewhere "renders the precise coordinates of the resulting legislative judgment virtually unreviewable. . . ." *FCC v. Beach Communications, Inc.*, supra, 508 U.S. at 315-316. Moreover, the Court has emphasized that, because "not every provision in a law must share a single objective," classifications that may appear to be irrational in terms of a law's "predomina[nt] . . . general objective" may nonetheless be found rational if the measure is viewed as one that also seeks "to achieve other desirable (perhaps even contrary) ends as well, thereby producing a law that balances objectives. . . ." *Fitzgerald v. Racing Assn. of Central Iowa*, 539 U.S. 103, 108-109 (2003) (upholding Iowa's higher tax on racetrack slot machines than on riverboat slot machines, for even if the law's primary purpose was to promote racetracks' economic interests by granting them the right to operate slot machines, the discriminatory tax treatment may have been designed to advance possible subsidiary goals, such as to aid river communities, promote riverboat history, or preserve local riverboats).

EXAMPLE

Example 6-I

The city council adopted an ordinance outlawing door-to-door sales in residential neighborhoods. The law contains an exemption for agents of the Bigelow Insurance Co., who are permitted to sell door-to-door in all parts of the city. Sherry, an agent for the Miller Insurance Co., was arrested and criminally charged with violating the ordinance. She has asked the court to dismiss the criminal action on the ground that the ordinance violates the Equal Protection Clause of the Fourteenth Amendment. How should the court rule?

EXPLANATION

Explanation

The ordinance is probably constitutional. Even if we have no idea why the city council adopted the measure, the classification will be upheld if there is any conceivable legitimate reason for treating Bigelow more favorably than other door-to-door sellers. The council may have believed that Bigelow agents are more polite than other door-to-door sellers. Or the council may have thought that Bigelow had been operating in the city longer than any other door-to-door company, giving it an equitable claim to favored treatment. Even if none of these hypothetical rationales was in fact what moved the city council, it is enough that the classification might have been adopted for one or more of these reasons. See *New Orleans v. Dukes*, 427 U.S. 297 (1976) (upholding exemption to ordinance barring most but not all pushcart vendors from certain parts of the city).

EXAMPLE

Example 6-J

For decades, the City funded sewer projects by apportioning a project's costs equally among all abutting lots. Lot owners could elect to pay the assessment in a lump sum or over time in installments. Sewer Project B involved 180 abutting lots. Forty of the lot owners affected by that project paid the assessment in full, while the remaining 140 opted to pay by installment. The debts were relatively small, and the monthly payments on the installments were in the range of $25 per month. The City later decided to abandon this funding model and to fund all future sewer projects through the issuance of bonds. As part of the new approach and in an effort to save administrative costs, the City forgave the remaining amounts owed to it by Project B lot owners who had elected to pay their apportioned fee in installments. The City did not, however, offer a refund to those Project B lot owners who had paid the assessment in full. The paid-in-full lot owners now claim that the City's refusal to provide an equivalent refund to them violated the Equal Protection Clause. How is a court likely to rule on their claim?

Explanation

Because the paid-in-full lot owners' claim does not involve a suspect or quasi-suspect classification and does not implicate a fundamental right, the City's decision not to offer them a refund will be upheld if there is any rational basis for the City's decision. The City could justify its choice as a cost-saving measure because the debt forgiveness will likely save the City the administrative cost of policing these relatively small debts. In other words, the City could rationally conclude that the cost of collection and administration no longer justified whatever incremental benefit the City might derive from collecting these small debts. As to the failure to offer an equivalent refund to the paid-in-full lot owners, the City might argue that offering them a refund would add more administrative costs to the City's effort to transition to a new funding model. Given these arguments, a court would likely conclude that the City acted rationally. See *Armour v. City of Indianapolis*, 566 U.S. 673 (2012) (so ruling on similar facts).

Example 6-K

The Territory Clause of the Constitution states that Congress may "make all needful Rules and Regulations respecting the Territory . . . belonging to the United States. . . ." Art. IV, § 3, cl. 2. Under the clause, Congress has broad authority to legislate with respect to the U.S. Territories, that is, American Samoa, Guam, the Northern Mariana Islands, the U.S. Virgin Islands, and Puerto Rico (also, the "Territories"). Exercising that authority, Congress sometimes legislates differently with respect to the Territories than it does with respect to the States, making policy judgments that account not only for the needs of the United States but also for the unique histories, economic conditions, social circumstances, independent policy views, and relative autonomy of the individual Territories. Congress must also decide how to structure federal taxes and benefits for residents of the Territories. In doing so, Congress has long maintained federal tax and benefits programs for residents of Puerto Rico and the other Territories that differ in some respects from the federal tax and benefits programs for residents of the 50 states. On the tax side, for example, residents of Puerto Rico are typically exempt from most federal income, gift, estate, and excise taxes. At the same time, residents of Puerto Rico generally pay Social Security, Medicare, and unemployment taxes. On the benefits side, residents of Puerto Rico are eligible for Social Security and Medicare. Residents of Puerto Rico are also eligible for federal unemployment benefits but are not eligible for Social Security benefits.

In 1972 Congress passed the Supplemental Security Income (SSI) program and President Nixon signed it into law. The SSI program provides benefits for, among others, those who are 65 or older, cannot financially support themselves, and are residents of the United States, which the statute defines as the 50 States and the District of Columbia. Thus, residents of Puerto Rico are not eligible for SSI. The federal government, though, provides supplemental income assistance to covered residents of Puerto Rico through a different benefits program.

José, originally a resident of New York, moved to Puerto Rico in 2013, where he continued to receive the SSI benefits he received while a resident of New York. When the U.S. government realized it had been providing José with benefits he wasn't entitled to under the SSI program, it sued José claiming restitution of $28,000. In response, José invoked the U.S. Constitution, arguing that Congress's exclusion of residents of Puerto Rico from the SSI program violated the equal protection component of the Fifth Amendment's Due Process Clause. How is a court likely to rule on the government's claim?

Explanation

EXPLANATION

In *United States v. Vaello Madero*, 596 U.S. 159 (2022), the Supreme Court held that the Constitution does not require Congress to extend SSI benefits to residents of Puerto Rico. Relying on *Califano v. Torres*, 435 U.S. 1 (1978), and *Harris v. Rosario*, 446 U.S. 651 (1980), the Court applied the deferential rational-basis test to uphold Congress's decision not to extend certain federal benefits to Puerto Rico, noting that because Congress chose to treat residents of Puerto Rico differently from residents of the States for purposes of tax laws, it could do the same for benefits programs. According to the Court, Congress's decision to exempt Puerto Rico's residents from most federal income, gift, estate, and excise taxes supplied a rational basis for likewise distinguishing residents of Puerto Rico from residents of the states for purposes of the SSI benefits program. *Valleo Madero*, supra, 596 U.S. at 165. According to the Court,

> Puerto Rico's *tax* status—in particular, the fact that residents of Puerto Rico are typically exempt from most federal income, gift, estate, and excise taxes—supplies a rational basis for likewise distinguishing residents of Puerto Rico from residents of the States for purposes of the Supplemental Security Income *benefits* program. In devising tax and benefits programs, it is reasonable for Congress to take account of the general balance of benefits to and burdens on the residents of Puerto Rico. In doing so, Congress need not conduct a dollar-to-dollar comparison of how its tax and benefits programs apply in the States as compared to the Territories, either at the individual or collective level. Congress need only have a rational basis for its tax and benefits programs. Congress has satisfied that requirement here.

Id. (emphasis in original). The Court further noted that the defendant's position "would usher in potentially far-reaching consequences. For one, Congress would presumably need to extend not just Supplemental

Security Income but also many other federal benefits programs to residents of the Territories in the same way that those programs cover residents of the States. And if this Court were to require identical treatment on the benefits side, residents of the States could presumably insist that federal *taxes* be imposed on residents of Puerto Rico and other Territories in the same way that those taxes are imposed on residents of the States. Doing that, however, would inflict significant new financial burdens on residents of Puerto Rico, with serious implications for the Puerto Rican people and the Puerto Rican economy. The Constitution does not require that extreme outcome." Id. at 165-166 (emphasis in original).

As the previous examples suggest, it is almost impossible for a legislatively drawn classification to be found unconstitutional under the traditional rational basis standard of review. As we will see later, there are occasions when the modern Court has struck down classifications ostensibly using the rational basis test. In these cases, however, the Court has at times applied a standard that is in fact more demanding than the traditional rational basis test. See §§ 6.7.2-6.7.4.

One of the few times a law may fail the mere rational basis test is if the legislature has clearly identified a specific purpose for a classification, leaving no room for a reviewing court to hypothesize or speculate about other conceivable bases that might have sufficed to uphold the measure. If the classification does not rationally advance the given or stated purpose, the law will be struck down. See *Nordlinger v. Hahn*, 505 U.S. 1, 14-16 (1992) (upholding California property tax scheme and distinguishing it from nearly identical scheme invalidated in *Allegheny Pittsburgh Coal Co. v. Webster County*, 488 U.S. 336 (1989), on basis that in the latter case, the purpose identified by state law precluded reliance on other conceivable purposes). A classification may also be invalidated under the rational basis test if it is clear that its actual purpose was an illegitimate one. See *United States Dept. of Agric. v. Moreno*, 413 U.S. 528, 534 (1973) (invalidating federal food stamp law where legislative history revealed that law's purpose was to "prevent so-called 'hippies' and 'hippie communes' from participating in the food stamp program").

Example 6-L

EXAMPLE

A city fire ordinance prohibits the operation of fraternity or sorority houses in residential areas of the city, on the stated ground that the occupants of such houses may have difficulty evacuating the building in the event of a fire. The city allows other types of group housing in residential areas, including regular student dormitories, boarding houses, senior citizen housing, and nursing homes. Is the city's discrimination against fraternity and sorority houses rationally related to a legitimate governmental purpose?

EXPLANATION

Explanation

Perhaps not. Unless the city can demonstrate that there is something about fraternity and sorority houses that exposes their occupants to special risk in time of fire, the discrimination is literally irrational. To meet its burden, the city would have to explain why, in terms of fire safety, it allows student dormitories, boarding houses, and senior citizen and nursing homes, while prohibiting fraternity and sorority houses. All would seem to be equally safe and equally risky in the event of a fire. In terms of equal protection, in the absence of any relevant distinction between the permitted uses and the prohibited use, the classification would not rationally advance the city's avowed interest in fire safety.

If the ordinance had not identified fire safety as the purpose of the ban, the city could more easily defend the measure against an equal protection attack by arguing that the discrimination against fraternity and sorority houses is rationally related to another legitimate governmental purpose—i.e., preserving residential tranquility. Since the occupants of fraternity and sorority houses are often particularly loud and boisterous, the ordinance's distinction between them and other types of group housing would rationally further the goal of maintaining peace in residential areas. However, the fact that the ordinance specifically identified fire safety as the purpose of the ban precludes any plausible inference that the reason for the discrimination was that of residential tranquility.

We now leave the rational basis test and turn to those classifications that trigger some form of heightened scrutiny under the equal protection provisions of the Fifth and Fourteenth Amendments. We will visit the rational basis test again, however, for, as noted above, the Court in certain circumstances has been willing to apply the test with somewhat greater rigor. See §§ 6.7.2-6.7.4.

§6.4 CLASSIFICATIONS ON THE BASIS OF RACE OR NATIONAL ORIGIN

§6.4.1 Race as a Suspect Classification

The Court's Early Treatment of Race

The driving force behind the adoption of the Fourteenth Amendment was a determination to prevent states from continuing to discriminate against the recently emancipated slaves. Under the Black Codes adopted at the end of the Civil War throughout most of the former Confederacy, ex-slaves were typically

> forbidden to appear in the towns in any other character than menial servants. They were required to reside on and cultivate the soil without the right to purchase or own it. They were excluded from many occupations of gain, and were not permitted to give testimony in the courts in any case where a white man was a party. It was said that their lives were at the mercy of bad men, either because the laws for their protection were insufficient or were not enforced.

Slaughter-House Cases, 83 U.S. (16 Wall.) 36, 70 (1872). While the Reconstruction-era Congress enacted a series of civil rights laws prohibiting mistreatment of the former slaves, Congress realized the importance of making these protections permanent and unrepealable by enshrining them in the Constitution. To this end, Congress approved the Fourteenth Amendment and sent it to the states for ratification. States that had joined the Confederacy were required to approve the Amendment as a condition for readmission to the Union.

The history of the Fourteenth Amendment makes clear that the "evil to be remedied" by its adoption was "[t]he existence of laws in the States where the newly emancipated negroes resided, which discriminated with gross injustice and hardship against them as a class. . . ." Id. at 81. Indeed, when the Supreme Court first construed the Equal Protection Clause of the Fourteenth Amendment in 1872, it expressed "doubt . . . whether any action of a State not directed by way of discrimination against the negroes as a class, or on account of their race, will ever be held to come within the purview of this provision." Id. It is not surprising that the Court in a number of early cases invoked the Equal Protection Clause to strike down state and local laws that discriminated against blacks. In *Strauder v. West Virginia*, 100 U.S. (10 Otto) 303 (1880), the Court thus used the clause to reverse the conviction of a black defendant because state law excluded blacks from the jury. Six years later the Court extended the clause to protect Chinese aliens living in this country, holding that the Fourteenth Amendment's protections are "universal in their application, to all persons within the territorial jurisdiction [of a state], without regard to any differences of race, of color, or of nationality. . . ." *Yick Wo v. Hopkins*, 118 U.S. 356, 369 (1886).

Despite its early promise as a shield against discrimination on the basis of race or national origin, the Equal Protection Clause suffered a near-crippling blow in *Plessy v. Ferguson*, 163 U.S. 537 (1896). There, the Supreme Court upheld a "Jim Crow" law enacted in 1890 by Louisiana that required railroads to "provide equal but separate accommodations for the white, and colored races. . . ." Id. at 540. *Plessy* explained that state laws forcibly segregating the races—whether in railroad cars, public schools, or marriage—do not offend the Equal Protection Clause because they are "reasonable regulation[s]" aimed at "the preservation of the public peace and good order." Id. at 550. If such state-mandated segregation "stamps the colored race with a badge of inferiority," said the Court, "it is not by reason of anything found in the act, but solely because the colored race chooses to put that construction upon it." Id. at 551. The "separate but equal" doctrine created by *Plessy* in effect treated laws imposing racial segregation as having no disproportionate impact on racial minorities and hence as not being subject to heightened scrutiny under the Equal Protection Clause. In the wake of *Plessy*, laws imposing racial segregation were typically upheld under a rational basis standard of review if the state provided some sort of separate facilities for blacks.

The tide began to turn during the 1940s, although it took decades to correct the approach. In *Korematsu v. United States*, 323 U.S. 214, 216 (1944), while the Court upheld the government's wartime evacuation of Japanese Americans from the West Coast, it observed that "all legal restrictions which curtail the civil rights of a single racial group are immediately suspect" and subject "to the most rigid scrutiny." Four years later in *Shelley v. Kraemer*, 334 U.S. 1 (1948), the Court invoked the Equal Protection Clause to overturn a state court's enforcement of a racially restrictive covenant. With *Brown v. Board of Education*, 347 U.S. 483 (1954), the Equal Protection Clause finally recovered from the blow sustained in *Plessy*. In *Brown* and its progeny, the Court emphatically rejected the doctrine of separate but equal. Instead, said the Court, laws that classify on the basis of race or national origin are "odious to a free people," and if "they are ever to be upheld, they must be shown to be necessary to the accomplishment of some permissible state objective, independent of the racial discrimination which it was the object of the Fourteenth Amendment to eliminate." *Loving v.Virginia*, 388 U.S. 1, 11 (1967).

In *Trump v. Hawaii*, 585 U.S. 667 (2018), the Court finally repudiated its ruling in *Korematsu*, a case whose rhetoric of "most rigid scrutiny" was not matched by its ruling which upheld the wartime internment of Japanese Americans. In the Court's words, "The forcible relocation of U.S. citizens to concentration camps, solely and explicitly on the basis of race, is objectively unlawful and outside the scope of Presidential authority. . . . *Korematsu* was gravely wrong the day it was decided, has been overruled in the court of history, and—to be clear—'has no place in law under the Constitution.'" Id. at 710 (quoting *Korematsu*, supra, 323 U.S. at 248 (Jackson, J., dissenting)). And in *Students for Fair Admissions, Inc. v. President and Fellows of Harvard College*, 600 U.S. 181, 206 (2023), the Court reaffirmed that "the 'core purpose' of the Equal Protection Clause [is] 'do[ing] away with all governmentally imposed discrimination based on race.'"

The Rationale for Strict Scrutiny

The Court's determination to strictly scrutinize laws that discriminate against racial minorities is not only consistent with the goals of the Fourteenth Amendment but is also justified by principles of democratic theory. In a democratic society, most decisions are made through the give-and-take of the majoritarian political process. Individuals and groups debate and decide issues under a principle of majority rule. Even groups that are themselves too small to command a majority may prevail on a particular issue by forming alliances with other groups, whom they may in turn agree to support on other issues. It is inevitable in such a process that some will win and some will lose. It would be utterly destructive of democratic principles if the losers in this process could routinely turn to the courts to reverse the defeat they suffered in the political arena. For this reason, federal courts normally apply a strong presumption in favor of the constitutionality of state and federal laws.

There may be times, however, when the political process cannot be trusted to produce outcomes that are fair to all concerned. In footnote four of *United States v. Carolene Products Co.*, 304 U.S. 144, 152-153 n.4 (1938), Justice Stone identified a number of circumstances under which "more exacting judicial scrutiny" might be warranted. One of these involves legislation "directed at particular religious . . . or national . . . or racial minorities." As Stone observed, "[P]rejudice against discrete and insular minorities may be a special condition, which tends seriously to curtail the operation of those political processes ordinarily to be relied upon to protect minorities, and which may call for a correspondingly more searching judicial inquiry." Id. Where the political process has been skewed by prejudice against those who are targeted by a law, judicial deference is no longer warranted by the assumption that those who lost out in that process were given equal justice. Instead, because the political process may have malfunctioned, closer judicial review is warranted to ensure that the law in question was not based on mere animus or a desire to harm.

In the years since Justice Stone wrote footnote four, the Court and commentators have noted that several types of "prejudice" and related factors may distort the legislative process in ways that call for heightened scrutiny. In *Democracy and Distrust: A Theory of Judicial Review* (1980), John Hart Ely suggested a distinction between first-degree prejudice and second-degree prejudice. First-degree prejudice involves outright hostility, dislike, or a simple desire to harm a particular group. Second-degree prejudice refers to exaggerated negative generalizations or stereotypes about a certain group, such as the belief that all or most members of the group are stupid, dishonest, dangerous, or silly—when in fact these traits are shared by only a normal or relatively small portion of the group. If legislators harbor either of these forms of prejudice toward those burdened by a law, there is a good chance that the group's interests were undervalued or entirely ignored in the legislative process. Ely observed that the legislative process may also be distorted if the trait that defines the targeted group involves an immutable characteristic. In such cases, a legislator's ability to empathize with the burdened class may be curtailed by the fact that unless the trait is widely shared, most legislators will never have been in the group's shoes and need never fear being there. Like first and second-degree prejudice, the factor of immutability may sometimes cause the interests of the targeted group to receive minimal, if any, consideration in the legislative process. Moreover, if the immutable trait is one that is generally irrelevant to a person's ability, use of that trait as a classifying factor may suggest the presence of either first- or second-degree prejudice. Finally, some groups may simply have been excluded from the political process by laws that deny them the right to vote or that effectively undermine their ability to be heard within the political arena.

All of these suggested rationales for heightened scrutiny apply with respect to laws that disadvantage racial minorities. In terms of first-degree prejudice, this nation's history of black slavery and racial discrimination leaves no doubt that racial minorities have been and are often still the objects of hatred and vilification. Second-degree prejudice is likewise present in the form of widespread and exaggerated negative stereotypes about the intelligence, morality, industry, and honesty of racial minority groups. Next, race is an immutable characteristic; and since most legislators are white, there is a danger that laws singling out racial minorities for adverse treatment may have been adopted because of the legislature's inability to empathize with those targeted by the measure. In addition, race is irrelevant to a person's abilities. Finally, racial minorities have historically been excluded from the political process, initially by outright denial of the right to vote and later through such devices as literacy tests, poll taxes, and physical intimidation.

§6.4.2 Scrutiny as a Measure of Constitutionality

Laws or practices that draw distinctions on the basis of race or national origin are inherently suspect and are universally subject to strict scrutiny under the equal protection provisions of the Fifth and Fourteenth Amendments. See, e.g., *Johnson v. California*, 543 U.S. 499, 505 (2005) (strict scrutiny applies to all government-sponsored racial classifications). In *Johnson*, the Court specifically rejected an invitation to lower the strict standard of review in the context of an equal protection challenge to a state prison policy that housed inmates according to race. Instead, the *Johnson* Court refused "to make an exception to the rule that strict scrutiny applies to all racial classifications," regardless of context. Id. at 509. As we will see later, strict scrutiny is also applied to many classifications drawn on the basis of alienage and to classifications that bear on the exercise of a fundamental right. While the method of analysis is the same in all these areas, the strict scrutiny standard is applied with special rigor in cases that involve racial or national origin discrimination. More recently, in *Students for Fair Admissions, Inc. v. President and Fellows of Harvard College*, supra, 600 U.S. at 217 n.5, the Court suggested that Justice Jackson's dissent in that same case "candidly advocates abandoning the demands of strict scrutiny . . . (arguing the Court must 'get out of the way,' 'leav[e] well enough alone,' and defer to universities and 'experts' in determining who should be discriminated against)." See id. at 407-410 (Jackson, J., et al., dissenting). Whether that is a correct interpretation of Justice Jackson's dissent, strict scrutiny remains the standard where applicable. As the Court noted, "[a]ny exception to the Constitution's demand for equal protection must survive a daunting two-step examination known in our cases as 'strict scrutiny.' Under that standard we ask, first, whether the racial classification is used to 'further compelling governmental interests.' Second, if so, we ask whether the government's use of race is 'narrowly tailored'—meaning 'necessary'—to achieve that interest." Id. at 206-207 (internal citation omitted).

Thus, a law or practice that is subjected to strict scrutiny under the Equal Protection Clause will pass constitutional muster only if it can be demonstrated that the challenged classification is (1) justified by a compelling governmental interest and (2) narrowly tailored to furthering that interest. Unless both of these requirements are met, the classification will be struck down because of the danger that its real purpose is to harm those burdened by the law or to discourage them from exercising a fundamental constitutional right.

Compelling Interest

The first step in testing a classification under strict scrutiny is to determine whether it is justified by a compelling governmental interest. The notion of a *compelling* governmental interest implies that not all legitimate governmental interests are important enough to justify a classification that is subject to strict scrutiny. The Court has not developed any formula for distinguishing among legitimate, important, and compelling governmental interests. Yet it has at times held that a governmental interest, while legitimate, is not weighty enough to satisfy this part of the strict scrutiny test. For example, the Court has held that administrative convenience, although clearly a legitimate state interest, is not sufficiently important to warrant the "compelling" label. *Frontiero v. Richardson*, 411 U.S. 677, 690-691 (1973).

In some cases, the Court may doubt the intrinsic importance of the asserted state interest. In such instances, the Court may insist that the law's defender "advance a factual showing" that the classification addresses "a real, as opposed to a merely speculative, problem to the State." *Bernal v. Fainter*, 467 U.S. 216, 227-228 (1984). In the absence of such a showing, the Court may reject the alleged goal on the ground that it "lacks the weight we have required of interests properly denominated as compelling." Id. at 228.

Even if an asserted governmental interest is important enough to qualify as compelling, the defender of the law "must show that the alleged objective was the legislature's 'actual purpose' for the discriminatory classification," as opposed to engaging in mere "speculation about what 'may have motivated' the legislature." *Shaw v. Hunt*, 517 U.S. 899, 908 n.4 (1996). Moreover, it is not enough to show that "some legislators" had the asserted purpose in mind; instead, it must be demonstrated that the purpose was one that motivated enough legislators to cause the legislation to be adopted. Id. at 910.

Finally, even if an asserted governmental interest might otherwise qualify as compelling, the Court may conclude that any harm to that interest is too minor to justify the classification in question. Thus, in *Nyquist v. Mauclet*, 432 U.S. 1 (1977), New York claimed that denying scholarships to aliens who did not intend to become citizens furthered the compelling interest of educating the electorate, since the money denied to these aliens was paid instead to persons eligible to vote. The Court rejected the state's argument, noting that because only a small number of aliens were disqualified under this law, including them would have only "an insubstantial impact" on the state's otherwise compelling goal. Id. at 11-12 n.15.

Narrowly Tailored

If, under the first part of the strict scrutiny test, a court accepts that a classification was designed to further a compelling governmental interest, the measure will be upheld only if it is also narrowly tailored to furthering that interest. Narrowly tailored means that "the classification at issue must 'fit'" the alleged compelling interest "with greater precision than any alternative means." *Wygant v. Jackson Bd. of Educ.*, 476 U.S. 267, 280 n.6 (1986). If there were other means available to the government that would have achieved the asserted goal better, it becomes doubtful that the classification was really designed to further that goal. Instead, the inadequacy of the "fit" confirms our initial suspicion that the measure was designed for the improper purpose of harming the affected group or discouraging the exercise of a fundamental constitutional right.

Consider this analogy. After a clothing store was robbed, the police stop a man who was running down the street carrying an expensive suit. They suspect that the suit was stolen from the store, but the man claims it is his. The officers ask the man to try the suit on. If, when he does so, the suit is narrowly tailored and fits him well, the officers are likely to accept the man's assertion that the suit belongs to him. If, on the other hand, the fit is poor—e.g., the cuffed pants are too long and the sleeves are too short—the fact that the suit is not narrowly tailored to its alleged owner tends to confirm the suspicion that it was designed for someone else.

The "fit" of a statutory classification is likewise described in terms of how well it is tailored to its asserted goal. If the measure covers persons or activities that are irrelevant in terms of the alleged goal, the classification is said to be overinclusive (i.e., too big). If, on the other hand, the statute does not apply to persons or activities one would expect it to cover, the classification is underinclusive in relation to its goal (i.e., too small). Some laws are both overinclusive and underinclusive in terms of their underlying goals. If it would have been relatively easy to draft the measure so that it was more closely tailored to the alleged goal, the fact that the fit is so poor strongly suggests that the measure was really designed with some other purpose in mind.

The Court sometimes describes the strict scrutiny equal protection test in terms of whether there is a less discriminatory alternative available for attaining the government's asserted purposes. By "less discriminatory," the Court means alternatives that are not as overinclusive or underinclusive as the means chosen by the government and that will, therefore, accomplish the state's goal with less of a disproportionate impact on the affected group. If such less discriminatory alternatives exist, then under strict scrutiny, the government must use them rather than the poorly tailored measure it has adopted.

EXAMPLE

Example 6-M

A state law requires that hospital emergency room personnel have been born in the United States. This law creates a suspect classification based on national origin. It was challenged by Carlos, a naturalized U.S. citizen who was born in Mexico and who, because of the law, was refused a job in a local emergency room. The state has defended the law on the ground that it furthers a compelling interest in health and safety by assuring that emergency room personnel speak and understand English well enough to communicate perfectly with patients and medical staff. If the court accepts this interest as being compelling, will the law survive Carlos's equal protection challenge?

EXPLANATION

Explanation

Under the "narrowly tailored" prong of the strict scrutiny test, this law must "fit" its alleged health and safety purpose better than any feasible alternative. The law is overinclusive in relation to its goal, for it applies to persons of foreign origin who speak and understand English perfectly. The law is also underinclusive, since it apparently allows anyone born in the United States to work in an emergency room even if that person's English is poor. If the state was really concerned about English fluency in hospitals, it could have achieved its goal as well or better by requiring all prospective employees to pass an English proficiency exam. The facts that the law is so poorly tailored to its alleged goal and that a less discriminatory alternative is available strongly suggest that the asserted health goal is a sham and that the law's real purpose is simply to burden people of foreign origin on the basis of prejudice or dislike. This law would, therefore, be found to violate the Equal Protection Clause.

As this example suggests, the second prong of the strict scrutiny equal protection analysis serves the same purpose as the first prong. Both are designed to ascertain whether the government was discriminating for an illicit purpose. In the words of the Court,

> the purpose of strict scrutiny is to "smoke out" illegitimate uses of race by assuring that the legislative body is pursuing a goal important enough to warrant use of a highly suspect tool. The test also ensures that the means chosen "fit" this compelling goal so closely that there is little or no possibility that the motive for the classification was illegitimate racial prejudice or stereotype.

City of Richmond v. J. A. Croson Co., 488 U.S. 469, 493 (1989).

We turn now to an examination of how the strict scrutiny standard has been applied to classifications based on race or alienage. In the next chapter, we will return to the strict scrutiny standard and look at its application in cases that involve discrimination tied to the exercise of a fundamental constitutional right.

§6.4.3 Racial Segregation of Public Schools

Brown v. Board of Education

In *Brown v. Board of Education*, 347 U.S. 483 (1954) (*Brown I*), the Court invoked the Fourteenth Amendment's Equal Protection Clause to strike down laws in Kansas, South Carolina, Virginia, and Delaware that required or permitted racial segregation of the public schools. Laws in each of these states provided for assignment of pupils to schools based on race, with the result that most schools were largely all-black or all-white in composition.

Since *Brown I* is widely regarded as one of the first cases in which the modern Court applied strict scrutiny to a race-based classification, it is interesting that the Court did not actually apply the strict scrutiny test. There was no discussion of whether the states had a compelling interest in creating racially segregated schools or of whether the states' pupil assignment laws were narrowly tailored. These omissions are explained by the fact that the states never suggested that they had a legitimate, much less compelling, reason for segregating their public schools. Instead, the states in effect argued that the plaintiffs had failed to make out a prima facie case of racial discrimination. The intent element of the prima facie case was established by the fact that the statutes in each of the four states were racially discriminatory on their face. However, the states relied on the "separate but equal" doctrine of *Plessy v. Ferguson*, 163 U.S. 537 (1896) (see § 6.4.1), to deny the existence of any disproportionate impact on black children who were forced to attend all-black schools.

Though the Supreme Court in *Brown I* was asked to overrule *Plessy*, it stopped short of doing so. Instead, the Justices applied the "separate but equal" doctrine in the context of public education and concluded that "[s]eparate educational facilities are inherently unequal." 347 U.S. at 495. The Court agreed that "the Negro and white schools involved have been equalized . . . with respect to buildings, curricula, qualifications and salaries of teachers, and other 'tangible' factors." Id. at 492. Yet despite this ostensible equalization, the Court concluded that the education provided in segregated schools was inherently unequal for two reasons. First, the intangible qualities that make a school great are "incapable of objective measurement." Id. at 494. Second, forced segregation in public education harms black schoolchildren. "To separate them from others of similar age and qualifications solely because of their race generates a feeling of inferiority as to their status in the community that may affect their hearts and minds in a way unlikely ever to be undone." Id. For these reasons, said the Court, "in the field of public education the doctrine of 'separate but equal' has no place." Id. at 495. Since the states did not attempt to justify their purposeful racial discrimination, the Court held that the discrimination violated the Equal Protection Clause of the Fourteenth Amendment. In *Bolling v. Sharpe*, 347 U.S. 497, 500 (1954), a companion case decided the same day as *Brown I*, the Court held that the Fifth Amendment—which contains no Equal Protection Clause—likewise barred the federal government from segregating schools in the District of Columbia because this "constitute[d] an arbitrary deprivation of . . . liberty in violation of the Due Process Clause."

The Court's opinion in *Brown I* at least implied that in settings other than public education, government-imposed racial segregation might not violate the Equal Protection Clause if it did not result in any measurable harm to racial minorities. Yet in a series of per curiam orders issued in the years following *Brown I*, the Court held that racial segregation of public facilities was unconstitutional even in settings where *Brown I*'s psychological impairment rationale was clearly inapplicable. These decisions—involving segregation of public beaches, bathhouses, golf courses, parks, municipal buses, athletics contests, and courtroom seating—made it clear that *Plessy*'s doctrine of separate but equal had been overruled sub silentio. Today, the Equal Protection Clause prohibits the government from mandating racial segregation of any public facilities.

Implementing Brown

It was initially unclear what duty *Brown I* imposed on school boards that had operated racially segregated schools. In a remedial decision handed down a year after *Brown I*, the Court suggested that the goal was "to achieve a system of determining admission to the public schools on a nonracial basis." *Brown v. Board of Education*, 349 U.S. 294, 300-301 (1955) (*Brown II*). Some states construed this command as one of "desegregation, not integration." Under this approach, it was enough for a state to cease forcing students to attend racially segregated schools, but the state was under no duty to dismantle its dual system of schools and bring about a unitary, integrated school system. Under this "desegregation, not integration" approach, states adopted freedom-of-choice plans that let students decide which school they would attend. Not surprisingly, this scheme left many schools largely all-white or all-black.

In *Green v. County School Board*, 391 U.S. 430, 436 (1968), decided 14 years after *Brown I*, the Court emphatically rejected the "desegregation, not integration" formula and held that "[t]he transition to a unitary, nonracial system of public education was and is the ultimate end to be brought about. . . ." School boards that had been guilty of operating racially segregated public schools were "charged with the affirmative duty to take whatever steps might be necessary to convert to a unitary system in which racial discrimination would be eliminated root and branch." Id. at 437-438.

Green identified six parts of a school system that a court must examine to determine whether a dual school system has been converted to unitary status. For a school district to be in full compliance with *Brown II*, each of these six aspects of the system must be free of racial discrimination. The first of the *Green* factors is the pattern of student attendance—i.e., the racial composition of each school. In *Swann v. Charlotte-Mecklenburg Board of Education*, 402 U.S. 1 (1971), the Court noted that the goal is to bring about a racial balance in every school that is roughly comparable to the racial composition of the school district as a whole. If, as in *Swann*, the district as a whole is 71 percent white and 29 percent black, each school in the district should ideally have a racial balance of 71-29 percent; the Court warned, however, that such ratios should be used as targets, not as strict quotas. The five other *Green* factors are faculty allocation, staff allocation, student transportation, extracurricular activities, and physical facilities. Some courts have added an additional factor: the overall quality of education.

To implement the commands of *Brown I*, *Brown II*, and their progeny where a school district has been found to have engaged in de jure segregation, a federal court must fashion remedies that address all these components of a school system and assure that each component is no longer tainted by racial discrimination. The process of federal judicial supervision frequently lasted for decades and encompassed such court-ordered measures as redrawing school attendance zones, busing students to schools outside their neighborhoods, repairing buildings, reassigning and upgrading the quality of teachers and staff, equalizing extracurricular programs, closing schools, and constructing new schools. The Supreme Court stressed that while the specific content of the desegregation remedy would necessarily vary from case to case, the "decree must indeed be *remedial* in nature, that is, it must be designed as nearly as possible 'to restore the victims of discriminatory conduct to the position they would have occupied in the absence of such conduct.'" *Milliken v. Bradley*, 433 U.S. 267, 280 (1977) (emphasis in original).

It is important to remember that federal courts may intervene to redress violations of the Equal Protection Clause only if plaintiffs have first established a prima facie case by proving both intent and impact. These requirements were easily met in *Brown I* and many other early school desegregation cases because the intent to discriminate was clear from the face of state laws providing for racially segregated schools. It was more difficult for plaintiffs to make out a prima facie case in states outside the South, where there was often no statute requiring or authorizing segregation. In these cases, while discriminatory impact was established by showing that a district's schools were racially imbalanced, "the Constitution is not violated by racial imbalance in the schools, without more." Id. at 280 n.14. As was noted previously, proving purpose or intent to discriminate can often be difficult. See § 6.2.2.

§6.4.4 Interdistrict Remedies

Even where a de jure violation has been proved, there are limits on the remedies a federal court may impose. One of these limits concerns the geographic scope of a court's remedial order. The Supreme Court has repeatedly held that "the nature of the desegregation remedy is to be determined by the nature and scope of the constitutional violation." *Milliken v. Bradley*, supra, 433 U.S. at 280. Metropolitan areas have frequently been divided by the state into dozens of independent school districts, each run by its own local school board. If an equal protection violation has been proved with respect to one district, this does not itself establish a violation on the part of adjacent or surrounding districts. In the absence of proof of an interdistrict violation—i.e., a violation that caused segregation in more than one district—a federal court's remedial orders must be limited to the district against which a constitutional violation has been proved. In other words, an intradistrict violation can be redressed only through an intradistrict remedy.

EXAMPLE

Example 6-N

Adams County is divided into five school districts, each run by an independent school board. The public school population in the county as a whole is 80 percent white and 20 percent black. District 1 is 80 percent black and 20 percent white; Districts 2 through 5, located in the surrounding suburbs, are each 90 percent white and 10 percent black. A suit was filed in federal court against the District 1 board, alleging that as a result of the board's purposeful acts, most children in District 1 attend one-race schools. If the judge orders District 1's board to integrate the schools there, each school will still be 80 percent black. May the court add the other four school boards as defendants and then order an interdistrict remedy that will result in each school being approximately 80 percent white and 20 percent black?

EXPLANATION

Explanation

Even if the other boards are added to the suit, the scope of the remedy is limited by the scope of the proven violation. Unless the plaintiffs show that a constitutional violation caused segregation between these adjoining districts, the court cannot order an interdistrict remedy and must confine its relief to District 1. See *Milliken v. Bradley*, 418 U.S. 717 (1974).

Proving an Interdistrict Violation

Plaintiffs may be able to prove an interdistrict violation in several ways. One approach is to show that the state, an adjacent school district, or some other governmental body was guilty of purposeful discriminatory acts that had interdistrict effects. However, in proving the element of discriminatory purpose, plaintiffs cannot use the *Keyes* presumption to transfer intent between different governmental actors. Just because one school board was guilty of purposeful racial discrimination does not make it reasonable to infer that the actions of other entities were also animated by segregative intent. Instead, plaintiffs must independently prove the element of intent as to each separate governmental body.

EXAMPLE

Example 6-O

In Example 6-N, how else might the plaintiffs prove an interdistrict violation?

Explanation

The plaintiffs might prove such a violation if they could show that the state drew or redrew the school district lines for Districts 1 through 5 with a purpose of segregating the schools—i.e., for the purpose of concentrating most of the county's blacks in District 1 while minimizing their presence in Districts 2 through 5. Or plaintiffs might be able to show that the state, for segregative reasons, allowed white children living in District 1 to attend schools in the surrounding suburbs even though students are usually required to enroll in their own district. An interdistrict violation might also exist if the state or an adjacent suburb adopted racially discriminatory housing policies that encouraged whites to move from District 1 to the suburbs, while at the same time making it difficult for racial minorities to do so. Proof of an interdistrict violation by any of these means would allow a federal court to fashion an interdistrict remedy that could require busing of students across district boundary lines.

In each of the prior examples, an interdistrict violation was established by showing that a governmental actor in addition to the targeted school district engaged in purposeful discriminatory conduct. An interdistrict violation may also be proved where the unconstitutional actions of the targeted district itself had segregative effects in other school districts. However, it must be shown that any such interdistrict effects were "significant" and "directly caused" by the constitutional violation.

Example 6-P

In Example 6-O, suppose that the plaintiffs could show that the District 1 school board decided to reduce funding for all schools in the district on account of the fact that the district was heavily minority in composition. As a result, many white families fled to adjacent suburbs, where the schools were better funded. Might this suffice to prove an interdistrict violation?

Explanation

Perhaps. The District 1 board's racially motivated funding decision arguably had significant and direct segregative effects between school districts, for the "white flight" caused by the board's action exacerbated the racial imbalance existing between District 1 and the surrounding suburban districts. This interdistrict violation would allow a federal court to impose an interdistrict remedy that might include busing students across district lines.

These examples of how plaintiffs may establish an interdistrict violation might make it appear simple for a federal court to order interdistrict relief. In reality, plaintiffs are seldom able to make the showing necessary for a court to impose desegregation remedies that cross school district lines.

Responding to White Flight

In the absence of proof of an interdistrict violation, a federal court may encounter severe difficulties in dealing with white flight. The term *white flight* refers to the process by which white families remove their children from a public school. Either the children are sent to a private school, or the family moves to a surrounding district where the public schools are predominately white. The Supreme Court has recognized that "implementation of a desegregation remedy may result in 'white flight'. . . ." *Missouri v. Jenkins*, 515 U.S. 70, 95 n.8 (1995). White parents, who were content to have their children attend segregated neighborhood schools, may balk either at integration or at the forced busing that it often entails. Because of white flight, judicial efforts to integrate the public schools may be self-defeating, for the composition of the district may become so heavily minority that any significant degree of integration is impossible.

A dramatic example of white flight was documented by the Court in *Missouri v. Jenkins*, involving the Kansas City, Missouri, School District (KCMSD). Until 1954, Missouri mandated racial segregation in its public schools; at that time, 18.9 percent of KCMSD's students were black. After *Brown I* was decided in 1954, the state stopped enforcing its school segregation laws; in 1977, the federal court initiated a plan to integrate KCMSD's schools. Between 1954 and 1985, the percentage of KCMSD's students who were black increased steadily, as follows: 1961-1962: 30 percent black; 1965: 40 percent black; 1975-1976: 60 percent black; 1985-1986: 68.3 percent black. While the overall enrollment in the district declined once the integration plan was adopted, white enrollment declined at a much faster rate than that for blacks. *Missouri v. Jenkins,* supra, 515 U.S. at 76, 94 n.6. By 1985, even if every school in the KCMSD were fully integrated, blacks would have comprised more than two-thirds of the students at each school.

Where white flight results from a court's attempt to integrate an urban school district, this does not create an interdistrict violation that would allow the court to include in its remedial decree the surrounding districts to which the white students have fled, for the Supreme Court has held such white flight is a consequence of "desegregation, not de jure segregation." Id. at 95. In other words, the interdistrict segregative effects caused by such white flight cannot serve as the basis for an interdistrict remedy. This does not prevent plaintiffs from trying to prove a direct causal link in some other manner (see Example 6-P), but such proof will ordinarily be difficult.

In response to the threat of white flight, federal courts may be reluctant to push remedies like mandatory busing beyond a certain point, even if this means settling for a less-than-optimal racial balance in some schools. Rather than impose remedies that are likely to be self-defeating, courts have increasingly ordered school districts to adopt programs that are designed both to keep white children from leaving the public schools and to draw them out of private schools back into the public system. One common program of this type involves the use of magnet schools, which offer high-quality, distinctive curricula that are frequently superior to anything found even in the private sector.

Yet in ordering a school district to adopt programs that are designed to retain and attract white students, a federal court must be careful that its decree does not go beyond what is necessary to remedy the proven constitutional violation. If the court requires a district to adopt programs designed to attract nonminority students *from surrounding school districts* to which they may have fled, the court is in effect imposing an interdistrict remedy that is invalid unless there was a proven interdistrict violation.

Example 6-Q

The Central City School District is 32 percent white. Before integration efforts began five years ago, the district was 80 percent white. This decline was largely the result of white flight to the suburbs and enrollment in private schools within the city. The only constitutional violation proved was confined to the city itself. To remedy this intradistrict violation, the federal court has ordered the city to develop a program of magnet schools designed, in part, to attract white students from the suburban districts to the Central City public schools. Is the remedial decree valid?

Explanation

To the extent that the program's purpose is to draw students back into the city from adjacent school districts, it involves the pursuit of an *interdistrict goal* that is beyond the scope of the *intradistrict violation* being remedied. Since the district court could not have directly mandated the interdistrict transfer of students, it may not accomplish the same goal indirectly. On the other hand, the magnet school program would be valid to the extent that it can be justified by the need to limit any further withdrawal of white students from the city's schools and/or by the desire to draw white students out of private schools located within the district. See *Missouri v. Jenkins*, 515 U.S. 70 (1995).

§6.4.5 Remedying Segregation at the College Level

If a state is found to have purposefully racially segregated its public colleges or universities, the remedies available to a court for such de jure segregation will differ from those usually applied to elementary and secondary schools. At the elementary and secondary levels, one of the primary goals in remedying racial segregation is to achieve a racial balance in each school that roughly matches the makeup of the district as a whole. The objective, in other words, is to racially *integrate* a district's schools, not merely to cease segregating them. At the college level, such a goal is impracticable for several reasons. First, a state's colleges are usually geographically dispersed throughout the state. To insist that each college or university be racially balanced would mean that students might be forced to attend a school hundreds of miles—rather than just a few miles—from their homes, a requirement that would be economically prohibitive for many and perhaps also subject to other constitutional challenges.

In addition, unlike most elementary and secondary schools, a state's colleges usually are not fungible or the functional equivalent of one another. Each college may have unique goals, programs, course offerings, and faculty expertise. To force a student to attend a college other than one of her choice would significantly interfere with an individual's ability to shape her education. While the latter problem might be solved by making the state's colleges and universities essentially identical, this could severely constrict the breadth of the state's educational offerings by forcing the state to jettison programs that could not feasibly be provided at every school.

For these reasons, if a federal court finds that a state has deliberately maintained a racially segregated system of colleges or universities, the court cannot simply order the state to integrate these schools, as could be done at the elementary or secondary level. However, the federal court may compel the state to abandon any policies, practices, or requirements that meet the following four conditions:

1. The policy was part of or is traceable to the prior de jure segregated system;
2. The policy continues to have segregative effects, such as influencing student enrollment decisions in a racially discriminatory way;
3. The policy lacks a sound educational justification; and
4. The policy can practicably be eliminated.

If the plaintiff carries the burden of establishing that the first two conditions are met as to a particular policy, the policy must be eliminated unless the state demonstrates that the policy is supported by a sound educational justification or that it cannot practicably be eliminated. See *United States v. Fordice*, 505 U.S. 717, 728-731 (1992).

EXAMPLE

Example 6-R

A state operates four colleges—two in the north (N-1 and N-2) and two in the south (S-1 and S-2). The state was found to have purposefully segregated these colleges based on race, so that N-1 and S-l were primarily white institutions, while N-2 and S-2 were historically black colleges. To be admitted to N-1 or S-l, a student had to score at least 15 on the ACT college admission test; about 70 percent of white applicants met this requirement as compared with 30 percent of blacks. On the other hand, to be admitted to N-2 or S-2, a student needed an ACT score of only 13 or higher. N-1 and N-2 duplicate many courses and programs; the same is true of S-l and S-2. The combined student population at all four colleges is 60 percent white and 40 percent black. What might a federal court do to remedy the state's racial discrimination?

EXPLANATION

Explanation

While the court cannot order the state to achieve a 60-40 percent racial balance at each college, it can insist on the elimination of many policies that support the present segregated scheme. For example, the use of a higher minimum ACT score for admission to N-1 and S-l than for admission to N-2 and S-2 might have to be abandoned, for the policy has a clear segregative effect, may lack a sound educational justification, and could practicably be eliminated. Indeed, the state might have to abandon rigid adherence to even a uniform ACT minimum score if it were shown that a more flexible formula that considers a student's high school grades would serve the state's legitimate admissions goals.

The state might also have to end any unnecessary duplication of programs and courses between N-1 and N-2 and between S-l and S-2. Unnecessary duplication has a racially segregative effect, for if students in the northern part of the state could pursue a particular program only at N-l or N-2, but not both, students of all races who wished to take that program would end up attending the same school. Therefore, unless the state can offer a sound educational justification for such duplication, the practice would have to be eliminated. See *United States v. Fordice*, 505 U.S. 717 (1992).

§6.4.6 Other Limitations on Desegregation Orders

Minimizing the Degree of Federal Interference

When federal courts use their equitable powers to impose remedies in desegregation cases, they "must take into account the interests of state and local authorities in managing their own affairs, consistent with the Constitution." *Milliken v. Bradley*, supra, 433 U.S. at 280-281. This principle, which reflects notions of comity and federalism, dictates that federal courts exercise their authority in a manner that avoids unnecessary interference with or intrusion on state and local governmental functions.

Example 6-S

In Example 6-Q, assume that the federal district court ordered the Central City School District to develop a program of magnet schools aimed at keeping students in the city's public schools and at drawing students who live in the city into the public system from private schools. The cost of this program is estimated to be $10 million. The Central City School District receives most of its operating expenses from a property tax that it is authorized to impose under state law. However, the state constitution prohibits the district from raising this tax by an amount sufficient to pay for the desegregation program. May the federal court order an increase in the local property tax?

Explanation

The court must use the least intrusive form of relief that will effectively achieve its remedial goal. For a federal court itself to impose a state tax is a drastic and, in this case, unnecessary interference with local governmental authority. The court can achieve the same end by ordering the school district to raise the property tax by the requisite amount and by enjoining operation of the state constitutional provision that would otherwise bar the district from exercising this power. See *Missouri v. Jenkins*, 495 U.S. 33 (1990).

The same principle applies to a federal court's exercise of its contempt power in enforcing desegregation orders against recalcitrant state or local officials. While the contempt power may be used for these purposes in the desegregation context, the court must proceed cautiously, exercising "[t]he least possible power adequate to the end proposed. . . ." *Anderson v. Dunn*, 19 U.S. (6 Wheat.) 204, 231 (1821).

Example 6-T

In Example 6-S, assume that the Central City School Board, which runs the school district, refused to comply with the federal court's order that it increase the local property tax. After warning the district that failure to comply would result in the imposition of contempt sanctions, the court issued an order providing that if the school board did not vote to raise the property tax before September 1, individual board members would be imprisoned by the U.S. marshal and fined $500 a day for each day of noncompliance. Is this order valid?

Explanation

The order is probably invalid because it is more intrusive than necessary to secure compliance with the desegregation order. Before threatening individual board members with imprisonment and fines, the court could first have tried imposing fines on the school district itself. If this failed to produce compliance within a reasonable time, it might then have been appropriate for the court to increase the pressure by proceeding against the board members individually. See *Spallone v. United States*, 493 U.S. 265 (1990).

Duration of Federal Desegregation Orders

The goal of federal judicial intervention in desegregation cases is to remedy the constitutional violation to the extent practicable and then "restore state and local authorities to the control of a school system that is operating in compliance with the Constitution." *Freeman v. Pitts*, 503 U.S. 467, 489 (1992). Federal oversight is "intended as a temporary measure to remedy past discrimination." *Board of Educ. v. Dowell*, 498 U.S. 237, 247 (1991). The Court has stressed that "[r]eturning schools to the control of local authorities at the earliest practicable date is essential to restore their true accountability in our governmental system." *Freeman v. Pitts*, supra, 503 U.S. at 490. As a practical matter, the period of federal judicial tutelage may last for decades as the court seeks to eliminate the vestiges of past discrimination in all aspects of the school system. Yet a district that has complied in good faith with the court's decree is eventually entitled to partial or complete relief from further federal supervision.

The proper duration of a federal desegregation decree is closely tied to the legitimate scope of that decree. A federal court may retain jurisdiction over a school district solely for the purpose of assuring that "the vestiges of past discrimination [have] been eliminated to the extent practicable." Id. at 492. The court may not continue to exercise supervisory authority to redress problems that are "not traceable, in a proximate way, to the prior violation." Id. at 494. For example, a federal court may not maintain control over a school district with the goal of bringing the quality of the educational program up to national norms in all grade levels unless these deficiencies are clearly attributable to a past constitutional violation. See *Missouri v. Jenkins*, 515 U.S. 70 (1995).

Even if a particular problem being addressed by a federal decree was at one time traceable to prior de jure segregation, the passage of time may have eliminated any causal link between current conditions and the constitutional violation, in which case the condition is no longer one the federal court can insist on rectifying. Instead, the court may well have to relinquish jurisdiction, at least with respect to that particular area of school operations.

EXAMPLE

Example 6-U

Fifteen years ago, a federal court ruled that the Dixon School Board had segregated the district's schools. In its desegregation decree, the court ordered the board to achieve an approximate racial balance of 65 percent white and 35 percent black at each school, matching the composition of the district as a whole. The board achieved compliance with this decree ten years ago by adjusting attendance zones, creating magnet schools, and adopting a busing plan. In the past few years, however, four schools in the southern part of the district have become more than 80 percent black, though the district as a whole remains 65 percent white and 35 percent black. The plaintiffs seek an order requiring the board to remedy the racial imbalance in these four schools. May the court order this relief?

EXPLANATION

Explanation

The federal court may redress this condition only if it is in fact a vestige of the prior de jure system. If the board can show that the current racial imbalance in the four schools is not traceable to past segregation but is instead a result of demographic shifts in population, the racial imbalance would be beyond the court's remedial powers. Not only would the court lack authority to redress this problem, but the board might also be entitled to have the court relinquish remedial control over the student assignment facet of the school system or even have the entire desegregation case finally dismissed. See *Freeman v. Pitts*, 503 U.S. 467 (1992); *Pasadena City Bd. of Educ. v. Spangler*, 427 U.S. 424 (1976).

In the previous example, if the federal court terminated its jurisdiction over the Dixon School Board, releasing the board from the desegregation plan, the board would be free to make any operational changes it wished without needing authorization from a federal court. Such changes might entail dismantling the busing program or closing the magnet schools, programs that had been critical to maintaining an integrated system. While these changes may well produce new racial imbalance in the district's schools, the board's action would violate the Constitution only if the plaintiffs could establish a new prima facie case of de jure segregation. In proving a prima facie case, the plaintiffs could invoke the *Keyes* presumption to establish discriminatory intent on the basis of the board's earlier de jure violation. However, the board might rebut this presumption by noting that it acted in good faith for many years since the past violation occurred, or by demonstrating that the program changes were made for budgetary or other reasons that had nothing to do with race. Thus, once a federal court relinquishes control over a school district, as it must at some point, there remains "the potential for discrimination and racial hostility . . . and its manifestations may emerge in new and subtle forms after the effects of *de jure* segregation have been eliminated." *Freeman v. Pitts*, supra, 503 U.S. at 490. Yet this danger does not justify a federal court's retaining perpetual jurisdiction over a school district simply because the district once violated the Constitution.

A federal desegregation decree usually covers a number of different facets of a school system, as identified by the *Green* factors. The court may order a partial withdrawal of its supervision in those areas where a school district has achieved compliance with the court's desegregation plan, even though other areas have not yet been brought into compliance. In *Freeman v. Pitts*, supra, 503 U.S. at 491, the Court held that such an incremental relinquishment of jurisdiction is permissible if three requirements are satisfied:

1. There has been full and satisfactory compliance with the desegregation decree in those aspects of the school system where supervision is to be withdrawn;
2. Retaining control is not necessary or practicable to achieve compliance in other facets of the school system; and
3. The school district has shown its good-faith commitment to the entire desegregation plan for a reasonable period of time.

EXAMPLE

Example 6-V

In Example 6-U, assume that the Dixon School Board has moved the court to relinquish control over student assignment policies on the ground that the board has achieved full compliance with this component of the desegregation plan. Two other facets of the system—achieving racial balance in teacher allocation and upgrading athletic facilities at two formerly black schools—are not yet in full compliance, though considerable progress has been made in these areas. May the court grant the motion to partially withdraw supervision?

EXPLANATION

Explanation

The court could probably grant the motion to relinquish control over the assignment of students to schools. First, if the current racial imbalance in the four schools in the south end of the district was caused by demographic shifts and is not traceable to the prior constitutional violation, the board remains in full compliance with the aspect of the court's decree requiring racial balance in student assignments. Second, it appears that withdrawing control over student assignment policies will not impair the court's ability to secure compliance in the two other areas dealing with teacher assignments and athletic facilities. Third, since the board reached compliance in the area of student assignments ten years ago, if the court is satisfied that the board has demonstrated a genuine commitment to the principle of racial equality in its efforts to comply with other aspects of the desegregation plan, partial withdrawal of control would be appropriate. On the other hand, if the board's efforts in the two remaining areas have been halting or lackluster, casting doubt on its good-faith commitment to integration, the court should not relinquish even partial control until the board has attained full compliance with all aspects of the court's decree for a reasonable period of time.

§6.4.7 Affirmative Action

In the previous sections, we have examined cases in which the government used race in a manner designed to harm a racial minority. The standard of review was consistently strict scrutiny. Sometimes, however, the government uses race to provide a benefit to a member of a racial minority group. For example, a government agency might use an applicant's race as a positive factor in making a hiring decision, the goal being either to remediate past discrimination against members of that race or to promote racial diversity in government employment. Or a state university might use race as a factor in an admissions decision. Such race-based uses of "affirmative action" have been challenged as being inconsistent with the equal protection guarantee. This section examines the Court's approach to resolving such challenges.

Strict Scrutiny for Affirmative Action

In *City of Richmond v. J. A. Croson Co.*, 488 U.S. 469 (1989), the Supreme Court held that all laws that purposefully discriminate based on race are subject to strict scrutiny under the Equal Protection Clause, including laws that discriminate against whites. *Croson* resolved a debate that had been simmering in the Court for more than a decade. In *Regents of the University of California v. Bakke*, 438 U.S. 265 (1978), Justice Brennan and three of his colleagues had urged that since whites are not a "discrete and insular minority" needing special protection from the majoritarian political process, only intermediate scrutiny should be applied to laws that discriminate against whites for benign purposes. Id. at 359-362. Justice Powell, on the other hand, had argued that strict scrutiny is required in all race discrimination cases, since the guarantee of equal protection is a personal right that "cannot mean one thing when applied to one individual and something else when applied to a person of another color." Id. at 289-290. In *Croson*, a majority of the Court adopted the position staked out by Justice Powell in *Bakke*. The *Croson* majority noted that strict scrutiny is necessary to assure that allegedly benign classifications are not "in fact motivated by illegitimate notions of racial inferiority or simple racial politics," and to assure that they do not inflict "stigmatic harm" on those they are intended to benefit. 488 U.S. at 493. Applying strict scrutiny, *Croson* struck down a Richmond, Virginia, plan that required prime contractors awarded city construction contracts to subcontract at least 30 percent of the work to minority business enterprises (MBEs).

Croson's strict scrutiny principle was limited to affirmative action undertaken by state and local governments. In an earlier case, *Fullilove v. Klutznick*, 448 U.S. 448 (1980), the Court had applied a more relaxed standard of review in upholding a similar MBE set-aside program adopted by Congress. In *Metro Broadcasting, Inc. v. FCC*, 497 U.S. 547, 564-565 (1990), decided a year after *Croson*, the Court again rejected the use of strict scrutiny for "benign race-conscious measures mandated by Congress" and ruled that such measures should be tested under the less-searching intermediate standard of review employed for gender discrimination. See § 6.6. The Court defended its use of different standards of review under the Fifth and Fourteenth Amendments on the ground that Congress, as a coequal branch, was deserving of special deference from the federal courts. Id. at 563-566.

Metro Broadcasting proved short-lived. The decision was overruled in *Adarand Constructors, Inc. v. Pena*, 515 U.S. 200 (1995), which held that principles of "skepticism," "consistency," and "congruence" were violated by relaxing the standard of review for race-based affirmative action programs adopted by Congress when all other racial classifications are subject to strict scrutiny. Instead, said the Court, all racial classifications must be viewed skeptically; there should be consistency in the standard of review regardless of which race is burdened; and there should be congruence between the equal protection analyses employed under the Fifth and Fourteenth Amendments. Id. at 222-227. *Adarand* restored these principles by holding that "all racial classifications, imposed by whatever federal, state, or local governmental actor, must be analyzed by a reviewing court under strict scrutiny. In other words, such classifications are constitutional only if they are narrowly tailored measures that further compelling governmental interests." Id. at 227; see also *Fisher v. University of Texas* (I), 570 U.S. 297, 310 (2013) (affirming that all racial classifications are inherently suspect and subject to strict scrutiny); but see

Gratz v. Bollinger, 539 U.S. 244, 298, 301 (2003) (Ginsburg, J., with whom Souter, J., joined, dissenting) (rejecting proposition that "the same standard of review controls judicial inspection of all official race classifications" and suggesting that a relaxed standard should be employed "where race is considered for the purpose of achieving equality"); *Parents Involved in Community Schools v. Seattle School District No. 1*, 551 U.S. 701, 823, 836-837 (2007) (Breyer, J., with whom Stevens, J., Souter, J., and Ginsburg, J., joined, dissenting) (endorsing a "contextual approach" to scrutiny under which benign uses of "race-conscious criteria to achieve positive race-related goals" would be subject to "a standard of review that is not 'strict' in the traditional sense of the word").

While a majority of the Court had endorsed strict scrutiny as the appropriate measure of all racial classifications, it noted that such "scrutiny is not 'strict in theory, but fatal in fact.' . . . When race-based action is necessary to further a compelling governmental interest, such action does not violate the constitutional guarantee of equal protection so long as the narrow-tailoring requirement is also satisfied." *Grutter v. Bollinger*, 539 U.S. 306, 327 (2003); accord *Fisher v. University of Texas (I)*, supra, 570 U.S. at 310-313. Where race was taken into account for benign purposes, it fared better than when it was designed to harm a particular group. In *Grutter*, the Court explained:

> Context matters when reviewing race-based governmental action under the Equal Protection Clause. . . . Not every decision influenced by race is equally objectionable, and strict scrutiny is designed to provide a framework for carefully examining the importance and the sincerity of the reasons advanced by the governmental decisionmaker for the use of race in that particular context.

539 U.S. at 327.

In *Students for Fair Admissions, Inc. v. President and Fellows of Harvard College*, 600 U.S. 181 (2023), the Court revisited the issue of using race for benign purposes in college admissions. There, the Court held that to comply with the Equal Protection Clause, the race-based admission program of a state university or of a private college receiving federal funds: (1) must be justified by a compelling interest sufficiently measurable to permit strict scrutiny; (2) must be supported by a meaningful connection between the means used and the diversity goals sought to be achieved; (3) cannot use race as a stereotype or negative; and (4) cannot lack a logical end-point. Id. at 213-215, 217-221, 224. The Court clarified that the opinion did not apply to military academies. Id. at 213 n.4. See also *Students for Fair Admissions, Inc. v. United States Military Academy at West Point*, 144 S. Ct. 716 (2024) (mem.) (denying application for writ of injunction pending appeal because of undeveloped record before the Court).

Compelling Interests

In many instances of affirmative action, the government's goal is compensatory in nature—i.e., the government is taking positive steps to remedy or make up for wrongs that were perpetrated against racial minorities in the past. In some affirmative action cases, however, the goal may be something other than remedial, such as achieving racial diversity in the schools or in the workforce. Justice Powell, who in *Bakke* applied strict scrutiny to overturn a medical school's special admissions program, suggested that a variety of interests might suffice to justify affirmative action, including eliminating the effects of past discrimination or attaining a diverse student body. Powell did not seem to envision a closed universe of compelling interests; instead, whether or not a particular goal was compelling would depend on the facts of the specific case.

The Supreme Court initially took a narrower view of what interests would be sufficient to justify the use of race-based affirmative action. It acknowledged that remedying the present effects of identified past discrimination qualifies as a compelling interest, but for many years it appeared this might be the only governmental interest that a majority of the Court would find adequate to uphold a race-based classification. See *City of Richmond v. J. A. Croson Co.*, supra, 488 U.S. at 493 (plurality opinion); id. at 511 (Stevens, J., concurring).

In *Grutter v. Bollinger*, supra, decided in 2003—25 years after *Bakke*—the Court expressly rejected the argument that "the only governmental use of race that can survive strict scrutiny is remedying past discrimination," and held that the Law School had "a compelling interest in attaining a diverse student body." 539 U.S. at 328. In upholding the University of Michigan Law School's race-based diversity admissions program, the Court stated that "[t]he Law School's educational judgment that such diversity is essential to its educational mission is one to which we defer." Id. Such respect is warranted, said the Court, by the "complex educational judgments" involved, and is "in keeping with our tradition of giving a degree of deference to a university's academic decisions, within constitutionally prescribed limits." Id. And in *Gratz v. Bollinger*, 539 U.S. 244, 268-270 (2003), a companion case, the Court agreed that "the interest in educational diversity" may also justify the use of race at the college undergraduate admissions level under a properly tailored plan.

Years later, along the same lines, the Court explained that "[c]onsiderable deference is owed to a university in defining those intangible characteristics, like student body diversity, that are central to its identity and educational mission," *Fisher v. University of Texas* (II), 579 U.S. 365, 388 (2016), for "enrolling a diverse student body 'promotes cross-racial understanding, helps to break down racial stereotypes, and enables students to better understand persons of different races' Equally important, 'student body diversity promotes learning outcomes, and better prepares students for an increasingly diverse workforce and society.'" Id. at 381 (internal citations omitted).

Thus, where a race-based admissions program was defended as having been designed to achieve a diverse student body, "good faith on the part of a university" was presumed absent a showing to the contrary. *Grutter v. Bollinger*, supra, 539 U.S. at 329. This enhanced deference to the state prompted the four dissenters in *Grutter* to suggest that "[a]lthough the Court recites the language of our strict scrutiny analysis, its application of that review is unprecedented in its deference." Id. at 380 (Rehnquist, C.J., et al., dissenting). However, the Court thereafter made clear that any relaxation of the strict scrutiny standard in *Grutter* "relied upon considerations unique to institutions of higher education," and that no such relaxation was appropriate with respect to "race-based assignments in elementary and secondary schools." *Parents Involved in Community Schools v. Seattle School District No. 1*, supra, 551 U.S. at 724-725.

Recently, though, the Court's approach to race-based college admissions has radically changed. In *Students for Fair Admissions, Inc. v. President and Fellows of Harvard College*, 600 U.S. 181 (2023), the Court granted certiorari on three questions: (1) whether the Court should overrule *Bakke*, *Grutter*, and *Fisher*; or, alternatively, (2) whether the University of North Carolina's admissions program is narrowly tailored, and (3) whether Harvard's admissions program is narrowly tailored. Picking none of these alternatives, the Court decided to "consider whether the admissions systems used by Harvard College and the University of North Carolina . . . are lawful under the Equal Protection Clause of the Fourteenth Amendment." Id. at 190-191. But see id. at 307 (Gorsuch, J., concurring) ("the Court today cuts through the kudzu."); see also id. at 352 (Sotomayor, J., with whom Kagan, J. and Jackson, J., joined, dissenting) ("In reality, however, 'the Court today cuts through the kudzu' and overrules its 'higher-education precedents' following *Bakke*.").

Under *Students for Fair Admissions*, to pass Equal Protection Clause muster, the programs would have to survive strict scrutiny, i.e., they would have to be supported by a "compelling governmental interest," and narrowly tailored to achieve that end. Revisiting the compelling-governmental-interest requirement as articulated in *Grutter*, the Court now concluded that a racial diversity rationale cannot meet that standard. More specifically, the Court discarded the interest in "better educating [college] students through diversity" as "not sufficiently coherent," "elusive," "standardless," and "imponderable," for it was unclear how courts would measure such a goal and determine whether it has been reached. Id. at 214-215. Similarly, the interests in "training future leaders in the public and private sectors," "preparing graduates to 'adapt to an increasingly pluralistic society,'" "producing new knowledge stemming from diverse outlooks," "promoting the robust exchange of ideas," "broadening and refining understanding," "fostering innovation and problem-solving," "preparing engaged and productive citizens and leaders," and "enhancing appreciation, respect, and empathy, cross-racial understanding, and breaking down stereotypes," were all discarded as "not sufficiently coherent for purposes of strict scrutiny." Id. at 214.

By contrast, said the Court, using race as a factor in the context of racial violence in a prison, or to respond to workplace discrimination is different, for in those contexts,

> courts can ask whether a race-based benefit makes members of the discriminated class "whole for [the] injuries [they] suffered." And in school segregation cases, courts can determine whether any race-based remedial action produces a distribution of students "compar[able] to what it would have been in the absence of such constitutional violations."
>
> . . . Unlike discerning whether a prisoner will be injured or whether an employee should receive backpay, the question whether a particular mix of minority students produces "engaged and productive citizens," sufficiently "enhance[s] appreciation, respect, and empathy," or effectively "train[s] future leaders" is standardless. The interests that respondents seek, though plainly worthy, are inescapably imponderable.

Id. at 215 (internal citations omitted). The Harvard College and University of North Carolina race-based admission programs were thus found to be in violation of the Equal Protection Clause. Id. at 230.

In contexts other than college admissions, where the government contends that a racial classification was adopted for a benign remedial purpose, two requirements must be met to satisfy the compelling interest prong of the analysis. First, the classification must seek to rectify the effects of identified racial discrimination within the entity's regulatory jurisdiction. The discrimination may have been that of the entity itself or of private parties subject to its authority. Thus, a city council may be entitled under state law to adopt ordinances that bar racial discrimination both by city government and by individuals and businesses within the city. However, "an effort to alleviate the effects of [past] *societal* discrimination is not a compelling interest," as this is too amorphous a basis for employing a racial classification. *Shaw v. Hunt*, 517 U.S. 899, 909-910 (1996) (emphasis supplied). Second, the entity adopting the remedial scheme must have a "'strong basis in evidence' to conclude that remedial action was necessary, '*before* it embarks on an affirmative action program.'" Id. (emphasis in original). In other words, prior to adopting the remedial scheme, the entity must have gathered evidence that factually demonstrates "a prima facie case of a constitutional or statutory violation" that needs to be redressed. *City of Richmond v. J.A. Croson Co.*, supra, 488 U.S. at 500. Unless both requirements are satisfied, the Court will find that the government did not have a compelling interest in remedying the effects of past discrimination.

Example 6-W

The faculty of Baxter State College adopted an affirmative action plan for faculty hiring after finding that racial minorities were severely underrepresented on the college staff. Under the plan, faculty are to be hired on an alternating basis so that every other faculty member hired must be a black or Latino, until the percentages of blacks and Latinos on the Baxter faculty reach the percentages these groups occupy in the state's population. The faculty adopted the plan after a U.S. Justice Department study found that the nation's colleges and universities had a long history of racial discrimination in faculty recruitment. Mary was turned down for a job in Baxter's history department because she is white. She has sued the college, claiming a violation of the Equal Protection Clause. Can Baxter establish that its action was warranted by a compelling interest in remedying past discrimination?

Explanation

The college probably cannot prove that it had a compelling interest in adopting the affirmative action plan for remedial purposes. As to the first requirement, even if Baxter was guilty of past racial discrimination in faculty hiring, it is doubtful that state law gives the college faculty, as opposed to the college's board of trustees or other governing body, the legal authority to adopt such a hiring plan.

The second requirement might not be met for several reasons. The fact that there are few minority faculty members at Baxter does not by itself establish a constitutional violation; proof of discriminatory intent would also be needed. In short, Baxter must make findings establishing a prima facie case that it had violated the Equal Protection Clause *before* adopting the plan. Instead, the faculty seems to have relied solely on a federal study that probably did not address the specific conduct of Baxter State College. Even if many or most of the nation's colleges engaged in illegal discrimination, this does not establish that Baxter did so. On the other hand, if the faculty had first gathered evidence of Baxter's past unconstitutional discrimination in faculty hiring, the second requirement would presumably be met.

Example 6-X

In Example 6-W, Baxter College sought to defend its race-based faculty-hiring plan on the ground that it was designed to remedy a violation of the Equal Protection Clause. Suppose that Baxter's remedial plan was instead adopted by its board of trustees on the basis that the college's past faculty hiring practices had violated Title VII of the 1964 federal Civil Rights Act, which prohibits employment practices having a racially disproportionate impact whether or not there was a racially discriminatory purpose. If the college has a "strong basis in evidence" showing that its earlier hiring practices had a racially discriminatory impact in violation of Title VII, would this then give the college a compelling interest for adopting its race-conscious remedial hiring plan?

Explanation

The finding of past discrimination and the adoption of the plan were made by the college's board of trustees, a body that presumably had the legal authority to take such action, thus satisfying the first of our two requirements, i.e., that the classification sought to rectify the effects of identified racial discrimination within the entity's regulatory jurisdiction. As to the second requirement—that the entity adopting the remedial scheme must have "a strong basis in evidence" to conclude that remedial action was necessary before embarking on an affirmative action program—the Court in *City of Richmond v. Croson* said that a race-based remedial scheme could be adopted if the factual evidence demonstrates "a constitutional *or statutory* violation" that calls for redress. 488 U.S. at 500 (emphasis supplied). See also *Students for Fair Admissions*, supra, 600 U.S. at 207 ("Outside the circumstances of these cases, our precedents have identified only two compelling interests that permit resort to race-based government action. One is remediating specific, identified instances of past discrimination that violated the Constitution *or a statute*." (Emphasis added.)).

Our example would appear to meet this test, for Baxter has shown that its past hiring practices violated Title VII of the 1964 Civil Rights Act. However, this assumes that a governmental entity is as free to adopt race-conscious remedies for past federal *statutory* violations as it is for past *constitutional* violations, for *Croson* and *Students for Fair Admissions* seemed to equate the two. See also *Students for Fair Admissions*, supra, 600 U.S. at 198, n.2; but cf. id. at 308-309 (Gorsuch, J., concurring) (emphasizing the differences between the Equal Protection Clause and Title VI). However, the Supreme Court cast doubt on Congress's ability to authorize—and the states' ability to employ—race-based remedies for state and local governmental conduct that falls short of violating the Equal Protection Clause. In *Ricci v. DeStefano*, 557 U.S. 557 (2009), a Title VII case challenging the City of New Haven's race-based promotion plan for firefighters, the Court held that the plan was improper under Title VII because there was no "strong basis in evidence" that the city's past practices had violated the act. Id. at 585. The Court was careful to note that "[o]ur statutory holding does not address the constitutionality of the measures taken here in purported compliance with Title VII. We also do not hold that meeting the strong-basis-in-evidence standard would satisfy the Equal Protection Clause in a future case." Id. at 584.

In the redistricting context, the Court has held that a race-based remedial plan adopted by a state legislature to comply with the Voting Rights Act of 1965 also complied with the Equal Protection Clause. *Bethune-Hill v. Virginia State Bd. of Elections*, 580 U.S. 178, 196 (2017). There, after the 2010 census, the Virginia State Legislature drew new lines for 12 state legislative districts to ensure that each district had a black voting-age population of at least 55 percent. Certain voters sued, claiming that the new districts violated the Fourteenth Amendment's Equal Protection Clause. While for 11 of the districts the voters had not shown that race was the predominant factor motivating the legislature's decision to place a significant number of voters within or without a particular district, the Court found that as to the 12th district, race predominated but that the lines were constitutional because the legislature's use of race was narrowly tailored to a compelling state interest. Under the strong-basis-in-evidence standard, the Court noted that such a basis "exists when the legislature has '*good reasons* to believe' it must use race in order to satisfy the Voting Rights Act, 'even if a court does not find that the actions were necessary for statutory compliance.'" Id. at 194 (emphasis in original).

Narrowly Tailored

Even if the government can show that its affirmative action plan is justified by a compelling interest, the scheme will be invalidated unless the government also shows that the measure is narrowly tailored and necessary to achieving its goal. As the Court has explained, "The purpose of the narrow tailoring requirement is to ensure that the means chosen fit the compelling goal so closely that there is little or no possibility that the motive for the classification was illegitimate racial prejudice or stereotype." *Grutter v. Bollinger*, supra, 539 U.S. at 333 (internal quotation marks omitted). We will look at how the Court has applied this "narrowly tailored" requirement first in the remedial setting and then in the educational diversity context.

When an affirmative action plan is adopted for remedial purposes, there are two requirements: (1) The government must demonstrate that the race-conscious remedy was adopted as a last resort after all race-neutral remedies were examined and found inadequate, and (2) the use of race must be no more extensive than necessary to redress the past wrongs.

As to the first requirement, the Court has emphasized that the proper remedy for past racial discrimination is ordinarily to take appropriate measures against those guilty of discriminating and/or to provide relief to the specific victims of that discrimination. These steps and any other race-neutral remedies that may fit a particular case must have been explored and found wanting before the government may choose a remedy that classifies based on race. Otherwise, the use of affirmative action is not *necessary* to achieve the government's remedial goal.

EXAMPLE

Example 6-Y

In Example 6-W, suppose that Baxter College met the compelling interest part of the strict scrutiny test through evidentiary findings that it was guilty of past racial discrimination in faculty hiring. Will the college be able to satisfy the first part of the narrowly tailored requirement?

EXPLANATION

Explanation

The college's use of a race-based affirmative action plan will be constitutional only if there is evidence that the college considered and for good reason rejected any seemingly viable race-neutral means of remedying the effects of its past misconduct.

There are several race-neutral remedies that might have achieved the state's remedial goal instead of the race-based affirmative action hiring plan adopted by the faculty. First, the state or the college might have punished or otherwise sanctioned those faculty and staff who engaged in acts of racial discrimination and warned that similar action will be taken in the future against anyone who engages in similar acts. Second, the state or the college might have sought to identify all applicants for teaching positions who were rejected because of their race and offered them jobs and/or paid them damages. Third, the college might have tried to hire more minority faculty by recruiting at universities that have a significant number of minority graduates. Unlike the faculty's affirmative action hiring plan, none of these alternatives employs a racial classification. The college would have to show that it had considered these and any other race-neutral options a court might think of and demonstrate why they were rejected as inadequate. This would be a difficult showing to make.

Even if a race-conscious remedy is justified by the lack of adequate race-neutral alternatives, the remedy must also be narrowly tailored in the way it employs race. In other words, the race-based remedy must not be overinclusive in terms of its duration or its scope. The scheme must be temporary, lasting no longer than the discriminatory effects it seeks to eliminate. In addition, any numerical set-asides or goals contained in the plan must be reasonable. The remedy must be confined to those racial groups that were victims of past discrimination, rather than randomly including all racial minority groups. The plan must be designed so that it does not stigmatize those it seeks to help. In addition, the remedy must be applied flexibly; this may require including a waiver for situations where rigid adherence to the plan would prove harsh or unreasonable. It may also be necessary to provide an opportunity for individualized determinations as to whether specific beneficiaries have suffered from the effects of past discrimination.

EXAMPLE

Example 6-Z

In Example 6-W, if Baxter College shows that there are no race-neutral means of adequately remedying the effects of its past discrimination in faculty hiring, will its race-conscious plan satisfy the second part of the narrowly tailored requirement?

EXPLANATION

Explanation

For this requirement to be met, the college must demonstrate that the plan's use of race is narrowly tailored to the remedial goal. While the plan is temporary, it may still be excessive because it is tied to achieving percentages of blacks and Latinos equal to their representation in the state's total population. Where, as here, special qualifications are required for a job, the relevant statistical pool is those who are qualified to take the job—in this case, college graduates or perhaps those with Ph.D.'s. The percentages of blacks and Latinos may be much lower in these two pools than in the state's population as a whole. Thus, the plan's duration and percentage goals may not be narrowly tailored because they are tied to achieving a higher representation of blacks and Latinos than is necessary to redress the effects of past discrimination.

The plan may also fail because it includes both blacks and Latinos; if the college previously discriminated against only one of these groups, the plan is overinclusive by including the other.

The plan may be too rigid to pass muster. It in effect sets aside 50 percent of all new teaching jobs for racial minorities. While this number may not be excessive since it is temporary, there appears to be no waiver provision for situations in which there are no qualified minority applicants. Nor does there seem to be a procedure for making individualized determinations that would weed out minority applicants who were in no way harmed by any past discrimination.

The program may also stigmatize minority teachers if it does not hold them to the same hiring qualifications required of nonminority applicants; if this is the case, a black or Latino teacher at Baxter State College may be judged by others to be inferior because he or she was hired under less rigorous standards. For any or all of these reasons, the college's affirmative action faculty hiring plan may not be narrowly tailored.

We have been looking at the narrowly tailored requirement as it applies to racial discrimination in the remedial context. Turning now to the educational diversity setting, the inquiry is somewhat different. Here, "the narrow-tailoring inquiry" is one that "must be calibrated to fit the distinct issues raised by the use of race to achieve student body diversity," since "the very purpose of strict scrutiny is to take such 'relevant differences into account.'" *Grutter v. Bollinger*, supra, 539 U.S. at 333-334. The Court suggested that a race-conscious diversity admissions program would be found to be narrowly tailored only if it satisfied five requirements. First, the program could not employ a quota system that insulated certain categories of applicants with desired qualifications from competition with others, such as by reserving a set number or proportion of the available seats for the favored group. Instead, race could be used only as a "plus" factor in an applicant's case, but without insulating the applicant from comparison with all other applicants.

Second, the use of race as a "plus" factor could never be weighted so heavily that it became the defining feature of an individual's application. While in a particular case race might tip the diversity balance in an applicant's favor, there had to be "other diversity factors besides race that can make a real and dispositive difference for nonminority applicants as well." Id. at 338. Race thus could not be used as *the* decisive factor (e.g., as a tie-breaker) in cases where it came into play, so that it became "determinative standing alone." *Parents Involved in Community Schools v. Seattle School District No. 1*, supra, 551 U.S. at 723.

Third, there had to be a "serious, good faith consideration of workable race-neutral alternatives that will achieve the diversity the university seeks." *Grutter v. Bollinger*, supra, 539 U.S. at 339. Only in this way could it be seriously maintained that the use of racial classifications was necessary to achieving the asserted compelling interest. This did not mean that a university ought to have actually tried these alternatives as opposed to having genuinely considered them, for "[n]arrow tailoring does not require exhaustion of every conceivable race-neutral alternative." Id. Nor did a university have to employ race-neutral schemes, such as a lottery or lower admissions standards, that might produce greater diversity but at the expense of other legitimate goals, such as maintaining the academic quality of its student body. The extent to which race-neutral alternatives had to be considered, however, might depend on the benefits the state received from its use of a race-conscious scheme, for the fewer those benefits, the greater the likelihood that other means would be equally effective. See *Parents Involved in Community Schools v. Seattle School District No. 1*, supra, 551 U.S. at 704 ("the minimal impact of the districts' racial classifications on school enrollment casts doubt on the necessity of using such classifications").

Fourth, the race-conscious admissions program could not "unduly burden" those who were not members of the favored racial group, but should be designed to "work the least harm possible to other innocent persons competing for the benefit." *Grutter v. Bollinger*, supra, 539 U.S. at 341. A program that used race as the sole diversity criterion would clearly fail this requirement, in contrast to one that considered an array of pertinent diversity elements, including factors having nothing to do with race.

Finally, "race-conscious admissions policies had to be limited in time." Id. at 342. This did not mean that such programs had to have a fixed expiration date, as long as it was clear that they would be terminated as soon as practicable. While the Court did not prescribe a fixed durational limit, it did say: "We expect that 25 years from now, the use of racial preferences will no longer be necessary to further the interest approved today." Id. at 343; but cf. id. at 376 n.13 (Thomas, J., and Scalia, J., dissenting) (viewing this as a "holding that racial discrimination in admissions will be illegal in 25 years," rather than as merely a "hope" or a "forecast").

The Court made it clear that the deference given to university administrators with respect to the compelling-interest prong of the analysis, i.e., the benefits derived from having a diverse student body, did not relax the rigor with which the narrow-tailoring requirement had to be applied. "Strict scrutiny does not permit a court to accept a school's assertion that its admissions process uses race in a permissible way without a court giving close analysis to the evidence of how the process works in practice." *Fisher v. University of Texas* (I), supra, 570 U.S. at 313 (reversing court of appeals decision that had adopted a deferential standard in applying the narrow-tailoring requirement).

In *Students for Fair Admissions, Inc. v. President and Fellows of Harvard College*, 600 U.S. 181 (2023), however, the Court marked the end of any deferential approach to universities and their assessment, and revisited the "narrowly tailored" requirement as originally described in *Grutter*. As to the deference owed to universities, the Court held that this cannot come at the expense of violating the Constitution. Id. at 217. See also id. at 256 (Thomas, J., concurring) ("In fact, it is error for a court to defer to the views of an alleged discriminator while assessing claims of racial discrimination."). Regarding the "narrowly tailored" prong, instead of applying the five *Grutter* requirements noted above, the Court required: (1) that there be a meaningful connection between the means adopted and the goals sought to be achieved; (2) that race not be used as a "negative" or operate as a stereotype; and (3) that there be a logical end-point to the race-admission program.

Concerning (1), the Court demanded a "meaningful connection" between the means higher institutions employ and the goals they pursue.

Id. at 215. Although this "meaningful connection" requirement might seem easier to satisfy than *Grutter's* five requirements, it is, in fact, quite challenging. The higher education institution must now demonstrate how the means used are meaningfully connected to goals that are concrete and objectively measurable. Not surprisingly, Harvard College and the University of North Carolina failed to meet the "meaningful connection" requirement. Among other things, the Court noted that the universities could not meet this requirement, or their goal of avoiding underrepresentation of minorities, because they measured the racial composition of their classes using "imprecise," "plainly overbroad," or "underinclusive" racial categories—Asian; Native Hawaiian or Pacific Islander; Hispanic; White; African-American; Native American. Id. at 216. By using these categories and focusing on underrepresentation, explained the Court,

> respondents would apparently prefer a class with 15% of students from Mexico over a class with 10% of students from several Latin American countries, simply because the former contains more Hispanic students than the latter. Yet, "[i]t is hard to understand how a plan that could allow these results can be viewed as being concerned with achieving enrollment that is 'broadly diverse' . . . [or] how courts are supposed to scrutinize the admissions programs that respondents use.

Id. at 217 (internal citations omitted).

Regarding (2), the Court insisted that race not be used as a "negative" or operate as a stereotype. Id. at 218. However, by providing a benefit to some applicants and not to others, observed the Court, the race-based admissions program necessarily advantaged the former group at the expense of the latter, thus functioning as a negative for the disadvantaged group. Id. at 218-219. And accepting race-based admissions programs in which some students obtained preference based on race alone meant stereotyping, the very thing that *Grutter* rejected, yet which both admissions programs at Harvard College and North Carolina University seemed to allow. Id. at 219-221. Of course, universities may still consider an applicant's discussion of how race affected his or her life, to the extent that the application essays or other means do not end up reintroducing the system that the *Students for Fair Admissions* Court held to be unconstitutional. Id. at 230.

Finally, as to (3), the Court, reading *Grutter* as "impos[ing] a final [time] limit on race-based admissions programs," id. at 212, concluded that the race-based admissions programs must have a "logical end point," which the Harvard College and North Carolina University programs lacked. Id. at 221-225. Such a logical end point would be necessary even if, as here, the programs were subject to periodic review to determine their continuing necessity. Id. at 225.

Example 6-AA

Suppose that in addition to its affirmative action plan for faculty hiring, Baxter State College adopted a policy designed to produce a more diverse student body. Under the policy, the college uses a selection index on which an applicant may score a maximum of 150 points. Those whose point totals are 100 or above are certain to be admitted; those with fewer than 75 points are likely to be rejected; and those with between 75 and 99 points may or may not be accepted, the likelihood of admission increasing with their scores. Of the 150 possible points, up to 110 may be awarded for academic performance factors, including high school grade point average, standardized test scores, and quality of the high school. Up to 40 additional points may be assigned for other, nonacademic factors, such as in-state residency, alumni relationships, personal essay, and personal achievement or leadership. Most of these nonacademic factors carry a low number of points (e.g., 3 for an outstanding essay, 5 for personal achievement or leadership, and 10 for in-state residency). However, any applicant who is an "underrepresented minority," defined as including African Americans, Hispanics, and Native Americans, automatically receives 20 additional points. As a result, virtually every qualified applicant from these racial groups has been admitted to the college. Does the Baxter College student diversity policy violate the Equal Protection Clause of the Fourteenth Amendment?

Explanation

It is very likely that a court would find Baxter College's admissions program violative of the Equal Protection Clause. Since the policy overtly considers an applicant's race, it will be subject to strict scrutiny. Under *Students for Fair Admissions*, the goal of obtaining a more diverse student body, although commendable, may still fail the "compelling governmental interest" test as revisited by the Court. In view of *Students for Fair Admissions*, a court might find the interest not subject to meaningful judicial review, especially in view of the racial classifications used by the College, which the Court considered "imprecise" and "opaque." As to the "narrowly tailored" requirement, it would be hard to find the meaningful connection between the goal sought to be achieved and the means used to achieve it, for here, as in *Students for Fair Admissions*, both the goal and the means would be hard to measure. Also, a court would likely find that the automatic attribution of 20 additional points for race only, which has led to the admission of every qualified applicant from the "underrepresented minority," uses "race" as a stereotype and as a "negative" for applicants not belonging to "underrepresented minorities." Finally, the College's program doesn't have an end point.

EXAMPLE

Example 6-BB

State X University (SXU) has a two-part admissions policy. Under the state's "Top 10% Law," any student who graduated in the top 10 percent of their state X high school class is guaranteed admission to SXU. These students comprise about 75 percent of each year's incoming freshman class. The remaining 25 percent of the entering class is selected based on consideration of an applicant's SAT score and their Personal Achievement Index (PAI). The PAI is a numerical score based on a holistic review of an applicant's essays, leadership and work experience, extracurricular activities, community service, and other "special circumstances." As originally adopted, special circumstances did not include an applicant's race. However, after operating for seven years under this system, SXU found that blacks and Hispanics were still seriously underrepresented despite SXU's extensive outreach efforts to attract minority students. After a year-long study, SXU decided to consider an applicant's race as an additional special circumstances factor in calculating the PAI. While those preparing an applicant's PAI know the applicant's race, those who make the final admissions decision do not. In some cases, an applicant's race can sufficiently alter the PAI score to make a difference in terms of whether the applicant is accepted or rejected. Under this new system which it periodically reassesses, SXU's Hispanic enrollment increased from 11 percent to 17 percent, and its African American enrollment rose from 3.5 percent to 7 percent. Hispanics and African Americans together comprise about 58 percent of state X's population. Does the SXU admissions policy violate the Equal Protection Clause of the Fourteenth Amendment?

EXPLANATION

Explanation

The admissions policy will still likely fail under *Students for Fair Admissions*. Because the policy overtly discriminates based on race, it will be subject to strict scrutiny. As to a compelling governmental interest, if framed as improving the educational experience of students through diversity, although commendable, this would still not qualify as "compelling" in light of *Students for Fair Admissions*' conclusion that it is not measurable. If SXU uses the racial classifications of African American and Hispanic to assess diversity, those classifications would be considered "imprecise" and "opaque." As to the "narrowly tailored" requirement, it would be hard to find the meaningful connection between the goal sought to be achieved and the means used to achieve it, because here again, as in *Students for Fair Admissions*, both the goal and the means are immeasurable. The fact that an applicant's race may be considered as an additional special circumstance that affects whether the applicant is accepted or rejected amounts to using "race" as a stereotype, and as a "negative" for the applicants not benefitting from the race factor. Although race is not given the dominant role in the admission process that it played in Example AA, it is still considered per se and not as part of that more holistic assessment—e.g., how race affected the applicant's life through discrimination, inspiration or otherwise—that was validated by the *Students for Fair Admissions* Court. Finally, even if SXU periodically reassesses its admissions program to determine whether consideration of race is still needed to promote diversity, the program is fatally flawed because it doesn't have an end point.

The foregoing discussion should make it clear that after *Students for Fair Admissions*, a university may no longer consider race as a "plus factor" in the admissions process. Instead, it may only consider race holistically when assessing "how race affected [an applicant's] life, be it through discrimination, inspiration, or otherwise." *Students for Fair Admissions*, supra, 600 U.S. at 230.

While the Equal Protection Clause now prohibits higher education institutions from adopting an admissions policy that doesn't meet the requirements of *Students for Fair Admissions*, under the same clause, a state's voters remain free to totally prohibit their state universities from using race as a factor in admissions, at least when there has been no showing of de jure discrimination by that university. *Schuette v. Coalition to Defend Affirmative Action*, 572 U.S. 291 (2014).

So far, we have been considering the remedial use of race by governmental entities and actors other than courts. It appears, however, that the Supreme Court will be equally demanding in its scrutiny of race-based remedies that are imposed by state or lower federal courts. The compelling interest component of strict scrutiny is presumably satisfied in such a case by the court's evidentiary findings of a constitutional or federal statutory violation. The problem may arise as to whether the remedy is narrowly tailored, including the requirement that the lower court have first explored every potential race-neutral alternative before ordering the race-conscious remedy. Even prior to the 1995 decision in *Adarand*, the Court had in a number of cases subjected lower federal court orders in race discrimination cases to very searching review. *Adarand*, in rejecting the notion that Congress as a coequal branch is entitled to special leeway when using race for remedial purposes, made it clear that "*all* racial classifications, *imposed by whatever federal, state, or local governmental actor*, must be analyzed by a reviewing court under strict scrutiny." *Adarand Constructors, Inc. v. Pena*, supra, 515 U.S. at 227 (emphasis supplied). This language is so all-embracing as to seemingly cover the actions of state and lower federal court judges. Thus, outside of well-established settings such as school desegregation, it may become increasingly rare that federal courts (or state courts for that matter) are permitted to order race-conscious remedies even in cases of proven past racial discrimination.

§6.5 CLASSIFICATION ON THE BASIS OF ALIENAGE

§6.5.1 The Standard for State and Local Laws

The Reason for Strict Scrutiny

State and local laws that discriminate based on alienage are, like laws based on race or nationality, generally deemed to involve a suspect classification and are thus subject to strict scrutiny. The Court has long recognized that the Fourteenth Amendment protects all persons who are within the jurisdiction of the United States, citizens as well as aliens. See *Yick Wo v. Hopkins*, 118 U.S. 356 (1886). Most classifications based on alienage are suspect for many of the same reasons that strict scrutiny applies to laws that discriminate on the basis of race or national origin (see § 6.4.1). As "foreigners," aliens are often the objects of first and second-degree prejudice. And though alienage is not an immutable condition since aliens may become naturalized citizens, the condition is mutable in only one direction; legislators will, therefore, not be restrained from placing special burdens on aliens by the possibility that they might one day find themselves in the same category. Moreover, aliens are totally excluded from the political process since they are not allowed to vote in either state or national elections.

There is a further reason for subjecting state laws that discriminate against aliens to strict judicial scrutiny, namely, to prevent states from interfering with the national government's exclusive authority to regulate the terms and conditions on which aliens are admitted to the United States. If states were free to discriminate against aliens subject only to rational basis review from the courts, states could make the lives of aliens so difficult as to in effect nullify the federal government's decision giving these individuals permission to live in the United States. The Court has thus recognized that "aliens lawfully within this country have a right to enter and abide in any State in the Union 'on an equality of legal privileges with all citizens under non-discriminatory state laws.'" *Graham v. Richardson*, 403 U.S. 365, 378 (1971).

Example 6-CC

EXAMPLE

Paul is a French citizen who was admitted to the United States on a student visa. He attends Baxter State College and plans to return to France after receiving his degree. A state law denies student financial aid to aliens unless they intend to become U.S. citizens. Because Paul has no such intention, the state denied him a scholarship. The state defended the measure on the grounds that it encourages aliens to become citizens, promotes the goal of educating those who are or will become members of the electorate, and limits scarce resources to citizens. Has the state violated Paul's constitutional right to equal protection?

EXPLANATION

Explanation

The law is most likely unconstitutional. It discriminates on the basis of alienage even though it denies financial aid to some, but not all, aliens; what is critical is that the law is directed at aliens, and only aliens are harmed by it. The measure is, therefore, subject to strict scrutiny. The goal of encouraging aliens to become citizens is probably not a valid *state* goal, since the federal government possesses exclusive authority over immigration and naturalization. Moreover, if this were accepted as being a valid and compelling state goal, it would justify virtually all forms of state discrimination against aliens.

The goal of educating the electorate may in theory be compelling, but it will be implicated here only if the state can show that including aliens would significantly impair this goal; if the number of aliens excluded by the law is small, the impact may be too trivial for this goal to come into play. See § 6.4.2. Yet even if this goal is accepted as compelling, the statute is probably not narrowly tailored. The law is overinclusive in that it denies aid to aliens who will remain in the community and who will thus help to shape its future other than at the ballot box. The law is also underinclusive, for it does not withhold aid from those who are or may become citizens, but who plan to move to another state or country.

Finally, the claimed interest in reserving scarce resources to citizens is not compelling. In *Graham v. Richardson*, supra, 403 U.S. at 376, which struck down state laws that denied welfare benefits to aliens, the Court held that there is no "special public interest" in reserving to citizens "tax revenues to which aliens have contributed on an equal basis with the residents of the State." The same result is called for with respect to the distribution of scholarship funds. See *Nyquist v. Mauclet*, 432 U.S. 1 (1977) (state statute that barred certain resident aliens from receiving state financial assistance for higher education violated Equal Protection Clause).

Governmental or Political Functions

The principal reason that classifications based on race, national origin, and alienage are inherently suspect is that they tend to be irrelevant to any *legitimate* state goal. Strict scrutiny in such cases serves as a way of uncovering any hidden improper purposes. Yet there are two exceptional circumstances in which state laws that discriminate against aliens are more likely to have been adopted for valid reasons. In these two areas, the Court, therefore, applies only a rational basis standard of review rather than strict scrutiny.

The first area involves the so-called governmental functions or political functions exception, which permits a state to reserve certain jobs or positions exclusively for those who are citizens. This exception applies to classifications that bar aliens from elective or nonelective "positions intimately related to the process of democratic self-government." *Bernal v. Fainter*, 467 U.S. 216, 220 (1984). It is justified on the theory that every government should be able to "limit the right to govern to those who are full-fledged members of the political community." Id. at 221.

The political function exception will apply if three requirements are satisfied:

1. The classification that excludes aliens must be fairly specific as to the positions that are involved rather than a disqualification aimed at a wide range of positions;
2. The position must involve broad discretionary authority in the formulation or the execution of public policies; and
3. The authority exercised must have an important impact on the citizen population.

Jobs that are essentially ministerial or clerical in nature and that call for little exercise of discretion do not meet the second requirement of this exception. Thus, the political function exception does not apply to notaries public. *Bernal v. Fainter*, 467 U.S. 216 (1984). A police officer's job, on the other hand, easily falls within the exception, since it entails broad discretion in the execution of public policies that significantly affect people's lives. *Foley v. Connelie*, 435 U.S. 291 (1978).

EXAMPLE

Example 6-DD

Pursuant to a law that bars aliens from taking any job with the State District Attorney's Office, Cheryl was denied a position as a prosecutor because she is not a U.S. citizen. Is the state's refusal to hire Cheryl subject to strict scrutiny, or does the political function exception lower the standard of review to rational basis?

EXPLANATION

Explanation

The position of state prosecutor is almost surely one to which the political function exception applies. Prosecutors wield tremendous discretion in enforcing criminal laws, with grave consequences for people's lives. In *In re Griffiths*, 413 U.S. 717 (1973), the Court held that states may not bar aliens from becoming members of the bar, but because of the political function exception, the position of prosecutor would probably be treated differently.

Yet the political function exception might still not apply here because of the first requirement of the test. The statutory exclusion of aliens from *any* job in the State District Attorney's Office is arguably so overinclusive as to defeat the exception. The ban seems to cover paralegals, secretaries, mail clerks, and maintenance personnel—positions that do not involve any discretionary authority in formulating or executing public policy. On the other hand, if the state courts have construed the statute as excluding aliens only from serving as prosecutors, the political function exception would probably apply, and the exclusion would be upheld under a rational basis standard of review.

Undocumented Aliens

The second area in which state alienage discrimination is subject to mere rational basis review rather than strict scrutiny involves laws that discriminate against undocumented aliens. The Court has held that "[u]ndocumented aliens cannot be treated as a suspect class because their presence in this country in violation of federal law is not a 'constitutional irrelevancy.'" *Plyler v. Doe*, 457 U.S. 202, 223 (1982). This exception is also defended on the basis that if a state discriminates against undocumented aliens, it is not encroaching as seriously on the federal domain, since those whom the state is burdening have, by definition, violated federal law.

These rationales for employing a mere rational basis standard of review for classifications aimed at undocumented aliens are not entirely satisfactory. Undocumented aliens as a class are often the objects of severe first and second-degree prejudice. At the same time, they are totally unable to protect themselves in the political process, since they cannot vote. Moreover, despite their undocumented status, some aliens in this group in fact have a right to remain in the United States as a matter of federal immigration law (e.g., because they may qualify for political asylum). If the purpose of heightened scrutiny is to afford added judicial protection to those who face a risk of serious harm from the political process, state laws that target undocumented aliens should be subject to something more than rational basis review. As we will see in the next chapter, the Court has been willing to apply a standard of review that is more searching than rational basis to at least some state laws that discriminate against undocumented alien children. See § 7.8.3. State laws that discriminate against undocumented aliens in general, however, are—at least for now—subject only to rational basis review.

Example 6-EE

In Example 6-CC, after a court held that the state may not constitutionally limit student financial aid to those aliens who intend to become U.S. citizens, the state amended its law to provide that "no financial aid shall be awarded for college study to any undocumented alien, i.e., an alien who is present in the United States in violation of federal immigration laws." Paul, a 22-year-old citizen of France, was admitted to this country on a student visa that expired two months ago. Baxter State College has denied him a scholarship based on the new state law. Has the college violated Paul's Fourteenth Amendment right to equal protection of the laws?

Explanation

The new state law discriminates solely against undocumented aliens. Thus, the measure is subject to mere rational basis review. Since the law pertains only to college students, it is unlikely that Paul could obtain a more elevated standard of review on the theory that this is a law discriminating against undocumented alien children. Under the rational basis test, the law is virtually certain to be upheld as rationally related to the state's legitimate interest in discouraging an influx of undocumented aliens.

§6.5.2 The Standard for Federal Laws

As we have seen, state and local discrimination against lawfully admitted aliens is subject to strict judicial scrutiny. By contrast, federal laws that discriminate against aliens are reviewed under a rational basis standard. This relaxed scrutiny of federal alienage classifications stems from the fact that

> the responsibility for regulating the relationship between the United States and our alien visitors has been committed to the political branches of the Federal Government. . . . The reasons that preclude judicial review of political questions also dictate a narrow standard of review of decisions made by the Congress or the President in the area of immigration and naturalization.

Mathews v. Diaz, 426 U.S. 67, 81-82 (1976). This deferential approach to federal alienage classifications marks one of the few areas where there is a lack of congruence between the equal protection standards applied under the Fifth and Fourteenth Amendments.

While the Court generally accords great deference to federal alienage classifications, this applies only if the classification was adopted by Congress, by the President, or by a federal agency that is charged with responsibility for protecting the nation's interest in immigration and naturalization. Otherwise, there is less reason for "presuming that the rule was actually intended to serve that interest," and strict scrutiny will be applied. *Hampton v. Mow Sun Wong*, 426 U.S. 88, 103 (1976). In *Hampton*, the Court thus invalidated on equal protection grounds a federal Civil Service Commission rule that barred aliens from most federal government jobs. The Court strongly suggested that the rule would have been upheld had it been mandated by Congress or the President, or had it been issued by a federal agency that, unlike the Civil Service Commission, has "direct responsibility" for immigration and naturalization matters.

§6.6 CLASSIFICATION ON THE BASIS OF GENDER OR LEGITIMACY

§6.6.1 Gender as a Quasi-Suspect Classification

Laws that classify on the basis of a person's gender are "quasi-suspect" and are subject to so-called intermediate or mid-level scrutiny under the equal protection provisions of both the Fifth and the Fourteenth Amendments. Such discrimination is unconstitutional unless it is shown to be supported by an "exceedingly persuasive justification." *Mississippi Univ. for Women v. Hogan*, 458 U.S. 718, 731 (1982). At one point, four members of the Court urged that gender classifications be regarded as "inherently suspect" and subject to the same "strict judicial scrutiny" that is accorded to classifications based on race, national origin, or alienage. *Frontiero v. Richardson*, 411 U.S. 677, 688 (1973) (Brennan, J., Douglas, J., White, J., and Marshall, J.). In later years, however, the Court settled on an intermediate standard falling somewhere between the extremes of strict scrutiny and rational basis review.

Gender classifications are subject to heightened scrutiny for some of the same reasons that call for strict scrutiny of laws that discriminate based on race, national origin, or alienage. While first-degree prejudice or animus has probably not been a significant factor in the legislative process, second-degree prejudice has played a major role in the history of discrimination against women. Male-dominated legislatures have frequently enacted laws that burden or limit the opportunities of women based on exaggerated negative stereotypes concerning the talents, capacities, preferences, and proper role of women. In terms of their participation in the political process, women did not win the constitutional right to vote until the Nineteenth Amendment was ratified in 1920, half a century after the Fifteenth Amendment sought to bar disenfranchisement based on race. Even though women today are not a "discrete and insular minority," since they comprise roughly half the electorate, many laws still on the books are relics of an era when women were totally excluded from the political process. In addition, like race and national origin, gender is, for most people at least, an immutable trait, which may make it easy for male-controlled legislatures to enact measures that burden women, since such laws can never be applied against the males who voted for them. Finally, while gender is a characteristic that is frequently irrelevant to any legitimate legislative objective, because there are certain physical differences between men and women, gender is somewhat more likely than race to be a legitimate basis of distinction. For these reasons, gender has been treated as a "quasi-suspect," rather than as a fully "suspect," basis of classification.

Gender classifications are subject to mid-level scrutiny even if they appear to burden men rather than women. In 1982, the Court declared that the fact that a law "discriminates against males rather than against females does not exempt it from scrutiny or reduce the standard of review." *Mississippi University for Women v. Hogan*, supra, 458 U.S. at 723. This pronouncement in effect repudiated the approach employed in several earlier cases where laws discriminating against males were subjected to less demanding scrutiny. See *Michael M. v. Superior Court*, 450 U.S. 464 (1981) (upholding California statutory rape law that punished only males); *Rostker v. Goldberg*, 453 U.S. 57 (1981) (upholding Military Selective Service Act requirement that males register for the draft).

It may seem odd to apply heightened scrutiny to classifications that discriminate against men. After all, male-dominated legislatures surely harbor no first or second-degree prejudice against men, nor do they lack empathy for their own kind. Nor have males as a class ever been excluded from the political process. However, stereotypes about the proper role of men implicitly rely on stereotypes about the proper role of women. Moreover, the Court's insistence that the standard of review not be reduced for laws that discriminate against males stems from the difficulty of determining which sex is burdened by a particular gender-discriminatory law. In *Mississippi University for Women v. Hogan*, supra, for example, Mississippi barred males from enrolling in a state-run school of nursing. On its face, this law discriminated against males like Joe Hogan who wished to attend nursing school. Yet the law could also be viewed as discriminating against women, for it helped perpetuate the stereotypical view that nursing is "woman's work," with the result that nurses have long been underpaid. Similarly, in *Schlesinger v. Ballard*, 419 U.S. 498 (1975), a male Navy officer challenged a federal statute that required the discharge of male officers who had gone without a promotion for 9 years, while female officers were given 13 years to obtain a promotion. This statute discriminated against males who faced dismissal at the nine-year mark, yet it also discriminated against women by making it easier for the Navy to delay their promotion. Even though it may not be correct "that all discriminations between the sexes ultimately redound to the detriment of females, because they tend to reinforce 'old notions' restricting the roles and opportunities of women," *Craig v. Boren*, 429 U.S. 190, 220 n.2 (1976) (Rehnquist, J., dissenting), there is enough truth in this that the Court today will apply intermediate scrutiny to all gender classifications.

A law that requires or permits *individuals* to be treated differently on account of their sex will be deemed to involve gender discrimination even if it happens that in the aggregate, men and women *as groups* are treated equally. In *J.E.B. v. Alabama*, 511 U.S. 127 (1994), a case involving the use of gender-based peremptory challenges, the state struck nine men and one woman from the jury panel, while the defendant struck nine women and one man. Even though men and women were treated equally as groups (each lost ten members), every individual juror who was removed because of gender was denied the right to be treated as an equal without regard to his or her sex. The *J.E.B.* Court, therefore, held that a prima facie case of gender discrimination had been established and proceeded to invalidate the government's use of gender-based peremptory challenges under the intermediate scrutiny test.

§6.6.2 Mid-Level Scrutiny as a Measure of Constitutionality

Once the plaintiff has established a prima facie case of gender discrimination, a court will evaluate the classification under an intermediate standard of review which, in recent years, has become increasingly rigorous even though it may not yet be quite as strict as that employed in race and national origin cases.

A law that classifies on the basis of gender will be found to violate the Equal Protection Clause unless its defender can establish an "exceedingly persuasive justification" for the classification. *United States v. Virginia*, 518 U.S. 515, 531 (1996). As the Court in that case explained, "[t]he burden of justification is demanding" and requires the defender of the measure to convincingly demonstrate that:

1. The classification serves "important governmental objectives" that do not rely on archaic or "overbroad generalizations about the different talents, capacities, or preferences of males and females";
2. These objectives are "genuine" in the sense that they "describe actual state purposes, not rationalizations for actions in fact differently grounded"; and
3. The discriminatory means employed are "substantially related" to the achievement of these objectives.

Id. at 531-534. We will look at how the Court has applied each of these elements of the mid-level gender discrimination test.

Important and Legitimate Objectives

Gender discrimination will be upheld only if it furthers an important governmental objective. However, the Court has been reluctant to reject a proffered state goal as too intrinsically unimportant to support a gender classification. Thus, unlike race cases, which are examined under strict scrutiny, remedying past societal discrimination is an objective that may sometimes justify a classification that favors women. In short, this part of the test is likely to be met as long as the government's objective is a *legitimate* one. An exception is found in Chief Justice Rehnquist's concurring opinion in *United States v. Virginia*, where he rejected Virginia's claim that excluding women from the Virginia Military Institute (VMI) served the important interest of maintaining VMI's so-called adversative method. Without "evidence in the record that an adversative method is pedagogically beneficial," Rehnquist concluded that such a goal was not sufficiently important to satisfy this part of the test. 518 U.S. at 564.

However, the Court has at times rejected state objectives as not being legitimate because they relied on overly broad generalizations about differences in the talents, character, or roles of men and women. For example, in *Orr v. Orr*, 440 U.S. 268, 279-280 (1979), the Court struck down an Alabama law that imposed alimony obligations on husbands, but not on wives. The state defended this discrimination partly on the ground that it reinforced a family model "under which the wife plays a dependent role"; the Court rejected this asserted objective as reflecting the "'old notion' that 'generally it is the man's primary responsibility to provide a home and its essentials.' . . ." See also *Michael M. v. Superior Court*, supra, 450 U.S. at 472 n.7 (suggesting that a law subjecting only males to prosecution for statutory rape could not be defended on the ground that it protected the virtue and chastity of young women, since this goal reflected "archaic stereotypes" about women).

Proof of Actual Purpose

If the Court has not placed a great deal of stress on the "importance" of a proffered state objective, the same cannot be said of its insistence that the objective be a "genuine" and "actual state purpose" rather than one "hypothesized or invented *post hoc* in response to litigation." *United States v. Virginia*, supra, 518 U.S. at 533, 535. In some cases, the legislature may have recorded its purpose in either the text or the legislative history of a law; if it has not, the classification's defender must produce other evidence demonstrating that the alleged goal was in fact the actual purpose for the challenged gender discrimination.

EXAMPLE

Example 6-FF

Joe was denied admission to the State School of Nursing under a law providing that only women may attend the school. Joe challenged the state's refusal to admit him as violating the Equal Protection Clause. The state defended its admissions policy on the ground that it serves the important objective of remedying past societal discrimination against women in the workplace by offering professional training that will assure women a job. Will the court accept the state's argument?

EXPLANATION

Explanation

Remedying past societal discrimination against women is an objective that may justify a gender classification. However, for this compensatory goal to suffice, several requirements must be met, including proof that this was the actual objective of the law. In the absence of any evidence to this effect in the state statute or its legislative history, a court would be skeptical of the state's benign goal. This skepticism would be compounded if Joe shows that the nursing school is part of a state university that has been limited to women since it was created a century ago. Moreover, the fact that nursing is one of the few professional fields from which women have not been excluded would cast further doubt on the state's alleged remedial goal. While women may need special assistance in gaining access to fields such as law, medicine, or engineering, there is no similar need in the field of nursing. It is thus doubtful a court would accept the state's proffered remedial goal as being the real objective of its discriminatory admissions plan. See *Mississippi Univ. for Women v. Hogan*, 458 U.S. 718 (1982).

Means Substantially Related to Goal

Once it is shown that a gender classification was adopted to achieve an important and genuine governmental purpose, the defender must also demonstrate that the discriminatory means are substantially related to that objective. Under this part of the test, the Court has required the government to show that it was necessary to discriminate to achieve the goal—i.e., that there were no gender-neutral alternatives that might have accomplished the objective equally well. If nondiscriminatory alternatives were available, then the government gained nothing by discriminating. The gender classification, in other words, is gratuitous and unnecessary, in which case the discrimination is not substantially related to furthering the state's goals. As the Court said in *Orr v. Orr*, supra, 440 U.S. at 283, "Where, as here, the State's . . . purposes are as well served by a gender-neutral classification as one that gender classifies and, therefore, carries with it the baggage of sexual stereotypes, the State cannot be permitted to classify on the basis of sex."

EXAMPLE

Example 6-GG

A state law makes it a crime for a male to have sexual intercourse with a female who is under the age of 18 unless the couple is married. Only the male partner is criminally punishable for such conduct. The state defends this gender classification on the ground that it is substantially related to the important goal of preventing illegitimate teenage pregnancies. According to the state, female minors would be less likely to file a complaint if they could then be prosecuted. Assuming that the court accepts the state's claimed objective as being both important and genuine, what should the state have to show to meet the "substantially related" requirement?

EXPLANATION

Explanation

The state should have to persuasively demonstrate that its gender-discriminatory law is more effective in achieving the state's goal than would be a gender-neutral law under which both partners are potentially subject to criminal prosecution. While it is no doubt true that there would be fewer complaints filed by female minors if they were subject to punishment, the state's goal was not to maximize the number of complaints filed, but to reduce the number of teenage pregnancies. A gender-neutral law might have a much stronger deterrent effect than a law that threatens only males with punishment. The state should have the burden of proving that its gender-discriminatory approach actually has a greater deterrent effect than would a gender-neutral law.

This example is taken from *Michael M. v. Superior Court*, 450 U.S. 464 (1981), where the Court upheld California's statutory rape law by applying what amounted to rational basis review. The plurality opinion by Justice Rehnquist did not require the state to prove that its gender-discriminatory law "is any more effective than a gender-neutral law would be in deterring minor females from engaging in sexual intercourse." Id. at 496 (Brennan, J., dissenting). *Michael M.* would probably be decided differently under the standard of review applied by the Court today.

EXAMPLE

Example 6-HH

Under the Immigration and Nationality Act (INA), a child born overseas to unmarried parents, only one of whom is a U.S. citizen, will be deemed to be an American citizen at birth if certain statutory requirements are met. One of these requirements is that the citizen parent must have resided in the United States for a specified number of years prior to the child's birth. However, it is harder for such a child to qualify as a citizen if their citizen parent was the father rather than the mother, for the INA, which originally required both citizen fathers and citizen mothers to have resided in the United States for at least five years prior to the child's birth, was then amended to make an exception for citizen mothers who had resided here continuously for one year before that birth. 8 U.S.C. §§ 1401(g), 1409(c).

Luis was born in the Dominican Republic in 1962 to a U.S. citizen father and a Dominican mother. His father was born in the United States but left this country as a child after having lived here just 20 days shy of the five-year minimum residency requirement. As a result, Luis did not qualify for U.S. citizenship at birth. In 1975, when he was 13 years old, Luis moved to the United States and has lived here ever since. He was recently ordered deported to the Dominican Republic, based on several past state court criminal convictions. Luis objected that he was not deportable because he is a U.S. citizen by birth. He contends that the provisions of the INA, insofar as they impose additional burdens on those, like him, who were born to citizen fathers rather than to citizen mothers, violate the equal protection guaranty of the Fifth Amendment.

In response, the government argued that the gender-based differential helps ensure that a child born abroad has a sufficiently strong connection to the United States to warrant the conferral of citizenship at birth. Since unwed fathers are often indifferent to their children, imposing a longer residency requirement on them helps to ensure the child's continuing connection to the United States. The government also contends that Congress adopted this gender distinction because there is a much greater danger foreign-born children will be born stateless if it is their mother rather than their father who is the U.S. citizen. There is little in the congressional record to suggest that either of these alleged purposes was in fact what led Congress to enact this differential scheme.

Are the INA provisions invalid as constituting forbidden gender discrimination? If they are, what is the appropriate remedy—i.e., should the court require that citizen fathers and citizen mothers both get the benefit of the one-year rule, or should both now be required to satisfy the five-year rule?

Explanation

The INA facially discriminates on the basis of gender, for it makes it more difficult for citizen fathers to transfer American citizenship to their children than for citizen mothers to do so. The government may argue that intermediate scrutiny should not apply because the Court traditionally shows deference to the political branches in cases involving immigration and naturalization. However, this case involves the acquisition of citizenship at birth and thus does not concern either immigration (the terms on which aliens may be admitted to or remain in the United States) or naturalization (the process by which persons may obtain citizenship after birth). Thus, the mid-level standard of review should not be relaxed.

Under the applicable mid-level-scrutiny standard, the government must show that its gender-based classification is substantially related to achieving an important governmental interest—i.e., that a gender-neutral law would not achieve its goals as well as this gender discriminatory measure. As to the goal of trying to ensure a strong connection between the child and the United States, there is no reason to believe that a citizen mother who has spent as few as 12 consecutive months here will necessarily maintain that connection after her child is born. Nor is there any reason to assume that because an unwed citizen father has spent fewer than five years in this country, his child will fail to develop such a connection. Nor is there any basis for assuming that all unmarried men need more time than all unmarried women to absorb U.S. values and hence be able to transmit them to their children. Even if this is an important governmental objective, the differential residency requirement is both overinclusive and underinclusive in terms of its goal, resting on unfounded stereotypes about the differences between unmarried men and unmarried women. Under intermediate scrutiny, the government would thus have to show that no gender-neutral alternatives—e.g., individualized parental assessments—would have attained its objectives, a showing that would be very difficult to make.

As to the second goal, it is far from clear that foreign-born children of unwed U.S. citizen mothers in fact face a greater risk of statelessness than those born abroad to unwed citizen fathers. Experts have found that "the risk of parenting stateless children abroad . . . remains today . . . substantial for unmarried U.S. fathers, a risk perhaps greater than for unmarried U.S. mothers." To the extent this is true, it would warrant complete gender neutrality rather than the discriminatory scheme adopted here.

We have thus far assumed that these asserted goals are ones a court would in fact consider in applying mid-level scrutiny. Yet the Supreme Court has stated that under the mid-level scrutiny called for in gender discrimination cases, the government's asserted objectives must be "genuine" in the sense that they describe "actual state purposes, not rationalizations for actions in fact differently grounded." *United States v. Virginia*, supra, 518 U.S. at 531-534. Here, the congressional record contained little if any evidence that the goals advanced in court were goals that Congress was in fact pursuing when it adopted the challenged provision. While a court might not feel comfortable rejecting the government's arguments on this basis alone, it seriously weakens any argument the government might make concerning the statute's ostensible goals.

Finally, there is the question of remedy. In equal protection cases involving statutory benefits or entitlements, if a court finds the challenged provision to be unconstitutionally discriminatory, it may either declare the statute a nullity so that no one receives the benefit in question, or it can extend statutory coverage to those aggrieved by the exclusion. Thus, equal treatment can be achieved here either by *withdrawing* the citizenship benefit from the favored class (i.e., from citizen mothers who lived here for a continuous period of at least one year but fewer than five years prior to the child's birth), or by *extending* the benefit to the disfavored class (i.e., to citizen fathers who lived here for less than five years but for at least 12 continuous months prior to his child's birth). While courts in such cases usually favor extension rather than nullification, the question is ultimately one of the legislature's presumed intent. Luis will argue in favor of giving fathers the benefit of the shorter residence requirement, while the government will respond that this would allow the exception to consume the rule, contrary to what Congress presumably intended.

In *Sessions v. Morales-Santana*, 582 U.S. 47 (2017), the Court on similar facts held that the INA violated the Fifth Amendment. Based on its best guess as to congressional intent, the Court ruled that the proper remedy was to preserve the basic five-year rule and abrogate the one-year exception for mothers. Luis's claim that he was a U.S. citizen was thus rejected and his removal to the Dominican Republic affirmed. See *Sessions v. Morales-Santana*, 706 Fed. Appx. 40 (2d Cir. 2017).

The "substantially related" requirement, by insisting that the government not resort to gender discrimination if gender-neutral alternatives are available, means that gender may not be used as a proxy for other factors that are gender-neutral. For example, while it is statistically true that women on average live longer than men, this gender stereotype is not true of all women or all men; some women live fewer years than the average man, while some men live longer than the average woman. Thus, to use gender as a predictor of longevity is to employ a classification that is both overinclusive and underinclusive. Instead of relying on gender stereotypes, the state must look beyond the surface to gender-neutral factors that may affect an individual's life span. The use of gender stereotypes will probably survive the "substantially related" requirement only if the government can prove "that gender alone is an accurate predictor" of the matter in question. *J.E.B. v. Alabama*, supra, 511 U.S. at 139. Rarely, if ever, will such a showing be possible.

Example 6-11

A state law requires female workers to pay higher annual premiums to the state retirement fund than men, on the theory that, because they live longer, women will draw retirement benefits for a longer time. The state has justified this discrimination on the basis that it needs to maintain the fiscal integrity of its pension plan. Is this gender discrimination valid?

Explanation

The goal of preserving the fiscal soundness of the state pension fund is no doubt an important state goal. Yet the means chosen are not substantially related to that objective, since the state could achieve its ends without engaging in gender discrimination. The state could maintain the fiscal integrity of its plan by charging men and women the same premium, with the total premiums collected being the same as they would have been under a gender-discriminatory plan.

If, on the other hand, the state wishes to vary premiums based on an individual's projected life span, it may not use gender as a proxy for longevity. Instead, the state must look beyond gender to other factors that influence life span, such as smoking, drinking, diet, exercise habits, and the like. See *City of Los Angeles v. Manhart*, 435 U.S. 702 (1978) (invalidating similar pension scheme under Title VII of the 1964 Civil Rights Act).

The prohibition against using gender stereotypes is another way of saying that the government may not employ a presumption that all members of a sex share a characteristic that may have statistical validity for the group as a whole, but that is not true of each member of the group. Virtually every law is based on stereotypes and presumptions. A speed limit law stereotypes those driving over the speed limit as dangerous drivers even though this presumption is not true of all speeders. Similarly, a law setting a minimum driving age of eighteen presumes that those under eighteen are unfit to drive even though this stereotype is not true in all cases. Stereotypes or presumptions based on group characteristics are the stuff of the law. They are problematic and generally prohibited only when the stereotype involves a trait such as race, national origin, or gender that calls for heightened scrutiny. In these cases, there is a danger that the government is using a racial or gender stereotype—in lieu of other more accurate factors—as a subtle way of harming the group in question. In addition, reliance on such stereotypes usually reinforces negative perceptions about racial minorities or women. See § 5.7.1 (Rebuttable and Irrebuttable Presumptions).

There is a difference, however, between classifications that use gender itself as a stereotype and classifications that are based on traits disproportionately or exclusively associated with one gender. While the former practice is usually prohibited, the latter type of classification may survive the "substantially related" test if it is not a pretext for gender stereotyping.

EXAMPLE

Example 6-JJ

The prosecution in a paternity case used all of its peremptory challenges to excuse from the jury ten men who had previously been defendants in paternity actions. Does the prosecutor's action violate the Equal Protection Clause?

EXPLANATION

Explanation

In *J.E.B. v. Alabama*, 511 U.S. 127 (1994), the state in a paternity suit used all but one of its peremptory challenges to remove men from the jury out of fear that male jurors would sympathize with the defendant. The Court held that such use of gender as a proxy for bias was unconstitutional; instead of employing "stereotypical and pejorative notions about a particular gender," id. at 143, the state was required to "look beyond the surface" to discover possible bias based on gender-neutral factors. Id. at 139 n.11. However, the Court in *J.E.B.* noted that "strikes based on characteristics that are disproportionately associated with one gender could be appropriate, absent a showing of pretext." Id. at 143 & n.16.

In our example, the prosecutor has not employed a stereotype about men in general or presumed that men will be biased toward the defendant. Instead, the prosecutor excused only those potential jurors who had been sued for paternity. While this group by definition consists only of men, it was not a juror's sex that led to exclusion, but rather the fact that he had been sued for paternity. Such conduct by the prosecutor does not constitute gender discrimination if the jurors were excused in spite of, not because of, their sex. See § 6.2.2. In other words, if the prosecutor had a good-faith concern about the jurors' prior involvement in paternity cases rather than about their being males, this would rebut any prima facie case of gender discrimination by defeating the purpose element. To be sure, the prosecutor relied on the stereotype that those sued for paternity will be biased toward the defendant in a paternity suit; but since this presumption rests on a trait or characteristic—prior involvement in a paternity suit—that does not call for heightened scrutiny, reliance on the presumption is constitutionally unobjectionable. The prosecutor's action would, therefore, not violate the Equal Protection Clause because it probably does not involve gender discrimination.

Comparing the Tests for Gender and Race Discrimination

As we have seen, the standard of review employed in gender discrimination cases today is extremely demanding and may approach the strict scrutiny test, which governs race, national origin, and many alienage discrimination cases. In *United States v. Virginia*, supra, the Court stated that it was not "equating gender classifications, *for all purposes*, to classifications based on race or national origin," implying that at least in some cases the level of scrutiny is the same. 518 U.S. at 532 (emphasis supplied). However, assuming that this is true, the Court has noted several circumstances under which its approach to gender and racial discrimination might lead to different results. One involves laws that draw distinctions based on the "[p]hysical differences between men and women," for while "[s]upposed 'inherent differences' are no longer accepted as a ground for race or national origin classifications," id. at 533, they may suffice to allow, for example, separate restrooms and living facilities for men and women in state colleges.

A second possible difference between the Court's approaches to gender and race classifications involves affirmative action. In the race setting, as we have seen, such programs are subject to the strictest scrutiny, whereas in gender cases they are more easily justified. Thus, whereas remedying past societal discrimination is not a sufficient interest to allow a race-conscious remedial scheme, this may be an adequate objective in the gender setting.

Finally, the Court has left open the possibility that the principle of "separate but equal" may allow a state to operate separate undergraduate institutions for men and women even though the maintenance of racially segregated schools and colleges is clearly unconstitutional. In

United States v. Virginia, the state defended its exclusion of women from the Virginia Military Institute (VMI) on the basis that single-sex colleges further the goal of providing diversity in educational opportunities. The Court rejected this argument because offering diversity in educational approaches was not the actual goal of VMI's male-only admissions policy. The Court added that even if this had been the state's goal, since there were no separate—much less equal—facilities for women, the "separate but equal" doctrine would not have justified the exclusion of women from VMI. However, the Court then went out of its way to emphasize that "[w]e do not question the Commonwealth's prerogative evenhandedly to support diverse educational opportunities," id. at 533 n.7, suggesting that in a different factual setting, states might provide single-sex colleges for men and women.

§6.6.3 Legitimacy

The intermediate or mid-level standard of review is also applied to laws that classify based on legitimacy and that thus discriminate against children born to unmarried parents. The use of intermediate scrutiny for laws aimed at nonmarital children may be justified on several bases. At one time at least, illegitimate children were the objects of considerable scorn and moral censure, as is suggested by the word "bastard," the dictionary definition of which is "counterfeit, sham, or inferior." Even though such first-degree prejudice against nonmarital children is probably rare today, our basic sense of fairness suggests that it is wrong for the law to heap burdens on a person because of a relationship over which he or she had no control. Moreover, while the condition of illegitimacy is not completely immutable since a child can become legitimized, the condition—like that of alienage—is alterable in only one direction, thus reducing the extent to which empathy might otherwise temper the legislative process.

The Court has described the standard of review for laws that discriminate based on legitimacy as requiring that the "statutory classification . . . be substantially related to an important governmental objective." *Clark v. Jeter*, 486 U.S. 456, 461 (1988). This is the same verbal formula that has long been used in gender cases. The Court has thus noted that "intermediate scrutiny . . . generally has been applied to discriminatory classifications based on sex or illegitimacy," id., suggesting that the standards are the same. However, with the recent strengthening of the gender discrimination standard to the point where it often approaches strict scrutiny, the standard of review applied in legitimacy cases is probably less rigorous than that now employed in gender cases.

The illegitimacy standard is, nevertheless, demanding. The requirement that the discrimination serve an important governmental objective bars the state from employing "classifications that burden illegitimate children for the sake of punishing the illicit relations of their parents, because 'visiting this condemnation on the head of an infant is illogical and unjust.'" Id. The government cannot categorically exclude illegitimate children from receiving benefits that would be paid to them if they were legitimate. On the other hand, the government has an important interest in minimizing the problems often associated with proving paternity. Time limits on an illegitimate child's attempt to prove paternity as a precondition to receiving various benefits will thus be upheld if they are substantially related to the state's interest in avoiding litigation of stale or fraudulent claims. However, the time limits must be reasonable and not appreciably shorter than necessary to achieve the state's goal.

Example 6-KK

EXAMPLE

State law provides that a father need not pay support on behalf of an illegitimate child unless paternity is established in an action filed prior to the child's fifth birthday; if paternity is so established, the father's support obligation shall not exceed 50 percent of the amount that would be owed to a legitimate child. Is this statute constitutional?

Explanation

EXPLANATION

Insofar as the statute limits the support that must be paid on behalf of an illegitimate child to 50 percent of what would be paid to a legitimate child, the statute is surely unconstitutional. It is difficult to imagine any reason for the 50 percent limitation other than a desire to punish the mother and her child for the child's having been born out of wedlock.

The five-year statute of limitations for filing a paternity action is also problematic. The state may argue that this rule bars stale or fraudulent paternity claims brought at a time when the putative father can no longer defend himself. The Court has recognized the importance of this state interest but has held that to meet the "substantially related" test, the state must allow a reasonable time for those interested in the well-being of such children to sue on their behalf. Moreover, the time limit here may be shorter than necessary to protect the state's interest. Given the fact that scientific evidence is now often able to prove and disprove claims of paternity, the harm to the putative father of allowing suit after the child's fifth birthday is likely to be minimal. Thus, the five-year limitations period is probably also unconstitutional. See *Clark v. Jeter*, 486 U.S. 456 (1988) (invalidating six-year limitation on paternity suits as a condition for receiving child support).

§6.7 OTHER POSSIBLY DISFAVORED BASES OF CLASSIFICATION

§6.7.1 The Rejection of New "Suspect" and "Quasi-Suspect" Classes

The Supreme Court has been unwilling to recognize any new bases of classification as being "suspect" or "quasi-suspect" for equal protection purposes. As a result, the list of "suspect" classifications that will trigger strict scrutiny is limited to race, national origin, and alienage, while only gender and legitimacy are deemed to be "quasi-suspect" and subject to intermediate scrutiny.

The Court has expressly rejected claims that discrimination based on age, mental retardation, or poverty should receive some form of heightened scrutiny. See *Massachusetts Bd. of Retirement v. Murgia*, 427 U.S. 307 (1976) (age classifications receive rational basis review); *City of Cleburne v. Cleburne Living Center*, 473 U.S. 432 (1985) (rejecting mental retardation as a quasi-suspect classification); *Harris v. McRae*, 448 U.S. 297, 323 (1980) (poverty or wealth not a suspect classification). *Cleburne* strongly implied that no new "suspect" or "quasi-suspect" classes will be recognized. The Court there stated that if mental retardation were granted "quasi-suspect" status,

> it would be difficult to find a principled way to distinguish a variety of other groups who have perhaps immutable disabilities setting them off from others, who cannot themselves mandate the desired legislative responses, and who can claim some degree of prejudice from at least part of the public at large. One need mention in this respect only the aging, the disabled, the mentally ill, and the infirm. We are reluctant to set out on that course, and we decline to do so.

473 U.S. at 445-446. Thus, the list of classifications that will be deemed to be "suspect" or "quasi-suspect" appears, for now at least, to be frozen.

While the Court has refused *formally* to recognize additional bases of classification that call for heightened scrutiny, it has not always applied the rational basis test in its customarily toothless manner. In certain situations, the rational basis standard seems to take on added rigor, with the result that the challenged classification is sometimes held to violate the Equal Protection Clause. Because the Court in these cases does not *acknowledge* that it is applying anything other than the traditional rational basis test, it is difficult to state with certainty that a more demanding standard was employed. Yet the fact that a law fails the rational basis test is itself a powerful indicator that something more than ordinary rational basis review was employed. We will examine several settings in which the Court appears to have elevated the standard of rational basis review. In each instance, the group discriminated against was politically powerless or politically unpopular.

§6.7.2 Discrimination Against Out-of-Staters

State laws that discriminate against persons from other states are often subject to challenge under the Commerce Clause (see Christopher N. May, Allan Ides & Simona Grossi, *Constitutional Law: National Power and Federalism*, ch. 8 (9th ed. 2022)); under the Privileges and Immunities Clause of Article IV, § 2 (see id., ch. 9); or as impairing the right to travel under the Equal Protection Clause or the Privileges or Immunities Clause of the Fourteenth Amendment (see § 7.4). There are times, however, when none of these approaches will work to invalidate discrimination against out-of-staters. In these instances, a litigant may wish to challenge such laws as being arbitrary and unreasonable under the Equal Protection Clause.

There is a strong argument that for equal protection purposes, discrimination against people from other states should receive heightened scrutiny because the group targeted is not represented in the political process that produced the measure in question. While the Court has not used strict or intermediate scrutiny in this setting, it has occasionally employed an enhanced rational basis test to review laws that discriminate against current or former out-of-staters. See, e.g., *Metropolitan Life Ins. Co. v. Ward*, 470 U.S. 869 (1985) (rational basis equal protection test barred Alabama from taxing out-of-state companies at higher rate than domestic companies); *Zobel v. Williams*, 457 U.S. 55 (1982) (rational basis equal protection test barred Alaska from paying new residents lower annual dividends than are paid to long-term residents). See § 7.4.3.

EXAMPLE

Example 6-LL

Norman moved from Illinois to Vermont shortly after buying a car in Illinois. Vermont requires its citizens to pay a use tax upon registering a car that was purchased in another state. However, Vermont grants an exemption from the use tax for any sales tax paid to another state if, at the time of purchase, the registrant was a Vermont citizen. When Norman registered the car in Vermont, the state charged him the full use tax, with no credit for the sales tax he had paid to Illinois, because at the time of purchase, he was not a Vermont citizen. Did Vermont violate the Equal Protection Clause by discriminating against people, such as Norman, who were recently citizens of another state?

EXPLANATION

Explanation

Under the traditional rational basis test, Vermont's tax would easily be upheld. The difference in treatment may have been based on the assumption that those who lived in another state when they bought a car benefited from that state's roads. Since they will derive benefits from the roads in two states, it is not unfair that they pay taxes to two states. By contrast, those who were Vermonters when they bought a car in another state may have derived little benefit from the other state's roads and thus should not have to pay taxes to two states. This sort of speculation affords a rational basis for the Vermont law. However, in *Williams v. Vermont*, 472 U.S. 14, 22 (1985), the Court, ostensibly applying the traditional rational basis test, invalidated this Vermont tax scheme as creating "an arbitrary distinction that violates the Equal Protection Clause." One explanation for the result is that the Court applied an enhanced form of rational basis review.

§6.7.3 Discrimination Against the Mentally Retarded

As we noted earlier, in *City of Cleburne v. Cleburne Living Center*, 473 U.S. 432, 442 (1985), the Supreme Court expressly refused to treat mental retardation as a "quasi-suspect classification" that calls for "intermediate-level scrutiny," and held that "[i]n such cases, the Equal Protection Clause requires only a rational means to serve a legitimate end." See § 6.7.1. Yet the Court then ruled that by denying permission to operate a group home for the mentally retarded, the City of Cleburne had violated the Equal Protection Clause "[b]ecause in our view the record does not reveal any rational basis" for the denial. Id. at 448. Instead, said the Court, the city's action "appears to us to rest on an irrational prejudice against the mentally retarded. . . ." Id. at 450. Under the ordinary rational basis test, however, there need not be anything in the record to support the classification in question; mere speculation will suffice. Justices Marshall, Brennan, and Blackmun thus objected to the majority's "refusal to acknowledge that something more than minimum rationality review is at work here." Id. at 459. As Justice Marshall wrote, "[P]erhaps the method employed must hereafter be called 'second order' rational-basis review rather than 'heightened scrutiny.' But however labeled, the rational-basis test invoked today is most assuredly not the [traditional] rational-basis test. . . ." Id. at 458.

The fact that the Court in *Cleburne* struck down the city's ordinance does not necessarily mean that all laws discriminating against the mentally retarded are invalid. In *Cleburne*, there was considerable evidence to bolster the Court's conclusion that the ban on group homes for the mentally retarded was a product of "irrational prejudice," including language in the ordinance itself that barred homes "'*for the* insane or *feeble-minded* or alcoholics or drug addicts.'" Id. at 436 n.3 (emphasis in original). In other words, there were strong indications that the *actual* goal of the ordinance was an illegitimate one, causing the Court to show less than usual deference to the *hypothetical* purposes offered by the measure's defenders. Where evidence of "irrational prejudice" or another illegitimate purpose is lacking, the Court has upheld classifications that burden the mentally retarded. See *Heller v. Doe*, 509 U.S. 312 (1993) (upholding Kentucky involuntary commitment procedures that made it easier to commit the mentally retarded than the mentally ill).

The *Cleburne* Court's willingness to more closely examine classifications that appear to be based on "irrational prejudice" against a disfavored group was not unique. In *United States Department of Agriculture v. Moreno*, 413 U.S. 528 (1973), the Court invoked the equal protection component of the Fifth Amendment to overturn a federal law that denied food stamps to households containing unrelated members. The Court concluded that the aim of the classification was "to prevent so-called 'hippies' and 'hippie communes' from participating in the food stamp program." Id. at 534. Though only rational basis review was called for, said the Court, "if the constitutional conception of 'equal protection of the laws' means anything, it must at the very least mean that a bare congressional desire to harm a politically unpopular group cannot constitute a *legitimate* governmental interest." Id. (emphasis in original).

§6.7.4 Discrimination on the Basis of Sexual Orientation

The Court in *Romer v. Evans*, 517 U.S. 620 (1996), showed a similar willingness to enhance the rational basis test where necessary to protect a politically unpopular group. *Romer* involved Colorado's Amendment 2, a constitutional provision that rescinded all state and local laws protecting gays and lesbians and that prohibited any legislative, executive, or judicial action designed to protect these groups in the future. The Colorado Supreme Court held the provision unconstitutional under the Fourteenth Amendment's Equal Protection Clause, applying strict scrutiny on the ground that the measure infringed on the fundamental right of gays and lesbians to participate in the political process. The U.S. Supreme Court affirmed, but on the ground that the provision "lacks a rational relationship to legitimate state interests." Id. at 632.

The rational basis test relied on in *Romer* was not the usual toothless version of the standard. Instead, the Court invalidated Amendment 2 for two reasons, neither of which would normally cause a classification to fail under the traditional rational basis test: First, the measure imposed such an "unprecedented," "broad and undifferentiated disability on a single named group"—i.e., gays and lesbians—as to render it "an invalid form of legislation"; second, the law lacked "a rational relationship to a legitimate governmental purpose" because it "inflict[ed] . . . immediate, continuing, and real injuries that outrun and belie any legitimate justifications that may be claimed for it," thus "rais[ing] the inevitable inference that the disadvantage imposed is born of animosity toward the class of persons affected." Id. at 632-635. Yet the fact that a classification is sweeping or unprecedented is usually not enough to doom it under the rational basis standard test. Nor, under that standard, does a court normally test a classification to see how well it fits the proffered goals. To the contrary, the Court's traditional rational basis standard of review tolerates measures that are imprecise, illogical, and ill-suited to their supposed purposes. Testing the closeness of the fit is characteristic of heightened—not rational basis—scrutiny.

One might conclude that *Romer* employed an enhanced version of the rational basis test. On the other hand, *Romer* could be seen as one of those rare cases in which a law fails the rational basis test because of overwhelming evidence that the measure was enacted for an illegitimate purpose. Whichever view one takes, the critical factor was the Court's conviction that Amendment 2 was "inexplicable by anything but animus toward the class it affects. . . ." Id. at 632. In this respect, the case is quite similar to *Moreno* (see § 6.7.3), a decision the Court cited with approval, which struck down a federal law aimed at "hippies."

It remains unclear to what extent other laws discriminating on the basis of sexual orientation will be subject to a similarly enhanced rational basis review. At this point, we can only pose questions rather than answer them. Is *Romer* limited to settings in which the government has imposed a "broad and undifferentiated disability" on gays and lesbians, or will the enhanced standard be triggered whenever a court believes that the discrimination was the product of anti-homosexual animus? If the latter is true, how is a court to ascertain the presence of animus? It is not a satisfactory response to say that enhanced scrutiny will be applied whenever the poorness of the fit casts doubts on a classification's asserted goals, for a court has no business testing the fit in this way unless it has first decided that some mode of enhanced scrutiny is called for. If, instead, mere suspicion of animus is enough to trigger enhanced scrutiny, what must the suspicion rest on? Is mere intuition enough? Unlike *Moreno*, where the Court cited specific legislative history in finding an animus against "hippies," *Romer* did not cite or rely on any background materials showing that Colorado's Amendment 2 was motivated by hostility toward gays and lesbians.

These uncertainties would be eliminated if the Court were explicitly to hold that because of widespread first- and second-degree prejudice against gays and lesbians, all laws that discriminate against these groups are subject to heightened scrutiny. However, as the Court has carefully avoided making such a determination, it is unclear what standard of review is to be applied in these cases. In *Lawrence v. Texas*, 539 U.S. 558, 574-575 (2003), the Court, in striking down a Texas statute that criminalized sodomy only if it was engaged in "with another individual of the same sex," expressly declined to address the equal protection issue and instead relied upon the Due Process Clause to invalidate the state law. See § 2.5.5. Justice O'Connor, in her separate concurring opinion, voted to invalidate the state statute relying solely on the Equal Protection Clause. In doing so, however, she applied only a rational basis standard of review, without discussing the question of whether a stricter standard of review might have been appropriate.

Later, in *Obergefell v. Hodges*, 576 U.S. 644 (2015), the Court struck down state marriage laws that discriminated against gays and lesbians. See § 2.5.1. It found that such laws were inconsistent with the Due Process and Equal Protection Clauses of the Fourteenth Amendment. The central holding of that case was that the fundamental right to marry fully extends to same-sex couples on both liberty and equality grounds. And see *Pavan v. Smith*, 582 U.S. 563 (2017) (per curiam) (under *Obergefell*, the state may not discriminate against married same-sex couples by listing only the birth mother on a child's birth certificate, when for married opposite-sex couples, the state requires listing both the mother and her male spouse, whether or not the latter is the child's biological father). *Romer*, *Obergefell*, and *Pavan* expressed no view as to whether classifications based on sexual orientation where no fundamental right is involved are subject to heightened scrutiny, but the tone of the majority opinion in *Obergefell* could be interpreted as at least requiring a closer look at laws that discriminate on this basis.

CHAPTER 7

Equal Protection: Fundamental Rights

§7.1 INTRODUCTION AND OVERVIEW

In the previous chapter, we examined application of the Equal Protection Clause in situations that call for mere rational basis review and in situations where the basis of classification was "suspect," "quasi-suspect," or otherwise such as to call for some form of heightened scrutiny. We turn now to an examination of the Equal Protection Clause in settings where the basis of the classification is unproblematic, but where the law discriminates in such a way as to impinge on a fundamental constitutional right. After exploring this fundamental-rights branch of the equal protection doctrine, this chapter will conclude by looking briefly at an alternative approach to equal protection that Justice Thurgood Marshall advocated as a replacement for the Court's three-tier model that we have been discussing.

§7.2 EQUAL PROTECTION AND FUNDAMENTAL RIGHTS

Laws that classify in ways that infringe on the exercise of a fundamental constitutional right will be upheld only if they survive the same strict scrutiny test that is applied to suspect classifications. In other words, the defender of the law must demonstrate that the discrimination is narrowly tailored to serve a compelling governmental interest. See § 6.4.2.

Example 7-A

Roger is 18 years of age and the father of a 3-year-old girl who was born out of wedlock. Two years ago, Roger was ordered to pay child support in the amount of $200 per month. Because he has been unemployed, Roger has not paid child support and owes an arrearage of almost $5,000. Roger recently applied for a marriage license. The license was denied under a state law that prohibits anyone from marrying who has not met his or her child-support obligations. Roger sued, alleging that the license denial violates his rights under the Equal Protection Clause. How should the court rule?

Explanation

The right to marry is a fundamental constitutional liberty. *Loving v. Virginia*, 388 U.S. 1 (1967). In this case, the state has created a classification that allows some people to marry, while denying that right to others. The classifying trait—payment of child support—is not one that calls for heightened scrutiny. However, because the law substantially interferes with a person's fundamental constitutional right to marry, the law is subject to strict scrutiny.

The state might argue that its discrimination against those who fail to support their children serves the compelling interest of assuring that minor children are cared for. Even if this is a sufficiently compelling interest to justify interference with the right to marry, the state must show that the marriage ban is narrowly tailored to that goal in the sense that it is neither overinclusive nor underinclusive. Here, the ban is overinclusive because it applies even when preventing a marriage will in no way further the state's child-support goal. Whether or not Roger gets married, it is unlikely he can pay child support. The state thus gains nothing by impairing Roger's constitutional rights. The law, therefore, violates the Equal Protection Clause because it creates a classification that burdens the fundamental right to marry without being narrowly tailored to the state's interest in seeing that children are adequately supported. See *Zablocki v. Redhail*, 434 U.S. 374 (1978).

Example 7-B

State X has refused to issue a marriage license to a same-sex couple on the grounds that State X law limits marriage to a union between a man and a woman. Is the State X law unconstitutional as a matter of equal protection?

Explanation

Yes. In *Obergefell v. Hodges*, 576 U.S. 644 (2015), the Supreme Court held that the fundamental right to marry extends to same-sex couples as part of the liberty protected by the Fourteenth Amendment. Since the discrimination here bears on the exercise of that fundamental right, it will also be subject to strict scrutiny under the Equal Protection Clause. In fact, the Court in *Obergefell* relied on both the Due Process Clause and the Equal Protection Clause in striking down state laws virtually identical to the State X law at issue here. In the Court's words:

> It is now clear that the challenged laws burden the liberty of same-sex couples, and it must be further acknowledged that they abridge central precepts of equality. Here the marriage laws enforced by the respondents are in essence unequal: same-sex couples are denied all the benefits afforded to opposite-sex couples and are barred from exercising a fundamental right. Especially against a long history of disapproval of their relationships, this denial to same-sex couples of the right to marry works a grave and continuing harm. The imposition of this disability on gays and lesbians serves to disrespect and subordinate them. And the Equal Protection Clause, like the Due Process Clause, prohibits this unjustified infringement of the fundamental right to marry.

Id. at 675. And see *Pavan v. Smith*, 582 U.S. 563, 564 (2017) (per curiam) ("the Constitution entitles same-sex couples to civil marriage 'on the same terms and conditions as opposite-sex couples'") (quoting *Obergefell*, supra, 576 U.S. at 676). Hence, in the absence of a compelling justification for this discrimination, the State X law will be struck down.

Rights that are considered fundamental for equal protection purposes are of two types. The first embraces *due process liberties*—i.e., interests that qualify as fundamental liberties under the Due Process Clauses of the Fifth and Fourteenth Amendments. These due process liberties include rights that are *enumerated* in the Constitution, such as freedom of speech and religion, as well as certain *unenumerated* interests that the Court has deemed to be fundamental, such as the freedom to marry, the freedom to choose whether to bear or beget a child, and the right to determine one's family living arrangements. See Chapter 2. The second type of fundamental liberty that may trigger strict scrutiny under the Equal Protection Clause is what we might call *equal protection liberties*. These consist of certain implied liberty interests that are deemed to be fundamental for equal protection purposes even though they do not enjoy fundamental liberty status under the Due Process Clause. These so-called equal protection liberties include the right to vote, the freedom to travel, and perhaps the liberty to obtain a basic education.

For strict scrutiny to be triggered when a law discriminates with respect to a fundamental constitutional liberty, the Court sometimes insists that the impairment of that right exceed a minimum threshold—i.e., the classification must infringe or impinge on the right in question by substantially interfering with it. This requirement was easily satisfied in Example 7-A, since the state totally barred people such as Roger from getting married. Suppose, however, that the state instead required parents who had not met their child-support obligation to obtain financial counseling before they could marry. If the counseling requirement did not significantly delay the ability to marry, a court might conclude that the classification is not subject to strict scrutiny because the state has not infringed or impinged upon the right to marry.

§7.3 THE RIGHT TO VOTE

§7.3.1 The Absolute versus the Equal Right to Vote

There are two distinct senses in which the Constitution protects the right to vote. First, in a few instances, the Constitution confers an *absolute right to vote* for a particular office by requiring that the office be filled through a popular election rather than by appointment or some other means. There are only two provisions in the Constitution that expressly guarantee the right to vote in this absolute sense: Article I, § 2, cl. 1 requires that members of the House of Representatives be "chosen . . . by the People," and the Seventeenth Amendment, cl. 1, commands that U.S. senators be "elected by the people." While "the people" thus have a federal constitutional right to vote for members of the House and the Senate, both Article I, § 2, and the Seventeenth Amendment leave it up to the states to decide *which people* shall enjoy this right. These constitutional provisions merely insist that the qualifications to vote for members of Congress be the same as the state establishes "for electors of the most numerous branch of the State legislature." As we shall see, however, other constitutional provisions limit the states' ability to determine voter qualifications.

One might argue that the Republican Form of Government Clause (Art. IV, § 4) implicitly confers an absolute right to vote for key state government officials, but the Supreme Court has never construed the clause in this way. It could also be argued that the references in Article I, § 2 and the Seventeenth Amendment to "*electors* of the most numerous branch of the State legislature" implicitly require that this state body be popularly elected, but again the Court has never so held. Thus, while the Constitution guarantees the people a right to vote for members of Congress, it "does not confer the right to vote in state elections. . . ." *Harris v. McRae*, 448 U.S. 297, 322 n.25 (1980). For example, nothing in the Constitution would prevent the City of Los Angeles from abolishing its practice of popularly electing the mayor and providing that the mayor shall instead be appointed by the city council. See *Rodriguez v. Popular Democratic Party*, 457 U.S. 1 (1982) (upholding Puerto Rico law under which legislative vacancies were filled by the legislator's political party rather than by popular election); *Fortson v. Morris*, 385 U.S. 231 (1966) (upholding Georgia law allowing state legislature in certain circumstances to choose state governor).

The second sense in which the Constitution protects the franchise is by guaranteeing people an *equal right to vote* for those federal and state officials who are chosen by popular election. Four constitutional amendments expressly protect the right to vote in this way by prohibiting the federal and state governments from selectively denying the franchise on certain bases: the Fifteenth Amendment (race), the Nineteenth Amendment (sex), the Twenty-fourth Amendment (failure to pay a tax), and the Twenty-sixth Amendment (age). In *Rice v. Cayetano*, 528 U.S. 495, 499 (2000), the Court thus struck down a Hawaii constitutional provision that limited the right to vote for trustees of a state agency to descendants of certain races, holding that the voting restriction was "a clear violation of the Fifteenth Amendment."

In addition, the Court has construed the Equal Protection Clause of the Fourteenth Amendment as implicitly protecting the equal right to vote. The Fourteenth Amendment right to vote is the "right to participate in the electoral process equally with other qualified voters." *Harris v. McRae*, supra, 448 U.S. at 322 n.25. Because this is a fundamental right, state and local laws that distribute the franchise on a selective basis or in an unequal manner are usually subject to strict scrutiny. It makes sense for the courts to closely scrutinize laws that discriminate in this way, for those who are burdened by such laws are, by definition, harmed in terms of their access to "those political processes which can ordinarily be expected to bring about repeal of undesirable legislation. . . ." *United States v. Carolene Products Co.*, 304 U.S. 144, 152 n.4 (1938). See § 2.3.2.

The Fourteenth Amendment confers only a "right to participate in elections on an equal basis with other citizens in the jurisdiction," *Dunn v. Blumstein*, 405 U.S. 330, 336 (1972); it does not confer the right to vote in an absolute sense. The Fourteenth Amendment right to vote, therefore, comes into play only when some *other* provision of law requires that a particular federal, state, or local office be filled by popular election. In such cases, laws that discriminate with respect to the franchise will generally be subject to strict scrutiny, requiring the state to show that the measure is narrowly tailored to serve a compelling state interest. The Fourteenth Amendment right to vote is thus a fundamental right for *equal protection* purposes, but not for *due process* purposes.

Example 7-C

The state has passed a law providing that the state attorney general shall be appointed by the governor rather than elected by the people. May state citizens successfully challenge the statute on the ground that it violates the Fourteenth Amendment Due Process Clause by impairing their fundamental liberty interest in voting?

Explanation

The suit should be dismissed. There is no such fundamental liberty under the Due Process Clause. The Fourteenth Amendment protects only the right to vote on an equal basis with other citizens. This right is not violated when all citizens are deprived of the right to choose the attorney general.

Six types of laws or practices may potentially infringe on the equal right to vote so as to trigger strict scrutiny: (1) selective denial of the franchise, (2) individual vote dilution, (3) group vote dilution, (4) assignment of voters to districts predominantly on the basis of their race, (5) denial of access to the ballot, and (6) the unequal counting of votes. We will consider each of these in turn. However, because judicial intervention shortly before an election could be extremely disruptive, the Supreme Court has cautioned "that lower federal courts should ordinarily not alter the election rules on the eve of an election." *Republican Nat'l Comm. v. Democratic Nat'l Comm.*, 589 U.S. 423, 424 (2020) (staying district court injunction that had extended time to count absentee ballots by six days, where injunction was issued only five days before the election). Thus, while federal courts can rule on the validity of voting and election laws, they must do so in a way that does not unduly disrupt the electoral process.

§7.3.2 Selective Denial of the Franchise

The most obvious way that a state might infringe on the Fourteenth Amendment's fundamental right to vote is by imposing conditions whose effect is to deny completely the vote to selected people. The Court has held that "any classification restricting the franchise on grounds *other than residence, age, and citizenship* cannot stand unless the . . . State can demonstrate that the classification serves a compelling state interest." *Hill v. Stone*, 421 U.S. 289, 297 (1975) (emphasis supplied). Later cases have described the test as involving a more flexible "balancing approach" under which "a court evaluating a constitutional challenge to an election regulation [must] weigh the asserted injury to the right to vote against the 'precise interests put forward by the State as justifications for the burden imposed by its rule.'" *Crawford v. Marion County Election Board,* 553 U.S. 181, 190 (2008) (plurality). The inquiry calls for a "sliding-scale balancing analysis: the scrutiny varies with the effect of the regulation at issue." Id. at 210 (Souter, J., and Ginsburg, J., dissenting, but agreeing with plurality as to use of a balancing analysis). Under this approach, there is no "litmus test for measuring the severity of a burden. . . . However slight that burden may appear . . . it must be justified by relevant and legitimate state interests 'sufficiently weighty to justify the limitation.'" Id. at 191 (plurality). Depending on the severity of the burden, the sliding-scale approach may call for the strictest of judicial scrutiny, as was employed in *Hill v. Stone* itself, where a city law limited the right to vote in certain elections exclusively to registered property owners.

We first consider the three exceptions noted in *Hill v. Stone* where the standard of review is mere rational basis. Denial of the franchise to nonresidents and noncitizens of the state is subject only to rational basis review. This follows from the fact that state and local governments have a legitimate interest in limiting the vote to those with a stake in the community. Otherwise, the fate of a state or a town could be decided by busloads of outsiders who swarm in on election day just to cast a ballot. States and cities may therefore restrict the vote to those who are citizens and bona fide residents of the jurisdiction. Such denials are subject only to rational basis review. While a citizenship restriction involves discrimination against aliens, the political function exception applies to the act of voting, and thus strict scrutiny would not be triggered. See § 6.5.1 ("Governmental or Political Functions").

It is one thing for a city or state to impose a bona fide residence requirement for voting. It is another matter to deny the vote to those bona fide residents who have not lived in the city or state for a prescribed period. Such durational residency requirements for voting are subject to strict scrutiny, since they temporarily deny the vote to persons who are in fact bona fide residents of the jurisdiction. See *Dunn v. Blumstein,* 405 U.S. 330 (1972) (invalidating Tennessee law that conditioned right to vote on residence in the state for one year and in the county for three months prior to the election). As we will see in § 7.4, durational residency requirements may also trigger strict scrutiny because of their impact on the fundamental equal protection right to travel.

Age restrictions on voting, like bona fide residence requirements, are subject to mere rational basis review under the Equal Protection Clause of the Fourteenth Amendment. However, under the Twenty-sixth Amendment, the vote may not be denied on account of age to anyone 18 years of age or older. Thus, while a state could deny the vote to those under 16, it could not impose an age restriction that denied the vote to 18-, 19-, or 20-year-olds, or to those over 70. Except for residence, citizenship, and age qualifications, all restrictions on the franchise must satisfy a potentially strict sliding-scale balancing test.

Example 7-D

A state law provides that anyone who owes back taxes or fines to the state may not vote. Elmer, who has been out of work for two years, owes the state $35 in personal property taxes on his automobile and $300 in unpaid traffic tickets. As a result, he was barred from voting in a recent election to pick members of Congress and members of the state legislature. Were Elmer's constitutional rights violated?

Explanation

Insofar as the state kept Elmer from voting for the state's delegation to Congress because of his failure to pay property taxes, the state violated the Twenty-fourth Amendment. That Amendment, which applies only to federal elections (i.e., a primary or regular election to select the President, Vice-President, or members of Congress), prohibits denying the vote "by reason of failure to pay any poll tax or other tax."

Though the Twenty-fourth Amendment does not protect Elmer's right to vote for state officials, Elmer can also invoke the Fourteenth Amendment Equal Protection Clause. The strictest scrutiny is called for here since the state is selectively denying the vote to those who owe back taxes or fines — obligations they may be unable to pay and that will therefore result in an absolute denial of the right to vote. The state would have to show that this discrimination was necessary to achieve a compelling state interest. While the state has an overriding interest in preserving the integrity of the election process, a person's failure to pay taxes or fines in no way threatens this goal. And even if the state has a compelling interest in collecting revenue, since there are numerous other ways of achieving this purpose, it is unnecessary to deny the vote as a collection device. See *Hill v. Stone*, 421 U.S. 289 (1975); *Harper v. Virginia Bd. of Elections*, 383 U.S. 663 (1966).

Example 7-E

A state enacted a voter ID law providing that anyone wishing to vote in person on election day or wishing to cast a ballot in person at the state court clerk's office before election day, must present a photo identification issued by the state or federal government, such as a driver's license, a state-issued ID card, or a federal passport. It is estimated that 90 percent or more of the state's voting-age population possess one of these forms of ID. Those unable to present such identification may cast a provisional ballot at the polls but must within ten days then go to the local court clerk's office and present a valid photo ID, or sign an affidavit that they are indigent and unable to obtain a photo ID because they cannot afford to pay for the necessary supporting documents. Those over 18 who are not licensed drivers may, with proper proof of identity, obtain a free photo ID card from the state. The state Democratic Party sued challenging the voter ID law on its face, claiming that it violated party members' right to vote under the Equal Protection Clause. If the Party has standing to bring this action, how should the court rule on the merits of its claim?

Explanation

None of the *Hill v. Stone* rational basis exceptions apply here, for this law does not simply condition the right to vote on residence. Instead, it requires proof of residence in a particular manner that will arguably keep some bona fide residents from being able to vote. We must therefore use a sliding-scale balancing approach, under which a court must first assess the extent of the burden that the measure imposes on an individual's right to vote. Unlike the state law in Example 7-D, the law here does not absolutely deny the right to vote to anyone, but rather conditions it on an individual's ability to prove they are a state resident who is entitled to vote. The ten-day post-election grace period eases the burden on those who forgot to bring a photo ID to the polls, who might have lacked such ID at the time they voted, or whose indigence prevented them from obtaining the documents necessary to get a photo ID. While the burdens imposed by this law would not appear to be great for most people, it may have the practical effect of preventing some from voting, such as (1) those who for reasons of time, distance, expense, age, or disability cannot make a post-voting trip to the local courthouse, or (2) those non-indigents who cannot assemble the necessary documents within ten days after an election. While the burdens imposed by this law are not great for most people, its practical effect may be severe on some.

On the state's side of the balance, the court must look at the interests advanced and determine whether they are sufficiently weighty to justify the burden imposed. The state defends its photo-ID law on two related grounds: protecting the integrity and reliability of the electoral process, and safeguarding voter confidence so people will participate in the democratic process. Both goals are furthered by a system that will help deter and detect voter fraud. While the plaintiff notes that there have been no documented instances of voter fraud in this state, other states have experienced the problem, and the issue has begun to draw national attention. While allowing universal use of absentee ballots would eliminate the burdens imposed by this measure, such voting is much more susceptible to fraud than the system the state has adopted.

The case is arguably a close one. The state has strong justifications for the measure, even though it may well have the effect of disenfranchising some otherwise eligible voters in at least one election, after which they may be able to get the documents necessary to allow them to vote in the future. *Crawford v. Marion County Election Board*, 553 U.S. 181, 202 (2008) upheld a similar Indiana statute on the basis that plaintiffs had failed to prove that the measure "imposes 'excessively burdensome requirements' on any class of voters." In rejecting what was brought as a facial challenge, the plurality concluded that "application of the statute to the *vast majority* of Indiana voters is amply justified by the valid interest in protecting 'the integrity and reliability of the electoral process.'" Id. at 204 (emphasis supplied). The Court left open the possibility that, in contrast to this facial attack, an as-applied challenge brought on behalf of a specific class of voters such as the indigent, upon whom the law was shown to impose an unacceptable burden, might succeed. Id. at 202-203. In such a case, however, the statute could be enjoined only as applied to that group, rather than being facially invalidated so that it could not be applied to anyone.

The rule that selective denials of the franchise are subject to potentially strict scrutiny under a sliding-scale balancing test applies only to elections for public entities that perform "normal governmental" functions. With respect to special limited-purpose entities that do not exercise general governmental authority, laws that restrict the vote to those persons who are principally affected by the entity's actions will receive only rational basis review under the Fourteenth Amendment. *Salyer Land Co. v. Tulare Lake Basin Water Storage Dist.*, 410 U.S. 719, 726-730 (1973) (upholding California law that allowed only landowners to vote in water storage district elections). However, in *Rice v. Cayetano*, 528 U.S. 495 (2000), the Court refused to extend the special-purpose-district exception to denials of the franchise based on ancestry or race. In that case, the Hawaii constitution restricted the right to vote for trustees of the Office of Hawaiian Affairs (OHA) to "native Hawaiians" and "Hawaiians," groups defined as being descendants of the "peoples" who inhabited the islands in 1778. The OHA is a statewide agency whose mission is to better the conditions of these Hawaiians. The Court held that even if the OHA qualified as a special purpose district for purposes of an Equal Protection Clause challenge, this would not excuse compliance with the "race neutrality command of the Fifteenth Amendment. . . . The Fifteenth Amendment has independent meaning and force. A State may not deny or abridge the right to vote on account of race, and this law does so." Id. at 522.

§7.3.3 Individual Vote Dilution: "One Person, One Vote"

The Problem: Unequal Weighting of Votes

A more subtle way to abridge a person's right to vote than outright denial is by employing an electoral scheme in which some people's votes count less than others. For example, state law might provide that in a state or local election (i.e., an election to fill positions at the state or local government level), a person shall receive an *extra* ballot for every $10,000 he or she paid in state income taxes during the previous year. Under this system, no one is completely denied the right to vote, but people's votes are not weighted equally. A person who paid $40,000 in state income tax may cast five votes (one regular and four extra), while an individual who paid no state income tax may cast only one vote. This involves individual vote dilution in that some people's votes carry less weight than those of others. Such a scheme is normally unconstitutional except in rare instances where the election involves a special limited-purpose entity that does not "administer such normal functions of government as the maintenance of streets, the operation of schools, or sanitation, health, or welfare services." *Ball v. James*, 451 U.S. 355, 366 (1981) (upholding a "one acre, one vote" voting scheme for electing directors of a water reclamation district). And see *League of United Latin American Citizens v. Edwards Aquifer Authority*, 937 F.3d 457 (5th Cir. 2019), *cert. denied*, 140 S. Ct. 2717 (2020) (upholding system for electing 15 board members of limited-purpose aquifer water authority where members were allocated among counties according to their per-capita water usage rather than by their population, in what amounted to a "one-gallon, one-vote," rather than a "one-person, one-vote," system).

Individual vote dilution is not usually as blatant as the last hypothetical suggests. Instead, vote dilution typically results from the fact that electoral districts are drawn in such a way that they do not include the same number of people even though each district elects the same number of officials. Consequently, those who live in larger population districts cast a vote that is diluted in relation to the vote of those residing in smaller districts.

EXAMPLE

Example 7-F

A town of 60,000 people is run by a three-member town council. The town is divided into districts A, B, and C, each of which elects one member to the council. District A consists of 40,000 people, district B of 15,000 people, and district C of 5,000 people. See Figure 7-1. Are some people's votes diluted in comparison with the votes of others?

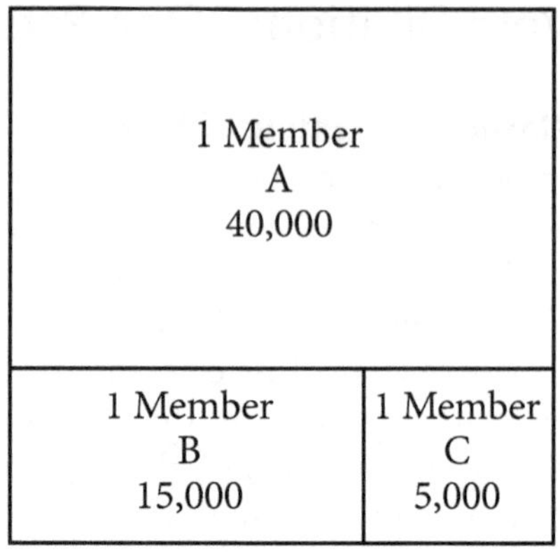

Figure 7-1.

Explanation

Yes. The 5,000 people who live in district C have the same representation and the same influence on the council as the 40,000 people in district A. When the people in district C cast ballots for a council member, they each in effect have a 1/5,000th say in the outcome of the election, while the people of district A each have a 1/40,000th say. Because the votes of those who live in district C carry eight times the weight of those who live in district A, the votes of those living in district A are *diluted* in comparison with the votes of those living in district C. To avoid individual vote dilution, each of the three districts would need to contain the same number of people—i.e., 20,000 (60,000/3 = 20,000).

The extent to which individual vote dilution has occurred is described in terms of the maximum (or overall) population deviation. This figure measures the difference between the largest district and the smallest district in terms of the percentage by which each exceeds or falls short of the ideal population. In Example 7-F, the ideal district contains 20,000 people. District A, the largest district, is 100 percent larger than it should be ((40,000 − 20,000)/20,000 = 20,000/20,000 = 1, or 100 percent). District C, the smallest district, is 75 percent smaller than it should be ((20,000 − 5,000)/20,000 = 15,000/20,000 = 0.75, or 75 percent). If you picture a thermometer on which the largest district's deviation from the ideal is marked as a temperature above zero, while the smallest district's deviation falls below zero, the maximum population deviation is the distance between these two points—in this case, 175 percentage points (i.e., the distance between +100 percent and −75 percent). If this example seems grotesque, the maximum population deviation between Georgia's congressional districts in 1963 was 140 percent. See *Wesberry v. Sanders*, 376 U.S. 1, 2 (1964).

The fact that voting districts contain unequal populations does not necessarily mean that there is individual vote dilution. The key lies in whether there is a disparity between districts in terms of the *ratio of elected officials to population*. Such a disparity existed in Example 7-F, since the ratio of elected officials to population was 1 to 40,000 in district A as compared with 1 to 5,000 in district C.

Example 7-G

In Example 7-F, suppose that the town were divided into only two districts, A and B. See Figure 7-2. District A contains 40,000 people and elects two members to the town council, while district B contains 20,000 people and elects one council member. Does vote dilution occur under this districting scheme?

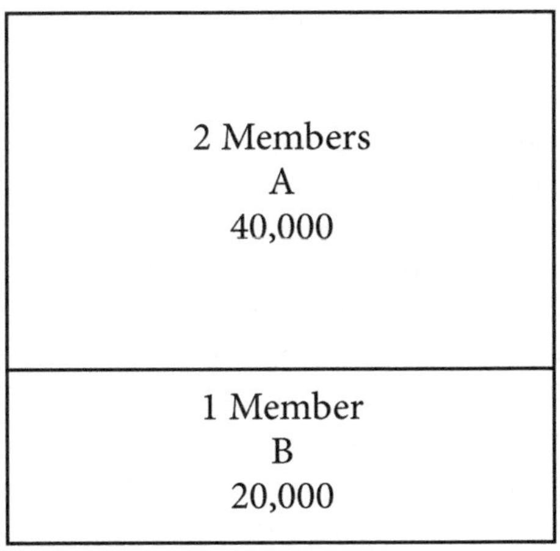

Figure 7-2.

Explanation

No. Even though the two districts are of unequal population, no vote dilution has occurred, since in both districts, the ratio of elected officials to population is the same—i.e., 2/40,000 = 1/20,000. In this example, the city has used a combination of a single-member district and a multimember district in a manner that does not cause any individual vote dilution.

"One Person, One Vote"

Individual vote dilution is subject to strict scrutiny. Under the Constitution, each person is entitled to cast a vote that carries substantially the same weight as that of other voters in the same election. The Court has derived this principle of "one person, one vote" from two distinct sources. In the case of elections for the U.S. House of Representatives, the Court has read the requirement of Article I, § 2, cl. 1—representatives are to be chosen "by the People"—as mandating substantial equality of population among the various districts established by a state legislature for the election of members of Congress. With respect to state and local elections, the Court has extracted the same principle from the Equal Protection Clause. Under that Clause, "an individual's right to vote for state [officials] is unconstitutionally impaired when its weight is in a substantial fashion diluted when compared with votes of citizens living in other parts of the State." *Reynolds v. Sims*, 377 U.S. 533, 568 (1964).

When governmental officials are elected on a district-by-district basis, compliance with the principle of "one person, one vote" requires that state and local governments "make an honest and good faith effort to construct districts . . . as nearly of equal population as is practicable." Id. at 577. In other words, each elected official must represent the same number of people. Thus, in Example 7-F, to cure the individual vote dilution so that each person's vote carries the same weight, the town would need to redraw the boundaries of its three election districts so that they are apportioned equally in terms of population by having roughly 20,000 people each.

In applying the "one-person, one-vote" principle, the longstanding national and state practice has been to use a state's or a municipality's total population, as determined by the last decennial census. Insofar as the U.S. House of Representatives is concerned, this "total population" principle is mandated by the Fourteenth Amendment, § 2, which provides that House seats "shall be apportioned among the several States according to their respective numbers, counting *the whole number of persons* in each State, excluding Indians not taxed." (Emphasis added.) At the state and local governmental levels, although the Constitution does not expressly address the question, all fifty states and many municipalities have long used the "total population" basis for apportioning seats in their own legislative bodies. In *Evenwel v. Abbott*, 578 U.S. 54 (2016), the Supreme Court addressed the question of whether a state's use of the "total population" principle to apportion seats in its state senate violated the Equal Protection Clause because the districts so drawn, while containing equal numbers of state *residents*, did not contain equal numbers in terms of *voter-eligible population*. Those challenging the Texas apportionment scheme argued that only the latter would produce true "voter equality." The Court rejected this challenge, noting that "history, precedent, and practice demonstrate [that] it is plainly *permissible* for jurisdictions to measure equalization by the total population of state and local legislative districts." Id. at 64 (emphasis added). At the same time, the Court was careful to leave open the question of whether states may, if they choose, draw their own legislative districts to equalize voter-eligible population rather than total population. Id. at 74-75. It appears that the question is still an open one.

Another unresolved question is whether in allocating seats in the House of Representatives, it is permissible to exclude from a state's population "aliens who are not in a lawful immigration status." On July 21, 2020, President Trump issued a Presidential Memorandum announcing this to be the new policy of the United States for purposes of "reapportionment of Representatives following the 2020 census." It was estimated that under Trump's plan, California, Florida, and Texas would each lose one congressional seat, compared to what they would otherwise have had. A three-judge federal court enjoined the plan as being in violation of several federal statutes, but the Supreme Court reversed and ordered the case dismissed on standing and ripeness grounds. *New York v. Trump*, 485 F. Supp. 3d 422 (S.D.N.Y.), *vacated*, 592 U.S. 125 (2020). President Biden, on his first day in office, revoked Trump's plan, stating that it was unconstitutional. Exec. Order No. 13986, 86 Fed. Reg. 7015, 2021 WL 229391(Pres.) (Jan. 20, 2021).

At-Large Election Schemes

An alternative means of satisfying the principle of "one person, one vote" is to choose an elected body at large—i.e., on a citywide, countywide, or statewide basis—rather than on a district-by-district basis. Under an at-large election scheme, everyone in the jurisdiction votes for the same set of officials, and each official represents everyone in the jurisdiction. In Example 7-F, the town might thus have complied with "one person, one vote" by abandoning its system of electing the council on a district basis and instead electing it at large. Under an at-large system, each voter would have the right to vote for three council members, and each council member would represent the same number of persons—i.e., all 60,000 people of the city. Each person's vote would now carry equal weight, for each has a 1/60,000th interest in each of the three council members.

The U.S. Senate is an example of a body that is elected on an at-large basis. Each of a state's two senators represents everyone in that state, and every qualified voter in the state can vote for each senator. By contrast, members of the U.S. House of Representatives are usually chosen on a district basis. If a state has only one representative in the House, then that state will elect its member at large. Otherwise, a state that has more than one representative in Congress must divide itself into as many districts as it has representatives, each district electing one member. Under the principle of "one person, one vote," it becomes imperative that the state's congressional districts be drawn so that they are apportioned on an equal population basis.

Reapportionment

Even if a districting scheme met the "one person, one vote" requirement when it was first established, individual vote dilution may gradually occur over time because of demographic changes that alter the population balance between districts. In Example 7-F, had the town initially created three council districts of 20,000 people each, this equality could eventually be destroyed because of an uneven pattern of births, deaths, and migration. At the congressional level, reapportionment may also be required if, because of the latest decennial census, there is a change in the number of representatives the state is entitled to in the House. For example, because of the 2020 census, Texas's authorized congressional delegation increased by two, necessitating that the state be divided into 38—rather than the previous 36—congressional districts. At the same time, six states each lost one seat in the House, including Montana that went from two districts to one, eliminating the need to draw district lines.

To remain in compliance with the Constitution, it is, therefore, necessary to reapportion electoral districts on a periodic basis. However, the Constitution does not require "daily, monthly, annual or biennial reapportionment. . . ." *Reynolds v. Sims,* supra, 377 U.S. at 583. Any attempt to enforce compliance with the "one person, one vote" principle on such a frequent basis would be totally unworkable. Instead, it is sufficient if reapportionment at the federal, state, and local governmental levels occurs once every ten years, following the decennial census taken pursuant to Article I, § 2, cl. 3. Under some circumstances, a state legislature may wish to engage in a second round of redistricting after an initial plan has been implemented. This might happen, for example, if the political composition of the state legislature were to change dramatically during the interim. Although redistricting "mid-decennial" is unusual, there is no per se rule against doing so. See, e.g., *League of United Latin American Citizens v. Perry,* 548 U.S. 399 (2006).

The degree of mathematical precision that must be achieved in the reapportionment process depends on the purpose of the districting in question. When a state engages in districting to elect state or local governmental officials, the Court will tolerate greater deviations from perfect equality than it will for congressional districting. "[S]tate reapportionment statutes are not subject to the same strict standards applicable to reapportionment of congressional seats." *White v. Regester,* 412 U.S. 755, 763 (1973).

At the state and local levels, it is enough that there be "*substantial* equality of population among the various districts, so that the vote of any citizen is *approximately* equal in weight to that of any other citizen in the State." *Reynolds v. Sims,* supra, 377 U.S. at 579 (emphasis supplied). At the state and local levels, maximum population deviations as high as 10 percent may be deemed so "minor" as to be "insufficient to make out a prima facie case of invidious discrimination" and, therefore, require no justification whatsoever. *Gaffney v. Cummings,* 412 U.S. 735, 745-746 (1973); and see *White v. Regester,* supra, 412 U.S. at 763-764. More substantial deviations will be upheld if the state can show that they were necessary to realize legitimate districting goals, such as keeping districts compact and contiguous, respecting municipal boundaries, and avoiding contests between incumbents.

At the level of congressional districting, on the other hand, "there are no *de minimis* population variations," *Karcher v. Daggett*, 462 U.S. 725, 734 (1983), and the standard of review is always strict. The Constitution requires "that [congressional] districts be apportioned to achieve population equality 'as nearly as is practicable.'" Id. at 730. No matter how small a maximum population deviation the state might have achieved, a challenger can establish a prima facie case by showing that a smaller deviation was possible. Once this prima facie case is made, the state must "prove that the population deviations in its plan were necessary to achieve some legitimate state objective." Id. at 740. Moreover, in contrast to the state and local levels, it appears that a state will at best be able to justify only "minor population deviations" among congressional districts. Id. The Court has defended this very strict approach to congressional districting on the basis that at the national level, the need for equal representation "outweighs the local interests that a State may deem relevant in apportioning districts for representatives to state and local legislatures. . . ." Id. at 733. However, the Court has shown a somewhat greater tolerance for small deviations in congressional redistricting plans that are prepared long after the last census, rather than within a few years of it, because census figures become increasingly inaccurate with time. See *Abrams v. Johnson*, 521 U.S. 74, 100 (1997) (approving court-imposed congressional redistricting plan, despite deviation from perfect equality, partly on the basis that more than six years had elapsed since the prior census).

EXAMPLE

Example 7-H

Following the 2020 census, the state adopted redistricting plans for the state senate and assembly and for the state's congressional districts. The maximum population deviations under these plans were 7 percent for the state senate, 17 percent for the state assembly, and 0.7 percent for the congressional districts. The plaintiffs challenged these schemes by showing that alternative plans would have more closely achieved equality in all three governmental bodies. Are the state's plans constitutional?

EXPLANATION

Explanation

The maximum deviation for the state senate plan is well below 10 percent and is thus so small as to be de minimis; the plaintiffs have thus failed to establish a prima facie equal protection violation as to this plan. The maximum population variation in the state assembly plan is above the de minimis level and, therefore, must be justified under strict scrutiny. The same is true of the deviation in the congressional plan, which, though quite small, will not be ignored as de minimis since the plaintiffs have shown that the state could have achieved an even lower deviation. For the state assembly and congressional plans to be upheld, the state must prove that each of the plans was necessary to achieve a legitimate districting goal, such as maintaining compactness and contiguity, respecting the integrity of political subdivisions or communities, or avoiding contests between incumbents. In the absence of such proof, either or both plans will be struck down. See *Karcher v. Daggett*, 462 U.S. 725 (1983).

§7.3.4 Group Vote Dilution

Minimizing Group Voting Strength

We have been focusing on situations in which the government has impaired an individual's right to vote by either denying the vote entirely to some people or diluting the weight of their vote in comparison to that of others. There is a third way in which the government may violate the fundamental right to vote, and that is by seeking to minimize or cancel out the voting strength of an identifiable group. Such *group vote dilution* defeats the "basic aim of legislative apportionment," which is "the achieving of fair and effective *representation* for all citizens. . . ." *Reynolds v. Sims*, supra, 377 U.S. at 565-566 (emphasis supplied). Guaranteeing a citizen the right to vote and to cast an equal vote would be of little value if the government could then undermine the voting power of the groups with whom an individual has affiliated for voting purposes. Besides outlawing individual vote dilution, the Constitution bars the government from deliberately denying "a particular group . . . its chance to effectively influence the political process." *Davis v. Bandemer*, 478 U.S. 109, 132-133 (1986). Group vote dilution usually involves attempts to minimize the vote of minority racial groups. However, such claims may conceivably arise with respect to other groups that are politically cohesive, such as ethnic minorities, political parties, and religious communities.

Group vote dilution can be accomplished through any of several different mechanisms. First, a governmental body might be chosen on an at-large basis so that a majority group can outvote a minority group for every seat. Second, the body might be elected under a districting plan whose lines have been purposefully drawn so that a majority group controls the outcome in every district or in a disproportionate share of the districts. Third, a districting plan might use multimember rather than single-member districts, again with the goal of preventing a minority from realizing its voting potential. We will consider each of these group vote dilution devices initially in the context of minority racial groups. Thereafter, we will examine their application to other types of groups.

Dilution Through At-Large Elections

One of the easiest ways to bring about group vote dilution is using an at-large voting scheme. In an at-large scheme, as we noted earlier, the principle of "one person, one vote" is always satisfied, so there can be no individual vote dilution. Group vote dilution, however, is a very real danger.

Example 7-I

In Example 7-F, assume that the town's racial composition is 40,000 whites and 20,000 blacks. The neighborhoods are fairly segregated, with whites living in the northern and central parts of town and blacks living in the southern part. Assume, too, that voting takes place along racial lines, with whites generally voting for white candidates and blacks voting for black candidates. How would an at-large election scheme produce group vote dilution?

Explanation

Since blacks make up a third of the population, they might fairly expect to elect one member to the council. This would follow if the town used a districting scheme in which blacks had a clear majority in one of the three council districts. Thus, if the city created three council districts (A, B, and C) whose lines ran horizontally from east to west, whites would have a clear majority in the northern and central districts, while blacks would dominate the southern district. See Figure 7-3. Under this scheme, the council's

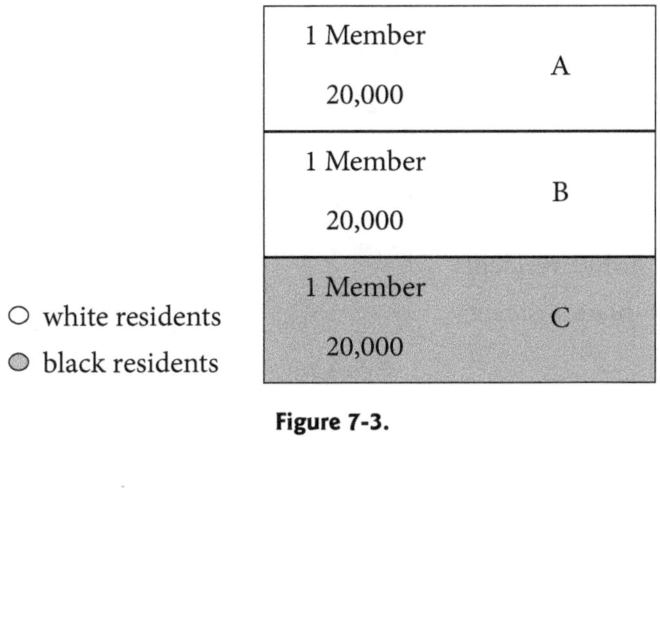

Figure 7-3.

membership would presumably reflect the racial composition of the city by containing two whites and one black.

However, whites could deliberately nullify the voting strength of black voters by deciding that the town council shall be elected at-large rather than from districts. Under this scheme, everyone in town would vote for all three council seats. If each candidate had to run for a specific seat and if a white opposed a black in each contest, whites would win all three seats, since they outnumber blacks in the town by a two-to-one margin. Through this purposeful scheme, blacks could be prevented from electing any candidates to the council even though they comprise a third of the town's population. See *Rogers v. Lodge*, 458 U.S. 613 (1982) (invalidating racially motivated at-large election scheme for Board of Commissioners of Burke County, Georgia).

Dilution Through Gerrymandering

A second means of diluting the voting strength of a minority group is through gerrymandering—i.e., purposefully drawing district lines so that the minority group will not have a majority in any district or in as many districts as it might otherwise have, or so that the group's political power is otherwise diminished.

Example 7-J

In Example 7-I, we noted that if the town had used a districting scheme in which district lines ran horizontally from east to west, blacks would be able to elect one member to the council. How might gerrymandering be utilized to dilute the voting strength of the town's black citizens?

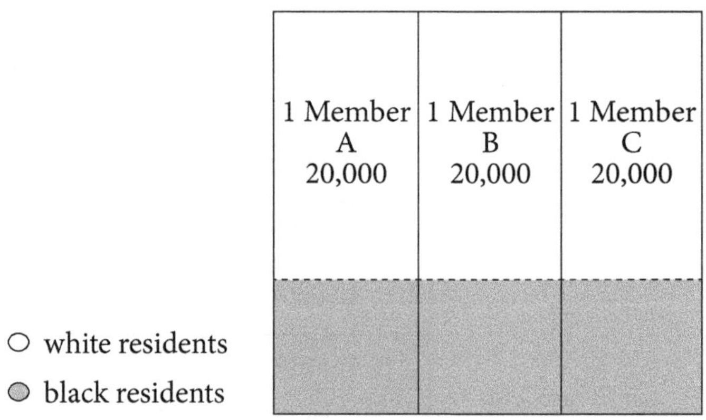

Figure 7-4.

EXPLANATION

Explanation

The districting scheme could instead be racially gerrymandered so that whites are assured of electing all three council members. This could be accomplished by drawing district lines vertically from north to south, rather than horizontally from east to west. See Figure 7-4. If each district contains 20,000 people, no individual vote dilution would occur. Yet by drawing district lines vertically rather than horizontally, since the northern and central portions of each district are virtually all-white, whites will have roughly a two-thirds majority in each district and thus be able to elect all three members of the council. Through this purposeful districting scheme, whites will have totally neutralized the voting strength of the town's sizable black minority.

Dilution Through Use of Multimember Districts

The third method of purposefully diluting a group's voting strength is to use multimember rather than single-member districts so that a district elects more than one representative. Multimember districts combine aspects of at-large elections and districting, for while districts exist, at least some of them elect more than one representative on a districtwide or at-large basis. Like at-large schemes, multimember districts operate on a "winner-take-all" principle that submerges minorities and overrepresents the majority. Yet the mere fact that multimember districts may deprive a racial minority of representation is not enough to invalidate their use. It must also be shown "that the political processes leading to nomination and election were not equally open to participation by the group in question — that its members had less opportunity than did other residents in the district to participate in the political processes and to elect legislators of their choice." *White v. Regester*, supra, 412 U.S. at 766.

EXAMPLE

Example 7-K

In Example 7-F, suppose that the town council consists of five rather than three members and that these five members are chosen from three council districts. See Figure 7-5. District A, which contains 12,000 people, elects one member, while districts B and C contain 24,000 people apiece and each elects two members. Since each council member represents exactly 12,000 people, the principle of "one person, one vote" is satisfied, and thus there is no individual vote dilution. How does this scheme cause group vote dilution?

Explanation

The districting plan makes it virtually impossible for blacks to elect a council member. District A contains 12,000 whites, while districts B and C (the two multimember districts) have each been drawn to contain 14,000 whites and 10,000 blacks. Assuming racial-bloc voting, a white candidate is certain to win the seat from all-white district A. Moreover, the two seats chosen from district B and the two seats chosen from district C are also likely to go to white candidates, since whites outnumber blacks in each of these districts by a margin of roughly 58 percent to 42 percent.

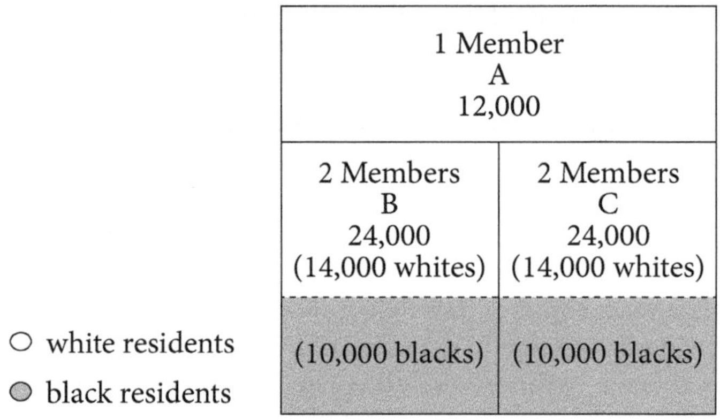

Figure 7-5.

It is important to emphasize that none of the three devices we have discussed in connection with group vote dilution is unconstitutional per se. At-large election schemes, districting schemes, and multimember districts are subject to strict scrutiny only if it can be shown by direct or circumstantial evidence that they were adopted for a suspect purpose, such as diluting the voting strength of a racial minority. Otherwise, these electoral devices, despite their discriminatory impact on minority groups, will receive only rational basis scrutiny and are certain to be upheld.

Vote Dilution and Nonracial Groups: Partisan Political Gerrymandering

The examples of group vote dilution that we have examined so far have all involved dilution aimed at minority racial groups. However, group vote dilution is objectionable not only when it is aimed at racial groups, but also when it is applied against groups defined in nonracial terms. The constitutional right to participate equally in the political process is a right that belongs to all citizens, not just to racial minorities. If an identifiable group shares interests that cause its members to vote on a cohesive basis, a deliberate attempt by the majority to minimize or destroy that group's voting power should be subject to strict scrutiny, whether the group consists of Italians, the poor, environmentalists, Hasidic Jews, senior citizens, or Democrats.

In *Rucho v. Common Cause*, 588 U.S. 684 (2019), the Court heard two group vote dilution cases that were filed in federal court to challenge the North Carolina and Maryland redistricting plans for electing members to the U.S. House of Representatives. Each plan was adopted by a Republican-controlled state legislature, and each overtly and admittedly discriminated against voters likely to support non-Republican candidates. The North Carolina plan thus divided the state into 13 congressional districts, each electing one of the state's members in the U.S. House of Representatives. Though the districts were equal in terms of population, they were deliberately drawn so as to maximize the number of Republican-controlled districts, thus ensuring that 10 of the state's 13 House seats would be filled by Republicans. As a result, while Republicans comprised 54 percent of the state's electorate, they controlled 77 percent of its House seats. The suits were brought by Democrats who reside in these states. The defendants moved to dismiss both actions on the ground that they presented a nonjusticiable political question.

One basis for finding that a case presents a political question is that there are no "judicially discoverable and manageable standards for resolving it. . . ." *Baker v. Carr*, 369 U.S. 186, 217 (1962). See Christopher N. May, Allan Ides & Simona Grossi, *Constitutional Law: National Power and Federalism* § 3.5 (10th ed. 2025) [hereinafter *National Power & Federalism*]. In *Rucho*, that concern arose both with respect to deciding whether there had been a constitutional violation, and if there had been, with respect to fashioning a judicial remedy. As to the first issue, the matter was complicated by the fact that the Court had previously recognized that states may, at least up to a point, "engage in constitutional political gerrymandering." *Hunt v. Cromartie*, 526 U.S. 541, 551 (1999). Given this judicially sanctioned leeway, how is a court is to decide whether a state has "gone too far" so as to give rise to a constitutional violation? One possibility is to say that where it is shown that political gerrymandering was a "predominant purpose" of the state's redistricting plan and that it had a "substantial effect" in terms of partisan vote dilution, the state has crossed the line between permissible and impermissible political gerrymandering. However, in these North Carolina and Maryland cases, there was arguably no need to formulate a rule as to what constitutes a "substantial effect," for the disparities were so extreme as to qualify as having gone "too far" under virtually any standard the Court might have adopted.

If a state were found to have "gone too far," the question then arises as to whether there is a judicially manageable remedy available. One might argue that the remedy in such cases is totally manageable, i.e., courts should simply redraw the district lines, as they do in "one-person, one-vote" cases. There, the lines are redrawn to create districts of equal population. Here, they would be redrawn so that the districts' majorities correspond to the parties' relative strengths in the electorate. Thus, for North Carolina, this would mean that 7 of its 13 congressional districts—i.e., 54 percent—would have Republican majorities, and the remaining 6 districts would have Democratic majorities. While this approach is certainly manageable, eliminating any political question concerns, nothing in the Equal Protection Clause or any other constitutional provision gives courts the authority to impose a precise proportionate representation requirement on the states since some political gerrymandering has always been allowable.

An alternative approach might be to say that if the "predominant purpose" and "primary effect" inquiries disclose a constitutional violation, it is not the court's job to redraw the district lines. Instead, that is a task for the state legislature. All that a court would need to do is enjoin use of the constitutionally infirm plan until the legislature comes up with a revised plan that is not based predominantly on political criteria. Under this approach, which had been widely employed by lower federal courts, judicially discoverable and manageable standards exist with respect to both identifying and rectifying a constitutional violation, with the result that such cases can proceed in federal court.

However, in a 5 to 4 decision, the *Rucho v. Common Cause* Court concluded that

> partisan gerrymandering claims present political questions beyond the reach of the federal courts. Federal judges have no license to reallocate political power between the two major political parties, with no plausible grant of authority in the Constitution, and no legal standards to limit and direct their decisions. "[J]udicial action must be governed by *standard*, by *rule*," and must be "principled, rational, and based upon reasoned distinctions" found in the Constitution or laws. Judicial review of partisan gerrymandering does not meet those basic requirements.

588 U.S. at 718 (emphasis in original) (internal citation omitted). As a result, the two cases were remanded with instructions that they be dismissed for lack of jurisdiction.

The Court nonetheless went on to say that "[o]ur conclusion does not condone excessive partisan gerrymandering." Id. at 719. Even though these suits cannot be brought in federal court, there are other ways of addressing state political gerrymandering. These may include filing suit in state courts (which are not bound by federal justiciability standards), perhaps with the guidance of state statutes or constitutional provisions that delineate the factors a legislature may and may not consider in the redistricting process. States can also amend their constitutions, as some have done, to take congressional and legislative districting decisions away from the state legislature and place them instead in the hands of independent multimember commissions. Finally, under the Elections Clause, Article I, § 4, cl. 1, Congress has the power to address this problem, such as by prescribing the manner in which states draw their congressional districts, requiring those districts to be created by independent commissions rather than by state legislatures, specifying the criteria to be used in the redistricting process, or simply banning partisan gerrymandering. Id. at 719-721. Thus, while the federal courts' doors are not open to these cases, there may be other viable means of addressing the problem of excessive political gerrymandering.

In ruling that partisan gerrymandering claims present a political question that is beyond the reach of the federal courts, *Rucho* suggested that such claims might be heard in state court. Yet nothing requires state courts to hear such claims. Thus, in *Harper v. Hall*, 384 N.C. 292, 300-301, 886 S.E.2d 393, 401 (2023), the North Carolina Supreme Court, "find[ing] the Supreme Court's analysis in *Rucho* insightful and persuasive," held that "partisan gerrymandering claims present a political question that is nonjusticiable under the North Carolina Constitution."

However, if state courts do treat such claims as being justiciable, there remains the potential for federal judicial review should a state court "so exceed the bounds of ordinary judicial review as to unconstitutionally intrude upon the role specifically reserved to state legislatures by Article I, Section 4 of the Federal Constitution." *Moore v. Harper*, 600 U.S. 1, 37 (2023). While state courts can thus apply constitutional restraints on their legislatures that exercise the power given to them by the Elections Clause, they cannot "arrogate to themselves the power vested in state legislatures to regulate federal elections." Id. at 36. Thus, while partisan political gerrymandering cases themselves involve political questions that federal courts cannot hear, there remains room for possible federal judicial review of the state judicial process to the extent that it adjudicates such claims.

§7.3.5 Nondilutional Race-Based Districting

We have seen that the fundamental right to vote may be violated by selective denials of the franchise, by individual vote dilution, or by group vote dilution. The fourth way in which the right to vote may be infringed is through race-based districting—i.e., where race is used as the predominant factor in assigning people to voting districts. In contrast to political gerrymandering, which states are free to pursue, "if a legislature gives race a predominant role in redistricting decisions, the resulting map is subjected to strict scrutiny and may be held unconstitutional." *Alexander v. South Carolina State Conference of the NAACP*, 144 S. Ct. 1221, 1233 (2024). Race-based districting is typically employed for the purpose of creating so-called majority-minority districts—i.e., districts in which a racial minority group constitutes a majority of the voters, thereby enhancing the group's chances of electing a representative of its own choosing.

EXAMPLE

Example 7-L

In Example 7-I, suppose that the three-member town council is chosen from three council districts, each containing 20,000 people. The town's population is one-third black and two-thirds white. If the town council wishes to make sure that blacks can elect one of the three council members, how might it achieve this goal?

EXPLANATION

Explanation

The council might employ race-based districting, drawing district lines so that people are assigned to districts based on their race. Thus, one of the three districts, district C, might be configured so that it consists almost entirely of blacks. District C would be a majority-minority district, for blacks — who constitute a minority of the town's population — would be a majority in this district. See Figure 7-3, above.

Race-based districting is sometimes referred to as a form of racial gerrymandering. Yet in contrast to traditional racial gerrymanders, race-based districting does not produce group vote dilution. Rather than minimizing or canceling out any group's *legitimate* voting strength, race-based districting often has the effect of helping minorities elect representatives in numbers that more closely match their proportion of the population. While such a scheme may mean that the majority is unable to elect as many representatives as it did before, the majority's representation is typically not reduced below its proportional share. Thus, in Example 7-L, if prior to race-based districting whites were able to elect all three members of the council, the new scheme still leaves whites with control of two of the three council districts, exactly matching their two-thirds makeup in the town's population. Nor does race-based districting entail individual vote dilution, for the districts are presumably of equal size, thus honoring the principle of "one person, one vote."

Race-based districting can also be employed to have the opposite effect of weakening a minority's ability to elect members to a legislative body. In Example 7-L, suppose that the town council, displeased with the fact that blacks were able to elect one of the council's three members, revises its Figure 7-3 districting plan so that blacks are now spread evenly among the three districts, as shown in Figure 7-4. Under this revised plan, since blacks would now constitute only a third of each district, it will be much harder for them to elect any black representatives to the council. Such a disadvantaging of black voters occurred in *Alexander v. South Carolina State Conference of the NAACP*, supra, where the Republican-controlled state legislature revised its congressional districting map to ensure that blacks, who voted overwhelmingly Democratic, could elect only one rather than two of the state's seven House Representatives; it did so by redrawing district lines to move some blacks out of a district that had been closely divided between Republicans and Democrats, thereby giving Republicans a clear majority there.

Whether race-based districting has the effect of strengthening or weakening a minority's political strength, it is subject to strict scrutiny. Even though it causes neither individual nor group vote dilution, the Court has identified three other types of injury that warrant the application of strict scrutiny. First, race-based districting may cause a *representational* harm, for if a district is created to benefit a particular racial group, this may send a message to elected officials "that their primary obligation is to represent only the members of that group, rather than their constituency as a whole." *Shaw v. Reno,* 509 U.S. 630, 648 (1993). Second, such districting may produce *stigmatic* injuries by operating on "the offensive and demeaning assumption that voters of a particular race, because of their race, 'think alike, share the same political interests, and will prefer the same candidates at the polls.'" *Miller v. Johnson,* 515 U.S. 900, 911-912 (1995). Finally, race-based districting may result in harm to society by threatening to "'balkanize us into competing racial factions. . . .'" Id. at 912.

To establish a prima facie case of race-based districting, the plaintiff must show that those who adopted the districting plan "subordinated traditional race-neutral districting principles," with the result "that race was the *predominant* factor motivating the . . . decision to place a significant number of voters within or without a particular district." Id. at 916 (emphasis added). In most race discrimination cases, it is enough to show that race was simply "a motivating factor." See § 6.2.2 ("Discriminatory Purpose"). However, the Court has rejected this standard in the race-based districting setting, for it could lead to excessive federal judicial interference in an area that is "primarily the duty and responsibility of the State." *Miller v. Johnson,* supra, 515 U.S. at 915. Since redistricting legislatures are invariably aware of racial demographics, the "a-motivating-factor" standard would make it too easy for a court to subject an apportionment plan to strict scrutiny. On the other hand, because a race-based districting claim "applies district-by-district," rather than "to a State considered as an undifferentiated 'whole'," it is enough for a plaintiff to show that a *particular* district's lines were drawn predominantly based on race, even if at the *state-wide* level, race would not qualify as having been the predominant factor. *Alabama Legislative Black Caucus v. Alabama*, 575 U.S. 254, 262-267 (2015).

In proving that race was "the predominant factor" in drawing a district's lines, "a plaintiff can rely upon either 'circumstantial evidence of a district's shape and demographics or more direct evidence going to legislative purpose'. . . ." *North Carolina v. Covington*, 585 U.S. 969, 977 (2018). Proof may thus consist of nothing more than the bizarreness of a district's shape and the statistics as to its majority-minority composition. In *Shaw v. Reno*, the Court held that a prima facie case of race-based districting was established simply by the fact that a North Carolina reapportionment plan containing "district boundary lines of dramatically irregular shape," 509 U.S. at 633, was "so bizarre on its face that it is 'unexplainable on grounds other than race.' . . ." Id. at 644. As *Shaw* suggests, the bizarreness of shape is not necessarily dispositive, for it may have been predominantly motivated by legitimate political concerns such as protecting incumbents or preserving partisan balance in the elected body, rather than by race. See *Hunt v. Cromartie*, 526 U.S. 541 (1999) (holding that bizarre shape, even when it coincides with racially defined precincts or neighborhoods, may be explicable in political rather than racial terms where there is a high degree of correlation between racial composition and party preference). Yet even regularly shaped districts are open to challenge if, by "more direct evidence going to legislative purpose," the plaintiff can show that race was the predominant factor in drawing district lines. *Miller v. Johnson*, supra, 515 U.S. at 916. And the fact that a state plan was also motivated by traditional districting considerations, such as compactness, contiguity, or incumbency protection, will not defeat the application of strict scrutiny if a court finds that these "legitimate districting principles were 'subordinated' to race." *Bush v. Vera*, 517 U.S. 952, 959 (1996) (applying strict scrutiny in a mixed motive case where race was found to have predominated over traditional goal of incumbency protection).

The Court has made it clear that plaintiffs face a stiff challenge in trying to establish that race was the predominant factor in a legislative districting scheme. In undertaking this inquiry, "we start with a presumption that the legislature acted in good faith." *Alexander v. South Carolina State Conference of the NAACP*, supra, 144 S. Ct. at 1233. In *Easley v. Cromartie*, 532 U.S. 234 (2001), the Court for the fourth time looked at North Carolina's efforts at congressional reapportionment following the 1990 census. The question was whether the evidence adduced at trial was sufficient to support a three-judge district court's finding that race was a predominant factor in North Carolina's reapportionment effort. The Court emphasized the "demanding" burden a plaintiff must satisfy to establish that a legislative districting plan is, in fact, a racial gerrymander. Id. at 241. "Race must not simply have been '*a* motivation for the drawing of a majority minority district,' but '*the predominant* factor motivating the legislature's districting decision.' Plaintiffs must show that a facially neutral law is 'unexplainable on grounds other than race.'" Id. at 241-242 (emphasis in original) (internal citations omitted). This burden is particularly hard to satisfy when, as was the case in North Carolina, "racial identification is highly correlated with political affiliation. . . ." Id. at 243. In the end, despite application of the deferential clearly erroneous standard of review, the Court concluded that the district court's finding of a predominant racial motivation in that case lacked sufficient evidentiary support:

> We concede the record contains a modicum of evidence offering support for the District Court's conclusion. . . . The evidence taken together, however, does not show that racial considerations predominated in the drawing of District 12's boundaries. That is because race in this case correlates closely with political behavior. The basic question is whether the legislature drew District 12's boundaries because of race *rather than* because of political behavior (coupled with traditional, nonracial districting considerations).

Id. at 257 (emphasis in original).

The *Cromartie* Court suggested that in cases with little direct evidence of discriminatory legislative intent, the party challenging the state's districting scheme must submit an alternative plan demonstrating that there were indeed "districting alternatives [that] would have brought about significantly greater racial balance." Id. at 258. The Court reiterated this point in *Alexander*: "Without an alternative map" — one "showing that a rational legislature sincerely driven by its professed partisan goals would have drawn a different map with greater racial balance" — "it is difficult for plaintiffs to defeat our starting presumption that the legislature acted in good faith." 144 S. Ct. at 1235.

Example 7-M

In Example 7-L, if blacks are concentrated in the southern end of town, district C, the majority-black district is probably not bizarre or irregular in shape. See Figure 7-3, above. What is the likelihood of proving the existence of race-based districting?

Explanation

Such a showing would be difficult. The plaintiffs would have to prove, through evidence other than the district's shape, that race was the predominant factor in creating district C. If the town council admitted that it had taken race into account in creating the reapportionment plan, this would still not be enough to prove that other factors were subordinated to race. The council might also have been motivated by a desire to keep districts compact or by a desire to preserve the community of interest that exists in the south end of town. A court might well find that these race-neutral factors played a large enough role to preclude a finding that race was the predominant consideration in creating district C.

While plaintiff's burden in nondilutional race-based districting cases is a heavy one, it is not impossible to carry, especially if there is some direct evidence of discriminatory intent. Sixteen years after *Cromartie* was decided, the Court in *Cooper v. Harris*, 581 U.S. 285 (2017), again had occasion to look at a North Carolina congressional redistricting plan—i.e., the plan that was drawn up following the 2010 census. This time, the Justices agreed with the district court that the state had acted unconstitutionally.

> Uncontested evidence in the record shows that the State's mapmakers . . . purposefully established a racial target: African-Americans should make up no less than a majority of the voting-age population. . . .
>
> Faced with this body of evidence—showing an announced racial target that subordinated other districting criteria and produced boundaries amplifying divisions between blacks and whites—the District Court did not clearly err in finding that race predominated in drawing District 1.

Id. at 299-301. The fact that state lawmakers were also seeking to concentrate African Americans in as few districts as possible to give Republicans control of eleven of the state's thirteen congressional districts did not save the redistricting plan, for the Court concluded that "race, not politics" was the predominant motivating factor. Id. at 309-310. And see id. at 342 (Thomas, J., concurring) (noting that in 2010, just prior to the adoption of the new redistricting plan, Democrats won 7 of the state's 13 House seats, while under the new plan, Democrats in 2016 won only 3 of them).

The *Cooper* Court also said that *Cromartie*'s seeming requirement that plaintiffs produce an alternative districting map showing that the districts in question could have been drawn with lesser racial disparities did not apply in cases such as that one where plaintiffs had offered abundant direct evidence of the legislature's racially discriminatory intent. "That evidence, the District Court plausibly found, itself satisfied the plaintiffs' burden of debunking North Carolina's 'it was really politics' defense; there was no need for an alternative map to do the same job." Id. at 322. But since a plaintiff can rarely rely with certainty on direct evidence of discriminatory intent, failure to present an alternative plan may well prove fatal. This proved to be the case in *Alexander v. South Carolina Conference of the NAACP*, supra, where the Court ruled that

> the District Court . . . critically erred by failing to draw an adverse inference against the Challengers for not providing a substitute map that shows how the State "could have achieved its legitimate political objects" . . . while producing "significantly greater racial balance." . . . For that reason, . . . when all plaintiffs can muster is "meager direct evidence of a racial gerrymander," "only [an alternative] map of that kind" can "carry the day."

144 S. Ct. at 1249. As the Court recognized, this "adverse inference may be dispositive in many, if not most, cases where the plaintiff lacks direct evidence or some extraordinarily powerful circumstantial evidence" of discriminatory intent. Id. at 1250. At the same time, the Court also cautioned that an alternative map may still not save the day in cases where plaintiff seeks to prove their race-based districting claim based on circumstantial evidence alone:

> Although we have never invalidated an electoral map in a case in which the plaintiff failed to adduce any direct evidence, we have, at least in theory, kept the door open for those rare instances in which a district's shape is "so bizarre on its face that it discloses a racial design" absent any alternative explanation.
>
> A circumstantial-evidence-only case is especially difficult when the State raises a partisan-gerrymandering defense. That is because partisan and racial gerrymanders "are capable of yielding similar oddities in a district's boundaries" when there is a high correlation between race and partisan presence. And that is the situation in this case, as the 2020 Presidential election illustrated. Exit polls found that at least 90% of black voters voted for the Democratic candidate in South Carolina and throughout the Nation. When partisanship and race correlate, it naturally follows that a map that has been gerrymandered to achieve a partisan end can look very similar to a racially gerrymandered map. . . . If either politics or race could explain a district's contours, the plaintiff has not cleared its bar.

Id. at 1235 (internal citations omitted). The door in these circumstantial-evidence-only cases thus remains open "at least in theory" — but perhaps only in theory.

If, as in *Cooper*, a plaintiff is able to make out a prima facie case of race-based districting through direct or "extraordinarily powerful" circumstantial evidence that a plan was predominantly motivated by race, "then the burden shifts to the State to prove that the map can overcome the daunting requirements of strict scrutiny." *Alexander v. South Carolina Conference of the NAACP*, supra, 144 S. Ct. at 1236. The plan will then be found unconstitutional unless the defendant can show that it was adopted to further a compelling state interest, and that "the State's use of race is 'narrowly tailored' — *i.e.*, 'necessary' — to achieve that interest," id., a very difficult showing to make. A plaintiff who manages to get this far is thus quite likely to succeed.

Example 7-N

EXAMPLE

Suppose that in Example 7-M a court found that race was the predominant factor in creating district C. How might the council defend the constitutionality of this majority-minority district?

EXPLANATION

Explanation

It might be able to show that the plan was necessary to eradicate the effects of past discrimination. As we saw earlier (§ 6.4.7 ("Compelling Interests")), this will constitute a compelling interest if there is proof that it was the actual goal behind the plan and that at the time the council adopted the plan it had a strong basis in evidence to support a finding of past discrimination. *Shaw v. Hunt*, 517 U.S. 899, 907-911 & n.4 (1996). The plan might thus be upheld if there is evidence that the town had previously used racial gerrymandering, literacy tests, poll taxes, or other devices to prevent blacks from electing members to the council, and if it is also shown that because whites still vote as a racial bloc, creating a majority-black district is necessary to eliminate the present effects of this past discrimination.

In seeking to defend their creation of majority-minority districts, states have sometimes argued that the U.S. Department of Justice had insisted that this was necessary in order to comply with the 1965 federal Voting Rights Act (VRA). The Court has recognized that if a state has adequate reason to believe that § 2 of the VRA requires the drawing of a majority-minority district, this will constitute a compelling state interest for purposes of the Equal Protection Clause. *Cooper v. Harris*, supra, 581 U.S. at 292 ("one compelling interest is complying with the operative provisions of the Voting Rights Act of 1965"). Even if the Justice Department, which is charged with enforcing the VRA, has given the state its approval, the Court will not automatically defer to the department's interpretation of the VRA. Instead, the Court will decide for itself whether the act in fact required race-based districting, and whether the state's use of race was narrowly tailored to that end. See *Shaw v. Hunt*, 517 U.S. 899 (1996), and *Bush v. Vera*, 517 U.S. 952 (1996) (applying strict scrutiny to invalidate race-based districting by North Carolina and Texas even though the Justice Department had insisted upon the creation of additional majority-black congressional districts under the VRA).

Independent judicial scrutiny likewise applies where a state seeks to defend its voluntary creation of majority-minority districts on the ground that doing so was necessary to avoid a *possible* violation of the VRA. In this setting, the Court has given the states some leeway.

> Since the Equal Protection Clause restricts consideration of race and the VRA demands consideration of race, a legislature attempting to produce a lawful districting plan is vulnerable to 'competing hazards of liability.' To harmonize these conflicting demands, we have assumed that compliance with the VRA may justify consideration of race in a way that would not otherwise be allowed. In technical terms, we have assumed that complying with the VRA is a compelling state interest, and that a State's consideration of race in making a

> districting decision is narrowly tailored and thus satisfies strict scrutiny if the State has "good reasons" for believing that its decision is necessary in order to comply with the VRA.

Abbott v. Perez, 585 U.S. 579, 587 (2018) (internal citations omitted). If a state can "establish that it had 'good reasons' to think it would transgress the Act if it did *not* draw race-based district lines," it has the "'breathing room' to adopt reasonable compliance measures that may prove, in perfect hindsight, not to have been needed." *Cooper v. Harris*, supra, 581 U.S. at 293 (emphasis in original). However, absent such a showing, a state's voluntary creation of majority-minority districts will fail. Thus, in *Cooper v. Harris*, North Carolina's effort to defend one of its majority-minority congressional districts on this basis rang hollow. The record showed that for the past 20 years, though African Americans made up less than 50 percent of the district in question, it "was 'an extraordinarily safe district for African-American preferred candidates'," who, because of "a long pattern of white crossover voting," consistently received anywhere from 59 percent to 70 percent of the total vote. 581 U.S. at 302-304. In fact, the state's attempt to use race in creating the district was designed to weaken, rather than strengthen, the African American voice—a predominantly Democratic one—in electing North Carolina's congressional delegation. Id. at 343-346 (Thomas, J., concurring).

In *Abbott v. Perez*, supra, Texas's efforts to defend its voluntary racial gerrymandering likewise fell short. The Court found that the evidence Texas cited—a complaint from the Mexican American Legal Caucus that the district's Latino population was too low, and the results from two primary elections—constituted "too thin a reed to support the drastic decision to draw lines in this way." 585 U.S. at 620-621. Cf. *Bethune-Hill v. Virginia State Bd. of Elections*, 580 U.S. 178 (2017) (upholding Virginia's creation of a majority-minority congressional district where state had "good reasons" to believe it would otherwise violate the VRA, based on extensive legislative study and analysis).

More recently, in *Wisconsin Legislature v. Wisconsin Elections Commission*, 595 U.S. 398 (2022), the Supreme Court reviewed a state legislative districting plan adopted by Wisconsin's governor. That plan included a seventh deliberately drawn majority-black district, overriding a race-neutral plan approved by the legislature that contained six majority-black districts. The Wisconsin Supreme Court upheld the plan, stating that while "'[W]e cannot say for certain on this record that seven majority-Black assembly districts are required by the VRA . . . we see good reasons to conclude a seventh majority-Black district *may* be required.' (emphasis added)." Id. at 403-404. However, while *Cooper* gave the states "breathing room to make reasonable mistakes," the state must have "strong basis in evidence" for concluding "that the Act *demanded* such steps." Id. at 404 (emphasis in original). Moreover, that evidence must be part of a careful "pre-enactment analysis with justifiable conclusions." Id.

at 403. Hence, it was not enough for the Wisconsin state court to conclude "that the VRA *might* support race-based districting"; rather, there must have been strong evidence for concluding "that the statute required it." Id. at 403 (emphasis in original). In addition, the state's pre-enactment record must show that it first considered districting schemes that did not include race-based considerations, and evidence that those race-neutral plans would not have passed muster under § 2 of the Voting Rights Act. Id. at 406. Since Wisconsin's high court did not undertake this analysis, the Supreme Court remanded the case for further consideration. On remand, the Wisconsin court concluded that because "there is 'not a strong basis in evidence' that the VRA requires the use of race to draw majority-Black legislative districts," there is therefore no basis "to justify drawing state legislative districts on the basis of race." *Johnson v. Wisconsin Elections Comm'n*, 972 N.W.2d 559, 565, 571 (Wis. 2022).

§7.3.6 Access to the Ballot

In contrast to the fundamental right to vote, there is no fundamental right of access by a potential candidate to the ballot. Strict scrutiny is therefore not automatically triggered whenever the government regulates or restricts a person's ability to run for public office. Since states have no choice but to regulate elections, "to subject every voting regulation to strict scrutiny . . . would tie the hands of States seeking to assure that elections are operated equitably and efficiently." *Burdick v. Takushi*, 504 U.S. 428, 433 (1992) (citing *Bullock v. Carter*, 405 U.S. 134, 143 (1972), and *Anderson v. Celebrezze*, 460 U.S. 780, 788 (1983)). But ballot access restrictions still warrant heightened scrutiny if they interfere with the fundamental equal protection right to vote for a candidate who reflects one's views, or with one's First Amendment right to associate with others.

In ballot-access equal protection cases, courts apply a "flexible standard" whose rigor turns on the extent to which a law burdens First and Fourteenth Amendment rights. *Burdick v. Takushi*, supra, 504 U.S. at 434. Courts "weigh 'the character and magnitude of the asserted injury' . . . against 'the precise interests put forward by the State as justifications for the burden imposed by its rule,' taking into consideration 'the extent to which those interests make it necessary to burden the plaintiff's rights.'" Id.

In *Bullock v. Carter*, supra, the Court struck down a Texas statute that imposed candidate filing fees as high as $8,900, and in *Lubin v. Panish*, 415 U.S. 709 (1974), a California law that set candidate filing fees at 2 percent of the position's annual salary which in plaintiff's case amounted to just over $700. The effect of these laws was to prevent less affluent groups from being able to vote for a candidate who shared their views. Due to the severity of the impairment, under its "flexible standard," the

Court applied rigorous scrutiny. In both cases, it held that there were less discriminatory ways to achieve the states' goals of controlling ballot length and discouraging frivolous candidacies without denying indigent candidates access to the ballot. One such alternative is requiring that candidates collect a specified number of signatures before their names may appear on the ballot. Signature requirements are typically upheld since "States may require persons to demonstrate 'a significant modicum of support' before allowing them access to a general election ballot, lest it become unmanageable," the same being true with respect to "access to a primary ballot." *New York State Board of Elections v. Lopez Torres*, 552 U.S. 196, 204 (2008) (state could require independent candidates seeking access to primary ballot for state judicial position to obtain signatures of 500 party members or 5 percent of the party's members, whichever is less, during a 37-day period prior to filing deadline). See also *Jenness v. Fortson*, 403 U.S. 431 (1971) (state could condition minor party candidate's access to ballot on obtaining signatures from 5 percent of the eligible voters within a 180-day period).

Signature requirements may nevertheless trigger heightened scrutiny if their effect is to keep independent candidates and minor parties from appearing on the ballot. In *Graveline v. Benson*, 992 F.3d 524 (6th Cir. 2021), the court struck down a Michigan law that allowed independent candidates running for statewide office to appear on the general election ballot only if: (1) they submit a qualifying petition with at least 30,000 valid signatures comprised of at least 100 registered voters from at least half of Michigan's 14 congressional districts; (2) the signatures are submitted at least 110 days before the general election; and (3) the signatures are obtained within 100 days immediately preceding the filing deadline. By contrast, candidates from the three major political parties (Democratic, Libertarian and Republican), rather than having to collect signatures, need only be nominated at a party convention. Because those conventions could be held as close as 60 days before the general election, a would-be independent candidate may not know who the major party nominees will be before their own filing deadline. Since voter support for an independent candidate will often hinge on who the primary party candidates are, the combined effect of these requirements was to impose a severe burden on independent candidates' ability to access the ballot. Applying the *Anderson-Bullock* framework, the *Graveline* court applied "strict-scrutiny review" and struck down the 30,000-signature requirement as not being the least restrictive means of achieving the state's compelling interests in avoiding voter confusion, ballot overcrowding, and frivolous candidacies. Moving the filing deadline closer to the date of the major parties' conventions and/or lowering the 30,000 figure were less discriminatory means of achieving the state's legitimate goals.

Strict scrutiny will not be applied to other types of ballot access restrictions that may keep *specific individuals* off the ballot as long as, in contrast to *Graveline*, they do not prevent any *groups of voters* from fielding a candidate of their choice. Thus, an ordinance requiring elected city officials to be residents of the city is probably constitutional, for while it will bar certain would-be candidates from running for office, the requirement is unlikely to infringe on any group's ability to vote for a candidate of its choice. See *Burrell v. Tipton County Election Comm'n*, 2022 WL 10225146 (6th Cir. Oct. 18, 2022) (applying relaxed "reasonably necessary" scrutiny to uphold town's requirement that to run for the office of mayor or alderman, a candidate must have been a bona fide resident of the town for six months preceding the election).

§7.3.7 Unequal Vote Count

In *Bush v. Gore*, 531 U.S. 98 (2000), the Court held that the Equal Protection Clause was violated when the methods of recounting presidential votes within the State of Florida differed from county to county. The presidential election of 2000 came down to the popular vote count in Florida. Whichever candidate won that vote would win in the electoral college. After the initial count of the Florida presidential votes, candidate Bush's margin of victory was less than one-half of 1 percent. Hence, under Florida law an automatic machine recount was required. After that recount, the margin of victory was smaller still and candidate Gore requested a hand recount in certain Florida counties, as he was permitted to do under Florida law. A major political/legal contretemps developed over the hand recounts, including an intense debate over exactly what should count as a vote on an insufficiently perforated machine ballot—does one count a hanging or dimpled chad or not? Eventually, on December 8, 2000, the Florida Supreme Court ordered a hand recount in all Florida counties in which there were "undervotes"—i.e., ballots for which voting machines had failed to tabulate a vote for president and that had not yet been manually recounted. The state high court did not, however, specify the standards for the recount other than ascertainment of "the intent of the voter." Hence, what might count as a vote could differ from county to county and might differ even within a single county. The U.S. Supreme Court, on a petition filed by Bush and his running mate, stayed the order of the Florida Supreme Court and granted certiorari.

In then holding that Florida's manual recount procedures violated the Equal Protection Clause, the Court relied on four facts: (1) the use of variable standards in measuring the intent of the voter; (2) the failure to recount "overvotes" (i.e., those ballots on which a voter may have mistakenly voted for more than one presidential candidate); (3) the certification of some partial recounts; and (4) the lack of training for the vote counters. Id. at 106-109. Instead of remanding to the state supreme court for the creation of uniform standards, the U.S. Supreme Court simply reversed the state court's recount order, essentially ending the recount process. Id.

In terms of doctrinal development, the Supreme Court described its ruling as limited to those circumstances in which "a court orders a statewide remedy. . . ." Id. at 109. It is possible that the Court's equal counting principle could be applied under other circumstances, but the Court seemed to suggest otherwise: "Our consideration is limited to the present circumstances, for the problem of equal protection in election processes generally presents many complexities." Id. Yet if a state permitted counties to use different methods for counting votes in statewide elections—e.g., relatively inaccurate punch card machines in one county and highly accurate computers in another—then a statewide vote could be seen as favoring voters in the "computer" counties. One expects that for the time being the Court will leave the choice of voting machines to political determination. Id. at 104 ("After the current counting, it is likely legislative bodies nationwide will examine ways to improve the mechanisms and machinery for voting."). See, e.g., *Southwest Voter Registration Educ. Project v. Shelley*, 344 F.3d 914 (9th Cir. 2003) (en banc) (refusing to enjoin discriminatory use of punch card machines in statewide election).

§7.4 THE RIGHT TO TRAVEL

One of the fundamental rights protected by the Fourteenth Amendment is the right to travel—i.e., the right to move to a state and establish residence there. Laws that discourage or penalize exercise of this right by discriminating against newcomers to the state are subject to strict scrutiny under either the Equal Protection Clause or the Fourteenth Amendment's Privileges or Immunities Clause, or both. The right to travel secured by the Fourteenth Amendment is something of a misnomer. What is protected is not the right to simply visit or pass through a state, but the right to migrate and change one's domicile and to then be treated as an equal with other residents of the state. The right to visit or pass through a state, whether for business or for pleasure, may be protected by other constitutional provisions, including the Commerce Clause, and the Privileges and Immunities Clause of Article IV. See *National Power & Federalism*, supra, chs. 8 and 9.

The Supreme Court initially used the Equal Protection Clause to protect newcomers of a state against laws that discriminate against them. The right to travel was deemed to be a fundamental right for equal protection purposes. As such, not all laws discriminating against new residents of the state were subject to strict scrutiny; rather, strict scrutiny came into play only if the state's adverse treatment of newcomers was sufficient to discourage or penalize migration to the state. Forms of discrimination that were deemed to be too incidental or insignificant did not impinge on the right to travel (see § 7.2), and therefore did not trigger strict scrutiny.

Without disavowing its equal protection right to travel cases, the Court in *Saenz v. Roe*, 526 U.S. 489 (1999), has since held that the right to travel is also protected by the Privileges or Immunities Clause of the Fourteenth Amendment. See *National Power & Federalism*, supra, at § 9.2. One of the privileges or immunities of national citizenship is "the right of the newly arrived citizen" to be "treated like other citizens of that State. . . ." *Saenz v. Roe*, supra, 526 U.S. at 500, 502. Under the Privileges or Immunities Clause, a state law that "discriminates against some of its citizens because they have been domiciled in the State for less than" a specified period of time is subject to strict scrutiny, even if it "affects the right to travel only 'incidentally' . . . ." Id. at 504-505. This is not to say that all such laws are necessarily unconstitutional.

Today, laws that discriminate against new residents of a state may thus be challenged under the Fourteenth Amendment, using either the Equal Protection Clause or the Privileges or Immunities Clause. Yet because it is more difficult to trigger strict scrutiny using the equal protection analysis due to its impingement requirement, a litigant would almost always prefer to challenge such discrimination by invoking the Privileges or Immunities Clause. While it is too early to tell, the Court's equal protection right to travel line of cases may fall into desuetude, much like a road that is abandoned after the construction of a modern highway.

In the balance of this section we examine the right to travel in the context of several different types of residency requirements—i.e., durational residency requirements, fixed-point and fixed-date residency requirements, and bona fide residency requirements. Not all of these implicate the right to travel protected by the Fourteenth Amendment.

§7.4.1 Durational Residency Requirements

One type of law that may trigger strict scrutiny under both the Equal Protection and the Privileges or Immunities Clauses is a durational residency requirement or waiting period. Such measures deny new residents a benefit or privilege that is available to other residents of the state until the newcomers have lived in the state and/or the county for a requisite period. If the benefit is sufficiently vital or important, the state's discrimination between new and old residents will be deemed to impinge on the right to travel and will receive strict scrutiny under the Equal Protection

Clause. Durational residency requirements for welfare benefits, medical care, and voting are thus subject to strict scrutiny, for they penalize the right to travel by imposing substantial burdens exclusively on those who recently moved to the state. Where less critical benefits are at stake, strict scrutiny is not necessarily called for under the Equal Protection Clause, although strict scrutiny will still be employed under the Privileges or Immunities Clause.

EXAMPLE

Example 7-O

A California law provides that during their first year in the state, new residents who apply for welfare may receive a monthly grant no higher than what they would have been eligible for in the state from which they moved. The purpose of the statute is to reduce the state's welfare budget by $11 million a year. The law was challenged by several California residents who qualified for welfare benefits but who, within the previous year, had moved to California from states with lower benefit levels. As a result, the plaintiffs receive welfare grants that are from $200 to $400 a month less than those received by Californians who have lived in the state for a longer time. Does this California durational residency requirement violate the Equal Protection Clause, or the Privileges or Immunities Clause?

EXPLANATION

Explanation

Even though it imposes a one-year waiting period, the California law might not be subject to strict scrutiny under the Equal Protection Clause. In contrast to the one-year durational residency requirements for welfare struck down in *Shapiro v. Thompson*, 394 U.S. 618 (1969), California does not withhold all welfare benefits from newcomers; instead, they receive the same cash benefits they were receiving or would have received in their home states. In addition, the disparity between the benefits paid new residents and older residents is partially offset by additional housing assistance and food stamp allowances. Thus, the impact on the fundamental right to travel may be too incidental to trigger strict scrutiny under the Equal Protection Clause.

Strict scrutiny would nevertheless be applied under the Privileges or Immunities Clause, which has no similar impingement requirement. Under strict scrutiny, the law is unconstitutional. The state's interest in reducing welfare costs is important but probably not compelling. Even if it were, the state's discrimination against newcomers is not necessary to achieving the state's goal. It could save the same amount of money by instead reducing all welfare grants—for new residents and old residents alike—by 72 cents a month. See *Saenz v. Roe*, 526 U.S. 489 (1999) (invalidating identical California welfare statute under Privileges or Immunities Clause).

Example 7-P

State law provides that, to file a divorce action, a plaintiff must have been a resident of the state for one year immediately prior to filing the action. Carol moved to the state five months ago and would like to bring a divorce action there so that she can marry Ralph. If Carol challenges the validity of the state's one-year durational residency requirement, will strict scrutiny apply under the Equal Protection Clause?

Explanation

This law classifies residents based on their length of residence in the state. Carol will argue that by denying her access to the divorce court for a year, the state is penalizing her for having recently exercised her right to travel. The state will respond that, unlike waiting periods for welfare benefits, medical care, and voting, a divorce decree is not a vital governmental benefit and the harm caused by the waiting period is not irreparable. Once the durational residency requirement has been satisfied, Carol will receive the same benefit she seeks now—a dissolution of her marriage. By contrast, in the welfare, medical care, and voting contexts, benefits denied during the waiting period are irretrievably lost. On this basis, the state will argue that the one-year waiting period does not impinge on either the fundamental right to travel or the fundamental right to marry and that strict scrutiny should, therefore, not be applied. See *Sosna v. Iowa*, 419 U.S. 393 (1975) (upholding one-year waiting period for filing a divorce action under the Equal Protection Clause, without applying strict scrutiny).

The result in this example might have been different had the state imposed a much longer waiting period—e.g., ten years rather than one year. Even though the nature of the benefit or privilege would be the same, the harm inflicted during the interim might in many respects now be irreparable. In other words, whether a durational residency requirement impinges on the equal protection right to travel may be a function of both the nature of the benefit and the length of time it is withheld. For a truly vital benefit, such as welfare or medical care, even a short waiting period may be enough to trigger strict scrutiny; for less critical benefits, it may take a long waiting period before one could conclude that the right to travel was being penalized. The Court in *Sosna* implied as much, noting that most states imposed waiting periods for divorce of between six months and two years and that Iowa's one-year period was the most common period prescribed. Id. at 404-405.

If the one-year waiting period for a divorce in Example 7-P were instead challenged under the Privileges or Immunities Clause, strict scrutiny would have applied since the law discriminates against new residents of the state. Yet the measure might not be found unconstitutional. In *Saenz v. Roe*, supra, the Court suggested that a state may be allowed to impose a durational residency requirement when there is a danger that immediate eligibility "will encourage citizens of other States to establish residency for just long enough to acquire some readily portable benefit, such as divorce or a college education, that will be enjoyed after they return to their original domicile." 526 U.S. at 505. The Court contrasted the welfare benefits at issue in *Saenz*, noting that they would be entirely consumed while the new resident was still living in the state. Yet, as Chief Justice Rehnquist remarked in his *Saenz* dissent,

> this "you can't take it with you" distinction is more apparent than real. . . . Welfare payments are a form of insurance, giving impoverished individuals and their families the means to meet the demands of daily life while they receive the necessary training, education, and time to look for a job. The cash itself will no doubt be spent in California, but the benefits from receiving this income and having the opportunity to become employed or employable will stick with the welfare recipients if they stay in California or go back to their true domicile. Similarly, tuition subsidies are "consumed" in-state but the recipient takes the benefits of a college education with him wherever he goes. A welfare subsidy is thus as much an investment in human capital as is a tuition subsidy, and their attendant benefits are just as "portable." . . . [T]he line drawn by the Court borders on the metaphysical, and requires lower courts to plumb the policies animating certain benefits like welfare to define their "essence" and hence their "portability."

Id. at 519-520. The "portability" argument may enable states to salvage some durational residency requirements despite the fact that they are subject to strict scrutiny under the Privileges or Immunities Clause; for as we shall see in the next section, some courts have invoked "portability" to uphold fixed-point residency requirements.

Besides making a "portability" argument, a state might be able to defend a relatively short durational residency requirement on the ground that it is necessary to assure that an individual has in fact become a bona fide resident of the state. In *Saenz*, the Court expressly alluded to this possibility, noting that, because it was undisputed that the plaintiffs there were citizens of California, "[w]e thus have no occasion to consider what weight might be given to a citizen's length of residence if the bona fides of her claim to state citizenship were questioned." Id. at 505.

§7.4.2 Fixed-Point and Fixed-Date Residency Requirements

Besides durational residency requirements, there are two other types of residency requirements that may trigger strict scrutiny because of their impact on the right to travel. One is a fixed-point residency requirement: To receive a particular governmental benefit or privilege, persons must have been a resident of the state at a specified point in time, such as when they were born, when they turned 21, or when they graduated from college. The other is a fixed-date residency requirement, which conditions a benefit or privilege on a person's having resided in the state on a specific date, such as on January 1, 2020. Like durational residency requirements, both fixed-point and fixed-date residency requirements draw distinctions among residents of the state; moreover, they usually have the effect of discriminating against newer residents of the state. In contrast to durational requirements, however, the burdens imposed by fixed-point and fixed-date requirements are permanent, for no matter how long a person waits, he or she will never be treated the same as other state residents. Because of their permanent impact, it may be easier than with durational residency requirements to find that fixed-point or fixed-date requirements impinge on the right to travel so as to trigger strict scrutiny under the Equal Protection Clause. To the extent that they discriminate against newer state residents, they should in any event receive strict scrutiny under the Privileges or Immunities Clause.

Example 7-Q

Under state Z law, those who were residents of state Z when they graduated from high school are entitled to free tuition at the state university. Ted is 25 years old and has been a resident of state Z for the last six years. He was admitted to the state university but was advised that he must pay tuition of $10,000 per year because when he graduated from high school he was a resident of state X. Ted has challenged state Z's tuition policy under the Equal Protection Clause and the Privileges or Immunities Clause. Will the policy be struck down?

Explanation

The state tuition policy involves a fixed-point residency requirement because to receive the benefit of free tuition, one must have been a state resident at a fixed point in one's life. This is not a fixed-date residency requirement, since the relevant date will vary in each individual case. Nor has the state employed a durational residency requirement or waiting period, for no matter how long Ted resides in state Z, he will never qualify for free tuition.

The Court has suggested that *durational* residency requirements for reduced tuition at a state university do not impinge on the equal protection right to travel. See, e.g., *Vlandis v. Kline*, 412 U.S. 441, 452-454 (1973); *Starns v. Malkerson*, 326 F. Supp. 234 (D. Minn. 1970), *aff'd*, 401 U.S. 985 (1971). Here, though, the state has employed a *fixed-point* requirement that has the effect of permanently relegating newcomers to a status inferior to that of older residents. The permanency of the disqualification may cause a court to find that state Z's residency requirement penalizes exercise of the right to travel and must, therefore, be subject to strict scrutiny. See *Attorney General of N.Y. v. Soto-Lopez*, 476 U.S. 898 (1986) (plurality opinion) (applying strict scrutiny to invalidate a fixed-point residency requirement for receipt of a civil service veteran's preference, noting that while the benefit was not as important as welfare, medical care, or voting, denial of the benefit was permanent rather than temporary).

Under the Privileges or Immunities Clause, strict scrutiny should be called for since this law discriminates against Ted as a relative newcomer to the state. While the law involves a fixed-point rather than a durational residency requirement, the state is still denying a relative newcomer the right to be treated like native-born or longer-term residents of the state.

But if the Court adopts the "portability" argument discussed earlier, this law might be upheld, for a college education is totally portable. One might respond that the portability discussion in *Saenz* was in the context of a temporary, one-year delay in providing a benefit to newcomers, and that the chances someone will "take the benefit and run" diminish the longer they have lived in the state. As such, even if this concern might justify some type of durational residency requirement, "portability" should not be the basis for permanently denying a benefit to someone like Ted who has already resided in the state for six years.

Yet in *Harris v. Hahn*, 827 F.3d 359 (5th Cir. 2016), the Court of Appeals invoked the "portability" argument to uphold a Texas program that provides tuition waivers at public universities to resident veterans who lived in Texas at the time they enlisted in the military. The plaintiff was a veteran who had resided in Texas for the previous six years but did not reside there when he enlisted in the Army at age 18. In ruling that this did not violate the Privileges or Immunities Clause, the court invoked *Saenz*'s caveat, stating that "the residency requirement . . . is justified because the benefit in question, unlike the benefits considered in other right to travel cases, is a portable benefit that can be received in Texas and enjoyed long thereafter if the recipient chooses to immediately leave the state." Id. at 370. Moreover, said the court, "the new veteran migrant to Texas has lost nothing that he would have received in his prior state of residence," for that state had no comparable program. Id. at 371. The court then upheld the residency requirement under a rational basis test, noting that it encouraged Texas students to complete high school, to enlist in the military, and to attend college. Id. at 367-369.

§7.4.3 The Equal Protection Alternative to Strict Scrutiny

Under the Equal Protection Clause, if a state law that discriminates against newcomers impinges on the right to travel, it will be subject to strict scrutiny and invalidated unless the measure is shown to be necessary to achieve a compelling state interest. If there is no infringement of the right to travel, so that strict scrutiny is not triggered, the standard of equal protection review will not necessarily drop to the "toothless" rational basis test. As we noted earlier, discrimination against those who recently moved to the state is sometimes reviewed under an enhanced version of the rational basis test. See § 6.7.2.

Example 7-R

State B gives residents an annual $10 recreation credit for each year they have lived in the state since reaching age 21. The credit can be used to reduce any fee charged by the state for admission to a park, beach, or campground and to reduce state fees for recreational fishing and hunting licenses. Ted, who is 51 and has lived in state B all his life, receives a $300 annual recreation credit, reflecting the fact that he has resided in the state for 30 years since reaching age 21. Sam, who is also 51, moved to the state five years ago and thus receives only a $50 credit. Has state B violated Sam's rights under the Equal Protection Clause?

Explanation

The recreation credit discriminates against newer residents of state B, who receive smaller credits than their counterparts, such as Ted, who have lived in state B all their lives. The credit involves a form of durational residency requirement, for state benefits are tied to how long one has lived in the state; however, unlike typical durational residency requirements, there is no point at which the relative newcomer will ever be treated as a full equal to longer-term residents. Yet for equal protection purposes, it is not clear that this durational residency scheme deters or penalizes exercise of the right to travel; instead, it may encourage adults to move to state B and rewards them for doing so.

Even if it does not infringe on the right to travel, the credit discriminates on the basis of when a person established residence in the state; moreover, the discrimination is permanent, for Sam will never catch up with people such as Ted. The Court might, therefore, apply an enhanced version of the rational basis test. Under this standard, while the state may argue that the recreation credit scheme furthers the interest of encouraging people to move to the state and to remain there, this might not justify the creation of "fixed, permanent distinctions between . . . concededly bona fide residents, based on how long they have been in the State." *Zobel v. Williams*, 457 U.S. 55, 59 (1982) (invalidating Alaska scheme that paid annual dividends based on the number of years a person had lived in the state).

Zobel was decided before the Court in *Saenz v. Roe* placed the right to travel under the umbrella of the Privileges or Immunities Clause. Today, the recreation credit scheme set forth in this example, as well as the dividend scheme challenged in *Zobel*, would most likely be subject to strict scrutiny and invalidated under the Privileges or Immunities Clause.

§7.4.4 Bona Fide Residency Requirements

It is important to distinguish durational, fixed-point, and fixed-date residency requirements, all of which may impinge on the right to travel, from bona fide residency requirements. A bona fide residency requirement merely insists that a person in fact be a resident of the state to receive a benefit or engage in some activity. Thus, whereas durational, fixed-point, and fixed-date residency requirements draw distinctions *among residents* of the state on the basis of when they took up residence there, bona fide residency requirements draw distinctions *between residents and nonresidents* of the state. Such requirements do not discourage or penalize exercise of the right to travel, but rather encourage people to move to the state and reward them for doing so. Once a person exercises this right by becoming a bona fide resident, he or she is instantly treated just like—and entitled to the same benefits as—all other residents of the state. Since bona fide residency requirements do not impinge on the right to migrate to the state, they are not subject to strict scrutiny equal protection review. Nor do they trigger scrutiny under the Privileges or Immunities Clause. See, e.g., *McCarthy v. Philadelphia Civil Serv. Comm'n*, 424 U.S. 645 (1976) (per curiam) (upholding requirement that city employees must be city residents, in suit brought by city employee who was terminated after moving his residence to a neighboring state). But because bona fide residency requirements discriminate against citizens of other states in favor of the state's own citizens, they may be subject to fairly demanding review under the dormant Commerce Clause and under the Privileges and Immunities Clause of Article IV, § 2. See *National Power & Federalism*, supra, at chs. 8 and 9.

The fact that bona fide residency requirements do not raise right to travel concerns indicates that the right is narrower in scope than we have so far suggested. The Court has described the right to travel as the right to migrate, as opposed to the right simply to travel about. Yet even this formulation is too broad, for it is only the right to *immigrate* or *move to* the state—not the right to *emigrate* or *leave* the state—that is protected by the right to travel under the Equal Protection Clause and the Privileges or Immunities Clause. If the right to emigrate were part of the fundamental right to travel, even bona fide residency requirements might trigger strict scrutiny, since they might discourage or penalize the decision to move out of the state.

Example 7-S

State A's medical school, which is one of the best in the nation, provides free tuition to all bona fide residents of the state. Students who attend the school, but do not maintain a permanent residence in the state, are charged full tuition. Sonya was a resident of state A when she began medical school, but during her second year, she and her family moved to state B. As a result, Sonya has now been charged out-of-state tuition of $25,000 per year. Has state A violated Sonya's constitutional right to travel?

Explanation

Sonya's right to travel has not been violated. State A has merely imposed a bona fide residency requirement to receive free tuition. Because the requirement encourages people to move to the state, it does not burden the right to travel under either the Equal Protection Clause or the Privileges or Immunities Clause. The state has not created a classification that treats new residents less favorably than older residents but has instead drawn a distinction between residents and nonresidents. Since the right to travel is not implicated, a court would at best apply enhanced rational basis review under the Equal Protection Clause. The residency requirement would be upheld on the ground that it rationally furthers the state's goal of underwriting the education of those most likely to provide medical care to residents of the state after graduation.

Nor does state A's residency requirement violate the Commerce Clause or Article IV's Privileges and Immunities Clause. Even if the requirement discriminates against interstate commerce because of the burden it places on out-of-state students, the state's operation of the medical school is exempt from the dormant Commerce Clause under the market participant doctrine. See *National Power & Federalism*, supra, at § 8.12. And, under the Privileges and Immunities Clause, the state has leeway to favor its residents by giving them free access to the state-owned medical school. See id. at § 9.5.2.

§7.5 ACCESS TO THE COURTS

Under very limited circumstances, the Equal Protection Clause may require that indigents be provided with equal access to the courts. In these situations, the government may be obligated to furnish counsel, waive fees, and pay litigation costs for those who would otherwise be unable to participate effectively in the legal process on a basis comparable to that of more affluent litigants. However, the Court has stopped far short of recognizing a broad-based fundamental right of equal access to the judicial process. Outside of the criminal context, the few cases in which the Court has required states to provide indigents with effective access to the legal system have often relied at least in part on substantive or procedural due process as well as the Equal Protection Clause.

In the criminal context, the Court has held that a state is obligated to provide indigent defendants with a free trial transcript and appointed counsel to take advantage of a first appeal of right, a process sometimes referred to as first-tier, nondiscretionary review. *Gideon v. Wainwright*, 372 U.S. 335 (1963); *Griffin v. Illinois*, 351 U.S. 12 (1956). This right does not extend to second-tier discretionary review by a state supreme court. *Ross v. Moffitt*, 417 U.S. 600, 610-612 (1974). It does, however, apply to first-tier discretionary review when the scope of that discretion turns on the merits of the defendant's petition for review. *Halbert v. Michigan*, 545 U.S. 605 (2005).

Since the state is not constitutionally required to provide a system of appellate courts or a right of appellate review, the above decisions are best understood as resting on a limited equal protection right of equal access to the appellate courts. *M.L.B. v. S.L.J.*, 519 U.S. 102, 120 (1997). However, the Court has construed this right narrowly, emphasizing that the Equal Protection Clause does not require the state "to duplicate the legal arsenal that may be privately retained by a criminal defendant . . . but only to assure the indigent defendant an adequate opportunity to present his claims fairly in the context of the State's appellate process." *Ross v. Moffitt*, supra, 417 U.S. at 616.

In *M.L.B. v. S.L.J.*, the Court extended its holdings from the criminal context to a civil proceeding that terminated a parent's rights in her two minor children. In that case, the Mississippi Supreme Court dismissed the mother's appeal because she was unable to pay record preparation fees of $2,352.36. The U.S. Supreme Court reversed. It emphasized that though such proceedings may be civil in nature, they have devastating and irretrievable consequences for a parent, setting them "apart from mine run civil actions, even from other domestic relations matters such as divorce, paternity, and child custody," which are usually "modifiable at the parties' will or based on changed circumstances. . . ." 519 U.S. at 127-128. Accordingly, said the Court, the Equal Protection Clause required the state to provide the indigent parent with a record of sufficient completeness to allow proper appellate consideration of her claim. Though the Court's decision rested on equal protection principles, it also noted that the case directly implicated a parent's fundamental interest in the relationship with her children. Id. at 116-118.

In most other civil contexts, the Constitution does not require a state to waive court fees or other costs for those unable to pay them. The *M.L.B.* Court stressed that it was not disturbing the "general rule . . . that fee requirements ordinarily are examined only for rationality" and that a "State's need for revenue to offset costs, in the mine run of cases, satisfies the rationality requirement. . . ." Id. at 123. See, e.g., *Mendoza v. Strickler*, 51 F.4th 346 (9th Cir. 2022) (Oregon's suspension of driver's license for nonpayment of traffic fines, despite individual's inability to pay, triggers only rational basis review, for unlike M.L.B., the state did not impair access to any judicial processes).

The few other civil cases that have departed from this rule have, like M.L.B., usually involved the presence of a fundamental right; and most of them have thus rested at least in part on substantive or procedural due process, as well as equal protection principles. In *Boddie v. Connecticut*, 401 U.S. 371 (1971), for example, the Court held that a state was constitutionally obligated to waive court fees and costs for an indigent who wished to file a divorce action. Since the state retained a monopoly over the means of adjusting marital relationships, the fee requirement operated as an absolute ban on divorce and remarriage for indigents. Under substantive due process, such a direct infringement on the fundamental right to marry is invalid because fee requirements are not necessary to achieve any compelling state interest. And as a matter of procedural due process, the fee requirement impaired an indigent's fundamental liberty in the marital decision without affording an opportunity to be heard.

Any thought that *Boddie* established a general right of equal access to the courts in civil cases was quickly put to rest by *United States v. Kras*, 409 U.S. 434 (1973). The Court there upheld a federal law requiring all bankruptcy petitioners to pay fees and costs of $50. Though the effect of this requirement was to deny indigents access to the bankruptcy court, *Boddie* did not compel the government to waive the fee. The *Kras* Court explained that, in contrast to *Boddie*, no fundamental interest was involved and thus only rational basis review was called for under substantive due process. With respect to procedural due process, while inability to pay the fee could impair a debtor's property interests, it was not clear that such a deprivation would occur. Unlike the situation in *Boddie*, the government has no monopoly over how indigents may protect their property interests: "[B]ankruptcy is not the only method available to a debtor for the adjustment of his legal relationship with his creditors." Id. at 445. Finally, under the equal protection component of the Fifth Amendment, since no fundamental right was involved and since poverty is not a suspect or quasi-suspect basis of classification (see § 6.7.1), only a rational basis was needed to justify the fee requirement.

M.L.B., *Boddie*, and *Kras* all involved the question of whether the government had to waive fees that would otherwise keep an indigent from getting into a trial or an appellate court. A related issue concerns when persons who are already in court are entitled to have the government pay certain of their litigation expenses. The issue is not one of access to the courts as such, but one of *meaningful* access. The Court has often approached this issue in terms of procedural due process rather than equal protection. If, on a case-by-case basis, a litigant's inability to pay a specific litigation expense is likely to harm an important interest, the state may be required to pay that expense. Compare *Little v. Streater*, 452 U.S. 1 (1981) (procedural due process required state to pay for blood tests in a paternity suit where, without them, an indigent faced a serious risk of erroneously being adjudged the father) with *Lassiter v. Department of Social Servs.*, 452 U.S. 18 (1981) (procedural due process did not require state to appoint counsel for indigent mother in parental termination suit where issues and evidence were such that counsel would not have made a significant difference).

The question of what procedures are necessary to comport with the requirements of procedural due process is explored in § 5.5. For a discussion of the right of access to courts under substantive due process, see § 2.6.3.

§7.6 WELFARE AND SUBSISTENCE

The Supreme Court has rejected the proposition that for equal protection purposes, there is a fundamental interest in the basic necessities of life. Though "[t]he administration of public welfare assistance . . . involves the most basic economic needs of impoverished human beings," it is, nonetheless, subject to the same standard of review as "state regulation of business or industry." *Dandridge v. Williams*, 397 U.S. 471, 485 (1970). Consequently, classifications employed in determining eligibility for welfare, food stamps, housing, and medical care typically call for only a rational basis review under the Equal Protection Clause. To be sure, governmental decisions involving the basic necessities of life must accord with procedural due process. See § 5.2.2. And such decisions will be subject to strict scrutiny if they impinge on some *other* fundamental liberty—e.g., the right to travel—or discriminate based on race or alienage. But the interest in subsistence itself is not fundamental for purposes of either the Due Process or the Equal Protection Clause.

EXAMPLE

Example 7-T

A state provides a monthly welfare grant to needy families. The grant is based in part on the number of unmarried children below age 21 living in the household. The Smith family's grant has been reduced by $150 per month because Sam, their 19-year-old son, was recently married. Sam and his new wife live in the Smith household. Did the state violate the Equal Protection Clause by reducing the Smiths' grant?

EXPLANATION

Explanation

Since wealth or poverty is not a suspect or quasi-suspect basis of classification, heightened scrutiny is not called for on this basis. Nor is the interest in subsistence benefits a fundamental right that would trigger strict scrutiny. The Smiths may argue that strict scrutiny is required because reducing the grant discriminates against the family because of Sam's exercise of his fundamental right to marry. However, a court would probably reject this argument on the ground that the state's conduct was not sufficient to impinge on Sam's freedom to marry. See § 2.4.4. The state did not directly prohibit him from marrying, and it would claim that the indirect effect of a $150 per month loss does not substantially impair the exercise of this fundamental liberty. On the other hand, if the Smiths could show that the impact of this welfare rule on the fundamental liberty interest in marriage is more severe (e.g., that unless the full grant is restored, Sam and his wife will have to divorce), strict scrutiny might be triggered, and the state would have to show that its discrimination against families with married children is necessary to serve a compelling state interest. See *Bowen v. Gilliard*, 483 U.S. 587 (1987) (upholding welfare laws under rational basis equal protection test after rejecting argument that the law impinged on a fundamental liberty interest); *Lyng v. Castillo*, 477 U.S. 635 (1986) (same).

The Court's reluctance to find that the withholding of subsistence benefits impinges on a fundamental liberty interest makes it easy for government to use its control over these benefits to in effect "buy up" people's constitutional rights. The government may accomplish this by conditioning benefits such as welfare and medical care on a recipient's surrender of such rights. At one time, under the *doctrine of unconstitutional conditions*, any such conditioning of governmental benefits would have been subject to strict scrutiny. The Court subsequently narrowed this doctrine. As a result, the discriminatory denial of benefits to those who exercised protected liberties contrary to the government's wishes were often upheld under a rational basis standard of review.

EXAMPLE

Example 7-U

As we saw in § 2.5.4, a woman has a fundamental liberty interest to decide whether to abort a fetus. The Due Process Clause would thus bar a state from directly interfering with this decision by making it a crime to have an abortion during the first six months of pregnancy. *Planned Parenthood v. Casey*, 505 U.S. 833 (1992). Suppose that the state instead seeks to influence this decision indirectly by refusing to pay the medical expenses of having an abortion, while agreeing to pay the medical costs associated with childbirth. Does this discrimination against women who exercise their liberty by choosing an abortion trigger strict scrutiny under the Equal Protection Clause?

Explanation

The answer depends on whether a court finds that this discriminatory denial of benefits is sufficient to impinge on a woman's fundamental right to choose between childbirth and abortion. In *Harris v. McRae*, 448 U.S. 297 (1980), the Court held that such discrimination in the administration of the federal Medicaid program did not trigger strict scrutiny, even where the abortion was medically necessary. In the Court's view, while such a selective denial of medical benefits may influence an indigent woman's decision in favor of childbirth, the denial did not infringe on or penalize her exercise of the fundamental liberty to choose an abortion. The Court proceeded to uphold the discriminatory eligibility rule under the rational basis standard of review.

There are signs that the modern Court may be taking a more hospitable view of the unconstitutional conditions doctrine. See, e.g., *Oil States Energy Services, LLC v. Greene's Energy Group, LLC*, 584 U.S. 325, 342 n.4 (2018) ("the unconstitutional-conditions doctrine" "prevents the Government from using conditions 'to produce a result which it could not command directly'"); *Agency for Int'l Development v. Alliance for Open Society*, 570 U.S. 205 (2013) (the "unconstitutional conditions" doctrine invalidates federal requirement that entities receiving certain federal funds must have a policy agreeing with the Government's position opposing prostitution and sex trafficking); *Koontz v. St. John's River Water Mgmt. Div.*, 570 U.S. 595, 604 (2013) (endorsing, in the context of land use permits, the "overarching principle, known as the unconstitutional conditions doctrine, that vindicates the Constitution's enumerated rights by preventing the government from coercing people into giving them up"); *Legal Services Corp. v. Velazquez*, 531 U.S. 533 (2001) (federal law barring attorneys who worked for federally-funded legal services programs from challenging the validity of state or federal welfare statutes violated First Amendment as an unconstitutional condition on use of those funds). Restoration of the doctrine would open the door to due process and equal protection claims where public benefits are denied to those who have exercised a constitutional right.

§7.7 ACCESS TO A BASIC EDUCATION

The interest in education is a protected liberty under the Due Process Clause. *Pierce v. Society of Sisters*, 268 U.S. 510, 534-535 (1925) (parents' liberty to direct "education of children"); *Meyer v. Nebraska,* 262 U.S. 390, 399 (1923) (liberty "to acquire useful knowledge"). See § 2.3.1. However, education is not a *fundamental* right under either the Due Process or the Equal Protection Clause. Consequently, state and local laws that adversely impact an individual's ability to obtain an education generally receive only rational basis due process and equal protection review. If the situation were otherwise, federal judges might in effect become overseers of the nation's public schools. Virtually every decision by state or local education officials would be subject to judicial examination under the lens of strict scrutiny, with the result that many educational policies would be invalidated because a federal court decided they were not narrowly tailored to serve a compelling state interest. Such intrusion would be contrary to the Court's frequent recognition that education is an area that falls peculiarly within the province of local government.

Yet there is a difference between the interest in education in general and the interest in acquiring a minimally adequate education. The Supreme Court has left open the possibility that the interest in acquiring "a minimally adequate education is a fundamental right" under the Equal Protection Clause, so that laws that "discriminatorily infringe that right should be accorded heightened equal protection review." *Papasan v. Allain,* 478 U.S. 265, 285 (1986). If the Court were to recognize such a fundamental right, laws that deny children in some schools the opportunity to acquire a basic education, while affording that opportunity to other children, would be subject to strict scrutiny under the Equal Protection Clause. Under such an approach, not all laws that discriminate concerning education would be subject to strict scrutiny. Nor would heightened scrutiny apply simply because some children's educational opportunities were inferior to those of others. Strict scrutiny would come into play only where the impact of a discriminatory law is so severe as to constitute a "radical denial of educational opportunity," such as where "schoolchildren . . . are not taught to read or write" or "receive no instruction on even the educational basics. . . ." Id. at 284, 286.

The rationale for applying heightened equal protection scrutiny in these circumstances was suggested in *Plyler v. Doe,* 457 U.S. 202 (1982), a case where the Court struck down a Texas law that excluded undocumented alien children from public schools. The Court agreed that education is not a "fundamental right" and that, therefore, "a State need not justify by compelling necessity *every variation* in the manner in which education is provided to its population." Id. at 223 (emphasis supplied). Yet as we will see in §7.8.3, the *Plyler* Court applied intermediate rather than rational basis review, partly because of the special role that a basic education plays in promoting equality. Justice Brennan, speaking for the majority, noted that a complete "denial of education to some isolated group of children poses an affront to one of the goals of the Equal Protection Clause: the abolition of governmental barriers . . . to advancement on the basis of individual merit." Id. at 221-222. In a separate concurrence, Justice Blackmun observed that "certain interests, though not constitutionally guaranteed, must be accorded a special place in equal protection analysis." Id. at 233. For example, he said, the "right to vote . . . is, in equal protection terms, an extraordinary right" because it assures "individual political equality. . . ." Id. The right to a basic education plays a similar role by helping to assure economic and social equality. Thus, a discriminatory "denial of an education is the analogue of denial of the right to vote: the former relegates the individual to second-class social status; the latter places him at a permanent political disadvantage." Id. at 234. Under this approach, while neither the Due Process nor the Equal Protection Clause would prevent a state from abolishing the right to vote for certain offices or from closing the public schools, a *discriminatory* withdrawal of either of these rights could trigger strict or intermediate equal protection scrutiny because the interests at stake—voting, and access to a basic education—are fundamental to the preservation of equality.

The cases in which the modern Court has upheld education laws under a mere rational basis standard are not inconsistent with a finding that the interest in a minimally adequate education is a fundamental equal protection right. The prior cases all involved situations where the discrimination in question, though it reduced the educational opportunities for some children, stopped short of denying anyone a minimally adequate education. See, e.g., *Kadrmas v. Dickinson Public Schools*, 487 U.S. 450, 459-460 (1988) (upholding state law allowing some school boards to charge fee for school bus transportation where this did not prevent any child from attending school); *Papasan v. Allain*, 478 U.S. 265 (1986) (upholding state law that resulted in a $75 per pupil funding disparity among schools); *San Antonio Indep. School Dist. v. Rodriguez*, 411 U.S. 1 (1973) (upholding state system of school financing that resulted in a 40 percent difference in per-pupil funding among schools). And see *A.C. by Waithe v. McKee*, 23 F.4th 37 (1st Cir. 2022) (distinguishing *Papasan* and applying rational basis test where plaintiffs alleged only a failure to provide K-12 students with "an adequate *civics* education" (emphasis added)).

Example 7-V

EXAMPLE

The Elm City School Board adopted a policy requiring all students attending city public schools to wear a prescribed uniform that cost $50. The policy was adopted to reduce gang violence. As a result of the policy, the three Jones children were forced to withdraw from school because their parents cannot afford to buy them uniforms. Does the city's uniform policy violate the Equal Protection Clause?

Explanation

Since wealth is not a suspect classification, the fact that the policy discriminates against the poor will not trigger heightened equal protection scrutiny. While the effect of the policy is to totally deny some children the opportunity to acquire a basic elementary education, the Supreme Court has yet to hold that this constitutes a fundamental equal protection right. If the court here were to conclude that such a right does exist, the policy would then be subject to strict scrutiny, for it clearly impinges on that right. Alternatively, a court following *Plyler* might subject the policy to intermediate scrutiny. Whichever the case, the policy is unlikely to pass muster as applied to children who cannot afford to buy uniforms. While the state presumably has a compelling interest in preventing gang violence, this is not the least discriminatory means of achieving that goal; the city could instead buy uniforms for those children who cannot afford them.

Example 7-W

Students at several Detroit public schools have sued the state officials who supervise Michigan's public schools, alleging that defendants violated their fundamental right to a basic minimum education that will provide them with "access to literacy." Plaintiffs allege that while most Michigan public grammar and high school students receive an adequate education, they do not. They cite a significant shortage of qualified teachers; unsanitary and dangerous conditions at school facilities; and a lack of grade-appropriate learning materials (if any). Plaintiffs cite data showing that illiteracy is the norm at their Detroit schools and that zero or a near-zero percentage of these students have subject-matter proficiency. Defendants moved to dismiss on the ground that only rational basis review applies and that under that test, plaintiffs failed to show any irrational behavior on the officials' part. How should the court rule on the motion to dismiss?

Explanation

Plaintiffs have alleged facts which, if proven at trial, would appear to show that they have been denied the "minimally adequate education" *Papasan v. Allain* suggested would qualify for strict scrutiny under the Equal Protection Clause. According to plaintiffs' complaint, students at their schools, unlike those in other Michigan public schools, are not receiving an education that will enable them to read, write, or obtain other minimally adequate basics. If a court makes good on the dictum in *Papasan*, the motion to dismiss should be denied and defendants should be forced to show "that this deprivation is narrowly tailored to advance a compelling state interest." See *Gary B. v.*

Whitmer, 957 F.3d 616, 661 (6th Cir. 2020) (so holding on these facts), *vacated by granting of reh'g en banc*, 958 F.3d 1216 (6th Cir. 2020).

§7.8 A SLIDING-SCALE APPROACH TO EQUAL PROTECTION

§7.8.1 Problems with the Three-Tier Model

As we have seen, the Supreme Court's approach to the Equal Protection Clause generally involves application of a three-tier model. Under this model, classifications that are "suspect" or that involve discrimination with respect to a fundamental right are subject to strict scrutiny, quasi-suspect classifications based on gender or legitimacy are subject to intermediate scrutiny, and most other classifications are subject to rational basis review.

The three-tier model has become static and rigid because of the Court's unwillingness to add to the lists of suspect and quasi-suspect classifications and its reluctance to recognize new fundamental rights. To be sure, in some rational basis cases the Court has applied a slightly more demanding form of review than the model would seem to dictate, but the Court has done so without acknowledging that any change was being made to the traditional three-tier framework.

§7.8.2 Marshall's Sliding-Scale Approach

Justice Thurgood Marshall consistently urged the Court to abandon its three-tier equal protection model in favor of a more flexible analysis that would be capable of considering differences that are masked by a ritualistic focus on "suspect classifications" and "fundamental rights." As Marshall wrote, "All interests not 'fundamental' and all classes not 'suspect' are not the same; and it is time for the Court to drop the pretense that, for purposes of the Equal Protection Clause, they are." *Massachusetts Bd. of Retirement v. Murgia*, 427 U.S. 307, 321 (1976) (Marshall, J., dissenting). In place of the majority's stratified model, Marshall urged the Court to employ a "variable standard" of review whose intensity would depend on (1) the basis or character of the classification and (2) the importance of the interest adversely affected. The greater the significance of these factors, the greater the government's burden of justifying the classification in question.

Marshall's first factor, the character of the classification, in some ways tracks the Court's concern with whether the classifying trait is "suspect" or "quasi-suspect." However, his suggested approach is more flexible, recognizing that there are groups besides the handful that have qualified under the Court's model that, because of prejudice, stereotypes, or a history of discrimination, require added protection from the political process. On this basis, Marshall advocated giving some heightened scrutiny to laws that discriminate against groups such as the poor, the mentally retarded, and the elderly.

Marshall's second factor, the nature of the interest affected by the classification, reflects the majority's focus on "fundamental rights," but again with the difference that it is more flexible than the Court's all-or-nothing approach. The fact that an interest does not qualify for the very strictest scrutiny does not necessarily mean it is worthy of no protection at all under a mere rationality test. Marshall urged that each interest be placed on a spectrum by considering the extent to which rights guaranteed by the Constitution depend on it. "As the nexus between the specific constitutional guarantee and the nonconstitutional interest draws closer, the nonconstitutional interest becomes more fundamental and the degree of judicial scrutiny applied when the interest is infringed on a discriminatory basis must be adjusted accordingly." *San Antonio Indep. School Dist. v. Rodriguez*, 411 U.S. 1, 102-103 (1973) (Marshall, J., dissenting). Following this approach, Marshall would have given some special protection to interests such as subsistence, housing, medical care, employment, and education—all of which affect a person's ability to participate in a democratic society and to exercise the civil and political rights conferred by the Constitution.

§7.8.3 *Plyler v. Doe*

To date, the Supreme Court has not rejected the three-tier model of equal protection review; nor has it adopted the sliding-scale approach that Marshall advocated. Yet the Court has at times shown increased flexibility in resolving equal protection cases—flexibility of the type that Marshall championed. Thus, at a doctrinal level, what began as a two-tier model consisting of only strict scrutiny and rational basis review has evolved into a three-tier model with the addition of intermediate scrutiny for classifications created on the basis of gender or legitimacy. Moreover, as we have seen, the Court has at times appeared to apply an enhanced version of the rational basis test, though without acknowledging that anything other than minimal scrutiny was being employed.

Perhaps the closest the Court has come to using Marshall's flexible sliding-scale approach was in *Plyler v. Doe*, 457 U.S. 202 (1982), where the Court struck down a Texas law that denied undocumented alien children the free public education that the state provided to other children. Justice Brennan, writing for the majority, carefully set out the Court's traditional three-tier equal protection model. He agreed that the case did not qualify for strict scrutiny: "Undocumented aliens cannot be treated as a suspect class. . . . Nor is education a fundamental right. . . ." Id. at 223. And Texas had not discriminated based on gender or legitimacy, criteria that would have warranted application of intermediate scrutiny. "But," said Brennan, "more is involved in these cases than the abstract question whether [the statute] discriminates against a suspect class, or whether education is a fundamental right. [The Texas statute] imposes a lifetime hardship on a discrete class of children not accountable for their disabling status." Id. The Court felt compelled to take these realities into account and, to the dissent's dismay, refused to apply the rational basis standard called for by the three-tier model. Instead, the Court employed a form of intermediate scrutiny, insisting that "the State must demonstrate that the classification is reasonably adapted to '*the purposes for which the state desires to use it*.'" Id. at 226 (emphasis in original) (internal citation omitted). To satisfy this test the state had to demonstrate that its discrimination actually "furthers some substantial state interest." Id. at 230. Texas was unable to make such a showing, and the statute was accordingly held to violate the Equal Protection Clause. As the dissent accurately noted, the majority departed from the Court's traditional approach to equal protection cases; "by patching together bits and pieces of what might be termed quasi-suspect-class and quasi-fundamental-rights analysis, the Court spins out a theory custom-tailored to the facts of these cases." Id. at 244 (Burger, C.J., White, J., Rehnquist, J., and O'Connor, J., dissenting).

The *Plyler* Court came very close to employing the mode of analysis that Marshall had long advocated. The majority noted that the basis of the classification was a trait over which the law's victims had no control. Moreover, it stressed that the interest at stake, "basic education," was vitally important to both the individual and society. Justice Marshall in fact joined Brennan's majority opinion, yet Marshall wrote a one-paragraph concurrence subtly urging that the Court *formally* reject its "rigidified approach to equal protection analysis" and instead adopt "an approach that allows for varying levels of scrutiny. . . ." Id. at 231. While Brennan and the majority demonstrated the kind of flexibility and sensitivity to context that lay at the heart of Marshall's sliding-scale approach, they nonetheless paid continued lip service to the three-tier equal protection model.

CHAPTER 8

The First Amendment: Freedom of Speech and of the Press

§8.1 INTRODUCTION AND OVERVIEW

As usual, we begin with the text. The words of the First Amendment are simple and straightforward: "Congress shall make no law . . . abridging the freedom of speech, or of the press." There is power in this simplicity. The blunt proscription would seem to preclude any legislation that limits or punishes the protected activities. No law. But as the length of this chapter attests, the simplicity of text does not translate into a paucity of doctrine, and the doctrines rarely, if ever, speak in terms of absolutes. Rather, the freedoms of speech and press are, like other rights protected by the Constitution, both contextual and contingent, providing a range of possibilities as varied as the human imagination. The text, though, is not meaningless. The seemingly absolute proscription, at the very least, describes a powerful constitutional commitment to the freedoms of speech and press. That is our starting point.

This commitment stems from a variety of philosophical perspectives, some emphasizing the importance of freedom of expression to human growth or self-realization, others noting the essential role of free expression within a political democracy, and still others seeing this freedom as the only method through which falsehood can be exposed and some approximation of transient truth discovered. Given the wide range of First Amendment doctrines, it is not too surprising that each of these perspectives can find some voice in the Court's opinions. The predominant theme of those opinions, however, is the centrality of political speech to the core purposes of the First Amendment, not because political speech is inherently more valuable than other types of speech, but because our system of self-governance is dependent on free inquiry and debate and because a centralized governmental power has the potential to constrict knowledge and to distort that debate through the suppression of opposing viewpoints. In the Court's words, therefore, the First Amendment represents "a profound national commitment to the principle that debate on public issues should be uninhibited, robust, and wide-open. . . ." *New York Times v. Sullivan*, 376 U.S. 254, 270 (1964).

Political speech does not represent a rigidly defined category. Rather, in practice, all speech is treated with the same dignity as that afforded political speech unless the speech at issue falls into a specifically defined category of less protected expression—obscenity being an obvious example. Thus, the freedoms of speech and press fully protect commentary and debate on an almost boundless range of topics from the profound to the mundane. Political speech is simply the nucleus around which these other categories revolve.

In terms of analysis, you will find that the doctrines of freedom of speech and press share much with the analysis applied to problems involving equal protection and due process. Thus, content-based restrictions on political speech are subject to strict scrutiny, requiring both a compelling state interest and the application of the least restrictive means test. And as speech strays from the core values of the First Amendment, the level of scrutiny will decrease in a manner similar to the three-tiered or the sliding-scale model of equal protection. Commercial speech, therefore, receives something like mid-level scrutiny. Moreover, the analytical tie to these other constitutional provisions applies even in those contexts in which special First Amendment doctrines have been developed to address particular types of problems. The specialized jargon of these doctrines often reflects a particular instance of strict, mid-level, or rational basis scrutiny.

Similarly, one will see the strands of substantive due process analysis in the treatment of governmental regulations that burden speech in a content-neutral fashion. Although the precise test used—time, place, and manner—speaks in terms of burdens on speech, the elements of the test are closely allied with the familiar balancing formula of due process.

§8.2 INTRODUCTORY THEMES

§8.2.1 Defining Terms: Speech and Press

The Speech and Press Clause prohibits the abridgement of "freedom of speech, or of the press." Literally this proscription includes only the spoken and the printed word. But in practice, does it embrace a wider array of expressive activities? For example, does it include the public display of a painting such as Picasso's *Guernica?* Or a public performance of Stravinsky's *Rite of Spring?* Does postmodern architecture qualify as speech? How about a protest demonstration in which blood is poured on the steps of Congress? The answer to each of these questions is yes (or at least probably yes). Each is a form of expression protected, at least to some extent, by the First Amendment. Indeed, the phrases "freedom of speech" and "freedom of the press" are often used interchangeably with the more inclusive phrase "freedom of expression."

In general, a wide variety of expressive activity or conduct—i.e., conduct intended to communicate a message and reasonably understood to communicate that message—is included within the broad reach of the Speech and Press Clause. As the Court observed in *Texas v. Johnson*, 491 U.S. 397 (1989), the protections of the First Amendment do "not end at the spoken or written word." Id. at 404. Nor do they end with the media of communication available to the founding generation. Thus, under appropriate circumstances, such diverse media as dance, music, art, architecture, photography, performance art, bumper stickers, parades, sit-ins, advertisements, radio, motion pictures, video games, and reruns of *South Park* all qualify for First Amendment solicitude. This does not mean that such activities are absolutely protected. It means only that they are embraced within the broad concept of freedom of expression and therefore might qualify as being "expressive" of ideas so as to trigger a First Amendment analysis.

A good example of the Court's approach to expressive activity is found in *Spence v. State of Washington*, 418 U.S. 405 (1974). In that case, a college student affixed a peace symbol to a U.S. flag and displayed the flag from the window of his apartment. His purpose was to protest the then-recent invasion of Cambodia and the killing of students at Kent State University. He was charged and convicted under a statute that criminalized the "improper use" of a U.S. flag.

The Court reversed his conviction as inconsistent with the First Amendment. In explaining why the student's actions were a form of protected expression, the Court focused on two factors: the *nature* of the conduct and the *context* within which that conduct occurred. As to the nature of the conduct, flags have been traditionally used and accepted as a form of communication, and the use here was consistent with that tradition. Id. at 410. In terms of context, given the temporal proximity of the flag display to the invasion of Cambodia and the killings at Kent State University, "it would have been difficult for the great majority of citizens to miss the drift of appellant's point at the time that he made it." Id. Given this combination of nature and context, the student's actions were clearly expressive and, therefore, would be treated as speech within the meaning of the First Amendment.

However, the variety of expressive activity or conduct entitled to First Amendment protection is not limitless. As the Court said in *United States v. O'Brien*, 391 U.S. 367, 376 (1968), the Court suggested that not all expressive activity will be treated as speech: "We cannot accept the view that an apparently limitless variety of conduct can be labeled 'speech' whenever the person engaging in the conduct intends thereby to express an idea." In practice, however, the Court has usually accepted the claim that the conduct at issue was "expressive conduct protected to some extent by the First Amendment." *Clark v. Community for Creative Non-Violence*, 468 U.S. 288, 293 (1984). In *O'Brien*, for example, the Court "assumed" that burning a draft card on the steps of a courthouse as a protest against the military draft was speech within the meaning of the First Amendment—a fair assumption given both the nature of the activity and the context in which it occurred. See also *Clark v. Community for Creative Non-Violence*, 468 U.S. 288, 293 (1984) (Court "assume[s] for present purposes" that overnight sleeping in Lafayette Park as part of a demonstration of the plight of the homeless is speech). Sometimes, though, the Court takes a slightly stricter view, as one of the two examples below suggests.

EXAMPLE

Example 8-A

A California statute prohibits the sale or rental of "violent video games" to minors. The statute covers games "in which the range of options available to a player includes killing, maiming, dismembering, or sexually assaulting an image of a human being, if those acts are depicted." Are such video games expressive activity within the protective reach of the First Amendment?

EXPLANATION

Explanation

Yes. A video game is a type of entertainment that is dependent on the communication of ideas. This fact alone establishes the expressive nature of the activity and entitles that activity to some degree of First Amendment protection. As the Supreme Court recently observed, "Like the protected books, plays, and movies that preceded them, video games communicate ideas—and even social messages—through many familiar literary devices (such as characters, dialogue, plot, and music) and through features distinctive to the medium (such as the player's interaction with the virtual world). That suffices to confer First Amendment protection." *Brown v. Entertainment Merchants Ass'n*, 564 U.S. 786, 790 (2011).

EXAMPLE

Example 8-B

A state law prohibits a legislator from voting on a matter over which she has a conflict of interest. Is the legislator's vote expressive activity within the reach of the First Amendment?

EXPLANATION

Explanation

One could argue in the affirmative that a legislative vote is expressive activity because the vote itself conveys the idea of the legislator's position on a particular measure. Stated slightly differently, the vote reflects the legislator's beliefs and, as such, communicates those beliefs to the electorate. On the other hand, one can characterize a legislative vote as part of a governmental process that reflects not the belief of the legislator, but only that legislator's apportioned share of the legislative power; it is a tool of governing, not a tool of communication. The fact that the vote may be exercised pursuant to a belief does not alter the fact that the vote itself is nothing more than a part of the mechanics of governing. The potentially communicative nature of the act, therefore, does not transform the act into expressive activity. The Supreme Court adopted this latter view in *Nevada Comm'n on Ethics v. Carrigan*, 564 U.S. 117 (2011).

The fact that a law has an effect on speech does not necessarily mean it will be treated as being a regulation of speech for purposes of triggering First Amendment scrutiny. Thus, a law that bars employers from discriminating in hiring based on gender will not by itself be deemed a regulation of speech, even if as a practical matter its effect is to induce an employer to take down a sign reading, "Only Men Need Apply." Similarly, a municipal ordinance requiring delis to offer sandwiches for $10 does not constitute a regulation of speech, even though most delis will post the $10 price or print it on their menus. In both of these examples, the "law's effect on speech would be only incidental to its primary effect on conduct, and 'it has never been deemed an abridgment of freedom of speech or press to make a course of conduct illegal merely because the conduct was in part initiated, evidenced, or carried out by means of language, either spoken, written, or printed.'" *Expressions Hair Design v. Schneiderman*, 581 U.S. 37, 47 (2018) (quoting *Rumsfeld v. Forum for Academic and Inst'l Rights, Inc.*, 547 U.S. 47, 62 (2006)). By contrast, the First Amendment would be implicated if state law required companies to include the statement, "We do not discriminate on the basis of gender," in all their job ads, or if delis had to print or post their $10 prices. See, e.g., *Barr v. American Ass'n of Political Consultants, Inc.*, 591 U.S. 610 (2020) (law that aided collection of debts owed to the federal government by allowing collectors of those debts to make robocalls to cell phones, when most other robocalls to cell phones were banned, was not a regulation of nonspeech commercial activity that placed only "incidental burdens" on speech, but was instead a law aimed at speech itself); *Expressions Hair Design*, supra, 581 U.S. at 48 (statute "regulating the communication of prices, rather than prices themselves, regulates speech" for purposes of the First Amendment).

In short, laws that only incidentally affect speech—i.e., that do not seek to regulate either its content, or the time, place, or manner of its expression—are ordinarily not subject to anything more than rational basis review under the First Amendment. See *Glickman v. Wileman Bros. & Elliott, Inc.*, 521 U.S. 457, 469-470, 477 (1997); *Barr v. American Ass'n of Political Consultants, Inc.*, 591 U.S. 610, 641 (2020) (Breyer, J., et al., concurring and dissenting). However, this will not be the case if the conduct in question, though normally not thought of as being speech, was engaged in for expressive purposes. In addressing the problem of expressive conduct, the Court has sometimes drawn a distinction between pure speech and symbolic speech, the latter being a term of art referring to nonverbal methods of communication. The distinction can be exemplified by using the facts of the *O'Brien* case. Suppose that an individual wishes to protest the draft. He can deliver a speech espousing his views, or as was done in *O'Brien*, he can burn his draft card as a symbolic gesture of opposition. The former is an example of pure speech; the latter is an example of symbolic speech (or expressive conduct). Are both forms of speech entitled to the same level of First Amendment scrutiny? The answer is yes, although there is some language in the Court's decisions that could lead one to conclude otherwise.

In *O'Brien*, the Court purported to describe a special test for the constitutional assessment of infringements on symbolic speech:

> [W]e think it clear that a government regulation is sufficiently justified if it is within the constitutional power of the Government; if it furthers an important or substantial governmental interest; if the governmental interest is unrelated to the suppression of free expression; and if the incidental restriction on alleged First Amendment freedoms is no greater than is essential to the furtherance of that interest.

391 U.S. at 377. Applying this test, the Court concluded that the First Amendment did not prevent the government from punishing O'Brien for burning his draft card. On the record before it, the Court saw the regulation as designed to advance important governmental interests in preserving the integrity of the draft and as not designed to punish draft protestors for the message they conveyed. Implicitly O'Brien was free to communicate his message in other forms that would not tread on these governmental interests. Since the government could not have punished O'Brien for simply speaking out against the draft, it would seem that pure speech is entitled to greater protection than symbolic speech. Not so.

The *O'Brien* test is nothing more than the standard time, place, and manner test (albeit worded slightly differently) that the Court generally applies to content-neutral regulations of speech. See *Clark v. Community for Creative Non-Violence*, supra, 468 U.S. at 298 & n.8 (noting the parallels between the two tests). Both tests apply mid-level scrutiny if the governmental regulation is not directed at the content of the speech, and neither test is used if the regulation is content-based. O'Brien's burning of his draft card was punishable, in other words, because the punishment was premised not on the message O'Brien attempted to convey, but on the *way* he conveyed it. Had O'Brien spray-painted the words "Stop the draft" on the walls of a courthouse, the "pure" form of his speech would no more have protected him from punishment for damaging public property than did the "symbolic" nature of his actual speech. In both cases, the focus of the government would be on the manner, and not the content, of the speech. On the other hand, if the government's reason for punishing O'Brien had stemmed from its opposition to the message he sought to convey, the fact that his speech was "symbolic" rather than pure would not allow the government to punish him. In short, the symbolic speech doctrine is merely a restatement of the time, place, and manner test that we will discuss in § 8.4. Do not, therefore, fall into the trap of thinking that symbolic speech is a less protected form of speech.

In fact, the supposed distinction between pure speech and symbolic speech is tenuous at best. All speech is symbolic. Take the word "hippopotamus." It represents a verbal shorthand we use when referring to a rather large, herbivorous, semi-aquatic mammal with a huge head, thick skin, and short legs. Calling it a hippopotamus is easier and more fun. The word "hippopotamus," however, is not a hippopotamus; it is a verbal symbol of the animal we are trying to describe. A picture of a hippopotamus is also not a hippopotamus; it, too, is a symbol. Indeed, *Webster's Third New World Dictionary* uses both words and a picture to define the word "hippopotamus." Both the word and the picture are symbolic, and both are speech, and both are entitled to the same First Amendment protections. (Beware. Some professors and some judges still think there is a special symbolic speech doctrine. If you cannot show them the error of their ways, simply apply the *O'Brien* test, described above, and pretend that you have actually done something meaningful.)

In summary, the parts of the Speech and Press Clause work together to protect a broad realm of freedom of expression. That realm includes both conventional and unconventional modes of communication. Obviously the more conventional one's method is, the more likely it is that a court will see the expressive component of the conduct. But it remains true, nonetheless, that once the expressive activity qualifies as speech, the full range of First Amendment protections will apply.

Throughout this chapter, unless a more precise approach is warranted, we will use the word "speech" to include the vast array of communicative activities that fall within the protection of the First Amendment.

§8.2.2 Protected and Unprotected Speech

Not all types of speech or expression qualify for protection under the First Amendment. Certain discrete categories of speech have been held by the Court to be proscribable because they fall entirely outside the First Amendment umbrella. As a result, they are generally entitled to no constitutional protection. These proscribable categories of speech include "fighting words," obscenity, child pornography, and false or misleading commercial speech. However, as we will see, there are some circumstances under which governmental restrictions on generally proscribable speech may, nonetheless, run afoul of the First Amendment. See § 8.3.9.

In approaching a First Amendment problem, it is often a good idea to first determine whether the speech at issue is speech that the First Amendment protects. If the result of this analysis is that the speech is of a constitutionally unprotected type—e.g., obscenity—the First Amendment analysis is normally over. If, on the other hand, the speech is of a type that falls under the First Amendment umbrella, it is then necessary to decide under the applicable First Amendment test whether the government has a right to punish or restrict it. For example, as we will see shortly, political speech, which lies at the core of the First Amendment, may be punished if the requirements of the clear and present danger test are satisfied. See § 8.3.2.

When reading the Court's opinions, be alert to the fact that the term *unprotected speech* is often used in two quite different senses. The term sometimes refers to speech, such as fighting words or obscenity, that is proscribable because the entire category of speech does not qualify for First Amendment protection. On other occasions, the term is used to describe speech that is generally entitled to First Amendment protection, but that is punishable under the particular circumstances of the case. In this chapter, unless otherwise indicated, the term *unprotected speech* will be used to describe speech such as obscenity that falls entirely outside the First Amendment umbrella.

§8.2.3 The Distinction Between Matters of Public and Private Concern

The key function of the Speech and Press Clauses of the First Amendment is to protect robust debate on matters of public concern. Consequently, and as will be examined further below, limitations imposed on speech pertaining to a matter of public concern will be subject to the most exacting scrutiny. In contrast, speech on a matter of purely private concern is entitled to less judicial solicitude. This variable treatment is premised on the notion that

> restricting speech on purely private matters does not implicate the same constitutional concerns as limiting speech on matters of public interest: "[T]here is no threat to the free and robust debate of public issues; there is no potential interference with a meaningful dialogue of ideas"; and the "threat of liability" does not pose a risk of "a reaction of self-censorship" on matters of public import.

Snyder v. Phelps, 562 U.S. 443, 452 (2011) (quoting *Dun & Bradstreet, Inc. v. Greenmoss Builders, Inc.*, 472 U.S. 749, 760 (1985)). In determining whether a matter is of public concern, the Court considers if the speech at issue pertains to a matter of political, social, or other concern to the community and, similarly, if the speech is newsworthy or of general interest to the community. *Snyder v. Phelps*, supra, 562 U.S. at 452-455. These are not bright-line tests, but instead require a consideration of the "content, form, and context" of the speech in question. Id. at 453.

The decision in *Dun & Bradstreet* provides a classic example of a matter of private concern. At issue in that case was whether erroneous information published by a credit-reporting agency to private subscribers triggered the First Amendment protections applicable in certain defamation cases. See § 8.3.4 ("Free Speech Limitations on Defamation (and Other Torts)"). The answer to that question depended, in part, on whether the publication involved a matter of public concern. The Court concluded that such information "concerns no public issue" and that it was of interest only to the speaker and a small group of subscribers. *Dun & Bradstreet*, supra, 472 U.S. at 762.

Example 8-C

EXAMPLE

Members of the Westboro Baptist Church lawfully picketed the military funeral of a soldier who had died in combat. The church members believe that the death of a soldier represented God's just punishment for America's toleration of homosexuality. To reflect this belief, they carried signs that included messages such as "Thank God for Dead Soldiers," "God Hates Fags," and "Fags Doom Nations." Do the expressive activities of the church members involve a matter of public concern? Does the potential offensiveness of the message play a role in determining whether the speech is a matter of public concern?

Explanation

Yes (as to the first question). The content of the signs address a moral issue with obvious political, social, and cultural dimensions, and the pickets convey a particular viewpoint on that issue. In addition, the form of the speech—picketing—is a traditional method of conveying information to the public in a public arena. In addition, the context of the speech activity—a military funeral—does not in any manner alter the public nature of the speech. By way of contrast, in *Dun & Bradstreet*, the context of the speech was a private disclosure to a small group of subscribers, thus supporting the conclusion that the speech there was not a matter of public concern. Here, the context is a public arena in which the message is directed broadly to anyone who is present, including the news media. As to the second question, the potential offensiveness of the speech plays no role in determining whether it involves a matter of public concern. See *Snyder v. Phelps*, 562 U.S. 443 (2011) (so holding under similar facts).

§8.2.4 The Special Problem of Prior Restraints

Historically courts have been more suspicious of prior restraints than they have been of other governmental restrictions on expression. Typically, prior restraints occur in one of two contexts: (1) governmental licensing or permit schemes and (2) injunctions against publication. The key to identifying a prior restraint is to focus on the timing of the government's intervention. If the government intervenes to prevent an expressive act—i.e., if the intervention takes place *before* a communication occurs—then the government's action is a prior restraint. For example, suppose that the government seeks and is granted a judicial order enjoining a newspaper from publishing certain classified information. By seeking and obtaining an injunction prior to publication, the government has interposed the force of law between a potential publisher and the act of publication. This is a classic prior restraint. The intervention precedes the communication.

An important distinction is drawn between prior restraint and subsequent punishment. The latter is a governmental restriction on expressive activity in which the government intervenes *after* the act of communication. In other words, a speech is made, and the speaker is "subsequently" punished. Suppose, for example, that a statute makes it a felony to publish classified information. A newspaper publisher who violates this proscription would be subject to a subsequent punishment—i.e., to potential criminal sanctions imposed after the act of publication. Although the statute is designed to prevent publication of classified information, the government's intervention takes place only after the publication has occurred. This subsequent punishment is not, by definition, a prior restraint.

EXAMPLE

Example 8-D

The City of Metrolex has created a Motion Picture Licensing Board. The board is empowered to "license" the public performance of motion pictures within the city. No such performance is permitted in the absence of a board-issued license. To qualify for a license, a motion picture must be submitted to the board for review. A license will be denied only if the submitted motion picture is deemed to be "obscene." By way of contrast, the neighboring City of Ruralex has passed an ordinance that makes the public performance of any "obscene" motion picture a felony. This ordinance is enforced by the local city attorney through criminal prosecution. Does the Metrolex scheme operate as a prior restraint?

EXPLANATION

Explanation

Yes. The reason is simple. Before a motion picture can be performed in public, it must be submitted to the board for review and approval. Since the intervention by the government precedes any public performance of the motion picture, the licensing scheme is a prior restraint. The Ruralex ordinance, on the other hand, operates only as a subsequent punishment. Although the ordinance is designed to prevent the screening of obscene motion pictures and although it may be quite effective in doing so, the governmental intervention comes only after an obscene motion picture has been screened. The restriction on speech is, therefore, subsequent.

In short, the critical distinction between a prior restraint and a subsequent punishment is the timing of the governmental intervention vis-à-vis the act of communication. Only an intervention that precedes an act of communication is a prior restraint.

Although both prior restraints and subsequent punishments are subject to First Amendment scrutiny, it is generally presumed that prior restraints present the more serious invasion of First Amendment liberties. While it remains in effect, a prior restraint completely suppresses the attempted communication. In essence, the government acts as a censor when it issues a prior restraint. Of course, the threat of criminal sanctions presumably operates as a strong and effective deterrent on speech or publication, and under some circumstances, the threat of prosecution may just as effectively prevent publication as would a prior restraint. Nonetheless, the deterrent effect is not considered a prior restraint, and prior restraints remain the most disfavored type of restriction on expressive activity.

One reason prior restraints are particularly disfavored is that a person who violates an injunction or other prior restraint on speech is ordinarily subject to punishment even if the speech activity was constitutionally protected; in other words, it is usually no defense to the violation of a prior restraint that the restraint was unconstitutional. Ordinarily, the only way to challenge the constitutionality of a prior restraint is to comply with it while challenging its validity in court; this may, of course, result in a lengthy postponement of the desired speech activity. By contrast, a statute that merely criminalizes certain speech may be violated by a speaker who is confident that the statute is unconstitutional. In the subsequent criminal prosecution, the First Amendment may be raised as a complete defense. In other words, while the First Amendment may shield a speaker who violates a criminal proscription on speech, the Amendment usually will not protect one who violates a prior restraint.

The judicial antipathy toward prior restraints is demonstrated in two leading cases. The first is *Near v. Minnesota*, 283 U.S. 697 (1931). In that case, a county attorney brought an action to enjoin the publication of a "malicious, scandalous and defamatory newspaper" known as *The Saturday Press*. Id. at 703. The newspaper had published a series of highly charged, possibly defamatory articles accusing local police and governmental officials of various derelictions, including corruption in office. After a trial, the publication of the newspaper was abated as a public nuisance, and its publishers were "perpetually enjoined . . . 'from producing, editing, publishing, circulating, having in their possession, selling or giving away any publication whatsoever which is a malicious, scandalous or defamatory newspaper. . . .'" Id. at 706. Any violations of the injunction would subject the publishers to being held in contempt of court.

Although the injunction was a product of the previously published issues of the newspaper, the order of the lower court was not a punishment for those publications. Rather, it was directed toward the future publishing activities of the defendants. With respect to those future publications, the government's intervention preceded the publication. It suppressed any such publications. The order was, therefore, a prior restraint, and as such, the lower court's order was highly suspect. This was so because, in the Supreme Court's view, both historically and as a matter of sound jurisprudence, prior restraints were highly disfavored, particularly in the context of critical commentary on public officials. Id. at 713-717. Subsequent punishments did not, however, receive that same disapproval from the *Near* Court.

> The fact that for approximately one hundred and fifty years there has been almost an entire absence of attempts to impose previous restraints upon publications relating to the malfeasance of public officers is significant [evidence] of the deep-seated conviction that such restraints would violate constitutional right. Public officers, whose character and conduct remain open to debate and free discussion in the press, find their remedies for false accusations in actions under libel laws providing for redress and punishment, and not in proceedings to restrain the publication of newspapers and periodicals.

Id. at 718-719. In short, while a subsequent punishment might pass constitutional muster, only under the most exceptional circumstances will a prior restraint do so. To this end, the Court described what is now referred to as the "troopship exception" for prior restraints: "No one would question but that a government might prevent actual obstruction to its recruiting service or the publication of the sailing dates of transports or the number and location of troops." Id. at 716. By analogy, this "exception" can be seen as the rough equivalent of a very strict scrutiny test.

New York Times v. United States, 403 U.S. 713 (1971), presents a much more dramatic application of the heavy presumption against prior restraints. In that case, commonly referred to as the *Pentagon Papers Case*, the executive branch of the U.S. government sought to enjoin the *New York Times* and the *Washington Post* from publishing the contents of a classified study entitled *History of U.S. Decision-Making Process on Viet Nam Policy*. At the time, the Vietnam War was far from over, and the government claimed that publication of the study would jeopardize the United States' war efforts. The Court nevertheless refused to sanction the injunction. In a cryptic three-paragraph per curiam opinion, the Court noted the "heavy presumption" against the constitutional validity of prior restraints and declared that the government had not met its "heavy burden of showing justification for the imposition of such a restraint." Id. at 714. Thus, even the government's claims of national security in the context of an ongoing military action were insufficient to satisfy the so-called troopship exception. Despite this ruling, several Justices suggested that this same judicial reluctance would not necessarily apply to post-publication criminal prosecutions. Id. at 733-740 (White, J., and Stewart, J., concurring); id. at 752 (Burger, C.J., dissenting); id. at 759 (Blackmun, J., dissenting).

The per curiam opinion in the *Pentagon Papers Case* was crafted to resolve that precise case and virtually no others. Separate opinions by the Justices do, however, shed some light on the appropriate standards. Two Justices, Black and Douglas, endorsed what was tantamount to an absolute prohibition against prior restraints. Id. at 714, 720. Justice Brennan used language suggestive of a very strict scrutiny: "Thus, only governmental allegation and proof that publication must inevitably, directly, and immediately cause the occurrence of an event kindred to imperiling the safety of a transport already at sea can support even the issuance of an interim restraining order." Id. at 726-727. Other Justices were somewhat more flexible. While both Justices White and Stewart agreed that publication could not be enjoined under the facts presented because of the "extraordinary protection against prior restraints enjoyed by the press under our constitutional system," their reluctance stemmed in part from the absence of a statute authorizing the requested injunction. Id. at 730. Justice Marshall's opinion also emphasized the lack of statutory authorization. Id. at 742-743. Of course, the three dissenters were willing to uphold the injunction against publication. These numbers certainly do not add up to anything like an absolute prohibition against prior restraints. The judgment does, however, represent a recognition of the "heavy presumption" against prior restraints. How that presumption is to be interpreted and applied remains somewhat vague.

Example 8-E

Modern Mercenary, a monthly periodical, is about to publish an article entitled "Five Easy Steps to Making Your Own Thermonuclear Device." The author of the piece, G.I. Jones, is a nuclear physicist who gathered most of his information from unclassified sources. But the article does disclose for the first time how several seemingly unrelated concepts must be brought together to construct a thermonuclear device. The government seeks to enjoin this publication pursuant to a section of the federal Atomic Energy Act that authorizes injunctive relief against anyone who would disclose "restricted data with reason to believe such data will be utilized to injure the United States or to secure an advantage to any foreign nation." Although the government doubts that Jones's article will lead to the basement construction of nuclear weapons, governmental experts claim that publication will possibly provide sufficient information to allow a medium-sized nation to move faster in developing a thermonuclear weapon. Assuming Jones's article contains "restricted data" within the meaning of the Atomic Energy Act, should the district court grant the requested relief?

Explanation

Since the government's intervention precedes the publication of the article, the injunction, if granted, would be a prior restraint. Like all prior restraints, this one comes with a heavy presumption against its validity. If one adopts an absolutist position, this case is relatively simple—no prior restraints. However, the absolutist position has never commanded a majority of the Court. Yet a similar result would probably obtain under Justice Brennan's near absolute position. At best the government has shown that "possibly" a medium-sized nation will speed up its nuclear capabilities because of this article. This speculative outcome can hardly be described as inevitable, direct, and immediate. Some current members of the Court might well adopt Justice Brennan's approach. On the other hand, the injunction is authorized by statute, and the potential harm is quite serious. A district court judge could reasonably conclude that under such circumstances, the troopship exception has been satisfied, and that conclusion *might* be upheld by the Court. See *United States v. Progressive, Inc.,* 467 F. Supp. 990 (W.D. Wis.), *appeal dismissed,* 610 F.2d 819 (7th Cir. 1979) (issuing an injunction under similar circumstances). Arguably there were at least five votes in the *Pentagon Papers Case* supportive of this conclusion.

The vagaries of the "heavy presumption" standard were somewhat ameliorated in *Nebraska Press Ass'n v. Stuart*, 427 U.S. 539 (1976). A state trial court judge, in anticipation of a trial for multiple murders, issued an order restraining the news media "from publishing or broadcasting accounts of confessions or admission made by the accused. . . ." Id. at 541. The purpose of the gag order was to preserve the accused's Sixth Amendment right to a fair and impartial jury. The Supreme Court held that despite this strong state interest, the judge's order could not withstand constitutional scrutiny. Prior restraints are highly disfavored, particularly in the context of reporting the news in a timely fashion. Id. at 560-561. Consequently, and in a manner strikingly similar to an intense strict scrutiny analysis, the Court examined the state's interest, the scope of the judge's order, and alternatives to that order that were less intrusive on First Amendment principles. In essence, the Court concluded that the order was not necessary to advance the purported state interest.

Outside of the news-reporting context, the formidability of the presumption against prior restraints depends on the nature of the speech activity being restrained. Recall Example 8-D—the Metrolex licensing scheme designed to prevent the public performance of obscene motion pictures. The licensing procedure described in that example is a prior restraint. However, as we will learn, obscenity, as defined by the Supreme Court, is a genre of speech that is unprotected by the First Amendment. See § 8.4.4. Hence, local communities are afforded substantial leeway in the way they may choose to regulate or proscribe matters deemed obscene. Accordingly, a prior restraint such as that described in the Metrolex scheme would be upheld if certain procedural safeguards were incorporated into the scheme: (1) The board must have the burden of proving that the motion picture is obscene under constitutional standards; (2) the procedure for making that determination must be of the shortest possible duration; and (3) immediate judicial review of the obscenity decision, including some assurance of a speedy resolution of the controversy, must be available. *City of Littleton v. Z.J. Gifts D-4, LLC*, 541 U.S. 774, 778-781 (2004); *Freedman v. Maryland*, 380 U.S. 51, 58-60 (1965). In essence, the presumption against prior restraints may be rebutted by a combination of the disfavored status of the speech and the presence of procedural safeguards designed to ensure that only disfavored speech will be suppressed.

§8.2.5 The Overbreadth and the Vagueness Doctrines

The overbreadth doctrine creates a special First Amendment exception to the normal rules of standing, which bar a litigant from asserting the constitutional rights of third parties. See Christopher N. May, Allan Ides & Simona Grossi, *Constitutional Law: National Power & Federalism* § 3.4.5 (10th ed. 2025) [hereinafter *National Power & Federalism*]. The overbreadth doctrine allows an individual as to whom the application of a law may in fact be constitutional to challenge the constitutionality of the law on its face, on the theory that as applied to other persons or under other circumstances, the measure violates the First Amendment. The essence of an overbreadth argument is that even though the challenged law may have some constitutional applications, its broad sweep encompasses protected speech activities and chills First Amendment rights of persons not before the Court to such an extent that the entire law must be struck down.

Since application of overbreadth requires the complete or facial invalidation of a law that may have some constitutional applications, courts are reluctant to apply the "strong medicine" of this doctrine. Accordingly, there are a number of restrictions on application of the overbreadth doctrine. First, if a law is subject to a reasonable, limiting construction that comports with the Constitution and that avoids the overbreadth concern, the law will not be invalidated. The Court will not, however, accept a narrowing construction that appears to be fabricated for purposes of the pending case. (Note that while the Supreme Court may limit the statutory scope of a federal law, any narrowing construction of state law must be premised on state court decisions.)

Second, the law in question must usually be *substantially* overbroad. While this is a vague requirement, it means that a law will not be struck down under the overbreadth doctrine if there are only a handful of circumstances in which its application would be unconstitutional. Instead, the statute's overbreadth must "be *substantial*, not only in an absolute sense, but also relative to the statute's plainly legitimate sweep." *United States v. Williams*, 553 U.S. 285, 292 (2008) (emphasis in original). In measuring substantiality, how one defines the scope of the relevant law may be critical. For example, if a city ordinance bars speech in a public park, "it might be dispositive whether [that] ordinance . . . is analyzed alone or as one element of the combined policies governing expression in public schoolyards, municipal cemeteries, and the city council chamber." *Virginia v. Hicks*, 539 U.S. 113, 125 (2003) (Souter, J., concurring). Moreover, the Court has sometimes been reluctant to find any overbreadth to be "substantial" based on mere possibilities or factual assumptions unsupported by evidence; instead, the extent of the overbreadth may have to be factually established on the record. *Washington State Grange v. Washington State Republican Party*, 552 U.S. 442, 454-458 (2008). However, in *Americans for Prosperity Foundation v. Bonta*, 594 U.S. 595, 615-618 (2021), the Court relaxed the substantiality requirement and facially invalidated a law as being overbroad due to the "risk" it would have a chilling effect on the right of association, though there was no evidence that such an effect would occur in a "substantial proportion" of its applications. Id. at 623, 624-625 (Sotomayor, J., et al., dissenting).

Third, overbreadth challenges will rarely succeed unless the law in question is "specifically addressed to speech or conduct necessarily associated with speech (such as picketing or demonstrating)," as opposed to conduct, such as trespassing, that is not inherently expressive but that may sometimes be engaged in for such purposes. *Virginia v. Hicks*, supra, 539 U.S. at 124 (opinion of the Court). See *Los Angeles Police Dep't v. United Reporting Publishing Corp.*, 528 U.S. 32 (1999) (overbreadth not available in challenge to a statute limiting access to certain police records since the claim is not premised on "speech"). Finally, overbreadth is usually invoked only when a litigant has engaged in some type of expressive activity; the Court has left "for another day" the question of whether it may be invoked by someone whose conduct did not involve any form of expressive activity but where the law in question does reach protected speech. *Virginia v. Hicks*, supra, 539 U.S. at 124.

Example 8-F

A federal statute makes it a crime for anyone to knowingly "create, sell, or possess a depiction of animal cruelty" if done "for commercial gain" in interstate or foreign commerce. The statute defines a depiction of "animal cruelty" as one "in which a living animal is intentionally maimed, mutilated, tortured, wounded, or killed" if that conduct violates "any" federal or state law where "the creation, sale, or possession" takes place. Robert was charged with violating this statute based on his possession of several videos that depict dog fighting. He has challenged the constitutionality of the statute on overbreadth grounds, arguing that the statute includes within its coverage a vast array of protected speech, including videos depicting hunting, fishing, and the slaughter of livestock. Assess the validity of his argument.

Explanation

The literal text of the statute appears to embrace a large array of common activities, such as videos portraying hunting, fishing, and the slaughtering of livestock. The possession of such videos would be presumptively protected by the First Amendment, yet they might fall within the proscriptive scope of the statute even if they merely depict the wounding or killing of an animal where no cruelty was involved. Although the referenced activities are legal in many parts of the United States, they are not legal under all circumstances, e.g., the hunting of specified species or the use of certain weapons may be banned in some states, out-of-season hunting or fishing is illegal everywhere, and specific slaughtering practices may be deemed inhumane and illegal in certain states. Hence, a video that portrayed the mere killing of an animal and that was possessed in a state or locality that banned the practice being depicted would—even though made in a state where the conduct was lawful—fall within the scope of the statutory proscription. On similar facts, the Supreme Court concluded that the statute at issue suffered from overbreadth in that it prohibited a substantial amount of otherwise protected speech. *United States v. Stevens*, 559 U.S. 460, 471-477 (2010). The Court left open the question of whether a statute that was limited to the depiction of extreme animal cruelty would pass muster. The dissent argued that the Court should have construed the federal statute narrowly to include only depictions of animal cruelty and hence exclude hunting videos and the like from its coverage. Id. at 482-499 (Alito, J., dissenting). Under this interpretation, the statute would not suffer from overbreadth because its coverage would be limited to a narrow category of arguably proscribable speech. But see § 8.3.8 (depictions of animal cruelty not categorically excluded from scope of First Amendment). Notice how the resolution of the overbreadth question was completely dependent on how broadly (or narrowly) the Justices interpreted the statute.

Turning from overbreadth to vagueness, the void for vagueness doctrine requires that all criminal statutes adequately describe the activities they prohibit. The doctrine is premised on two concerns rooted in the Due Process Clause—that a person potentially subject to the proscription be given fair notice of that which is proscribed, and that officers charged with enforcing the law not be vested with arbitrary enforcement discretion. *Holder v. Humanitarian Law Project*, 561 U.S. 1, 18-25 (2010); *Papachristou v. City of Jacksonville*, 405 U.S. 156, 162 (1972). Statutes that use open-ended terms such as "annoying or offensive conduct" are particularly suspect because they implicate both of the above concerns.

With respect to the adequacy of notice, a party challenging a statute purely on vagueness grounds may not rely on hypothetical circumstances to which the statute might be applied but must instead demonstrate that the statute is vague with respect to the precise conduct she has engaged in or proposes to engage in. In other words, the question is whether the statute is vague with respect to its coverage of the specific conduct at issue and not with respect to other conduct not before the court. *Expressions Hair Design v. Schneiderman*, supra, 581 U.S. at 47-48; *Holder v. Humanitarian Law Project*, supra, 561 U.S. at 18-25. This is, of course, quite unlike the overbreadth doctrine.

Example 8-G

A federal statute makes it a crime to "knowingly provide material support or resources to a foreign terrorist organization." The statute defines "material support or resources" as including the provision of "training," or "expert advice or assistance." The statute applies regardless of whether the material support directly advances the terrorist mission of the organization. In other words, it covers all material support, including support for the lawful activities of the terrorist organization. A group of plaintiffs brought a pre-enforcement challenge to this statute, arguing, among other things, that it was vague. The specific activities the plaintiffs wanted to engage in were to train members of a specified terrorist organization on how to use humanitarian and international law to peacefully resolve disputes, and to teach members of that organization how to petition various representative bodies such as the United Nations for humanitarian relief. Is the material-support statute vague as to its potential coverage of the proposed activities?

EXPLANATION

Explanation

No. First, the language used in the statute is a far cry from open-ended terms such as "annoying or offensive conduct" that have run afoul of the vagueness principle. Next, putting hypothetical scenarios to the side, plaintiffs' proposed conduct falls squarely within the scope of the statutory terms. Plaintiffs wish to "train" members of the terrorist organization on the use of humanitarian and international law; presumably they will provide "expert advice or assistance" in doing so. In short, as to these plaintiffs, the statute is not vague. It clearly covers their proposed conduct. See *Holder v. Humanitarian Law Project*, 561 U.S. 1 (2010) (so holding under similar facts).

The fact that "close cases can be envisioned" in terms of whether particular conduct falls within a criminal statute's prohibition does not itself render the statute vague in the constitutional sense, for "[c]lose cases can be imagined under virtually any statute." *United States v. Williams*, 553 U.S. 285, 306 (2008). "Close" questions of that type are dealt with by the requirement that in criminal cases, guilt be proved beyond a reasonable doubt. The vagueness that will render a criminal statute infirm "is not the possibility that it will sometimes be difficult to determine whether the incriminating fact it establishes has been proved; but rather the indeterminacy of precisely what that fact is." Id. at 306. Thus, a statute "that tied criminal culpability to whether the defendant's conduct was 'annoying' or 'indecent'—wholly subjective judgments without statutory definitions"—would be void for vagueness since it is not clear what the statute's incriminating facts—"annoying" and "indecent"—mean. Id. By contrast, a law that criminalized the use of "fighting words," defined as those "which by their very utterance inflict injury or tend to incite an immediate breach of the peace," *Chaplinsky v. New Hampshire*, 315 U.S. 568, 572 (1942), is not unconstitutionally vague, even though in a particular case it may be a close question whether the words a defendant used fell within the statutory definition. See § 8.3.3.

In the context of potentially vague statutes that may tread on First Amendment rights, however, these due process concerns take on special significance. A vague statute that may include protected speech activity within its amorphous scope potentially runs afoul of the overbreadth doctrine by chilling that protected speech. Under such circumstances, the overbreadth and void for vagueness arguments merge since it is the vagueness that creates the overbreadth. In addition, a vague statute that may be applied to speech activity and that vests enforcement officers with arbitrary authority to define the scope of the proscription runs a risk of permitting discriminatory enforcement on the basis of the favored or disfavored content of the speech. The vesting of such arbitrary authority is itself unconstitutional. In the First Amendment setting, a vague statute, like a substantially overbroad one, is facially invalid.

In *NAACP v. Button*, 371 U.S. 415, 432-433 (1963) (internal citations omitted), the Court described the constitutional significance of these doctrines to the First Amendment:

> The objectionable quality of vagueness and overbreadth does not depend upon absence of fair notice to a criminally accused or upon unchanneled delegation of legislative powers, but upon the danger of tolerating, in the area of First Amendment freedoms, the existence of a penal statute susceptible of sweeping and improper application. These freedoms are delicate and vulnerable, as well as supremely precious in our society. The threat of sanctions may deter their exercise almost as potently as the actual application of sanctions. Because First Amendment freedoms need breathing space to survive, government may regulate in the area only with narrow specificity.

Example 8-H

A City of Rockville ordinance prohibits "any person from engaging in any disturbing or offensive conduct" while on the grounds of City Park. On a crisp autumn afternoon, while strolling through the park, Billy decides to express his oneness with nature by tearing his clothes off and prancing through the falling leaves. He is arrested for violating the city ordinance. Assuming that a precisely drawn law, such as a prohibition of public nudity, could proscribe the expressive activity engaged in by Billy, may Billy, nonetheless, mount a successful overbreadth or vagueness challenge to this ordinance?

Explanation

To successfully invoke the overbreadth doctrine, Billy must establish that the ordinance is substantially overbroad. He may well succeed on this score. The words "disturbing or offensive" are subject to very broad applications that would include much protected speech. For example, a Republican may find almost any speech by a Democrat disturbing or offensive even though the Democrat has every right to engage in such speech. In this sense, the potential overbreadth is a product of vagueness. Given the words used—"disturbing or offensive"—the actual scope of the proscription is unclear, providing both inadequate notice to potential violators and an opportunity for discriminatory, content-based enforcement. Therefore, in the absence of a reasonable and narrowing construction that would confine the scope of the ordinance to unprotected speech, the statute violates the principle of overbreadth and is void for vagueness; thus, it will be facially invalidated.

As Example 8-H suggests, a state or local law that may be unconstitutionally vague or overbroad as written can sometimes be saved from invalidation if it is given a reasonable and narrowing construction by the state high court. If a federal court has been asked to rule on the constitutionality of such a state measure, the court may, under the *Pullman* doctrine, have the discretion to temporarily abstain from ruling on the validity issue until a state court is given a chance to clarify the measure's meaning or scope. See *National Power & Federalism*, supra, § 4.4.1.

§8.3 CONTENT-BASED RESTRICTIONS ON SPEECH

§8.3.1 What Constitutes a Content-Based Restriction?

"Government regulation of speech is content based if a law applies to particular speech because of the topic discussed or the idea or message expressed." *Reed v. Town of Gilbert*, 576 U.S. 155, 163 (2015). In *Near v. Minnesota*, for example, the lower court's injunction was directed toward the future publication of any "malicious, scandalous, or defamatory" newspaper, characterizations that can only emanate from the substance or content of an intended publication. Similarly, in the *Pentagon Papers Case*, the injunction sought by the government was directed toward preventing the defendant newspapers from publishing specific information—a content-based imposition.

By way of contrast, in *City of Austin v. Reagan National Advertising of Austin, LLC*, 596 U.S. 61 (2022), the Court held that an ordinance that discriminated between on-site and off-site signs, regulating the latter more heavily, was not content-based even though the determination of whether a sign was on- or off-site required a minimal inquiry into the "content" of the sign. In so holding, the Court rejected "the view that *any* examination of speech or expression inherently triggers heightened First Amendment concern. Rather, it is regulations that discriminate based on 'the topic discussed or the idea or message expressed' that are content based. The sign code provisions challenged here do not discriminate on those bases." Id. at 73-74 (emphasis in original) (internal citation omitted).

In addition to the above, a content-based restriction on speech must be "materially adverse action" that is capable of deterring a speaker from exercising their First Amendment rights. *Houston Community College System v.Wilson*, 595 U.S. 468, 479 (2022). In that case, the Court held that a school board's public censure of an elected board member, albeit content-based, did not amount to a restriction of that member's First Amendment rights for two reasons. First, as the Court put it, "[i]n this country, we expect elected representatives to shoulder a degree of criticism about their public service from their constituents and their peers—and to continue exercising their free speech rights when the criticism comes." Id. at 478. "Second, the only adverse action at issue before us is itself a form of speech from Mr. Wilson's colleagues that concerns the conduct of public office. The First Amendment surely promises an elected representative like Mr. Wilson the right to speak freely on questions of government policy. But just as surely, it cannot be used as a weapon to silence other representatives seeking to do the same." Id.Content-based restrictions are considered a most serious infringement of First Amendment liberties, since the government is using the force of law to distort public discourse by suppressing, through either prior restraint or subsequent punishment, those messages perceived by the government to be somehow objectionable. Always begin with the presumption that a content-based restriction on speech is suspect. The strength of that presumption (and scrutiny) may diminish, however, if the type of expression at issue falls into a less protected category of speech. Or the Court may avoid the strict scrutiny triggered by a seemingly content-based restriction by interpreting statutory language in a manner that eliminates the content-based issue. See, e.g., *National Endowment for the Arts v. Finley*, 524 U.S. 569 (1998) (construing as merely advisory and not regulatory a statutory directive to the National Endowment for the Arts to consider "general standards of decency" in awarding grants).

Restrictions on speech may qualify as content-based in several different ways. One involves restrictions aimed at specific subjects or topics—e.g., a city ordinance that regulates signs based on the type of information the signs convey. A second type of content-based regulation involves restrictions aimed at specific viewpoints—e.g., a law prohibiting criticism of the war effort or banning the teaching of evolution. Another type of content regulation involves restrictions resulting from the speaker's identity—e.g., a law barring labor organizers or religious groups from using a public auditorium. This list is not exclusive; content-based restrictions can take other forms as well. See *U.S. v. Alvarez*, 567 U.S. 709 (2012) (federal statute that prohibits false claims of having been awarded military decorations imposes a content-based restriction) (plurality); *Holder v. Humanitarian Law Project*, 561 U.S. 1, 27 (2010) (content-based restrictions are those that depend on what the speaker says); *Shurtleff v. City of Boston*, 596 U.S. 243 (2022) (city's refusal to allow the display of a religiously themed flag on a flagpole in a public forum when the city would permit the display of a flag with a secular message operates as a content-based restriction on speech).

Example 8-I

Members of the Westboro Baptist Church picketed the military funeral of a soldier who had died in combat. The church members believe that the death of a soldier represented God's just punishment for America's toleration of homosexuality. To reflect this belief, they carried signs that included messages such as, "Thank God for Dead Soldiers," "God Hates Fags," and "Fags Doom Nations." In response, the father of the slain soldier sued the church and several of its members for intentional infliction of emotional distress. A jury awarded the father over $2 million in damages. Does this award of damages operate as a content-based restriction on speech?

Explanation

Yes. The father's understandable emotional distress is a direct product of the viewpoint expressed by the picketers. His lawsuit seeks redress for the consequences that resulted from the expression of that viewpoint. Hence, the damage award is a content-based restriction, as it flows directly from the viewpoint expressed by the church members. The fact that the speech took place at a particular location (the funeral) does not alter the content-based nature of the restriction. Regardless of location, the message triggered the harm, and the message was the focal point of the remedy sought. See *Snyder v. Phelps*, 562 U.S. 443 (2011).

Example 8-J

In 2015 Congress amended the Telephone Consumer Protection Act to make an exception to its general ban on robocalls placed to cell phones. The exception allowed such calls to be made by authorized debt collectors to collect on debts owed to or guaranteed by the federal government. Is this a content-based restriction on speech?

Explanation

Yes. The exception is a content-based law for three reasons. First, it allows calls relating only to certain subjects, i.e., government debt collection; calls made to address other topics are not permitted. Second, it allows only those calls that express a certain viewpoint on the matter of government debt, thereby favoring speech to collect a debt over speech that might urge debtors to instead give their money to charity or to a political campaign. Third, it distinguishes permissible from impermissible speech based on the caller/speaker's identity; calls made by authorized debt collectors are permitted while calls from others are banned. See *Barr v. American Ass'n of Political Consultants, Inc.*, 591 U.S. 610 (2020) (2015 amendment to Telephone

Consumer Protection Act imposed a content-based restriction on speech that violated the First Amendment).

Example 8-K

The Federal Lanham Act prohibits the registration of any "immoral or scandalous" trademarks. Erik is an artist who founded a clothing line that uses the trademark FUCT, which he says is pronounced by its four individual letters: F-U-C-T. When he applied to register this as a federal trademark, his application was denied on the ground that despite his view as to how the mark should be pronounced, a substantial segment of the public would find it to be "highly offensive and vulgar." Erik has challenged the "immoral or scandalous" ban under the First Amendment, alleging that it constitutes viewpoint discrimination such as to render it per se invalid. The government argues that the statute, properly construed, is viewpoint-neutral, for it merely bans lewd, sexually explicit, or profane marks, a standard that deals merely with the "*mode* of expression, independent of any *view* that may be expressed." How should the court characterize this ban for purposes of First Amendment analysis?

Explanation

If the statute were read as the government urges to simply prohibit those trademarks that are lewd, sexually explicit, or profane, the ban would arguably operate independently of any viewpoint expressed in the trademark. In other words, while the registration's prohibition would be content-based, it would be viewpoint-neutral in that it does not depend on the ideas or opinions being conveyed. However, this reading is much narrower than what is suggested by the words the statute uses, i.e., "immoral or scandalous." The latter terms go far beyond the words or images employed and require a judgment to be made as to the ideas, messages, or opinions being conveyed. On that basis, the Lanham Act trademark ban, as written, is clearly one that is viewpoint-based. See *Iancu v. Brunetti*, 588 U.S. 388, 396-399 (2019) (holding that Lanham Act's ban on "immoral or scandalous" marks was viewpoint discriminatory, and declining government's invitation that Court narrowly construe the Act as in effect asking it "not to interpret the statute Congress enacted, but to fashion a new one.").

It may be difficult to decide what type of content-based restriction is involved in a particular case. For example, is a law that outlaws the showing of indecent films a subject or topic restriction, or does it entail a viewpoint restriction on the theory that it seeks to restrict the expression of a certain attitude toward sex? As we will see later, it is sometimes necessary to decide what type of content-based restriction is involved, for viewpoint restrictions in certain circumstances are treated more severely by the Court than other types of content restrictions. Indeed, in recent years, it has been said that laws deemed to be viewpoint discriminatory are invalid per se. See *Iancu v. Brunetti*, supra, 588 U.S. at 399 ("The Court's finding of viewpoint bias ended the matter."). Second, such statutes cannot be saved by arguing that they are not *substantially* overbroad. "[T]his Court has never applied that kind of analysis to a viewpoint-discriminatory law." Id. at 398-399. See § 8.2.5. Finally, as we will see later, even though the government has considerable leeway to restrict speech in a nonpublic forum (i.e., government property that has not been opened to the public for speech purposes), it is still barred from engaging in viewpoint discrimination there. See § 8.5.3.

A law that would otherwise appear to be content based in any of the senses we have just described may, nonetheless, be treated by the Court as being content neutral if the government can show that the law was aimed at the *secondary effects* of the speech. Secondary effects are those other than the impact of the speech on a listener. For example, a law prohibiting the showing of indecent movies because such films are thought to promote marital infidelity imposes a content-based restriction, since it is aimed at the impact on those who view them. If, on the other hand, the same law had been enacted to protect surrounding neighborhoods from the crime that sometimes accompanies so-called adult theaters, then under the secondary effects doctrine the law would be deemed content neutral, since it was enacted to combat the secondary effects of indecent movies.

The extent to which the secondary effects doctrine will be applied in contexts other than those involving pornography remains to be seen. Compare *City of Renton v. Playtime Theatres, Inc.*, 475 U.S. 41 (1986) (applying secondary effects doctrine to uphold prohibition against adult theaters), with *Boos v. Barry*, 485 U.S. 312 (1988) (rejecting application of secondary effects doctrine in case involving political speech). In *Packingham v. North Carolina*, 582 U.S. 98 (2017), the Court was confronted with the similar question of what standard of review to apply to a state statute that made it a felony for registered sex offenders to gain access to certain social media websites. The statue was content neutral insofar as it did not select the covered websites based on their content. Yet it was arguably content based since it targeted only a subset of speakers—i.e., registered sex offenders. Speaker identity is a traditional way of deeming a law to be content based, but the Court has suggested that this principle does not apply unless the distinction among speakers is "a subtle means of exercising a content preference"; otherwise "such speaker distinctions are not presumed invalid under the First Amendment." *Turner Broadcasting, Inc. v. FCC*, 512 U.S. 622, 645 (1994). In *Packingham*, the state invoked *Turner*, arguing that it had targeted registered sex offenders, not because of any views they might have or wish to express on social media, but rather because of the risk that they would use the Internet for sexual predation purposes. In its decision, the Court did not resolve this issue but instead proceeded on "the assumption that the statute is content neutral and thus subject to intermediate scrutiny," a standard of review that nevertheless proved fatal to the North Carolina law. *Packingham*, supra, 582 U.S. at 105.

In the sections that follow, we will examine several doctrines designed to assess the constitutionality of various content-based restrictions on speech. These doctrines are the product of the Court's treatment of recurring problems that arise in the context of freedom of speech. Keep in mind that each of these doctrines reflects the underlying First Amendment values at stake, creating variable standards of scrutiny depending on the proximity of the speech to what the Court perceives as core values of the First Amendment.

As we will see, there are basically three different types of tests the Court employs in assessing the validity of content-based restrictions on speech. The first involves application of a *specialized* or *doctrinal test* that has been created for a particular type of protected speech. For example, the clear and present danger test is used to assess restrictions on speech that advocates unlawful conduct, while the commercial speech test is used mainly for restrictions on commercial advertising. A second approach involves determining whether the speech in question falls into a category of constitutionally *unprotected or proscribable speech;* examples of this approach include the "fighting words" doctrine and the test for obscenity. Finally, if no specialized or doctrinal test exists and if the speech is of a type entitled to First Amendment protection, the Court may employ an *ad hoc balancing test* in which it determines whether the restriction can be defended on the ground that it is narrowly tailored to achieve a compelling governmental interest.

§8.3.2 Advocacy of Unlawful Conduct: The Clear and Present Danger Test

The clear and present danger test is the Court's earliest First Amendment doctrine. It is most clearly applicable to laws restricting advocacy of unlawful conduct, but it has also been applied in the more general contexts of laws restricting either social protest or commentary on public issues. As now configured, the clear and present danger test operates as a specialized form of strict scrutiny, permitting restrictions on speech only when necessary to advance a substantial, overriding governmental interest and only when the danger presented by the speech is such that the government has no other option but to punish the speaker.

The doctrine began inauspiciously. In *Schenck v. United States*, 249 U.S. 47 (1919), two defendants were charged with various violations of the Espionage Act of 1917. The charges stemmed from their distribution of leaflets exhorting potential conscripts to resist the draft. At trial, the defendants claimed a First Amendment right to distribute the leaflets. They were, nonetheless, convicted. The Supreme Court affirmed, treating their First Amendment defense with almost casual indifference. In the words of Justice Holmes:

> We admit that in many places and in ordinary times the defendants in saying all that was said in the circular would have been within their constitutional rights. But the character of every act depends upon the circumstances in which it is done. The most stringent protection of free speech would not protect a man in falsely shouting fire in a theatre and causing a panic. . . . The question in every case is whether the words used are used in such circumstances and are of such a nature as to create a clear and present danger that they will bring about the substantive evils that Congress has a right to prevent. It is a question of proximity and degree. When a nation is at war many things that might be said in time of peace are such a hindrance to its effort that their utterance will not be endured so long as men fight and that no Court could regard them as protected by any constitutional right. . . . The statute of 1917 . . . punishes conspiracies to obstruct as well as actual obstruction. If the act, (speaking, or circulating a paper,) its tendency and the intent with which it is done are the same, we perceive no ground for saying that success alone warrants making the act a crime.

Id. at 52. The Court did not apply any clear and present danger standards to the facts before it. There was no examination of proximity, degree, or context. Rather, the Court simply assumed that the circumstances warranted the conviction and punishment. It was apparently enough that the leaflets might have had a bad tendency.

The week after deciding *Schenck*, the Court issued two more opinions upholding similar convictions under the Espionage Act. Justice Holmes authored both opinions, and in neither did he allude to the clear and present danger language he had used in *Schenck*. In the first, *Frohwerk v. United States*, 249 U.S. 204 (1919), it was sufficient to uphold the defendant's conviction that it "*might* . . . have been found that the circulation of the paper was in quarters where a little breath would be enough to kindle a flame and that the fact was known and relied upon by those who sent the paper out." Id. at 209 (emphasis supplied). And in the second, *Debs v. United States*, 249 U.S. 211 (1919), the defendant was convicted for delivering a speech in which he praised individual draft resisters for their courage and sacrifice. His criminality derived from the inference that his listeners should follow the same course of conduct. The First Amendment discussion was relegated to a cryptic citation to *Schenck*.

At this point, "clear and present danger" would seem to have been no more than a passing phrase in an opinion that gave little regard to the freedom of expression. A significant change was, however, on the horizon. Hints of that change appeared just six months after the decisions in *Schenck*, *Frohwerk*, and *Debs*. The vehicle was yet another Espionage Act case—*Abrams v. United States*, 250 U.S. 616 (1919). Again, the Court rejected the proffered First Amendment defense. Yet despite the parallels between the facts of *Abrams* and those of the preceding cases, Justice Holmes, joined by Justice Brandeis, dissented:

> Every year if not every day we have to wager our salvation upon some prophecy based upon imperfect knowledge. While that experiment is part of our system I think that we should be eternally vigilant against attempts to check the expression of opinions that we loathe and believe to be fraught with death, unless they so *imminently* threaten *immediate* interference with the *lawful and pressing purposes* of the law that an immediate check is required to save the country. . . . Only the emergency that makes it immediately dangerous to leave the correction of evil counsels to time warrants making any exception to the sweeping command, "Congress shall make no law . . . abridging the freedom of speech."

Id. at 630-631 (emphasis supplied). Despite his protestation to the contrary, i.e., that *Schenck*, *Frohwerk*, and *Debs* "were rightly decided" (id. at 627), Holmes's dissent reflected a new, speech-protective perspective on the freedom of expression. From this new perspective, speech advocating unlawful conduct would be protected unless that speech "imminently" threatened "immediate" interference with a "lawful and pressing" governmental purpose. In other words, unless the restrictive law is narrowly tailored to advance an important purpose, the freedom of speech must prevail.

Justice Brandeis took these emerging themes a step further in his eloquent concurring opinion in *Whitney v. California*, 274 U.S. 357, 372 (1927) (Brandeis, J., joined by Holmes, J., concurring). See also *Gitlow v. New York*, 268 U.S. 652, 672 (1925) (Holmes, J., joined by Brandeis, J., dissenting). Brandeis proposed a test that was highly speech-protective and, most important, enforceable by courts on an as-applied basis.

> To justify suppression of free speech there must be reasonable ground to fear that serious evil will result if free speech is practiced. There must be reasonable ground to believe that the danger apprehended is imminent. There must be reasonable ground to believe that the evil to be prevented is a serious one. . . . [E]ven advocacy of [law] violation, however reprehensible morally, is not a justification for denying free speech where the advocacy falls short of incitement and there is nothing to indicate that the advocacy would be immediately acted on. The wide difference between advocacy and incitement, between preparation and attempt, between assembling and conspiracy, must be borne in mind. In order to support a finding of clear and present danger it must be shown either that immediate serious violence was to be expected or was advocated, or that the past conduct furnished reason to believe that such advocacy was then contemplated.

Whitney, supra, 274 U.S. at 376.

The standards suggested by Brandeis in *Whitney*—incitement, immediacy or imminence, and seriousness of harm—were adopted and applied by the Court in *Herndon v. Lowry*, 301 U.S. 242 (1937). In *Herndon*, the defendant was convicted for soliciting membership in the Communist Party, an organization whose aim was, in part, the forcible overthrow of the government, admittedly a serious evil. While the defendant had participated in public meetings and had distributed communist literature, there was no evidence that he had in any fashion endorsed *immediate* unlawful action. Thus, although the evidence established that the defendant had engaged in *advocacy* of a doctrine that itself embraced unlawful action, there was no evidence that he had *incited* anyone to take such action or that as an *immediate* result of his activities such unlawful action was *imminent*. The Supreme Court reversed his conviction, finding that the absence of incitement and imminence was fatal to the conviction. Id. at 260-264. In short, there was no clear and present danger sufficient to overcome the presumptive protection for speech provided by the First Amendment.

After *Herndon*, the Court began to apply the clear and present danger test beyond the context of unlawful advocacy. See, e.g., *Terminiello v. Chicago*, 337 U.S. 1, 4-5 (1949) (breach of peace); *West Virginia State Bd. of Educ. v. Barnette*, 319 U.S. 624, 633-634 (1943) (refusing to salute the flag); *Cantwell v. Connecticut*, 310 U.S. 296, 308-309 (1940) (religious proselytizing); *Thornhill v. Alabama*, 310 U.S. 88, 104-105 (1940) (labor picketing). In one such case, the Court described the "minimum compulsion" of the First Amendment as requiring that "the substantive evil must be extremely serious and the degree of imminence extremely high before utterances can be punished." *Bridges v. California*, 314 U.S. 252, 263 (1941). Holmes's passing observation in *Schenck* had thus become a relatively formidable and widely applicable doctrine, inherent in which was a strong presumption in favor of freedom of expression.

Example 8-L

Shannon was convicted of assaulting nonunion truck drivers as part of an effort to force those truck drivers to join a union. In a presentencing hearing, Shannon's lawyer requested that Shannon be placed on probation as a first-time offender. In response to this request and prior to sentencing, the leading local newspaper ran an editorial describing Shannon as a "goon and a thug" and calling for imposition of the maximum sentence. The editorial ended with this observation: "Judge Scott will make a serious mistake if he grants probation to Shannon. The community needs the example of Shannon's assignment to the rock pile." Based on this editorial, Judge Scott held the newspaper in contempt and assessed a fine of $1,000. In so ruling, Judge Scott explained that the editorial threatened the "impartial adjudication of a pending case." Applying the modern clear and present danger test, may this contempt citation be upheld?

EXPLANATION

Explanation

Probably not. Although interference with the impartial adjudication of a pending case is a most serious evil and one that the government is fully empowered to prevent, on these facts there is little evidence that the cited newspaper editorial would cause the occurrence of this evil, much less that the evil was imminent. To say that a judge will make a "serious mistake" would seem to fall well within the right of a newspaper to comment on matters of public interest. Stated somewhat differently, one should be able to assume that a judge is sufficiently hearty to be able to withstand such criticism and veiled threats. See *Bridges v. California*, supra, 314 U.S. at 271-275 (arriving at a similar conclusion under similar facts); accord *Craig v. Harney*, 331 U.S. 367 (1947) and *Pennekamp v. Florida*, 328 U.S. 331 (1946).

Yet one can certainly argue to the contrary. The purpose of the editorial was clearly to put pressure on the judge, and if one adds the fact that the judge was soon to be up for reelection, the potential for interference becomes more plausible and the threat more imminent. This is especially true if the newspaper enjoys either prestige or power within the community. So, too, if the trial had been particularly notorious. From this perspective, there may well be a clear and present danger to the administration of justice—a substantial possibility that the judge will conform his or her decision to the dictates of the editorial. *Bridges v. California*, supra, 314 U.S. at 299-300 (Frankfurter, J., dissenting). The presumptive strength of the First Amendment, however, has generally prevailed over such arguments.

The foregoing example should demonstrate at least two important points. First, as it has evolved, the modern clear and present danger test values freedom of expression over even very weighty government interests. Only specific facts proving an imminent danger to such an interest will permit interference with the freedom of expression. The parallel with strict scrutiny is obvious. Speech may be restricted only to prevent an extremely serious evil—a compelling government interest—and only if the occurrence of that evil is an imminent result of the speech. Moreover, the law must be narrowly drawn to advance the government's interest in the least restrictive or least intrusive manner. Second, and closely related, the clear and present danger test, and, therefore, implicitly any protection afforded by the First Amendment, is intensely fact driven. Context is everything; therefore, what is said in any particular case must be filtered through the specific facts of that case.

The critical importance of context can be seen in *Dennis v. United States*, 341 U.S. 494 (1951), a case in which the clear and present danger test seemed to veer away from the speech-protective model described above. The defendants in *Dennis* were convicted under the Smith Act of conspiring to create an organization, the Communist Party of the United States, that advocated the unlawful overthrow of the U.S. government. There was no evidence, however, that the defendants were devising specific plans to overthrow the government or to engage in acts of sabotage. Rather, the evidence established only that the defendants had conspired to form a group to teach and advocate the creed of communism as espoused by Marx, Lenin, and Stalin, included within which was the propriety and inevitability of violent overthrow and industrial revolution. The defendants claimed a First Amendment right to teach these doctrines.

In a plurality opinion, which has been treated by the Court as authoritative on several occasions, Chief Justice Vinson purported to endorse what he described as the Holmes-Brandeis version of clear and present danger, but he in fact applied a formula that was more deferential to governmental interests. "In each case [courts] must ask whether the gravity of the 'evil,' discounted by its improbability, justifies such invasion of free speech as is necessary to avoid the danger." 341 U.S. at 510 (quoting *United States v. Dennis*, 183 F.2d 201, 212 (2d Cir. 1950) (Chief Judge Learned Hand)). In other words, under this formula, the more substantial the potential evil is, the less likely its realization must be for the government to restrict speech promoting that evil.

Quite obviously, the violent overthrow of governmental and social institutions is a substantial evil. In the plurality's words, "[T]his is the ultimate value of any society, for if a society cannot protect its very structure from armed internal attack, it must follow that no subordinate value can be protected." 341 U.S. at 509. As to imminence, any lack of immediacy—indeed, there was no showing of immediacy—was far outweighed by a combination of the substantiality of the evil and the perception that the illegal action would occur whenever the time for action was deemed propitious. In the plurality's words, clear and present danger "cannot mean that before the Government may act, it must wait until the *putsch* is about to be executed, the plans have been laid and the signal is awaited." Id. Given the context of the emerging Cold War and the perceived threat posed by the worldwide communist movement, the Court found that a clear and present danger existed sufficient to affirm the defendants' convictions. The Court made no attempt to distinguish *Herndon v. Lowry*, supra, but presumably the defendant there was seen as an isolated actor, and not part of a nationwide conspiracy. Presumably, too, the context of the Cold War altered perceptions about the threat posed by the communist movement.

Example 8-M

Lester is an anti-government man. He believes that all forms of government are a massive conspiracy designed to suppress freedom and individualism. Lester also believes that violence is a legitimate method to combat the forces of this unconscionable leviathan. To promote his views, Lester has written a pamphlet that describes his philosophy, and in which he advocates the use of stealth and violence to combat the forces of government. He gives, as an example, the bombing of public buildings. At least once every week Lester stands outside public buildings and hands out free copies of his pamphlet. Based on this activity, Lester is charged with violating a statute that makes it a crime "to advocate the use of violence to overthrow or physically attack any institution of government." Does the clear and present danger test protect Lester under these circumstances?

Explanation

If one applies the pre-*Dennis* version of clear and present danger, requiring both an extremely serious evil and an extremely high probability of imminence, then, in the absence of more evidence, Lester's activities would seem to be protected. Although the evil is extremely serious, the facts do not show any degree of imminence. At best there is the possibility that someone in the future may act on Lester's proselytizing. Stated somewhat differently, Lester has engaged not in incitement, but in protected advocacy. Thus, this would appear to be an instance in which the remedy of more speech remains readily available. On the other hand, if one applies the *Dennis* balancing formula, a contrary result may obtain. Given the seriousness of the evil, combined with very real concerns about domestic terrorism, the relative lack of probability may not sufficiently "discount" the evil to prevent prosecution for this advocacy.

But should *Dennis* apply to facts such as those described in Example 8-M? Some insight into a potential answer can be found in Justice Jackson's concurring opinion in *Dennis*. Justice Jackson thought that the clear and present danger test was useful as a judicial tool to measure the constitutionality of prosecutions of discrete acts of protest: "a hot-headed speech on a street corner, or circulation of a few incendiary pamphlets, or parading by some zealots behind a red flag, or refusal of a handful of school children to salute our flag. . . ." 341 U.S. at 568. Under such circumstances, a judge can examine the facts and make the appropriate determination of evil and immediacy. But with respect to a "well-organized, nation-wide conspiracy," such as the Communist Party, the "judge-made verbal trap" of clear and present danger requires the appraisal of "imponderables." Id. at 568-570. Consequently, Jackson thought the test was simply inapplicable under such circumstances.

If one adopts Jackson's approach, Lester's circulation of incendiary pamphlets would seem to qualify for application of the stricter pre-*Dennis* clear and present danger test, for his activities were not part of a well-organized, nationwide conspiracy. If this is true, it suggests that there are two somewhat different strains of the clear and present danger test.

That this may be the case is suggested by the Court's decision in *Brandenburg v. Ohio*, 395 U.S. 444 (1969). There, the Court returned to the version of clear and present danger described by Justice Brandeis in *Whitney*, though, oddly enough, without ever using the phrase "clear and present danger." In *Brandenburg*, a Ku Klux Klan leader was convicted of violating a state law that made it unlawful to advocate "the duty, necessity, or propriety of crime, sabotage, violence, or unlawful methods of terrorism as a means of accomplishing industrial or political reform. . . ." Id. at 444-445. The conviction was premised on two speeches made by the defendant at Klan gatherings. In one, he stated, "We're not a revengent organization, but if our President, our Congress, our Supreme Court, continues to suppress the white, Caucasian race, it's possible that there might have to be some revengeance taken." Id. at 446. And in the other, he made racist comments about blacks and Jews. The Court reversed his conviction, ruling that the advocacy of unlawful conduct cannot be punished "except where such advocacy is directed to inciting or producing imminent lawless action and is likely to incite or produce such action." Id. at 447.

Brandenburg did not, however, overrule *Dennis*. Instead, *Brandenburg* represents an implicit acceptance and application of the distinction recognized by Justice Jackson in his *Dennis* concurring opinion. In those contexts in which the speech is *public and overt*, the formula of Justice Brandeis's *Whitney* concurrence provides a good judicial measure of constitutionality. In contexts in which the speech is *covert*—i.e., part of some type of an organized, clandestine conspiracy—the balancing test applied by the *Dennis* majority may well provide the most serviceable method for assessing the countervailing interests at stake. Of course, one could argue that a case involving the Klan should fit into the latter category. But the charges against the defendant in *Brandenburg* did not involve covert or clandestine operations; rather, they were premised on the defendant's public declarations of his organization's philosophy, made in the presence of a television film crew.

Example 8-N

EXAMPLE

In Example 8-M, suppose that instead of being a lone pamphleteer, Lester was the leader of American Liberation Now (ALN), an organization whose purpose was to establish, through crime and violence, an independent state within the United States. Suppose, too, that ALN had several hundred members who met in secret to discuss philosophy and strategy and to train for independence. These members were pledged to achieve their goal of independent statehood as soon as the circumstances were propitious. If, based on his leadership of this organization, Lester were charged with conspiring to advocate the unlawful overthrow of the government of state X and if he relied on the First Amendment as a defense to those charges, which version of clear and present danger should (or would) a court apply?

EXPLANATION

Explanation

One argument would be that there is only one version of clear and present danger—namely, the one applied in *Brandenburg*, the Court's most recent foray into this context. Under that test, Lester's potential conviction could be upheld only if imminence of unlawful conduct were established. In the absence of such a showing, the appropriate remedy is more speech. This is true regardless of whether the speech on which the charges rest is public or clandestine. The other argument would look to the *Dennis* balancing formula as presenting the more appropriate measure. This argument is founded on the assumption that the charges are premised not on public statements made by Lester (such as those at issue in *Brandenburg*), but on Lester's speech-related involvement in the covert and clandestine activities of the ALN. According to this view—which is similar to that espoused by Justice Jackson in *Dennis*—the covert and clandestine nature of the activities at issue makes application of the more traditional clear and present danger test both impractical and unsound. The government should not have to wait "until the *putsch* is about to be executed." Rather, in determining whether Lester may be punished, the court must balance the substantiality of the evil against its improbability. The outcome is obviously both subjective and fact dependent.

To sum up, the clear and present danger test is contextual. The formulas described in *Dennis* and *Brandenburg* are both designed to balance the weightiness of the government's interest against the individual's right of free expression. Which test to apply and how rigorously to apply it will depend on the facts, the perceived dangers, and the government's opportunities to prevent the very real harms that may be caused by the advocacy of unlawful conduct.

§8.3.3 Fighting Words, True Threats, and Hate Speech

Fighting words are defined as those words "which by their very utterance inflict injury or tend to incite an immediate breach of the peace." *Chaplinsky v. New Hampshire*, 315 U.S. 568, 572 (1942). Such words are presumed to play little or no part in the exposition of ideas and are, therefore, deemed to be a type of speech that falls outside the First Amendment umbrella. Id. Yet despite a definition that focuses on the inherently harmful or provocative nature of the words themselves, in practice the applicability of the fighting words doctrine depends largely, if not completely, on the context in which the presumably harmful or provocative words are used. There are, therefore, no words that automatically fall into this category. *Cohen v. California*, 403 U.S. 15, 22-26 (1971) (the word "fuck" may not be excised from the lexicon on the theory that it is "inherently likely to cause violent reaction"). Moreover, words that one normally would not consider to be fighting words may warrant that label if delivered under particularly volatile circumstances and in a manner likely to cause a violent reaction.

Example 8-O

Al is a card-carrying liberal. He has a strong aversion to anything to the right of the New Deal, and he finds conservative talk show hosts particularly loathsome. One evening while taking a stroll, Al happens upon Bush Limbo, the well-known (and sometimes rotund) host of a conservative talk-radio show. Al races up to Bush and screams in his face, "You're a big fat idiot!" Just before Bush is about to land the first blow, a police officer intervenes and arrests Al for causing a breach of the peace. Were the words uttered by Al "fighting words" and, therefore, unprotected by the First Amendment?

Explanation

Perhaps. The mere offensiveness of the words used will not automatically qualify them as fighting words, but given the circumstances and the manner of delivery, a court might find that Al's intemperate epithet was delivered in a manner likely to invite an unthinking, violent response. See *Chaplinsky v. New Hampshire*, 315 U.S. 568 (1942) (epithets "God damned racketeer" and "damned Fascist" delivered in a face-to-face confrontation with a police officer held to be fighting words). If so, the "fighting words" label may be applied, and the speech will be unprotected. The relatively mild nature of Al's invective may, however, render the application of the doctrine somewhat questionable. Had the words used been more provocative—e.g., so-called four-letter words—the "fighting words" label would more easily attach because of the increased likelihood that the use of such words in an angry face-to-face confrontation would lead to a breach of the peace.

Suppose instead that Al publishes a book entitled *Bush Limbo Is a Big Fat Idiot*. Even if this pejorative epithet might qualify as fighting words in a face-to-face confrontation, it would not be so considered as the title to a book. The context simply lacks the necessary immediacy associated with the fighting words doctrine. This would remain true even if the book title contained highly provocative four-letter words.

As one can discern from the prior example, the fighting words doctrine may be thought of as merely a specific application of the clear and present danger test. *Feiner v. New York*, 340 U.S. 315, 319-320 (1951); *Terminiello v. Chicago*, 337 U.S. 1, 2 (1949). The use of offensive or provocative language will be punishable according to that doctrine only if the words are delivered in a manner and under circumstances likely to cause an immediate and serious harm—typically, a violent reaction stemming from a face-to-face confrontation. Given this reality, a number of commentators have suggested that the fighting words nomenclature should be abandoned. They argue that instead of treating fighting words as a form of speech that falls outside the First Amendment, such words should be recognized as a form of speech that falls under the First Amendment umbrella but that is, nonetheless, punishable where the requirements of the clear and present danger test are met. The Court, however, continues to refer to "fighting words" as a separate category of unprotected speech. See, e.g., *United States v. Alvarez*, 567 U.S. 709, 717 (2012); *Brown v. Entertainment Merchants Assn*, 564 U.S. 786, 791 (2011).

The Court has also held that "true threats" are unprotected by the First Amendment. A "true threat" occurs when an individual "means to communicate a serious expression of an intent to commit an act of unlawful violence to a particular individual or group of individuals." *Virginia v. Black*, 538 U.S. 343, 359 (2003). The harm caused by a true threat is not, as in the case of fighting words, the imminent outbreak of violence but the reasonable fear that such violence might occur. Thus, a true threat can be seen as a variation on the fighting words theme that does not require an actual face-to-face confrontation. "Intimidation in the constitutionally proscribable sense of the word is a type of true threat, where a speaker directs a threat to a person or group of persons with the intent of placing the victim in fear of bodily harm or death." Id. at 360. Hence, burning a cross on someone's front lawn as a means of intimidation might well qualify as an unprotected true threat, even if the resident was not home at the time. See *Counterman v. Colorado*, 600 U.S. 66, 75-78 (2023) (to establish that speech qualifies as a proscribable true threat, it must be shown that the speaker was subjectively aware of the threatening nature of the speech under a recklessness standard).

Closely related to the fighting words doctrine is the problem of hate speech. In recent years, several communities—particularly college communities—have attempted to regulate the use of language that ridicules or demeans racial minorities, women, gays and lesbians, and other groups deemed particularly susceptible to verbal abuse. Proponents of such regulations argue that the designated groups are victims of deeply ingrained patterns of prejudice, patterns that are only exacerbated by a permissive attitude toward verbal abuse. Hate speech as such is not, however, an unprotected category of speech; and since state-imposed limitations on hate speech are content based, they must satisfy rigorous First Amendment standards. Consequently, courts have been reluctant to uphold such measures. See, e.g., *Doe v. University of Michigan*, 721 F. Supp. 852 (E.D. Mich. 1989) (striking down the University of Michigan's speech code). Similarly, in *R.A.V. v. City of St. Paul*, 505 U.S. 377 (1992), the Supreme Court struck down a city ordinance that prohibited the display of any symbol that "arouses anger, alarm or resentment in others on the basis of race, color, creed, religion or gender. . . ." Id. at 380. Even though the state limited the scope of the ordinance to fighting words, an unprotected category of speech, the Court held that the law was facially invalid as a content-based restriction on speech, since the proscription depended on the message being communicated by the fighting words. Id. at 391-393. See § 8.3.9.

§8.3.4 Free Speech Limitations on Defamation (and Other Torts)

The Court's landmark decision in *New York Times v. Sullivan*, 376 U.S. 254 (1964), rejected an entrenched judicial assumption that the common law of defamation was categorically exempt from limits imposed by the First Amendment. In the post-*Sullivan* jurisprudence of the First Amendment, the law of defamation is no longer the sole bailiwick of the states. Instead, the *Sullivan* Court proclaimed, "a profound national commitment to the principle that debate on public issues should be uninhibited, robust, and wide-open, and that it may well include vehement, caustic, and sometimes unpleasantly sharp attacks on government and public officials" (id. at 270), under which the common law of defamation and other speech-premised torts (e.g., intentional infliction of emotional distress) must at times give way to the expanding constitutional law of free speech.

The decision in *Sullivan* grew out of a controversy surrounding a full-page advertisement published in the *New York Times*. The ad solicited support for the civil rights movement and described, among other things, certain anti-civil rights actions said to have taken place in Montgomery, Alabama, under the auspices of the local sheriff's department. In response, the sheriff of the City of Montgomery sued the *New York Times* (and others) for defamation, alleging that he had been libeled by certain factual errors contained in the ad. Under Alabama law as it stood, a publication was deemed "libelous per se" if the publication was "of and concerning" the plaintiff and if it tended to injure the plaintiff "in his reputation" or "bring [him] into public contempt." Id. at 267. Once libel per se was established, the defendant could prevail only on proof that the matters published were true. The ad at issue in

Sullivan did contain factual errors regarding the events said to have occurred in Montgomery, and under Alabama law, those falsehoods could be treated as pertaining to the sheriff. After a trial, a jury awarded the sheriff $500,000 in damages.

The Supreme Court reversed, holding that the First Amendment "prohibits a public official from recovering damages for a defamatory falsehood relating to his official conduct unless he proves that the statement was made with 'actual malice'—that is, with knowledge that it was false or with reckless disregard of whether it was false or not." Id. at 279-280. Moreover, the actual malice element must be established with "convincing clarity." Id. at 285-286.

The Court's rationale for this relatively tough standard focused on the importance of public debate in a democratic society. If that debate is to be uninhibited, robust, and wide-open, the participants must be free to risk the publication of factual error in their exploration for truth or consensus and in their quest for democratic accountability. To conclude otherwise would be to impose a dangerous chill on both the terms and the scope of public discourse. In short, the risk of transient error was far outweighed by the risk of enforced silence.

This risk of error does not, however, encompass the knowing or reckless falsehood, since neither contributes to a good-faith willingness to participate in public discourse. Thus, under *Sullivan*, in the context of criticism of public officials, the knowing or reckless falsehood is without First Amendment value and hence without First Amendment protection. The actual malice standard was designed to ensure that, in the context of public debate, only this unprotected speech remained subject to the law of defamation.

The Burdens Imposed by the Actual Malice Standard

In cases in which it applies (a subject to which we will return), the actual malice standard injects a scienter element into the plaintiff's prima facie case. The standard has nothing to do with "malice" as that word is commonly understood. Rather, it requires only that a plaintiff alleging defamation prove that the defendant published a defamatory falsehood either with knowledge of falsity or with reckless disregard for the truth. The phrase "knowledge of falsity" means what it says—the defendant must have known that the published defamation was false. "Reckless disregard for the truth" is only a small step removed. That language requires proof that the defendant "in fact entertained serious doubts as to the truth of his publication" (*St. Amant v. Thompson*, 390 U.S. 727, 731 (1968)) or that the publication was made "with 'a high degree of awareness of . . . probable falsity'. . . ." *Harte-Hanks Communications v. Connaughton*, 491 U.S. 657, 667 (1989) (quoting *Garrison v. Louisiana*, 379 U.S. 64, 74 (1964)). Mere negligence or failure to follow professional standards is not enough to satisfy either standard. 491 U.S. 664-666. Proof of actual malice must be clear and convincing (id. at

657), a standard that falls somewhere between a preponderance of the evidence and proof beyond a reasonable doubt.

Example 8-P

Olive was a candidate for the position of city court judge. The local newspaper, the *Blade-Gazette,* supported her rival, the incumbent. One week prior to the election, the incumbent's clerk was indicted on several counts of bribery in connection with cases pending before the city court. The next day, the *Blade-Gazette* published an article in which it quoted "an anonymous informant" as claiming to have been bribed by Olive to make false accusations against the indicted clerk. The informant was quoted accurately, but her description of Olive's complicity was completely false. Olive had never spoken to her and was not involved with any type of bribery. With a limited amount of investigation, the *Blade-Gazette* would have discovered these facts. Among other things, the prosecutor would have told the newspaper that there was both physical evidence and several other witnesses that corroborated the informant's testimony against the clerk, and that Olive had played no role in the affair. Was the falsehood regarding Olive published "knowingly" or with "reckless disregard for the truth"?

Explanation

It depends. The fact that the *Blade-Gazette* was careless and even unprofessional in its investigation will not, standing alone, be sufficient to establish actual malice. The limited (or nonexistent) investigation may, however, support an inference that the newspaper doubted the veracity of the informant and did not wish to have those doubts verified. This inference, standing alone, is still not *clear and convincing* evidence of actual malice. If, on the other hand, Olive can prove that the *Blade-Gazette* was aware of facts tending to discredit the informant's story and failed to pursue obvious leads to that effect, the case for actual malice would be much stronger. This is especially true when one factors in the *Blade-Gazette*'s support for the incumbent. Under such circumstances, it might fairly be said that the *Blade-Gazette* published the falsehood with a high degree of awareness of its probable falsity. See *Harte-Hanks Communications,* supra, 491 U.S. at 685-693 (affirming a finding of actual malice on similar grounds).

Implicit in the actual malice standard is a requirement that the plaintiff prove the falsity of the defamatory statement. Knowledge of falsity can only be established if the defamatory assertion was in fact false; reckless disregard for the truth also implies the publication of a false statement. In other words, truth is not a defense in an actual malice case; instead, lack of truth—i.e., falsity—is an element of the plaintiff's cause of action. The burden of proof on this element, however, is merely a preponderance of the evidence. In Example 8-P, therefore, Olive would be required to prove by a preponderance of the evidence that she had not bribed the informant.

The falsity element also requires that the alleged defamation involve an assertion of *fact* and not a mere statement of *opinion*. While a factual assertion can be false, an opinion, regardless of how ridiculous or pernicious, cannot be. Consequently, statements of opinion are absolutely protected. If, however, the supposed opinion reasonably implies the existence of certain false and defamatory facts, it will be treated as a factual assertion. In other words, courts will not allow a defendant to disguise a factual assertion as an opinion. The claim in Example 8-P that Olive bribed a potential witness is a statement of fact. Had the published account quoted the informant as "being of the opinion" that Olive was involved in such a scheme, the conclusion would be the same. The former asserts the fact of bribery; the latter reasonably implies it. See *Milkovich v. Lorain Journal Co.*, 497 U.S. 1 (1990).

A similar treatment is given to hyperbole and parody. In those contexts in which the actual malice standard applies, both genres are absolutely protected unless the publication can be reasonably said to imply a false statement of facts. Thus, in *Hustler Magazine v. Falwell*, 485 U.S. 46 (1988), a particularly nasty parody regarding a well-known televangelist and his mother was held not actionable, since no reasonable person could have interpreted the parody—which was labeled as such—as making any assertion of fact, implied or otherwise. The *Hustler* case is also noteworthy because the underlying tort was not defamation, but intentional infliction of emotional distress. Nonetheless, the *Sullivan* standard applied, and recovery could be premised only on the plaintiff's proof of falsity and actual malice.

The Contexts in Which the Actual Malice Standard Applies

First, the actual malice standard applies to speech-premised tort claims, such as defamation or intentional infliction of emotional distress, when such claims are brought by *public officials*. The latter term is broadly defined to include all elected officials as well as any individual running for elective office—such as Olive in the example above. It includes as well any person employed by the government who holds a position that permits him or her to exercise discretion over the conduct of governmental affairs or whose position is such that the public would have "an independent interest in the qualifications and performance of the person who holds it. . . ." *Rosenblatt v. Baer*, 383 U.S. 75, 85-86 (1966) (supervisor of a county-owned ski resort deemed a public official). This definition excludes public employees such as custodians, filing clerks, and typists, but it just as clearly includes public school teachers, police officers, playground supervisors, social workers, and the like.

The actual malice standard also applies when such claims are brought by *public figures*—i.e., persons who are "intimately involved in the resolution of important public questions or, by reason of their fame, shape events in areas of concern to society at large." *Curtis Publishing Co. v. Butts*, 388 U.S. 130, 164 (1967) (Warren, C.J., concurring). The Court has subsequently recognized two types of public figures for purposes of this rule. First are those who "occupy positions of such persuasive power and influence that they are deemed public figures for all purposes. More commonly, those classed as public figures have thrust themselves to the forefront of particular public controversies in order to influence the resolution of the issues involved." *Gertz v. Robert Welch, Inc.*, 418 U.S. 323, 345 (1974). Notice that under this standard, the status of being a public figure derives largely from a personal choice by the "public figure" to become involved in public affairs. The Court has stated that the case of the truly involuntary public figure will be rare indeed.

Example 8-Q

Bill "Big Boy" Butz is the head coach of the New York Knockablockers, a newly franchised NFL football team. A New York sportswriter has written several articles about Butz and his unorthodox training methods, including an accusation that Butz promotes the use of illegal steroids. If Butz sues the sportswriter for defamation, will Butz be deemed a public figure?

Explanation

Probably. A person who has accepted a high-profile position such as that occupied by Butz is a public figure for purposes of any publications pertaining to the position from which that status derives. See *Curtis Publishing Co. v. Butts*, 388 U.S. 130 (1967).

Suppose, however, that Butz's wife, Beverly, files for divorce and that the same reporter writes an article describing Beverly as a "prime candidate for the Betty Ford Clinic." Suppose, too, that Beverly holds a news conference explaining why she has decided to leave Butz. Is Beverly a public figure? Not likely. Beverly's marriage to a public figure does not automatically make her a public figure, and this is true regardless of how interesting the public or the press may find her marriage and divorce. What is important is that nothing in these facts indicates that Beverly occupies a position of persuasive power and influence. Nor has she thrust herself to the forefront of a *public* controversy. As long as the news conference is not being used to influence the outcome of the divorce proceedings, it will not transform Beverly into a public figure. See *Time, Inc. v. Firestone*, 424 U.S. 448 (1976).

The Standards for Private-Plaintiff Lawsuits

At one time, some members of the Court sought to extend the actual malice standard to any speech related to a matter "of public or general interest." *Rosenbloom v. Metromedia, Inc.*, 403 U.S. 29, 43 (1971) (plurality opinion). Thus, the standard would apply regardless of the status of the plaintiff. The Court, however, has rejected that view, limiting the application of actual malice to cases in which the plaintiff is either a public official or a public figure. *Gertz v. Robert Welch, Inc.*, 418 U.S. 323 (1974). Specifically, in *Gertz*, the Court held that in defamation suits brought by private plaintiffs—i.e., plaintiffs who are neither public officials nor public figures—liability for *actual damages* could be established, consistent with the First Amendment, if the plaintiff proves that the defendant had, with negligence, published a false statement of fact regarding the plaintiff. See also *Philadelphia Newspapers, Inc. v. Hepps*, 475 U.S. 767, 768 (1986). The award of punitive damages or presumed damages, however, would require a showing of actual malice. *Gertz*, supra, 418 U.S. at 349. See also § 8.2.3 ("The Distinction Between Matters of Public and Private Concern").

The First Amendment and Speech-Premised Torts Generally

The First Amendment standards adopted in the context of defamation are not the exclusive measures of the constitutionality of speech-premised torts. Those standards are most directly relevant to torts under which the truth or falsity of statement is critical to establishing liability. More generally, however, whenever civil liability for a tort is premised on the content of protected speech, the standards of the First Amendment applicable to the type of speech at issue must be applied. Hence, political speech that potentially gives rise to a tort will be protected under the most rigorous standards.

EXAMPLE

Example 8-R

Members of the Westboro Baptist Church picketed the military funeral of a soldier who had died in combat. The church members believe that the death of a soldier represents God's just punishment for America's toleration of homosexuality. To reflect this belief, they carried signs that included messages such as, "Thank God for Dead Soldiers," "God Hates Fags," and "Fags Doom Nations." In response, the father of the slain soldier sued the church and several of its members for intentional infliction of emotional distress. To succeed on his claim under the applicable state law, the father was required to show that the defendants intentionally engaged in "extreme and outrageous" conduct that caused plaintiff to suffer severe emotional distress. (We have previously concluded that the picketing at issue here was a matter of public concern (Example 8-C, supra) and that the imposition of liability for the picketing would amount to a content-based restriction on speech (Example 8-I, supra). Is the father's lawsuit likely to survive a First Amendment challenge?

Explanation

No. The fact that the picketing may qualify as extreme and outrageous cannot serve as a premise for restricting what is, in essence, political speech. The risk that the speech will be punished because of the offensiveness of the content is simply too great. As the Court stated in *Snyder v. Phelps*, the case on which this problem is based, "Such speech cannot be restricted simply because it is upsetting or arouses contempt. 'If there is a bedrock principle underlying the First Amendment, it is that the government may not prohibit the expression of an idea simply because society finds the idea itself offensive or disagreeable.'" *Snyder v. Phelps*, 562 U.S. 443, 458 (2011) (quoting *Texas v. Johnson*, 491 U.S. 397, 414 (1989)).

The Court has also applied the First Amendment in the context of civil fraud actions. For example, in *Illinois ex rel. Madigan v. Telemarketing Associates*, 538 U.S. 600 (2003), the State of Illinois filed a civil fraud action against a for-profit fundraising organization (Telemarketers) that had been retained to raise funds for a nonprofit veterans organization (VietNow). Under the agreement, Telemarketers was to retain 85 percent of the gross receipts from Illinois donors. According to the Illinois Attorney General's complaint, during the fundraising campaign Telemarketers represented that a significant amount of each dollar donated would go directly to VietNow. Further, one potential donor was told that 90 percent of the donations would go to the vets, while another was told that her donation would not be used for labor expenses because "all members are volunteers." Id. at 608. The question before the Supreme Court was whether this civil fraud action could proceed in light of the First Amendment right to engage in charitable solicitations.

The Court began its analysis by reaffirming a trio of cases that had struck down state laws that imposed specific percentage limitations on the amount of money a for-profit fundraiser could retain when soliciting funds for a nonprofit organization. *Schaumburg v. Citizens for a Better Environment*, 444 U.S. 620 (1980) (25 percent); *Secretary of State of Maryland v. Joseph H. Munson Co.*, 467 U.S. 947 (1984) (25 percent with the possibility of a waiver); and *Riley v. National Fed. of the Blind of North Carolina, Inc.*, 487 U.S. 781 (1988) (rebuttable presumption that 35 percent was too high). In essence, the Court explained, this trilogy held that the imposed limitations impermissibly invaded a charitable organization's First Amendment right to raise funds. The Court, however, reiterated that the First Amendment did not protect fraudulent activity or the intentional lie. In fact, "*Schaumburg*, *Munson*, and *Riley* took care to leave a corridor open for fraud actions to guard the public against false or misleading charitable solicitations." *Illinois ex rel. Madigan*, supra, 538 U.S. at 617.

In upholding the Attorney General's authority to proceed with its fraud action, the Court described the Illinois law as follows:

> False statement alone does not subject a fundraiser to fraud liability. As restated in Illinois case law, to prove a defendant liable for fraud, the complainant must show that the defendant made a false representation of a material fact knowing that the representation was false; further, the complainant must demonstrate that the defendant made the representation with the intent to mislead the listener and succeeded in doing so. Heightening the complainant's burden, these showings must be made by clear and convincing evidence.

Id. at 620 (internal citation omitted). The Court then observed: "Exacting proof requirements of this order, in other contexts, have been held to provide sufficient breathing room for protected speech." Id. (citing *New York Times v. Sullivan*, supra). In short, consistent with the First Amendment, "States may maintain fraud actions when fundraisers make false or misleading representations designed to deceive donors about how their donations will be used." Id. at 624.

§8.3.5 Campaign Financing, Campaign Advocacy, and Restrictions on the Initiative Process

Campaign Financing and Campaign Advocacy

The First Amendment has been interpreted as limiting the authority of the government to regulate the financing of political campaigns. See generally *Buckley v. Valeo*, 424 U.S. 1 (1976). Expenditures in support of or against candidates for elective office are thought to be inextricably tied to the underlying message of the campaign and are thus treated as political speech. Consequently, such expenditures (e.g., taking out a newspaper ad supporting the candidate) are entitled to the most stringent protections of the First Amendment. These same protections apply to expenditures made in support of referendum measures. *Citizens Against Rent Control v. Berkeley*, 454 U.S. 290 (1981). As one Justice cynically observed, for purposes of the First Amendment, "money talks. . . ." 424 U.S. at 262 (White, J., concurring and dissenting).

Although the Court has recognized the importance and legitimacy of the government's interest in preventing corruption or the appearance of corruption in the electoral and referendum processes, the Court has rarely found that interest sufficient to justify restrictions on direct expenditures made by a candidate or a candidate's supporters. The net result is that no government—federal, state, or local—may limit the amount of money a political candidate may spend toward his or her own election. Nor may the government, instead of capping a candidate's total personal expenditures, penalize wealthy candidates who spend more of their own money than their opponents can, such as by giving the opponent certain statutory fundraising advantages that are withheld from the wealthier candidate. *Davis v. Federal Election Comm'n*, 554 U.S. 724 (2008) (invalidating federal law that relaxed statutory private contribution limits for opponents of wealthy candidates whose personal contributions to their own campaign exceeded a specified minimum). Neither may the government provide matching funds to a publicly financed candidate to offset expenditures over a specified threshold by a privately funded candidate. *Arizona Free Enterprise Club's Freedom Club PAC v. Bennett*, 565 U.S. 721 (2011) (so holding). Similarly, direct expenditures by individuals or independent political groups in support of a candidate (or a cause) may not be restricted if the expenditures are "independent" and not disguised contributions to the candidate. *Federal Election Comm'n v. National Conservative Political Action Comm.*, 470 U.S. 480, 493 (1985). To be "independent," the expenditures must not have been made at the request of or coordinated with the endorsed candidate.

At one time, the Court permitted the government to restrict political expenditures made by profit-based and some nonprofit corporations, on the basis that the government has a compelling interest in protecting the integrity of the marketplace of ideas from the corrosive influence of aggregated corporate wealth. See *Austin v. Michigan State Chamber of Commerce*, 494 U.S. 652 (1990) (allowing the government to require such corporations to make any such expenditures from "segregated" funds generated by voluntary contributions). But in *Citizens United v. Federal Election Comm'n*, 558 U.S. 310 (2010), the Supreme Court overruled *Austin* and held that "the Government may not suppress political speech on the basis of the speaker's corporate identity. No sufficient governmental interest justifies limits on the political speech of nonprofit or for-profit corporations." Id. at 365. In short, a corporation is fully entitled to make unlimited, independent expenditures on behalf of or in opposition to a candidate for political office.

There is, however, an important distinction between political expenditures and political contributions. While the authority of the government to restrict expenditures in political campaigns is severely limited by the First Amendment and thus subject to strict scrutiny, the authority to impose restrictions on the amount of a person's contributions to political campaigns is broader and subject to a less demanding standard of review. *Buckley v. Valeo*, supra, 424 U.S. at 20-21; see also *Nixon v. Shrink Missouri Government PAC*, 528 U.S. 377 (2000) (upholding state contribution limitations under the *Buckley* standard). The same is true of contribution limitations imposed on corporations, including nonprofit advocacy corporations. *Federal Election Comm'n v. Beaumont*, 539 U.S. 146 (2003). As the Court has said, "restrictions on political contributions have been treated as merely 'marginal' speech restrictions subject to relatively complaisant review under the First Amendment, because contributions lie closer to the edges than to the core of political expression." Id. at 161.

This relaxed scrutiny of contribution limitations reflects the fact that the political message conveyed by a monetary contribution is at best opaque. And, in terms of the impact on speech by the candidate, a restriction on contributions does no more than force that candidate to rely on a broader base of support. The distinction also reflects the fact that for the individual contributor, a contribution is at best speech by proxy (furthering the ability of the person receiving the contribution to speak) and a rough but imperfect measure of the strength of a potential association. Both are more derivative interests for the individual than is the interest in creating and disseminating speech oneself (which is what independent expenditures foster). As a result, "instead of requiring contribution regulations to be narrowly tailored to serve a compelling governmental interest, a contribution limit involving 'significant interference' with associational rights passes muster if it satisfies the lesser demand of being 'closely drawn' to match a 'sufficiently important interest.'" Id. at 162 (internal citations omitted). Under this approach, the government's interest in preventing corruption or the appearance of corruption is usually sufficient to override any marginal effects on the freedom of speech.

However, do not be misled into thinking that the lower standard of review applied to contribution limitations will invariably lead to their validation. In *Randall v. Sorrell*, 548 U.S. 230 (2006), the Court struck down what can be fairly described as relatively low contribution limitations imposed by the State of Vermont. A three-person plurality noted that the state's limitations were "substantially lower than both the limits we have previously upheld and comparable limits in other States. These are danger signs that [the law's] contribution limits may fall outside tolerable First Amendment limits." Id. at 253. For example, under Vermont law, the amount a person, corporation, or political action committee could contribute to a gubernatorial candidate during any election cycle was, in effect, $200 per campaign, about 1/20th the size of the limitations upheld in *Buckley*. Id. In ruling that these limits ran afoul of the First Amendment, the plurality explained that imposition of such low limits posed a significant risk of undermining "the ability of a candidate running against an incumbent officeholder to mount an effective *challenge*." Id. at 255 (emphasis in original).

In *Thompson v. Hebdon*, 589 U.S. 1, 4 n.* (2019), the Supreme Court in a per curiam decision held that the plurality opinion in *Randall* should be treated as binding precedent. On that basis, the *Thompson* Court reversed a Ninth Circuit opinion that had ignored *Randall* and upheld Alaska's $500-per-year-individual-to-candidate contribution limit. In remanding the case for reconsideration in light of *Randall*, the Court observed that Alaska's limit was "substantially lower" than limits previously upheld, that it was "substantially lower" than comparable limits in other states, and that since it did not adjust for inflation it would inevitably become too low with time.

The Court's most recent examination of contribution limits arose in the context of a federal law that limited a political candidate's ability to use post-election campaign contributions to repay the candidate's personal campaign loans. The Court, without endorsing a specific standard of review, held that this limitation burdened core political speech, lacked adequate justification, and therefore violated the First Amendment. *Federal Election Comm'n v. Cruz*, 596 U.S. 289 (2022).

Note that the protections afforded independent *expenditures* created a rather easy method for circumventing any restriction on *contributions*. Amounts that cannot be contributed *to* a candidate can be spent *in support of* that candidate, if the expenditures are "independent." *Federal Election Comm'n v. National Conservative Political Action Comm.*, 470 U.S. 480 (1985); see also *Colorado Republican Federal Campaign Comm. v. Federal Election Comm'n*, 518 U.S. 604 (1996) (*Colorado I*) (expenditures by a political party used to attack rival party's candidate, but before its own candidate's nomination, deemed independent and fully protected). Of course, if a third party's expenditures on behalf of a candidate are not independent—i.e., if they are coordinated with that candidate—then those expenditures will be treated as the functional equivalent of a contribution and subjected to the appropriate Federal Election Campaign Act (FECA) limitations.

In *Federal Election Commission v. Colorado Republican Federal Campaign Committee*, 533 U.S. 431 (2001) (*Colorado II*), the Colorado Republican Party challenged a provision of FECA that treated a political party's coordinated expenditures on behalf of a congressional candidate as the functional equivalent of contributions to that candidate. The Party argued that its coordinated expenditures should receive the same constitutional protection as its independent expenditures. Cf. *Colorado I*, supra (political party's truly independent expenditures protected). Unlike other supporters of a political candidate, whose nonindependent expenditures are subject to FECA, the Party explained that the sole reason for a political party's existence is to support candidates for office. Hence, in the Party's view, a political party's expenditures on behalf of an affiliated candidate, regardless of the independence of those expenditures, go to the very heart of the Party's mission, which is to engage in political speech. The government argued that treating a political party's coordinated expenditures as contributions was necessary to prevent circumvention of FECA's legitimate limitations on contributions. "A party's right to make unlimited expenditures coordinated with a candidate would induce individual and other nonparty contributors to give to the party in order to finance coordinated spending for a favored candidate beyond the contribution limits binding on them." Id. at 446. The Court, concluding that the facts supported the government's contention and that there was no reason to treat political parties differently from individuals whose coordinated expenditures were politically motivated, held "that a party's coordinated expenditures, unlike expenditures truly independent, may be restricted to minimize circumvention of contribution limits." Id. at 465.

A similar approach was adopted by the Court in *McConnell v. Federal Election Commission*, 540 U.S. 93 (2003). *McConnell* involved a constitutional challenge to the Bipartisan Campaign Reform Act of 2002 (BCRA). One of the issues before the Court involved Title I of BCRA, which imposes a package of restrictions prohibiting national political parties from "soliciting, receiving, directing, or spending any soft money." Id. at 133. Prior to the adoption of BCRA, one of the most significant loopholes in the regulation of federal election financing involved the distinction drawn between so-called hard and soft money. Under the Federal Election Campaign Act (FECA), "hard money" referred to direct contributions to a federal candidate's campaign. Such contributions were strictly limited by FECA. "Soft money," on the other hand, referred to contributions to a national or local *political party* that might be used by the party for state and local races or for mixed purposes such as get-out-the-vote efforts. These funds were essentially unrestricted by FECA. Over time, this soft money began to be used to indirectly finance and support the election of federal candidates. For example, a party might use soft money to pay for an "issue ad" that included the candidates' names and noted their positions on a particular issue but that did not expressly ask the recipient of the message to vote for or against either candidate. Not surprisingly, "[a]s the permissible uses of soft money expanded, the amount of soft money raised and spent by the national political parties increased exponentially." Id. at 124. By 2000, soft money accounted for 42 percent of spending by the Republican and Democratic parties. Id. Moreover, soft-money contributions tended to be significantly larger per donor than those permitted for hard money.

BCRA took the national parties "out of the soft money business" by adopting a package of restrictions that rendered such contributions illegal. Id. at 133. However, some of the restrictions imposed by Title I of BCRA were phrased in such a way as to also include limitations on the expenditure of soft money by national parties. In other words, some of the provisions in effect said that a national party could neither "receive nor spend" money from certain sources. The Court nevertheless treated those "expenditure" restrictions as mechanisms designed to prevent the party from circumventing BCRA's limitation on the contribution of soft money, the idea being that if any such money could not be spent, there would be less of an incentive for a party to receive it. Id. at 138-139. Since these were not limits on the total amount of money that parties could spend—not, that is, "expenditure" restrictions—the more lenient standard of review applicable to contribution limitations was used to assess the constitutionality of this entire package of soft-money restrictions. Applying that standard, the *McConnell* Court upheld the restrictions, concluding that there was "substantial evidence to support Congress' determination that large soft-money contributions to national political parties give rise to corruption and the appearance of corruption." Id. at 154.

Restrictions on Judicial Elections

Some states provide for judicial elections. The Court has taken a somewhat more solicitous approach to laws that restrict the financing of judicial campaigns. Although such restrictions are subject to strict scrutiny review, that standard is more easily met in this context than it is in the context of campaign financing for political office. Thus, in *Williams-Yulee v. Florida Bar*, 575 U.S. 433 (2015), the Court found that a law that prohibited candidates for elective judicial office from personally soliciting donations "advances the State's compelling interest in preserving public confidence in the integrity of the judiciary, and it does so through means narrowly tailored to avoid unnecessarily abridging speech. This is therefore one of the rare cases in which a speech restriction withstands strict scrutiny." Id. at 444. In so concluding, the Court explained that its decisions restricting campaign financing in the context of political elections had little bearing on the resolution of the question presented here:

> [A] State's interest in preserving public confidence in the integrity of its judiciary extends beyond its interest in preventing the appearance of corruption in legislative and executive elections. . . . States may regulate judicial elections differently than they regulate political elections, because the role of judges differs from the role of politicians. Politicians are expected to be appropriately responsive to the preferences of their supporters. Indeed, such "responsiveness is key to the very concept of self-governance through elected officials." The same is not true of judges. In deciding cases, a judge is not to follow the preferences of his supporters or provide any special consideration to his campaign donors. A judge instead must "observe the utmost fairness," striving to be "perfectly and completely independent, with nothing to influence or control him but God and his conscience." Address of John Marshall, in Proceedings and Debates of the Virginia State Convention of 1829–1830. . . . [T]herefore, our precedents applying the First Amendment to political elections have little bearing on the issues here.

Id. at 446-447 (internal citations omitted).

Restrictions on the Initiative Process

Most state laws are enacted through a process that involves a measure's being approved by the state's legislature and signed by the governor. However, under the so-called initiative process, laws in some states may be enacted directly by the people who vote to approve or reject a proposed measure that gathered enough signatures to appear on the state-wide election ballot. The Constitution is neutral with respect to whether a state may implement a ballot initiative process, and if a state chooses to adopt such a process, it retains "considerable leeway to protect the integrity and reliability of the initiative process." *Buckley v. American Constitutional Law Foundation*, 525 U.S. 182, 191 (1999). However, to the extent that state restrictions on the initiative process interfere with political expression, those restrictions are subject to strict scrutiny under the First Amendment. Id. at 191 & n.12. We have already noted that state-imposed contribution limitations in this context are subject to First Amendment scrutiny. *Citizens Against Rent Control v. Berkeley*, 454 U.S. 290 (1981). Similarly, certain restrictions on the process through which a measure qualifies for the ballot may also be subjected to strict scrutiny if those restrictions limit core political speech.

The two leading cases are *Meyer v. Grant*, 486 U.S. 414 (1988), and *Buckley v. American Constitutional Law Foundation*, supra. In *Meyer*, the Court invalidated a ban on the use of paid petition circulators, concluding that the ban unconstitutionally diminished core political speech by inhibiting the ability of the measure's supporters to communicate their message. Id. at 422-423. The state's justifications for this imposition—promoting grass roots support for initiatives and leveling the playing field—did not survive the standards of strict scrutiny. Id. at 425-428. In *Buckley*, the Court also applied strict scrutiny to invalidate three restrictions on the signature-gathering process: a requirement that petition circulators be registered voters, a requirement that they wear personal identification badges displaying their names, and a reporting requirement that mandated disclosure of each circulator's name, address, and the total amount paid to that circulator. The Court found that each of these requirements restricted political speech by substantially diminishing the number of persons willing to circulate petitions, thus reducing the initiative's proponents' ability to convey their message. The Court further concluded that the state's primary justification for these measures—protecting the integrity of the initiative process—was either inadequately advanced or could be served by less restrictive means. *Buckley*, supra, 525 U.S. at 195-196, 203-204. The *Buckley* Court did conclude, however, that a state may "legitimately require[] sponsors of ballot initiatives to disclose who pays petition circulators, and how much." Id. at 205. But see *Doe v. Reed*, 561 U.S. 186 (2010) (state law that mandates public disclosure of the names of referendum signers does not facially violate the First Amendment).

§8.3.6 Commercial Speech

At one time, commercial speech—i.e., speech whose purpose is to propose a commercial transaction—was completely unprotected by the First Amendment. In essence, commercial speech was equated with commercial activity. As a result, federal, state, and local governments were free to restrict commercial speech to the same extent they could restrict commercial activity. In *Valentine v. Chrestensen*, 316 U.S. 52 (1942), for example, the Court saw no constitutional objection to a content-based ordinance that completely prohibited distribution of leaflets advertising a for-profit exhibition of a submarine. The state was free to regulate this "occupation" without reference to any countervailing First Amendment concerns. Id. at 54.

The Court's categorical exclusion of commercial speech from the protection of the First Amendment was eventually criticized, then limited, and finally rejected. *Cammarano v. United States*, 358 U.S. 498, 514 (1959) (Douglas, J., concurring); *Bigelow v. Virginia*, 421 U.S. 809 (1975); *Virginia Bd. of Pharmacy v. Virginia Consumer Council*, 425 U.S. 748 (1976). As will be developed below, the Court eventually adopted a type of mid-level scrutiny to measure the constitutionality of content-based restrictions on commercial speech. More recently, however, the Court seems to be moving toward a standard akin to strict scrutiny. See *Sorrell v. IMS Health Inc.*, 564 U.S. 552 (2011).

The Definition of Commercial Speech

The mere fact that a speaker seeks to profit from expressive activity, however, does not necessarily transform that activity into commercial speech. For example, a good many motion pictures are made for the primary purpose of economic gain. Yet motion pictures are not automatically treated as commercial speech. *Joseph Burstyn, Inc. v. Wilson*, 343 U.S. 496, 501 (1952). Nor are books or newspapers, most of which are published with a profit motive, deemed to involve commercial speech. *New York Times v. Sullivan*, 376 U.S. 254, 266 (1964); *Smith v. California*, 361 U.S. 147, 150 (1959). With respect to these media, the profit motive usually runs parallel with an expressive content that is not necessarily commercial. Thus, a movie made for profit may tell the story of a little pig and her friends on the farm. It is that expressive content that defines the character of the speech.

The Court has had difficulty coming up with a satisfactory definition of commercial speech. It has variously described commercial speech as "expression related *solely* to the economic interests of the speaker and its audience," *Central Hudson Gas & Elec. v. Public Serv. Comm'n*, 447 U.S. 557, 561 (1980) (emphasis supplied), or as "speech which *does* 'no more than propose a commercial transaction,'" *Virginia Bd. of Pharmacy v. Virginia Consumer Council*, 425 U.S. 748, 762 (1976) (emphasis supplied). More recently it has sought to narrow the definition by stating that "the proposal of a commercial transaction [is] '*the* test for identifying commercial speech.'" *City of Cincinnati v. Discovery Network, Inc.*, 507 U.S. 410, 423 (1993) (emphasis in original). Yet none of these descriptions is meant to be technical; rather, they provide a common-sense basis for determining whether any speech at issue can be deemed commercial. Essentially, if the *purpose and content* of a message, taken as a whole, are "strictly business"—i.e., designed to propose or facilitate a commercial transaction—then the speech conveying that message is commercial. *Friedman v. Rogers*, 440 U.S. 1, 11 (1979). If not, the commercial label may be inappropriate.

Price advertising for a specific product is an obvious instance of this category, just as political advertising, even when it seeks monetary contributions, is not. The former invites the listener or reader to buy a product; the latter invites the recipient to invest in a political debate. Between these alternatives are several subtle variations in which the invitation to transact business may not be explicit, but is, nonetheless, at the heart of the speech; or in which that invitation is so closely tied to a matter of public import as to negate any inference that the speech is merely commercial; or in which clearly commercial speech is combined with speech that is noncommercial in nature. There is no precise test for measuring these variations, and, unfortunately, the Court often applies the "commercial speech" label in a question-begging fashion. As mere mortals, however, we must assess the facts of each case with an eye toward discovering the precise speech values at stake. Common sense is often the key.

EXAMPLE

Example 8-S

Mercury, Inc., is in the business of producing and marketing an extensive line of athletic shoes and apparel. The company's logo is a slashing bolt of lightning; its motto is "Your turn." Currently Mercury is running three different types of advertisements on television. The first features a well-known professional basketball player. In the ad, he talks about the special line of shoes Mercury has developed for him. As the ad ends, he holds one of the shoes toward the camera and says, "Your turn." The second ad features a series of visually stunning vignettes of athletes engaged in fierce competition. The only direct allusion to Mercury comes at the end of the ad, with a cut to a graphic of the Mercury logo and motto. The third ad features scenes of several young girls involved in different sports. The voice-over talks about the importance of athletic competition for young girls, stressing such things as building self-esteem, avoiding teen pregnancy, achieving good grades, and maintaining personal health. The ad ends with the same graphic of the Mercury logo and motto. Which, if any, of these ads is commercial speech?

EXPLANATION

Explanation

The first advertisement is commercial speech. Although the celebrity does not expressly invite the viewer to purchase the shoes, the message of the commercial is plainly to propose a commercial transaction: Buy these shoes. Nor is there any doubt that the purpose of this ad is to promote sales of the new line of shoes. In short, there is a common-sense congruity between content and purpose, both being "strictly business."

The second advertisement is more subtle in its sales pitch. Standing alone, the vignettes propose no business transaction. They are artistic depictions of athleticism. As such, they should be entitled to the full protection of the First Amendment. But does the juxtaposition of the vignettes with the Mercury logo and motto alter this conclusion? In other words, does the commercial character of this advertisement overwhelm the artistic character? Probably so. When one considers both the implicit message created by the juxtaposition and the clear overall purpose to promote the Mercury label, a conclusion that the advertisement as a whole is commercial speech seems sensible. In *Board of Trustees of the State University of New York v. Fox*, 492 U.S. 469 (1989), for example, the Court held that the presence of noncommercial speech at a commercial Tupperware party—the speech involved financial responsibility and efficient homemaking—did not sanitize the commercial nature of the enterprise. The party was in essence a sales pitch. Id. at 473-475. Moreover, the commercial and noncommercial aspects of the speech at the party were not "inextricably intertwined" such that the one could not be communicated without the other. Id.

The third advertisement is more subtle still. It does promote the Mercury company, but it does so only by associating the company with what is in essence a public service announcement. There is no direct sales pitch. And although Mercury may profit from this advertised association, that does not necessarily transform the communication into commercial speech. In *Bigelow v. Virginia*, 421 U.S. 809, 822 (1975), for example, the Court held that the for-profit aspects of an advertisement for abortion services did not transform the ad into commercial speech, since the advertisement also included noncommercial information of "public interest" regarding the general availability of abortions. The third Mercury ad likewise contains information of public interest. Arguably, therefore, this ad is not commercial speech. The proposal of a commercial transaction, if any, is at best an indirect product of the public service provided by the message. On the other hand, the noncommercial and commercial aspects of the ad are not inextricably intertwined. The importance of girls' participating in athletics can be communicated without any reference to Mercury. One could certainly argue, therefore, that the use of a public service message as a prologue to the real ad—the familiar logo and motto—should not be allowed to transform the commercial nature of this ad into a more protected form of speech. Yet if one takes the latter approach, a television documentary on world hunger might be relegated to the category of commercial speech by virtue of the fact that it is sponsored by General Foods Corporation. Ultimately, you must decide whether the third ad is closer to the Tupperware party in *Fox* or the abortion ad in *Bigelow*. The "correct" answer is at best elusive.

The foregoing examples should illustrate that commercial speech is relatively easy to spot in those situations in which the "strictly business" aspect of the speech is obvious and is not interwoven with other types of speech—e.g., the free-standing offer to sell or purchase goods or services for a fee, the publication of prices, and so on. As the content or context of the message becomes more ambiguous and more complex, the commercial components of the speech may be outweighed by First Amendment concerns that require a more exacting level of scrutiny. The only measure here is one of careful judgment, common sense, and effective argument.

The Rationale for Protecting Commercial Speech

Having defined commercial speech (to the extent a definition is possible), we must next examine the constitutional standard against which restrictions on commercial speech are measured. The two leading cases are *Virginia Board of Pharmacy v. Virginia Consumer Council*, 425 U.S. 748 (1976), and *Central Hudson Gas & Electric v. Public Service Commission*, 447 U.S. 557 (1980). The first established commercial speech as a constitutionally protected form of speech and provided a rationale for that protection; while the second examined the law that had developed under *Virginia Board* and organized that law into a test for measuring the constitutionality of laws restricting commercial speech.

At issue in *Virginia Board* was a state law that prohibited licensed pharmacists from publishing the prices of prescription drugs. The prohibited speech was commercial. As the Court phrased it, "Our pharmacist does not wish to editorialize on any subject, cultural, philosophical, or political. . . . The 'idea' he wishes to communicate is simply this: 'I will sell you the X prescription drug at the Y price.'" 425 U.S. at 761. The question before the Court was whether the commercial character of this speech automatically divested it of the protections of the First Amendment.

The Court examined this question from three perspectives: the advertiser, the consumer, and society at large. As to the first, the mere fact that the speaker had an economic motivation did not deprive the speech of First Amendment protection. In numerous other contexts, speech that was economically motivated was, nonetheless, protected—labor disputes being a prime example. Id. at 762-763. Second, "[a]s to the particular consumer's interest in the free flow of commercial information, that interest may be as keen, if not keener by far, than his interest in the day's most urgent political debate." Id. at 763. The Court noted that "the poor, the sick, and particularly the aged" would find this information not only useful, but perhaps critically important. Id. at 763-764. Finally, from the perspective of society at large, much commercial advertising contains information of interest to the general public, and, even more importantly, the free flow of commercial information is indispensable to making intelligent economic choices in our free enterprise economy. Id. at 764-765. In short, commercial speech plays a vital role within our socioeconomic system, and, as a consequence, such speech is entitled to the protections of the First Amendment.

In holding that the First Amendment protects commercial speech, the Court did not completely insulate commercial speech from governmental regulation. For example, the Court saw "no obstacle to a State's dealing effectively with" the problem of "false or misleading" advertising. Id. at 771-772. Similarly, the Court emphasized that the price advertisements at issue before it did not propose transactions that were "illegal in any way." Id. at 772. The Court in *Virginia Board* did not, however, propose any standard for measuring the constitutionality of restrictions on commercial speech that is not false or misleading and that does not propose an illegal transaction. Some Justices and commentators have taken this to mean that commercial speech not falling into either of the latter categories should be fully protected. See *44 Liquormart, Inc. v. Rhode Island,* 517 U.S. 484, 518 (1996) (Thomas, J., concurring). The Court, however, has not adopted this view.

The Central Hudson *Test*

Laws that regulate commercial speech are now measured under the *Central Hudson* test, a "four-part analysis" described by the Court in *Central Hudson Gas & Electric v. Public Service Commission,* supra, 447 U.S. at 561-566. The test is essentially a modified version of mid-level scrutiny. Under the first part of the test, one asks whether the commercial speech at issue is either misleading or related to an unlawful activity. If the speech falls into either of these categories, the First Amendment offers no protection for the speech, and the government may regulate or even prohibit that speech entirely. Thus, a law that prohibits newspapers from running advertisements for prostitution would be upheld without resort to First Amendment analysis (assuming prostitution is illegal within the jurisdiction). If, however, the commercial speech is neither misleading nor related to unlawful activity, the government may regulate the speech only if three additional standards are satisfied:

- The government interest in doing is substantial;
- The regulation directly advances that interest; *and*
- A more limited restriction on speech will not serve that interest.

In *Central Hudson,* for example, public utilities were banned from advertising to promote the use of electricity. Since the ban was not directed toward advertisements that were misleading or that promoted unlawful activity, the constitutionality of the ban depended on the satisfaction of the above three standards.

The substantial governmental interest requirement invites a value judgment regarding the relative importance of the governmental interest. This prong can be satisfied by any nontrivial governmental interest. In *Central Hudson,* the interests in energy conservation and the maintenance of a fair utility rate structure were both deemed substantial. More generally, laws designed to protect the health, safety, or welfare of citizens and residents will easily meet this standard. If, however, the Court deems the asserted interest to be illusory or a post hoc rationalization, this element will not be satisfied. *Linmark Assoc., Inc. v. Township of Willingboro*, 431 U.S. 85 (1977) (record did not support government's claim that ordinance was adopted to decrease white flight). Few laws are struck down for failure to satisfy the substantial governmental interest requirement.

The third and fourth requirements of *Central Hudson* measure the "fit" of the law with the interest it is said to promote. Under the directly advances requirement, a regulation of commercial speech will not be upheld if it is either ineffective or remote in sustaining the government's interest. There is no mathematical measure for this requirement. The *Central Hudson* Court found that the ban on promotional advertising did directly advance the state's interest in energy conservation, citing what the Court perceived as an "immediate connection between advertising and demand for electricity." 447 U.S. at 569. However, the connection between promotional advertising and the goal of maintaining a fair rate structure was deemed far too speculative. Id. There was simply no showing that increased demand would alter the fairness of the rate structure.

The fourth element requires that the law be narrowly tailored to advance the government's interest. If the law is perceived as excessively sweeping in its coverage or if there are other equally effective, but substantially less speech-restrictive alternatives, the law will not be upheld. The advertising ban in *Central Hudson* was struck down under this standard, since the ban prohibited the promotion of even energy-efficient uses of electricity—i.e., it was broader than necessary to advance the goal of energy conservation, and there were less speech-restrictive alternatives to a complete ban on all promotional advertising. This fourth element does not, however, require that the state employ the "least restrictive means." *Board of Trustees of the State Univ. of N.Y. v. Fox*, 492 U.S. 469, 475-481 (1989). Rather, the standard is one of reasonable fit, a measure that is more flexible than least restrictive means, but less deferential than rational basis. *Florida Bar v. Went for It, Inc.*, 515 U.S. 618 (1995).

As a general matter, the Court has not been consistent in the manner in which it has applied the *Central Hudson* standards. At times, the Court has used a "reasonableness" overlay to permit states broader leeway in the regulation of commercial speech, while at other times, the Court has approached the standards as creating a strong presumption against such regulations. Thus, the Court's relatively straightforward application of the "four-part analysis" in *Central Hudson* should not lead you to conclude that this test has led to obvious results or even to a coherent body of results. As was true in the context of equal protection, mid-level scrutiny is somewhat more malleable than its strict scrutiny and rational basis counterparts, and the commercial speech case law bears this out.

EXAMPLE

Example 8-T

Puerto Rico permits gambling in licensed casinos. While the casinos are allowed to advertise to promote tourism, they are not allowed to engage in promotional advertising "to the public of Puerto Rico." The purpose of this limitation is to reduce the demand for gambling by Puerto Rican residents and to thereby protect their health, safety, and welfare. More specifically, the goal of the limitation is to prevent increases in local crime, such as prostitution and public corruption; to avoid the infiltration of organized crime; and to preserve the moral and cultural identity of Puerto Rico. Is this limitation a legitimate regulation of commercial speech?

EXPLANATION

Explanation

The answer depends on the rigor with which one applies the *Central Hudson* test. The first two steps in the analysis would be noncontroversial. Since the ban applies to advertisements that are neither misleading nor related to unlawful activities, Puerto Rico could not premise its defense of the regulation on this first element of the test. Similarly, there would be general agreement that the interests asserted by Puerto Rico are substantial. The prevention of crime is one of the paramount purposes of government. The difficulty arises in the application of the third and fourth elements. Does the regulation directly serve the interests asserted by Puerto Rico? And if so, would a more limited restriction on speech advance those interests equally well?

From a perspective that is more deferential to governmental prerogatives, one could argue that the advertising ban *directly advances* the interests asserted by the government. If, as was recognized in *Central Hudson*, advertising increases demand for a product, the ban on local advertising should prevent increased demand for casino gambling by residents, and the absence of that increased demand should diminish the pressure to commit those crimes associated with casino gambling. Next, since "some" advertising would diminish the effectiveness of the across-the-board ban, a more limited restriction on speech would not as adequately advance the government's interest. This is essentially the approach a five-person majority of the Court took in upholding such a ban in *Posadas de Puerto Rico Assocs. v. Tourism Co.*, 478 U.S. 328, 340-344 (1986).

On the other hand, from a more speech-protective perspective, the relationship between the government's aims and the advertising ban is "remote" at best. There is simply no way to know whether the ban will affect the amount of resident casino gambling, much less prevent in any significant way the types of crimes that are associated with casino gambling. Indeed, given the popularity of casino gambling and the fact that it will be promoted and developed for the tourist trade, the ban may be completely ineffective in reaching its goals. In addition, with respect to the fourth requirement, there are a number of less speech-restrictive ways in which Puerto Rico could advance its goals, among them an outright ban on casino gambling by residents. See *44 Liquormart, Inc. v. Rhode Island*, supra, 517 U.S. at 531-532 (a majority of the Court disapproves the *Posadas* analysis in two separate opinions).

The Court endorsed reasoning similar to that in the preceding paragraph when it held that a federal ban on casino advertising over the broadcast media could not be constitutionally applied to advertisements that were broadcast in a state where casino gambling was legal. *Greater New Orleans Broadcasting Assoc, Inc. v. United States*, 527 U.S. 173 (1999). Applying the "directly advance" element of *Central Hudson*, the Court noted that the government had failed to produce evidence that a ban on casino gambling advertising would actually reduce the demand for gambling and thereby ameliorate problems associated with gambling. Although the Court's holding did not rest on this "lack of evidence" point, the opinion did suggest that the government must do more than merely speculate about the potential relationship between an advertising ban and the interest the government seeks to promote. Id. at 189-190. The more fundamental flaw in this advertising ban, however, was the fact that it "and its attendant regulatory regime is so pierced by exemptions and inconsistencies that the Government cannot hope to exonerate it." Id. at 190. For example, the ban did not apply to gaming on Indian reservations. In essence, the lack of coherence in the ban made it impossible to conclude that it was properly tailored to advance the government's asserted interests. *Greater New Orleans Broadcasting* thus represents another example of the Court's recent move toward a stricter application of the *Central Hudson* test.

Although the *Central Hudson* test is easily described—at least as a verbal formula—its application remains subject to substantial variations, depending on the circumstances of the case and on one's perception of how strictly the test ought to be applied. However, it seems clear that the Court has moved toward a more speech-protective application of the test. In *44 Liquormart*, for example, it unanimously struck down a state law that banned the advertising of retail liquor prices. While there was no majority opinion, the overall tenor of the principal opinions reflected a relatively rigorous application of the *Central Hudson* standards. See also *Rubin v. Coors Brewing Co.*, 514 U.S. 476 (1995) (striking down federal ban on the disclosure of alcohol content on beer labels as not directly advancing government's interest in preventing strength wars).

EXAMPLE

Example 8-U

A state bar regulation prohibits personal injury lawyers from sending direct-mail solicitations to accident victims or their relatives for 30 days following the accident. The regulation is designed to protect the "flagging" reputation of the legal profession by preventing attorneys from engaging in a "deplorable" practice that intrudes on the "special vulnerability and private grief of victims or their families." Is this regulation constitutional under the First Amendment?

EXPLANATION

Explanation

We must first decide whether the state here is regulating *commercial speech*. Since direct-mail solicitations propose a commercial transaction between the lawyer and the potential client—essentially a business arrangement—the speech at issue is at least arguably commercial. Would the "commercial" label be appropriate, however, if the solicitation included language describing the legal rights of the victim, or explaining the importance of a prompt investigation or the wisdom of avoiding a precipitous settlement? Aren't the "solicitation" and the pertinent noncommercial information "inextricably intertwined," as was the case in *Bigelow v. Virginia?* Suppose, for example, that the solicitation arises out of an airline disaster. The airline will certainly procure legal counsel immediately and may even attempt to gain quick settlements. Under such circumstances, is the victim's interest in legal representation purely a commercial matter? In *Florida Bar v. Went for It, Inc.*, 515 U.S. 618, 622-623 (1995), a five-person majority concluded without any discussion that such direct-mail "advertisements" were commercial speech entitled only to "intermediate" scrutiny. The dissent objected that given the potential noncommercial overlay and the vital interest of victims in receiving that information, at the very least *Central Hudson* should be applied with additional rigor. Id. at 636-637.

Assuming the speech is commercial, we must next determine if the speech is either misleading or related to an illegal transaction. Since the state bar regulation draws no distinction between solicitations that are misleading and those that are not, or between legal and illegal transactions, the regulated speech cannot be characterized as either misleading or related to an illegal transaction. We must, therefore, apply the remaining three parts of the test described in *Central Hudson*.

Is the state's interest *substantial?* Certainly, the interest in enhancing the reputation of the legal profession by preventing members of that profession from engaging in an odious practice is nontrivial. Of course, this begs the question of whether direct-mail solicitations to the victims of a recent accident are odious. One's answer to that question depends on the relative importance one places on the information victims may receive from such solicitations. In other words, substantiality is premised on an assumption about the intrinsic value of the speech. The Court majority in *Florida Bar* concluded that the state's interest was substantial since, in general, states have a compelling interest in the practice of professions within their boundaries. Id. at 625. The dissent provided a more detailed discussion of the issue and concluded that the circularity of the state's argument was evidence that the regulation was "censorship pure and simple." Id. at 640. Thus, for the dissent, the element of substantiality was not satisfied.

Whether the regulation *directly advances* the state's interest depends on proof of the relationship between means and ends. If the state can establish that direct-mail solicitations of accident victims harm the reputation of the legal profession, then it would follow that a ban on such solicitations would ameliorate that harm. In *Florida Bar*, the majority and the dissent disagreed over whether the proof on this point was adequate, the majority finding that it was (id. at 627-629) and the dissent finding that it was not. Id. at 640-641.

Finally, the regulation must be *narrowly tailored* to advance the established purpose. The standard here is one of *reasonable fit*. Clearly there are numerous other ways to overcome the "ambulance chasing" image of lawyers. The state bar could thus place restrictions on the content of the direct mailings to ensure that any solicitation is consistent with professional standards. The majority in *Florida Bar* seemed to soft-pedal this issue by taking a relatively deferential approach to the judgment of the state bar. The limited temporal scope of the rule, combined with other channels of communication through which victims could learn of their rights, convinced the majority that the fit between the means and the end was reasonable. The dissent, on the other hand, argued that the regulation cast a broad net that captured commercial as well as noncommercial speech, thereby establishing the unreasonableness of the fit between means and ends.

This last example highlights what the Court has described as "the difficulty of drawing bright lines that will clearly cabin commercial speech in a distinct category." *City of Cincinnati v. Discovery Network, Inc.*, 507 U.S. 410, 419 (1993). Because commercial speech ostensibly receives only mid-level scrutiny, the inability to distinguish commercial from noncommercial speech threatens to dilute the protection afforded noncommercial speech. It is perhaps in response to this danger that the Court in recent years has narrowed the definition of commercial speech and at the same time strengthened the rigor with which the *Central Hudson* test is applied. See *Thompson v. Western States Medical Center*, 535 U.S. 357 (2002) (striking down federal ban on advertising designed to promote the sale of compounded drugs by pharmacies); *Lorillard Tobacco Co. v. Reilly*, 533 U.S. 525 (2001) (striking down state ban on cigar and smokeless tobacco advertising); *Greater New Orleans Broadcasting Ass'n, Inc. v. United States*, 527 U.S. 173 (1999) (striking down federal ban on broadcast advertising of casino gambling in those jurisdictions in which such gambling is legal). Moreover, several Justices have urged that truthful and nonmisleading commercial speech about lawful activities should be fully protected under the First Amendment. See *44 Liquormart, Inc. v. Rhode Island*, 517 U.S. 484, 518 (1996) (Thomas, J., concurring); *City of Cincinnati v. Discovery Network, Inc.*, supra, 507 U.S. at 431-438 (Blackmun, J., concurring). In a similar vein, the Court recently declined, at least for the time, to create a new category of "professional speech"—i.e., speech by licensed professionals who provide personal service to clients based on their expert knowledge—that would receive less First Amendment protection. *National Institute of Family and Life Advocates v. Becerra*, 585 U.S. 755, 766-773 (2018).

The trend toward imposing a strict scrutiny standard of review to assess the validity of commercial speech regulations continued in *Sorrell v. IMS Health Inc.*, 564 U.S. 552 (2011). There, a Vermont statute provided that state-regulated pharmacies "shall not [1] sell . . . regulated records containing prescriber-identifiable information, nor [2] permit the use of [such] records . . . for marketing or promoting a prescription drug, unless the prescriber consents." Id. at 558-559. The effect of this statute was to deprive pharmaceutical companies of data that could help them create better marketing strategies for the sale of patented drugs. Essentially, the pharmacies wanted to know the prescription patterns of individual doctors to tailor their sales pitch to each doctor's prescription practices. The Court first held that the regulation was content-based because it proscribed a particular category of speech—prescriber-identifiable information. Having so concluded, the Court then explained and reiterated that the regulation would be subject to "heightened judicial scrutiny." Id. at 557. Eventually, the Court arrived at the *Central Hudson* test but characterized that test as establishing the minimal standard a state would have to satisfy in the context of a commercial speech regulation. Id. at 571-572 ("State must show *at least* that the statute" meets the *Central Hudson* test) (emphasis supplied). Vermont attempted to meet that burden by showing that its law was designed "to protect medical privacy, including physician confidentiality, avoidance of harassment, and the integrity of the doctor-patient relationship." Id. at 572. The State also argued that the statute was "integral to the achievement of . . . improved public health and reduced healthcare costs." Id. The Court found that none of these interests was substantially advanced by what the Court characterized as a form of censorship of "disfavored speech." Id. at 577. Accordingly, it held the statute unconstitutional. In short, the opinion appeared to invite adoption of a strict scrutiny standard of review and, in practical effect, assessed the

Vermont law under a form of review that looked and operated much like strict scrutiny.

Mandatory Disclosure Requirements

Where the government has required that certain disclosures be made in the commercial speech setting, the Court has taken a more lenient approach than would otherwise be called for by *Central Hudson*, though the standard of review is by no means cursory. In *Zauderer v. Office of Disciplinary Counsel of Supreme Court of Ohio*, 471 U.S. 626 (1985), the Court upheld a state's right to discipline an attorney who had failed to make certain fee disclosures in ads he ran in local newspapers. Such disclosure requirements will be upheld if they: (1) apply only to "commercial advertising"; (2) require the disclosure only of "purely factual and uncontroversial information about the terms under which . . . services will be provided"; (3) are "reasonably related to the State's interest in preventing deception of consumers"; and (4) are not shown by the law's defender *not* to be "unjustified or unduly burdensome" (i.e., such measures will be presumed to be unjustified and unduly burdensome unless the state can show otherwise). Id. at 651. The Court has indicated that the "reasonably related" requirement will be met only if the harm the state is addressing is "potentially real not purely hypothetical," *Ibanez v. Florida Dep't of Business and Professional Regulation*, 512 U.S. 136, 146 (1994), and if the mandated disclosure is "no broader than reasonably necessary." *In re R.M.J.*, 455 U.S. 191, 203 (1982).

The Court recently addressed the constitutionality of such state-mandated disclosure requirements in *National Institute of Family and Life Advocates v. Becerra*, 585 U.S. 755 (2018), a case involving a California statute that required "crisis pregnancy centers"—i.e., clinics that primarily serve pregnant women—to provide certain public notices. Clinics that were state licensed had to notify women that California provides free or low-cost services, including abortions. This "licensed notice" had to be posted in the waiting room, printed and distributed to clients, or provided digitally at check-in. Centers that were not state licensed had to provide a government-drafted notice indicating that the facility was not licensed as a medical facility and that it has no medical providers. This "unlicensed notice" had to be conspicuously posted on site and included in all advertising materials. Depending on a county's population, the notices had to be in as many as 13 different languages. The purpose of this law was to "ensure that California residents make their personal reproductive health care decisions knowing their rights and the health care services available to them." Id. at 763. The Court held both notice requirements to be unconstitutional.

With respect to the "licensed notice" requirement, the Court held that the *Zauderer* standard was inapplicable here since the posted-notice mandate did not apply to commercial advertising as such, nor did it pertain to services that the *regulated center* was providing but rather to *state*-sponsored services that were available elsewhere. Nor was the requirement that these centers provide "information about . . . abortion, anything but an 'uncontroversial' topic." Id. at 769. In declaring the requirement to be unconstitutional, the Court, rather than applying strict scrutiny as one might have expected, invalidated the provision under an "intermediate scrutiny" standard. In doing so, it ruled that even if providing information about state-sponsored services qualifies as a "substantial state interest, the licensed notice is not sufficiently drawn to achieve it." Id. at 773. The measure was "wildly underinclusive," for it applied only to clinics that had the "primary purpose" of providing family planning. Id. at 774. It was also far more burdensome than necessary since the state could instead simply have launched its own public-information campaign, including posting information on public property near the crisis pregnancy centers. Id. at 775. The Court's use of intermediate rather than strict scrutiny may have been in response to an argument that the "professional speech" at issue here—i.e., speech by licensed professionals who provide personal service to clients based on their expert knowledge—should receive something less than strict scrutiny. While the Court said it had not found "a persuasive reason for treating professional speech as a unique category," id. at 773, by invoking only intermediate scrutiny here, it left the door open for a future Court to hold that this more deferential standard of review is all that is called for in cases involving restrictions on so-called professional speech.

Turning to the notice requirement imposed on unlicensed centers, the Court applied the *Zauderer* standard, even though this notice requirement did not apply only to the content of advertising materials. Instead, the statute also mandated that notice be posted conspicuously on site, both at the facility's entrance and in at least one waiting area. Since the latter postings have nothing to do with advertising, stricter scrutiny was arguably called for. But again, since the Court went on to invalidate the provision under a less demanding standard of review, though the choice of standards made no difference in this case, it could influence the approach taken in future cases where, as here, commercial and noncommercial speech are commingled. Under *Zauderer*, the Court quickly disposed of the "unlicensed notice" requirement, finding that the state had not carried its burden of proving that the notice was not "unjustified" and not "unduly burdensome." Instead, the state's attempted justification amounted to nothing "more than 'purely hypothetical.'" Id. at 776. The state also failed to carry its burden of showing that the requirement was not "unduly burdensome," particularly in those California counties where advertisement notices might have to be in as many as 13 different languages. Id. at 779. In striking down the provision, the Court left open the possibility that a "similar disclosure requirement that is better supported or less burdensome" might be upheld. Id.

§8.3.7 Sexually Explicit Speech—Obscenity and Pornography

Sexually explicit speech, whether it be in the form of visual depiction (live performances, motion pictures, photography, etc.) or verbal description (books, magazines, songs, etc.), has been relegated by the Court to a relatively low position in the First Amendment hierarchy. Various reasons have been asserted. Most typically, sexually explicit speech is said to contribute little or nothing to the exposition of ideas. Indeed, some would say that sexually explicit speech often conveys no ideas whatsoever, but merely operates as a sensual stimulus designed to generate an animalistic response. Critics have noted the obvious cultural bias in these assertions and suggest that the sexual content of speech should not diminish the protections of the First Amendment. See *Roth v. United States*, 354 U.S. 476, 508-514 (1957) (Douglas, J., and Black, J., dissenting). This more libertine attitude, however, has never commanded a majority of the Court.

A Definition of Obscenity

From a doctrinal perspective, a legal distinction is drawn between obscenity and pornography. Obscenity, which is defined below, is completely unprotected by the First Amendment, while pornography—i.e., sexually explicit speech that is not legally "obscene"—is entitled to constitutional protection. As you can imagine, the distinction between these categories is somewhat elusive, but quite important, since it often defines what separates the criminally punishable from the merely naughty.

After years of doctrinal confusion, the Court in *Miller v. California*, 413 U.S. 15 (1973), adopted the following test for defining obscenity:

> (a) whether "the average person, applying contemporary community standards" would find that the work, taken as a whole, appeals to the prurient interest; (b) whether the work depicts or describes, in a patently offensive way, sexual conduct specifically defined by the applicable state law; and (c) whether the work, taken as a whole, lacks serious literary, artistic, political, or scientific value.

Id. at 24 (internal citations omitted). Note that the complete focus of this definition is on the nature and quality of the speech, not on its intent, effect, or dangerous tendency. No clear and present danger of anything need be established—no actual malice, no substantial relationship, nothing. Rather, the harm is assumed to be implicit in the nature of the speech itself. The "doctrinal test" for the regulation of obscenity, therefore, simply defines a category of speech that falls completely outside the First Amendment. If the speech fits the definition, it may be regulated without further recourse to constitutional analysis. Understanding the definition is, therefore, critical.

The first two elements of the *Miller* definition are measured from the perspective of contemporary community standards, which are themselves defined as the standards of an average person residing within the *local,* not the national, community. These local standards, therefore, are largely a product of the geographic reach of the jury pool and of the perceptions of the selected venire. Those perceptions can be informed by the evidence at trial as well as by the court's instructions to the jury. However, the prosecution is not required to introduce expert testimony on the question of local standards.

In applying contemporary community standards, one must assess two things: whether the material appeals to the prurient interest in sex and whether it is patently offensive. Appeal to the prurient interest connotes the promotion of lasciviousness or lustful desire. The standard is satisfied if a reasonable juror, applying contemporary community standards, could conclude that the material induces inappropriate sexual longing—obviously a subjective and elastic standard. Similarly, whether the material describes or depicts sexual conduct in a patently offensive manner requires an equally subjective judgment by this same reasonable juror. Thus, what is quite acceptable in a large, urban setting may well be "patently offensive" to the members of a small, insular community.

The "prurient interest" and "patently offensive" elements of *Miller* are tempered somewhat by the further requirement that the material be fairly classifiable as "hard-core" pornography—i.e., the graphic and explicit representation of ultimate sex acts and the like. 413 U.S. at 25. In other words, the sensitivity of the local community is moderated by a nationally applicable minimum of tolerance. For example, in *Jenkins v. Georgia,* 418 U.S. 153 (1974), the Court held that a local jury could not, consistent with the *Miller* standard, conclude that the Mike Nichols film *Carnal Knowledge* was patently offensive. Although sex was the theme of the film, the treatment of the subject was far removed from the graphic style of hard-core pornography, thus precluding a finding that the film was obscene. Id. at 160-161.

The third element of *Miller*—whether the material lacks serious literary, artistic, political, or scientific value—is measured by a *national* reasonable person standard for which expert testimony is permissible, but not required. *Pope v. Illinois,* 481 U.S. 497 (1987). This standard quite often trumps the local community's perceptions of prurient interest and patent offensiveness. In *Luke Records, Inc. v. Navarro,* 960 F.2d 134 (11th Cir.), *cert. denied,* 506 U.S. 1022 (1992), for example, a district court found that 2 Live Crew's recording of "As Nasty as They Wanna Be" was obscene under *Miller,* but the court of appeals reversed on the ground that the state had failed to meet its burden of proof on the third element of the *Miller* test. The state's only evidence of obscenity was the recording itself. The defense, however, presented expert testimony by two pop music critics and a political science professor, each of whom endorsed the artistic and political value of the recording.

Note also that in determining whether the first and third elements of *Miller* are satisfied, the material must be "taken as a whole." That is, the work as a whole must appeal to a prurient interest in sex and must lack serious value. Therefore, an allegedly obscene segment of a larger artistic endeavor cannot be excised from the whole. Thus, in *Navarro,* the lyrics of "As Nasty as They Wanna Be" could not be isolated from the accompanying music. At the same time, an otherwise obscene motion picture will not be saved by a scene in which a couple fornicates while listening to a medley of John Philip Sousa's greatest hits, since the work as a whole must have serious value. The distinction is between the sham inclusion of "art" and a fully integrated artistic endeavor.

EXAMPLE

Example 8-V

The newly released film *Terminator* 2020: *A Violent Odyssey* is a box office smash. It stars Arnold Swartzenlocker, the popular bodybuilding gobernator hunk, in a sci-fi thriller about the past, the future, and a lot of stuff in between. In one scene, Arnold runs around naked, and in another, he makes love to an androgynous android. The scene, however, is filmed in a manner that makes it impossible to see anything but two large shapes bouncing around in what appears to be a rather large hamster habitat. The film does have plenty of violence though, including one scene of graphic and gruesome mayhem, at the end of which Arnold reprises his famous line, "I have every intention of returning to this locale, if the opportunity presents itself." The film is rated PG-13. The city attorney for the small town of Omigosh went to the local premiere of *Terminator* 2020. He has now charged the owner of the theater with violation of the town's anti-obscenity ordinance. Consistent with the *Miller* test, may a jury convict on these charges?

EXPLANATION

Explanation

Most likely not. Although the Court has adopted a local community standard to measure prurience and patent offensiveness, there remains a national minimum standard of explicitness that even a sensitive local community must tolerate. Regardless of what one thinks of Arnold's film, it is simply not the type of material the Court was considering when it created the *Miller* standard. Although the film may appeal to various base instincts, nothing in the above description suggests that the appeal is to a prurient interest in sex. Nor does the patent offensiveness of the film have anything to do with the graphic depiction of sexual conduct. Violence, no matter how gruesome, is not obscene (in the absence of a graphic sexual context).

Similarly, nudity, in and of itself, is not obscene. *Schad v. Borough of Mount Ephraim*, 452 U.S. 61, 66 (1981). In short, the local community standards, even if offended, would quite likely be trumped by the national minimum of tolerance. Finally, although one need not decide the point, given Arnold's earlier work, it seems quite likely that, taken as a whole, the film has tremendous literary, artistic, political, and even scientific value. Two thumbs up.

Example 8-W

Imagine, however, a somewhat different film—*Penetrator 2020: A Sexual Oddity*. It stars Jonny Hot, a cult hero among aficionados of pornography. The film has little plot. Mostly it is about sex, more sex, and even more sex, all of which is graphically portrayed in intimate detail. Several of the scenes are somewhat humorous as spoofs of popular sci-fi classics. But mostly the film is about Jonny Hot's never-ending sexual unions. Is this film obscene?

Explanation

Perhaps. *Penetrator* 2020 is surely meant to appeal to the viewer's interest in sex. Whether that interest is "prurient" will depend on the jury's perception of contemporary standards within the relevant local community. Similarly, patent offensiveness is also a question for the jury, applying contemporary community standards. However, the city's ordinance must have specifically defined the sexual conduct that allegedly is depicted in a patently offensive way. Moreover, in both determinations, the jury's judgment is limited by a national standard of minimum tolerance. But if the film can be fairly characterized as hard-core pornography—we would have to see it to know for sure—national standards will not trump the jury's determinations. Finally, the third element asks whether the work, taken as a whole, lacks serious literary, artistic, political, or scientific value. This is a national standard under which the jury would have to determine if the limited humor (or other production values) makes the film something other than raw, hard-core pornography.

It should be clear that the *Miller* definition of obscenity provides little more than a verbal screen for a highly subjective judgment. Justice Stewart's offhanded remark regarding obscenity—"I know it when I see it"—would seem to be equally as useful and, at the same time, less legally pretentious. *Jacobellis v. Ohio*, 378 U.S. 184, 197 (1964). Nevertheless, the *Miller* three-part formula remains both the definition and the standard for the regulation of obscenity.

Because speech that qualifies as obscene under *Miller* is completely unprotected by the First Amendment, it may, therefore, be suppressed through either the threat of subsequent punishment or the imposition of prior restraints. As to the former, there is a narrow (and shrinking) constitutional privilege for the possession of obscene material within one's own home. *Stanley v. Georgia*, 394 U.S. 557 (1969); but see *Osborne v. Ohio*, 495 U.S. 103 (1990) (refusing to extend the privilege to the possession of child pornography). Beyond that limited privilege, however, the government need only comply with applicable principles of criminal procedure to punish the production or dissemination of obscene material. If the government attempts to secure a prior restraint against the dissemination of obscene speech, the government must provide a prompt hearing in which it carries the burden of establishing obscenity. *Freedman v. Maryland*, 380 U.S. 51, 58-59 (1965). If the hearing is administrative in nature, the prior restraint may be continued only if the finding of obscenity is promptly affirmed by a judicial body. Id. See § 8.2.4.

Nonobscene Sexually Explicit Speech — Pornography

Pornography—i.e., communicative material that is sexually explicit but not legally obscene—is speech within the meaning and protections of the First Amendment. This remains true regardless of how "shabby, offensive, or even ugly" one may find it. *United States v. Playboy Entertainment Group Inc.*, 529 U.S. 803, 826 (2000). Thus, content-based restrictions on pornography will generally be evaluated under the traditional standards of strict scrutiny. Id. at 813.

In *Playboy Entertainment Group*, for example, the Court struck down a federal statute that, as a practical matter, required cable channels primarily dedicated to sexually oriented programming to limit their transmissions to hours when children were unlikely to be viewing (i.e., between 10 P.M. and 6 A.M.). The regulation was content based since it was triggered by the subject matter of the material being transmitted. Consequently, the government was required to establish that the regulation was narrowly tailored to advance a compelling government interest. The government's goal was to prevent viewing of sexually oriented material by children whose parents might object to such viewing. The problem it sought to address arose from the possibility that even nonsubscribers to a sexually oriented channel might occasionally experience "signal bleed," allowing the viewer to receive all or part of the programming. In the Court's view, however, the government failed to quantify the actual extent of the problem generated by signal bleed, and, in any event, had not selected the least restrictive means of accomplishing its goal. As to the latter, cable customers could be provided with blocking devices to prevent all transmission of the unwanted signal, leaving the channels free to transmit twenty-four hours a day. Having failed to satisfy this element of strict scrutiny, the statute was declared unconstitutional.

In two contexts, however, the Court has not applied strict scrutiny to content-based restrictions on nonobscene pornography. The first involves zoning laws that regulate the location of pornographic movie houses and bookstores. In essence, cities are free to impose restrictions on the location of such businesses, either forcing their dispersal to avoid creating a "red-light" district, *Young v. American Mini Theatres, Inc.*, 427 U.S. 50 (1976), or requiring their concentration to avoid the spread of perceived blight, *City of Renton v. Playtime Theatres, Inc.*, 475 U.S. 41 (1986). In short, as long as the city does not completely suppress so-called adult entertainment, it may impose special zoning requirements on purveyors of the medium. See *City of Los Angeles v. Alameda Books, Inc.*, 535 U.S. 425 (2002) (upholding city ordinance that prohibits the establishment of more than one "adult" entertainment business in a single building). Quite obviously neither type of regulation would be acceptable if it were applied to political speech. A zoning ordinance that required politically oriented bookstores to locate no closer than 1,000 feet from one another to avoid potential clashes between patrons would be subjected to the strictest scrutiny and easily struck down.

The second non-strict-scrutiny context involves a form of nonobscene pornography that is completely unprotected by the First Amendment. In *New York v. Ferber*, 458 U.S. 747 (1982), the Court held that the distribution of child pornography—i.e., sexually explicit motion pictures or photographs that are not legally obscene but that depict *actual children* engaged in sex acts—could be subject to criminal prosecution. The Court reasoned that given the "modest, if not de minimis," value of the speech—the portrayal of children engaged in lewd sexual conduct—and the substantial harm and abuse suffered by the actual children who are being photographed, "it is permissible to consider these materials as without the protection of the First Amendment." Id. at 764. Child pornography, therefore, even when not technically obscene under *Miller*, is entitled to no protection under the First Amendment. More recently, the Court explained that the rationale for treating child pornography as an unprotected category of speech was premised, in part, on the relationship between that speech and obscenity, which itself is unprotected, and, in part, because the "market for child pornography was 'intrinsically related' to the underlying abuse [of children] and was therefore 'an integral part of the production of such materials, an activity illegal throughout the Nation.'" *United States v. Stevens*, 559 U.S. 460, 471 (2010).

Example 8-X

The Child Pornography Prevention Act of 1996 (CPPA) makes it unlawful for anyone to distribute "any visual depiction, including any photograph, film, picture, or computer-generated image or picture that is, or appears to be, of a minor engaging in sexually explicit conduct." In other words, the CPPA prohibits the distribution of "virtual" as well as actual child pornography. Virtual child pornography could be created by adults portraying children, by animation, or by computer graphics. The statutory proscription does not require the government to establish that the materials at issue are obscene under *Miller v. California*. To the extent that it prohibits the distribution of nonobscene, virtual child pornography, does the CPPA violate the First Amendment?

Explanation

The key question is whether virtual child pornography, as defined by the CPPA, is unprotected under the First Amendment. The argument in favor of that view links the suppression of virtual child pornography to the rationale of *New York v. Ferber*. That rationale, however, focused on the fact that real children were abused in the making of actual child pornography. Distribution of such material caused harm to the child involved and also created an economic incentive for the future criminal exploitation of children. Because no actual children are used in the making of virtual child pornography, this rationale is not directly applicable to the CPPA. Indeed, given the illegality of actual child pornography, the availability of virtual child pornography creates a disincentive to create the illegal product.

The government might also argue that the ban on virtual child pornography is necessary because access to such materials could encourage pedophiles to engage in illegal conduct. Yet such an argument runs afoul of the First Amendment principle that the mere tendency of speech to foster unlawful acts is an insufficient basis on which to ban the speech. By contrast, in *Ferber*, the child pornography and the underlying criminality were inextricably linked.

In *Ashcroft v. Free Speech Coalition*, 535 U.S. 234, 256 (2002), the Court held that the CPPA prohibition on virtual child pornography violated the First Amendment by abridging "the freedom to engage in a substantial amount of lawful speech." The Court distinguished *Ferber* on the grounds noted above and found the government's justifications for the ban inadequate in light of the breadth of the prohibition, which, the Court hinted, might have included acclaimed contemporary films such as *Traffic* and *American Beauty*, both of which included scenes that portrayed teens who "appear[ed] to be" engaged in "sexually explicit conduct." Id. at 246-248.

A year after the Court decided *Ashcroft v. Free Speech Coalition*, Congress enacted a new statute aimed at curbing the proliferation of child pornography. Rather than criminalizing the possession of such materials, the 2003 Exploitation of Children Today Act, 117 Stat. 650, made it a crime to "knowingly" advertise, promote, present, distribute, or solicit material (or purported material) that contains "a visual depiction of an actual minor engaging in sexually explicit conduct." The statute's definition of the relevant material precisely tracked that held to be constitutionally proscribable in

New York v. Ferber and *Miller v. California*. Since the act had been "carefully crafted" to punish only "offers to provide or requests to obtain child pornography . . . categorically excluded from the First Amendment," the Court in *United States v. Williams*, 553 U.S. 285 (2008) rejected a facial challenge to the act, holding that it was neither overbroad nor impermissibly vague. The Court agreed that there might be situations where protected First Amendment activity fell within the coverage of the act—e.g., a case involving "documentary footage of atrocities being committed in foreign countries, such as soldiers raping young children." Id. at 302. While "the existence of that exception would not establish that the statute is *substantially* overbroad," said the Court, it "could of course be the subject of an as-applied challenge." Id. at 302-303 (emphasis in original). See § 8.2.5.

Indecent or Vulgar Speech

The use of indecent or vulgar language is protected by the First Amendment as long as the context in which the language is used does not trigger some other limiting First Amendment principle. Thus, if, taken as a whole, the material in which the indecent language appears is obscene under the *Miller* test, the protection is lost. Similarly, if the indecent language is uttered in a context likely to cause a public disturbance, the "fighting words" doctrine may come into play. On the other hand, if the language is merely offensive or used in a context that is deemed socially inappropriate, the full protections of the First Amendment should apply. As we shall see, however, special rules apply to the use of indecent language in the broadcast media.

The leading indecent speech case is *Cohen v. California*, 403 U.S. 15 (1971). There, the defendant was convicted of disturbing the peace for wearing a jacket bearing the words "Fuck the Draft." At the time of the incident, the defendant was in the corridor of a county courthouse and in the presence of women and children. Although some observers might have been offended, there was no evidence of any potential altercation. The Court reversed the conviction. In so doing, it alluded to a fairly sophisticated model of speech:

> [M]uch linguistic expression serves a dual communicative function: it conveys not only ideas capable of relatively precise, detached explication, but otherwise inexpressible emotions as well. In fact, words are often chosen as much for their emotive as their cognitive force. We cannot sanction the view that the Constitution, while solicitous of the cognitive content of individual speech has little or no regard for that emotive function which practically speaking, may often be the more important element of the overall message sought to be communicated.

Id. at 26. Premised on this view, the Court held that a state is not empowered "to cleanse public debate to the point where it is grammatically palatable to the most squeamish among us. . . . For, while the particular four-letter word being litigated here is perhaps more distasteful than most others of its genre, it is nevertheless often true that one man's vulgarity is another's lyric." Id. at 25.

The Court's solicitude for lyrical vulgarity was less charitable in *FCC v. Pacifica Foundation*, 438 U.S. 726 (1978). There, the Court adopted a particularly squeamish approach to an afternoon radio broadcast of George Carlin's satirical monologue on "dirty words." Based on a listener's complaint, the Federal Communications Commission (FCC) issued a "declaratory order" against the station for having broadcast an "indecent" monologue at a time of day when children were in the audience. The order put the station on notice that any further similar broadcasts could subject it to sanctions, including license revocation. The Court upheld the constitutionality of the order based on a combination of factors. Chief among them were the more limited First Amendment protections accorded the broadcast media (see § 8.8); the fact that children were in the audience at the time the broadcast occurred; the relative modesty of the sanction imposed; and from the Court's perspective, the sheer offensiveness and de minimis value of the language used. Id. at 742-751. See also *Iancu v. Brunetti*, 588 U.S. 388, 396-399 (2019), id. at 400-401 (Roberts, C.J., concurring and dissenting); id. at 401 (Breyer, J., concurring and dissenting); id. at 409 (Sotomayor, J., & Breyer, J., concurring and dissenting) (nine Justices suggesting that the government's refusal to register trademarks that are obscene, vulgar, or profane would be constitutional, in part because such marks can still be used even if they are not registered).

Indecent Speech and the Internet

The Supreme Court has made it clear that the First Amendment applies with full force in the context of communications undertaken via the Internet. *Reno v. ACLU*, 521 U.S. 844, 869-870 (1997). As the *Reno* Court phrased it, "[O]ur cases provide no basis for qualifying the level of First Amendment scrutiny that should be applied to this medium." Id. at 870. In the context of sexually explicit materials, this means that restrictions on the communication of nonobscene "indecent" speech will be subject to the compelling state interest test, including the requirement that the government adopt the least restrictive means. Id. at 874. In short, the somewhat diluted First Amendment protections accorded to the broadcast media have no application to the Internet.

At issue in *Reno* were two provisions of the Communications Decency Act of 1996 (CDA). The first made it a crime to use any telecommunications device, including the Internet, for the knowing transmission of "obscene or indecent" materials to anyone under the age of 18. The second provision made it a crime to use a computer to send or display to a person under the age of 18 any "patently offensive" material involving "sexual or excretory activities or organs." Id. at 857-861. Both sections applied to all commercial and noncommercial uses of the Internet, including e-mail, chat rooms, and Web pages. The CDA qualified its criminal proscriptions by providing two affirmative defenses. The first required a showing by the party charged with a violation of the CDA that they had "taken, in good faith, reasonable, effective, and appropriate actions . . . to restrict access by minors" to the objectionable material, while the second was triggered if the party charged had controlled access by "requiring use of a verified credit card, debit account, adult access code, or adult personal identification number." Id. at 861.

The Court held that both proscriptions were unconstitutional to the extent that they prohibited the communication of nonobscene material. In large part, the Court's ruling stemmed from the CDA's failure to define its operative terms. Because of the potential elasticity of the terms "indecent" and "patently offensive," a person could not "confidently assume that a serious discussion about birth control practices, homosexuality, . . . or the consequences of prison rape would not violate the CDA." Id. at 871. Thus, "[g]iven the vague contours of the coverage of the statute, it unquestionably silences some speakers whose messages would be entitled to constitutional protection." Id. at 874. Later in the opinion, the Court reiterated this point by observing, "The general, undefined terms 'indecent' and 'patently offensive' cover large amounts of nonpornographic material with serious educational or other value." Id. at 877.

The Court did recognize that the government had a legitimate interest in protecting minors from certain nonobscene but sexually explicit material. Nonetheless, given that adults had a right of access to that very same material, the *Reno* Court held that the CDA was unconstitutional:

> We are persuaded that the CDA lacks the precision that the First Amendment requires when a statute regulates the content of speech. In order to deny minors access to potentially harmful speech, the CDA effectively suppresses a large amount of speech that adults have a constitutional right to receive and to address to one another. That burden on adult speech is unacceptable if less restrictive alternatives would be at least as effective in achieving the legitimate purpose that the statute was enacted to serve.

Id. at 874. In finding that there were less restrictive alternatives, the Court credited the district court's conclusion that "currently available *user-based* software suggests that a reasonably effective method by which *parents* can prevent their children from accessing sexually explicit and other material which *parents* may believe is inappropriate for their children will soon be widely available." Id. at 877 (emphasis in original). The Court also rejected the government's argument that the CDA's affirmative defenses operated to narrowly tailor the act's proscriptions. Among other things, the affirmative defenses were either technologically unavailable or, at least for noncommercial users, economically unfeasible.

In response to the Court's decision in *Reno*, Congress in 1998 passed the Child Online Protection Act (COPA). COPA prohibits any person from "knowingly and with knowledge of the character of the material, in interstate or foreign commerce by means of the World Wide Web, making any communication for commercial purposes that is available to any minor and that includes any material that is harmful to minors." 47 U.S.C. § 231(a)(1). The act defines "material that is harmful to minors" by reference to the *Miller* test for obscenity as adjusted for minors. Hence, part one of the COPA-*Miller* test measures legality by asking whether "the average person, applying contemporary community standards, would find, taking the material as a whole *and with respect to minors*, [that the material] is designed to appeal to, or is designed to pander to, the prurient interest. . . ." Id. at § 231(e)(6)(A) (emphasis supplied). Thus, COPA differs from the CDA in at least two significant ways: (1) by applying only to commercial uses of the Internet and (2) by defining the offending material under a variation of the *Miller* standard for obscenity.

In a facial challenge to COPA, filed a month before the statute was to go into effect, a federal district court enjoined its enforcement on the ground that the organizations challenging it had established a likelihood of success on the merits. The Third Circuit affirmed, concluding that the "contemporary community standards" element of COPA rendered the statute overbroad by giving local communities a right to trump a national dialogue. The Supreme Court reversed on narrow grounds:

> We hold only that COPA's reliance on community standards [as borrowed from *Miller*] to identify "material that is harmful to minors" does not *by itself* render the statute substantially overbroad for purposes of the First Amendment. We do not express any view as to whether COPA suffers from substantial overbreadth for other reasons, whether the statute is unconstitutionally vague, or whether the District Court correctly concluded that the statute likely will not survive strict scrutiny analysis once adjudication of the case is completed below.

Ashcroft v. ACLU, 535 U.S. 564, 585-586 (2002) (emphasis in original). Six members of the Court, comprised of the concurring and dissenting Justices, expressed concern that a local community standard as applied to the Internet might well run afoul of the First Amendment. See id. at 586 (O'Connor, J., concurring); id at 589 (Breyer, J., concurring); id. at 591 (Kennedy, J., Souter, J., and Ginsburg, J., concurring); and id. at 602 (Stevens, J., dissenting). Determination of that question was, according to all but Justice Stevens, premature in a facial challenge.

On remand, the Third Circuit again affirmed the district court's entry of a preliminary injunction. In so doing, the circuit court credited the district court's conclusion that the plaintiffs were likely to succeed on the merits since, among other things, the government had failed to rebut plaintiffs' plausible claim that the restrictions imposed by COPA were not the least restrictive means available to advance the government's interest in protecting minors from access to indecent materials on the Internet. *American Civil Liberties Union v. Ashcroft*, 322 F.3d 240, 266-271 (3d Cir. 2003). The Supreme Court affirmed, agreeing that the district court had not abused its discretion. *Ashcroft v. ACLU*, 542 U.S. 656 (2004). The primary alternative at issue was filtering software. The Court concluded that filters were "less restrictive" than the measures employed by COPA and suggested that filters "also may well be more effective than COPA." Id. at 667. The Court did not, however, rule that COPA was unconstitutional. Rather, it held that given the government's failure to rebut this specific contention by the plaintiffs, the issuance of a preliminary injunction was not an abuse of discretion. The government would remain free to challenge the availability and effectiveness of filters at a trial on the merits. On remand, the District Court, after a trial on the merits, then held COPA to be unconstitutional, ruling that the government had not carried its burden of showing COPA to be a more effective and less restrictive alternative for achieving the act's purposes than the use of filters and the government's promotion of them. See *American Civil Liberties Union v. Mukasey*, 534 F.3d 181 (3d Cir. 2008), *cert. denied*, 555 U.S. 1137 (2009).

Another decision in this area involved a facial challenge to the Children's Internet Protection Act (CIPA). *United States v. American Library Association*, 539 U.S. 194 (2003). At the heart of the controversy were various federal spending measures granting public libraries financial assistance to help provide their patrons with Internet access. Under CIPA, all libraries receiving such federal assistance are required to install filtering software to block "visual depictions" that constitute obscenity or child pornography, or that are harmful to minors. CIPA does, however, permit the covered libraries to disable the filtering device "to enable access for bona fide research or other lawful purposes." The American Library Association challenged the constitutional validity of CIPA's "filtering" requirement on the ground that it violated the First Amendment. The Court rejected this facial challenge without issuing a majority opinion. The four-person plurality opinion, authored by Chief Justice Rehnquist, found no constitutional violation. According to the plurality, CIPA did not induce libraries to violate the rights of their adult patrons, because those patrons had no right to a library collection of any particular content. "Most libraries already exclude pornography from their print collections because they deem it inappropriate for inclusion. We do not subject these decisions to heightened scrutiny; it would make little sense to treat libraries' judgments to block online pornography any differently, when these judgments are made for just the same reason." 539 U.S. at 208. Moreover, any potential free speech violation was obviated by the statutory provision allowing libraries to disable the CIPA-required filtering devices under appropriate circumstances. Justice Kennedy concurred but noted that his agreement with the Court's judgment left open the possibility of an as-applied challenge premised on the ineffectiveness or unavailability of filter disabling services. Id. at 215. Justice Breyer's concurrence was to the same effect. Id. at 215-221. There were also two dissents, both of which saw CIPA as a content-based restriction on speech that was not narrowly tailored to advance the government's interest. Id. at 220 (Stevens, J., dissenting); id. at 231 (Souter, J., joined by Ginsburg, J., dissenting). Hence, given the concurrences and dissents, CIPA's filtering requirement remains subject to an as-applied challenge.

§8.3.8 Speech that Depicts Actual Violence or Cruelty

One can argue plausibly that visual depictions of extreme violence or cruelty ought to be treated in a fashion similar to that accorded obscenity and child pornography—i.e., such depictions ought to be treated as categorically beyond the protection of the First Amendment. This argument is especially strong with respect to films and videos that document actual violence and cruelty staged solely for the purpose of entertainment. Certainly, one can imagine a variation of the *Miller* obscenity test apropos to such speech:

> (a) whether the average person, applying contemporary community standards would find that the work, taken as a whole, appeals to an unhealthy interest in violence or cruelty; (b) whether the work depicts or describes, in a patently offensive way, violent or cruel conduct specifically defined by the applicable state law; and (c) whether the work, taken as a whole, lacks serious literary, artistic, political, or scientific value.

The question of whether the depiction of such staged violence or cruelty should be categorically denied First Amendment protection arose recently in *United States v. Stevens*, 559 U.S. 460 (2010), a case involving a federal statute that imposed a penalty of up to five years in prison for anyone who knowingly "creates, sells, or posseses a depiction of animal cruelty" (with certain exceptions and limitations). The statute defined a depiction of "animal cruelty" as one "in which a living animal is intentionally maimed, mutilated, tortured, wounded, or killed. . . ." Id. at 465.

The Government argued that the depictions of animal cruelty covered by the statute should be treated as categorically beyond the protection of the First Amendment because, much like obscenity, the speech at issue "lack[ed] expressive value. . . ." Id. at 469. In the Government's view, "Whether a given category of speech enjoys First Amendment protection depends upon a categorical balancing of the value of the speech against its societal costs."

Id. at 470. The Court described the Government's argument as "startling and dangerous." Id. While the Court agreed that there were some "historic and traditional categories" of speech beyond the reach of the First Amendment (such as obscenity), id. at 468, it disavowed any "freewheeling authority to declare new categories of speech outside the scope of the First Amendment." Id. at 472. In the Court's words:

> The First Amendment's guarantee of free speech does not extend only to categories of speech that survive an ad hoc balancing of relative social costs and benefits. The First Amendment itself reflects a judgment by the American people that the benefits of its restrictions on the Government outweigh the costs. Our Constitution forecloses any attempt to revise that judgment simply on the basis that some speech is not worth it.

Id. at 470. The Court went on to hold that the statute violated the First Amendment overbreadth principle, noting that even the government did not "seriously contest that the presumptively impermissible applications of [the statute] far outnumber any permissible ones." Id. at 481.

§8.3.9 Content Discrimination Within Categories of Unprotected Speech

We have noted that there are certain categories of speech—e.g., fighting words, true threats, obscenity, and child pornography—that fall outside the First Amendment and that, therefore, normally receive no constitutional protection. However, the Court has held that the government may not discriminate within a category of otherwise proscribable speech to favor some viewpoints or ideas over others. If the government does so, the First Amendment will come into play, and the measure will be struck down unless it is shown that the discrimination is necessary to achieve a compelling governmental interest.

It was on this basis that the Court in *R.A.V. v. City of St. Paul*, 505 U.S. 377 (1992), struck down a city ordinance that outlawed certain types of hate speech. Though the ordinance was limited to "fighting words," a category of generally unprotected speech, the city banned only those fighting words that provoked anger "on the basis of race, color, creed, religion or gender." By thus discriminating within the category of fighting words so as to disfavor some ideas and viewpoints over others, the ordinance triggered application of the First Amendment. Applying an ad hoc balancing test, the Court concluded that the ordinance was not necessary to achieve the city's compelling goal of combating racism, sexism, and bigotry, since a blanket ban on all fighting words would have achieved that goal equally well.

The *R.A.V.* Court did, however, recognize an exception to this nondiscrimination principle that would permit proscriptions of unprotected speech that do not ban the entire category of speech at issue. In the Court's words,

> When the basis for the content discrimination consists entirely of the very reason the entire class of speech at issue is proscribable, no significant danger of idea or viewpoint discrimination exists. Such a reason, having been adjudged neutral enough to support exclusion of the entire class of speech from First Amendment protection, is also neutral enough to form the basis of distinction within the class.

Id. at 388. Thus, the federal government could "criminalize only those threats of violence that are directed against the President . . . since the reasons why threats of violence are outside the First Amendment . . . have special force when applied to the person of the President." Id. Similarly, a state could choose to ban only the most hardcore obscenity on the theory that such obscenity does the most harm to the community. In other words, neither states nor the federal government must ban all proscribable speech to proscribe some of that speech. But if some proscribable speech is banned within a particular unprotected category, the basis for the ban must be premised on the aspect of that speech that makes it unprotected (e.g., on the threat or the obscenity) and not on any other message the speech seeks to convey.

Example 8-Y

Jones, in an effort to frighten his new African American neighbors into leaving the neighborhood, ignited a large wooden cross on their front lawn. Upon being apprehended, he was charged under a state law that provides: "It shall be unlawful for any person or persons, with the intent of intimidating any person or group of persons, to burn, or cause to be burned, a cross on the property of another, a highway or other public place." Does the First Amendment provide a defense to this charge?

Explanation

No. The burning of the cross was intended to convey a message of intimidation and fear. As such, it constitutes a true threat and thus falls into an unprotected category of speech. See § 8.3.3. The fact that the statute does not cover all true threats raises the possible applicability of *R.A.V.* because the statute "discriminates" within a proscribable category by making only some true threats unlawful. However, unlike the statute in *R.A.V.*, this statute does not proscribe only those cross burnings that convey a particular message beyond the intimidation. Rather, the focus on cross burnings can be seen as an example of a partial proscription of the category based on "the very reason the entire class of speech at issue is proscribable," namely, the particularly intimidating nature of cross burnings. As the Court observed in a factually similar case, "Unlike the statute at issue in *R.A.V.*, the Virginia statute does not single out for opprobrium only that speech directed toward 'one of the specified disfavored topics.'" *Virginia v. Black*, 538 U.S. 343, 362 (2003). Moreover, in the Court's view, the state was free to focus only on cross burnings "because burning a cross is a particularly virulent form of intimidation." Id. at 363. The dissent, however, saw the cross burning-statute as an impermissible content-based discrimination because, in its view, that proscription was premised on the ideological message generally associated with cross burnings. Id. at 380 (Souter, J., dissenting).

Note that the actual statute at issue in *Virginia v. Black* included a provision that treated a cross burning as prima facie evidence that the burning was done with the intent to intimidate. A plurality of four Justices concluded that this evidentiary presumption ran the risk of convicting a person who had not communicated a true threat but who had instead engaged in political speech. See id. at 363-367 (Part IV of Justice O'Connor's opinion). Justice Souter's concurring and dissenting opinion, which was joined by two other Justices, adopted a similar position. See id. at 384-387.

§8.3.10 Compelled Speech

In addition to imposing limitations on the government's authority to prevent or punish speech, the First Amendment restricts governmental efforts to compel speech. This issue arose earlier, in our discussion of commercial speech. See § 8.3.6. We saw there that the government may at times impose mandatory disclosure requirements with respect to the advertising of products and services. The standard of review in that setting is somewhat relaxed, though such requirements will still be stricken if they are "unjustified or unduly burdensome." *Zauderer v. Office of Disciplinary Counsel of Supreme Court of Ohio*, 471 U.S. 626, 651 (1985). Here, we look at compelled speech requirements in the noncommercial setting, where speech rights are fully protected.

Freedom of speech 'includes both the right to speak freely and the right to refrain from speaking at all." *Wooley v. Maynard*, 430 U.S. 705, 714 (1977). Thus, the government may not force anyone to affirm a particular ideological belief. See *West Virginia State Bd. of Educ. v. Barnette*, 319 U.S. 624 (1943) (holding compelled flag salute unconstitutional); § 9.5.2. Similarly, the government may not force an individual to use his or her property to convey an ideological message with which that person disagrees. In *Wooley v. Maynard*, for example, the Court upheld the First Amendment right of a Jehovah's Witness couple to refuse to display the state motto, "Live Free or Die," on their state-issued license plate. The couple cited religious, moral, and political objections to the motto. The Court held that the state could not compel them to be an instrument for disseminating the state's ideological message.

The Court purported to apply this principle in 303 *Creative LLC v. Elenis*, 600 U.S. 570 (2023). At issue in that case was a First Amendment challenge to a Colorado public accommodations law that precluded businesses open to the public from discriminating based on sexual orientation. The plaintiff, who had religious scruples against same-sex marriage, planned to operate a for-profit business that created websites for weddings. However, she did not want to create such websites for same-sex marriages, and she argued that requiring her to do so would violate her right to freedom of speech. The Court upheld her claim in part on the theory that enforcement of the public accommodations law would compel her to engage in expressive activity that went against her religious beliefs. Of course, no one was compelling her to do anything. Unlike the children in *Barnette* who were forced to attend school and to recite the pledge of allegiance daily under threat of expulsion and truancy, the plaintiff in 303 *Creative* was not required to run a business open to the public. Nor did the Colorado law require her to say anything about gay marriage.

The right to refrain from speaking includes "[t]he right to eschew association for expressive purposes. . . ." *Janus v. American Federation of State, County, and Municipal Employees*, 585 U.S. 878, 892 (2018). This right also extends to laws that would compel a person to provide financial support for another's speech. The Court in *Janus* applied these principles to hold that in the public employment setting, states and public-sector unions cannot, under an agency-shop arrangement, require nonmember employees to pay an "agency fee," or make any other contribution to the union, unless the employee has affirmatively consented to do so. Earlier, in *Abood v. Detroit Board of Education*, 431 U.S. 209 (1977), the Court had unanimously allowed the mandatory deduction from nonmembers' pay of that portion of a union's fees that was "germane" to its collective-bargaining activities, as distinct from union expenditures for political or ideological projects. In overruling *Abood*, the *Janus* Court held that regardless of the use to which union deductions are to be put, "[c]ompelling a person to *subsidize* the speech of other private speakers" goes to the heart of the First Amendment and cannot survive the "'exacting' scrutiny" required in such cases. 585 U.S. at 893-894 (emphasis in original). Neither of the interests advanced by the state to defend its agency-shop law—i.e., maintaining "labor peace" by assuring that workers would be represented by only one union, and avoiding the risk of "free riders"—survived this demanding test. Id. at 894-901. The Court's ruling in *Janus* was consistent with *Davenport v. Washington Education Association*, 551 U.S. 177 (2007), which had held that the First Amendment did not bar a state from requiring a public employees' union to obtain the affirmative consent of nonmembers, before their agency-shop fees could be used for political purposes, rather than placing the burden of objecting or opting out on the individual worker. After *Janus*, procuring such consent is not only required, but also applies to *all* of a union's agency-shop fees, not just that portion that might be used for political purposes.

Similar principles apply outside the union-dues setting. See *Keller v. State Bar of Cal.*, 496 U.S. 1 (1990) (compulsory state bar dues may not be used for political or ideological purposes); cf. *United States v. United Foods, Inc.*, 533 U.S. 405 (2001) (compelled subsidy for generic advertising of a food product, where the subsidy is not part of a larger regulatory or marketing program, violates First Amendment as being government-compelled speech); cf. *Johanns v. Livestock Marketing Ass'n*, 544 U.S. 550 (2005) (no violation of "compelled-subsidy" doctrine when the speech being funded is the government's own speech, as opposed to the speech of a private organization). See § 8.6.

EXAMPLE

Example 8-Z

State University imposes a mandatory student fee, part of which funds various student organizations, a number of which engage in political or ideological advocacy. Some students have challenged the fee on the basis that they are being forced to support political and ideological positions with which they disagree. Does the university's mandatory student fee violate the objecting students' First Amendment rights?

EXPLANATION

Explanation

Arguably yes. These fees are collected by the state university which then authorizes them to be distributed to and spent by private entities that engage in First Amendment activity. This is an even stronger case of state involvement than in the labor union setting, where it is a private entity that collects the fees, albeit pursuant to state authority. While First Amendment rights may be somewhat diluted at the elementary and secondary school levels, see § 8.5.4, this case involves the university setting where such rights operate at full or nearly full strength. The students will argue that under *Janus*, they cannot be compelled to subsidize the speech of other private speakers. The fact that their fees are distributed among a variety of groups, not all of whom may be objectionable to plaintiffs, does not undermine the fact that the groups to which they do object are receiving a portion of their fees. The university apparently has no procedure whereby a student can object to any part of their fees going to the support of specified student organizations. However, even such a procedure would put the onus on students to publicly reveal their political or ideological positions, thus violating their constitutional right to refrain from speaking at all.

To sustain this mandatory fee collection scheme, the university would need to satisfy *Janus*'s "exacting scrutiny" test. While the university will claim it has a compelling interest in supporting student organizations, this goal, even if compelling, can be achieved through means significantly less restrictive of associational freedom—e.g., allow students to select which if any organizations they wish to participate in and then pay a set fee to those groups, or have the university support student organizations out of its general fund, rather than using special student fees for this purpose. There is thus a good chance this mandatory student fee would be held unconstitutional. But see *University of Wisconsin System v. Southworth*, 529 U.S. 217 (2000) (upholding such a student-fee program in a case pre-dating the Supreme Court's decision in *Janus*).

As the first paragraph of this section noted, a different constitutional analysis applies depending on whether a mandatory disclosure requirement arises in a commercial speech rather than a noncommercial speech setting. Yet there will be times when the line separating these two realms is blurred. For example, suppose a state requires that certain specific disclosures be made in both advertising and in settings that are independent of any advertising. This was the case in *National Institute of Family and Life Advocates v. Becerra*, 585 U.S. 755 (2018), where California required that unlicensed pregnancy centers include a government-drafted notice in all of their advertising materials and that the same notice be posted at the centers' physical premises. Since the premises notices would presumably not qualify as being commercial speech, it was not surprising that "[t]he parties dispute whether the unlicensed notice is subject to deferential review under *Zauderer*." Id. at 776. The Court did not need to resolve that question because it found that the disclosure requirement was invalid even under the more relaxed commercial speech standard. See § 8.3.6. However, there may be times when the competing standards will lead to different outcomes, in which case the question of how to treat such a mixed-speech case setting will have to be addressed.

§8.3.11 Ad Hoc Balancing

If a content-based restriction on otherwise protected speech does not fall into one of the judicially recognized doctrinal patterns that we discussed earlier, its constitutionality will be measured by an ad hoc balancing test that asks whether the restriction is narrowly tailored to serve a compelling government interest. *Republican Party of Minnesota v. White*, 536 U.S. 765, 774-775 (2002). See, e.g., *R.A.V. v. City of St. Paul*, supra, § 8.3.9. To satisfy this test, the government must show that the restriction does not "unnecessarily circumscrib[e] protected expression." *Brown v. Hartlage*, 456 U.S. 45, 54 (1982). Although the ad hoc balancing test borrows its standards from equal protection strict scrutiny (see § 7.2), the test does vest a judge (and the Court) with some leeway in determining what constitutes a compelling government interest and under what circumstance a speech restriction will be deemed narrowly tailored to advance that interest.

Example 8-AA

The State A constitution provides for the popular election of all judges, including justices of the state supreme court. Candidates running for judicial office are, however, prohibited from announcing their "views on disputed legal or political issues." On the assumption that this "announce clause" prohibits judicial candidates from taking a public position as to how "disputed legal or political issues" should be decided in the future, does the restriction violate the First Amendment?

Explanation

Because this content-based restriction on judicial candidate speech does not fall into any specific doctrinal category, the measure of its constitutionality depends on whether the restriction can be properly characterized as narrowly tailored to advance a compelling government interest. In defending its announce clause, State A might assert that the judicial office differs from other elective offices to the extent that judges, in performing their duties, must be impartial and must maintain an appearance of impartiality. This requisite impartiality pertains both to specific cases and to a general attitude of open-mindedness. The restriction on candidate speech is designed to promote these interests by prohibiting only that type of speech that is most likely to undermine the principle of impartiality, namely, speech that appears to commit the candidate to a specific point of view on how particular cases should be decided.

The Court, by a 5 to 4 majority, rejected similar arguments in *Republican Party of Minnesota v.White*, 536 U.S. 765 (2002).The speech restriction at issue in *White* was both narrower and more complicated than the one given in this example, but the Court's reasoning in that case remains instructive. Justice Scalia, writing for the majority, agreed that the state had a compelling interest in promoting judicial impartiality toward parties but concluded that the announce clause was not narrowly tailored to advance that interest because it did not "restrict speech for or against particular *parties*, but rather speech for or against particular *issues*." Id. at 776 (emphasis in original). To the extent that impartiality pertains to a judge's legal views, the Court concluded that the interest in promoting this type of impartiality was not compelling. In the Court's words, "[a] judge's lack of predisposition regarding the relevant legal issues in a case has never been thought a necessary component of equal justice, and with good reason. For one thing, it is virtually impossible to find a judge who does not have preconceptions about the law." Id. at 777.

The dissenters in *White* saw the judicial office and the judicial election process as being sufficiently distinct from political office and the general election process to permit the state's restrictions on a judicial candidate's speech. 536 U.S. at 796 (Stevens, J., dissenting); id. at 803 (Ginsburg, J., dissenting).

One potentially troubling feature of ad hoc balancing is that it comes with a built-in flexibility that may allow for a somewhat diluted approach to strict scrutiny.

Example 8-BB

A federal statute makes it a crime to "knowingly provide material support or resources to a foreign terrorist organization." The proscription covers support for all the activities of such an organization, including its legal activities. The breadth of the proscription was a product of the congressional finding that any support for terrorist organization could ultimately, even if indirectly, support the organization's terrorist mission. The phrase "material support" includes engaging in political advocacy coordinated with a terrorist organization—i.e., the statute prohibits an individual from engaging in political advocacy in concert with a terrorist organization. The statute does not, however, prohibit an individual from engaging in independent political advocacy in support of a terrorist organization. To the extent that the material-support provision prohibits an individual from engaging in coordinated political advocacy, does it violate that individual's First Amendment rights?

Explanation

The restriction on coordinated political advocacy is a content-based prohibition on speech because it is triggered by both the message conveyed and the viewpoint expressed. As such, the government should be required to establish that the restriction represents a narrowly tailored means of advancing a compelling government interest. Certainly, the prevention of terrorism is a compelling government interest. As to narrowly tailored, one might argue that the statute's focus on coordinated political advocacy limits the scope of the proscription to those speech activities most likely to provide indirect support for a terrorist organization's terrorist mission. Moreover, the fact that the statute does not regulate independent political advocacy supports the view that Congress was trying to curtail as little speech as possible. The statute also might be sustained on the reasoning of *Dennis v. United States*, 341 U.S. 494 (1951), arguing that this somewhat limited restriction on speech is justified by the gravity of the evil discounted by its probability. See § 8.3.2.

On the other hand, it might be argued that there is no meaningful distinction between coordinated and independent political advocacy in terms of their respective impacts on a terrorist organization's terrorist mission. Both forms of advocacy run the risk of giving the organization a higher public profile and political legitimacy, and both would allow the terrorist organization to expend less effort and money on advocacy and more of both on illegal activities. However, to the extent Congress believed that independent advocacy posed less of a threat than coordinated advocacy, its decision not to punish the former is content neutral and imposes less of a burden on speech than would a total ban. See *Holder v. Humanitarian Law Project*, 561 U.S. 1 (2010) (upholding such a restriction under similar facts); see also id. at 40 (Breyer, J., dissenting).

§8.3.12 Free Speech Rights of Public Employees and Other Voluntary Participants in Government Programs

Public employees do not automatically lose their right to engage in free speech by virtue of their public employment. *Pickering v. Board of Education*, 391 U.S. 563 (1968). Their rights of free expression may, however, be somewhat more restricted than the rights of persons not so employed. For example, the Supreme Court has consistently upheld provisions of the Hatch Act that prohibit federal employees from active participation in political campaigns. *United States Civil Service Comm'n v. National Assn. of Letter Carriers AFL-CIO*, 413 U.S. 548 (1973). Obviously, such a restriction would be unconstitutional as applied to citizens generally, but with respect to public employees the notion is that the government could not operate effectively and fairly if civil servants were allowed to engage in partisan politics. On the other hand, the Court has struck down broad prohibitions on the speech activity of public employees when the government can assert no reasonable, employment-related grounds for the breadth of the prohibition. See *United States v. National Treasury Employees Union*, 513 U.S. 454 (1995) (law that prohibits federal employees from accepting any compensation for making speeches or writing articles, regardless of the relationship with the employee's official duties, held unconstitutional). As a general matter, where the government seeks to impose limits on public employees' speech rights, the Court has attempted to map out a middle ground in which the right of the public employee to comment on matters of public concern is balanced against the government's interest in promoting efficiency and effectiveness in the public workplace. Similar principles may apply in non-employment settings where the government seeks to restrict the free speech rights of those with whom it has entered a voluntary relationship.

Looking first at public employment, one area of recurring conflict involves restrictions on public employees' speech that is critical of their government employers. In *Pickering v. Board of Education*, supra, the Supreme Court upheld the First Amendment right of a public-school teacher to publish a letter critical of the administrative competence of his employer, the local board of education. The Court explained its ruling as follows: "[W]e hold that, in a case such as this, absent proof of false statements knowingly or recklessly made by him, a teacher's exercise of his right to speak on issues of public importance may not furnish the basis for his dismissal from public employment." 391 U.S. at 574. In part, the recognition of this right was premised on the public's legitimate interest in receiving such information.

More generally, a public employee's right of free speech—including the right recognized in *Pickering*—is subject to two important limitations. First, to be protected, the speech must relate to a matter of "public concern" and not merely involve a personnel issue internal to the workplace. *Connick v. Myers*, 461 U.S. 138, 145-146 (1983); see also *Borough of Duryea v. Guarnieri*, 564 U.S. 379 (2011) ("public concern" standard applies under the Petition Clause when a government employee's Petition Clause claim replicates a claim under the Speech Clause). Second, the employee's interest in the speech must outweigh the government's interest in maintaining an efficient and effective workplace. *Connick v. Myers*, supra, 461 U.S. at 146-147; *Rankin v. McPherson*, 483 U.S. 378, 388 (1987). As to the second element, assuming the speech pertains to a matter of public concern, the government must provide evidence that the employee's speech impairs efficiency or effectiveness in the workplace to trump the protection provided by the First Amendment. Id. at 388-389. This two-part test is sometimes referred to as the *Pickering/Connick* balancing test.

EXAMPLE

Example 8-CC

Romeo, a City of Sandy Ego police officer, made a video in which he stripped off a police uniform and engaged in explicit, autoerotic activity while purporting to issue a traffic citation. He sold copies of the video on the adults-only section of eBay, where he identified himself as a law enforcement officer. When the city learned of Romeo's activities, it fired him for engaging in conduct unbecoming a police officer. Romeo filed suit against the city in a federal court, claiming a violation of his First Amendment rights. The city has moved to dismiss on the strength of *Pickering* and *Connick*. How should the court rule?

Explanation

For his speech to qualify as protected under the First Amendment, Romeo must first show that the speech involved a matter of public concern. In other words, he must satisfy the first element of the *Pickering/Connick* test. Although there is no specific formula for determining whether any particular act of expression involves a matter of public concern, it seems highly unlikely that Romeo's videotaped exploits would qualify. The public concern element of *Pickering/Connick* was designed to allow public employees the ability to provide valuable information to the public. It may also include a public employee's more open-ended commentary on generic political matters. Romeo's speech does not qualify as either. The case should be dismissed.

On similar facts, the Supreme Court unanimously concluded that the speech at issue was not a matter of public concern: The officer's "activities did nothing to inform the public about any aspect of the [the police department's] functioning or operation." *City of San Diego v. Roe*, 543 U.S. 77, 84 (2004). Nor was there any hint of a larger political message. Thus, since his speech did not involve a matter of public concern, the officer had no grounds on which to assert a violation of the First Amendment. Moreover, even if the video had involved a matter of public concern, the *Roe* Court noted that the officer's activities were "detrimental to the mission and functions of [his] employer" (id.), strongly suggesting that the officer's claim also failed to satisfy the second element of the *Pickering/Connick* test.

The Supreme Court again addressed the *Pickering/Connick* balancing test in *Garcetti v. Ceballos*, 547 U.S. 410 (2006). In that case, a deputy district attorney claimed that his First Amendment rights were violated when he was subjected to a series of retaliatory employment actions after having written a memorandum to his supervisor regarding a potentially fraudulent affidavit that had been filed by a police officer in a pending case. The memorandum was not distributed to the public; rather, it was written as part of the deputy's official duties and directed to the deputy's supervisor. The Court concluded that the deputy's speech was not entitled to First Amendment protection since the memorandum was written pursuant to his official duties. As such, the employee's speech did not satisfy the "public concern" element of the *Pickering/Connick* test. "We hold that when public employees make statements pursuant to their official duties, the employees are not speaking as citizens for First Amendment purposes, and the Constitution does not insulate their communications from employer discipline." Id. at 421. The Court hinted that this bright-line test might not apply in the context of "expression related to academic scholarship or classroom instruction," given the critical role of the First Amendment in protecting academic freedom. Id. at 425. But beyond that specific context, the test appears to limit public employees' rights of free speech to communications made outside of the scope of their official duties.

The scope of *Garcetti* was later examined in *Lane v. Franks*, 573 U.S. 228 (2014). There, a government employee was fired in retaliation for giving subpoenaed testimony pertaining to corruption in the government program in which he was employed. The Court held that the employee's work-related testimony was not made pursuant to the employee's "official duties" within the meaning of *Garcetti*. Rather, such testimony was more properly characterized as the speech of a citizen on a matter of public concern. Id. at 228-241. The fact that the employee gathered the information during his employment was irrelevant. Thus, while the employee's testimony may have involved his work-related duties, the testimony itself was not within the scope of those duties. Consequently, the employee's "off duty" speech was entitled to First Amendment protection under the *Pickering/Connick* balancing formula. Id. at 242.

We have been dealing with laws that in some way *restrain or punish* government workers' speech. There is a critical distinction, however, between government-imposed restrictions on individuals' rights, and a government refusal affirmatively to assist people—be they government employees or citizens generally—in exercising those rights. While government restraints on speech trigger heightened scrutiny, the government's failure to assist people in exercising those rights does not violate the First Amendment. Since what is protected by the First Amendment is "the right to be free from government abridgment of speech," the government "is not required to assist others in funding the expression of particular ideas, including political ones. '[A] legislature's decision not to subsidize the exercise of a fundamental right does not infringe the right, and thus is not subject to strict scrutiny.' " *Ysursa v. Pocatello Education Assn.*, 555 U.S. 353, 358 (2009) (state law that banned public-employee payroll deductions to support labor union's political activities did not infringe on union's First Amendment rights and was therefore subject only to rational basis review).

The Court has extended the principles applicable to government employee speech to settings where private parties have voluntarily entered some other type of relationship with the government. In such cases, the *Pickering/Connick* balancing test may be used to determine whether a restriction on speech violates the First Amendment. In *Tennessee Secondary School Athletic Assn. v. Brentwood Academy*, 551 U.S. 291 (2007), the Court employed that test in a case involving the TSSAA, a nonprofit membership corporation that, on behalf of the state, regulated interscholastic sports among its 345 public and private Tennessee high school members. The Court held that TSSAA did not violate the First Amendment by sanctioning a member school for using "undue influence" in recruiting middle school students to its athletic program. "Just as the government's interest in running an effective workplace can in some circumstances outweigh employee speech rights, so too can an athletic league's interest in enforcing its rules sometimes warrant curtailing the speech of its voluntary participants." Id. at 299 (internal citations omitted). The Court was willing to assume that the school's coach, in his recruitment communications with the students, was "speaking as a citizen about matters of public concern" (id. at 300), thus satisfying the first prong of *Pickering/Connick*. Since the second prong of the test was thus triggered, TSSAA could impose "only those conditions on such speech that are necessary to managing an efficient and effective state-sponsored high school athletic league." Id. The Court found this requirement easily met, based on "TSSAA's commonsense conclusion that hard-sell tactics directed at middle school students could lead to exploitation, distort competition between high school teams, and foster an environment in which athletics are prized more highly than academics." Id. The school's First Amendment rights were therefore not infringed.

The Court again applied the *Pickering/Connick* balancing test in *Janus v. American Federation of State, County, and Municipal Employees Council*, 585 U.S. 878 (2018), to assess the constitutionality of an Illinois statute that authorized private labor unions to collect "agency fees" from nonconsenting public employees. See § 8.3.10.

§8.3.13 Government Coercion of Private Parties to Violate the Free Speech Rights of Others

"Government officials cannot attempt to coerce private parties to punish or suppress views that the government disfavors." *National Rifle Association v. Vullo*, 602 U.S. 175, 180 (2024). In *Vullo*, the superintendent of the New York Department of Financial Services allegedly pressured regulated entities to help her stifle the NRA's pro-gun advocacy by threatening enforcement actions against those entities that refused to disassociate themselves from the NRA and other gun-promotion advocacy groups. Id. The Court held that those allegations plausibly claimed a content-based restriction on the free speech rights of the NRA.

> A government official can share her views freely and criticize particular beliefs, and she can do so forcefully in the hopes of persuading others to follow her lead. In doing so, she can rely on the merits and force of her ideas, the strength of her convictions, and her ability to inspire others. What she cannot do, however, is use the power of the State to punish or suppress disfavored expression.

Id. at 188. Stated somewhat differently, "a government official cannot do indirectly what she is barred from doing directly," i.e., they "cannot coerce a private party to punish or suppress disfavored speech on her behalf." Id. at 190. While the Court did not provide a standard of review, given that the alleged coercion was directed at limiting the political speech of the NRA, strict scrutiny would presumably apply if the allegations of coercion were proved at trial.

§8.4 CONTENT-NEUTRAL RESTRICTIONS ON SPEECH: THE TIME, PLACE, AND MANNER TEST

The government sometimes regulates speech indirectly by imposing limitations that do not pertain to the content of speech, but that nonetheless affect the circumstances under which expressive activity may occur. These so-called time, place, and manner restrictions are, by definition, content neutral. They are focused not on the subject or message of the speech or on the speaker's identity, but on factors related to the circumstances under which the speech may be delivered. For example, an ordinance that prohibits the use of loudspeakers on city streets is a time, place, and manner restriction. It prohibits, at all *times*, in specified *places*, a particular *manner* of communicating, and the prohibition applies regardless of the identity of the speaker or the content of the message the speaker wishes to convey. Similarly, if a law that makes it a crime to deface governmental property is applied to an individual who spray paints a graffiti message on the walls of a governmental building, this law is properly characterized as a time, place, and manner restriction as long as the punishment is not premised on the message of the graffiti.

§8.4.1 Content Neutrality

Content-neutral restrictions are constitutional as long as they "are [1] justified without reference to the content of the regulated speech, . . . are [2] narrowly tailored to serve a significant governmental interest, and . . . [3] leave open ample alternative channels for communication of the information." *Clark v. Community for Creative Non-Violence*, 468 U.S. 288, 293 (1984). The first element of the test, content neutrality, is a key component of the analysis. A law is content neutral if it does not depend in any way on the subject or topic of the speech, the viewpoint being expressed, or the identity of the speaker. Stated somewhat differently, a content-neutral law focuses only on the time, place, or manner of a communication. See *City of Erie v. Pap's A.M.*, 529 U.S. 277 (2000) (plurality treats ban on public nudity as a content-neutral regulation of expressive conduct). However, as noted earlier, a law that appears to be content-based may still be treated as content neutral if it falls within the secondary effects doctrine. See § 8.3.1.

Frequently one will encounter statutes or regulations that appear to be focused on time, place, and manner concerns, but that also include a content-based trigger. Suppose, for example, that a state law prohibits the distribution of campaign literature within 100 feet of a polling place on election day. In a colloquial sense, this prohibition regulates the time (election day), the place (polling place), and the manner (distribution of literature) of the affected speech. But the trigger of the law's application is dependent on the political content of the literature being distributed. Therefore, the law cannot properly be characterized as a mere time, place, and manner restriction. Rather, it is a content-based restriction on political speech and is therefore subject to much more exacting scrutiny. See *Burson v. Freeman*, 504 U.S. 191 (1992).

Example 8-DD

A city ordinance prohibits picketing on public streets or sidewalks within 150 feet of a grade school or high school during hours when school is in session. Excluded from the ordinance is peaceful labor picketing. Is this ordinance properly characterized as a time, place, and manner restriction?

Explanation

No. Even though the ordinance does regulate the time, place, and manner of expression, the applicability of the ordinance is dependent on the content of the message conveyed by the picketing. Labor picketing will be allowed, while picketing with other messages will not. The ordinance, therefore, must be analyzed as a content-based restriction on speech. *Carey v. Brown*, 447 U.S. 455, 460-461 (1980); *Police Dep't of Chicago v. Mosley*, 408 U.S. 92, 95-96 (1972).

Example 8-EE

A Colorado statute makes it unlawful for any person within a 100-foot radius of a health care facility's entrance to "knowingly approach" within 8 feet of another person, without that person's consent, to pass out "a leaflet or handbill to, display a sign to, or engage in oral protest, education, or counseling with [that] person. . . ." The measure was passed, in part, as a response to problems of access to health care facilities caused by abortion protestors. The measure was designed, however, to apply to all health care facilities, including those having nothing to do with family planning, on the theory that the state has a strong interest in protecting ingress and egress to and from those facilities. Is this statute content neutral?

EXPLANATION

Explanation

The measure appears to be content neutral. The statute applies regardless of the general subject matter of the speech, the specific topic of that speech, the identity of the speaker, or the speaker's particular viewpoint. Nor does this appear to be a situation in which the government is seeking to suppress a particular message. Rather, Colorado has imposed a "place" regulation that applies regardless of the underlying message the speaker wishes to convey. Thus, unlike the situation presented in Example 8-DD, the statute's applicability here is not dependent on the content of the message being conveyed. One could argue, however, that the phrase "oral protest, education, or counseling" creates a content-based restriction since the statute covers only these forms of speech. A friendly greeting, therefore, would not be covered. In a similar case, the Court held that such language was not a content restriction, but merely designed to ensure that the statute applied only to the types of speech activity most likely to cause the consequences the government sought to prevent, namely, the harm caused by in-your-face harassment of patients and health care givers. *Hill v. Colorado*, 530 U.S. 703 (2000).

In a more recent decision, the Court considered the content-neutrality of a Massachusetts statute that made it a crime to knowingly stand on a "public way or sidewalk" within 35 feet of the entrance or driveway to any "reproductive health care facility," defined as "a place, other than within or upon the grounds of a hospital, where abortions are offered or performed." *McCullen v. Coakley*, 573 U.S. 464, 471 (2014). The Court concluded that the statute was content neutral since its application was in no way dependent on what a person said or on the speaker's identity, but rather only on where they were. Id. at 479-482. In addition, an exception that permitted employees of the facility to be within the buffer zone did not alter the Court's conclusion since the exception had nothing to do with the speech of those employees. Id. at 482-485. A law that may appear to discriminate based on speaker identity can avoid being so treated if the distinction among speakers is based on other factors, and "is not a subtle means of exercising a content preference. . . ." *Turner Broadcasting, Inc. v. FCC*, 512 U.S. 622, 645 (1994). See § 8.3.1. Would the conclusion in *McCullen* still have been the same if it were shown that the statute was enforced only against abortion protestors? Despite its facial neutrality, would the law then have been content based as applied?

The principle of content neutrality will be violated if a facially neutral time, place, and manner restrictions grants excessive discretion to administrators, for "such discretion has the potential for becoming a means of suppressing a particular point of view." *Heffron v. International Soc. for Krishna Consciousness*, 452 U.S. 640, 649 (1981). In *Shuttlesworth v. Birmingham*, 394 U.S. 147 (1969), for example, the Court struck down a city ordinance that gave a city commission the authority to grant or deny a parade permit on the basis of the commission's perception of the "public welfare, peace, safety, health, decency, good order, morals or convenience." Id. at 150. In the Court's view, these vague and subjective standards vested the commission with a "virtually unbridled and absolute power" over the granting of parade permits. Id. The potential for abuse passed the limits of constitutional tolerance. See § 8.2.5 (discussing vagueness). On the other hand, the Court has upheld parade permit requirements that limit the discretion of the issuing administrator to the imposition of reasonable time, place, and manner constraints designed to accommodate public safety and convenience. *Cox v. New Hampshire*, 312 U.S. 569 (1941).

§8.4.2 Narrowly Tailored to Advance a Significant Governmental Interest

The second element of the content-neutral test requires a familiar means/ends analysis with something of a variable bite—not unlike mid-level scrutiny. Is the restriction narrowly tailored to advance a significant governmental interest? The answer depends on a variety of fact-driven considerations, including:

- The nature of the speech activity being regulated;
- The perceived significance of the governmental interest;
- The scope of the restriction;
- The availability of effective, but less restrictive alternatives; and
- The court's judgment as to the actual effectiveness of the restriction in advancing the proffered interest.

As to the nature of the speech activity being regulated, be aware that the more traditional a mode of communication is, the more likely it is that the Court will be sympathetic to the claimed violation of First Amendment rights. The other considerations are self-evident in application.

The Court addressed each of these factors in *Watchtower Bible and Tract Society of New York, Inc. v. Village of Stratton*, 536 U.S. 150 (2002). In that case, two religious organizations brought a facial challenge to a village ordinance that prohibited any door-to-door solicitations or canvassing within the village, in the absence of preregistration with the mayor and the issuance of a permit.

The type of speech regulated by this content-neutral ordinance included commercial activities as well as religious proselytizing, political canvassing, and the distribution of noncommercial handbills. The Court struck down the ordinance as being inconsistent with the free speech guarantee of the First Amendment. "[A] law requiring a permit to engage in such speech constitutes a dramatic departure from our national heritage and constitutional tradition." Id. at 166.

The Court's rationale began by noting that the nature of the speech at issue was highly valued and at the core of First Amendment protections. Citing a long line of precedents, the Court emphasized "the historical importance of door-to-door canvassing and pamphleteering as vehicles for the dissemination of ideas." Id. at 162. Yet, because the village had significant and legitimate interests in "the prevention of fraud, the prevention of crime, and the protection of residents' privacy" (id. at 164-165), the protection of such door-to-door speech could not by its nature be absolute. Nonetheless, the Court concluded that, given the traditional and valued nature of this type of speech and the broad scope of this particular proscription, which apparently included even neighbor-to-neighbor political communications, the permit requirement was insufficiently tailored to advance those asserted interests. Specifically, the Court concluded that the interest in preventing fraud "provides no support for its application to petitioners [who did not solicit funds], to political campaigns, or to enlisting support for unpopular causes." Id. at 168. As to the interest in preventing crime, the Court observed, "[I]t seems unlikely that the absence of a permit would preclude criminals from knocking on doors and engaging in conversations not covered by the ordinance." Id. at 169. Finally, the Court explained that the privacy interests of residents were adequately protected by the less restrictive alternative of posting enforceable "No Solicitation" signs, which, "coupled with the resident's unquestioned right to refuse to engage in conversation with unwelcome visitors, provides ample protection for the unwilling listener." Id. at 168.

EXAMPLE

Example 8-FF

The City of Lost Angels prohibits the distribution of "handbills" on any street, sidewalk, or park within the city. "Handbill" is defined to encompass all forms of written literature, including circulars, leaflets, booklets, pamphlets, posters, and the like. The prohibition applies regardless of the content of the handbill. The asserted governmental interest is the prevention of littering. Is this ordinance narrowly tailored to advance a significant governmental interest?

Explanation

No. While the prevention of littering within the city may well be a significant governmental interest, the ordinance completely bans a time-honored mode of communication and does so in a manner much more intrusive than necessary to advance the proffered interest. Laws that punish a party who litters provide an effective and substantially less restrictive method to advance the city's goal. Given the breadth of the prohibition, the nature of the speech activity affected, and the availability of substantially less restrictive alternatives, this ordinance is unconstitutional. See *Schneider v. State*, 308 U.S. 147 (1939).

Example 8-GG

A federal regulation prohibits all forms of peaceful picketing on the public sidewalks that surround the grounds of the Supreme Court building. The purpose of the ban is to preserve the integrity of the Supreme Court grounds, to protect individuals having business with the Court, and to maintain proper order and decorum on those grounds. Is this regulation narrowly tailored to advance a significant governmental interest?

Explanation

Given the nature, function, and prestige of the Supreme Court, it certainly follows that the government has a strong and, therefore, significant interest in promoting safety, order, and decorum on the grounds surrounding the Supreme Court building. The question then is whether the total ban on peaceful picketing is "narrowly tailored" to advance those interests. It does not seem to be. The total ban is far more sweeping than necessary to advance the stated goals. Peaceful picketing, by definition, threatens neither persons nor property, nor would it seem to detract from the decorum of the Court, at least when practiced on the otherwise public sidewalks surrounding the Court. Moreover, there are numerous less restrictive alternatives to the total ban, such as limitations on the number of picketers, the size of signs, and so on. See *United States v. Grace*, 461 U.S. 171, 181-184 (1983) (arriving at an identical conclusion under virtually the same facts); see also *McCullen v. Coakley*, supra, 573 U.S. at 495 ("To meet the requirement of narrow tailoring, the government must demonstrate that alternative measures that burden substantially less speech would fail to achieve the government's interests, not simply that the chosen route is easier.").

Despite the apparent rigor of this mid-level scrutiny, application of the narrowly tailored test is not always fatal to the government's position. For example, *Clark v. Community for Creative Non-Violence*, 468 U.S. 288 (1984), involved a First Amendment challenge to a National Park Service (NPS) regulation that prohibited camping in national parks except in designated camping areas. No such areas are designated in the memorial parks located in Washington, D.C., including Lafayette Park and the Mall. The Community for Creative Non-Violence (CCNV), seeking to demonstrate the plight of the homeless, was granted a permit by NPS to erect temporary tent cities in Lafayette Park and the Mall. However, CCNV's request to sleep in the "symbolic tents" was denied on the basis of the content-neutral camping ban. The Supreme Court, assuming that sleeping in a symbolic tent was expression protected by the First Amendment, upheld the NPS regulation as being a valid time, place, and manner restriction. In the Court's words, "It is . . . apparent to us that the regulation narrowly focuses on the Government's substantial interest in maintaining the parks in the heart of our Capital in an attractive and intact condition, readily available to the millions of people who wish to see and enjoy them by their presence." Id. at 296. See also *Heffron v. International Soc'y for Krishna Consciousness*, supra, 452 U.S. at 650-656 (upholding regulation that prohibited face-to-face solicitations at state fair except in designated booths).

In essence, application of this means/ends analysis requires a careful marshaling of facts and a dose of common sense.

Example 8-HH

Reconsider the facts of Example 8-EE. At issue there was a Colorado statute that made it unlawful for any person within a 100-foot radius of a health care facility's entrance to "knowingly approach" within 8 feet of another person, without that person's consent, to pass out "a leaflet or handbill to, display a sign to, or engage in oral protest, education, or counseling with [that] person. . . ." Assume that the measure was adopted pursuant to the state's traditional police powers to protect the health and safety of its citizens. More particularly, the state wished to ensure unimpeded access to health care facilities and to avoid potential trauma to patients caused by in-your-face confrontational protests. Is this measure narrowly tailored to advance a significant government interest?

Explanation

The interests asserted by the state are undoubtedly significant. Individuals entering health care facilities often are struggling with a wide range of physical and emotional concerns. Eliminating the additional trauma of a personal confrontation would seem to be quite significant from a health perspective. (A good lawyer would, of course, want to present evidence on this point.) The speech being regulated, however, is political speech. A court must, therefore, carefully examine the restrictions to determine if they are narrowly tailored to advance the asserted interest. This depends largely on the scope of the restriction. Here the 8-foot restriction operates only within a specifically defined zone, namely, a 100-foot radius from the entrance of any health care facility. Moreover, the restriction does not prohibit all forms of speech within that zone. There are no restrictions on the content or manner of one's verbal communications or on the type of signs one might use. The only restriction is the 8-foot limitation on approach, and even this limitation does not prevent the speaker from offering a passerby a leaflet; the passerby is free, of course, to reject the offer or to reach outside the 8-foot limit and accept the leaflet. It would seem then that within the 100-foot zone itself there are ample opportunities to communicate virtually any message, even to those within the 8-foot zone, and there is nothing in the statute or in the facts that suggests any limitation on one's ability to communicate messages outside of that zone. Given the limited intrusion on the speaker's ability to convey a message and given that the statute effectively eliminates the problems caused by in-your-face confrontational communications, absent some creative alternative that is equally effective the measure would seem to be narrowly tailored to advance a significant interest. See *Hill v. Colorado,* 530 U.S. 703 (2000) (so holding under similar facts).

§8.4.3 Alternate Channels for Communication

The third element of the time, place, and manner test requires that the restriction leave open ample alternative channels for speech activity. Certainly, if the effect of a law is to leave no time, no place, and no manner under which the subject information can be communicated, this element of the test is not satisfied. Beyond this certainty, there is no set formula for determining exactly what range of alternatives will satisfy the standard. It appears, however, that the general availability of traditional means of communication will suffice. For example, in *Clark v. Community for Creative Non-Violence,* supra, the Court seemed to resolve this element by offhandedly observing that nothing in the record suggested that the "message concerning the plight of the homeless" could not be communicated through either the media or other means. 468 U.S. at 295.

Example 8-II

The Minnesota State Fair is an annual event designed to exhibit to the public a wide array of goods, services, entertainments, and other matters of interest. Exhibitors, of which there are approximately 1,400, are not allowed to sell goods or solicit funds anywhere in the fair except at their designated booths. The Krishnas have rented a booth at the fair; however, in addition to solicitations at the booth, they seek permission to engage in solicitations throughout the 125 acres of the fairgrounds. The fair administrators, relying on the neutral rule described above, declines to grant the requested permission. Assuming that this limitation on peripatetic solicitations is narrowly tailored to advance a significant state interest, does the restriction leave open ample alternative channels of communication?

Explanation

EXPLANATION

Yes. The restriction does not apply to any areas outside the fair, leaving a wide array of communicative opportunities available to the Krishnas, and even within the fair, the Krishnas remain free to make solicitations at their booth. This may not be the ideal system from the perspective of the Krishnas, but in the absence of a showing that the alternative channels are either illusory or demonstrably inadequate, this factor of the time, place, and manner test should be easily satisfied. See *Heffron v. International Soc'y for Krishna Consciousness*, supra, 452 U.S. at 654-655.

Where the speech in question is of a type that the Court treats as having relatively low value, the requirement that there be alternative channels of communication may be so diluted as to be meaningless. For example, in *City of Renton v. Playtime Theatres, Inc.*, 475 U.S. 41 (1986), a zoning ordinance relegated theaters that showed adult films to the outlying portions of the city. Even though application of the ordinance turned on the content of the movies being shown, the Court deemed the law to be content neutral on the basis that it was aimed at the secondary effects of such theaters on the surrounding neighborhoods. See § 8.3.1. Applying the time, place, and manner test, the Court found that the third part of the test was satisfied even though the theaters proved that as a practical matter, the 5 percent of the city where they were legally permitted to locate was not commercially viable. Thus, in the particular context of this adult pornography, the alternative channels of communication did not need to be ample or even available.

§8.4.4 Prior Restraints

Some time, place, and manner restrictions operate as prior restraints—e.g., a city ordinance that allows parades on city streets only after the sponsors of the parade have received a permit from a designated city office. Such content-neutral ordinances will be upheld if the discretion of those administering them is limited to imposing reasonable time, place, and manner restrictions. Compare *Cox v. New Hampshire*, supra, § 8.4.1 (upholding parade permit requirement), with *Watchtower Bible and Tract Society of New York, Inc.*, supra, § 8.4.2 (invalidating door-to-door solicitation permit requirement). However, if the ordinance grants the administrator arbitrary discretion with the potential for content-based discriminations, the ordinance will be struck down. See, e.g., *Shuttlesworth v. Birmingham*, supra, § 8.4.1.

§8.4.5 Injunctions

A court may issue an injunction that regulates the time, place, and manner of speech as long as the "provisions of the injunction burden no more speech than necessary to serve a significant government interest," and as long as the purpose of the injunction is not to suppress the message of the speakers. *Madsen v. Women's Health Center, Inc.*, 512 U.S. 753, 765 (1994). The Court has described this test as requiring a "somewhat more stringent application" of First Amendment principles than would be required by the standard time, place, and manner analysis. Id. The most recent applications of this test have involved injunctions issued against protestors at abortion clinics.

Example 8-JJ

The Family Planning Clinic (FPC) is a privately owned health care facility that performs abortions. For the past several years, the FPC has been involved in an ongoing conflict with abortion protestors who demonstrate daily on the grounds surrounding the clinic. The protests have included the blocking of driveways and entrances, aggressive confrontations with employees and patients, and occasional physical assaults. The FPC sought an injunction against the protestors to prevent them from interfering with the operations of the clinic. The trial court issued an injunction that imposed a 15-foot radius floating buffer zone around persons and vehicles seeking access to the clinic and a fixed 15-foot buffer zone around clinic doorways, driveways, and parking lot entrances. Protestors entering either of these zones would be subject to being held in contempt. Are these two aspects of the injunction acceptable time, place, and manner restrictions?

Explanation

Although the injunction focuses only on the activities of abortion protestors, the purpose of the injunction appears to be not the suppression of their point of view or their message, but rather the regulation of the secondary effects of their activities in terms of blocking access to the clinic. The injunction will, therefore, be treated as being content neutral.

As to the significance of the governmental interest, the standard is akin to that used in mid-level scrutiny, requiring that the government show that there is some important interest at stake. The interests in maintaining public safety and in protecting a woman's right to seek "pregnancy-related services" have been deemed significant in the context of abortion protests. *Schenck v. Pro-Choice Network of Western N.Y.*, 519 U.S. 357, 375-376 (1997).

The question then becomes whether either the floating buffer zone or the fixed buffer zone burdens more speech than necessary to advance these significant interests. Under similar facts, the Court in *Schenck* concluded that a floating buffer zone unduly intruded on basic speech rights by making it impossible to engage in a normal conversation or to hand out leaflets without potentially running afoul of the injunction. The fixed buffer zones were upheld, however, as appropriate devices to ensure safe and free access to the facility. Compare this conclusion with that described in Example 8-HH. How, in terms of being narrowly tailored, does a floating 15-foot radius buffer zone differ from one that makes it unlawful to knowingly approach within 8-feet of a person entering a health care clinic?

§8.4.6 The Special Problem of Copyrights

Under Article I, § 8, cl. 8 (the Copyright Clause), Congress has the power to grant to authors an "exclusive Right" to publish their writings for "limited Times." The copyright system enacted in 1976 granted natural persons federal copyright protection that would run from the work's creation and last until 50 years after the author's death. The Copyright Term Extension Act of 1998 (CTEA) enlarged the copyright protection of existing and future copyrights by an additional 20 years. In *Eldred v. Ashcroft*, 537 U.S. 186 (2003), the Court was asked to consider whether the CTEA, as applied to existing copyrights, exceeded the powers vested in Congress by the Copyright Clause and, if not, whether this exercise of the copyright power violated the First Amendment. As to the first question, the Court held that it was for Congress to determine what constituted a "limited time" for purposes of copyright protection and that the judgment of Congress would be upheld so long as it was rational. The Court cited "international concerns" and "demographic, economic, and technological changes" as providing sufficiently rational grounds for the passage of the CTEA. Id. at 205-206.

The plaintiffs in *Eldred* also argued that the CTEA extension violated First Amendment principles as an insufficiently justified, content-neutral regulation of speech. The Court rejected this argument, observing that "[t]he Copyright Clause and First Amendment were adopted close in time. This proximity indicates that, in the Framers' view, copyright's limited monopolies are compatible with free speech principles. Indeed, copyright's purpose is to *promote* the creation and publication of free expression." Id. at 219 (emphasis in original). In addition, the Court explained that "copyright law contains built-in First Amendment accommodations. First, it distinguishes between ideas and expression and makes only the latter eligible for copyright protection. . . . Second, the 'fair use' defense allows the public to use not only facts and ideas contained in a copyrighted work, but also expression itself in certain circumstances." Id. The Court did not hold that copyright law was "'categorically immune from challenges under the First Amendment.' But when, as in this case, Congress has not altered the traditional contours of copyright protection, further First Amendment scrutiny is unnecessary." Id. at 221 (internal citation omitted).

§8.5 THE NATURE OF THE PUBLIC FORUM

The previous discussion of content-based and content-neutral restrictions on speech assumed that the speech in question occurred in a setting where the First Amendment operates at full strength. Yet before one can proceed on that assumption, it is necessary to make a preliminary determination as to the nature of the property on which the expressive activity occurs. For these purposes, we must distinguish between private property and public property.

Where the government seeks to restrict speech on (or involving the use of) property that is privately owned—e.g., books, newspapers, billboards, movie theaters, or the front lawn of one's home—speech is protected to the fullest extent called for by the appropriate First Amendment test. In other words, content-based restrictions on protected speech are subject to strict scrutiny or to a specifically applicable doctrinal test, while content-neutral restrictions are subject to the standard time, place, and manner analysis.

On the other hand, where the expressive activity occurs on property owned by the government, the level of First Amendment protection depends on how the particular property is classified—i.e., as a *public forum*, a *designated public forum*, or a *nonpublic forum*. How a piece of public property is classified under this so-called forum doctrine is critical. While First Amendment protections operate at full strength in public fora and in designated public fora (just as they do with respect to private property), the protections are substantially diluted where the property in question is deemed to be a nonpublic forum.

A traditional public forum is a public facility that has, by long tradition, been dedicated to "the free exchange of ideas." *Cornelius v. NAACP Legal Defense & Educ. Fund*, 473 U.S. 788, 800-802 (1985). Falling squarely within this category are streets, sidewalks, and parks, which "have immemorially been held in trust for the use of the public and, time out of mind, have been used for purposes of assembly, communicating thoughts between citizens, and discussing public questions." *Hague v. CIO*, 307 U.S. 496, 515 (1939); see also *Frisby v. Schultz*, 487 U.S. 474, 481 (1988).

A designated public forum is a public facility that is not a traditional public forum, but one that the government has intentionally dedicated to expressive activity, such as a college meeting room or a municipal auditorium. While the government may limit the scope of the designated public forum (e.g., for use by enrolled students only), in which case it may be described as a *limited public forum*, or rescind the designation altogether, as long as the facility remains dedicated to expressive activity the full protections of the First Amendment apply within the legitimately defined scope.

A public facility, such as a welfare office or a courtroom, in which some expressive activity occurs, but which is neither a traditional nor a designated public forum is, by definition, a nonpublic forum, to which the protections of the First Amendment apply in only a limited fashion. In the words of the Court:

> Public property which is not by tradition or designation a forum for public communication is governed by different standards. We have recognized that "the First Amendment does not guarantee access to property simply because it is owned or controlled by the government." In addition to time, place, and manner regulations, the State may reserve the forum for its intended purposes, communicative or otherwise, as long as the regulation on speech is reasonable and not an effort to suppress expression merely because public officials oppose the speaker's view. . . . "[T]he State, no less than a private owner of property, has power to preserve the property under its control for the use to which it is lawfully dedicated."

Perry Educ. Ass'n v. Perry Local Educators' Ass'n, 460 U.S. 37, 46 (1983) (internal citations omitted). In short, within a nonpublic forum, the government is free to impose reasonable restrictions on speech, including most content-based restrictions, as long as the government maintains viewpoint neutrality—i.e., as long as the government does not grant or deny access on the basis of the favored or disfavored status of any particular message.

One final caveat. All of our discussion so far has dealt with constraints that the First Amendment imposes on the government's ability to regulate or prohibit speech by private parties. Where the government is itself the speaker, the Speech and Press Clauses do not come into play. Thus, under the "recently minted government speech doctrine," *Pleasant Grove City, Utah v. Summum*, 555 U.S. 460, 481 (2009) (Stevens, J., et al., concurring), the government may shape the content of its own message in any way it wishes, endorsing some views and rejecting others. Moreover, the forum in which the government chooses to speak does not affect the analysis. Thus, even on property that constitutes a public forum, while the First Amendment severely limits the government's ability to regulate *private* expression, the Speech and Press Clauses in no way constrain the government's ability to craft its own message.

§8.5.1 Traditional Public Forum

Given the more limited First Amendment protection applied to speech in a nonpublic forum, the determination of whether any particular facility is a public forum or a nonpublic forum is critical. Indeed, public forum analysis often presents a threshold issue in First Amendment cases. Examination of that issue begins with determining whether the forum qualifies as a traditional public forum. This breaks down into two propositions: The first covers those fora that are almost automatically included; the second focuses on the potential for further expansion of the category into more novel realms.

First, streets, sidewalks, and parks are generally considered traditional public fora to which the protections of the First Amendment fully apply. See *Frisby v. Schultz*, 487 U.S. 474, 481 (1988) (reaffirming standard as to residential streets). Therefore, if a case involves expressive activity on a street or a sidewalk or in a park, the public forum threshold is usually easily crossed. This generalization must, however, be qualified. If the street, sidewalk, or park has a special or limited use—i.e., it is not a generalized public thoroughfare or a general-use park—the traditional "public forum" label may not attach. Thus, a street on a military base is not a traditional public forum. *Greer v. Spock*, 424 U.S. 828, 835-837 (1976). Nor is a limited-use sidewalk resting completely on post office property and designed solely to provide access from a post office parking lot to a post office building. *United States v. Kokinda*, 497 U.S. 720, 727-728 (1990). Perhaps the same can be said of historic national parks designed for the special purpose of preserving our environment or heritage. Those qualifications aside, however, in general, public streets, sidewalks, and parks are traditional public fora. See *McCullen v. Coakley*, supra, 573 U.S. at 476-477 (reaffirming the general principle).

Next, while the category of traditional public fora may theoretically include a much wider array of public facilities than streets, sidewalks, and parks, in practice it does not, largely because the Court has been reluctant to expand the category beyond those specific contexts. But see *Edwards v. South Carolina*, 372 U.S. 229, 235 (1963) (arguably treating the grounds surrounding a state legislative house as a traditional public forum). The theoretical threshold for entry into the category is a showing that the property or facility at issue is of a type whose *principal and historic purpose* has been the free exchange of ideas. *Cornelius v. NAACP Legal Defense & Educ. Fund*, supra, 473 U.S. at 801-802. Of course, this is a somewhat peculiar test given that streets, sidewalks, and parks do not themselves meet this standard other than by ipse dixit—for example, one would think that the principal purpose of a street is to provide a thoroughfare for traveling from one place to another. The Court has also noted that one indicium of a traditional public forum is "unfettered access" by the public. *Arkansas Educ. Television Comm'n v. Forbes*, 523 U.S. 666, 678 (1998). As long as "principal and historical purpose" and "unfettered access" remain the standard, one should not expect any major additions to the category of traditional public forum. See *United States v. American Library Association*, 539 U.S. 194 (2003) (Internet access in public library creates neither a "traditional" nor a "designated" public forum).

EXAMPLE

Example 8-KK

Members of the Intergalactic Society of Enlightenment, known as Izzies, seek to promote their views by proselytizing wherever crowds gather. Their proselytizing includes the distribution of free literature and the solicitation of contributions. They have found airports to be particularly attractive venues for these activities, and several Izzies have regularly solicited funds at the Buena Vista International Airport, a city-owned facility located in Virginia. After complaints from numerous patrons of the airport, the city adopted an ordinance that prohibited all face-to-face solicitations on airport property. The Izzies challenged this ordinance, arguing that the airport is a traditional public forum. They premise their argument on a combination of factors: the similarity of airport thoroughfares to streets and sidewalks, the history of expressive activity at airports, and the similar history and tradition of expressive activity at other transportation centers, such as train and bus stations. In essence, they argue that freedom of speech is consistent with the general character of airports and that this consistency compels a finding that airports are traditional public fora. Evaluate these arguments.

EXPLANATION

Explanation

The arguments are certainly plausible. Anyone who has traveled by air transportation knows that expressive interactions, including the distribution of literature and face-to-face solicitations, do occur in airports in much the same fashion as those activities occur on city streets. Moreover, the analogy to city streets and sidewalks is especially strong given the plethora of shops and vendors that now line airport walkways. This argument, however, does not adequately address the somewhat more rigid focus of the traditional public forum inquiry. Applying the principal and historical purpose test, it would be difficult to sustain the proposition that one of the principal purposes of an airport is the free exchange of ideas. Although expressive activity clearly takes place in airports — e.g., commercial advertising by airlines and conversations among travelers — *the* principal purpose of an airport is the profitable facilitation of air travel. That being the test, the analogies to streets and sidewalks and to bus and train stations would seem inapt. See *International Soc'y for Krishna Consciousness, Inc. v. Lee*, 505 U.S. 672, 679-683 (1992).

There is one potential wrinkle to the analysis described in Example 8-KK. Since the 1992 decision in *International Society for Krishna Consciousness, Inc.*, supra, the Court's makeup has changed in a manner that may lead to a more flexible approach to traditional public forum analysis, akin to that argued for by the Izzies. In fact, four Justices in that case took a more pragmatic approach, urging that "[i]f the objective, physical characteristics of the property at issue and the actual public access and uses that have been permitted by the government indicate that expressive activity would be appropriate and compatible with those uses, the property is a public forum." 505 U.S. at 698 (Kennedy, J., joined by Blackmun, J., Stevens, J., and Souter, J., concurring). Thus, we should not assume that traditional public forum analysis will remain narrowly focused on the principal and historical purpose test. In short, your arguments in this context should consider the possibility of a more inclusive approach.

§8.5.2 Designated Public Forum

A public facility that does not qualify as a traditional public forum may, nonetheless, be characterized as a *designated* public forum. The test here focuses on the intent of the government. But here, too, the current Court has erected a somewhat substantial (albeit murky) barrier. If and only if the government *intends* to open a nontraditional public forum to a wide class of persons for expressive activity will the designated public forum status attach. As a consequence, a designated public forum cannot be created by inaction or by general public access to the forum, see *International Soc'y for Krishna Consciousness, Inc. v. Lee*, supra, 505 U.S. at 680, or even by a "selective" opening of the forum for expressive activity, *Perry Educ. Assn. v. Perry Local Educators' Assn.*, supra, 460 U.S. at 47. Thus, if a state university develops a policy under which classrooms are made available as meeting places for student clubs, the requisite intent to designate a public forum has been established. *Widmar v. Vincent*, 454 U.S. 263, 267 (1981). However, because the intent of the university was to open its classrooms only to student groups, the property is a *limited* public forum available only to those groups. If, on the other hand, student groups just happen to use classrooms without objection from the university, no public forum has been designated even as to them. Nor has such a forum been established if the university permits selective, nonsystematic use by student groups, though the difference between what is selective and what reflects a standing policy may be far from clear.

The facts of *Perry Education Association* are instructive. At issue in that case was the "forum" status of a school district's internal mail system. The system was dedicated largely to school purposes. Access was, however, granted to a labor union that had been elected as the exclusive bargaining agent for the teachers. In addition, certain civic groups, such as the Girl Scouts, the Cub Scouts, and the YMCA, were occasionally allowed access to the system. A rival union sought access to the internal mail system on the theory that the school district had created a designated public forum. The Court disagreed. The "selective access" granted to civic groups did not transform the internal mail system into a designated public forum. 460 U.S. at 47. The Court provided no elaboration, but presumably something more systematic would be required to establish the necessary intent to create a designated public forum. This judicial reluctance underscores the nature of the inquiry. A designated public forum will not be created by accident or by occasional practices that permit expressive activity to occur within the forum. Rather, a designated public forum will be created only if the government consciously and affirmatively intends to create one.

Example 8-LL

AETC is a public broadcasting station owned by the State of Arkansas. During the 1992 elections, the station decided to air a series of debates involving the candidates for various federal and state offices. One of the debates was to focus on the candidates for the state's Third Congressional District. AETC invited the Republican and Democratic candidates for that district but declined to invite Ralph Forbes, an independent candidate for the same congressional seat. In declining to invite Forbes, AETC cited his overall lack of support among the voters of the district. AETC believed that the limited amount of time available for the debate would be better served by focusing attention on the candidates from the two major parties. Are the AETC *debates* a traditional or a designated public forum?

Explanation

One could certainly argue in the abstract that the "principal and historical purpose" of a public broadcasting station is the free exchange of ideas. Of course, the historical vintage and the operation of such stations bear only the most remote comparison to streets, sidewalks, and parks. And the free exchange of ideas on such stations has always been tempered by the editorial judgment of the stations' managers. Perhaps most importantly, the public has never enjoyed "unfettered access" to airtime on public broadcasting stations. Similarly, even if we focus solely on the televised debates as traditional public fora, there is nothing in the history of such debates to suggest a generalized public right of access. It is quite unlikely that the Court would declare debates aired on public broadcasting stations to be a traditional public forum.

That brings us to the question of a designated public forum. Focusing solely on the televised debates, it would not seem that AETC's actions evidence an intent to open these debates to a wide class of persons for expressive purposes. Rather, AETC has at most selectively invited certain parties to engage in expressive activity in what would appear to be a nonpublic forum. The debates are thus neither a traditional nor a designated public forum. See *Arkansas Educ'l Television Comm'n v. Forbes*, 523 U.S. 666 (1998) (so holding under similar facts).

Even if a designated public forum has been created, the government may limit the use of that forum based on subject matter and speaker identity. *Rosenberger v. Rector and Visitors of Univ. of Va.*, 515 U.S. 819, 829 (1995) (designated public forum may be reserved "for certain groups or for the discussion of certain topics"). Such a *limited* public forum will be upheld "so long as the distinctions drawn are reasonable in light of the purpose served by the forum and are viewpoint neutral." *Lamb's Chapel v. Center Moriches Union Free School Dist.*, 508 U.S. 384, 392-393 (1993). Thus, a limited public forum created for the purpose of promoting the culinary arts need not be open to a discussion of general current events (as opposed to *currant* events). Nor must a limited public forum created for the use of students be open to nonstudents. In *Perry Education Association*, for example, the Court explained that even if access to the school district's mailing system by the various civic groups in that case had created a designated public forum, the scope of that forum would be limited to access by similar groups. 460 U.S. at 47.

The "viewpoint neutrality" principle was applied in *Lamb's Chapel*, supra. At issue in that case was a challenge to a public school district's policy that permitted the use of school facilities by the local residents for "social, civic, or recreational uses" but denied any use "for religious purposes." 508 U.S. at 387. Applying this policy, the school district refused to allow an evangelical group to show a film series that gave a Christian perspective on child rearing. The Court held that the school district's refusal amounted to unlawful viewpoint discrimination. As the Court put it, "[t]he film series involved here no doubt dealt with a subject otherwise permissible under [district policy], and its exhibition was denied solely because the series dealt with the subject from a religious standpoint." Id. at 394. Such viewpoint discrimination cannot stand in the absence of a compelling state interest.

By way of contrast, in *Christian Legal Society Chapter of the University of California, Hastings College of the Law v. Martinez*, 561 U.S. 661 (2010), the Court considered whether Hastings College of Law, a public university, violated the viewpoint neutrality standard when it required that all clubs seeking "official recognition" adopt an "all comers" membership policy under which any student must be allowed to join and fully participate in the club's activities regardless of that student's status or belief. The Court found that the policy was both reasonable in light of the school's nondiscriminatory educational mission and viewpoint neutral because the policy was justified without reference to the content or viewpoint of the challenged speech or expressive activity. Id. at 694-697.

Example 8-MM

Milford Central School (MCS) permits district residents to use its facilities after school for, among other things, instruction in education or the arts and for social, civic, recreational, and entertainment uses pertaining to the community's welfare. Under this policy, secular groups, such as the Boy Scouts, are allowed access to the facilities for such purposes as influencing a boy's moral development and spiritual growth. Darlene, a district resident, sponsors the Good News Club, a private Christian organization for children ages 6 to 12. She submitted a request to hold the club's weekly after-school meetings in the school. Darlene described the club meetings as follows:

> Each meeting begins with calling the roll. As each child's name is called, if the child recites a Bible verse, the child receives a treat. The club members then sing songs and engage in games that involve, among other things, learning Bible verses. I then read a Bible story and explain how it applies to club members' lives. The meeting closes with a prayer. Finally, I distribute treats and Bible verses for memorization.

MCS denied the request on the ground that the proposed use — to sing songs, hear Bible lessons, memorize scripture, and pray — was the equivalent of religious worship prohibited by the community use policy. Has MCS engaged in viewpoint discrimination?

Explanation

The answer depends on how one characterizes the activities of the Good News Club. If the activities of the club are designed to promote moral development and spiritual growth through Bible study, then it would appear that MCS has engaged in impermissible viewpoint discrimination because the school district does permit groups with a secular viewpoint to promote such values. Only the religious viewpoint is disfavored on this particular topic. A majority of the Supreme Court so held on similar facts. In the Court's words, "[w]hat matters for purposes of the Free Speech Clause is that we can see no logical difference in kind between the invocation of Christianity by the Club and the invocation of teamwork, loyalty, or patriotism by other associations to provide a foundation for their lessons." *Good News Club v. Milford Central School*, 533 U.S. 98, 111 (2001).

If, however, one views the activities of the Good News Club as religious worship or proselytizing, then the club's activities can be seen as different in kind from those of the secular groups that have been granted access. This was the view adopted by the dissent in *Good News Club*. In Justice Souter's words, "[i]t is beyond question that Good News intends to use the public school premises not for the mere discussion of a subject from a particular, Christian point of view, but for an evangelical service of worship calling children to commit themselves in an act of Christian conversion." Id. at 138 (Souter, J., et al., dissenting). Given the holding of the majority, however, one can safely assume that the Court, and lower federal courts, will be suspicious of any public-school policy pertaining to facilities access that appears to disfavor religious viewpoints. See also Example 9-J, examining this same problem under the Establishment Clause.

§8.5.3 Nonpublic Forum

Finally, if the public facility at which private expressive activity occurs is neither a traditional public forum nor a designated public forum, it is by default a nonpublic forum. (The Court also sometimes refers to a limited public forum as a nonpublic forum.) Thus, whether governmental property falls into this latter category is answered through a process of elimination. Private speech in a nonpublic forum, like speech in a limited public forum, may be limited under a mere reasonableness standard tied to the underlying purpose of the forum, as long as the restrictions imposed are viewpoint neutral. *Arkansas Educ'l Television Comm'n v. Forbes,* 523 U.S. 666, 682 (1998).

EXAMPLE

Example 8-NN

The Combined Way Drive (CWD) is an annual charity drive aimed at federal employees. Money raised through the program is distributed to participating organizations. Participation is limited to about 250 nonprofit charitable agencies that provide direct health and welfare services to individuals. Participating charities are carefully selected based on extensive admissions criteria that are designed to keep the number of participants at a manageable level. Each participating organization is permitted to "advertise" its needs in a CWD circular that is published as a part of the drive. Federal employees may then designate which of these charities will receive their contribution. Specifically excluded from the drive are legal defense and political advocacy organizations such as the Sierra Club and the NAACP Legal Defense Fund. One of the reasons given for this exclusion is that "a dollar spent on food and shelter is more beneficial than a dollar spent on litigation or political advocacy." The government also argues that the exclusion avoids the appearance of political favoritism. Several political advocacy groups have challenged the constitutionality of the exclusion as being a restriction on political speech. Is the CWD a nonpublic forum? If it is, will this content-based restriction withstand judicial scrutiny?

Explanation

As to the nature of the forum, the CWD is clearly not a traditional public forum. Nor does it appear to be a designated public forum, for the government has never opened the CWD to all charitable organizations even for the limited purpose of raising money, much less for other speech activities. Instead, the CWD's clear purpose and consistent practice has been to selectively choose which nonprofit organizations will be allowed to participate, and to limit their number to a manageable level (250 being a small fraction of the 850,000 nonprofit charitable entities then operating in the United States). Thus, the CWD, being neither a traditional nor a designated public forum, would appear to be a nonpublic forum.

Although the exclusion of political advocacy from the forum is a content-based restriction of political speech, the nonpublic status of the forum significantly lowers the level of judicial scrutiny. As long as the restriction is reasonable and viewpoint neutral, it will be upheld. This restriction appears to satisfy both standards. It is certainly reasonable to conclude that money spent directly on food and shelter is more beneficial than money spent on litigation or advocacy. This remains true even if there is an equally reasonable argument to the contrary. The same can be said of the political favoritism rationale. As to the requirement of viewpoint neutrality, nothing on the face of the exclusion indicates that the CWD is favoring one side or the other of a political controversy. An orientation toward litigation or political advocacy is not itself a viewpoint, but rather a means to advance a particular viewpoint. Therefore, unless it can be demonstrated that the restriction, either by design or as applied, reflects a bias against disfavored viewpoints, the restriction will be upheld. See *Cornelius v. NAACP Legal Defense & Educ. Fund*, 473 U.S. 788, 806-813 (1985) (holding, on similar facts, that the Combined Federal Campaign (CFC) was a nonpublic forum and that, under the applicable lower level of scrutiny, its exclusion of the NAACP and other legal defense and political advocacy groups did not violate the groups' First Amendment rights).

Example 8-OO

Minnesota law bars individuals from wearing a "political badge, political button, or other political insignia" inside a polling place on Election Day. The "political apparel ban" covers articles of clothing and accessories with political insignia on them. State election judges decide whether a particular item falls within the ban, and violators are subject to a civil penalty or prosecution for a misdemeanor. Andrew was turned away from the polls on Election Day for wearing a "Please I. D. Me" button, a T-shirt bearing the words "Don't Tread on Me," and a Tea Party Patriots logo. He and others challenged the statutory ban on its face, alleging that it violates voters' rights of free expression. He contends that the ban, even as later clarified by the state's "Election Day

Policy" manual, never defines the critical adjective "political." It is so broad and ambiguous that it could be read to prohibit wearing not only what he wore to the polls, but also a badge that says "VOTE!"; a shirt saying "Support Our Troops" (if any candidate had expressed a view on military funding to aid veterans); or an ACLU or Ben & Jerry's cap, if those groups had taken identifiable positions on an issue in the current election. The state responds that the ban serves the important purpose of maintaining a polling place "as an island of calm in which voters can peacefully contemplate their choices" during what should be a time for choosing, not for campaigning. Does a polling place qualify as a nonpublic forum? If it does, is the Minnesota law valid?

Explanation

The interior of a government-operated polling place clearly qualifies as a nonpublic forum. It has historically been a zone of quiet, a place where political speech, commercial speech, and indeed almost any other speech besides speaking with polling place personnel, have traditionally not been allowed. There is no evidence that the Minnesota law, which is being challenged facially rather than as applied, has ever been used to target people because of their political persuasion or the views they have expressed. As such, the apparel ban will pass muster so long as it is reasonable considering the purpose served by the forum—here, voting.

The state will argue that the political apparel ban is reasonable considering its important if not compelling purpose. To attempt to specifically delineate or define all of the particular messages and insignia that are prohibited in an election would entail an enormous amount of work and time, given all of the issues that might be raised—issues that will vary from office to office, from candidate to candidate, and from election to election. The state can also argue that its restriction on any individual's speech is extraordinarily limited in both space and time, applying only for the few minutes a year a person spends inside a polling place. As such, the state will urge that the statute easily passes muster under the reasonableness standard.

On the other hand, the Court has never measured the strength of First Amendment rights based on the number of words, pages, or minutes involved. And though this facial challenge is not dependent on how the law has been applied, its ambiguity creates a serious risk that those enforcing it at the state's hundreds of polling places on Election Day may do so in ways that discriminate against individuals whose views they disfavor. These dangers, coupled with the fundamental nature of the right to vote, underline the dangers of a statute that is so ambiguous as to be incapable of reasoned application. Finally, the state has other options that might achieve the same goal but in a less sweeping and less ambiguous manner—e.g., simply barring the display of information advocating for or against any candidate, measure, or political party at polling places on Election Day.

In *Minnesota Voters Alliance v. Mansky*, 585 U.S. 1 (2018), the Court applied the reasonableness test to what it agreed was a nonpublic forum and held that a Minnesota law essentially identical to that described here violated the First Amendment. Two Justices dissented, believing that the Court should have certified the case to the Minnesota Supreme Court for a definitive interpretation of the statute's political apparel ban, believing the state court might interpret the law in such a way as to bring it within constitutional bounds. Id. at 26-32 (Sotomayor, J., and Breyer, J., dissenting). See *National Power & Federalism*, supra, § 4.4.1 ("Abstention: The *Pullman* Doctrine").

§8.5.4 Student Speech in Public Schools

Earlier, we looked at speech in public schools in the context of determining whether school officials had created a designated public forum in which *outsiders* could use the school for speech-related purposes. See § 8.5.2. We turn now to the speech rights of public school students themselves. The question is to what extent the First Amendment protects their rights while they are at school or participating in school-sponsored functions. While the Court has made it clear that students do not "shed their constitutional rights to freedom of speech or expression at the schoolhouse gate," *Tinker v. Des Moines Independent Community School Dist.*, 393 U.S. 503, 506 (1969), school officials can more easily regulate student speech than the government may do in other settings.

The Court's cases suggest that the level of First Amendment protection for student school speech may vary depending on both the nature of the speech and the setting in which it occurs. Protection would appear to be at its highest when the student speech in question is political in nature and when it does not seriously disrupt school activities. In *Tinker*, the Court held that a public school could not discipline its students for wearing armbands to express their "disapproval of the Vietnam hostilities and their advocacy of a truce, to make their views known, and, by their example, to influence others to adopt them." Id. at 514. Such expression, clearly political in nature, was punishable only if school officials could reasonably believe it would "materially and substantially disrupt the work and discipline of the school." Id. at 513. Absent any basis for such concern, the "mere desire to avoid the discomfort and unpleasantness that always accompany an unpopular viewpoint," said the Court, could not justify suppressing student speech that involved the "silent, passive expression of opinion, unaccompanied by any disorder or disturbance. . . ." Id. at 508-509.

In *Bethel School District No. 403 v. Fraser*, 478 U.S. 675 (1986), the Court applied a less demanding standard of review in sustaining a public high school's right to discipline Fraser, a student who delivered a speech at a school assembly in which he used "an elaborate, graphic, and explicit sexual metaphor." Id. at 678. Had the case been analyzed under *Tinker*, as the lower federal courts did, there was clearly no basis for disciplining the student since no disruption was caused or threatened by his speech. However, the Supreme Court declined to apply the *Tinker* standard and held that the "School District acted entirely within its permissible authority in imposing sanctions upon Fraser in response to his offensively lewd and indecent speech." Id. at 685. While the Court failed to explain why *Tinker* did not govern the case, it did note the "marked distinction between the political 'message' of the armbands in *Tinker* and the sexual content of [Fraser's] speech. . . ." Id. at 680. To the extent the cases can be reconciled, *Fraser* suggests that though lewd and indecent speech falls within the First Amendment, it will receive considerably less protection in the public school setting than does political speech. This may be especially true where, as in *Fraser*, there is no suggestion that the speech is being punished because of disagreement with its content, but rather "to ensure that a high school assembly proceed in an orderly manner." Id. at 689 (Brennan, J., concurring in judgment).

Finally, the Court has made it clear that public school officials have a greater right to interfere with student speech when it is perceived as bearing the imprimatur of the school. In *Hazelwood School District v. Kuhlmeier*, 484 U.S. 260 (1988), students on a high school newspaper staff sued their school for refusing to publish two of their articles. The court of appeals, applying *Tinker*, ruled in favor of the students, finding that there was no evidence "the censored articles would have materially disrupted classwork or given rise to substantial disorder in the school." *Kuhlmeier v. Hazelwood School District*, 795 F.2d 1368, 1375 (8th Cir. 1986). The Supreme Court reversed, holding that "educators do not offend the First Amendment by exercising editorial control over the style and content of student speech in school-sponsored expressive activities so long as their actions are reasonably related to legitimate pedagogical concerns." 484 U.S. at 273.

Thus, in the setting of a public school student's speech, it is critical to first determine, as best one can from the Court's trilogy of cases, which standard of review should be applied: the strict standard used in *Tinker* or the far more deferential standards that were applied in *Fraser* and *Kuhlmeier*.

EXAMPLE

Example 8-PP

Frederick, a high school student, was suspended by the school principal after waving a banner at an off-campus, school-approved activity that took place during school hours. The event involved the 2002 Olympic Torch Relay, which passed along the street in front of the school. As the torchbearers and camera crews went by, Frederick and his friends, who were standing across the street from the school, unfurled a 14-foot banner that read "BONG HITS 4 JESUS." The principal immediately ordered the students to remove their banner. When Frederick refused to comply, the banner was confiscated, and he was suspended for ten days. The principal justified her action on the basis that she believed the banner to be encouraging illegal drug use, in violation of established school policy. The school board sustained the principal's action. It found that "'bong hits' is a reference to a means of smoking marijuana," and that Frederick was "advocating the use of illegal drugs. [His] speech was not political. He was not advocating the legalization of marijuana or promoting religious belief. He was displaying a silly message promoting illegal drug usage in the midst of a school activity, for the benefit of television cameras covering the Torch Relay." If Frederick challenges his suspension under the First Amendment, would a court find that the school violated his free speech rights?

Explanation

EXPLANATION

While the conduct for which Frederick was disciplined took place off school grounds, a court would likely find that he was still engaged in a school-sponsored function. This is so because it took place during school hours as part of the school's daily program, with the activity sanctioned and monitored by school officials. Frederick's activities would thus likely qualify as school speech. Had the events taken place at the same location but after school hours or on the weekend, without school supervision, this would clearly not be a school speech case and the First Amendment would apply in full force. Instead, as a school speech case, the level of protection is reduced.

The question then is how Frederick's speech should be characterized. If it can fairly be described as political speech, advocating the legalization of marijuana, then the case would seemingly be governed by the *Tinker* standard, under which Frederick would certainly prevail. From the evidence available, his refusal to take down the banner did not cause any material or substantial disruption of the school's classroom activities, which were suspended at the time, or even of this non-classroom activity that took place outside the school. It is possible Frederick could make the case that he was indeed engaged in political speech and/or that he was in some manner promoting Christianity. However, there is little evidence to suggest this and the school superintendent concluded that he was just trying to get some television coverage.

If Frederick's display of the banner does not qualify as political or religious speech, the level of protection falls dramatically. The case clearly does not fit into the third category, as there was no student newspaper or other school endorsement involved. The case therefore appears to fall into the second category, where the relatively lenient *Fraser* standard merely requires that the school's actions be "reasonably related to legitimate pedagogical concerns." That test would easily be met by the school's argument that it ordered Frederick to remove the banner to keep him from sending a message that the school was not all that serious about its student drug-use policy. See *Morse v. Frederick,* 551 U.S. 393 (2007) (so holding on essentially identical facts).

We have thus far been looking at student speech that takes place on a school campus or that occurs off campus as part of a school-sponsored activity. We turn now to the question of when school officials may discipline students based on their off-campus expression in settings that do not involve school-supervised affairs. In this context, a school's argument for infringing upon student free speech is much weaker, such that some courts took the position that in these cases, students' free speech rights always remain at full strength. In *Mahanoy Area School District v. B.L.*, 594 U.S. 180 (2021), the Supreme Court rejected that view, stating, "we do not believe the special characteristics that give schools additional license to regulate student speech always disappear when a school regulates speech that takes place off campus." Id. at 188. Yet the Court made it clear that in the off-campus context, "the leeway the First Amendment grants to schools in light of their special characteristics is diminished." Id. at 190. The Court declined to

> set forth a broad, highly general First Amendment rule stating just what counts as "off campus" speech and whether or how ordinary First Amendment standards must give way off campus to a school's special need to prevent, *e.g.*, substantial disruption of learning-related activities or the protection of those who make up a school community.

Id. at 189. Examples of student speech that might warrant lesser protection included:

> serious or severe bullying or harassment targeting particular individuals; threats aimed at teachers or other students; the failure to follow rules concerning lessons, the writing of papers, the use of computers, or participation in other online school activities; and breaches of school security devices, including material maintained within school computers.

Id. at 188. However, even in those settings, said the Court, any "First Amendment leeway" will not be automatic and will instead be "circumstance-specific. . . ." Id. at 190. Thus, in the off-campus context, any relaxation of students' First Amendment rights is permitted only in exceptional situations.

Example 8-QQ

Betty is a student at Mahanoy Public High School where she is a junior varsity cheerleader. At the end of her freshman year, she tried out for a position on the varsity cheerleading squad. The weekend after she was turned down for that position, Betty and her friends visited a local store where she used her smartphone to post two photos on Snapchat, a social media application that allows users to post photos that disappear after a set period. Betty's photos were accessible to about 250 of her Snapchat "friends" for a period of 24 hours. The photos and their captions were critical of the school and were crude but not obscene. On two occasions, some students discussed the postings for 5 or 10 minutes in an Algebra class taught by one of the cheerleading coaches. In response, the school suspended Betty from the junior varsity cheerleading squad for the upcoming year. The school defended its action based on its interests in teaching good manners, preventing disruption of school-sponsored extracurricular activities, and preserving team morale. Did the school's suspension of Betty violate her First Amendment rights?

Explanation

Since Betty's speech occurred off campus and was not part of any school-sponsored event, her First Amendment rights should operate at full strength. None of the exceptional circumstances suggested in *Mahanoy* for relaxing those protections are present here. There was no evidence that Betty's activities caused any disruption of learning-related activities or that they harmed or endangered anyone in the school community. The justifications offered by the school are weak. The interest in teaching good manners cannot suffice, for that would give the school unfettered discretion to regulate all of a student's off-campus speech, including that which has no connection to the school or any of its activities. The interest in preventing disruption of school-related activities, while certainly legitimate, was not implicated here, for the brief discussions of the posting were in a class taught by a cheerleading coach, a natural place for it to come up, and caused no apparent disruption. Finally, the interest in preserving team morale cannot suffice to warrant punishment for a student's off-campus speech. Were the rule otherwise, a school could punish any student speech anywhere, if the school perceived it as having a negative effect on student morale. The school's action therefore violated Betty's First Amendment rights. See *Mahanoy Area School District v. B.L.*, 594 U.S. 180 (2021) (so holding on these facts).

§8.6 GOVERNMENT SPEECH

We have thus far been dealing with situations where the speech the government seeks to regulate or prohibit on public property is speech engaged in by private actors. In that setting, under the forum doctrine, the First Amendment speech protections come into play even if the property is deemed to constitute a nonpublic forum, with the strength of the protection depending on how the property is characterized. However, if the speech in question is that of the government itself, the forum doctrine plays no role, for the Free Speech Clause was designed to shield *private speech* from governmental interference, not to limit the government's own speech. As the Court recently explained, "The Free Speech Clause restricts government regulation of private speech; it does not regulate government speech." *Pleasant Grove City, Utah v. Summum*, 555 U.S. 460, 467 (2009). As the Court has said,

> "[I]t is not easy to imagine how government could function" if it were subject to the restrictions that the First Amendment imposes on private speech. . . . [I]mposing a requirement of viewpoint-neutrality on government speech would be paralyzing. When a government entity embarks on a course of action, it necessarily takes a particular viewpoint and rejects others. The Free Speech Clause does not require government to maintain viewpoint neutrality when its officers and employees speak about that venture.

Matal v. Tam, 582 U.S. 218, 234 (2018) (internal citations omitted).

The same principle applies even if the government "receives assistance from private sources for the purpose of delivering a government-controlled message," since the use of private parties as the government's agents does not alter the fact that it is still the government that is speaking. *Pleasant Grove City*, supra, 555 U.S. at 467. See *Rust v. Sullivan*, 500 U.S. 173 (1991) (government may preclude doctors at government subsidized family planning clinics from discussing abortion with their patients at those clinics, on the basis that the government is using the doctors as its surrogates to convey the government's specific message).

Nevertheless, because the government-speech doctrine completely eviscerates the protections of the Free Speech Clause in cases where it is deemed to apply, the Court has exercised "great caution before extending" its application. *Matal v. Tam*, supra, 582 U.S. at 235. "[I]t is a doctrine that is susceptible to dangerous misuse. If private speech could be passed off as government speech by simply affixing a government seal of approval, government could silence or muffle the expression of disfavored viewpoints." Id. In *Matal*, the Court rejected an argument that trademarks are government rather than private speech. Id. at 238-239 It then proceeded to strike down the Lanham Act's prohibition on marks that may "disparage . . . or bring . . . into contempt" any "persons, living or dead, institutions, beliefs, or national symbols," as being facially invalid under the Free Speech Clause. Id. at 246-247. See *Kennedy v. Bremerton School District*, 597 U.S. 507 (2022) (post-game prayer led by a public-school coach was private speech protected by both the Free Exercise and Free Speech Clauses). The free-exercise aspect of the *Kennedy* decision is discussed in § 9.4.2.

Where the government has involved itself with private parties in speech-related activities, it may not always be clear whether the government has simply enlisted those parties in delivering *the government's* message, such that the Free Speech Clause does not apply, or whether the government is imposing restrictions on the speech rights of the private parties themselves, in which case the First Amendment is fully applicable.

EXAMPLE

Example 8-RR

The City of Pleasant Grove operates a public park that includes 15 permanent displays, 11 of which were donated by private groups or individuals. These include a historic granary, a wishing well, a September 11 monument, and a Ten Commandments monument given to the city in 1971 by the Fraternal Order of Eagles. All the monuments either directly relate to the city's history or were donated by those with longstanding city ties. Summum, a religious organization based outside Pleasant Grove, asked the city to accept and erect its gift stone monument that contained the Seven Aphorisms of Summum, similar in size to the Ten Commandments monument. When the city declined, on the ground that the monument did not meet its criteria, Summum sued the city, claiming that the park was a traditional public forum and that the city had violated the Free Speech Clause's ban on content discrimination by accepting the Ten Commandments monument while rejecting the Seven Aphorisms monument. Is the Free Speech Clause applicable in this setting?

EXPLANATION

Explanation

A municipal public park is a traditional public forum for purposes of speeches, parades, and other expressive actions. See § 8.5.1. Thus, if the permanent display of city-owned sculptures is the type of speech to which the forum analysis applies, the Free Speech Clause would come into play here, just as it would were the city to allow a Christian speaker to discuss the Ten Commandments at a park rally while denying a similar privilege to a Summum speaker. If, on the other hand, the display is viewed as being the city's own speech, Summum cannot complain that Pleasant Grove has violated the Free Speech Clause by discriminating among private speakers based on the content of their message. Nor would it matter that the city's speech takes place in what is otherwise a traditional public forum, or that it favors some religious views over others, since the Free Speech Clause simply does not come into play when the government rather than a private party is the speaker. Thus, the critical question here is how the city's display should be characterized—i.e., as the city's having provided a public forum for private speech or as the city having engaged in its own expression.

In *Pleasant Grove City, Utah v. Summum*, 555 U.S. 460 (2009), the Court on these facts held that the city's permanent monument display qualified as government speech. The eight-member majority noted that "[g]overnments have long used monuments to speak to the public." Id. at 470. That the monuments here were donated by private parties rather than commissioned and financed by the government itself made no difference, for in the end they conveyed what became the city's message. Moreover, said the Court, it was unlikely those viewing the monuments would think the "speaker" to be anyone other than the city itself, since it was the city that selected the pieces for its permanent collection. In doing so, the city used "such content-based factors as esthetics, history, and local culture. The monuments that are accepted, therefore, are meant to convey and have the effect of conveying a government message, and they thus constitute government speech." Id. at 472. And, unlike temporary speakers and temporary displays, where there may be virtually no limit on the number that can be accommodated by the park over time, "it is hard to imagine how a public park could be opened up for the installation of permanent monuments by every person or group wishing to engage in that form of expression." Id. at 479. Thus, said the Court,

> if public parks were considered to be traditional public forums for the purpose of erecting privately donated monuments, most parks would have little choice but to refuse all such donations. And where the application of forum analysis would lead almost inexorably to closing of the forum, it is obvious that forum analysis is out of place.

Id. at 480. Instead, under the government speech doctrine, the city's display was exempt from the constraints of the Free Speech Clause. See also *Walker v. Texas Division, Sons of Confederate Veterans*, 576 U.S. 200, 210-214 (2015) (concluding that, under *Summum*, the content of the specialty state plates constitutes government speech).

Justice Souter, concurring in the *Pleasant Grove* judgment, rejected the majority's categorical treatment of all public monuments as being government speech. However, he agreed that under a more flexible "reasonable observer test," the monuments in question here were such that "a reasonable and fully informed observer would understand the expression to be government speech, as distinct from private speech the government chooses to oblige by allowing the monument to be placed on public land." *Pleasant Grove*, supra, 555 U.S. at 487.

The facts presented in this problem also raise issues under the First Amendment Establishment Clause, issues the Court was not asked to address in *Pleasant Grove*. They were addressed, however, in an earlier decision, *Van Orden v. Perry*, 545 U.S. 677 (2005), involving a virtually identical Ten Commandments monument, also donated by the Fraternal Order of Eagles, this for display on the grounds of the Texas State Capitol. See § 9.2.4 ("Not Foster Excessive Entanglement with Religion" (discussing *Van Orden*)).

If the government, rather than engaging in its own speech, subsidizes or aids private speech, the subsidy program, rather than qualifying as government speech, may be viewed as equivalent to the government's having created a limited or nonpublic forum since public property (i.e., government money) is now being used by private parties for their own speech purposes. In such situations, the Free Speech Clause and its viewpoint neutrality principle apply in full force. For example, in *Shurtleff v. City of Boston*, 596 U.S. 243 (2022), the Court held that a city program that allowed private groups to temporarily display their flags on a city-owned flagpole did not constitute government speech. Hence, the First Amendment barred the city from engaging in viewpoint discrimination against a religious group that wanted to display a religiously themed flag.

Example 8-SS

The Legal Services Corporation (LSC) is a federally created entity that distributes funds appropriated by Congress to local organizations that provide legal services for the poor, including services pertaining to state and federal welfare programs. Since 1996, Congress has prohibited the LSC from funding any organization that represents clients who seek to challenge the constitutionality of state or federal welfare laws. In essence, lawyers from such grantee organizations are permitted to represent welfare clients only in routine benefit matters. If a constitutional issue arises in such a case, the LSC-funded lawyer must decline to address the issue and withdraw her representation. Does this prohibition on government-subsidized lawyer speech represent impermissible viewpoint discrimination? In other words, does the LSC funding program represent a subsidy for private speech so that the program is subject to the First Amendment's proscription against viewpoint discrimination, or, as in *Rust v. Sullivan* and *Pleasant Grove City, Utah v. Summum*, is the program simply a conduit for conveying the government's preferred message, in which case the Free Speech Clause is inapplicable?

EXPLANATION

Explanation

The Court, in *Legal Services Corp. v. Velazquez*, 531 U.S. 533 (2001), held that the LSC funding prohibition amounted to unlawful viewpoint discrimination with respect to private speech. The federal government was funding the private speech of lawyers within the context of what might be characterized as a limited or nonpublic forum, namely, the adversarial system of justice. The prohibition on challenging the constitutionality of a state or federal welfare statute constituted viewpoint discrimination since it precluded legal services lawyers from taking a particular advocacy position with respect to state and federal welfare laws. In essence, the "unconstitutionality" viewpoint was prohibited. Thus, unlike the situation in *Rust* and *Pleasant Grove City*, the government was not paying or drawing upon surrogates to help convey the government's own message. Rather, the government here was limiting the private speech of lawyers made on behalf of their clients and was doing so with respect to a forum—i.e., the courts—that was itself dependent on the speech of the participants. In holding that the measure was unconstitutional, the Court also noted that this prohibition on lawyer speech threatened a "severe impairment of the judicial function" by undermining the judiciary's ability to interpret and apply the law. 531 U.S. at 546.

You might sense that the distinction, at least between *Rust* and *Velazquez*, is somewhat elusive, for the doctors in *Rust* might be characterized—and viewed by the public—as being likewise engaged in private speech when they consult with their patients. This tension between the two decisions suggests that each case might have involved other policy concerns that transcend the First Amendment, namely, the underlying abortion controversy in *Rust* and a perception of interference with the judicial function in *Velazquez*. Hence, the presence or absence of a First Amendment issue in the context of a government subsidy will often depend on how the Court characterizes that subsidy—funding the government's message or subsidizing private speech—and that characterization may in turn be a product of non-First Amendment concerns.

§8.7 THE FIRST AMENDMENT RIGHT OF ASSOCIATION

The Court has referred to the constitutional right of association in two separate contexts. The first involves those intimate relationships that are protected by the right of privacy under the due process clauses—e.g., marriage, parent and child, and extended family. See §§ 2.5.1-2.5.3. The second, which is the topic of this section, protects the freedom of individuals to gather in small groups or to unite in larger organizations to engage in activities protected by the First Amendment, such as "speech, assembly, petition for the redress of grievances, and the exercise of religion." *Roberts v. United States Jaycees*, 468 U.S. 609, 618 (1984).

This First Amendment right of association, although not mentioned in the text of the Constitution, is implicit in the textual freedoms protected by the First Amendment. The exercise of those textual freedoms presumes the availability of opportunities for human dialogue and united action, without which the expressly provided rights would be meaningless. The right of association thus assures individuals the freedom to choose with whom, and for what causes, they will gather to exercise their First Amendment freedoms.

For purposes of analysis, the Court has divided laws that infringe upon the First Amendment right of expressive association into two categories—those that infringe directly and those that do so only indirectly. The first category embraces laws that mandate or prohibit association itself by regulating the membership of a group or prohibiting a group's existence. A law prescribing who must be a member of a group would fall into this category, as would one barring membership in the group, for the right to associate includes a corresponding right not to do so. By contrast, the second category involves laws that prescribe the terms and conditions on which association may occur, but without going so far as to compel or prohibit association itself. Thus, a law requiring certain expressive groups to file their membership lists with the state would fall into this second category, for it neither requires nor bars association as such. We will look at each of these categories in turn.

In the first category of direct infringement cases, courts apply "strict scrutiny." Under this standard of review, a law will pass constitutional muster only if the government can show that it was "adopted to serve compelling state interests, unrelated to the suppression of ideas, that cannot be achieved through means significantly less restrictive of associational freedoms." *Roberts*, supra, 468 U.S. at 623. See § 8.3.10 ("Compelled Speech").

EXAMPLE

Example 8-TT

The Hillside Board of Education requires all teachers to take an oath that they do not belong to any organization that "advocates the unlawful overthrow of the government." The purpose of the oath requirement is to protect the public education system from subversion by, among other things, keeping subversives out of the teaching ranks. Hayes, a member of the Masked Militia Movement (MMM), was fired from his job as a high school physical education teacher because he refused to take this oath. The MMM does advocate the violent overthrow of all government. Does Hayes's dismissal violate his right of association?

Explanation

Since the oath requirement in effect forbids membership in a particular group, it is subject to strict scrutiny. While the Board might claim a compelling interest in not having students taught to violently overthrow the government, this law would fail the second prong of the strict scrutiny analysis since there are less burdensome means of insuring that teachers do not convey such doctrines to their pupils. These would include interpreting the oath to apply only to active membership in such organizations, and then only when an individual has actual knowledge of the illegal aims of the organization and the specific intent to further those illegal aims. Alternatively, and even less burdensomely, the Board could simply insist that whatever a teacher's personal beliefs, such doctrines not be taught in class. See *Keyishian v. Board of Regents*, 385 U.S. 589, 606-610 (1967); *United States v. Robel*, 389 U.S. 258, 265-268 (1967).

In contrast to the first category, laws that fall into the second category infringe only indirectly on the right of association. Rather than mandating or prohibiting membership in any particular association, such measures impose some special hardship or burden on an expressive group. Examples would include laws compelling disclosure of a group's confidential membership lists, where doing so might discourage membership or jeopardize a group's existence; laws interfering with a group's internal operations; and laws creating barriers to a group's participation in the political process. Measures falling into this second category are subject to a less demanding "exacting scrutiny" standard of review. Under that test, the government must show that there is "'a substantial relation between the disclosure requirement and a sufficiently important governmental interest.' *Doe v. Reed*, 561 U.S. 186, 196 (2010)." *Americans for Prosperity Found.*, 594 U.S. 595, 607 (2021). In addition, the disclosure requirement "must be narrowly tailored to the interest it promotes, even if it is not the least restrictive means of achieving that end." Id. at 609-610. The test here is a flexible one that considers the "seriousness of the actual burden on First Amendment rights." Id. at 607. The greater the burden, the greater "the strength of the governmental interest" necessary to sustain it. Id. This exacting scrutiny test is somewhat weaker than strict scrutiny in several key respects. First, under exacting scrutiny, while the state's interest must be "sufficiently important," it need not be "compelling." Id. Second, while under exacting scrutiny the means chosen must be "narrowly tailored" to the state's interest, they need not "be the least restrictive means" available. Id. at 609-610. And third, while strict scrutiny is usually triggered only if it is shown that a law has "impinged on" a fundamental liberty, exacting scrutiny applies regardless of "the severity of any demonstrated burden." Id. at 610. Instead, merely "[t]he *risk* of a chilling effect on association is enough. . . ." Id. at 618-619 (emphasis added). And see § 2.4.4 ("The Concept of Impingement").

Example 8-UU

At the height of the civil rights movement, the Attorney General (AG) of Alabama brought an equity suit to enjoin the National Association for the Advancement of Colored People (NAACP) from conducting activities within the state. The AG argued that the organization had failed to qualify to do business within the state as required by Alabama law. The NAACP claimed a First Amendment right to engage in the contested activities. As part of the AG's lawsuit, a state court ordered the NAACP to turn over its membership lists to the AG. Fearing reprisal against its members, the organization refused to comply with the order. For this refusal, the NAACP was held in contempt. Would enforced disclosure under these circumstances violate the right of association of NAACP members?

Explanation

Under the Court's current standards, this case involves only an indirect (albeit serious) infringement on the NAACP and on its members' rights of association. For while the state's purpose may have been to destroy the NAACP, it did not outlaw the organization or prohibit membership in it. Compelled disclosure of affiliation with a group engaged in advocacy can have a chilling effect on a prospective member's willingness to join the group, and on the group's ability to convey its message. Here, the potential for reprisal was quite real, given the NAACP's "uncontroverted showing that on past occasions revelation of the identity of its rank-and-file members had exposed those members to economic reprisal, loss of employment, threat of physical coercion, and other manifestations of public hostility."

To uphold this compelled disclosure, the state must show that there is a substantial relation between the disclosure sought and an important state interest, and that the disclosure is narrowly tailored to that end. The state here claimed it needed the membership lists to determine whether the NAACP was conducting intrastate business in violation of Alabama's foreign corporation law. While this state interest might qualify as important, there is no substantial relation between it and the disclosures sought since that information was either irrelevant to the state's claimed need, already in the state's hands, or obtainable from the NAACP without having to access its membership lists. In *NAACP v. Alabama*, 357 U.S. 449, 463 (1958), the Court, without precisely defining the applicable standard of review, concluded that Alabama had not "demonstrated an interest in obtaining the disclosures . . . which is sufficient to justify the deterrent effect . . . these disclosures may well have on the . . . petitioner's members . . . right of association."

EXAMPLE

Example 8-VV

Under State X law, any charitable organization soliciting funds in the state must disclose the identities of its major donors by annually providing the state with a copy of the organization's federal IRS Schedule B, a form that contains this information. State X collects this information from about 60,000 charities each year. It claims that having this information on hand will make it easier to police misconduct by charities. However, it then consults the Schedule B only if it receives a complaint about a charity, something that has occurred fewer than a dozen times over the past 10 years. If the state wishes to investigate a charity, it could obtain this same information either by subpoena or by audit letter, though this could take more time and might tip off a charity under suspicion. Two charities have sued claiming that State X's Schedule B filing requirement violates their rights under the First Amendment. Have plaintiffs asserted a meritorious claim?

EXPLANATION

Explanation

The State X law only indirectly infringes on the right of association since it regulates a charity's activities rather than prohibiting its existence or membership in it. Thus, "exacting" rather than "strict" scrutiny applies. State X will argue that its goal is to prevent fraud by charitable organizations. While this is clearly an important interest, it must also show that the universal filing requirement is both substantially related and narrowly tailored to that end. State X will have difficulty making the substantially related showing, given the miniscule number of cases in which its copies of the Schedule B are in fact utilized. Nor is the requirement narrowly tailored to that end, for there are less burdensome ways of obtaining the requisite information in the relative handful of cases where it is needed. Though State X need not use the least burdensome means—which might be to rely entirely on other information without ever demanding the IRS Schedule B—the fact that there is the much less burdensome alternative of collecting the form only in cases where it is needed should be enough to invalidate a universal filing requirement that burdens 60,000 charities. As to its argument that this alternative would be less effective because it might slow things down or alert suspect groups, State X would have to offer evidence to support this claim. Moreover, any miniscule additional benefit in a tiny number of cases would still not justify the totally unnecessary burden the law imposes on those charities with respect to which the filing requirement renders the state no benefit at all. Finally, State X might argue that its requirement does not impinge on the right of association because the charities have already filed a Schedule B with the IRS, and because there is no evidence that it has had a chilling effect on anyone's right of association. Even if these allegations were true, in freedom of association cases such as this one, the "severity of any demonstrated burden" is not dispositive. "[T]he protections of the First Amendment are triggered not only by actual restraints on an individual's ability to join with others to further shared goals. The *risk* of a chilling effect on association is enough, because the First Amendment freedoms need breathing space to survive." See *Americans for Prosperity Found. v. Bonta*, 594 U.S. 595, 619 (2021) (emphasis added) (internal citation omitted) (facially invalidating identical California law as violating First Amendment right of free association).

The issue of compelled disclosure of affiliation has also arisen in the context of referendum petitions and other ballot initiatives where, pursuant to a public records act, a governmental entity has been asked to reveal the names of those who signed a particular ballot measure. The Court has held that disclosing the names of such referendum signers does not necessarily violate the First Amendment. See *Doe v. Reed*, 561 U.S. 186 (2010) (rejecting a facial attack claiming that the First Amendment right of association prohibits a state from *ever* releasing the names of referendum signers, but leaving open the possibility that signers might be able to show that as applied to them, disclosure would be unconstitutional).

Example 8-WW

EXAMPLE

The State of Washington allows its citizens to challenge enacted state laws by referendum. To put such a referendum petition on the state ballot, 4% of Washington voters must sign a petition that includes their names and addresses. The state's Public Records Act (PRA) authorizes private parties to obtain copies of government documents, including submitted referendum petitions. After Washington's governor signed into law SB 5688, a statute that expanded the rights of state-registered domestic partners including same-sex partners, the group Protect Marriage Washington (PMW) collected enough signatures to put a referendum (R-71) on the ballot that would allow the state's voters to themselves vote on SB 5688. While PRA then urged voters to reject SB 5688, the voters approved R-71, thus preserving SB 5688 as state law. When the state was asked to release copies of the R-71 petition, including the names and addresses of its 137,000 signers, PMW and some individual signers sued to enjoin the state from releasing any documents that would reveal the names or contact information of R-71's signers. Plaintiffs allege that such publication would violate their right of association because "there is a reasonable probability that the signatories . . . will be subject to threats, harassment, and reprisals." Would the state's release of this information violate the signers' First Amendment rights?

Explanation

Since the release of this information would impose only an indirect burden on plaintiffs' right of association, "exacting" rather than "strict" scrutiny will apply. Washington clearly has a "sufficiently important governmental interest" in releasing the information, since public access to it goes to the heart of democratic government and the need for preservation of political transparency. Just as legislators' individual identities and actions are a legitimate focus of public concern, so too are the identities of petition signers who, in the initiative process, act in the legislators' stead. There is also a "substantial relationship" between such releases and protecting electoral integrity, for without this information, the public cannot confirm that the referendum process was properly invoked. As to whether the disclosure is "narrowly tailored" to promoting these interests, for disclosure to serve the purpose of validating the initiative process there should be public access to as much of the signatory information as possible. A generalized, unsubstantiated concern about possible reprisals from the release of signers' names should thus not suffice to impose a blanket ban on making this information public, for that would totally defeat the state's interest. On the other hand, one might argue that if a particular individual can demonstrate that, as applied to them, there is a reasonable probability that disclosure of their personal information would subject them to threats, harassment, or reprisals, this might support case-specific relief. Yet if such relief were readily available to a large segment of the community, this would defeat the inherent need for transparency in the referendum process. There is thus a good argument that the state's universal disclosure mechanism is "narrowly tailored" to promoting its goal of political transparency, even without the possibility of individual exclusions.

In *Doe v. Reed*, supra, the Court on these facts rejected a facial challenge to a similar law but left the door open to an as-applied challenge. However, four concurring Justices suggested that even an as-applied challenge to a referendum disclosure law was unlikely to succeed. Id. at 214-215 (Sotomayor, J., et al., concurring); id. at 218 (Stevens, J., et al., concurring). On remand, the district court rejected plaintiffs' as-applied challenge, finding that the facts "do not rise to the level of demonstrating that a reasonable probability of threats, harassment, or reprisals exists as to the signers. . . ." *Doe v. Reed*, 823 F. Supp. 2d 1195, 1212 (W.D. Wash. 2011), *appeal dismissed as moot*, 697 F.3d 1235 (9th Cir. 2012). In short, the circumstances that allowed the state to refuse disclosure in *NAACP v. Alabama* will rarely if ever be found to exist in the referendum setting.

The right of association does not protect all associations, but only those related to First Amendment protected activity. Thus, a law partnership designed solely to promote the economic interests of its partners is not protected by the right of association, at least not to the extent the partnership is engaged in for-profit economic activity. The right to associate for economic gain has not been recognized as a First Amendment right, although the First Amendment does protect rights of commercial speech. On the other hand, if the purpose of a law partnership is to engage in political advocacy through litigation or lobbying, the protections would attach. Political advocacy is a quintessential First Amendment right, and the right of association is tailor-made to protect collective efforts to engage in that expressive activity. See, e.g., *NAACP v. Button,* 371 U.S. 415 (1963) (NAACP's sponsorship of civil rights litigation was expressive activity protected by the First Amendment).

But suppose our law partnership is somewhat more complicated. Although created primarily for economic purposes, it also engages in significant expressive advocacy by performing a substantial amount of pro bono litigation for the homeless. Does the firm's dominant economic purpose preclude application of the right of association, or does its expressive advocacy transform the economic enterprise into an expressive association? This same question applies to other groups that associate for a combination of economic, social, and expressive activities.

The Court has set a very low threshold for concluding that an association is entitled to First Amendment protection. "[A]ssociations do not have to associate for the 'purpose' of disseminating a certain message in order to be entitled to the protections of the First Amendment. An association must merely engage in expressive activity that could be impaired in order to be entitled to protection." *Boy Scouts of America v. Dale*, 530 U.S. 640, 655 (2000). If an organization engages in any protected expressive conduct, the Court will ask whether the alleged government infringement on associational rights impinges on that protected activity. Justice O'Connor argued for a more flexible test. In *Roberts v. United States Jaycees,* supra, she suggested that the right of association should attach only to organizations whose "activity is *predominantly* protected expression. . . ." 468 U.S. at 635-636 (emphasis supplied). While her approach poses the risk of underprotecting First Amendment associational activities, in most cases the results under the O'Connor approach and that adopted by the Court should be roughly similar.

Example 8-XX

The Junior Chamber of Commerce (JCC) is an all-male membership organization that promotes and practices the arts of good salesmanship and sound management. The JCC claims that the training provided to its members in these areas gives them an advantage in the business world. Aside from these training programs, one of the major activities of the JCC is the recruitment and sale of memberships in the organization. Over 80 percent of the national officers' time is devoted to recruiting new members, referred to generally as customers. The JCC at times takes advocacy positions on political and public issues. A JCC bylaw provides that one aim of the organization is to promote "genuine Americanism and civic virtue" in young men. The State of Minnesota, under its public accommodations law, has ordered the JCC to admit women as full voting members. The JCC objects that the forced admission of women would violate its male members' rights of association by impairing their right not to associate with women. May the JCC claim a First Amendment right of expressive association? If so, would that right be violated by application of Minnesota's public accommodations law?

Explanation

If one applies the approach endorsed by Justice O'Connor in *Roberts v. United States Jaycees*, supra, given the largely commercial nature of the JCC, the organization's collateral expressive activities might be insufficient to qualify it as a group to which the First Amendment right of association attaches. Under the more lenient approach adopted by the Court, however, one can presume that the right of association is at least implicated, since the organization engages in some protected First Amendment activity. The question then is not whether the JCC qualifies as an expressive association, but whether the forced association with women impermissibly infringes on the expressive component of its mission of fostering civic virtue and commercial success.

Because this law directly regulates an association's membership, it falls into the category of cases calling for strict scrutiny. Yet it should still pass muster. First, any infringement on the JCC's expressive activities is minimal. There is nothing to suggest that admitting women as full members will impede the JCC's ability to engage in its regular activities or to disseminate its preferred views on gender or any other topic. Second, the state's interest in eradicating gender discrimination is compelling and is unrelated to the suppression of ideas. Finally, the means chosen here are the least restrictive means of advancing the state's interest, since anything less than full membership would defeat its goal of ensuring gender equality. See *Roberts v. United States Jaycees*, 468 U.S. 609 (1984) (applying strict scrutiny on these facts to uphold Minnesota's action against the Jaycees). See also *Board of Directors of Rotary Int'l v. Rotary Club of Duarte*, 481 U.S. 537, 548-549 (1987) (applying strict scrutiny to uphold California's mandate that a Rotary Club admit women).

EXAMPLE

Example 8-YY

The Youth Club of America (YCA) is a private nonprofit organization engaged in instilling its system of values in young people. The YCA seeks to inculcate these values by having its adult leaders spend time with youth members, instructing and engaging them in activities like camping, archery, and fishing. The organization asserts that homosexual conduct is inconsistent with those values and with the YCA Oath, which requires youths to be "morally straight," and with YCA Law which requires that persons be "clean." The YCA does not specifically teach members about sex. Rather, youths are instructed to receive guidance on this topic from their parents, spiritual leaders, or professionals. The YCA has a written policy against having avowed homosexuals as adult leaders. That policy is based on a view that homosexuality is inconsistent with the YCA Oath and Law. Dale is an adult whose position as assistant director of a YCA club was revoked after the YCA learned he is an avowed homosexual and gay rights activist. Dale filed suit in state court, alleging that his dismissal violated the state's public accommodations law which bars discrimination on the basis of sexual orientation. The state supreme court upheld Dale's state law claim and ruled that application of that law did not violate the YCA's First Amendment right of expressive association. Is the YCA's right of expressive association implicated here? Assuming that it is, would that right be violated by application of the state's law requiring the YCA to accept Dale as an adult leader?

EXPLANATION

Explanation

The YCA will argue that it is an expressive association to which the First Amendment should apply since it engages in expressive activity as part of its efforts to instill values in its young members. For example, the YCA Oath declares, "On my honor I will do my best . . . To keep myself physically strong, mentally awake, and morally straight." The YCA Law states, "A YCA member is: . . . Thrifty, Brave, Clean, and Reverent." Many YCA activities focus on promoting these ideals. The YCA also urges that the ideals of being "morally straight" and "clean" include an admonition against homosexuality, and that its policy against homosexual adult leaders is premised on that admonition. Thus, if a homosexual were allowed to be a YCA leader, the implied endorsement of homosexuality would run counter to the message the YCA wishes to convey on that topic. Therefore, Dale's inclusion as a leader would substantially burden the YCA's right of expressive association.

On the other hand, one can argue that the YCA does not engage in any expressive activity regarding sexuality. Nothing in its Oath or Law addresses sexuality, nor does the YCA attempt to instill the value of heterosexuality through its youth activities. Instead, the YCA is largely silent on this matter, instructing its youth leaders to refer questions on these topics to parents, spiritual leaders, or professionals. That being the case, the sexual orientation of an adult leader would arguably have no discernible impact on the YCA's expressive activities. So viewed, application of the state public accommodations law would not implicate much less burden the YCA's expressive right of association, and the First Amendment therefore should not come into play.

In *Boy Scouts of America v. Dale,* 530 U.S. 640 (2000), the case on which this example is based, the Court deferred to the Boy Scouts of America's (BSA) characterization of its expressive mission as including an admonition against homosexuality. "The fact that the organization does not trumpet its views from the housetops, or that it tolerates dissent within its ranks, does not mean that its views receive no First Amendment protection." Id. at 656. The four dissenters focused on the fact that the BSA engaged in no expressive activity on the topic of sexuality, the same conclusion reached below by the New Jersey Supreme Court. *Dale v. Boy Scouts of America,* 734 A.2d 1196, 1223-1224 (N.J. 1999).

Once the Court concluded that the forced inclusion of Dale would "directly," "immediately," and "significantly affect" the BSA's right of expressive association, strict scrutiny rather than an "intermediate standard of review" was called for since the case involved an association's membership rules. 530 U.S. at 656, 659. The Court agreed that states have a compelling interest in eliminating discrimination, at least in "traditional places of public accommodation—like inns and trains." Id. at 656. It suggested that that interest grows weaker when such laws are extended to private membership organizations like the Boy Scouts, particularly when the extension was affected, as here, by a state supreme court's novel reading of a state statute, rather than explicitly by the legislature itself. Id. at 657. In its strict scrutiny analysis, the Court never asked whether the state had any less burdensome means of achieving its nondiscrimination goal. Instead, "[t]he state interests embodied in New Jersey's public accommodations law do not justify such a severe intrusion on the Boy Scouts' rights to freedom of association" Id. at 659. This suggests that in the Court's eyes, the state's interest did not rise to the level of "compelling," perhaps because it was not clearly set forth in a state statute, thus rendering any further strict scrutiny analysis unnecessary. Might the Court have reached a different conclusion had the statute expressly prohibited discrimination based on sexual orientation? A postscript: 15 years after it won this case, the BSA, faced with widespread criticism and loss of support, abandoned its blanket prohibition against gay leaders and instead allowed local troops to address this issue for themselves. See *Boy Scouts faring well a year after easing ban on gay adults* (apnews.com) (July 23, 2016).

The Right of Association and State Regulation of Elections

In the special context of state regulation of elections, the Court has adopted a variable standard of review for right-of-association cases. If the burden imposed on associational rights is deemed severe, strict scrutiny applies and the state regulation must be shown to be narrowly tailored to advance a "compelling" state interest. See, e.g., *Tashjian v. Republican Party of Conn.*, 479 U.S. 208 (1986) (applying strict scrutiny and striking down state law requiring that persons voting in a party's primary be members of that party, when party wished to open its primary to all voters as a way of attracting new members); *Eu v. San Francisco County Democratic Central Comm.*, 489 U.S. 214 (1989) (applying strict scrutiny and striking down state law that barred governing bodies of political parties from endorsing primary candidates and that dictated the organization and composition of a party's governing body). If, however, the burden is of a lesser character, "important regulatory interests" will suffice to sustain the measure, without any requirement that it be closely tailored to achieving those interests. *Timmons v. Twin Cities New Party*, 520 U.S. 351, 358-359 (1997). There is no bright-line test to measure the difference between a "severe" burden and a "lesser" one. Rather, the distinction turns on the degree to which a state regulation impairs the ability of a political party or candidate to exercise core First Amendment functions.

EXAMPLE

Example 8-ZZ

In 1996, a California ballot proposition, Proposition 198, changed the state's primary election from a closed primary, in which only a political party's members can vote on that party's nominees, to a blanket or open primary in which nonmembers of a party can cross over and vote for that party's nominee. Thus, a person registered in one party can participate in the nomination of a candidate for another party. The candidate of each party who wins the most votes is that party's nominee for the general election, even though many of those votes might have been cast by members of another party. Four political parties filed suit challenging the practice. Each party prohibits nonmembers from voting in its primary, the purpose of this requirement being to allow only party members to select the candidate who will then represent the views of the party in the general election. Does Proposition 198 impose a severe burden on the associational rights of these parties?

EXPLANATION

Explanation

Yes. Proposition 198 forces a political party to alter its candidate-selection process in a manner that allows nonmembers of the party, who may have different views from that of the party (and who may outnumber party members), to participate in the selection of the party's candidates for office. Since a nominee represents the collective views of those who vote for her, the blanket primary system could well have a severe impact on the party's ability to convey its viewpoint to the electorate during the general election. In fact, participation by nonparty members may alter the views of the party by nominating a candidate who does not share the views of the party's majority. This likely negative impact of Proposition 198 on political parties was supported by a district court record that included four days of expert testimony and many exhibits. *California Democratic Party v. Jones*, 984 F. Supp. 1288, 1292-1293 (E.D. Calif. 1997). Given its significant negative impact on political parties, Proposition 198 must therefore be narrowly tailored to advance a compelling state interest. See *California Democratic Party v. Jones*, 530 U.S. 567 (2000) (so holding under similar facts). The Court in *California Democratic Party* then concluded that the asserted interests of the state—producing elected officials who better represent the electorate, expanding candidate debate beyond the scope of partisan concerns, ensuring that disenfranchised persons enjoy the right to an effective vote, promoting fairness, affording voters greater choice, increasing voter participation, and protecting privacy—were not compelling under the circumstances. Id. at 582-586.

While the Court in *California Democratic Party* found that the law in question imposed a "severe" burden on the political parties' right of association, thus calling for the application of strict scrutiny, the Court has not hesitated in other case to characterize the burden as a "lesser" one, thus permitting a more lenient standard of review. See *Clingman v. Beaver*, 544 U.S. 581 (2005) (state law that allows political party to invite only its own members and registered independents to vote in primary does not impose severe burden on right of association); *Timmons v. Twin Cities Area New Party*, 520 U.S. 351, 363 (1997) (state law barring a candidate from appearing on the ballot as the nominee of more than one political party imposed burdens on party's associational rights that "though not trivial—are not severe").

Example 8-AAA

Suppose that after the Supreme Court decision in *California Democratic Party v. Jones* (see Example 8-ZZ), the State of Washington, whose primary election procedures were essentially identical to those struck down in *Jones*, amended its election law. Under the new Washington statute, there is still a single primary election. Each candidate files his or her own declaration as to their party preference. Their name and their designated party preference then appear on the ballot, no matter how repugnant they may be to the party with which they have chosen to affiliate themselves. Voters in the primary election may select any candidate listed on the ballot, regardless of the party preference of the candidates or of the voter. The candidates for each office with the highest and second-highest vote totals advance to the general election, regardless of their stated party preferences. Thus, the general election could pit two candidates with the same listed party preference against one another. Each candidate's party preference is listed on the general election ballot and may not be changed between the primary and general elections. Before any elections were held under the new law, the Democratic and Republican parties joined in a suit to declare the system unconstitutional. They claim that the new system severely burdens their right of association by usurping the parties' ability to nominate their own candidates and by forcing them to associate with candidates whom they may not in fact endorse. Plaintiffs contend that the statute is thus facially unconstitutional under *Jones*, since it allows primary voters who are unaffiliated with a party to choose the party's nominee. Is the new Washington procedure invalid under *Jones*, or are the two cases constitutionally distinguishable?

Explanation

EXPLANATION

In *Washington State Grange v. Washington State Republican Party*, 552 U.S. 442 (2008), the Court held that *Jones* did not control this case because Washington's primary election, unlike California's blanket primary, did not purport to select or designate the *political parties'* nominees. Instead, it merely registered *voter* preferences among the candidates who appeared on the ballot with the candidates' own self-described party affiliations. In the later general election, political parties remain free to endorse or not endorse any candidate chosen in the open primary, regardless of a candidate's self-described party affiliation. Nor does the statute or the primary ballot refer to candidates as being party nominees. Washington's election regulations also specifically state that the primary "does not serve to determine the nominees of a political party but serves to winnow the number of candidates to a final list of two for the general election." Parties thus remain free to nominate and promote their own candidates but must do so by means other than simply designating them as such on the primary election ballot.

The Court agreed that "it is *possible* voters will misinterpret the candidates' party-preference designation as reflecting endorsement by the parties. But," said the Court, "we cannot strike down [the statute] on its face based on the mere possibility of voter confusion." Id. at 455 (emphasis in original). Moreover, as to the likelihood of any such voter confusion, here, unlike *California Democratic Party v. Jones*, there was no evidentiary record from which to assess the statute's likely impact, for the district court here granted summary judgment for plaintiffs less than two months after the suit was filed. *Washington State Republican Party v. Logan*, 377 F. Supp. 2d 907 (W.D. Wash. 2005). As the Supreme Court noted, the measure might well be implemented in ways that would eliminate any possible voter confusion, such as by having the ballot contain "prominent disclaimers explaining that party preference reflects only the self-description of the candidate and not an official endorsement by the party." 552 U.S. at 456. Since there were "at least some ways" the law could be constitutionally applied, the statute "*on its face* does not impose a severe burden on political parties' associational rights. . . ." Id. at 457-458 (emphasis supplied). The plaintiffs' "arguments to the contrary rest on factual assumptions about voter confusion that can be evaluated only in the context of an as-applied challenge. . . ." Id. at 444. Employing a deferential standard of review, the Court then upheld the measure on the basis that it furthered "[t]he State's asserted interest in providing voters with relevant information about the candidates on the ballot. . . ." Id. at 458.

After the Supreme Court rejected the facial challenge to Washington's primary election procedures, the state implemented its primary election law in a manner consistent with the Supreme Court's suggestions for eliminating possible voter confusion. Not surprisingly, the constitutionality of that statute was then upheld in a subsequent as-applied challenge. See *Washington State Republican Party v. Washington State Grange*, 676 F. 3d 784 (9th Cir.), *cert. denied*, 568 U.S. 814 (2012).

§8.8 SPECIAL PROBLEMS OF THE MEDIA

The text of the First Amendment refers to the "freedom of speech" and "of the press." Although one Justice has suggested that the specific reference to the press indicates that the press should be entitled to special protections beyond those afforded the general public (see Potter Stewart, "Or of the Press," 26 *Hastings L.J.* 631 (1975)), the Court has never adopted this approach. Rather, both freedoms are seen as part of a more encompassing freedom of expression. In cases specifically involving the press, however, the Court has not ignored the special role played by the press in our system of freedom of expression. In this section, we will examine some specific problems that arise in the context of freedom of the press.

§8.8.1 Access to Information

From time to time, members of the press have argued for a right of access to information over which the government may enjoy a monopoly. The Court's decisions have made it clear, however, that the press enjoys no greater access to government-controlled information than that enjoyed by the public at large. *Saxbe v. Washington Post Co.*, 417 U.S. 843 (1974); *Pell v. Procunier*, 417 U.S. 817 (1974). In *Houchins v. KQED, Inc.*, 438 U.S. 1 (1978), however, the Court, in a three-one-three decision, held that the "equal" access granted the press and public must afford the press "effective" access and must, therefore, take into account the special needs of the press. For example, press access might include the use of microphones or other equipment under circumstances where the use of such equipment is denied to the public. This result, however, was a product of Justice Stewart's swing vote between the plurality and the dissent; as a consequence, the decision may be of very limited precedential value.

§8.8.2 Access to Criminal Proceedings

Despite the Court's reluctance to enforce a general right of access to government-controlled information, in *Richmond Newspapers, Inc. v. Virginia*, 448 U.S. 555 (1980), the Court held that both the public and the press have a First Amendment right to attend criminal trials. This right is premised on the historical tradition of open criminal trials and on the public's right to know what transpires in a criminal proceeding. As a consequence of this right, a criminal trial cannot be closed to the public or the press in the absence of specific findings that establish both a compelling governmental interest in closure—typically, fairness to the defendant or the protection of a witness—and a means narrowly tailored to advance that interest. *Globe Newspaper Co. v. Superior Court*, 457 U.S. 596, 606-607 (1982).

In *Globe Newspaper*, for example, the Court struck down a state law that required trial court judges to exclude the press and public from all criminal trials involving sexual offenses against persons under 18 years of age. The Court agreed that the state's interest in protecting minor victims of sex crimes from further trauma and embarrassment was compelling but concluded that the interest could be adequately served by a less burdensome nonmandatory law that assessed the propriety of closing trials on a case-by-case basis. Id. at 608. See also *Press-Enterprise Co. v. Superior Court*, 464 U.S. 501, 510-513 (1984) (applying same standard to jury voir dire).

Several commentators have suggested that the right of access to criminal trials established in *Richmond Newspapers* could serve as the foundation for a more inclusive "right to know" directed toward providing the public with the fullest possible access to government-controlled information. See, e.g., Anthony Lewis, "A Public Right to Know about Public Institutions: The First Amendment as Sword," 1980 *Sup. Ct. Rev.* 1. The Court has yet to accept that invitation.

§8.8.3 Gag Orders in Criminal Proceedings

A concomitant to the right of access to criminal trials is the right to publish information procured through that access. As a consequence, gag orders that prohibit the press from publishing accounts of ongoing criminal proceedings are highly suspect, this despite the potential conflict between the right to publish and the defendant's right to a fair trial. As the Court recognized in *Nebraska Press Assn. v. Stuart*, 427 U.S. 539, 559 (1976), a judicially imposed gag order is a prior restraint and is, therefore, subject to the strictest scrutiny—"prior restraints on speech and publication are the most serious and the least tolerable infringement on First Amendment rights." See § 8.2.4.

Although the *Nebraska Press* Court did not hold that such orders are per se invalid, the tenor of the Court's opinion, along with that of concurring opinions, suggests that the circumstances under which such orders will be permitted are rare to nonexistent. This does not mean that the First Amendment right to publish automatically trumps the Sixth Amendment guarantee of a fair trial. Rather, the heavy presumption against prior restraints requires that the trial court seek measures that will accommodate both rights. At a minimum, therefore, a trial court is required to make specific findings that there are no less intrusive means for protecting the integrity of the trial process. The *Nebraska Press* Court suggested a litany of such alternatives: change of venue, postponement of the trial, searching questioning of prospective jurors, the use of emphatic and clear instructions, and sequestration of jurors. Id. at 563-564. In the vast majority of cases, these alternatives will obviate any necessity to impose a gag order on the press.

The Court has not applied the rule of *Nebraska Press* to civil proceedings, and, therefore, gag orders may be more easily sustained in the civil context. See *Seattle Times Co. v. Rhinehart*, 467 U.S. 20 (1984) (upholding order restricting newspaper from disclosing information it had received as part of discovery in defamation case).

§8.8.4 The Publication of Truthful, Lawfully Obtained Information

The Court has consistently upheld the right of the press to publish truthful information lawfully obtained from public records. While the right is not absolute, any potential infringement on that right will be subject to what is in essence strict scrutiny. Thus, a newspaper or other mass-media instrument may be punished for such a publication only when the proscription on publication is "narrowly tailored to a state interest of the highest order. . . ." *Florida Star v. B.J.F.*, 491 U.S. 524, 541 (1989).

This is a difficult standard to satisfy. In *Florida Star*, for example, the state attempted to impose civil liability—negligence per se—for publication of the identity of a rape victim whose name had accidentally appeared in a police report. The Court agreed that protecting the privacy of a rape victim was an interest of the "highest order," but found that the means chosen by the state were not sufficiently tailored to meet the constitutional standard. Three reasons were given. First, the state could have protected the victim's privacy interest by excluding her name from the police report. Next, the negligence per se standard swept too broadly by imposing liability even when the victim's identity was well known throughout the community. And finally, the proscription was underinclusive, since it applied only to the mass media. See *Smith v. Daily Mail Publishing Co.*, 443 U.S. 97 (1979) (upholding right of press to publish lawfully obtained name of youth charged as a juvenile offender); *Cox Broadcasting v. Cohn*, 420 U.S. 469 (1975) (upholding right of press to publish name of rape-murder victim that had been lawfully obtained from court records).

Example 8-BBB

During collective bargaining negotiations between a teachers' union and a local school board, an unidentified individual illegally intercepted and recorded a conversation between two of the union's negotiators. During the intercepted conversation, one of the union negotiators stated, "We're gonna have to go to their homes to blow off their front porches." A tape of the intercepted conversation was passed on to a radio commentator who then played the entire tape on the air in connection with news reports about the settlement of the negotiations. The union negotiators sued the commentator for damages under a federal statute creating a private right of action against anyone who "intentionally discloses . . . to any other person the contents of any wire, oral, or electronic communication, knowing or having reason to know that the information was obtained through the interception of a wire, oral, or electronic communication. . . ." 18 U.S.C. §§ 2511(1)(c), 2520(c)(2). Assuming the elements of the statute have been satisfied, would application of it to these facts violate the First Amendment? In answering this question, consider what facts would be significant to a court confronted with this question and what interests might be advanced to justify punishing the publisher.

Explanation

These facts differ from those in *Florida Star v. B.J.F.* While both cases involve the publication of truthful information, the facts given here involve an illegal interception of a private conversation, albeit a conversation on a topic of legitimate public concern. Narrowly stated, the question is whether the privilege recognized in *Florida Star* should apply to the publication of truthful information of public concern by a person who lawfully obtained that information but who knew or should have known that the information was itself obtained through unlawful means. The Court, on similar facts, held that the publication was privileged. *Bartnicki v. Vopper*, 532 U.S. 514 (2001). Key factors for the Court were that the information was truthful, that the radio commentator did not participate in the illegal interception, that he in fact received the information through lawful means, and that the subject matter of the intercepted conversation was a topic of legitimate public concern.

The United States, which had intervened in the lawsuit to defend the constitutionality of the federal statute, proffered two justifications for the statutory ban—"first, the interest in removing an incentive for parties to intercept private conversations, and second, the interest in minimizing the harm to persons whose conversations have been illegally intercepted." Id. at 529. The Court rejected both justifications, at least as applied in this particular case. As to the first, the Court explained that in the vast majority of cases the interest in deterrence could be fully vindicated by punishing the wrongful interceptor. The incidental deterrent effect of punishing the subsequent publisher was insufficient to justify this restriction on pure speech. As to the second, the Court agreed that the interest in protecting privacy might be strong enough to overcome the First Amendment in some cases—e.g., those involving trade secrets or domestic gossip concerning matters of purely private concern. But in the context of the publication of a matter of public concern, as was the case here, the Court concluded that the interest of the government in protecting privacy must give way to the right to publish truthful information that had been lawfully obtained by the publisher.

§8.8.5 The Protection of Confidential Sources

In *Branzburg v. Hayes*, 408 U.S. 665 (1972), the Court rejected claims by news reporters that they had a First Amendment privilege to shield confidential sources when subpoenaed to testify before a grand jury engaged in a criminal investigation. The reporters argued that enforced disclosure violated their First Amendment right to gather information. Although they did not seek an absolute privilege, the reporters argued that the government could breach the privilege only by satisfying what was in essence the compelling state interest test. The Court completely rejected their claim, finding no such privilege in the context of good-faith grand jury investigations.

Post-*Branzburg*, reporters thus have no *constitutional* privilege to refuse to reveal confidential sources before a grand jury that is engaged in a good-faith criminal investigation. The Court did observe, however, that "wholly different issues" would be presented if the grand jury investigation were "conducted other than in good faith. . . . Official harassment of the press undertaken not for purposes of law enforcement but to disrupt a reporter's relationship with his news sources would have no justification." Id. at 707-708. Beyond this, any privilege enjoyed by reporters must be based on statutory "shield" laws. Many states have adopted such laws, some of which expressly give reporters an absolute privilege against having to disclose confidential sources in grand jury proceedings, civil and criminal actions, administrative and legislative hearings, or "any other kind of proceedings in which a person can be compelled by law to appear and give evidence." California Evid. Code §§ 901, 1070. And see, e.g., Alabama Code 1975, § 12-21-142; Kentucky Rev. Stat.

Ann. § 421.100; Nevada Rev. Stat. § 49.275, New York Civ. Rights Law § 79-h, and Ohio Rev. Code Ann. §§ 2739.04, 2739.12.

§8.8.6 Forced Access to the Press: Print Media

At issue in *Miami Herald Publishing Co. v. Tornillo*, 418 U.S. 241 (1974), was a state law requiring newspapers to provide reply space to political candidates they had criticized in their editorial pages. Proponents of the right of press access had argued that modern newspapers, along with their television and radio counterparts, exercise vast and almost monopolistic control over the information available to the public. Moreover, given economic realities, competition with these information magnates was all but impossible. The statutorily conferred right of access was designed to ensure that the public received a wider array of information than would otherwise be available through what was essentially a monopoly over information. The Court concluded, however, that the forced access operated as a substantial content-based restriction on the editorial judgment of the press, the net effect of which would be to dampen public debate by inducing the press to avoid controversy on important public issues. Without further consideration, the Court held the statute invalid.

The Court's opinion in *Tornillo* ended with the somewhat enigmatic observation, "It has yet to be demonstrated how governmental regulation of this crucial process can be exercised consistent with First Amendment guarantees of a free press as they have evolved to this time." Id. at 258. Despite this seeming invitation for further consideration, the doctrine of *Tornillo* has been treated as firmly established and relatively absolute, quite likely on the theory that governmental supervision of editorial judgment is simply inconsistent with the First Amendment. The government may not force the press to publish that which it does not wish to publish. The one possible exception arises in the context of defamation. Although the Supreme Court has not addressed the issue, it may be that a court-ordered retraction is a permissible remedy against the press once liability for defamation has been established under a fault standard. See id. at 258-259 (Brennan, J., with whom Rehnquist, J., joined, concurring). Arguably the government has a compelling interest in providing relief for the harm incurred, and in recognizing that the victim has a right of retraction may be a narrowly tailored means to that end.

One final point: The opinion in *Tornillo* made no reference to an earlier decision in which the Court had upheld a very similar right of access requirement as applied to the broadcast media, *Red Lion Broadcasting Co. v. FCC*, 395 U.S. 367 (1969). The differential treatment of these two media is presumably the result of characteristics peculiar to the broadcast media, a topic to which we now turn.

§8.8.7 The First Amendment and Modern Technologies

The Broadcast Media

The broadcast media, both radio and television, rely on electromagnetic frequencies to transmit their messages across the airwaves. On the basis of the theory that these frequencies represent a scarce commodity held in trust for the public, the federal government has developed a regulatory scheme through which the use of these frequencies is regulated to promote the "public interest, convenience or necessity." Communications Act of 1934, 47 U.S.C. § 309(a) (1988). The Court has accepted this scarcity theory, *National Broadcasting Co. v. United States*, 319 U.S. 190, 213 (1943), the consequence being that the broadcast media can be regulated in ways that would be unconstitutional if applied to the traditional print media. The Court has also accepted the theory that the "pervasive" nature of the broadcast media may raise privacy concerns not evident in other forms of communication. In essence, broadcast messages intrude on one's privacy by invading the home with little or no choice by the viewer other than to change the channel. This intrusive potential is of special concern when children may be in the audience.

The most obvious difference in treatment between broadcast and print media is that the former may be subjected to content-based licensing requirements that would violate the doctrine of prior restraints if imposed on the print media. See *City of Lakewood v. Plain Dealer Publishing Co.*, 486 U.S. 750 (1988) (upholding facial challenge to a permit scheme that granted mayor broad discretion to deny permits for use of news racks on city streets). Moreover, once a license is granted, the broadcaster is not free to use the assigned frequency in any manner it chooses but is subject to content-based regulations designed to promote the public interest, convenience, and necessity. See *FCC v. Pacifica Found.*, 438 U.S. 726 (1978) (upholding FCC's authority to regulate indecent language in radio broadcasts).

A good example of this disparate treatment can be seen by contrasting the Court's decision in *Miami Herald Publishing Co. v. Tornillo*, 418 U.S. 241 (1974), with its decision in *Red Lion Broadcasting v. FCC*, 395 U.S. 367 (1969). In the former case, the Court held that a state could not require a newspaper to print a response to a political editorial. Forced access was antithetical to the right of a newspaper to control the editorial content of its pages. In *Red Lion*, however, the Court had no difficulty in upholding the Federal Communications Commission's authority to impose a similar right of reply requirement on the broadcast media—specifically, the right to respond to personal attacks and to certain political editorials under the "fairness doctrine." In the Court's words, "Although broadcasting is clearly a medium affected by a First Amendment interest, differences in the characteristics of new media justify differences in the First Amendment standards applied to them." Id. at 386. The primary difference the Court relied on was the presumed scarcity of available frequencies. Because of that scarcity, the privilege of a broadcast license carried with it the responsibility to act in the public interest, and the FCC could reasonably conclude that a right of reply for personal attacks and political editorials reflected a proper balance of First Amendment concerns by ensuring that the fullest range of information is made available to the public with only a limited intrusion on the editorial prerogative of the broadcasters.

The *administrative* right of access upheld in *Red Lion* did not translate, however, into a *constitutionally mandated* right of access—i.e., a right of access that stemmed from the Constitution and that could be judicially enforced even in the absence of any statutory or administrative grant of such a right. Thus, in *Columbia Broadcasting System, Inc. v. Democratic National Committee,* 412 U.S. 94 (1973), the Court held that a broadcaster could, consistent with the First Amendment, adopt a policy of refusing to accept paid editorial advertisements on issues of public importance. Nothing in the First Amendment created a constitutionally mandated right of access, and no federal statute or regulation provided such a right. Id. at 121-132. Taken together with *Red Lion,* this means that while a broadcaster may be required to provide access under statutorily derived administrative regulations—the personal attack component of the fairness doctrine, for example—in the absence of such regulations, the broadcaster enjoys a relatively uninhibited editorial freedom to deny access to the use of its facilities.

Example 8-CCC

A federal statute provides that a broadcaster's license may be revoked "for willful or repeated failure to allow reasonable access to, or to permit purchase of reasonable amounts of time for the use of a broadcasting station . . . by a legally qualified candidate for Federal elective office on behalf of his [or her] candidacy." 47 U.S.C. § 312(a)(7). Frederica S. is the Republican candidate for the Eighty-fifth Congressional District in California. She has repeatedly attempted to purchase air time from a local television station but has been rebuffed in each instance. After receiving Ms. S.'s complaint, the FCC held an open hearing, upon the completion of which it held that the station had violated the above statutory proscription. As part of its judgment, the FCC ordered the station to sell Ms. S. a "reasonable amount of air time." Evaluate the station's claim that the order violates its First Amendment right to control the content of its programming.

Explanation

Ms. S. is not seeking a constitutional right of access. Rather, she is seeking access based on a congressional enactment. The most appropriate precedent, therefore, is *Red Lion*. Under that decision, the question is whether Congress has acted reasonably in balancing the First Amendment rights of the broadcaster, the candidate, and the public. Given the limited nature of the desired access—reasonable access for legally qualified candidates for federal elective office—along with the importance of the political speech involved, Congress has made a fair accommodation of the interests at stake by limiting the scope of the intrusion to the significance of the public's interest. As such, granting Ms. S. access under the federal statute would not violate the station's First Amendment rights. See *CBS, Inc. v. FCC*, 453 U.S. 367 (1981).

One should not take the foregoing discussion to mean that the government's power to impose content-based restrictions on the broadcast media is without limit. Aside from the federal government's authority to impose limited rights of access or to promote the discussion of public affairs, and excluding the special problem of indecent speech, other content-based restrictions on the broadcast media may well be subject to the same standards of review applicable to the print media. In *FCC v. League of Women Voters of California*, 468 U.S. 364 (1984), for example, the Court applied what was in essence strict scrutiny in striking down a federal statute that prohibited noncommercial television stations funded by the Corporation for Public Broadcasting from engaging in "editorializing" on issues of public importance. The heightened standard of review was mandated by the nature of the speech being regulated, namely, commentary on issues of public importance. The medium of communication did not in any fashion alter that standard. The Court distinguished the more deferential approach it had adopted in *Red Lion* as arising in a context in which the governmental intervention promoted more speech rather than less.

Developing Technologies — Cable Operators

The scarcity rationale, which is at the heart of the Court's broadcast media jurisprudence, has never been accepted uncritically. Today, the factual premise for that rationale is even more suspect. With the advent of cable television, fiber optics, and the ever-expanding information superhighway, the idea that there is a scarcity of "frequencies" on which broadcasters must rely is no longer tenable. Ultimately, this new factual reality should lead to a new jurisprudence, the most likely characteristic of which will be a merging of the standards applicable to electronic and print media, although one can expect some divergence on the basis of the different characteristics of the new technologies and the theory that old habits die hard. See Note, "The Message in the Medium: The First Amendment on the Information Superhighway," 107 *Harv. L. Rev.* 1062 (1994).

Turner Broadcasting System, Inc. v. FCC, 512 U.S. 622 (1994) (*Turner I*), addresses some preliminary issues in the First Amendment jurisprudence to be applied to emerging speech technologies. In that case, cable operators challenged the so-called must-carry provisions of the Cable Television Consumer Protection and Competition Act of 1992. Those provisions required cable operators to devote a specific number of their available channels to local broadcast stations. The government, in defending the provisions, argued that cable operators should be subject to the more relaxed First Amendment standards applicable to the broadcast media under *Red Lion*. The operators countered that the regulation operated as a content-based restriction thereby requiring application of strict scrutiny. The Court rejected both arguments.

The Court first held that cable operators did not share the physical characteristics that justified the more intrusive regulation of the broadcast media. Neither the scarcity rationale nor a frequency interference rationale applied. Consequently, any restriction on the speech engaged in by cable operators would be examined under "settled principles of our First Amendment jurisprudence," id. at 639, rather than under relaxed standards. That did not mean, however, that the special characteristics of cable would be ignored in applying those principles. Thus, the Court rejected the argument that *Miami Herald Publishing Co. v. Tornillo*, supra, required automatic invalidation of the must-carry provisions. The Court found the analogy between the print media and cable media inapt.

> [T]he asserted analogy to *Tornillo* ignores an important technological difference between newspapers and cable television. Although a daily newspaper and a cable operator both may enjoy monopoly status in a given locale, the cable operator exercises far greater control over access to the relevant medium. A daily newspaper, no matter how secure its local monopoly, does not possess the power to obstruct readers' access to other competing publications—whether they be weekly local newspapers, or daily newspapers published in other cities. Thus, when a newspaper asserts exclusive control over its own news copy, it does not thereby prevent other newspapers from being distributed to willing recipients in the same locale.
>
> The same is not true of cable. When an individual subscribes to cable, the physical connection between the television set and the cable network gives the cable operator bottleneck, or gatekeeper, control over most (if not all) of the television programming that is channeled into the subscriber's home. Hence, simply by virtue of its ownership of the essential pathway for cable speech, a cable operator can prevent its subscribers from obtaining access to programming it chooses to exclude. A cable operator, unlike speakers in other media, can thus silence the voice of competing speakers with a mere flick of the switch.

512 U.S. at 656. Ultimately, the Court concluded that as applied to cable operators, the must-carry provisions were content-neutral regulations of the *manner* of speech and that they were, therefore, subject to mid-level scrutiny under the time, place, and manner test. The case was remanded for application of that standard. On remand, the trial court upheld the must-carry provisions and the Supreme Court affirmed. *Turner Broadcasting System, Inc. v. FCC*, 520 U.S. 180 (1997) (*Turner II*).

The essential message of the *Turner Broadcasting* decisions is that settled principles of First Amendment law must be applied to emerging technologies, but with an eye toward applying those principles in a fashion that considers any special characteristics of the new technologies. Just as print is not broadcasting, cable is neither broadcasting nor print, and the Internet combines features of all these media as well as unique features of its own. In short, analogies with other forms of speech will be useful only to the extent that the old and new forms of speech share relevant First Amendment characteristics pertinent to the problem presented. Otherwise, the First Amendment principles to be applied must be considered in light of the special characteristics of the new medium.

Developing Technologies — Social Media

In 2001, Texas and Florida passed statutes that, among other things, restricted privately owned social media platforms, such as Facebook and YouTube, from censoring postings by their users. In essence, each law prevented the covered platforms from demoting, labeling, or removing content based on the viewpoint being expressed and thus regulated the editorial judgment of the subject platforms. NetChoice, an Internet trade association, sued each state in separate proceedings, arguing in each that both statutes were invalid on their face under the First Amendment. In proceedings involving preliminary injunctions, the Fifth Circuit held that Texas was likely to prevail on the merits, while the Eleventh Circuit found that the Florida statute violated the First Amendment. In *Moody v. NetChoice, LLC*, 144 S. Ct. 2383 (2024), the Court consolidated the cases and found that the statutes would likely be struck down under basic First Amendment doctrine. As the Court explained it:

> Despite the relative novelty of the technology before us, the main problem in this case—and the inquiry it calls for—is not new. . . . The platforms object that the law thus forces them to alter the content of their expression—a particular edited compilation of third-party speech. That controversy sounds a familiar note. We have repeatedly faced the question whether ordering a party to provide a forum for someone else's views implicates the First Amendment. And we have repeatedly held that it does so if, though only if, the regulated party is engaged in its own expressive activity, which the mandated access would alter or disrupt. So too we have held, when applying that principle, that expressive activity includes presenting a curated compilation of speech originally created by others.

Id. at 2399-2400. The Court relied on an array of opinions supportive of the above propositions. See, e.g., *Miami Herald Publishing Co. v. Tornillo*, 418 U.S. 241 (1974) (statute that required newspaper to grant a political candidate a right of reply violates First Amendment); *Pacific Gas & Elec. Co. v. Public Util. Comm'n of Cal.*, 475 U.S. 1 (1986) (statute that required public utility to include statement of a consumer advocacy group in the utility's newsletter violates the First Amendment); *Hurley v. Irish-American Gay, Lesbian and Bisexual Group of Boston, Inc.*, 515 U.S. 557 (1995) (law that compelled organizers of St. Patrick's Day parade to include a gay and lesbian group that wanted to express "gay pride" violates the First Amendment rights of the organizers).

Based on these precedents, the *Moody* Court concluded, "When the platforms use their Standards and Guidelines to decide which third-party content those feeds will display, or how the display will be ordered and organized, they are making expressive choices. And because that is true, they receive First Amendment protection." 144 S. Ct. at 2406. The Court then held that based on the current record, the Texas statute was unconstitutional and, implicitly, that the Eleventh Circuit's similar conclusion regarding the Florida statute was correct. However, because both cases involved disfavored facial rather than as-applied challenges, and because neither lower court addressed the question of whether each "law's unconstitutional applications are substantial compared to its constitutional ones" — a prerequisite for facial invalidation — both cases were remanded for further proceedings. Id. at 2394, 2408-2409.

The Court had earlier addressed the First Amendment in the context of social media in *Packingham v. North Carolina*, 582 U.S. 98 (2018). That case involved a state law that made it a crime for registered sex offenders to access specified websites, including social media websites like Facebook and Twitter. The Court prefaced its analysis as follows:

> While in the past there might have been difficulty in identifying the most important places (in a spatial sense) for the exchange of views, today the answer is clear. It is cyberspace—the "vast democratic forums of the Internet" in general, and social media in particular. Seven in ten American adults use at least one Internet social networking service. One of the most popular of these sites is Facebook. . . . Facebook has 1.79 billion active users. This is about three times the population of North America. . . .
>
> . . . [T]he Cyber Age is a revolution of historic proportions. . . . The forces and directions of the Internet are so new, so protean, and so far reaching that courts must be conscious that what they say today might be obsolete tomorrow.
>
> This case is one of the first this Court has taken to address the relationship between the First Amendment and the modern Internet. As a result, the Court must exercise extreme caution before suggesting that the First Amendment provides scant protection for access to vast networks in that medium.

Id. at 104-105. Yet rather than being daunted by the novelty of the setting in which the *Packingham* case arose, the Court—as it has been doing for more than 200 years in this and other constitutional law settings—proceeded to analyze the case in terms of its existing case law and principles, adapting them as necessary to the unique factual setting presented. These are the same principles that you've been reading about for more than four hundred pages now. So let's give it a shot!

EXAMPLE

Example 8-DDD

A state statute, § 14-202, makes it a felony for a registered sex offender to access a commercial social networking website when the sex offender knows the site permits minor children to become members, or to create or maintain personal webpages. The statute applies to about 20,000 people in the state, over 1,000 of whom have been prosecuted under it. Lester was a 21-year-old college student when he had sex with a 13-year-old girl. Because the offense, to which he pled guilty, qualified as "an offense against a minor," he was required by state law to register as a sex offender, thus barring him from gaining access to commercial social networking sites for as many as 30 years. Eight years later, after a state court dismissed a traffic ticket against him, Lester logged on to Facebook.com and posted a statement on his personal file that read: "Man God is Good! I got so much favor they dismissed the ticket before court even started. No fine, no court cost, no nothing spent! Praise be to GOD. Thanks JESUS!" A vigilant police officer traced the posting to Lester, who was then convicted under § 14-202. The state high court affirmed his conviction, rejecting Lester's argument that the statute violated his First Amendment rights. The Supreme Court has granted review. How should the Court rule and why?

EXPLANATION

Explanation

Section 14-202 is a restriction on speech since it denies affected individuals access to a critical portion of the Internet. See § 8.3.7 ("Indecent Speech and the Internet"). The first question is whether the statute should be treated as a content-based restriction, thus rendering it subject to the strictest of scrutiny, or whether it is instead a content-neutral regulation subject to a more relaxed time, place, and manner standard of review. One could certainly argue that this is content based since the prohibition applies only to certain Internet users—i.e., registered sex offenders. The Court has long said that speaker identity is one basis for deeming a law restricting speech to be content based. As such, the statute would be subject to strict scrutiny. On the other hand, the Court has also suggested that if a law targets a subset of speakers for reasons having nothing to do with the content of their speech, then it might not be deemed content based for purposes of First

Amendment analysis. See §§ 8.3.1, 8.4.1. Here, a good case can be made that § 14-202's limitation to registered sex offenders is not based on the views they may have or wish to communicate on social media, but rather due to the risk that they will use the Internet as a means to engage in further predatory behavior. As such, the statute would then be content neutral and subject to intermediate scrutiny under the time, place, or manner analysis.

If the Court were to apply strict scrutiny, the state would have to show that § 14-202 is narrowly tailored to achieving a compelling governmental interest, there being no other specialized First Amendment analysis that would be applicable to the harmless, nonobscene speech for which Lester was convicted. Under that test, the state surely has a compelling interest in protecting minors from the threat of harm by convicted child predators. The question thus comes down to whether the state has chosen the least restrictive means of achieving its goal. Because this inquiry is nearly identical to the narrowly tailored prong of the time, place, and manner analysis (see § 8.4.2), the outcome in this case will be essentially the same whether § 14-202 is deemed to be content based or content neutral.

On the narrowly-tailored point, the state will argue that its statute is narrowly tailored since it applies to only a narrow subclass of the population, and bars them from using only one means of communication—i.e., the major Internet websites. It leaves this group free to access other media to receive information (e.g., radio, television, newspapers, etc.), and allows them to communicate their thoughts by non-Internet means (e.g., by telephone, by U.S. mail, by personal conversation, etc.), and even allows them to use the Internet itself, as long as it does not involve a commercial social networking website.

Lester will respond that § 14-202 is far broader than necessary to protect the state's interest in safeguarding children from abuse. It bars people like him from using Amazon.com, many news websites, and websites that offer health-related resources—websites that are ill-suited for use in stalking or harming children since they offer little opportunity for conversations that could lead to abuse. Placing these websites categorically off limits to registered sex offenders thus bars them from receiving and engaging in speech that is fully protected by the First Amendment, while doing little to advance the state's goal of protecting children from recidivist sex offenders. Lester will argue that the state has not met its burden of showing that its broad prohibition is narrowly tailored to serve its goal. See *Packingham v. North Carolina*, 582 U.S. 98 (2017) (ruling 8-0 that this North Carolina statute violated the Free Speech Clause of the First Amendment).

CHAPTER 9

The First Amendment: Freedom of Religion

§9.1 INTRODUCTION AND OVERVIEW

The First Amendment provides, "Congress shall make no law respecting an establishment of religion, or prohibiting the free exercise thereof. . . ." The two clauses of this sentence, commonly referred to as the Establishment Clause and the Free Exercise Clause, ostensibly divide the constitutional principle of religious freedom into two doctrinal realms, each with its own particular principles and methods. Stated very generally, the Establishment Clause precludes the government from favoring any particular religion or group of religions, or from preferring religion over nonreligion (though the scope of this limitation is evolving rapidly), while the Free Exercise Clause limits the government's authority to interfere with religious beliefs and practices. Taken together, both clauses are designed to promote religious freedom by limiting the capacity of the government to become excessively involved in religious matters. Both clauses apply to the states through the Fourteenth Amendment.

As a preliminary matter, although "religion" is the protected subject under both the Establishment Clause and the Free Exercise Clause, the Court has never defined religion in a constitutional context. Typically, a court will accept any nonfrivolous claim that a particular set of beliefs constitutes a religion. Certainly, the term "religion" includes all organized systems of faith premised on either a supreme being or some similar transcendent authority. This is true regardless of how bizarre the belief system is or how recent its heritage. In a sense, religion is in the heart of the believer. Thus, although a court may inquire into the sincerity of one's religious beliefs, a court will not inquire into the legitimacy or believability of those beliefs. While the Court has stated that merely philosophical or personal beliefs do not qualify as a religion, the difference between a philosophy and a religion is far from clear, and the Court has never applied this distinction. Thus, presumably, something like existentialism is not a religion, although one could certainly make a case to the contrary.

In what follows, we examine the various doctrines the Court has developed under the Religion Clauses, focusing first on the Establishment Clause and then on the Free Exercise Clause. We will also note significant areas in which the clauses seem to overlap.

§9.2 THE ESTABLISHMENT CLAUSE: THEMES, THEORIES, AND TESTS

The Establishment Clause provides, "Congress shall make no law respecting an establishment of religion." Historically, these words have been interpreted as limiting governmental action of two types: Action that discriminates between religions; and action that promotes religion in general. While the first type of governmental action still falls within the clause's prohibition, it is no longer true that the government cannot promote religion. Instead, it may do so as long as it does not favor one denomination over another; any such favoritism would violate the still-operative nondiscrimination principle.

The current reading of the Establishment Clause marks the end of a long-running debate between two competing interpretations of the clause—separationism and nonpreferentialism. That debate was complicated by several compromise approaches that borrowed from each of these interpretive theories. Some familiarity with these particular theories and their variations will provide a deeper appreciation of that jurisprudence and what the current Court's reading of the clause means.

§9.2.1 Separationist Theory

Separationism, which is sometimes referred to as the separation of church and state, provided the dominant theme of Establishment Clause jurisprudence during the latter half of the twentieth century. The basic premise of separationism is that religion and government do not mix well, each presenting dangers to the other. *Everson v. Board of Education*, 330 U.S. 1, 9-16 (1947). In *Everson*, the Court relied heavily on the history of religious persecution and intolerance toward minority religions as support for the separationist thesis. From the perspective of this thesis, the Establishment Clause is sometimes described as creating a "wall of separation" between church and state—a metaphor borrowed from Thomas Jefferson.

The Court's reliance on separationism did not, however, create an impregnable barrier between church and state. From a realistic perspective, some interaction between government and religion was inevitable, and the developed separationist jurisprudence recognizes that inevitability. Thus, parochial schools are surely entitled to police and fire protection even though such protection assists, at least indirectly, the sectarian mission of the school. Overall, however, the theme of separationism is to keep separate, as much as reasonably possible, the realms of church and state. See *McCreary County v. ACLU*, 545 U.S. 844 (2005) (applying separationist model); *Lee v. Weisman*, 505 U.S. 577, 609 (1992) (Souter, J., concurring) (defending the separationist model). As applied, this meant that the government had no power to create an officially recognized church; to prefer one religion over another; to pass laws specifically designed to aid one religion or all religions; or to support, financially or otherwise, the teaching or practice of religion. *Everson v. Board of Education*, supra, 330 U.S. at 15-16.

§9.2.2 Nonpreferentialist Theory

Nonpreferentialist theory, on the other hand, rejects the "wall of separation" metaphor and is premised instead on the idea that the government may provide aid to religion and religious institutions—as long as the government does not favor or prefer any one religion or group of religions over others. Proponents of nonpreferentialism read the history of religious persecution and intolerance as indicative of a need to prevent discriminations between religions or religious sects, but not as requiring government to separate itself completely from the sphere of religion. They note that from the time of the First Congress the United States has promoted various religious activities, thus placing a gloss on the meaning of the Establishment Clause. For example, the First Congress, in a joint resolution passed a day after the First Amendment was proposed, urged President Washington to proclaim the Thanksgiving holiday as "a day of public thanksgiving and prayer, to be observed by acknowledging with grateful hearts the many signal favors of Almighty God." *Lynch v. Donnelly*, 465 U.S. 668, 675 n.2 (1984). In short, according to proponents of nonpreferentialism, while the government may not discriminate between religions, it is free to promote religion in general. See *McCreary County v. ACLU*, supra, 545 U.S. at 885 (Scalia, J., dissenting) (defending nonpreferentialist model); *Wallace v. Jaffree*, 472 U.S. 38, 91 (1985) (Rehnquist, J., dissenting) (same).

§9.2.3 Three Compromise Approaches

The Court has applied at least three compromise approaches to the Establishment Clause that slightly modified the competing theories of separationism and nonpreferentialism. First, the Court on occasion tempered the harsh strictures of separationism by limiting its scope to those governmental actions that could be described as creating an *endorsement of religion*. *Wallace v. Jaffree*, supra, 472 U.S. at 56. Thus, governmental action that assists religion in general, but that does not place the government's stamp of approval on religion will not violate this variation of separationism. See also *Lynch v. Donnelly*, 465 U.S. 668, 690 (1984) (O'Connor, J., concurring). From this perspective, a moment of silence at the beginning of the school day would provide an opportunity for students to pray but would not necessarily indicate any governmental endorsement of religion or of prayer.

Next, the Court sometimes applied a *coercion test* to limit the extent to which the government under the nonprefentialism approach might promote a seemingly neutral religious practice. In *Lee v. Weisman*, 505 U.S. 577 (1992), for example, the Court held that a public high school could not invite a religious cleric to recite a nondenominational prayer at a high school graduation because, given the context and the age of the participants, the recital of the prayer would coerce unwilling students into participating in a religious practice. See also *Santa Fe Independent School Dist. v. Doe*, 530 U.S. 290 (2000) (applying coercion test to strike down school-sponsored prayer at high school football games).

Third, the Court sometimes used *tradition and historical practice* to define and limit the prohibitions of the Establishment Clause, the idea being that the Establishment Clause should not be interpreted to void practices that have long been an accepted part of our social customs. For example, since the days of John Marshall, all sessions of the Supreme Court have opened with the proclamation, "God save the United States and this Honorable Court." It is quite unlikely that the Court would hold that this traditional practice violates the Establishment Clause. See, e.g., *Marsh v. Chambers*, 463 U.S. 783 (1983) (upholding state's power to pay a chaplain to open sessions of the legislature with a prayer); *Town of Greece v. Galloway*, 572 U.S. 565 (2014) (upholding town's power to begin monthly town board meetings with a prayer); *Kennedy v. Bremerton School District*, 597 U.S. 507, 510 (2022) ("this Court has instructed that the Establishment Clause must be interpreted by 'reference to historical practices and understandings.' ").

§9.2.4 The *Lemon* Test

In the early 1970s, the Court attempted to reduce its Establishment Clause jurisprudence to a simple three-part formula, which was commonly referred to as the *Lemon* test. *Lemon v. Kurtzman*, 403 U.S. 602 (1971). Under the *Lemon* test, governmental action

- Must have a secular purpose;
- Must have a primary effect that neither advances nor inhibits religion; and
- Must not foster an excessive governmental entanglement with religion.

The *Lemon* test was largely a product of separationist theory and thus a matter of considerable controversy for those members of the Court who favored the nonpreferentialist model. See, e.g., *McCreary County v. ACLU*, supra, 545 U.S. at 885 (Scalia, J., dissenting). And even though it was sometimes ignored by the Court, the *Lemon* test remained an important part of its overall Establishment Clause jurisprudence until quite recently.

Secular Purpose

The secular purpose element of the *Lemon* test required that a law have a non-religious purpose. This did not mean that the sole purpose of a challenged law had to be secular, but only that the government had to articulate a non-frivolous secular purpose for the law. Thus, a law enacted partly to advance religious doctrine was not necessarily invalid under this element if there was also a secular purpose for the law. In general, while the Court tended to be deferential toward the government in applying this element, this was not always the case. See, e.g., *Stone v. Graham*, 449 U.S. 39, 41 (1980) ("pre-eminent" purpose of a law requiring posting of the Ten Commandments in public classrooms was religious); *McCreary County v. ACLU*, supra, 545 U.S. at 863-864 (government-mandated display of the Ten Commandments in county courthouses violated secular purpose prong of *Lemon* test, which prong is not to be trivialized by permitting "any transparent claim to secularity").

Primary Effect That Does Not Advance, Endorse, or Inhibit Religion

In contrast to the relative rarity of secular purpose decisions, the second element of the *Lemon* test—i.e., that a law not have the primary effect of either advancing or inhibiting religion—often served as a basis for invalidating laws thought to violate the Establishment Clause. This was particularly true when this element was enhanced by asking whether a "reasonable observer" would consider the government's action to be an "endorsement" of religion." *County of Allegheny v. ACLU*, 492 U.S. 573, 593 (1989). There was no specific way to determine whether the effect of a law was "primary." As a consequence, this aspect of the *Lemon* test was quite subjective, making it a convenient surrogate for a more generalized judgment that a particular law or governmental action went too far in advancing nonsecular ends. In general, the more substantial and direct the government aid, the more likely a court would find a primary effect to advance religion.

Not Foster Excessive Entanglement with Religion

Finally, the excessive entanglement prong of the *Lemon* test was designed to ensure that any interaction between church and state was not such that the state became too heavily involved in the affairs of a church or religious institution. In determining whether there was an excessive entanglement, the Court examined the character of the religious institution involved; the nature of the governmental assistance (i.e., whether the aid is financial or in-kind services); and the resulting interaction between the religious institution and the government. The excessive entanglement element often put a state between a rock and a hard place when it came to assisting religious institutions. If the state did not take steps to ensure that its monies were being spent only for secular purposes, then there was a distinct possibility that a court would find that the primary effect of the state's program was to advance religion. Yet if the state did attempt to oversee public expenditures, the potential for excessive entanglement loomed large.

Because of these difficulties with the *Lemon* test, the Court often bypassed it and used some other available Establishment Clause approach. For example, in *McCreary County v. ACLU*, supra, the Court employed the *Lemon* test to strike down a state-mandated display of the Ten Commandments in county courthouses. On the same day, in *Van Orden v. Perry*, 545 U.S. 677 (2005), it held that the placement of a monument inscribed with the Ten Commandments on the grounds of the Texas state capitol did not violate the Establishment Clause. In contrast to *McCreary County*, however, none of the *Van Orden* Court's majority applied the *Lemon* test. Instead, a four-person plurality employed a nonpreferentialist analysis that emphasized our nation's religious heritage, id. at 685-694. A fifth Justice, who concurred in the judgment, also adopted this approach.

In *American Legion v. American Humanist Association*, 588 U.S. 29 (2019), the Court cast further doubt on the *Lemon* test, noting that while the original hope was that it

> would provide a framework for all future Establishment Clause decisions, [that] expectation has not been met. In many cases, this Court has either expressly declined to apply the test or has simply ignored it.
>
> This pattern is a testament to the *Lemon* test's shortcomings. . . . The test has been harshly criticized by Members of this Court, lamented by lower court judges, and questioned by a diverse roster of scholars.

Id. at 49 (internal citations omitted). While the *American Legion* Court stopped short of overruling *Lemon*, not a single Justice was willing to use that test to decide whether Maryland's display of a 32-foot-tall Latin cross, erected on public land in 1925, violated the Establishment Clause. Had *Lemon* been applied, the display of this "preeminent symbol of Christianity" would likely have been invalidated under the "effects" prong, since "a reasonable observer would view the [state's] ownership and maintenance of the monument as an endorsement of Christianity." Id. at 47. Instead, said the Court, "the Establishment Clause must be interpreted by reference to historical practices and understandings. . . ." Id. at 61. The Court acknowledged that while it "is undoubtedly a Christian symbol," id. at 66, which may have been installed in part for religious reasons, the display has taken on additional meaning over time, both as a war memorial and as an historic monument. "For all these reasons," said the Court, "the Cross does not offend the Constitution." Id.

§9.2.5 The Establishment Clause Today

In *Kennedy v. Bremerton School District*, 597 U.S. 507 (2022), the Supreme Court finally overruled *Lemon*. Justice Gorsuch, writing for a six-member majority, said that "the 'shortcomings' associated with this 'ambitiou[s],' abstract, and ahistorical approach to the Establishment Clause became so 'apparent' that this Court long ago abandoned *Lemon* and its endorsement test offshoot." Id. at 534. The Court now formally put that decision to rest, "overruling *Lemon* entirely and in all contexts." Id. at 572 (Sotomayor, J., et al., dissenting).

The question then was what approach should the Court take in future Establishment Clause cases? The *Kennedy* Court sought to answer this question as follows:

> In place of the *Lemon* and the endorsement test, . . . the Establishment Clause must be interpreted by "reference to historical practices and understandings." "[T]he line that courts and governments must draw between the permissible and the impermissible" has to "accor[d] with history and faithfully reflec[t] the understanding of the Founding Fathers." An analysis focused on original meaning and history, this Court has stressed, has long represented the rule rather than some "'exception' within the "Court's Establishment Clause jurisprudence."

Id. at 535-536 (internal citations omitted). As examples of how particular religious practices might fare under "[a]n analysis focused on original meaning and history," the Court cited three earlier cases that had employed that analysis—two that upheld Sunday closing laws and church tax exemptions, and one that invalidated religious test oaths. Id. at 536.

In the Establishment Clause discussion that follows, we will refer to the *Lemon* test from time to time, particularly in cases where an earlier court relied upon that approach. But don't forget that *Lemon* and the related endorsement test are no longer good law.

§9.3 THE ESTABLISHMENT CLAUSE APPLIED: DISCRIMINATION BETWEEN RELIGIONS

In the context of governmental action that discriminates between religions, there is general agreement that the government may not create an official religion, prefer one religion over others (which is tantamount to the same thing), or treat any religion less favorably than it does others. This was of course true of separationists. It is also true of proponents of nonpreferentialism since such discriminatory practices violate of the principle of neutrality among religions.

§9.3.1 The Ban on Officially "Established" Religions

The language of the Establishment Clause expressly divests Congress of any power to designate or adopt an official religion for the United States. Any such law would be a "law respecting an establishment of religion." In addition, the Establishment Clause appears to prevent the United States from interfering with state-established religions, of which there were several at the time the Bill of Rights was adopted. Indeed, one of the purposes of the Establishment Clause was to prevent such federal interference with state religions. Thus, a congressional enactment *disestablishing* the Church of England, the official religion of Virginia, would have been a "law respecting an establishment of religion" in violation of the Establishment Clause.

This latter aspect of the Establishment Clause is no longer relevant. With the incorporation of the Establishment Clause into the Fourteenth Amendment, the protection of the states' authority to establish an official religion has been transformed into a constitutional barrier that prevents the exercise of such an authority. But see *Town of Greece v. Galloway*, supra, 572 U.S. at 603-607 (Thomas, J., concurring) (suggesting that the Establishment Clause should still be treated as a principle of federalism, operating as a limitation on the federal government but not upon the states). Thus, just as Congress may not create an official religion for the United States, neither may state or local governments do the same within their respective jurisdictions.

§9.3.2 The Limitation on Conferring a Preferred Status

As one might suspect, problems involving the actual establishment of an official government religion are rare to nonexistent. Congress, for example, has never passed a law expressly establishing an official national religion. Modern instances in which states or local governments have attempted to do so are idiosyncratic at best. The Establishment Clause, however, goes beyond proscribing the creation of an official religion. It also prohibits the government from granting a preferred status to any religion or group of religions. Thus, the government may not impose a tax to support the ministers of any particular faith or spend money to promote certain religious practices or beliefs, or pass laws designed to conform government practices to the tenets of any particular religion. In each such case, the government would be conferring a preferred status on the religion so favored, which, although not accomplished through an express "establishment" of an official religion, is tantamount to the same thing.

Example 9-A

The Unity City School Board has decided, with overwhelming community support, to promote the religious doctrines of Christianity within its school system. Although students attending Unity City schools will not be required to profess their acceptance of Christianity, all students will be required to take courses on New Testament theology, and all classes will be taught with an underlying theme of Christian faith. Does this program violate the Establishment Clause?

Explanation

Yes. The Establishment Clause precludes the school board from taking this action. Although the school board has not expressly designated Christianity as the official local religion, it has granted Christianity a preferred status over other religions in violation of the Establishment Clause. Moreover, the government would be impermissibly making the observance of a religious practice *coercive*. See *Kennedy v. Bremerton School Dist.*, supra, 597 U.S. at 536-537 ("this Court has long held that government may not, consistent with a historically sensitive understanding of the Establishment Clause, 'make a religious observance compulsory.'").

As the foregoing discussion suggests, in the context of governmental action that confers a preferred status on a particular religion, there is in a sense only one theory. The government's conferral of a preferred status violates the Establishment Clause. To this extent, the analysis of "preferred status" problems is relatively simple. Once a preference is established, unconstitutionality is essentially a foregone conclusion.

The only difficulty in this context is in determining whether a challenged statute or governmental action does in fact grant a preferred status to a religion. There is no particular test for making such a determination. In fact, the label "preferred status" is merely a conclusion that is placed on a court's interpretation of the facts and circumstances presented. In approaching this issue, however, it may be helpful to frame the inquiry by asking whether the government's sole purpose in enacting a measure was to favor one religion or whether this is the primary effect of the law.

EXAMPLE

Example 9-B

Unity City has adopted a Sunday closing law that prohibits the operation of any "nonessential" businesses on Sundays. Most retail operations are included within the prohibition. Does this law violate the Establishment Clause as it grants a preferred status to a particular religion or group of religions?

EXPLANATION

Explanation

Arguably it does. Historically, Sunday closing laws were passed for the avowed purpose of promoting Sunday worship—a potential violation of the nonpreferentialism principle. Those religions that recognize Sunday as a day set aside for religious worship are seemingly preferred over those religions that do not by conferring a special benefit on Sunday worshipers.

On the other hand, a court could construe the Sunday closing law as promoting the secular purpose of rest and recuperation and as not directly preferring any particular religious practice. And even though such laws were at one time religiously premised, the modern basis for these laws has been secularized by practice, habit, and cultural change. On this basis, one could argue that as a matter of history and tradition, Sunday closing laws have long been deemed consistent with the First Amendment. Similarly, while some religions will benefit from this law, one could argue that the primary effect is as secularized as the purpose, namely, the promotion of rest and recuperation. Under this interpretation of the facts, no religion would be granted a preferred status. See *McGowan v. Maryland*, 366 U.S. 420 (1961) (upholding Sunday closing law against an Establishment Clause challenge); see also *Town of Greece v. Galloway*, supra, 572 U.S. at 581-586 (finding no religious preference in the practice of opening a monthly town board meeting with sectarian prayer).

§9.3.3 The Limitation on Imposing a Disfavored Status

Just as the government may not grant one religion a preferred status, the government may not impose a disfavored status on any religion. Such action is typically referred to as action discriminating against a religion. The underlying principle is virtually identical to that described in the discussion of preferred status. A law that grants one religion a preferred status obviously discriminates against all other religions. So, too, a law that discriminates against certain religions creates a preferred status for those religions not so burdened. Yet the two approaches serve distinct ends. The focus of preferred status cases is on a religion receiving a special benefit, while the focus of discrimination cases is on a religion receiving less favored treatment. The problem is the same: the government has established a preference. Since the problem is the same, it follows that the solution is the same whether we think of the matter in terms of preferred status or discriminatory treatment. Either way, such discriminatory laws violate the principle of nonpreferentialism.

This anti-discrimination principle was applied by the Court in *Fowler v. Rhode Island*, 345 U.S. 67 (1953). At issue in *Fowler* was a local ordinance that had been construed to prohibit preaching in a public park by a Jehovah's Witness minister but to permit Catholics and Protestants to hold religious services in that same park. The Court found that this discrimination violated the First Amendment because it was "merely an indirect way of preferring one religion over another." Id. at 70. The decision in *Fowler* underscores the similarity between governmental action that discriminates against a religion and governmental action that confers a preferred status on a religion. Each presents another perspective from which to examine the other.

Denominational preferences can also be assessed by reference to standards developed under the Equal Protection Clause. See § 7.2; *Larson v. Valente*, 456 U.S. 228, 246-251 (1982) (using equal protection standards to measure the constitutionality of a denominational preference under the Establishment Clause). As the Court in *Larson* explained it, when "a state law [grants] a denominational preference, our precedents demand that we treat the law as suspect and that we apply strict scrutiny in adjudging its constitutionality." Id. at 246. At issue in that case was a state law that exempted religious organizations from reporting under the state's charitable solicitations act, but only if the organization received more than half of its contributions from members or affiliated organizations. Since the Unification Church received the bulk of its contributions from nonmembers, it was deemed ineligible for the exemption. The Court explained that the state law created a denominational preference by providing a selective exemption for certain religious organizations. After examining the state's asserted justifications for this selective exemption, the Court concluded that the preference was not "'closely fitted' to further[ing] a 'compelling governmental interest.'" Id. at 251. The preference, therefore, violated the Establishment Clause.

The cases we have discussed thus far have all involved action taken at the state and local governmental levels. Yet the Establishment Clause applies to the federal government as well, as its text—"Congress shall make no laws respecting an establishment of religion"—makes clear. And though it is addressed specifically to Congress, the prohibition has been assumed to apply to federal executive branch actions as well. But depending on the circumstances, the clause may operate more leniently with respect to federal executive actions than it might in other settings. This proved to be the case in *Trump v. Hawaii*, 585 U.S. 667 (2018). There, the Court held that a presidential proclamation that indefinitely barred nationals from six predominantly Muslim countries from entering the United States did not violate the Establishment Clause. Though the proclamation was religiously neutral on its face, for it targeted individuals based on their country of origin rather than on their religion, plaintiffs contended that since most of the covered countries had Muslim-majority populations, "the primary purpose of the Proclamation was religious animus and that the President's stated concerns about vetting protocols and national security were but pretexts for discriminating against Muslims." Id. at 699.

The Court rejected this contention for several reasons. First, *Kleindeinst v. Mandel*, 408 U.S. 753 (1972), had held that when challenges are made to federal executive decisions to exclude foreign nationals, if the executive gives "a 'facially legitimate and bona fide' reason for its action," the judicial inquiry comes to an end. 585 U.S. at 703. That requirement was met here, for the proclamation was "expressly premised on legitimate purposes: preventing entry of nationals who cannot be adequately vetted and inducing other nations to improve their [vetting] practices." Id. at 706. The Court added that *Mandel*'s narrow standard of review "has particular force" in cases like this, for when "national security" and "foreign affairs" concerns overlap, separation of powers strongly counsels for judicial self-restraint. Id. at 704. Second, even if it were proper to go beyond *Mandel*'s exclusive focus on facial neutrality, judicial scrutiny would still involve only a "rational basis" equal protection review, a standard easily met here. The president's proclamation was based on a worldwide review process undertaken by members of the Cabinet that examined the distinct conditions in each country. Moreover, the proclamation provided for an ongoing reassessment process that allows a country's entry restrictions to be terminated and included an individual waiver program for people from the covered countries. Id. at 706-710. "Under these circumstances," said the Court, "the Government has set forth a sufficient national security justification to survive rational basis review." Id. at 710.

§9.4 THE ESTABLISHMENT CLAUSE APPLIED: THE DISCRIMINATORY PROMOTION OF RELIGION

As we have seen, with the Supreme Court's overruling of *Lemon* and its related principles of separationism and endorsement, the government is free to promote or assist religion as long as it does so in a nondiscriminatory and noncoercive way.

Nondiscriminatory promotion may take either of two forms. The first involves governmental action designed to promote the value of religion generally. An example of this type of governmental assistance would be a state law that mandates a moment of silence for prayer in public schools. Even though such a law is denominationally neutral, it still promotes religion and thus falls within this category. Second, governmental assistance to religion may be the product of a program that is not designed to promote religion in any manner, but that, nonetheless, has the effect of doing so. An example of this form of assistance would be a state-funded program that permits public schools to lend textbooks to private schools regardless of the private school's religious or nonreligious character. While religion is seemingly irrelevant to the state's plan, if private sectarian schools participate in the program, the government can be fairly described as providing support or assistance to those religious institutions.

Under the Court's nonpreferentialist approach, there is no limitation on the government's ability to promote religion or support religious institutions. The government is free to promote religion generally—i.e., to discriminate against nonreligion and to support religious institutions—as long as it does not create a preference for any particular religion or religious institution, and its promotional activities are not coercive so as to force participation.

Example 9-C

The Unity City School Board has adopted a policy that mandates "a moment of silent meditation or prayer" at the beginning of each school day. A student who is an atheist challenges this policy as one designed to promote prayer in public schools in violation of the Establishment Clause. She argues that although a mandated moment of "silent meditation" may have a secular purpose, the "or prayer" language has no purpose other than to promote religion in a public school setting. She also argues that the primary effect of this additional language is to advance a religious practice.

Explanation

While the student would have had a reasonably good argument under separationist theory and the *Lemon* test, those are no longer valid bases for objection. Under nonpreferentialist theory, her argument is unavailing. Even if the law does promote prayer in public schools, it does so in a neutral manner without preferring any religion. Our student's only hope is to somehow convince the court that a policy promoting silent prayer is not neutral and that it in fact confers a preferred or disfavored status on certain religions. Since no student is required to engage in prayer during the moment of silence, there appears to be no coercion. However, depending on the ages of the students and the grade level, an argument based on peer pressure and fear of nonconformity might suggest otherwise.

The most effective way to study this Establishment Clause jurisprudence is to examine some of the principal contexts in which issues involving the promotion of religion have arisen, with an eye on how they may run afoul of the nonpreferentialism or noncoercion limitations.

§9.4.1 Public Aid to Parochial Schools

For nearly 50 years, some form of separationism provided the dominant theme within the Court's decisions involving public aid to elementary and secondary parochial schools. *Everson v. Board of Education*, 330 U.S. 1 (1947). Of course, under an absolutely strict application of separationist theory, no such aid would be permitted under any circumstances. After all, so the argument goes, if one purpose of the Establishment Clause is to prevent the government from taxing and spending in support of religious institutions, then that purpose is potentially subverted whenever the government provides public assistance to sectarian institutions.

But the Court never adopted such a rigid view even in the heyday of separationism. Instead, separationist principles were moderated to permit some degree of governmental support for parochial schools, particularly when that support was either part of a general health and safety program or clearly directed toward the students and not the school itself. In short, separationism was tempered by a desire to avoid hostility toward religion.

Example 9-D

Unity City reimburses parents for the cost of their children's bus transportation to and from school. This reimbursement is available regardless of whether the children attend public or private school. A substantial portion of the money expended under this program will be used to reimburse parents who send their children to a local Catholic school. Does this program violate the Establishment Clause?

Explanation

The plan would pass muster under a nonpreferentialist approach since it does not appear to favor one religious private school over another.

Under the Court's current nonpreferentialist approach, virtually all forms of public aid to parochial schools will be allowed as long as that aid does not entail a preference for any particular religion or group of religions.

Before *Kennedy v. Bremerton School District*, supra, a pure nonpreferentialist approach had already been adopted in *Mitchell v. Helms*, 530 U.S. 793 (2000).

That case involved a program under which state and local educational agencies received federal money to purchase educational materials and equipment which they could then loan to public and private elementary and secondary schools within their respective jurisdictions. The federal funds could not be used to supplant current programs, but only to supplement the overall curriculum. Items that could be purchased included library materials such as general circulation books and reference materials, as well as computer software and hardware for instructional use. All items purchased under the program were required to be secular in nature and no item purchased under the program could be used for sectarian purposes. Thus, if a computer were purchased under the program, the computer could be lent to a parochial school, but the school was forbidden to use the computer to teach sectarian matters.

The Court upheld the program, but without a majority opinion. For the plurality, the potential for diversion of the equipment to sectarian uses by the parochial schools was constitutionally irrelevant. As long as the government itself did not participate in that diversion, there was no violation of the Establishment Clause. In essence, the plurality concluded that any diverted sectarian use would not be attributable to the government but to private actors at the recipient schools. Moreover, although not an issue in the case, the plurality hinted that even direct financial aid to sectarian schools might be permissible as long as the government itself was not promoting the sectarian mission of the school. Id. at 819 n.8. In short, the plurality endorsed an approach very similar to the pure nonpreferentialist position adopted by the Court in *Kennedy*, a non-parochial school setting.

Justice O'Connor's concurring opinion, which was joined by Justice Breyer, described the plurality's rationale as one of "unprecedented breadth." Id. at 837. She agreed that the aid program was constitutional but strongly disagreed with the "singular importance" the plurality had placed on neutrality, and with the plurality's assertion that diversion of government aid to sectarian use would be constitutionally permissible. The former was but one factor to consider in the "impermissible effect" analysis, and the latter would, in her estimation, amount to an unconstitutional endorsement of religion. For O'Connor, the constitutionality of the aid program resulted from the confluence of several factors: The neutral, secular criteria under which the aid was awarded; the fact that the aid supplemented and did not supplant the existing curriculum; the fact that no religious schools received the government funds; the fact that the items purchased and loaned were secular; the fact that evidence of any actual diversion was de minimis; and the inclusion in the program of adequate safeguards against diversion. Based on the foregoing, Justices O'Connor and Breyer concluded that the aid program did not have the effect of either advancing or endorsing religion.

The *Mitchell* dissent, authored by Justice Souter, joined by Justices Stevens and Ginsburg, provided a detailed rejection of the plurality's nonpreferentialism model and of the proposition that diversion of government aid to sectarian purposes might be constitutionally permissible. The dissent called for a multifactored analysis like the one adopted by Justice O'Connor, but with the key difference that, for the dissent, any potential for the aid to be diverted to sectarian uses was automatically fatal. The fact that a computer could easily be put to a religious use led the dissent to conclude that this type of aid was unconstitutional.

Thus, under the *Mitchell* plurality and concurring opinions, the government could, under some circumstances, provide parochial schools with aid that was potentially divertible to sectarian uses.

Years later, in *Trinity Lutheran Church v. Comer*, 582 U.S. 449 (2017), the Court implicitly reaffirmed *Mitchell*'s holding that for divertibility to be fatal under the Establishment Clause, there had to be actual proof of diversion rather than just a possibility. In *Comer*, the State of Missouri had refused to fund the purchase of a rubber playground surface at a religious preschool, under a state policy that disqualified religious entities from receiving playground grants. The Court summarily rejected the state's Establishment Clause defense to the school's claim that the state had violated its free exercise rights, for there was no evidence of actual diversion. Under such circumstances, "Missouri's policy preference for skating as far as possible from religious establishment concerns," said the Court, does not "qualify as compelling." The dissent disagreed, noting that "[t]he playground surface cannot be confined to secular use any more than lumber used to frame the Church's walls, glass stained and used to form its windows, or nails used to build its altar." Id. at 476 (Sotomayor, J. and Ginsburg, J., dissenting). In the dissent's view, it was enough that the playground could be used for religious activities, even if, to receive funds, the Church had to certify "that it will put program funds to only a secular use." Id. at 476 n.3. The disagreement between the majority and the dissent reflected a critical disagreement as to how high the wall of separation must be. After *Kennedy v. Bremerton School District*, though, for purposes of Establishment Clause analysis, there should be no difference between how we analyze government assistance to a religious entity's physical plant and infrastructure, and government support for activities that take place there, to the extent there is no preferentialism. See also § 9.2.

EXAMPLE

Example 9-E

There are over 75,000 students enrolled in the Inner City School District. The education provided by the district has, in recent years, been woefully inadequate. For example, only one in ten ninth graders within the system could pass a basic proficiency examination. Almost two-thirds of high school students either drop out or fail to graduate. To address these deficiencies the state has created four options for low-income families residing within the district. Under those options, such parents may choose to have their children (1) attend their local public school but receive grants up to $360 to cover 90 percent of the costs of tutorial assistance; (2) attend a participating private school within the district, with the state providing tuition assistance covering 90 percent of the tuition up to $2,250; (3) attend one of ten independent "community schools" within the district (i.e., a public school within the district that is empowered to set its own curriculum and academic standards and that is run by its own independent school board); or (4) attend one of 23 public magnet schools within the district. Under the tuition-assistance option, parents choose the private school their child will attend from a list of participating schools. The state makes no distinction between private schools that have a religious affiliation and those that do not; however, of the 56 private schools participating in the program, 46 (or 82%) were religiously affiliated. Private schools choosing to participate in the program may not discriminate on the basis of race, national origin, or religion. The tuition grants are administered by giving the parent a check for the amount of the grant, with the parent then endorsing that check to the chosen private school. The state funding for public schools, including community schools and magnet schools, is approximately twice as high per pupil as the tuition-assistance grants made available for attendance at private schools. In the most recent academic year, of the over 75,000 students residing within the district, 1,400 received grants for tutorial assistance, 3,700 received tuition assistance to attend private schools (with over 96% of those students enrolled in religiously affiliated schools), 1,900 attended community schools, and 13,000 attended magnet schools. Does the tuition-assistance program violate the Establishment Clause?

Explanation

EXPLANATION

Under a nonpreferentialist approach, the solution here is relatively simple. The tuition grant program is completely neutral in relation to religious and nonreligious schools. That being the case, the Establishment Clause is not in any fashion implicated by this religiously neutral program. Indeed, a strict nonpreferentialist would allow the state to even prefer religious schools over nonreligious schools so long as the state did not prefer any particular religion.

In terms of what the recipient religious schools may then do with the funds, there is nothing to prevent them from using them for purely religious purposes. The Court has examined divertibility along with other factors and has not treated it as necessarily fatal by itself. See, e.g., *Mitchell v. Helms*, supra. Nor would a coercion argument likely succeed here. Even in cases where the only realistic choice for parents is the religiously affiliated school option, the state's program has in no way increased the pressure to send their children to such a school, even though it has lightened their burden of doing so.

Example 9-E is based on the Court's decision in *Zelman v. Simmons-Harris*, 536 U.S. 639 (2002). The program there was instituted by the State of Ohio to address what was described as an unprecedented crisis in the Cleveland City School District. The Court, in an opinion by Chief Justice Rehnquist, upheld the program under the now-defunct *Lemon* test. However, the Court also addressed several factors that might still be relevant today. It stressed the fact that the money going to the private schools was the product of a "true private choice" made by the parents. Id. at 652-653. Moreover, that private choice was made in the context of a "neutral" state program that embraced both sectarian and nonsectarian private schools as well as a range of public school options. "[W]here a government aid program is neutral with respect to religion, and provides assistance directly to a broad class of citizens who, in turn, direct government aid to religious schools wholly as a result of their own genuine and independent private choice, the program is not readily subject to challenge under the Establishment Clause." Id. at 652. That the vast majority of the tuition grants ultimately went to sectarian schools was deemed irrelevant so long as the state program did not compel that result. Id. at 657-658. The four separationists on the Court—Justices Stevens, Souter, Ginsburg, and Breyer—dissented, arguing that the primary effect of the program was to advance religion, which was prohibited under the second prong of the now-defunct *Lemon* test.

Although the majority of the Court in *Zelman* did not endorse the strict nonpreferentialist view, the majority did adopt a more limited form of nonpreferentialism, namely, one in which the prohibitions of the Establishment Clause may be relaxed based on a state's neutrality in terms of how it treats similarly situated religious and nonreligious institutions. The Court followed this approach in *Espinoza v. Montana Department of Revenue*, 591 U.S. 464 (2020), which held that a state scholarship program that distributed funds to the parents of needy children to pay tuition at private sectarian or nonsectarian schools of their choice, did not violate the Establishment Clause. Citing *Zelman*, the Court noted that

> the Establishment Clause is not offended when religious . . . organizations benefit from neutral government programs. Any Establishment Clause objection to the scholarship program here is particularly unavailing because the government support makes its way to religious schools only as a result of Montanans independently choosing to spend their scholarships at such schools.

Id. at 474 (internal citations omitted).

§9.4.2 Prayer in Public Schools

Suppose that the Unity City School Board composes a prayer to be recited at the beginning of each school day by all students and faculty members who are willing to participate in the recital. The prayer is designed to be nondenominational: "Almighty God, we acknowledge our dependence upon Thee, and we beg Thy blessings upon us, our parents, our teachers, and our Country." Does the school board's action violate the Establishment Clause?

Under the Court's former separationist theory, the answer would be yes, and the Court so held in *Engle v. Vitale*, 370 U.S. 421 (1962). The reason was simple: The law directly promoted a religious practice and in so doing laid waste to the wall of separation between church and state. However, the Court no longer adheres to separationism. How would such a law be analyzed today? There are several ways to look at it. Under a nonpreferentialist approach, the constitutionality of the school board's action hinges in part on how one construes the board's prayer. If it is assumed to be nondenominational—i.e., to create no preferred status for any religion or group of religions—then the school board's action is constitutional. The board is free to promote religion as long as it does not discriminate in favor of or against any particular religion. On the other hand, if the prayer were construed as promoting only a particular set of religious beliefs, the board's action would run afoul of the principle of nonpreferentialism. In other words, the latter construction of the facts would take the problem out of this category and place it in the category of discrimination among religions, preferring some over others. As such, the school-endorsed recital of the prayer would be unconstitutional. See *Epperson v. Arkansas*, 393 U.S. 97 (1968) (invalidating religiously motivated law that prohibited teaching of evolution in public schools); *School Dist. of Abington Twp. v. Schemp*, 374 U.S. 203 (1963) (public school cannot require that the Lord's Prayer or passages from the Bible be recited at the beginning of each school day).

Suppose we clear the nonpreferentialism hurdle by changing the facts so that our school board does not endorse or promote any particular prayer or religion, but simply provides students an opportunity to pray if they wish, and to do so in any manner they choose. Would this still run afoul of the Establishment Clause? In *Wallace v. Jaffree*, 472 U.S. 38 (1985), the Court was confronted with an Alabama statute that authorized public grammar schools and high schools to conduct a period of silence "for meditation or voluntary prayer." Although the statute endorsed no particular religion and authorized no particular prayer, the Court held that it nonetheless violated the Establishment Clause under *Lemon*'s secular purpose element, as "the statute had *no* secular purpose" (id. at 56 (emphasis in original)) and therefore constituted an impermissible endorsement of religion. But since *Lemon* is no longer good law, would the moment of silence policy be upheld today? Justice Rehnquist's dissent in *Jaffree* helps us answer this question. He rejected the separationist model relied on by the majority as, in his view, the Establishment Clause was not designed to prevent government from taking action that favors religion over "irreligion." In a classic statement and application of the nonpreferentialist model, he said that the purpose of the clause was simply to prevent the creation of a government-sponsored religion and to preclude discrimination among sects. Since Alabama's moment of silence law did neither of these things, and instead promoted religion generally, it did not violate the Establishment Clause.

But before we conclude that our statute would pass constitutional muster today, is there any other basis on which it might still be found to violate the Establishment Clause? As to the grammar school students who fall within our statute, a good argument can be made that they may feel coerced by their peers to engage in prayer, or not fully understand that they have a choice in the matter. If so, the school's "voluntary" prayer statute might still be struck down today under the coercion test. In fact, in *Jaffree*, while the Court relied exclusively on *Lemon*'s secular purpose element to invalidate the law, plaintiffs also alleged that "minor children were exposed to ostracism from their peer group class members if they did not participate," 472 U.S. at 42, thus making what might have been a strong case for coercion. See § 9.2.3.

The court has since stressed the critical element of coercion in assessing the validity of prayer in the public-school context. In *Lee v. Weisman*, 505 U.S. 577 (1992), the Court held that the practice of inviting a cleric to recite a nonsectarian prayer at a high school or middle school graduation violated the Establishment Clause. While it might have invoked the separationist theory to reach this result, the majority ignored *Lemon* and relied on the coercion model instead—students attending the graduation were psychologically coerced to join in the prayer. Id. at 587-588. Justice Kennedy, writing for the *Lee* majority, stressed that "coercion" was the essence of an Establishment Clause violation, suggesting that without that element, the ceremony would have been constitutional. Id. at 591-594.

In 2022, in *Kennedy v. Bremerton School District*, supra, the Court reaffirmed Justice Kennedy's position in *Lee*, stating that "by 'including [a] clerical membe[r]' who publicly recited prayers 'as part of [an] official graduation ceremony' . . . the school had 'in every practical sense compelled attendance and participation in' a 'religious exercise.'" 597 U.S. at 541. Indeed, all nine members of the *Kennedy* Court recognized the critical and dispositive role of the coercion factor in school prayer cases, but the Court found no coercion under the circumstances because there was no evidence of coercion in the record. Id. at 539. Yet the dissenting opinion called for a more realistic assessment of the facts and an approach more consistent with the Court's precedent. See id. at 574-575 (Sotomayor, J., et al., dissenting) (noting that while the majority insisted upon evidence that students were "*directly* coerced to pray," "indirect coercion" should suffice as well) (emphasis in original).

Example 9-F

Prior to 1995, a student elected as Santa Fe High School's student council chaplain delivered a prayer, sometimes overtly Christian, over the school's public address system before the start of each home varsity football game. This practice was sanctioned and promoted by the school district and was part of school-sponsored pre-game activities. While most students were not required to attend games, attendance was mandatory for cheerleaders, members of the band, and team members. Santa Fe is a public school whose student body is heavily Southern Baptist. Its Mormon and Catholic students objected to the prayer practice and filed suit challenging it under the Establishment Clause. While the suit was pending, the school revised its policy to authorize two student elections, the first to determine by majority vote whether prayers should be delivered at football games, and the second to choose the individual who would select and deliver those prayers. Is the new policy unconstitutional?

Explanation

Looking first at the nonpreferentialism model, one might want more facts regarding the nature of the prayers. If they are sufficiently nondenominational, a nonpreferentialist would probably not find a violation of the Establishment Clause. However, if the prayers were overtly Christian and consistently so under the policy over a period of years, the principle of nonpreferentialism might be violated. Yet even if the prayers are distinctly sectarian, there might be no violation of the principle of government neutrality since the choice of prayer would probably not be attributable to the school but rather to the private individual chosen by the students to recite it. See *Zobrest v. Catalina Foothills School Dist.*, supra, and *Rosenberger v. Rector and Visitors of the Univ. of Va.*, supra (private choice of individual acted as a buffer between the state and the recitation of prayer so that the prayer was not attributed to the state).

Also, some members of the Court might find that prayers at high school football games are consistent with history and tradition, having become a recognized part of American culture, one in which the name of God is routinely invoked at governmental and public events and ceremonies. Under this approach, there would be no violation of the Establishment Clause to the extent these prayers are not coercive. Thus, we would need to ask whether students attending or participating in the game are being pressured into joining the prayer. The case for coercion is probably not as strong as in *Lee v. Weisman*, where the activity was a graduation ceremony in which attendance was essentially mandatory. On the other hand, for the players, cheerleaders, and band members who must attend the games, as well as for supporters who choose to attend, the pressure to conform in a mass gathering may be just as great as at a graduation. On this basis, the policy might violate the Establishment Clause.

In a similar case, the Court held that a school district's dual election system violated the Establishment Clause. *Santa Fe Independent School District v. Doe*, 530 U.S. 290 (2000). While it relied mainly on the now defunct *Lemon* and endorsement tests, based on *Lee v. Weisman*, the Court also concluded that the school-sponsored prayer prior to football games had the "improper effect of coercing those present to participate in an act of religious worship," in a setting where some students were compelled to be present due to their extracurricular responsibilities. Id. at 311-312.

EXAMPLE

Example 9-G

Joseph lost his job as a public high school football coach because he made a practice of kneeling at the 50-yard line after each game, bowing his head and quietly reciting a prayer that lasted about 30 seconds. Though some students and other coaches still remained on the field, they did not join him in these prayers and were instead engaged in unrelated informal postgame activities such as greeting family and friends. When the school became aware of Joseph's post-game prayers, it issued a policy barring him from engaging in "any overt actions that could appear to a reasonable observer to endorse prayer while he is on duty as a District-paid coach." The school's policy stemmed from a bona fide concern that allowing Joseph to engage in this practice would violate the Establishment Clause as a state endorsement of religion. When Joseph continued his post-game prayers, he was fired. He has now sued the school, claiming that the school's action violated his rights under the Free Exercise Clause. Assuming Joseph can make out a prima facie case that his free exercise rights were violated, can the school successfully defend on the ground that allowing him to continue his post-game prayer practice would make the school violate the Establishment Clause?

EXPLANATION

Explanation

If the school has infringed upon Joseph's First Amendment free exercise rights, strict scrutiny applies. The school must show that firing him served a compelling interest and that this was the least burdensome means of doing so. The school may argue that continuing to employ Joseph would have violated the Establishment Clause, for a public entity cannot engage in conduct that a reasonable observer would view as government endorsement of religion. Caught in a Catch-22 situation of either continuing to violate the Establishment Clause or denying Joseph's rights under the

Free Exercise Clause, the school chose to honor its Establishment Clause obligation. However, this argument ignores the fact that *Lemon* and the endorsement test were overruled in *Kennedy v. Bremerton School District*, supra. See § 9.2.4.

The school needs some other compelling interest. It might argue that it sought to protect its students from being coerced into prayer, surely a compelling interest. The facts do not suggest that Joseph directly coerced anyone into participating in the prayers. Yet, one might argue that the pressure of not joining might have exerted on the students some indirect coercion which, according to the justices dissenting in *Kennedy*, should suffice to find coercion. See *Kennedy v. Bremerton School District*, 597 U.S. 507, 574 (Sotomayor, J., et al., dissenting); see also *Carson v. Makin*, 596 U.S. 767, 778 (2002) ("The Free Exercise Clause . . . protects against 'indirect coercion or penalties on the free exercise of religion, not just outright prohibitions.'"); and see *Espinoza v. Montana Dep't of Revenue*, 591 U.S. 464, 478 (2020). Joseph might still argue that there are less burdensome ways of achieving the goal of avoiding a violation of the Establishment Clause than firing him, e.g., by requiring him to conduct his prayers after all students have left the field. The school might claim it had to fire Joseph to maintain order at football games. But there is no evidence that this was a problem, and even if it were, there are less burdensome ways of achieving that interest than imposing a "heckler's veto." It thus appears that firing Joseph was unconstitutional. See *Kennedy v. Bremerton School District*, supra (so holding on these facts).

Example 9-H

Milford Central School (MCS) permits local residents to use its facilities after school for, among other things, "instruction in education or the arts and for social, civic, recreational, and entertainment uses pertaining to the community welfare." Under this policy, a wide array of secular groups have used the school's facilities. Darlene, a district resident, sponsors the Good News Club, a private Christian organization for elementary school children ages 6 to 12. She submitted a request to hold the club's weekly after-school meetings in the school. To attend club meetings, children must have parental consent. Darlene described the club meetings as follows:

> Each meeting begins with calling the roll. As each child's name is called, if the child recites a Bible verse, the child receives a treat. The club members then sing songs and engage in games that involve, among other things, learning Bible verses. I then read a Bible story and explain how it applies to club members' lives. The meeting closes with a prayer. Finally, I distribute treats and Bible verses for memorization.

MCS denied the request on the ground that the proposed use—to sing songs, hear Bible lessons, memorize scripture, and pray—was the equivalent of religious worship such that granting the Club permission would violate the Establishment Clause. Is MCS correct?

Explanation

Probably not. Under a nonpreferentialist model, allowing the Club to use the facilities would not offend the Establishment Clause as long as access was religiously neutral—i.e., as long as the school lets other religiously affiliated groups use the premises as well. Nor would permission to use the facilities standing alone constitute a form of governmental coercion to join the Good News Club, for students could participate only with parental consent. Finally, it is not clear what a focus on history and tradition would show. It is not evident that there is a history of disallowing such use by religious groups when the facilities, as here, have been opened to outsiders as a limited public forum. In such instances, while the government can restrict who may use the forum, it cannot do so based on hostility to the viewpoints that will be expressed. For this factor to be dispositive, the school would need to show that history and tradition support excluding religious groups from facilities that are otherwise open to the public.

In *Good News Club v. Milford Central School*, 533 U.S. 98 (2001), a case with similar facts, the Court held that the school would not be in violation of the Establishment Clause were it to open its facilities to the Good News Club. Using nonpreferentialist terms, the Court said that "allowing the Club to speak on school grounds would ensure neutrality [toward religion], not threaten it. . . ." Id. at 114. The Court placed no independent significance on the fact that the school at issue was an elementary school with a possible coercive effect on young children, given that parental approval was necessary before children could engage in Club activities.

See also Example 8-MM, addressing the public forum aspects of this problem.

In sum, the Court's recent jurisprudence in the context of prayer in public schools has become somewhat more permissive. The Court will still not allow a public school itself to sponsor prayer in the classroom or at other school events, due to its coercive potential, even if those prayers can be characterized as being nondenominational. On the other hand, truly voluntary student-led prayers on public school campuses, as well as non-student prayer that does not in any way coerce students, will not run afoul of the Establishment Clause. Nor will the clause be violated by neutral access policies that permit similarly situated religious and nonreligious groups to use school facilities.

§9.4.3 Other Contexts

Establishment Clause challenges to governmental action that promotes or provides aid to religion or religious institutions may also arise in a variety of other contexts, including the public display of religious symbols (particularly during the holiday seasons), tax exemptions for religious institutions, released time from public school for religious studies, aid to sectarian colleges and universities, the participation of religious institutions in secular governmental programs, and the delegation of governmental power to religious institutions. The same themes, techniques, and debates that arise in the public school prayer and public aid to elementary and secondary schools contexts are present in these other settings as well. With the Court's rejection of *Lemon* and the endorsement test, however, *stare decisis* will not significantly affect the direction the Court will take in each of these subcategories.

EXAMPLE

Example 9-I

Several taxpayers have filed suit in federal court, challenging, on Establishment Clause grounds, the display of a nativity scene and a menorah in the rotunda of City Hall during the winter holiday season. The city permits such displays if the costs of constructing, maintaining, and dismantling them are not borne by the city. How will a court rule?

EXPLANATION

Explanation

In its strict separationism days, the Court would likely have invalidated the display under *Lemon* and the endorsement tests, for the purpose and primary effect of the display would appear to be government advancement of religion. The result might be different under today's approach. From the perspective of nonpreferentialism, as long as the city's policy is itself neutral with respect to the religious symbols that may be displayed, there is no Establishment Clause violation. And there would be no coercion since passersby in City Hall are not required to acknowledge the display in any manner. On this point, the Court in *Kennedy v. Bremerton School District*, supra, 597 U.S. at 535, said that the Establishment Clause does not "'compel the government to purge from the public sphere' anything an objective observer could reasonably infer endorses or 'partakes of the religious.'" This result would be consistent with tradition and history, placing such displays within an acceptable range of governmental action. Compare *Lynch v. Donnelly*, 465 U.S. 668 (1984) (upholding constitutionality of municipal policy that permitted a holiday display that included both sectarian and secular symbols) with *County of Allegheny v. American Civil Liberties Union*, 492 U.S. 573 (1989) (holding that display of a crèche on county courthouse grounds violates Establishment Clause).

EXAMPLE

Example 9-J

Through an executive order, the President has endorsed a Faith-Based and Community Initiative (FBCI) whose guiding principle is that "faith-based charities should be able to compete on an equal footing with other charities for public dollars to provide public services." Under FBCI, religiously affiliated organizations that provide social services to the needy are thus eligible to receive direct federal funding. However, a religious organization receiving federal money under FBCI may not use the federal dollars for religious worship, instruction, proselytizing, or the like. Moreover, religious activities by the organization must be kept separate from the funded activities, although both funded and religious activities can take place in the same location. For example, a federally funded job training program can take place in one room of a church hall while a Bible study group meets in another. Recipients of FBCI funding may not discriminate based on religious affiliation or require participants in the federally funded programs to participate in religious activities. But they may invite those participants to join in a religious service, including prayer, as long as it is clear that such participation is optional. Does FBCI violate the Establishment Clause?

EXPLANATION

Explanation

Note that FBCI differs from vouchers, for FBCI funding goes directly from the government to the religiously affiliated organization. Hence, the seemingly important private choice that directs government funds to a religious institution in the school voucher context, and that was present and apparently important in *Zelman v. Simmons-Harris*, is not present here. Instead, the money here goes directly to the religious institution.

Under the old *Lemon* and endorsement tests, a separationist would have argued that FBCI is unconstitutional because its primary effect is to advance the overall mission of the recipient religious institution, though this is certainly questionable. Under a nonpreferentialist approach, however, the program would most likely pass muster since it operates without regard to the possible religious affiliation of a recipient. But the conclusion might be different with respect to recipient programs that involve children who are asked to engage in prayer or other religious activity, for in that setting the program might be coercive. See *Hein v. Freedom from Religion Foundation, Inc.*, 551 U.S. 587 (2007) (ruling 5-4 that taxpayers lacked standing to challenge constitutionality of conferences held under President's FBCI program).

§9.5 THE FREE EXERCISE CLAUSE

The Free Exercise Clause provides, "Congress shall make no law . . . prohibiting the free exercise" of religion. This language has been interpreted as protecting the right of an individual to adhere to whatever religious doctrine or faith that individual chooses to believe. This protection of religious belief is, as a practical matter, absolute. A corollary of this freedom to believe is the right to profess one's chosen beliefs. Incursions on this right are generally examined under traditional, rigorous free speech standards.

The Free Exercise Clause also protects religiously motivated conduct, but not to the same extent as it protects the right to believe and to profess those beliefs. Although religiously motivated conduct was once protected under a strict scrutiny test, the current Court has adopted a less solicitous attitude toward most such conduct. Only laws that are specifically directed toward regulating conduct *because of* its religious nature are subject to heightened scrutiny. Laws that regulate conduct *despite* its religious nature are not subject to such exacting review.

In free exercise cases, the plaintiff bears the burden of proving that their rights under the Free Exercise Clause have been violated. If the plaintiff makes this showing, the burden shifts to the defendant to show that its actions were constitutional, which usually means proving that its actions were narrowly tailored to achieve a compelling governmental interest. *Kennedy v. Bremerton School Dist.*, 597 U.S. 507, 525 (2022).

§9.5.1 The Distinction Between Belief and Conduct

While the distinction between belief and conduct often plays a critical role in determining the appropriate level of judicial scrutiny to be applied under the Free Exercise Clause, there is no bright-line test for determining whether a law regulates belief or conduct. At times the distinction between belief and conduct is less than obvious. For example, in *McDaniel v. Paty*, 435 U.S. 618 (1978), a state law disqualified "ministers of the Gospel" from participating in a state constitutional convention. Although seven members of the Court agreed that the provision violated the Free Exercise Clause, there was no majority opinion for the Court. Three Justices thought that the law impinged on an individual's beliefs, since its application depended on the intensity of those beliefs—i.e., beliefs that were sufficiently intense to cause one to choose the ministry. These Justices, therefore, concluded that the law transgressed the absolute protection afforded religious belief. Four Justices, however, thought that the law was directed primarily toward religious conduct—i.e., action taken in the capacity of a minister—and that it was, therefore, not subject to the same strict level of protection as that afforded religious belief. Yet they did agree that the law violated the Free Exercise Clause, but under a slightly more deferential standard.

Although there is no bright-line test for determining whether a particular law regulates belief or conduct, an effective way to measure the distinction is to examine the regulatory focus of the challenged law. If the regulatory focus of the law is on an individual's *thought processes* or on the *mental conclusions* the individual may have derived from those processes, then the law is belief-centered and subject to the absolute prohibition imposed by the Free Exercise Clause. On the other hand, if the regulatory focus of the law is directed toward *external actions* triggered by those thought processes and mental conclusions, the law is conduct-centered and not subject to the absolute prohibition. In most cases, the distinction between thought processes and external action will be apparent from the interaction between the challenged law and the particular facts presented.

Example 9-K

Dickie is a member of a religious group that absolutely prohibits the use of violence toward fellow human beings. On the basis of his religious beliefs, Dickie refused to sign an oath affirming the duty of all citizens to defend with arms the Constitution of the United States. Because of this refusal, Dickie was denied a position as a public school teacher. If Dickie were to challenge the government's action under the Free Exercise Clause, would the case be treated as involving a regulation of belief or of conduct?

Explanation

Although the act of signing (or refusing to sign) an oath can be fairly characterized as conduct, the government's attention is focused not so much on the refusal to sign as on what that refusal signifies, namely, a particular belief. Ultimately, Dickie is being denied a job because of what he believes. The government's action, therefore, runs afoul of the absolute prohibition against the regulation of belief.

On the other hand, if Dickie were drafted to fight in a war (assuming that he was not entitled to statutory conscientious objector status) and refused to serve based on his religious beliefs, any punishment for that refusal to fight would presumably involve a regulation of his conduct. Although Dickie's refusal was premised on belief, the focus of the government's attention is not on Dickie's beliefs, but on his external action. The punishment for refusing to fight applies regardless of a person's motivation and would have been the same had Dickie's refusal stemmed from cowardice. The government's action, therefore, would not run afoul of the absolute prohibition against the regulation of belief and would be evaluated under the less stringent standard that applies to religiously motivated conduct.

§9.5.2 The Protection of Religious Belief

The protection afforded religious belief is essentially absolute. Individuals or groups are entitled to believe anything they choose to believe, no matter how improbable, pernicious, or plain silly that belief may be. As the Court has observed,

> The free exercise of religion means, first and foremost, the right to believe and profess whatever religious doctrine one desires. Thus, the First Amendment obviously excludes all "governmental regulation of religious *beliefs* as such." The government may not compel affirmation of religious belief, punish the expression of religious doctrines it believes to be false, impose special disabilities on the basis of religious views or religious status, or lend its power to one or the other side in controversies over religious authority or dogma.

Employment Division v. Smith, 494 U.S. 872, 877 (1990) (emphasis in original) (internal citations omitted).

One of the most important cases arising in this context is *West Virginia State Board of Education v. Barnette*, 319 U.S. 624 (1943). In that case, a group of Jehovah's Witnesses brought suit, seeking to enjoin a West Virginia law that required all public school students to participate daily in the salute to the flag and in the recital of the Pledge of Allegiance. The Witnesses objected to the compelled flag salute and Pledge recital as contravening the Bible's Exodus, Chapter 20, verses 4 and 5, which state: "Thou shalt not make unto thee any graven image, or any likeness of anything that is in heaven above, or that is in the earth beneath, or that is in the water under the earth; thou shalt not bow down thyself to them nor serve them." The Witnesses believed that both the salute and the Pledge violated these Biblical admonitions.

Although the challenged law was in a sense directed toward conduct—saluting the flag and reciting the Pledge—the Court interpreted the state law as primarily directed toward the public affirmation of what an individual believed. As a consequence, the Court held that the state law violated the First Amendment by compelling the Witnesses to affirm a belief they did not share with the community. The Court declared:

> If there is any fixed star in our constitutional constellation, it is that no official, high or petty, can prescribe what shall be orthodox in politics, nationalism, religion, or other matters of opinion or force citizens to confess by word or act their faith therein. If there are any circumstances which permit an exception, they do not now occur to us.

Id. at 642. The holding and principles of *Barnette* have been consistently followed, particularly in the context of religious belief. See *Torcaso v. Watkins*, 367 U.S. 488, 495-496 (1961) (holding unconstitutional a state law that required an individual to affirm a belief in God to obtain a governmental commission).

EXAMPLE

Example 9-L

Pete was indicted for mail fraud on the basis that he used the mail to promote beliefs that were false. The indictment charged a scheme to defraud on the basis of Pete's promotion of the "I Can" movement and his asserted belief that he was the appointed messenger of God, that he had shaken hands with Jesus, and that he had the divine power to cure incurable diseases. Could the jury, consistent with the First Amendment, convict Pete on the basis of its conclusion that his claimed religious beliefs were in fact false?

EXPLANATION

Explanation

No. Although a jury could examine Pete's good faith in asserting these beliefs—i.e., whether Pete actually entertained the professed beliefs—it could not attempt to determine the truth or falsity of those beliefs. To do so would undermine the freedom of religion by giving government the power to determine the truth of religious belief and doctrine and to then punish those found to hold "false" beliefs. See *United States v. Ballard*, 322 U.S. 78 (1944).

In the above example, as in *Barnette*, the determination of unconstitutionality was premised on a single inquiry—i.e., whether the contested governmental action was aimed at a religious belief. An affirmative answer to that inquiry led directly to a finding of unconstitutionality. There was no balancing of interests, strict or otherwise. The protection of belief is, in this sense, absolute.

The Right to Profess Religious Beliefs

The protection of religious belief also includes the right to profess one's beliefs freely and openly. In *Cantwell v. Connecticut*, 310 U.S. 296, 304 (1940), the Court observed, "No one would contest the proposition that a State may not, by statute, wholly deny the right to preach or to disseminate religious views." And just as the government may not declare any particular religious belief to be false or heretical, the government may not outlaw the expression of unpopular or offensive religious views merely because those views do not comport with some generally accepted notion of what is true from a religious perspective.

However, the right to profess one's religious beliefs is not absolute. It stands on the same footing as the First Amendment right to profess one's political beliefs. In neither case may the government suppress the expression of those beliefs simply because the beliefs are deemed to be false, pernicious, or even dangerous. Yet the government may sometimes restrict such expression if it is able to satisfy a very strict standard of judicial review. See Chapter 8. Speech professing one's religious beliefs or promoting religious dogma is thus not protected under all circumstances. In general, the protection afforded religious expression differs little, if at all, from the protection afforded speech generally, and a content-based restriction on an individual's ability to express religious ideas will be subject to the same searching scrutiny as would a content-based restriction on political speech.

Example 9-M

Cantwell is a Jehovah's Witness. He believes it is his duty to proselytize his faith and to demonstrate the corruption of organized religions. Consistent with these beliefs, Cantwell introduced himself to two strangers on a street corner and with their permission played a recording for them that was highly critical of the Catholic Church. Though both individuals were highly incensed by what was said on the recording and threatened to strike Cantwell unless he went away, no violence ensued. Cantwell was, nonetheless, convicted of inciting a breach of the peace. Did Cantwell's conviction violate his free speech or free exercise rights?

Explanation

The conviction violated Cantwell's free speech rights. In a case with similar facts, the Supreme Court reversed the defendant's conviction, holding that since he had done no more than express an idea that his listeners found offensive, he could not be convicted consistent with the free speech guarantee of the First Amendment. The Free Exercise Clause, though mentioned by the Court in passing, added nothing to its analysis. *Cantwell v. Connecticut*, supra, 310 U.S. at 307-311.

However, like political speech, religious speech that does present a clear and present danger to public safety may be subject to governmental restriction.

Example 9-N

The Cult of the Avenging Angel is a modern apocalyptic religion that believes the path to salvation will be found in swift vengeance on its enemies. Members of the cult are taught that each one of them has a duty to seek vengeance on any person who harms the cult in any manner. May the government outlaw the teaching of this belief?

EXPLANATION

Explanation

It depends. The government may not outlaw the teaching of this belief merely because it represents an evil or pernicious doctrine. But if the government can show that the circumstances under which this doctrine is being taught are such as to create a clear and present danger of imminent harm, such as specific harm to a particular individual, then consistent with both the Free Speech and the Free Exercise Clauses, the teaching of this belief can be proscribed or punished. See § 8.3.2.

Similarly, just as content-based restrictions on religious speech must satisfy strict scrutiny, content-neutral restrictions are subject to time, place, and manner standards. See § 8.4.

EXAMPLE

Example 9-O

The Knights of Columbus, a religious organization affiliated with the Roman Catholic Church, wishes to sponsor an interfaith parade celebrating the theme "Religion in America." The city in which the Knights hope to hold the parade requires parade sponsors to apply for and obtain a parade permit and, should the permit be granted, to comply with various regulations designed to promote the safe and efficient use of city streets while the parade is in progress. What First Amendment standards should be applied to assess the constitutionality of the parade permit requirement?

EXPLANATION

Explanation

Because both the permit application process and the regulations appear to be content-neutral, the proper standard for assessing the city's permit procedures and regulations is the time, place, and manner test applicable to parades generally. The religious nature of the message to be conveyed by this planned parade does not alter those standards.

The congruity between the freedom of speech and the freedom to profess one's religious beliefs also means that religious speech cannot be treated less favorably than other protected speech. Thus, in *Rosenberger v. Rector & Visitors of the University of Virginia*, 515 U.S. 819 (1995), the Court held that a state university cannot refuse to fund a student publication merely because that publication espouses a religious viewpoint. The religious nature of the proposed publication does not lessen the protections afforded by the First Amendment guarantee of free speech. Here, the state's refusal was not viewpoint-neutral and, as a consequence, violated the strict standards that protect speech in a designated public forum. See § 8.5.2. The Court also found that funding the publication, under neutral principles, does not violate the Establishment Clause. See § 9.4.1. See also *Watchtower Bible and Tract Soc'y of New York, Inc. v. Village of Stratton*, 536 U.S. 150 (2002) (applying free speech principles to a restriction on door-to-door canvassing by a religious organization).

Ecclesiastical Disputes

The protection afforded religious belief is also implicated when the government attempts to insinuate itself into an ecclesiastical dispute within a church hierarchy. For example, in *Presbyterian Church v. Hull Church*, 393 U.S. 440 (1969), a general church organization became involved in a dispute with two local churches that had been members of the general church. The dispute involved the ownership of certain property that the local churches held in trust for the general church. The controversy arose when the local churches withdrew from the general church and then claimed ownership of the property, their theory being that the general church had abandoned certain doctrinal tenets, thereby relinquishing its interest in the property. This theory was consistent with state law, and after a trial in state court, the position of the local churches was sustained by a jury. The Supreme Court reversed, holding that a court may not become embroiled in a property dispute within a church if resolution of that dispute requires the court to resolve a controversy over religious doctrine. Whether the general church had abandoned previously held doctrinal tenets fell directly within that category and was not, therefore, subject to judicial resolution by a state or federal court.

Similarly, the Free Exercise Clause precludes courts from becoming embroiled in conflicts involving the internal operations of a church or religion, at least in the absence of some showing of fraud or deceit. The Court applied this principle in *Hosanna-Tabor Evangelical Lutheran Church and School v. E.E.O.C.*, 565 U.S. 171 (2012), in which it held that the antidiscrimination provisions of the Americans with Disabilities Act (ADA) were subject to a "ministerial exception" because of the limitations imposed by the Religion Clauses. Applying that exception, the Court held that a decision by a religious school to rescind the ministerial status of a teacher who had developed narcolepsy (and fire her) was not actionable under the ADA. In reaching that conclusion, the Court found that four factors were satisfied: First, the teacher had the title of minister; second, she had received a significant degree of religious training followed by a process of commission; third, she held herself out as a minister of the church; and fourth, her job duties reflected a role in conveying the church's message and carrying out its mission.

Eight years after *Hosanna-Tabor*, the Court significantly expanded the ministerial exception to bar two Catholic elementary school teachers from suing their schools under the federal Age Discrimination in Employment Act and the Americans with Disabilities Act. In *Our Lady of Guadalupe School v. Morrissey-Berru*, 591 U.S. 732 (2020), the Court held that the teachers' jobs fell within the exception, even though they met only one or two of the *Hosanna-Tabor* factors. Neither teacher had a religious title; neither had much religious training; neither was a minister or official of the church, and one was not even a "'practicing' member of the religion with which the employer is associated." Id. at 761. However, said the Court, the four factors do not constitute mandatory "checklist items" or a "rigid formula. Id. at 757-758. Instead, "[w]hat matters, at bottom, is what an employee does." Id. at 753. Here, that fourth factor was satisfied, for "their core responsibilities as teachers of religion were essentially the same" as those of the teacher in *Hossana-Tabor*. Id. at 757. In dissent, Justices Sotomayor and Ginsburg charged the majority with "rewriting *Hossana-Tabor*" to "expand[] the ministerial exception far beyond its historic narrowness," thereby stripping over 100,000 religious institution employees of protection against "employment decisions because of a person's skin color, age, disability, sex, or any other protected trait for reasons having nothing to do with religion." Id. at 772, 784.

Example 9-P

The Holy Synod of the Serbian Orthodox Church removed and defrocked the Bishop for the American Canadian Diocese of that church. The removed bishop challenged this action as being procedurally and substantively defective under the internal regulations of the Mother Church and therefore arbitrary and invalid as a matter of church law. He filed suit in state court, seeking reinstatement. May a court grant the requested relief?

Explanation

Even assuming the church acted arbitrarily in applying its own internal regulations, the First and Fourteenth Amendments preclude a state or federal court from interfering with the church tribunal's decision when, as here, resolution of the dispute cannot be made without extensive inquiry into religious law and polity, at least where there has been no showing of fraud, collusion, or deceit on the tribunal's part. *Serbian Eastern Orthodox Diocese v. Milivojevich*, 426 U.S. 696 (1976).

Of course, the mere fact that a church is involved in a legal controversy does not disable the judiciary or the government generally from resolving that controversy. The First Amendment is implicated only when the resolution of such a controversy requires the judiciary or the government to become embroiled in a religious doctrinal dispute or a dispute over the application of the internal rules and regulations of a church. See *Jones v. Wolf*,

443 U.S. 595 (1979), *opinion after remand*, 244 Ga. 388, 260 S.E.2d 84 (1979), *cert. denied*, 444 U.S. 1080 (1980) (resolving dispute over church property following schism in local Georgia church affiliated with hierarchical church organization by applying Georgia common law principle of presumptive majority rule).

§9.5.3 The Protection of Religiously Motivated Conduct

As we noted earlier, the Free Exercise Clause also protects religiously motivated conduct, though the protection may not be as strong as that afforded religious beliefs. The phrase "religiously motivated conduct" denotes action taken in compliance with one's religious beliefs, such as drinking wine as part of a Catholic Mass or ingesting peyote in compliance with the tenets of the Native American Church. A Quaker's scripture-based refusal to bear arms against a fellow human being is another example of religiously motivated conduct. The key factor in each of these examples is the presence of a religious motivation for the action undertaken or refused. In the absence of such a motivation, the consumption of wine, the ingestion of peyote, and the refusal to bear arms would constitute purely secular conduct and would be entitled to no protection under the Free Exercise Clause.

If a law governing religiously motivated conduct is specifically designed to suppress or burden that conduct *because* of its religious nature, then the law is not "neutral." And if the law applies only to specific individuals or religious groups *because* of their religious practice, then the law is not "generally applicable." A law regulating religiously motivated conduct which is not neutral and of general applicability will be invalidated under the Free Exercise Clause unless the law passes the strict scrutiny test. See also *Kennedy v. Bremerton School District*, supra, 597 U.S. at 526.

Laws that potentially infringe on religious conduct can be divided into three categories: (1) laws that regulate, prohibit, or decline to fund religious conduct *because* of its religious nature or only when that conduct is engaged in for religious purposes; (2) laws that regulate religious conduct *despite* its religious nature; and (3) laws that regulate nonreligious conduct, but that incidentally *burden* religious practices. In the sections that follow we will assess each of these types of laws under the Free Exercise Clause.

The Purposeful Suppression or Selective Nonfunding of Religiously Motivated Conduct

The Free Exercise Clause severely limits the government's authority to enact a law that regulates religiously motivated conduct specifically *because* of that conduct's religious nature, or only when that conduct is engaged in for religious purposes. Such a law is not neutral within the meaning of the Free Exercise Clause since the law uses religion as a criterion for the application of governmental power. This lack of neutrality creates a presumption of invalidity that can only be rebutted through satisfaction of the strict scrutiny test. Thus, only if the government can demonstrate that the challenged law advances a compelling interest through the least restrictive means available will the law be upheld. The instances in which this test will be satisfied under the Free Exercise Clause are extraordinarily rare.

Not all laws that regulate religiously motivated conduct fall into this category. The key question is whether the government's action is purposefully aimed at religion. For example, a law that by its specific terms prohibits the *sacramental* drinking of wine regulates conduct because of its religious nature, while a law that prohibits the consumption of wine regardless of the circumstances under which it is consumed does not. The first example describes a law that is purposefully directed toward the suppression of a religious practice, while the second describes a neutral law that happens to sweep a religious practice within its scope. The free exercise implications for this latter type of law are discussed in the next subsection.

One of the leading cases involving the deliberate regulation of religious conduct is *Church of the Lukumi Babalu Aye, Inc. v. City of Hialeah*, 508 U.S. 520 (1993). At issue there was a series of city ordinances that prohibited the ritual or sacrificial killing of animals within city limits. The ordinances were facially neutral in that they did not mention or appear to target any particular religious group. The Santerian church brought suit in federal court to enjoin enforcement of the ordinances, alleging that despite their facial neutrality, the laws violated the Free Exercise Clause because they were adopted with the discriminatory purpose of prohibiting a religious ritual that was integral to Santeria but distasteful to city residents. The key question for the Court was whether these ordinances, though facially neutral, were in fact adopted *because* of the religious nature of the practices at issue. If they were, then the ordinances would be subject to a rigorous and presumptively fatal application of the strict scrutiny test.

The Court approached this "because of" inquiry from two perspectives, each designed to determine whether the law's real purpose was to suppress a religious practice. First, the Court considered whether the city ordinances were neutral in the sense that their adoption was independent of the religious nature of the practice being prohibited. The ordinances did not satisfy this test. Both the text of the ordinances, which used religious terms such as *ritual* and *sacrifice*, and the events leading up to their adoption, which indicated an animosity for the Santeria religion, made it clear that the object of these ordinances was the suppression of a religious practice. The ordinances also included an exemption for licensed slaughterhouses, seeming to favor the secular killing of animals and further demonstrating a lack of neutral purpose.

Second, the Court considered whether, in terms of their practical effect, the ordinances could be considered laws of general applicability. In other words, the Court asked whether the scope of these ordinances encompassed a wide array of related activities to advance a legitimate legislative purpose or whether they placed their entire burden on activities of a religious nature. In the latter case, it could be inferred that the measures were enacted because of their impact on this religious practice. Here, the Court noted that if, as the city suggested, the purpose of these ordinances was to prevent the inhumane treatment of animals and promote public health, the ordinances were substantially underinclusive, since the proscription of the laws only applied when those interests were threatened by religiously motivated conduct. As a consequence, the ordinances could not be fairly characterized as laws of general applicability.

Since the ordinances were neither neutral nor of general applicability, the Court concluded that they were enacted because of, not despite, their impact on a religious practice. The Court, therefore, applied the strict scrutiny test. The purported interests of the city—the humane treatment of animals and public health—although perhaps compelling in the abstract, were not deemed compelling under the circumstances since the ordinances did so little to advance those interests. So, too, the ordinances were both overbroad and underinclusive, and hence not narrowly tailored to advance the city's purported interests. In short, the ordinances failed the strict scrutiny test.

Church of the Lukumi Babalu Aye was an unusual case, for the facts and circumstances made it obvious that the city's actions were in fact designed for the specific purpose of suppressing the religious practices of the Santeria religion. A similar case, where the facts and circumstances made clear that the government's action was infected by hostility towards an individual because of his religious beliefs, was presented in *Masterpiece Cakeshop, Ltd. v. Colorado Civil Rights Commission*, 584 U.S. 617 (2018). There, a baker, who was a devout Christian, refused on religious grounds to prepare a wedding cake for a same-sex couple. The couple then brought an action before the state Civil Rights Commission, alleging violation of the state's Anti-Discrimination Act. In defense, the baker asserted that compelling him to bake a cake under such circumstances would violate his rights under the Free Exercise Clause. After the Commission ruled against the baker and the state courts affirmed, the baker obtained review in the Supreme Court. In setting aside the Commission's order, the Court explained that "[t]he Free Exercise Clause bars even 'subtle departures from neutrality' on matters of religion." Id. at 638 (quoting from *Church of the Lukumi Babalu Aye*). Because the record made clear that "the Commission's consideration of Phillips' case was neither tolerant nor respectful of Phillips' religious beliefs," and that his "religious objection was not considered with the neutrality that the Free

Exercise Clause requires," the Commission proceedings were held to be unconstitutional. Id. at 639.

Example 9-Q

In Example 9-G, supra, Joseph lost his job as a public high school football coach because he prayed on the field after each game had ended. When the school fired him for engaging in this practice, Joseph sued the school claiming that it had violated the Free Exercise Clause. Can he carry his burden of making a prima facie showing that the school violated his free exercise rights?

Explanation

To carry this burden, Joseph must show that the school infringed upon a sincere religious practice pursuant to a policy that is not neutral or generally applicable. There seems no question as to the sincerity of his post-game prayers, for he has regularly engaged in this practice for many years. Nor is the school's policy neutral, for it sought to restrict Joseph's actions because of their religious character; indeed, the religious nature of the prohibited activities is expressly set forth in the school's policy. Finally, the policy is not of general applicability in terms of how it treats members of the coaching staff since it bars those like Joseph from engaging in post-game religious activity while other coaches can remain on the field and engage in social activities with players, families, and friends. Joseph can thus make out a prima facie case that the school violated his rights under the Free Exercise Clause. See *Kennedy v. Bremerton School District*, 597 U.S. 507, 523-527 (2022) (so holding).

Example 9-R

During the COVID-19 pandemic, the governor of New York issued an emergency order that imposed severe attendance restrictions on houses of worship in areas identified as "red" or "orange" zones. In red zones, no more than 10 people may attend each religious service; in orange zones, attendance is capped at 25. The order treats houses of worship more harshly than comparable secular facilities which, whether or not deemed "essential," may generally decide for themselves how many people to admit. The order was challenged by the Roman Catholic Diocese of Brooklyn and by Agudath Israel, an organization that represents Orthodox Jews. Both groups have operated their facilities at 25 percent or 33 percent of capacity for months, without a single COVID outbreak. Does the governor's order violate plaintiffs' rights under the Free Exercise Clause?

Explanation

The state here specifically targeted religiously motivated conduct, i.e., attending houses of worship. Even if the governor's action was not based on a desire to suppress or harm religion in general or target specific religious groups, it nonetheless treats houses of worship differently from all other places where people gather. In contrast to *Church of the Lukumi Babalu Aye*, it is clear from the face of the order that it was intended to target religious practices. Moreover, its practical effect is limited to such entities. The conclusion is thus inescapable that the order was enacted because of—not in spite of—its impact on houses of worship. As such, it is subject to the strictest of scrutiny.

While the state will claim a compelling interest in stemming the spread of COVID-19, it must show that the order is "narrowly tailored" to achieving that goal. This means it has the burden of demonstrating that the order is neither underinclusive in terms of those whom it reaches nor overly burdensome in terms of the restrictions it imposes. The order clears neither of these hurdles. First, it is grossly underinclusive since it applies only to religious gathering places. While the state may argue that such venues are different from other places where people assemble, it would have to demonstrate what those germane differences are. Second, even if houses of worship are deemed to fall into a special category, there are less burdensome alternatives available to the state. For example, it might have limited its restrictions just to entities that have had documented cases of COVID-19 infection, rather than burdening those like plaintiffs whose own efforts seemed to have successfully addressed the problem. In addition, for entities that are covered by its restrictions, the state might have used a variable attendance cap tied to the seating capacity of a particular church or synagogue, thereby letting entities with higher capacities to seat more people. The order is thus more burdensome than necessary as applied to larger houses of worship. On these facts, the Supreme Court enjoined New York's governor from enforcing these occupancy limits, finding that they violated the Free Exercise Clause. *Roman Catholic Diocese of Brooklyn v. Cuomo*, 592 U.S. 14 (2020).

More typically, free exercise challenges to governmental action that proscribes or burdens religiously motivated conduct arise in settings where it is harder to prove that the state's purpose was to suppress a religious practice, rather than further some legitimate goal. Such cases often arise in settings where the government, instead of regulating or prohibiting religiously based conduct, has chosen to withhold financial or other support from an individual or entity due to their religious affiliation or the religious nature of their activities. The Court's thinking in this context has evolved.

EXAMPLE

Example 9-S

The State of Washington awards "Promise Scholarships" to students who qualify for them based on their high school grades, family income, and attendance at an accredited college in the state. The scholarships may be used at both sectarian and nonsectarian schools. Joshua was awarded a Promise Scholarship and enrolled in an accredited college within the state. However, his scholarship, which amounted to just under $3,000, was then rescinded after he declared his major to be devotional theology. The state defends its action on the ground that state funding for religious instruction is barred by state law. Does this action by the state violate Joshua's rights under the Free Exercise Clause?

EXPLANATION

Explanation

Notice that this problem is in a sense the converse of the problem addressed in Example 9-E and the materials following that example. There, the question was whether the Establishment Clause barred a government entity from *providing* funding for sectarian education through the indirect method of a voucher system driven by parental choice. Under facts similar to that example, the Court in *Zelman v. Simmons-Harris*, 536 U.S. 639 (2002), found no Establishment Clause violation, largely because the program was technically neutral as between sectarian and nonsectarian institutions. See § 9.4.1. Here, the question is whether a government entity that provides tuition assistance for nonsectarian studies at private colleges can *withhold* funding for sectarian studies at those same institutions—i.e., whether it must be neutral in relation to religion and nonreligion when it funds private education.

On similar facts, the Supreme Court found no violation of the Free Exercise Clause. *Locke v. Davey*, 540 U.S. 712 (2004). Although the Promise Scholarship Program was not facially neutral with respect to religion, the Court declined to apply the presumption of unconstitutionality it had established in *Church of the Lukumi Babalu Aye*. Rather, in the Court's view, the state's lack of neutrality reflected neither hostility to religion nor a desire to suppress it, but rather a legitimate desire to promote the antiestablishment value of avoiding taxpayer support for religious institutions and practices. The Court distinguished its *Lukumi* decision with the following observations:

> In *Lukumi*, the city of Hialeah made it a crime to engage in certain kinds of animal slaughter. We found that the law sought to suppress ritualistic animal sacrifices of the Santeria religion. In the present case, the State's disfavor of religion (if it can be called that) is of a far milder kind. It imposes neither criminal nor civil sanctions on any type of religious service or rite. It does not deny to ministers the right to participate in the political affairs of the community.

> And it does not require students to choose between their religious beliefs and receiving a government benefit. The State has merely chosen not to fund a distinct category of instruction.

Locke v. Davey, supra, 540 U.S. at 720-721 (internal citations omitted). And, consistent with the current Court's focus on "original meaning and history" in construing the Religion Clauses, "opposition to such funding 'to support church leaders' lay at the historic core of the Religion Clauses," *Trinity Lutheran Church of Columbia, Inc. v. Comer*, 582 U.S 449, 465 (2017) (quoting *Locke*, supra, 540 U.S. at 722), and that most early state constitutions prohibited the expenditure of tax dollars to support the clergy. 540 U.S. at 722-723. The net result of the Court's reasoning was that strict scrutiny did not apply, and the state's spending program was upheld despite its seeming lack of neutrality.

The *Locke* majority also suggested that to trigger the Free Exercise Clause, the burden imposed on that right may have to exceed some de minimis level. The two-year scholarship at issue there totaled less than $3,000—what the Court described as a "far milder" burden than the criminal penalty involved in *Lukumi*. Such a threshold requirement would mirror the concept of "impingement" that applies in the substantive due process area. See § 2.4.4. The *Locke* dissenters objected to the Court's importing a "threshold quantum-of-harm requirement" into the First Amendment free exercise area. See *Locke v. Davey*, supra, 540 U.S. at 731-732 (Scalia, J., and Thomas, J., dissenting).

Example 9-T

EXAMPLE

The State of Missouri adopted a Scrap Tire Program that provides grants to public and private schools and nonprofit daycare centers to help them purchase rubber playground surfaces made from recycled tires. The program serves the twin goals of recycling and child safety. The state has a blanket rule that categorically disqualifies churches and other religious organizations from receiving grants under this program, based on a state constitutional provision that bars Missouri from spending money "in aid of any church, sect or denomination of religion." Trinity Lutheran Church operates a preschool and daycare center on church property. The center includes a playground area, most of which was covered by coarse pea gravel. Seeking to make the area safer for children, the church applied for a grant under the Scrap Tire Program. The grant was denied on the ground that the program could not provide financial assistance directly to a church. Does the state's action violate the church's rights under the Free Exercise Clause?

Explanation

Under *Locke v. Davey*, one would argue that the program should not be subject to strict scrutiny and therefore likely upheld, for despite its facial discrimination against religious entities, the program is designed to serve the legitimate goal of ensuring a separation of church and state. As in *Locke*, no entity or individual is barred from engaging in any particular activity. Rather, the state has simply declined to fund these activities for reasons that, unlike *Lukumi Babalu*, reflect no apparent hostility towards religion.

However, the church might argue that *Locke* is distinguishable on the basis that there, no individual or entity was categorically disqualified from receiving state funding because of *who* they were. Instead, the denial was based on *what* the would-be recipient proposed to do with the money. Here, by contrast, there is simply no way Trinity Lutheran can receive assistance under the Scrap Tire Program because of who or what it is—i.e., a church. Only by renouncing its religious character and becoming a secular entity could it receive benefits under the program. This is arguably a much more severe intrusion on the church's rights than was the burden imposed in *Locke*, where Joshua did not have to renounce his religious beliefs to receive a state scholarship, even one to a religious school where he could take devotional theology classes so long as he did not pursue a degree in that subject. On this reasoning, the Missouri law should be subjected to strict scrutiny. The state's only asserted interest is in assuring a greater separation of church than is required by the Establishment Clause. That interest cannot qualify as sufficiently compelling as to justify a violation of the Free Exercise Clause.

On these facts, the Court in *Trinity Lutheran Church v. Comer*, 582 U.S. 449 (2017), in a 7 to 2 decision, held that Missouri's policy violated the Free Exercise Clause. The Court's reasoning tracked the church's argument above. However, two members of the majority found the Court's attempt to distinguish *Locke* based on "the status-use distinction" unconvincing. Id. at 469-470 (Gorsuch, J., and Thomas, J., concurring). In their view, "the endorsement in *Locke* of even a 'mild kind' of discrimination against religion remains troubling"; they therefore suggested that *Locke* be reconsidered in an appropriate case, something the Court was not asked to do here. Id. at 468 (Thomas, J., and Gorsuch, J., concurring in part). But, in contrast to *Locke*, no member of the Court touched on an "impingement" requirement that, depending on the size of the grant at issue here, might have avoided application of strict scrutiny.

The *Trinity Lutheran* dissent urged a more flexible approach to the Free Exercise Clause, one that would give government greater leeway to maintain separation between church and state. It noted that there is a strong "historical pedigree"—as evidenced by state practices dating back to the time of the framing—for "a prophylactic rule against the use of public funds for houses of worship" such as the one Missouri enacted in this case. Id. at

487 (Sotomayor, J., and Ginsburg, J., dissenting). In the dissent's view, "[a] State's decision not to fund houses of worship does not disfavor religion; rather, it represents a valid choice to remain secular in the face of serious establishment and free exercise concerns. . . . It means only that the State has 'established neither atheism nor religion as its official creed.'" Id. at 493.

Example 9-U

The Montana legislature enacted a scholarship program for needy children who attend private schools, whether the schools are religious or secular. The program gives a state tax credit of up to $150 to anyone who donates to certain charitable organizations. Those organizations in turn give scholarships to financially eligible parents whose children attend private schools. After the program was in place, the Montana Department of Revenue barred the scholarships from being used at religious schools, based on a "no-aid" provision in the state constitution which guarantees "all Montanans that their government will not use state funds to aid religious schools." Parents of children who qualified for the scholarships and wished to use them at religious grammar schools sued in state court to determine the validity of the religious school exclusion. The Montana Supreme Court held that the program violated the "no-aid" provision of the state constitution and its goal of separating church and state, a goal that also protects taxpayers who do not want their money spent to support religion. The parents have petitioned the U.S. Supreme Court for review, claiming that the state's invocation of the "no-aid" provision to exclude religious schools and families from the scholarship program violates the Free Exercise Clause. How should the Court rule?

Explanation

Montana will argue that this case is controlled by *Locke v. Davey*, 540 U.S. 712 (2004). (See Example 9-S.) As in that case, the state has denied scholarship assistance to students who plan to use the money to attend sectarian schools, on the ground that funding for religious education is barred by state law. Petitioners will respond that *Locke* is distinguishable. There, state scholarships were generally available for use at sectarian schools, and it was only the fact that Joshua wanted to use the money to major in religious studies that led the state to withhold assistance. Here, by contrast, there is no indication the money will be used for anything other than getting a grammar school education, albeit one where religious instruction will be part of but by no means the sole or predominant focus of the program. And in contrast to *Locke*, where there was a "historical pedigree" for states' declining to fund the training of religious clergy, states have long provided financial support for private elementary and secondary schools, including religious ones.

Petitioners will then argue that since *Locke* is distinguishable, the case is controlled by *Trinity Lutheran* (see Example 9-T). As in that case, the state here disqualified otherwise eligible recipients from a public benefit solely because of the recipient school's religious character. And, as there, would-be recipients were disqualified solely because of *who* they were, not because of *what* they might do with the money. If the money given to the religious schools was in fact used for religious purposes, that could be the basis for a separate challenge, but no such showing was made here. Under *Trinity Lutheran*, Montana's no-aid provision would have to survive strict scrutiny. The state's claimed interest in separating church and state "more fiercely" than may be required by the First Amendment is unavailing, for by doing so, the state is violating petitioners' rights under the Free Exercise Clause. The same is true of the state's desire to protect taxpayers who do not want their money spent in a way that might support religion.

On these facts, the Court in *Espinoza v. Montana Department of Revenue*, 591 U.S. 464 (2020), ruled 6 to 3 that Montana's invocation of its "no-aid" provision to deny religious schools access to the state scholarship program violated the Free Exercise Clause. The Court made it clear that the standard of review in such cases is strict in theory and virtually fatal in fact: "When otherwise-eligible recipients are disqualified from a public benefit 'solely because of their religious character,' we must apply strict scrutiny." Id. at 2260. Moreover, "[t]hat 'stringent standard' is not 'watered down but really means what it says.' To satisfy it, government action 'must advance interests of the highest order and must be narrowly tailored in pursuit of those interests.'" Id. (internal citations omitted). Montana could not make that showing here.

The *Espinoza* dissent would have upheld the exclusion under a more "flexible, context-specific," "'play-in-the-joints' doctrine" which recognizes that the states need some leeway to navigate between the competing demands of the Free Exercise and Establishment Clauses. Id. at 2281-2282, 2288 (Breyer, J., and Kagan, J., dissenting); id. at 2295-2297 (Sotomayor, J., dissenting). The dissent also suggested that a more relaxed standard of review should be applied when, as here, a government benefit—rather than a government restraint—is at issue. Id. at 2288-2291 (Breyer, J., and Kagan, J., dissenting).

Two years after *Espinoza* was decided, the Court in *Carson v. Makin*, 596 U.S. 767 (2022), reached a similar result in a case where the state of Maine withheld secondary school tuition assistance from families whose children went to sectarian rather than nonsectarian private schools. In another 6-to-3 decision the Court wrote: "The 'unremarkable' principles applied in *Trinity Lutheran* and *Espinoza* suffice to resolve this case." Id. at 780. For a state "to 'disqualify some private schools' from funding 'solely because they are religious . . . must be subjected to 'the strictest of scrutiny'" and "'will survive strict scrutiny only in rare cases.'" Id. at 780-781 (internal citation omitted). Rejecting Maine's argument that its actions were warranted by an effort to steer clear of the Establishment Clause, the Court said that "such an interest in separating church and state 'more fiercely' than the Federal Constitution . . . 'cannot qualify as compelling' in the face of the infringement of free exercise.'" Id. at 781 (quoting from *Espinoza*). The same Justices who dissented in *Espinoza* again dissented here, largely repeating the arguments they made in the earlier case.

Thus, if an individual can show that the government has taken regulatory action specifically designed to suppress or burden a religious practice (the law is not neutral) and that the regulatory action applies to specific individuals or religious groups because of their religious practice (the law is not of general applicability), the governmental action will be subject to strict scrutiny under the Free Exercise Clause, requiring both a compelling governmental interest and the least restrictive means to advance that interest. If, on the other hand, the challenged regulatory action can be fairly described as being neutral or of general applicability but happens to reach some religious activity, this rigorous constitutional standard for regulatory action will not apply. The rigorous strict scrutiny standard will likewise apply to governmental spending programs that facially discriminate between religious and nonreligious activities.

The Nonpurposeful Regulation of Religiously Motivated Conduct

As discussed in the previous section, a law specifically directed toward the proscription of a religious practice "prohibits" the free exercise of religion within the meaning of the Free Exercise Clause. But can a law that is facially neutral from the perspective of the Free Exercise Clause, but that nonetheless sweeps within its ambit some conduct of a religious nature, likewise be deemed a law "prohibiting" the free exercise of religion?

For example, suppose that a statute proscribes the ingestion of peyote under all circumstances. If one wishes to ingest peyote for religious purposes, as would a member of the Native American Church, the law prohibits that ingestion. As such, the law literally "prohibits" a religious practice even if its purpose was not to suppress a religious practice as such. Does this type of nonpurposeful prohibition—i.e., one emanating from an otherwise neutral law of general applicability—nevertheless run afoul of the Free Exercise Clause?

In *Wisconsin v. Yoder*, 406 U.S. 205 (1972), it applied strict scrutiny to a neutral statute that had the effect of punishing religiously motivated conduct, but then in *Employment Division v. Smith*, 494 U.S. 872 (1990), it concluded that strict scrutiny is not warranted in such cases. The Court has since resolved this conflict. Today, a neutral law of general applicability will not be subject to strict scrutiny merely because it happens to sweep religiously motivated conduct within its coverage.

Wisconsin v. Yoder involved a free exercise challenge to the state's compulsory school-attendance law that required all children residing within the state to attend public or private school until age 16. Amish parents whose children were subject to this law refused to send their children to school past the eighth grade, claiming that to do otherwise would violate fundamental principles of their religion by risking the spiritual salvation of their children. The Supreme Court held that enforcement of the compulsory school-attendance law against the Amish parents violated their free exercise rights.

Yoder involved neither the regulation of belief nor the purposeful suppression of religiously motivated conduct. Nonetheless, the Court held that the Wisconsin compulsory school-attendance law could not be applied to Amish children unless the state established that doing so would advance "interests of the highest order" that could not be "otherwise served" by measures that did not encroach on the religious freedom of the Amish (406 U.S. at 215)—in essence, unless the state could overcome the standards of strict scrutiny.

Yoder and the cases following it did not, however, establish a blanket immunity for all religiously motivated conduct. The heightened scrutiny described in *Yoder* was not necessarily fatal to the law being challenged. For example, in *United States v. Lee*, 455 U.S. 252 (1982), a member of the Old Order Amish claimed that paying Social Security taxes as an employer violated the principles of his religion. Despite the clash between religion and state, the Court found no violation of the Free Exercise Clause. "The state may justify a limitation on religious liberty by showing that it is essential to accomplish an overriding governmental interest." Id. at 257. In general, however, under *Yoder*, governmental action that regulated or prohibited conduct of a religious nature was subject to some form of heightened scrutiny under the Free Exercise Clause, even if the government did not purposefully target religious activity.

EXAMPLE

Example 9-V

The Unity City School Board has voted to expand the school week from five days to six days, to make better use of overcrowded school facilities. Under the new plan, all students will be required to attend classes on Saturdays at least two-thirds of the school year. To avoid charges of favoritism, the board has refused to recognize any exceptions to this Saturday attendance rule. Several students have objected to the new policy on the ground that their religion commands them not to work on Saturday, their Sabbath. Does the board's policy violate the Free Exercise Clause?

EXPLANATION

Explanation

Although the board's policy regulates conduct and not belief, and although it is neutral and of general application, the policy, nonetheless, impairs the free exercise of religion by requiring the students to take action inconsistent with their religious beliefs. Under *Yoder*, the policy can be applied to these students only if the board can establish that the law serves an interest of the highest order and does so in a manner essential to advance that interest. It is unlikely that the board could make such a showing in this case.

All of this changed with the Court's decision in *Employment Division v. Smith*, 494 U.S. 872 (1990). *Smith* involved an Oregon statute that criminalized the possession of peyote, a hallucinogenic drug derived from certain cactus plants. Members of the Native American Church challenged the constitutionality of this statute as applied to their religious use of peyote within the church's religious ceremonies. There was no claim that the law was specifically designed to suppress the religious practices of the Native American Church. The statute was concededly neutral and of general applicability. The religious practices of the church just happened to fall within the general proscription of the law, as had the practices of the Amish parents in *Yoder*. The *Smith* Court held that the Free Exercise Clause was not implicated, however, since the law being challenged was "not specifically directed" at the religious practices of the Native American Church. Id. at 878. Under *Smith*, the free exercise protection for religiously motivated conduct is limited to circumstances, such as those present in *Church of the Lukumi Babalu Aye*, where a law is specifically and deliberately directed at the suppression of a religious practice.

Smith's reinterpretation of the Free Exercise Clause was premised in part on a policy judgment regarding the proper scope of that clause within a pluralistic society. According to the Court,

> because "we are a cosmopolitan nation made up of people of almost every conceivable religious preference," and precisely because we value and protect that religious divergence, we cannot afford the luxury of deeming *presumptively invalid*, as applied to the religious objector, every regulation of conduct that does not protect an interest of the highest order.

494 U.S. at 888 (quoting *Braunfeld v. Brown*, 366 U.S. 599, 606 (1961) (emphasis in original)). The price of this policy judgment is that the

values and practices of a minority religion—such as the Native American Church—may be ignored in the majoritarian political process. Thus, although under *Smith* the practices of a minority religion may not be deliberately suppressed, such practices may fall victim to the majority's unwitting interference with a religious practice that the members of that majority do not share. The Court has since reaffirmed *Smith*'s narrow reading of the reach of the Free Exercise Clause. In *Trinity Lutheran Church v. Comer*, supra, 582 U.S. at 460, it thus wrote: "In recent years, when this Court has rejected free exercise challenges, the laws in question have been neutral and generally applicable without regard to religion. We have been careful to distinguish such laws from those that single out the religious for disfavored treatment."

EXAMPLE

Example 9-W

The City has passed a law prohibiting the intentional killing of any animal regardless of the circumstances under which the killing takes place. The purpose of the ordinance is to protect animals and promote a healthy, vegetarian lifestyle. In passing this law, the city council was aware that members of the Santeria Church engaged in animal sacrifice within the city limits. Does the ordinance violate the Free Exercise Clause?

EXPLANATION

Explanation

Under *Smith*, the Free Exercise Clause will not protect members of the Santeria Church unless they can establish that the ordinance was specifically designed to prohibit their religious practices. The city council's mere awareness that the ordinance would apply to the Santerians is not adequate to establish such a lack of neutrality. Given the apparent neutrality and general applicability of the ordinance, the Free Exercise Clause does not come into play and will not prevent application of this ordinance to the practices of the Santeria Church.

Employment Division v. Smith thus radically changed the law. Until that 1990 ruling, neutral laws of general applicability that happened to prohibit religious practices were generally subject to strict scrutiny, while after *Smith*, the Free Exercise Clause is no longer even triggered by such laws. Oddly enough, *Yoder* was not overruled. Instead, the Court distinguished *Yoder* as involving a hybrid situation in which the Free Exercise Clause was joined with another fundamental constitutional right—that of parents to direct the education of their children—a rather obvious revision of the rationale of the *Yoder* decision. Under *Smith*, free exercise claims challenging neutral laws that happen to regulate or prohibit religiously motivated conduct will therefore be subject to heightened scrutiny only if such claims are joined with the claimed violation of another fundamental right.

EXAMPLE

Example 9-X

Revisiting the facts of Example 9-V, suppose that the students seek an exemption from the school district requirement that they attend classes on Saturday. They assert that such attendance would conflict with their religious beliefs and practices. Assuming that an appropriate case is filed on their behalf, will they prevail on this claim?

EXPLANATION

Explanation

Under *Smith*, the students have no free exercise claim since the school policy requiring them to attend school on Saturdays is neutral and of general applicability, and the district's requirement does not impair any of the students' other fundamental constitutional rights.

However, if the parents of these same students sought to prevent their children from attending school on Saturdays, the *parents'* fundamental right to direct the education of their children (see § 2.3.1), coupled with the underlying free exercise claim, might well trigger heightened scrutiny as a "hybrid" case under the *Smith* revision of *Yoder*.

As we have seen, to qualify for *Smith's* hands-off approach under the Free Exercise Clause, a law must be neutral and of general applicability—a requirement that was concededly satisfied in *Smith* itself. However, a law that might appear to meet this test will be subject to strict scrutiny if it allows individual exceptions to be made, for it is then no longer a law of general applicability. In *Fulton v. City of Philadelphia*, 593 U.S. 522 (2021), the Court on this basis applied strict scrutiny to invalidate a city's refusal to renew its foster care contract with Catholic Social Services (CSS) unless CSS, despite its religious objection to doing so, agreed to certify same-sex couples as foster parents. Because the city in its contract retained the authority to make exceptions to the same-sex-couples requirement, this law was no longer one of general applicability. *Smith's* hands-off approach is likewise inapplicable if a law does not reach all "comparable" secular activities, thereby treating some secular activities more favorably than the included religious exercises. In such cases, the Free Exercise Clause is fully applicable. The key question here is deciding what constitutes "comparable" secular activity.

EXAMPLE

Example 9-Y

In response to the COVID-19 pandemic, California issued a regulation that prohibits all in-home private gatherings that bring together people from more than three households. The regulation has been challenged by plaintiffs who wish to hold Bible studies and communal worship gatherings of more than three households in their homes. Is the Free Exercise Clause triggered in this case?

EXPLANATION

Explanation

At first blush, it might seem that the clause should not come into play here. The regulation appears to be religiously neutral and of general applicability insofar as it applies to all in-home gatherings of more than three households, regardless of their purpose; the limitation applies whether the gathering is to watch a televised football game or engage in religious activity. Nor does it exempt any "comparable" in-home secular activities. Finally, there is no indication that it was adopted for the purpose of suppressing religious gatherings.

Yet one might argue that given the regulation's public health rationale, it makes no sense to limit the "comparability" focus just to gatherings in the home. If the state's goal is to limit indoor activities that pose a risk of spreading COVID, comparable activities should include other settings where people from more than three households gather indoors, such as hair salons, retail stores, movie theatres, and restaurants. Under the latter approach, the regulation is not neutral or of general applicability, for it treats some "comparable" indoor secular activities more favorably than it does religious gatherings. On this basis, the Free Exercise Clause should come into play and the regulation struck down unless the state can show that the less restrictive measures it uses to protect public health in other comparable settings would be less effectual in the indoor residential context. See *Tandon v. Newsom*, 593 U.S. 61 (2021) (per curiam) (enjoining similar California law pendente lite).

Tandon appears to have given the Court a way of limiting the reach of *Smith's* "general applicability" rule, thereby expanding the range of cases in which the Free Exercise Clause may be invoked. Under *Tandon*, even if a law that regulates religious practices was drafted in religiously neutral terms, the clause will still come into play if the measure does not reach other secular activity that is deemed "comparable" to the regulated religious activity. As the Court said in *Tandon*, "government regulations are not neutral and generally applicable, and therefore trigger strict scrutiny under the Free Exercise

Clause, whenever they treat *any* comparable secular activity more favorably than religious exercise." *Tandon*, supra, 593 U.S. at 62 (emphasis in original). And see *Kennedy v. Bremerton School District*, supra, 597 U.S. at 526 ("government policy will fail the general applicability requirement if it 'prohibits religious conduct while permitting secular conduct that undermines the government's asserted interests in a similar way,' or if it provides 'a mechanism for individualized exemptions'"). Since comparability is an elastic concept, it may not prove that difficult for courts to invoke *Tandon* as a way around the hands-off approach established in *Smith*.

Fulton and *Tandon* both narrowed *Smith*'s hands-off approach to the Free Exercise Clause. Though *Smith* has not yet been overruled, ten Justices—including six members of the current Court—have openly questioned its soundness. See *Fulton v. City of Philadelphia*, supra, 593 U.S. at 626 (Gorsuch, J., et al., concurring). Indeed, in *Fulton*, one of the questions on which the Court granted cert was: "Whether *Employment Division v. Smith* should be revisited." Id. at 551 (Alito, J., et al., concurring). The *Fulton* majority avoided answering this question by concluding that the city's policy fell outside *Smith*, but Justices Alito, Thomas, and Gorsuch all urged that *Smith* be overruled, while Justices Barrett and Kavanaugh expressed sympathy with that position. Id. at 616-618 (Alito, J., et al., concurring); id. at 618, 626-627 (Gorsuch, J., et al., concurring); id. at 543-544 (Barrett, J., et al., concurring).

While the Supreme Court has the last word as to what the Constitution means, Congress may by statute confer rights that go beyond the minimum that the Court has found to be constitutionally protected. Though Congress cannot take away constitutional rights recognized by the Court, it may be able to augment those rights in settings where it thinks the Court got it wrong. In 1993 Congress sought to do just that by adopting the Religious Freedom Restoration Act (RFRA), 42 U.S.C. § 2000bb. This statute bars the federal government from imposing substantial burdens on religious exercise, even if the law imposing those burdens is a neutral one of general applicability. In adopting RFRA, Congress described *Smith* as a case where "the Supreme Court virtually eliminated the requirement that the government justify burdens on religious exercise imposed by laws neutral toward religion. . . ." Id. at 2000bb(a)(4). The purpose of RFRA, said Congress, was "(1) to restore the compelling interest test as set forth in *Sherbert v. Verner* . . . and *Wisconsin v. Yoder* . . . ; and (2) to provide a claim or defense to persons whose religious exercise is substantially burdened by government." Id. at 2000bb(b). When the Court was later asked to apply RFRA in a case against an FBI agent, it noted approvingly that

> RFRA secures Congress' view of the right to free exercise under the First Amendment, and it provides a remedy to redress violations of that right. Congress passed the Act in the wake of this Court's decision in [*Smith*]. . . .

> RFRA sought to counter the effect of that holding and restore the pre-*Smith* "compelling interest test" . . . .

Tanzan v. Tanvir, 592 U.S. 43, 45 (2020).

One final note. If you have good recall, you may have noticed that RFRA is the same statute the Court struck down in *City of Boerne v. Flores*, 521 U.S. 507 (1997), on the basis that it exceeded Congress' Fourteenth Amendment § 5 lawmaking authority. See § 1.5.2. However, because *Tanzan* involved RFRA's application to federal employees rather than to a state or a city, it was well within Congress' Article I, § 8 powers, without any need to invoke § 5. To this limited extent, RFRA thus survived *City of Boerne*. See *Kikumura v. Hurley*, 242 F.3d 950, 958-959 (10th Cir. 2001) (so holding).

The Incidental Burdening of Religiously Motivated Conduct

A law that does not itself *prohibit* or *regulate* religiously motivated conduct as such may still have the effect of making it more difficult for an individual to engage in a religious practice. Such a law can be said to indirectly burden the free exercise of religion. For example, a state law that requires an individual seeking unemployment compensation to be available for work Monday through Saturday burdens the religious practices of anyone whose religion requires abstinence from work on Saturdays. While the law does not require anyone to work on Saturdays, it does impose a severe burden on individuals whose religion deems Saturday a sacred day reserved for rest and worship. That burden is a product of the choice forced by the law—the individual must either violate their religious principles or forgo a vital governmental benefit. In these "unconstitutional conditions" cases, a person must violate a tenet of their religious beliefs to qualify for some government benefit. The question is whether such burdens are tantamount to the "prohibition" of a religious practice and, therefore, are sufficient to trigger the protections of the Free Exercise Clause? See also §§ 5.2, 5.6.

In *Sherbert v. Verner*, 374 U.S. 398 (1963), the Court answered this question in the affirmative. The facts of *Sherbert* are described in the preceding paragraph. The suit was brought by a Seventh-day Adventist who claimed that the state violated the Free Exercise Clause by forcing her to violate the precepts of her religion to be eligible for unemployment compensation. The Court agreed that this choice imposed a *substantial burden* on claimant's free exercise rights and that it could be justified only by a "compelling state interest." Id. at 406. Finding no such interest at stake, the Court held that the plaintiff could not be denied unemployment compensation solely on the basis of her unavailability to work on Saturdays. In so ruling, the Court rejected the state's argument that because unemployment benefits are a mere statutory "privilege" rather than a constitutional right, constitutional protections do not apply: "It is too late in the day to doubt that the liberties of religion and expression may be infringed by the denial of or the placing of conditions upon a benefit or privilege." Id. at 404. This is the doctrine of "unconstitutional conditions."

Yet, while constitutional protections are triggered in such cases, the government may sometimes be able to show that it has a sufficiently compelling interest to justify the infringement. See, e.g., *Locke v. Davey*, 540 U.S. 712 (2004) (states' historic interest in not funding training of clergy was sufficiently compelling to uphold its refusal to grant scholarships for the training of ministers); *Bob Jones University v. United States*, 461 U.S. 574 (1983) (government's interest in eradicating racial discrimination sufficiently compelling to justify denying tax-exempt status to religious organization that claimed a religious right to discriminate on the basis of race).

Example 9-Z

Thomas, a Jehovah's Witness, was employed in a foundry that fabricated sheet metal for industrial uses. When the foundry was closed, he was transferred to a department that produced military weapons. Thomas believed that he could not work in that department consistent with his religious convictions. Since all remaining departments of the company were involved in the production of military weapons, he asked to be laid off. When this request was denied, Thomas quit and applied for unemployment insurance. His application was denied, despite a finding that he quit his job for religious reasons, because his religious motivation was not considered "good cause" for voluntary termination within the meaning of state law. Applying *Sherbert*, does Thomas have a good claim?

Explanation

Under *Sherbert*, the state's refusal to grant Thomas unemployment compensation burdened his ability to honor his religious convictions. To justify this denial of these critical benefits, the state must demonstrate that it has chosen "the least restrictive means of achieving some compelling state interest." *Thomas v. Review Bd.*, 450 U.S. 707, 718-719 (1981) (rejecting state's asserted justifications as not being "sufficiently compelling to justify the burden upon Thomas's religious liberty").

The approach adopted in *Sherbert* does not apply every time the government takes regulatory or spending action inconsistent with an individual's religious beliefs. Rather, *Sherbert* applies only if the effect of the government's action is so severe as to coerce an individual to violate his or her religious principles. See *Locke v. Davey*, 540 U.S. 712 (2004) (no coercion found in state scholarship program that precludes the use of scholarship funds for the study of "devotional theology").

Moreover, the Free Exercise Clause does not require the government to conduct its purely internal operations in a way that conforms with or promotes an individual's religious precepts. See *Bowen v. Roy*, 476 U.S. 693 (1986) (government may use an individual's Social Security number even if the individual insists that in doing so the government violates precepts of his religion).

EXAMPLE

Example 9-AA

The U.S. Forest Service has announced plans to construct a paved road through a national forest. The road will cause serious damage to sacred areas necessary to the religious practices of several Native American tribes. The tribes claim that the construction of the road will violate the Free Exercise Clause by making it impossible for their members to engage in sacred religious ceremonies. Will the tribes' claim be upheld?

EXPLANATION

Explanation

Their claim will be denied. Despite the substantial impact on the sacred practices of these tribes, the Free Exercise Clause does not limit the government's power to use its own land in a manner that may happen to conflict with a body of religious principles. The government has not regulated or prohibited any religious practices, nor has it coerced anyone to violate their religious beliefs as a condition of receiving a governmental benefit. *Lyng v. Northwest Indian Cemetery Protection Assn.*, 485 U.S. 439 (1988).

In short, under *Sherbert*, a law will be subjected to strict scrutiny only if it burdens an individual's ability to comply with religious precepts by forcing the individual to choose between receiving a valuable governmental benefit and adhering to religious principle. Otherwise, governmental action that does not itself prohibit or regulate religious practices is not subject to review under the Free Exercise Clause even though it may make it somewhat more difficult for an individual to practice his or her religion.

The question remains whether *Sherbert* survived the decision in *Employment Division v. Smith*, supra. As we saw earlier, *Smith* held that a neutral criminal law of general applicability does not implicate the Free Exercise Clause, even if a religious practice like the use of peyote happens to fall within its prohibition. Rather than overruling *Sherbert*, *Smith* distinguished that case on the basis that a law is not of *general* applicability for these purposes if it provides "a mechanism for individualized exemptions." 494 U.S. at 884. And that turns out to have been the case with the unemployment benefits statute at issue in *Sherbert*, for it contained a "good cause" exemption "that permitted government to grant exemptions based on the circumstances underlying each application." *Fulton v. City of Philadelphia*, 593 U.S. 522, 534 (2021) (describing *Sherbert*). When a law contains "a system of individual exemptions," said Court, then it is not "generally applicable" and the state "may not refuse to extend that system to cases of 'religious hardship' without compelling reason." *Smith*, 494 U.S. at 884. In other words, if a law allows for any exceptions, it must then include one that accommodates an individual's religious convictions. Also, principles underlying the unconstitutional conditions doctrine may offer additional protection, particularly where the RFRA or state equivalents are in effect. The interplay between these doctrines remains a complex and evolving area of constitutional law.

Under *Smith*'s reformulation of *Sherbert v. Verner*, limiting the principle to cases where the law in question allows some exceptions, would strict scrutiny still apply in *Thomas v. Review Board*, 450 U.S. 707 (1981) (Example 9-Z)?

In this section, we have been discussing laws that only *incidentally* burden religious conduct. By contrast, if a law facially discriminates based on religion or religiously motivated conduct, it is not subject to *Sherbert*'s caveat and can be challenged under the Free Exercise Clause even if it does not allow exceptions. See, e.g., *Carson v. Makin*, 596 U.S. 767 (2022) (state law that withheld school tuition assistance from students who attended private sectarian schools subject to strict scrutiny even though it contained no apparent exceptions).

§9.6 THE ACCOMMODATION OF RELIGION

Under *Employment Division v. Smith*, the First Amendment does not require the government to provide exemptions from laws of general applicability for individuals who claim a religiously premised right to engage in conduct otherwise prohibited by those laws. However, the Court in *Smith* also made it clear that the government is free to create such religious exemptions if it chooses to do so. Thus, the Constitution neither requires nor precludes the reasonable accommodation of religious beliefs and practices. In the context of *Smith*, this means that while the Constitution did not require Oregon to recognize an exemption from its criminal drug laws for Native American Church members who ingest peyote, Oregon could, nonetheless, grant an exemption for the religious use of peyote if it wished to do so.

However, although the accommodation of a religious practice may be generated by a desire to promote the free exercise of religion, any accommodation of a religious practice runs the risk of violating the Establishment Clause by granting the accommodated religion a preferred status. In order for the government's voluntary accommodation of religion to pass muster under the Establishment Clause, three requirements must therefore be satisfied, each of which will be discussed in turn.

First, the accommodation of religion must do no more than offset or alleviate a special burden that the government has imposed by law. *Cutter v. Wilkinson*, 544 U.S. 708, 720 (2005); *Board of Educ. of Kiryas Joel v. Grumet*, 512 U.S. 687, 705-707 (1994). An exemption for the religious use of peyote or other controlled substances would satisfy this principle since the exemption merely removes a burden that the state itself imposed by the criminal law. *Gonzales v. O Centro Espirita Beneficente Uniao Do Vegetal*, 546 U.S. 418 (2006).

Example 9-BB

All residents of the village of Hasidim are members of a strict, orthodox Jewish sect. Most of the children who live there attend private sectarian schools within the village. A few children with learning disorders attend a nearby public school where special education programs are available, but their parents have expressed concern that attendance at the public school will have an adverse impact on the children's religious upbringing. In response to these concerns, the state has created a new school district just for the village. The purpose of this new school district is to create a state-funded special education program for village children with learning disabilities. Does the creation of this new school district represent an acceptable accommodation of religion, or does it violate the Establishment Clause?

Explanation

The state's action is probably unconstitutional. Rather than alleviating a burden imposed by the state, this governmental action appears to confer a special benefit on a particular religious sect by granting that sect governmental powers to advance the religious aims of the sect. *Board of Educ. of Kiryas Joel v. Grumet*, supra, 512 U.S. at 706 (holding that a similar arrangement violated the Establishment Clause).

Second, the accommodation must be denominationally neutral. *Larson v. Valente*, 456 U.S. 228 (1982). To do otherwise would violate the nondiscrimination principle of the Establishment Clause. A denominational discrimination is quite unlikely to satisfy the principle of nonpreferentialism. Similarly, it is unlikely that such a discrimination would satisfy the equal protection standard of strict scrutiny. See § 7.2. Thus, an exemption for the religious use of peyote that applied only to the Native American Church would potentially violate this principle by discriminating against other religions that used peyote as part of their religious ceremonies.

Finally, the Court has sometimes insisted that in order not to violate the Establishment Clause, the accommodation must be neutral as between religion and nonreligion. See *Texas Monthly, Inc. v. Bullock*, 489 U.S. 1 (1989) (holding unconstitutional a tax exemption that only applied to religious publications). However, in *Corporation of Presiding Bishop v. Amos*, 483 U.S. 327 (1987), the Court, applying a relaxed version of then applicable *Lemon* test, upheld an exemption to Title VII of the 1964 Civil Rights Act that permitted religious organizations, unlike other employers, to use religion as a criterion for hiring and firing employees. In the Court's words, "Where . . . government acts with the proper purpose of lifting a regulation that burdens the exercise of religion, we see no reason to require that the exemption come packaged with benefits to secular entities." Id. at 338; accord *Cutter v. Wilkinson*, supra, 544 U.S. at 724. Under today's nonpreferentialist approach, the result would be the same, for an exemption that benefits all religions creates no preference for any particular religion.

Example 9-CC

The Unity City School Board has adopted a "released time" program to permit public school students to leave public school premises each day to receive religious instruction. Only students who will attend a program of religious instruction are released. Is this program a lawful accommodation of religion?

Explanation

First, does the program alleviate a state-imposed burden on religion? Perhaps. Since students are required to attend school and since students who attend public schools may not receive religious instruction on the public school campus, a program that permits public school students to leave campus for religious instruction does alleviate a burden imposed by the mandatory attendance requirement. The burden, however, does not prevent students from practicing their religions; it merely restricts the time during which they can receive religious instruction. The burden is, therefore, rather slight.

Second, does the program discriminate between religions? No, the program appears to be denominationally neutral. While it does favor religion over nonreligion since that is the only basis for getting released time, under the Court's nonpreferentialist approach, this discrimination is not fatal to the program since it treats all religions alike. See *Zorach v. Clauson*, 343 U.S. 306 (1952) (upholding similar released time program that could be "initiated by any religious organization. . . ." *Zorach v. Clauson*, 303 N.Y, 161, 167, 100 N.E.2d 463, 464 (N.Y. 1951)).

Finally, it would be difficult to argue that this program involves coercion, for it is unlikely that peer pressure or other factors would induce students who would not otherwise have done so to take time off to receive religious instruction. On the other hand, one might argue that some students will do anything "to get out of school," in which case this might be more problematic. If there were a parental consent requirement here, that might alleviate any coercion concern. See Example 9-H.

In short, the government may choose to accommodate a religious belief or practice to permit the free exercise of religion, but in so doing, it cannot violate the underlying principles of the Establishment Clause. The Court has adopted a nonpreferentialist approach to the Establishment Clause by permitting the government to accommodate a religious practice if it does so in a religiously neutral way, while at the same time not requiring that similar benefits be granted to parallel nonsectarian practices. But as we saw in *Trinity Lutheran Church*, supra (Example 9-T), there may be times when the government, though it might prefer not to extend benefits to religious organizations, may be required to do so under the Free Exercise Clause if similar benefits have been afforded nonsectarian entities. As the Court there said, while the Establishment Clause "does not prevent Missouri from including Trinity Lutheran in the Scrap Tire Program," the decision to "deny[] a generally available benefit solely on account of religious identity imposes a penalty on the free exercise of religion that can be justified only by a state interest 'of the highest order.'" 582 U.S. at 458.

CHAPTER 10

The Right to Keep and Bear Arms

§10.1 INTRODUCTION AND OVERVIEW

The text of the Second Amendment provides, "A well regulated Militia, being necessary to the security of a free State, the right of the people to keep and bear Arms, shall not be infringed." In interpreting this text, the critical question is whether the language establishes the general right of an individual "to keep and bear Arms" for private, non-militia uses or, instead, creates only a particularized right, limited in scope to the needs of a well-regulated militia. Until recently, the Supreme Court endorsed the latter, narrower view. Thus, in the leading case of *United States v. Miller*, 307 U.S. 174 (1939), the defendants were indicted for shipping a sawed-off shotgun in interstate commerce, in violation of the National Firearms Act. They argued, among other things, that the indictment infringed their Second Amendment right to bear arms. The Court disagreed, explaining that the "obvious purpose" of the Second Amendment was "to assure the continuation and render possible the effectiveness of [militia] forces" trained by the states and subject to regulation by the federal government. Id. at 178. In other words, the right to bear arms was a means of advancing the interest of the several states in self-preservation through the maintenance of a militia of armed citizens. Id. at 179. In the Court's view, the highly individualized claim of the *Miller* defendants did not fall within that intended scope:

> In the absence of any evidence tending to show that possession or use of a "shotgun having a barrel of less than eighteen inches in length" at this time

> has some reasonable relationship to the preservation or efficiency of a well regulated militia, we cannot say that the Second Amendment guarantees the right to keep and bear such an instrument.

Id. at 178. The fair import of the *Miller* decision was that the right to keep and bear arms was tied to the collective preservation of the community and not in any manner to an individual's independent interest in the possession or ownership of a firearm.

The practical result of *Miller* was that the Second Amendment provided little or no protection for an individual's right to bear arms. In addition, since the Court had previously held that the Fourteenth Amendment did not incorporate the Second Amendment, state laws regulating gun ownership were completely immune from Second Amendment challenges. See § 1.3. Essentially, from an individual rights perspective, during the nineteenth and twentieth centuries, the Second Amendment was of little pragmatic consequence.

The *Miller* Court's interpretation of the Second Amendment, however, was not without controversy. During the latter half of the twentieth century, gun-rights advocates argued that the Second Amendment should be more broadly construed as encompassing an independent right of the individual to keep and bear arms, without regard to any state interest in maintaining a militia. In *District of Columbia v. Heller*, 554 U.S. 570 (2008), the Court reconsidered *Miller* and adopted this more encompassing view. In this chapter, we examine the *Heller* decision and some of its potential consequences. Keep in mind, however, that the right to keep and bear arms post-*Heller* is a new and evolving area of constitutional jurisprudence that necessarily remains somewhat of a moving target.

§10.2 *DISTRICT OF COLUMBIA v. HELLER*

§10.2.1 Interpreting the Second Amendment

At issue in *District of Columbia v. Heller* was whether a District of Columbia law that prohibited "the possession of usable handguns in the home violate[d] the Second Amendment to the Constitution." 554 U.S. at 573. The answer to that question depended largely on how the Court interpreted the Second Amendment:

> The two sides in this case have set out very different interpretations of the Amendment. [The District of Columbia] . . . believe[s] that it protects only the right to possess and carry a firearm in connection with militia service. [Heller] argues that it protects an individual right to possess a firearm unconnected

> with service in a militia, and to use that arm for traditionally lawful purposes, such as self-defense within the home.

Id. at 577. According to the five-person *Heller* majority, the choice between these interpretive options remained open to the Court since, in the majority's view, *United States v. Miller* "did not even purport to be a thorough examination of the Second Amendment." Id. at 623.

The majority, in an opinion by Justice Scalia, began its analysis of the Second Amendment by dividing the text of that amendment into what it described as a "prefatory clause" ("A well regulated Militia being necessary to the security of a free State") and an "operative clause" ("the right of the people to keep and bear arms, shall not be infringed"). Id. at 577. The Court then proceeded to examine, word by word and phrase by phrase, each of these clauses, beginning with the operative clause, on which it placed the most weight. With respect to the term "arms," the Court rejected, as "bordering on the frivolous," the argument that "only those arms in existence in the 18th century are protected by the Second Amendment." Id. at 582. Rather, "the Second Amendment extends, prima facie, to all instruments that constitute bearable arms, even those that were not in existence at the time of the founding." Id. After engaging in a detailed analysis of the text of that clause, and of historical background materials, the Court concluded that the operative clause recognized and guaranteed a preexisting right of all Americans to carry arms for the purpose of confrontation and self-defense. As the Court summarized its conclusion, "Putting all of these textual elements together, we find that they guarantee the individual right to possess and carry weapons in case of confrontation. This meaning is strongly confirmed by the historical background of the Second Amendment." Id. at 592.

Next, the Court examined the prefatory clause to determine whether that clause was consistent with the meaning assigned to the operative clause, and whether the prefatory clause in any fashion limited the scope of the operative clause. Id. at 595-600. The Court concluded that the two clauses were consistent with one another and that while the prefatory clause offered an explanation for the codification of the right to bear arms—the preservation of state militias—that explanation did not limit the right to keep and bear arms to militia-related usages. In other words, the prefatory clause was itself non-operative.

> It is therefore entirely sensible that the Second Amendment's prefatory clause announces the purpose for which the right was codified: to prevent elimination of the militia. The prefatory clause does not suggest that preserving the militia was the only reason Americans valued the ancient right; most undoubtedly thought it even more important for self-defense and hunting.

Id. at 599. Thus, the Court majority concluded that the Second Amendment prohibited the infringement of a preexisting right to keep and bear arms and that that right was not limited to military usages, but included all traditionally lawful uses of arms, including self-defense. Indeed, the Court described self-defense, and particularly self-defense in the home, as "central to the Second Amendment right." Id. at 628.

The Court completed its discussion of the Second Amendment with an important caveat:

> Like most rights, the right secured by the Second Amendment is not unlimited. From Blackstone through the 19th-century cases, commentators and courts routinely explained that the right was not a right to keep and carry any weapon whatsoever in any manner whatsoever and for whatever purpose. For example, the majority of the 19th-century courts to consider the question held that prohibitions on carrying concealed weapons were lawful under the Second Amendment or state analogues. Although we do not undertake an exhaustive historical analysis today of the full scope of the Second Amendment, nothing in our opinion should be taken to cast doubt on longstanding prohibitions on the possession of firearms by felons and the mentally ill, or laws forbidding the carrying of firearms in sensitive places such as schools and government buildings, or laws imposing conditions and qualifications on the commercial sale of arms.

Id. at 626-627 (internal citations omitted). In a footnote appended to the above paragraph, the Court further observed, "We identify these presumptively lawful regulatory measures only as examples; our list does not purport to be exhaustive." Id. at 627 n.26. In short, while the Second Amendment protects an individual's right to keep and bear arms for personal use, the scope of the right can be limited, consistent with tradition, under appropriate circumstances and particularly so when the possession or use at issue transcends the central value of self-defense.

The four-person dissent, authored by Justice Stevens, would have limited the protections of the Second Amendment to the militia context. In arriving at this opposite conclusion, the dissent, like the majority, relied on an array of textual and historical arguments:

> The Second Amendment was adopted to protect the right of the people of each of the several States to maintain a well-regulated militia. It was a response to concerns raised during the ratification of the Constitution that the power of Congress to disarm the state militias and create a national standing army posed an intolerable threat to the sovereignty of the several States. Neither the text of the Amendment nor the arguments advanced by its proponents evidenced the slightest interest in limiting any legislature's authority to regulate private civilian uses of firearms. Specifically, there is no indication that the Framers of the Amendment intended to enshrine the common-law right of self-defense in the Constitution.

Id. at 637 (Stevens, J., et al., dissenting). Ironically, both the majority and the dissent purported to be offering an originalist view of the Second Amendment. It is for the reader to determine which is the more persuasive and whether "originalism" is an adequate measure of constitutional meaning in the twenty-first century.

Two years after *Heller* was decided, the Court in *McDonald v. City of Chicago*, 561 U.S. 742 (2010), overruled its 124-year-old decision in *Presser v. Illinois*, 116 U.S. 252 (1886), which had ruled that the Second Amendment was not part of the liberty protected by the Fourteenth Amendment. In *McDonald*, the Court rejected *Presser* and held that the Second Amendment is now incorporated by the Fourteenth Amendment and is therefore fully enforceable against state action. See § 1.3. Hence, the principles adopted in *Heller* apply to both federal and state laws.

§10.2.2 Applying the Second Amendment

Having established that the Second Amendment protected an individual's right to possess a gun in the home for purposes of self-defense, it remained for the Court to examine the constitutionality of the District of Columbia law restricting such possession. As the Court described it, that law "totally bans handgun possession in the home" and "also requires that any lawful firearm in the home be disassembled or bound by a trigger lock at all times, rendering it inoperable." *District of Columbia v. Heller*, 554 U.S. 570, 628 (2008). Essentially, the law disarmed the resident gun owner. From this perspective, the Court had little difficulty in concluding that both the prohibition on handguns, and the requirement of inoperability as to other firearms, transgressed the Second Amendment. As to the first, said the Court,

> the inherent right of self-defense has been central to the Second Amendment right. The handgun ban amounts to a prohibition of an entire class of "arms" that is overwhelmingly chosen by American society for that lawful purpose. The prohibition extends, moreover, to the home, where the need for defense of self, family, and property is most acute. Under any of the standards of scrutiny that we have applied to enumerated constitutional rights, banning from the home "the most preferred firearm in the nation to 'keep' and use for protection of one's home and family," would fail constitutional muster. . . .
>
> It is no answer to say, as petitioners do, that it is permissible to ban the possession of handguns so long as the possession of other firearms (*i.e.*, long guns) is allowed. It is enough to note . . . that the American people have considered the handgun to be the quintessential self-defense weapon. There are many reasons that a citizen may prefer a handgun for home defense: It is easier to store in a location that is readily accessible in an emergency; it cannot easily be redirected or wrestled away by an attacker; it is easier to use for those without the upper-body strength to lift and aim a long gun; it can be pointed

> at a burglar with one hand while the other hand dials the police. Whatever the reason, handguns are the most popular weapon chosen by Americans for self-defense in the home, and a complete prohibition of their use is invalid.

Id. at 628-629. As to the inoperability provision, the Court arrived at a similar conclusion, stating that that requirement for firearms "makes it impossible for citizens to use them for the core lawful purpose of self-defense and is hence unconstitutional." Id. at 630.

Quite clearly, the caveat issued by the Court, in which it recognized the possible constitutional validity of restrictions on the possession of firearms, was not broad enough to sustain a law that absolutely prohibited the in-home possession of a firearm traditionally used as a means of self-defense.

§10.3 DEVELOPMENTS SINCE *HELLER*

§10.3.1 The Range of Protected Arms

In *Caetano v. Massachusetts,* 577 U.S. 411 (2016), the Court was presented with a case involving a relatively new, nontraditional weapon, i.e., a stun gun. This is a small electronic device with two metal prongs and a switch; when the prongs are placed in direct contact with a person and the switch is thrown, the gun will stun them. Jaime Caetano, who was carrying a stun gun for self-defense purposes while out in public, was convicted under a state law that barred possession of such weapons. She invoked her Second Amendment right to bear arms, but the state court rejected that defense on three grounds. First, it said, stun guns "'were not in common use at the time of the Second Amendment's enactment.'" Id. at 411. Second, *Heller* recognized as one limitation on the right to carry arms "the historical tradition of prohibiting the carrying of 'dangerous and unusual weapons'"—a category into which Jaime's stun gun allegedly fell. Id. at 412. And third, nothing in the record suggested that stun guns "'are readily adaptable to use in the military'." Id.

In a five-paragraph per curiam opinion, the Supreme Court reversed, rejecting each of the Massachusetts state court's grounds for decision. As to the first, said the Court, *Heller* expressly held that the Second Amendment extends to arms "that were not in existence at the time of the founding." Id. at 412. Second, to fall within *Heller*'s "dangerous and unusual" exception, it is not enough that a weapon be dangerous since virtually all weapons fit that description. It must also be shown that the weapon is "unusual" in a contemporary sense, not simply that it might have been thought unusual at the time of the framing. Otherwise, as the concurring opinion noted, the Second Amendment would be limited to the few weapons that existed in 1789. Thus, as the concurring opinion noted, the relevant inquiry as to "unusual" is "whether stun guns are commonly possessed by law-abiding citizens for lawful purposes *today*." Id. at 420 (Alito, J., and Thomas, J., concurring) (emphasis in original). The answer to that question was clearly yes, for stun guns are widely owned and were legal in 45 states. Finally, said the Court, it does not matter whether stun guns are readily adaptable for military use since *Heller* flatly rejected the proposition "that only those weapons useful in warfare are protected." Id. at 412. Having concluded that stun guns fall within the scope of the Second Amendment, the Court remanded the case for further proceedings, without addressing the question of whether the Amendment protected Jaime's right to carry the stun gun outside her home as she was doing at the time of her arrest.

Cases in which weapons, ammunition, and related items have been found to fall entirely outside the Second Amendment are relatively rare. But see *United States v. Cox*, 906 F.3d 1170, 1185 (10th Cir. 2018), *cert. denied*, 139 S. Ct. 2690 (2019) ("possession of short-barreled rifles falls outside the Second Amendment's guarantee"). If the question is at all close, courts typically assume that the weapon is protected, and then go on to decide whether the restriction passes muster under the appropriate level of scrutiny. See, e.g., *Duncan v. Bonta*, 19 F.4th 1087, 1102-1103 (9th Cir. 2021) (finding "significant merit" in argument that "large-capacity magazines lack Second Amendment protection because they are similar to '"M-16 rifles and the like," i.e., "weapons that are most useful in military service,"'" but then "assuming, without deciding, that California's law implicates the Second Amendment"), *vacated on other grounds*, 142 S. Ct. 2895 (2022); *New York State Rifle & Pistol Ass'n, Inc. v. Cuomo*, 804 F.3d 242, 256-257 (2d Cir. 2015), *cert. denied sub nom. Shew v. Malloy*, 579 U.S. 917 (2016) (where unclear from record whether semiautomatic assault weapons and large capacity magazines are "typically possessed by law-abiding citizens for lawful purposes" and hence not "unusual," court "proceed[s] on the assumption that these laws ban weapons protected by the Second Amendment"); *Teter v. Conners*, 460 F. Supp. 3d 989, 1000 (D. Haw. 2020) (where record unclear whether butterfly knives, while clearly "dangerous," are also "unusual," court "assumes without deciding that [they] are protected 'arms' within the scope of the Second Amendment").

One court of appeals has rejected *Caetano's* common-use approach, as least as it applies to "M-16 rifles and the like," holding that regardless of their popularity or common use, these weapons fall "outside the ambit of the Second Amendment." *Kolbe v. Hogan*, 849 F.3d 114, 135-136 (4th Cir.) (en banc), *cert. denied*, 583 U.S. 1007 (2017). To reach that conclusion, the court read *Heller's* "most useful for military service" language as creating a balancing test under which if a weapon's military utility outweighs its utility for other purposes, "[t]here is no Second Amendment protection for [it]." Id. at 136-137, 142. The *Kolbe* approach was an anomaly and has been rejected by most other courts. See, e.g., *Worman v. Healey*, 922 F.3d 26, 35 (1st Cir. 2019) (rejecting the test). Moreover, *Kolbe* then analyzed the case on the alternative assumption that the M-16 is protected by the Second Amendment. 849 F.3d at 138-141.

Example 10-A

The National Firearms Act makes it unlawful for any person "to receive or possess a firearm that is not registered to him or her in the National Firearms Registration and Transfer Record." The Act defines the term "firearm" as a "destructive device," which in turn is defined to include "any explosive . . . bomb." David was prosecuted and convicted of aiding and abetting the unlawful possession of a pipe bomb, in violation of these provisions. At trial, he objected to his prosecution as constituting a violation of the Second Amendment. The district court overruled his objection and David has appealed. How should the court rule on David's Second Amendment claim?

Explanation

The court should affirm the judgment of the district court. As *Heller* explained, "the right secured by the Second Amendment is not unlimited," and is "not a right to keep and carry any weapon whatsoever in any manner whatsoever and for whatever purpose." 554 U.S. at 626. *Heller* made clear that the Second Amendment does not protect "the carrying of 'dangerous and unusual weapons.'" Id. at 627. While pipe bombs would surely have been deemed "unusual" in 1791, the pertinent question—as *Caetano* explained—is whether they are "unusual" by contemporary standards. Here, unlike the handgun in *Heller* or the stun gun in *Caetano*, pipe bombs are still "unusual" even under today's standards, for they are not typically possessed by law-abiding citizens for lawful purposes. Thus, it is very unlikely that a pipe bomb, surely a dangerous and unusual weapon, would be deemed protected by the Second Amendment. See *United States v. Tagg*, 572 F.3d 1320 (11th Cir. 2009) (so ruling on similar facts); see also *United States v. Fincher*, 538 F.3d 868, 870, 873-874 (8th Cir. 2008), *cert. denied*, 555 U.S. 1174 (2009) (possession of machine gun not protected by Second Amendment).

§10.3.2 The Spatial Aspect of the Right to Bear Arms

Heller established the right to keep an operable handgun within one's home for purposes of self-defense. The Court also recognized that in contrast to the home, there were some "sensitive places," such as schools and government buildings, where the right to carry a handgun might be restricted.

554 U.S. at 626. More generally, whether the Second Amendment protected an individual's right to carry a firearm in public—a so-called right to "open carry"—remained unresolved until recently. Lower federal courts provided a variety of answers.

Several lower courts ruled that the Second Amendment guarantees a right to openly carry weapons outside the home for self-defense purposes. See, e.g., *Wrenn v. District of Columbia*, 864 F.3d 650, 663-664 (D.C. Cir. 2017) ("the individual right to carry firearms beyond the home for self-defense . . . falls within the core of the Second Amendment's protections"); *Moore v. Madigan*, 702 F.3d 933, 935 (7th Cir. 2012) ("the constitutional right of armed self-defense is broader than the right to have a gun in one's home"). While these courts recognize that the government may impose some limits on this right—e.g., training requirements, limiting the right to responsible persons, or banning guns in certain places—the basic right to carry a weapon in public was in their view one of fundamental constitutional dimension.

A larger number of Federal Courts of Appeals concluded either that there is no constitutional right to bear arms outside the home, or that any such right receives but minimal protection. See, e.g., *Young v. Hawaii*, 992 F.3d 765, 821 (9th Cir. 2021) (en banc) ("There is no right to carry arms openly in public; nor is any such right within the scope of the Second Amendment."); *Malpasso v. Palozzi*, 767 F. Appx. 525 (4th Cir. 2019), *cert. denied*, 141 S. Ct. 109 (2020) (imposing a "good cause" requirement in order to bear arms outside the home does not violate Second Amendment); *Gould v. Morgan*, 907 F.3d 659 (1st Cir. 2018), *cert. denied*, 141 S. Ct. 108 (2020) (limiting right to carry firearms in public to those who have shown "good reason" for doing so does not violate Second Amendment).

The Supreme Court resolved this conflict in *New York State Rifle & Pistol Association, Inc. v. Bruen*, 597 U.S. 1 (2022). At issue in *Bruen*, was a New York statute that required applicants for "open carry" permits to "demonstrate a special need for self-protection distinguishable from that of the general community." Id. at 12 (internal citation omitted). The Court had little difficulty in concluding that "the Second and Fourteenth Amendments protect an individual's right to carry a handgun for self-defense outside the home." Id. at 10. Nor did the Court endorse a diluted form of protection for open-carry laws.

In short, *Heller* established that the Second Amendment protects an individual's right to keep arms within the home for purposes of self-defense. *Bruen* extended that holding to include an individual's right to bear arms in public for purposes of self-defense.

Of course, the right to bear arms is not absolute. Hence, having established that the Second Amendment applied to New York's open-carry law, the remaining question was whether that law could survive Second Amendment scrutiny. To make that determination, the Court articulated a new standard of review, a point to which we now turn.

§10.4 THE *BRUEN* STANDARD OF REVIEW

In the wake of *Heller*, lower federal and state courts had adopted a variety of standards for applying the Second Amendment. See *State v. Misch*, 256 A.3d 519 (Vt. 2021) (discussing various standards of review employed by federal and state courts in right to bear arms cases). Most of these involved a two-step inquiry modeled on traditional individual rights analysis. The *Bruen* Court described that approach as follows:

> Since *Heller* and *McDonald*, the two-step test that Courts of Appeals have developed to assess Second Amendment claims proceeds as follows. At the first step, the government may justify its regulation by "establish[ing] that the challenged law regulates activity falling outside the scope of the right as originally understood." The Courts of Appeals then ascertain the original scope of the right based on its historical meaning. If the government can prove that the regulated conduct falls beyond the Amendment's original scope, "then the analysis can stop there; the regulated activity is categorically unprotected." But if the historical evidence at this step is "inconclusive or suggests that the regulated activity is *not* categorically unprotected," the courts generally proceed to step two.
>
> At the second step, courts often analyze "how close the law comes to the core of the Second Amendment right and the severity of the law's burden on that right." The Courts of Appeals generally maintain "that the core Second Amendment right is limited to self-defense *in the home*." If a "core" Second Amendment right is burdened, courts apply "strict scrutiny" and ask whether the Government can prove that the law is "narrowly tailored to achieve a compelling governmental interest." Otherwise, they apply intermediate scrutiny and consider whether the Government can show that the regulation is "substantially related to the achievement of an important governmental interest." Both respondents and the United States largely agree with this consensus, arguing that intermediate scrutiny is appropriate when text and history are unclear in attempting to delineate the scope of the right.

597 U.S. at 18-19 (emphasis in original) (internal citations omitted).

The *Bruen* Court rejected this two-step approach, along with any form of means-ends analysis applicable to the right to bear arms. Instead, the Court devised a unique constitutional standard that measures constitutional validity based solely on historical analogies. In the words of the *Bruen* Court:

> Despite the popularity of this two-step approach, it is one step too many. Step one of the predominant framework is broadly consistent with *Heller*, which demands a test rooted in the Second Amendment's text, as informed by history. But *Heller* and *McDonald* do not support applying means-end scrutiny in the Second Amendment context. Instead, the government must affirmatively prove that its firearms regulation is part of the historical tradition that delimits the outer bounds of the right to keep and bear arms.

Id. at 19. The *Bruen* Court further described its newly endorsed approach as follows:

> The test that we set forth in *Heller* and apply today requires courts to assess whether modern firearms regulations are consistent with the Second Amendment's text and historical understanding. In some cases, that inquiry will be fairly straightforward. For instance, when a challenged regulation addresses a general societal problem that has persisted since the 18th century, the lack of a distinctly similar historical regulation addressing that problem is relevant evidence that the challenged regulation is inconsistent with the Second Amendment. Likewise, if earlier generations addressed the societal problem, but did so through materially different means, that also could be evidence that a modern regulation is unconstitutional. And if some jurisdictions actually attempted to enact analogous regulations during this timeframe, but those proposals were rejected on constitutional grounds, that rejection surely would provide some probative evidence of unconstitutionality.

Id. at 26-27. In short, a modern firearms regulation can only be justified if that regulation is supported by a regulatory analogue that existed at or around the time of the adoption of the Bill of Rights in 1791 or ratification of the Fourteenth Amendment in 1868. Note that by endorsing this historical-analogue test and abandoning any form of means-ends analysis, the Court has essentially ruled that even a compelling government interest today will not justify a limitation on the right to bear arms if that limitation lacks a demonstrable historical analogue. The Court insisted that its "analogical" approach was not a "regulatory straightjacket." Id. at 30. Yet, as we examine below, its demanding application of this novel methodology suggests that modern regulations of firearms will face an intense—and often fatal—form of historical scrutiny.

§10.5 THE *BRUEN* STANDARD APPLIED

As noted in § 10.3.2, the *Bruen* Court readily concluded that the Second Amendment protected an individual's right to bear arms for purposes of self-defense outside the home. Also as noted, the *Bruen* Court then endorsed an historical-analogue standard for measuring the constitutionality of modern firearms regulations that interfered with that right. The final question for the *Bruen* Court was whether New York's "special-need" (or probable-cause) restriction on the right to bear arms could survive the new standard of review.

In terms of application, the basic question under *Bruen* is simple: Whether, during the periods of time roughly contemporaneous with the adoption of the Constitution and the Fourteenth Amendment, there existed firearms regulations sufficiently similar to the regulation being challenged to sustain the validity of the latter. The simplicity of the question should not belie the complexity of the interpretive enterprise, including the fact that neither justices nor judges nor lawyers are necessarily trained as historians.

In assessing this basic question, the *Bruen* Court considered "sources from the late 1200s to the early 1900s," dividing these into five historical periods: "(1) medieval to early modern England; (2) the American Colonies and the early Republic; (3) antebellum America; (4) Reconstruction; and (5) the late-19th and early-20th centuries." 597 U.S. at 34. Then, over the course of 38 pages in the U.S. reports (id. at 32-70), the Court, acting as an historical arbiter, interpreted a wide range of public-carry provisions, finding each to be insufficiently analogous to New York's special-needs requirement.

In summary fashion, the Court concluded that materials from medieval and early modern English history were "ambiguous at best" and "not sufficiently probative to defend New York's proper cause requirement." Id at 39-40. As to the Colonial era and early years of the American Republic, the Court discussed several statutes and common law provisions, but concluded that they provided "little evidence of an early American practice of regulating public carry by the general public." Id. at 46. The Court next surveyed the ante-bellum period and found no laws from that era that "imposed a substantial burden on public carry analogous to the burden created by New York's restrictive licensing regime." Id. at 50. As for the postbellum Reconstruction years, the Court concluded that with the exception of Texas, "public carry for self-defense remained a central component of the protection that the Fourteenth Amendment secured for all citizens." Id. at 60. With regard to Texas, said the Court, "We acknowledge that the Texas cases support New York's proper-cause requirement," but these were "outliers" compared to what other states were doing. Id. at 65. "In the end, . . . we will not give disproportionate weight to a single state statute and a pair of state-court decisions." Id. Finally, the Court placed no weight on late nineteenth century proscriptions on public carry in the Western Territories or in Kansas. The Territorial laws were temporary, were not part of the American tradition, and applied to only "miniscule" populations. Id. at 66-69. And in Kansas, its 1881 law barring the public carry of firearms applied in only three cities, hardly "demonstrate[ing] a broad tradition of States doing so." Id. at 69-70.

The dissent rejected the Court's "rigid history-only approach. . . ." Id. at 107 (Breyer, J., Sotomayor, J., and Kagan, J., dissenting). While they agreed that "history can often be a useful tool in determining the meaning and scope of constitutional provisions, . . . the Court's near-exclusive reliance on that single tool today goes much too far." Id. at 102-103. In the dissent's view, such a reliance is both unjustifiable and unworkable, for a number of reasons. "Courts are, after all, staffed by lawyers, not historians. Legal experts typically have little experience answering contested historical questions or applying those answers to resolve contemporary problems." Id. at 107. Moreover, as the majority's opinion demonstrates, historical evidence is highly manipulative, for the Court "offers a laundry list of reasons to discount seemingly relevant historical evidence," thereby "giv[ing] judges ample tools to pick their friends out of history's crowd." Id. at 112. And, "even under ideal conditions, historical evidence will often fail to provide clear answers to difficult questions," especially with respect to "modern cases presenting modern problems." Id. at 112-113. As the dissent then made clear, this case "demonstrated the very pitfalls" that can result from use of a "history-only test":

> The historical evidence reveals a 700-year Anglo-American tradition of regulating the public carriage of firearms in general, and concealed or concealable firearms in particular. The Court spends more than half of its opinion trying to discredit this tradition. But, in my view, the robust evidence of such a tradition cannot be so easily explained away. Laws regulating the public carriage of weapons existed in England as early as the 13th century and on this Continent since before the founding. Similar laws remained on the books through the ratifications of the Second and Fourteenth Amendments through to the present day. Many of those historical regulations imposed significantly stricter restrictions on public carriage than New York's licensing requirements do today. Thus, even applying the Court's history-only analysis, New York's law must be upheld. . . .

597 U.S. at 115. That is not to say that the dissent's interpretation of the historical materials was correct, but it does suggest that an exclusively historical test will not ensure consistency or coherence or even conformity to historical reality; nor will it insulate the judiciary from the effects of personal predilection or bias on the part of individual judges and justices.

The Court most recently applied its Second Amendment historical-analogue test in *United States v. Rahimi*, 144 S. Ct. 1889 (2024). Problem 10-B is premised on that decision.

EXAMPLE

Example 10-B

Zachey's former girlfriend procured a domestic restraining order that included a finding that he had engaged in domestic violence against her and that he posed a credible threat to her physical safety. While he was subject to that order, the police discovered several firearms in his apartment. Federal law prohibits an individual subject to a domestic violence restraining order from possessing a firearm if that order includes a finding that he "represents a credible threat to the physical safety of [an] intimate partner." 18 U.S.C. § 922(g)(8). Consequently, Zachey was charged with a violation of § 922(g)(8). He defended on Second Amendment grounds. In support of the constitutionality of the statute, the government cited two sets of laws from the founding era that arguably provided historical analogues to § 922(g)(8), i.e., surety laws and going-armed laws. Surety laws were a form of "preventive justice" that authorized magistrates to require individuals suspected of future misbehavior to post a bond. If an individual failed to post a bond, he would be jailed. If the individual did post a bond and then broke the peace, the bond would be forfeited. Surety laws could be invoked to prevent all forms of violence, including spousal abuse. The government also cited going-armed laws, which provided a mechanism for punishing those who had menaced others with firearms. Under these laws, individuals were prohibited from going armed with dangerous or unusual weapons to terrify members of the public. Were these historic analogues sufficient to sustain the validity of § 922(g)(8)?

Explanation

Yes. In *United States v. Rahimi*, supra, an 8-member majority, applying a somewhat relaxed version of *Bruen*, so held. "Taken together, the surety and going armed laws confirm what common sense suggests: When an individual poses a clear threat of physical violence to another, the threatening individual may be disarmed. Section 922(g)(8) is by no means identical to these founding era regimes, but it does not need to be. Its prohibition on the possession of firearms by those found by a court to present a threat to others fits neatly within the tradition the surety and going armed laws represent." Id. at 1901 (internal citations omitted). Justice Thomas, the author of *Bruen*, dissented, arguing that "[n]ot a single historical regulation justifies the statute at issue." Id. at 1930 (Thomas, J., dissenting).

At this point, the history-analogue standard is difficult to pin down. It was applied strictly in *Bruen* (and in Justice Thomas's dissent in *Rahimi*), but more generously by the majority in *Rahimi*. The latter result may suggest a softening of the strict *Bruen* approach, or it may be the result of the consequences the Court perceived would follow from a ruling sustaining Rahimi's Second Amendment challenge. Ironically, the latter possibility suggests that some form of means-ends analysis may have crept back into the doctrine, albeit silently.

Table of Cases

A.C. by Waithe v. McKee, 23 F.4th 37 (1st Cir. 2022), 365
A.C. ex rel. Park v. Cortez, 34 F.4th 783 (9th Cir. 2022), 136
Abbott v. Perez, 585 U.S. 579 (2018), 345
Abigail Alliance for Better Access to Developmental Drugs v. Eschenbach, 495 F.3d 695 (D.C. Cir. 2007), 119
Abood v. Detroit Board of Education, 431 U.S. 209 (1977), 450
Abrams v. Johnson, 521 U.S. 74 (1997), 329
Abrams v. United States, 250 U.S. 616 (1919), 397-398
Adamson v. California, 332 U.S. 46 (1947), 12, 86
Adarand Constructors, Inc. v. Pena, 515 U.S. 200 (1995), 282, 287
Adickes v. Kress & Co., 398 U.S. 144 (1970), 15, 25-26
Adkins v. Children's Hospital, 261 U.S. 525 (1923), 69, 722
Agency for International Development v. Alliance for Open Society, 591 U.S. 430 (2020), 2-3
Agins v. City of Tiburon, 477 U.S. 255 (1980), 148
Alabama Legislative Black Caucus v. Alabama, 575 U.S. 254 (2015), 329
Alexander v. South Carolina State Conference of the NAACP, 144 S. Ct. 1221 (2024), 337-343
Aliessa ex rel. Fayad v. Novello, 96 N.Y.2d 418, 754 N.E.2d 1085 (N.Y. 2001), 92
Allegheny Pittsburgh Coal Co. v. Webster County, 488 U.S. 336 (1989), 248
Allen v. Cooper, 589 U.S. 248 (2020), 206
Allgeyer v. Louisiana, 165 U.S. 578 (1897), 9, 68, 82-83, 85, 128
Allied Structural Steel Co. v. Spannaus, 438 U.S. 234 (1978), 175-176, 181-182, 185-187
Amalgamated Food Employees Union v. Logan Valley Plaza, 391 U.S. 308 (1968), 19
American Civil Liberties Union v. Ashcroft, 322 F.3d 240 (3d Cir. 2003), 443
American Civil Liberties Union v. Mukasey, 534 F.3d 1032 (3d Cir. 2008), 445
American Legion v. American Humanist Association, 588 U.S. 29 (2019), 524-525
American Manufacturers Mutual Insurance Co. v. Sullivan, 526 U.S. 40 (1999), 17, 19, 28, 33, 205
Americans for Prosperity Foundation v. Bonta, 594 U.S. 595 (2021), 364, 467, 469
Ancata v. Prison Health Services, 769 F.2d 700 (11th Cir. 1985), 21
Anderson v. Celebrezze, 460 U.S. 780 (1983), 346
Anderson v. Dunn, 19 U.S. (6 Wheat.) 204 (1821), 267
Andrews v. Ballard, 498 F. Supp. 1038 (S.D. Tex. 1980), 119
Andrus v. Allard, 444 U.S. 51 (1979), 158
Anonymous v. City of Rochester, 13 N.Y.3d 35, 915 N.E.2d 593 (2009), 132
Apartment Association of Los Angeles County v. City of Los Angeles, 10 F.4th 905 (9th Cir. 2021), 189
Aptheker v. Secretary of State, 378 U.S. 500 (1964), 84, 130
Arizona Free Enterprise Club's Freedom Club PAC v. Bennett, 565 U.S. 721 (2011), 415
Arkansas Educational Television Commission v. Forbes, 523 U.S. 666 (1998), 473, 477, 479
Arkansas Fish and Game Commission v. United States, 568 U.S. 23 (2012), 154
Armour v. City of Indianapolis, 566 U.S. 673 (2012), 243-244, 246
Arnett v. Kennedy, 416 U.S. 134 (1974), 209
Ashcroft v. American Civil Liberties Union, 535 U.S. 564 (2002), 444
Ashcroft v. American Civil Liberties Union, 542 U.S. 656 (2004), 445
Ashcroft v. Free Speech Coalition, 535 U.S. 234 (2002), 440
Atkins v. Virginia, 536 U.S. 304 (2002), 139

Table of Cases

Attorney General of New York v. Soto-Lopez, 476 U.S. 898 (1986), 355
Austin v. Michigan State Chamber of Commerce, 494 U.S. 652 (1990), 415

Bains LLC v. Arco Products Co., 405 F.3d 764 (9th Cir. 2005), 81-82
Baker v. Carr, 369 U.S. 186 (1962), 335
Ball v. James, 451 U.S. 355 (1981), 323
Barancik v. County of Marin, 872 F.2d 834 (9th Cir. 1988), 165
Barr v. American Association of Political Consultants, Inc., 591 U.S. 610 (2020), 375-376, 393
Barron v. Mayor & City Council of Baltimore, 32 U.S. (7 Pet.) 243 (1833), 2, 7, 12
Bartnicki v. Vopper, 532 U.S. 514 (2001), 508-509
Bell v. Maryland, 378 U.S. 226 (1964), 23
Bellotti v. Baird, 443 U.S. 622 (1979), 97
Benton v. Maryland, 395 U.S. 784 (1969), 13-14
Bernal v. Fainter, 467 U.S. 216 (1984), 254-255, 290
Bert Co. v. Turk, 298 A.3d 44 (Pa. 2023), 80
Betancourt v. Bloomberg, 448 F.3d 547 (2d Cir. 2006), 130
Bethel School District No. 403 v. Fraser, 478 U.S. 675 (1986), 482-483
Bethune-Hill v. Virginia State Board of Elections, 580 U.S. 178 (2017), 279
Bigelow v. Virginia, 421 U.S. 809 (1975), 245, 421, 423, 429
Bishop v. Wood, 426 U.S. 341 (1976), 206-207
Blum v. Yaretsky, 457 U.S. 991 (1982), 20
BMW of North America, Inc. v. Gore, 517 U.S. 559 (1996), 76
Board of Directors of Rotary International v. Rotary Club of Duarte, 481 U.S. 537 (1987), 115, 499
Board of Education v. Dowell, 498 U.S. 237 (1991), 268
Board of Education of Kiryas Joel v. Grumet, 512 U.S. 687 (1994), 474
Board of Regents of State Colleges v. Roth, 408 U.S. 564 (1972), 202, 206-207
Board of Trustees of the State University of New York v. Fox, 492 U.S. 469 (1989), 423, 426
Board of Trustees of the University of Alabama v. Garrett, 531 U.S. 356 (2000), 56-57
Bob Jones University v. United States, 461 U.S. 574 (1983), 571
Boddie v. Connecticut, 401 U.S. 371 (1971), 218, 360
Bolling v. Sharpe, 347 U.S. 497 (1954), 258
Boos v. Barry, 485 U.S. 312 (1988), 395
Borough of Duryea v. Guarnieri, 564 U.S. 379 (2011), 456
Bowen v. Gilliard, 483 U.S. 587 (1987), 362
Bowen v. Roy, 476 U.S. 693 (1986), 572
Bowers v. Hardwick, 478 U.S. 186 (1986), 117
Boy Scouts of America v. Dale, 530 U.S. 640 (2000), 498, 500,
Brandenburg v. Ohio, 395 U.S. 444 (1969), 403-404
Branzburg v. Hayes, 408 U.S. 665 (1972), 509
Braunfeld v. Brown, 366 U.S. 599 (1961), 565-566
Bray v. Alexandria Women's Health Clinic, 506 U.S. 263 (1993), 46
Brentwood Academy v. Tennessee Secondary School Athletic Association, 531 U.S. 288 (2001), 16, 39-40
Bridges v. California, 314 U.S. 252 (1941), 399-400
Brown v. Board of Education (Brown I), 347 U.S. 483 (1954), 257-260, 351
Brown v. Board of Education (Brown II), 349 U.S. 294 (1955), 259-260
Brown v. Entertainment Merchants Association, 564 U.S. 786 (2011), 374, 406
Brown v. Hartlage, 456 U.S. 45 (1982), 453
Brown v. Legal Foundation of Washington, 538 U.S. 216 (2003), 152-153
Brumfield v. Cain, 576 U.S. 305 (2015), 136
Buckley v. American Constitutional Law Foundation, 525 U.S. 182 (1999), 420
Buckley v. Valeo, 424 U.S. 1 (1976), 414-415
Bullock v. Carter, 405 U.S. 134 (1972), 346-347
Burdick v. Takushi, 504 U.S. 428 (1992), 346
Burrell v. Tipton County Election Commission, 2022 WL 10225146 (6th Cir. Oct. 18, 2022), 348
Burson v. Freeman, 504 U.S. 191 (1992), 461
Burton v. Wilmington Parking Authority, 365 U.S. 715 (1961), 27-29, 32, 41
Bush v. Gore, 531 U.S. 525 (2000), 348-349
Bush v. Vera, 517 U.S. 952 (1996), 340, 344

Caetano v. Massachusetts, 577 U.S. 411 (2016), 582-584
Calder v. Bull, 3 U.S. (3 Dall.) 386 (1798), 70
Califano v. Jobst, 434 U.S. 47 (1977), 105
California Democratic Party v. Jones, 984 F. Supp. 1228 (E.D. Cal. 1997), 503
California Democratic Party v. Jones, 530 U.S. 567 (2000), 503-504
Cammarano v. United States, 358 U.S. 498 (1959), 421
Campbell v. State Farm Mutual Automobile Insurance Co., 98 P.3d 409 (Utah 2004), 80
Cantwell v. Connecticut, 310 U.S. 296 (1940), 399, 548-549
Caperton v. Massey, 556 U.S. 868 (2009), 219
Carey v. Brown, 447 U.S. 455 (1980), 461
Carey v. Population Services International, 431 U.S. 678 (1977), 94
Carson v. Makin, 596 U.S. 767 (2022), 541, 562, 573
CBS, Inc. v. FCC, 453 U.S. 367 (1981), 513
Cedar Point Nursery v. Hassid, 594 U.S. 139 (2021), 153, 155
Central Hudson Gas & Electric Corporation v. Public Service Commission of New York, 447 U.S. 557 (1980), 421, 424-432
Chaplinsky v. New Hampshire, 315 U.S. 568 (1942), 389, 404-405
Chicago, Burlington & Quincy Railroad Co. v. Chicago, 166 U.S. 226 (1897), 10
Christian Legal Society Chapter of the University of California, Hastings College of the Law v. Machine, 561 U.S. 661 (2010), 477
Christopher v. Harbury, 536 U.S. 403 (2002), 135
Church of Lukumi Babalu Aye, Inc. v. City of Hialeah, 508 U.S. 520 (1993), 554-555, 557-560, 565
Citizens Against Rent Control v. Berkeley, 454 U.S. 290 (1981), 414-415, 420
Citizens United v. Federal Election Commission, 558 U.S. 310 (2010), 415
City of Akron v. Akron Center for Reproductive Health, Inc., 462 U.S. 416 (1983), 97
City of Austin v. Reagan National Advertising of Austin, LLC, 586 U.S. 61 (2022), 391
City of Boerne v. Flores, 521 U.S. 507 (1997), 52-56, 58, 570
City of Chicago v. Morales, 527 U.S. 41 (1999), 130
City of Cincinnati v. Discovery Network, Inc., 507 U.S. 410 (1993), 421, 430-431
City of Cleburne v. Cleburne Living Center, 473 U.S. 432 (1985), 306, 308-309
City of Erie v. Pap's A.M., 529 U.S. 277 (2000), 460
City of Grants Pass v. Johnson, 144 S. Ct. 2202 (2024), 138
City of Lakewood v. Plain Dealer Publishing Co., 486 U.S. 750 (1988), 511
City of Littleton v. Z.J. Gifts D-4, LLC, 541 U.S. 774 (2004), 385
City of Los Angeles v. Alameda Books, Inc., 535 U.S. 425 (2002), 439
City of Los Angeles v. David, 538 U.S. 715 (2003), 216
City of Los Angeles v. Manhart, 435 U.S. 702 (1978), 301
City of Monterey v. Del Monte Dunes at Monterey, Ltd., 526 U.S. 687 (1999), 157, 168, 170, 174
City of Renton v. Playtime Theatres, Inc., 475 U.S. 41 (1986), 395, 439, 468
City of Richmond v. J. A. Croson Co., 488 U.S. 469 (1989), 257, 271, 274, 276
City of Rome v. United States, 446 U.S. 156 (1980), 59-60
City of San Diego v. Roe, 543 U.S. 77 (2004), 457
City of Santa Barbara v. Adamson, 27 Cal. 3d 123, 610 P.2d 436 (1980), 116-117
City of West Covina v. Perkins, 525 U.S. 234 (1999), 208-209
Civil Rights Cases, 109 U.S. 3 (1883), 43-45
Clark v. Chrysler Corp., 436 F.3d 594 (6th Cir. 2006), 81
Clark v. Community for Creative Non-Violence, 468 U.S. 288 (1984), 374, 376, 460, 465, 467
Clark v. Jeter, 486 U.S. 456 (1988), 306
Cleveland Board of Education v. Loudermill, 470 U.S. 532 (1985), 209, 212, 214, 219
Clingman v. Beaver, 544 U.S. 581 (2005), 503
Cohane v. National Collegiate Athletic Association, 215 Fed. Appx. 13 (2d Cir. 2007), 39
Cohen v. California, 403 U.S. 15 (1971), 405, 441-442
Cohen v. Cowles Media Co., 501 U.S. 663 (1991), 24

Colorado Republican Federal Campaign Committee v. Federal Election Commission, 518 U.S. 604 (1996), 417
Columbia Broadcasting System, Inc. v. Democratic National Committee, 412 U.S. 94 (1973), 512
Columbus Board of Education v. Penick, 443 U.S. 449 (1979), 234
Commonwealth v. Hairston, 249 A.3d 1046 (Pa. 2021), 140
Connecticut Department of Public Safety v. Doe, 538 U.S. 1 (2003), 213
Connick v. Myers, 461 U.S. 138 (1983), 456-459
Conservatorship of Wendland, 26 Cal.4th 519, 110 Cal. Rptr.2d 412 (2001), 122
Cooper v. Harris, 581 U.S. 285 (2017), 342-345
Cooper Industries, Inc. v. Leatherman Tool Group, Inc., 532 U.S. 424 (2001), 76-77
Coppage v. Kansas, 236 U.S. 1 (1915), 68, 71
Corfield v. Coryell, 6 F. Cas. 546 (C.C.E.D. Pa. 1823), 5
Cornelius v. NAACP Legal Defense & Education Fund, 473 U.S. 788 (1985), 471, 473, 480
Corporation of Presiding Bishop v. Amos, 483 U.S. 327 (1987), 575
Counterman v. Colorado, 600 U.S. 66 (2023), 406
County of Allegheny v. American Civil Liberties Union, 492 U.S. 573 (1989), 523-524
Cox v. New Hampshire, 312 U.S. 569 (1941), 463, 468
Cox Broadcasting v. Cohn, 420 U.S. 469 (1975), 508
Craft v. Vanderbilt University, 18 F. Supp. 2d 786 (M.D. Tenn. 1998), 31
Craig v. Boren, 429 U.S. 190 (1976), 294
Craig v. Harney, 331 U.S. 367 (1947), 400
Crawford v. Marion County Election Board, 553 U.S. 181 (2008), 319, 322
Cruzan v. Director, Missouri Department of Health, 497 U.S. 261 (1990), 93, 122-127
Curtis Publishing Co. v. Butts, 388 U.S. 130 (1967), 411
Culley v. Marshall, 601 U.S. 377 (2024), 215
Cutter v. Wilkinson, 544 U.S. 709 (2005), 574-575

Dale v. Boy Scouts of America, 734 A.2d 1196 (1999), 501
Dandridge v. Williams, 397 U.S. 471 (1970), 109, 244, 361
Daniels v. Williams, 474 U.S. 327 (1986), 206
Davenport v. Washington Education Association, 551 U.S. 177 (2007), 450-451
Davidson v. Cannon, 474 U.S. 344 (1986), 133
Davidson v. City of New Orleans, 96 U.S. 97 (1878), 64, 70
Davis v. Bandemer, 478 U.S. 109 (1986), 330
Davis v. Federal Election Commission, 554 U.S. 724 (2008), 415
Dayton Board of Education v. Brinkman, 443 U.S. 526 (1979), 238
Debs v. United States, 249 U.S. 211 (1919), 397-398
Demore v. Hyung Joon Kim, 538 U.S. 510 (2003), 129
Dennis v. Sparks, 449 U.S. 24 (1980), 25, 27, 38
Dennis v. United States, 341 U.S. 494 (1951), 401-402, 455
Department of Homeland Security v. Regents of the University of California, 591 U.S. 1 (2020), 236
Department of Homeland Security v. Thuraissigiam, 591 U.S. 103 (2020), 3
Department of State v. Muñoz, 144 S. Ct. 1812 (2024), 109, 196
DeShaney v. Winnebago County Department of Social Services, 489 U.S. 189 (1989), 92, 133-134, 138
DeVillier v. Texas, 601 U.S. 285 (2024), 145
District of Columbia v. Heller, 554 U.S. 570 (2008), 578-583
Dobbs v. Jackson Women's Health Organization, 141 S. Ct. 2619 (2021), 100
Dobbs v. Jackson Women's Health Organization, 597 U.S. 215 (2022), 89, 90, 94, 95, 100-102
Doe v. Bolton, 410 U.S. 179 (1973), 97
Doe v. Bonta, 101 F.4th 633 (9th Cir. 2024), 137
Doe v. Reed, 561 U.S. 186 (2010), 420, 496
Doe v. Reed, 823 F. Supp. 2d 1195 (W.D. Wash. 2011), 497
Doe v. University of Michigan, 721 F. Supp. 852 (E.D. Mich. 1989), 407
Dolan v. City of Tigard, 512 U.S. 374 (1994), 172-174
Dred Scott v. Sandford, 60 U.S. (19 How.) 393 (1857), 4, 67

Dun & Bradstreet, Inc. v. Greenmoss Builders, Inc., 472 U.S. 749 (1985), 379-380
Duncan v. Bonta, 19 F.4th 1087 (9th Cir. 2021), 583
Duncan v. Louisiana, 391 U.S. 145 (1968), 12-14, 86
Dunn v. Blumstein, 405 U.S. 330 (1972), 317, 319
Dusenberry v. United States, 534 U.S. 161 (2002), 208

Easley v. Cromartie, 532 U.S. 234 (2001), 340-341
Eastern Enterprises v. Apfel, 524 U.S. 498 (1998), 177
Edmonson v. Leesville Concrete Co., 500 U.S. 614 (1991), 41
Edwards v. South Carolina, 372 U.S. 229 (1963), 473
Eisenstadt v. Baird, 405 U.S. 438 (1972), 94-95
El Paso v. Simmons, 379 U.S. 497 (1965), 183
Eldred v. Ashcroft, 537 U.S. 186 (2003), 470-471
Employment Division v. Smith, 494 U.S. 872 (1990) 52, 547, 563, 565-566, 569, 572-573
Energy Reserves Group, Inc. v. Kansas Power & Light Co., 459 U.S. 400 (1983), 170
Engle v. Vitale, 370 U.S. 421 (1962), 537
Engquist v. Oregon Department of Agriculture, 553 U.S. 591 (2008), 232
Epperson v. Arkansas, 393 U.S. 97 (1968), 537
Espinoza v. Montana Department of Revenue, 591 U.S. 464 (2020), 536, 541, 562
Eu v. San Francisco County Democratic Central Committee, 489 U.S. 214 (1989), 502
Evans v. Abney, 396 U.S. 435 (1970), 24
Evenwel v. Abbott, 578 U.S. 54 (2016), 326
Everson v. Board of Education, 330 U.S. 1 (1947), 521, 532
Ewing v. Mytinger & Casselberry, Inc., 339 U.S. 594 (1950), 215
Expressions Hair Design v. Schneiderman, 581 U.S. 37 (2018), 375, 388
Exxon Shipping Co. v. Bakery, 554 U.S. 471 (2008), 81

FCC v. Beach Communications, Inc., 508 U.S. 307 (1993), 244
FCC v. Fox Television Stations, Inc., 567 U.S. 239 (2012), 209
FCC v. League of Women Voters of California, 468 U.S. 364 (1984), 513
FCC v. Pacifica Foundation, 438 U.S. 726 (1978), 442
Federal Election Commission v. Beaumont, 539 U.S. 146 (2003), 415-416
Federal Election Commission v. Colorado Republican Federal Campaign Committee, 533 U.S. 431 (2001), 417-418
Federal Election Commission v. Cruz, 596 U.S. 289 (2022), 415
Federal Election Commission v. National Conservative Political Action Committee, 470 U.S. 480 (1985), 415, 417
Feiner v. New York, 340 U.S. 315 (1951), 406
Ferguson v. Skrupa, 372 U.S. 726 (1963), 74-75
First English Evangelical Lutheran Church of Glendale v. County of Los Angeles, 482 U.S. 304 (1987), 167-168
Fisher v. University of Texas (I), 570 U.S. 297 (2013), 272, 283
Fisher v. University of Texas (II), 579 U.S. 365 (2016), 274
Fitzgerald v. Racing Association of Central Iowa, 539 U.S. 103 (2003), 244
Flagg Brothers v. Brooks, 436 U.S. 149 (1978), 19, 34-35
Flax v. DaimlerChrysler Corp., 272 S.W.3d 521 (Tenn. 2008), 82
Fletcher v. Peck, 10 U.S. (6 Cranch) 87 (1810), 191
Florida Bar v. Went for It, Inc., 515 U.S. 618 (1995), 426, 429
Florida Prepaid Postsecondary Education Expense Board v. College Savings Bank, 527 U.S. 627 (1999), 56
Florida Rock Industries, Inc. v. United States, 18 F.3d 1560 (Fed. Cir. 1994), 163-164
Florida Rock Industries, Inc. v. United States, 45 Fed. Cl. 21 (1999), 164
Florida Star v. B.J.F., 491 U.S. 524 (1989), 507-508
Foley v. Connelie, 435 U.S. 291 (1978), 290
Fortson v. Morris, 385 U.S. 231 (1966), 317
44 Liquormart, Inc. v. Rhode Island, 517 U.S. 484 (1996), 425, 428, 431
Fowler v. Rhode Island, 345 U.S. 67 (1953), 529
Freedman v. Maryland, 380 U.S. 51 (1965), 385, 438
Freeman v. Pitts, 503 U.S. 467 (1992), 268-270

Friedman v. Rogers, 440 U.S. 1 (1979), 421
Frisby v. Schultz, 487 U.S. 474 (1988), 471, 473
Frohwerk v. United States, 249 U.S. 204 (1919), 397-398
Frontiero v. Richardson, 411 U.S. 677 (1973), 254, 293
Fuentes v. Shevin, 407 U.S. 67 (1972), 195
Fullilove v. Klutznick, 448 U.S. 448 (1980), 272
Fulton v. City of Philadelphia, 593 U.S. 522 (2021), 567, 569, 571-572

Gaffney v. Cummings, 412 U.S. 735 (1973), 328
Garcetti v. Ceballos, 547 U.S. 410 (2006), 457-458
Garrison v. Louisiana, 379 U.S. 64 (1964), 408
Gary B. v. Whitmer, 957 F.3d 616 (6th Cir. 2020), 366-367
Gasperini v. Center for Humanities, Inc., 518 U.S. 415 (1996), 14
General Motors, Inc. v. Romein, 503 U.S. 181 (1992), 176, 177-179
Georgia v. McCollum, 505 U.S. 42 (1992), 41
Gertz v. Robert Welch, Inc., 418 U.S. 323 (1974), 411, 412
Gideon v. Wainwright, 372 U.S. 335 (1963), 359
Gilbert v. Homar, 520 U.S. 924 (1997), 217
Gitlow v. New York, 268 U.S. 652 (1925), 398
Glickman v. Wileman Brothers & Elliott, Inc., 521 U.S. 457 (1997), 376
Globe Newspaper Co. v. Superior Court, 457 U.S. 596 (1982), 506
Goldberg v. Kelly, 397 U.S. 254 (1970), 203, 219
Gonzales v. O Centro Espirita Beneficente Uniao Do Vegetal, 546 U.S. 418 (2006), 574
Good News Club v. Milford Central School, 533 U.S. 98 (2001), 478-479, 542
Goss v. Lopez, 419 U.S. 565 (1975), 206
Gould v. Morgan, 907 F.3d 659 (1st Cir. 2018), 585
Graham v. Richardson, 403 U.S. 365 (1971), 288, 289
Gratz v. Bollinger, 539 U.S. 249 (2003), 272-273, 274
Graveline v. Benson, 992 F.3d 524 (6th Cir. 2021), 347-348
Greater New Orleans Broadcasting Association, Inc. v. United States, 527 U.S. 173 (1999), 428, 431
Green v. Biddle, 21 U.S. (8 Wheat.) 1 (1823), 175
Green v. County School Board, 391 U.S. 430 (1968), 259
Greenholtz v. Nebraska Penal Inmates, 442 U.S. 1 (1979), 128
Greer v. Spock, 424 U.S. 828 (1976), 473
Gregg v. Georgia, 428 U.S. 153 (1976), 139
Griffin v. Breckenridge, 403 U.S. 88 (1971), 46
Griffin v. Illinois, 351 U.S. 12 (1956), 359
Griswold v. Connecticut, 381 U.S. 479 (1965), 85-88, 90-91, 94, 95
Grutter v. Bollinger, 539 U.S. 306 (2003), 273-275, 279, 282-284

H.L. v. Matheson, 450 U.S. 398 (1981), 97
Hague v. CIO, 307 U.S. 496 (1939), 471
Halbert v. Michigan, 545 U.S. 605 (2005), 359
Hall v. Oklahoma, 488 U.S. 878 (1988), 139
Hampton v. Mow Sun Wong, 426 U.S. 88 (1976), 225, 292
Harper v. Hall, 384 N.C. 292, 886 S.E.2d 393 (2023), 337
Harper v. Virginia State Board of Elections, 383 U.S. 663 (1966), 320
Harris v. Hahn, 827 F.3d 359 (5th Cir. 2016), 355
Harris v. McRae, 448 U.S. 297 (1980), 138, 306, 316-317, 363
Harris v. Rosario, 446 U.S. 651 (1980), 247
Harte-Hanks Communications, Inc. v. Connaughton, 491 U.S. 657 (1989), 408-409
Hawaii Housing Authority v. Midkiff, 467 U.S. 229 (1984), 146
Haywood v. Drown, 556 U.S. 729 (2009), 49
Hazelwood School District v. Kuhlmeier, 484 U.S. 260 (1988), 483
Heart of Atlanta Motel, Inc. v. United States, 379 U.S. 241 (1964), 42-43
Heffron v. International Society for Krishna Consciousness, 452 U.S. 640 (1981), 462-463, 466, 468
Heights Apartments, LLC v. Walz, 30 F.4th 720 (8th Cir. 2022), 189-190
Hein v. Freedom from Religion Foundation, Inc., 551 U.S. 587 (2007), 544
Heller v. Doe, 509 U.S. 312 (1993), 309

Herndon v. Lowry, 301 U.S. 242 (1937), 399, 401
Hewitt v. Helms, 459 U.S. 460 (1983), 128
Hill v. Colorado, 530 U.S. 703 (2000), 462, 467
Hill v. Stone, 421 U.S. 289 (1975), 318-319, 320, 321
Hodes & Nauser, MDs, P.A. v. Kobach, 551 P.3d 37 (Kan. 2024), 102
Holder v. Humanitarian Law Project, 561 U.S. 1 (2010), 388, 389, 392, 455
Holly v. Scott, 434 F.3d 287 (4th Cir. 2006), 21
Homar v. Gibert, 63 F. Supp. 2d 559 (M.D. Pa. 1999), 217
Home Building & Loan Association v. Blaisdell, 290 U.S. 398 (1934), 186, 188-189, 190
Horne v. Department of Agriculture, 576 U.S. 350 (2015), 146, 151
Hosanna-Tabor Evangelical Lutheran Church and School v. E.E.O.C., 565 U.S. 171 (2012), 551-552
Houchins v. KQED, Inc., 438 U.S. 1 (1978), 505
Houston Community College System v. Wilson, 595 U.S. 468 (2022), 391-392
Hudgens v. NLRB, 424 U.S. 507 (1976), 19
Hudson v. Palmer, 468 U.S. 517 (1984), 214
Hudson Water Co. v. McCarter, 209 U.S. 349 (1908), 184
Hunt v. Cromartie, 526 U.S. 541 (1999), 335, 340
Hunter v. Underwood, 471 U.S. 222 (1985), 234, 242
Hurley v. Irish-American Gay, Lesbian and Bisexual Group of Boston, Inc., 515 U.S. 557 (1995), 516
Hurst v. Florida, 577 U.S. 92 (2016), 139
Hurtado v. California, 110 U.S. 516 (1884), 11, 14
Hustler Magazine, Inc. v. Falwell, 485 U.S. 46 (1988), 410
Hutchins v. District of Columbia, 188 F.3d 531 (D.C. Cir. 1999), 132

Iancu v. Brunetti, 588 U.S. 388 (2019), 394, 395, 442
Ibanez v. Florida Department of Business and Professional Regulation, 512 U.S. 136 (1994), 432
Illinois ex rel. Madigan v. Telemarketing Associates, 538 U.S. 600 (2003), 413-414
In re A.G., 181 Cal. App. 4th 989 (Ct. App. 2010), 132
In re Employment Discrimination Litigation Against the State of Alabama, 198 F.3d 1305 (11th Cir. 1999), 51
In re Griffiths, 413 U.S. 717 (1973), 290
In re R.M.J., 455 U.S. 191 (1982), 432
Ingraham v. Wright, 430 U.S. 651 (1977), 215
International Society for Krishna Consciousness, Inc. v. Lee, 505 U.S. 672 (1992), 474, 475
Iten v. County of Los Angeles, 81 F.4th 979 (9th Cir. 2023), 175-176

Jackson v. Metropolitan Edison Co., 419 U.S. 345 (1974), 19
Jacobellis v. Ohio, 378 U.S. 184 (1964), 437
Jacobson v. Massachusetts, 197 U.S. 11 (1905), 121
Janus v. American Federation of State, County, and Municipal Employees, 585 U.S. 878 (2018), 450, 459
J.E.B. v. Alabama, 511 U.S. 127 (1994), 294-295, 301, 302
Jenkins v. Georgia, 418 U.S. 153 (1974), 435
Jenness v. Fortson 403 U.S. 431 (1971), 347
Johanns v. Livestock Marketing Association, 544 U.S. 550 (2005), 451
Johnson v. California, 543 U.S. 499 (2005), 253
Johnson v. California, 545 U.S. 162 (2005), 232
Johnson v. State, 731 P.2d 993 (Okla. Ct. Crim. App. 1987), 140
Johnson v. United States, 576 U.S. 591 (2015), 209
Johnson v. Wisconsin Elections Commission, 972 N.W.2d 559 (Wis. 2022), 345
Jones v. Alfred H. Mayer Co., 392 U.S. 409 (1968), 43-44
Jones v. Wolf, 443 U.S. 595 (1979), 552-553
Joseph Burstyn, Inc. v. Wilson, 343 U.S. 496 (1952), 421

Kadrmas v. Dickinson Public Schools, 487 U.S. 450 (1988), 365
Kaley v. United States, 571 U.S. 320 (2014), 215
Karcher v. Daggett, 462 U.S. 725 (1983), 329, 330
Katzenbach v. McClung, 379 U.S. 294 (1964), 43
Katzenbach v. Morgan, 384 U.S. 641 (1966), 47, 51-53, 55, 59
Keller v. State Bar of California, 496 U.S. 1 (1990), 451

Kelo v. City of New London, Conn., 545 U.S. 469 (2005), 147-148
Kennedy v. Bremerton School District, 597 U.S. 507 (2022), 488, 522, 525, 527, 532, 534, 538, 541, 543, 545, 553, 556
Kennedy v. Louisiana, 554 U.S. 407 (2008), 139
Kerry v. Din, 576 U.S. 86 (2015), 197
Keyes v. School Dist. No. 1, 413 U.S. 189 (1973), 232, 238-240, 242, 261, 270
Keyishian v. Board of Regents, 385 U.S. 589 (1967), 493
Keystone Bituminous Coal Association v. DeBenedictis, 480 U.S. 470 (1987), 158, 160, 185, 187, 189
Kikumura v. Hurley, 242 F.3d 950 (10th Cir. 2001), 570
Kimel v. Florida Board of Regents, 528 U.S. 62 (2000), 56
Kleindeinst v. Mandel, 408 U.S. 753 (1972), 530
Kligler v. Attorney General, 198 N.E.3d 1228 (Mass. 2022), 126
Knick v. Township of Scott, 588 U.S. 180 (2019), 145
Kolbe v. Hogan, 849 F.3d 114 (4th Cir. 2017), 583-584
Koontz v. St. Johns River Water Management District, 570 U.S. 595 (2013), 169, 170-171, 363
Korematsu v. United States, 323 U.S. 214 (1944), 251
Kuhlmeier v. Hazelwood School District, 795 F.2d 1368 (8th Cir. 1986), 483
Kwong Hai Chew v. Colding, 344 U.S. 590 (1953), 3

L.W. ex rel. Williams v. Skrmetti, 83 F.4th 460 (6th Cir. 2023), 120-121
Lamb's Chapel v. Center Moriches Union Free School District, 508 U.S. 384 (1993), 477
Lane v. Franks, 576 U.S. 228 (2014), 458
Larson v. Valente, 456 U.S. 228 (1982), 529, 574
Lassiter v. Department of Social Services, 452 U.S. 18 (1981), 361
Lassiter v. Northampton Election Board, 360 U.S. 45 (1959), 51
Lawrence v. Texas, 539 U.S. 558 (2003), 93, 95, 106, 117-118, 310
League of United Latin American Citizens v. Edwards Aquifer Authority, 937 F.3d 457 (5th Cir. 2019), 323
League of United Latin American Citizens v. Perry, 548 U.S. 399 (2006), 328
Lee v. Weisman, 505 U.S. 577 (1992), 521, 522, 538, 539-540
Legal Services Corporation v. Velazquez, 531 U.S. 533 (2001), 363, 491
Lemon v. Kurtzman 403 U.S. 602 (1971), 522-526, 530, 531, 536, 537, 538, 540-541, 543, 544, 575
Lincoln v. Case, 340 F.3d 283 (5th Cir. 2003), 82
Lindsey v. Normet, 405 U.S. 56 (1972), 138
Lingle v. Chevron U.S.A., Inc, 544 U.S. 528 (2005), 148, 163
Lindke v. Freed, 601 U.S. 187 (2024), 37
Linmark Associates, Inc. v. Township of Willingboro, 431 U.S. 85 (1977), 426
Little v. Streater, 452 U.S. 1 (1981), 361
Lloyd Corp. v. Tanner, 407 U.S. 551 (1972), 18, 19
Lochner v. New York, 198 U.S. 45 (1905), 67-73, 74, 76, 82-83, 84, 85, 86, 90, 121, 133
Locke v. Davey, 540 U.S. 712 (2004), 558-562, 571
Loretto v. Teleprompter Manhattan CATV Corp., 458 U.S. 419 (1982), 151-153
Lorillard Tobacco Co. v. Reilly, 533 U.S. 525 (2001), 431
Los Angeles Police Dept. v. United Reporting Publishing Corp., 528 U.S. 32 (1999), 387
Louisiana v. New Orleans, 109 U.S. 285 (1883), 177
Loving v. Virginia, 388 U.S. 1 (1967), 103, 104, 251, 314
Lubin v. Panish, 415 U.S. 709 (1974), 326
Lucas v. South Carolina Coastal Council, 505 U.S. 1003 (1992), 156, 159, 162-164, 165, 166, 167
Lugar v. Edmondson Oil Co., 457 U.S. 922 (1982), 17, 32-33, 34, 39, 41, 42
Lujan v. G&G Fire Sprinklers, Inc., 532 U.S. 189 (2001), 217-218
Luke Records, Inc. v. Navarro, 960 F.2d 134 (11th Cir. 1992), 435-436
Lynch v. Donnelly, 465 U.S. 668 (1984), 521, 522, 543

Lynch v. Household Finance Corp., 405 U.S. 538 (1972), 76
Lyng v. Castillo, 477 U.S. 635 (1986), 108-109, 362
Lyng v. Northwest Indian Cemetery Protection Association, 485 U.S. 439 (1988), 572

Madison v. Alabama, 586 U.S. 265 (2019), 139
Madsen v. Women's Health Center, Inc., 512 U.S. 753 (1994), 469
Mahanoy Area School District v. B.L., 594 U.S. 180 (2021), 485, 486
Malloy v. Hogan, 378 U.S. 1 (1964), 14
Malpasso v. Palozzi, 767 F. Appx. 525 (4th Cir. 2019), 585
Manhattan Community Access Corp. v. Halleck, 587 U.S. 802 (2019), 22, 30, 37
Marbury v. Madison, 5 U.S. (1 Cranch) 137 (1803), 58
Marsh v. Alabama, 326 U.S. 501 (1946), 18-19
Marsh v. Chambers, 463 U.S. 783 (1983), 522
Massachusetts Board of Retirement v. Murgia, 427 U.S. 307 (1976), 306, 367
Masterpiece Cakeshop, Ltd. v. Colorado Civil Rights Commission, 584 U.S. 617 (2018), 555-556
Matal v. Tam, 582 U.S. 218 (2018), 487-488
Mathews v. Diaz, 426 U.S. 67 (1976), 129, 292
Mathews v. Eldridge, 424 U.S. 319 (1976), 210-216, 218
McCarthy v. Philadelphia Civil Service Commission, 424 U.S. 645 (1976), 357
McConnell v. Federal Election Commission, 540 U.S. 93 (2003), 417-419
McCreary County v. American Civil Liberties Union, 545 U.S. 844 (2005), 521-524
McCullen v. Coakley, 573 U.S. 464 (2014), 462, 465, 473
McCulloch v. Maryland, 17 U.S. (4 Wheat.) 316 (1819), 47, 48, 59
McDaniel v. Paty, 435 U.S. 618 (1978), 545
McDonald v. City of Chicago, 561 U.S. 742 (2010), 13-14, 581, 586
McDonald v. Santa Fe Trail Transportation Co., 427 U.S. 273 (1976), 46
McGowan v. Maryland, 366 U.S. 420 (1961), 528
Meachum v. Fano, 427 U.S. 215 (1976), 128
Melendez v. City of New York, 16 F.4th 992 (2d Cir. 2021), 176, 191
Melendez v. City of New York, 668 F. Supp.3d 184 (S.D.N.Y. 2023), 191
Members of Medical Licensing Board of Indiana v. Planned Parenthood Great Northwest, 211 N.E.3d 957 (Ind. 2023), 102
Memphis v. Greene, 451 U.S. 100 (1981), 46
Memphis Light, Gas & Water Division v. Craft, 436 U.S. 1 (1978), 208-209
Mendez v. County of San Bernardino, 540 F.3d 1109 (9th Cir. 2008), 81
Mendoza v. Strickler, 51 F.4th 346 (9th Cir. 2022), 359-360
Metro Broadcasting, Inc. v. FCC, 497 U.S. 547 (1990), 272
Metropolis Theatre Co. v. Chicago, 228 U.S. 61 (1913), 244
Metropolitan Life Insurance Co. v. Ward, 470 U.S. 869 (1985), 307
Meyer v. Grant, 486 U.S. 414 (1988), 420
Meyer v. Nebraska, 262 U.S. 390 (1923), 82-83, 84, 85, 86, 110, 364
Miami Herald Publishing Co. v. Tornillo, 418 U.S. 241 (1974), 510-512, 514, 516
Michael H. v. Gerald D., 491 U.S. 110 (1989), 110-111
Michael M. v. Superior Court, 450 U.S. 464 (1981), 294, 296, 298
Milkovich v. Lorain Journal Co., 497 U.S. 1 (1990), 410
Miller v. California, 413 U.S. 15 (1973), 434-441, 444, 446
Miller v. Johnson, 515 U.S. 900 (1995), 233, 339-340
Milliken v. Bradley, 418 U.S. 717 (1974), 261
Milliken v. Bradley, 433 U.S. 267 (1977), 260, 267
Mississippi University for Women v. Hogan, 458 U.S. 718 (1982), 58-59, 293, 294, 297
Minnesota Voters Alliance v. Mansky, 585 U.S. 1 (2018), 481
Missouri v. Jenkins, 495 U.S. 33 (1990), 267
Missouri v. Jenkins, 515 U.S. 70 (1995), 263, 264, 269
Mitchell v. Helms, 530 U.S. 793 (2000), 532-534, 535
M.L.B. v. S.L.J., 519 U.S. 102 (1997), 359-360
Moody v. NetChoice, LLC, 144 S. Ct. 2383 (2024), 515-516
Moore v. City of East Cleveland, 431 U.S. 494 (1977), 90, 107, 108, 109, 110
Moore v. Harper, 600 U.S. 1 (2023), 337

Moore v. Madigan, 702 F.3d 933 (7th Cir. 2012), 585
Moore v. Texas 581 U.S. 1 (2017), 139
Moose Lodge v. Irvis, 407 U.S. 163 (1972), 27-28, 29
Morris v. Brandenburg, 376 P.3d 836 (N.M. 2016), 126
Morrissey v. Brewer, 408 U.S. 471 (1972), 199
Morrow v. Balaski, 719 F.3d 160 (3d Cir. 2013), 134-135
Morse v. Frederick, 351 U.S. 393 (2007), 485
Mt. Healthy School District Board of Education v. Doyle, 429 U.S. 274 (1977), 221
Mugler v. Kansas, 123 U.S. 623 (1887), 68
Mullane v. Central Hanover Bank and Trust Co., 339 U.S. 306 (1950), 207-208
Muller v. Oregon, 208 U.S. 412 (1908), 69-70, 73
Munn v. Illinois, 94 U.S. 113 (1877), 68, 74, 75
Murr v. Wisconsin, 582 U.S. 383 (2017), 160, 161, 162
Murray's Lessee v. Hoboken Land & Improvement Co., 59 U.S. (18 How.) 272 (1856), 64

NAACP v. Alabama, 357 U.S. 449 (1958), 494, 497
NAACP v. Button, 371 U.S. 415 (1963), 390, 498
National Aeronautics and Space Administration v. Nelson, 562 U.S. 134 (2011), 136
National Broadcasting Co. v. United States, 319 U.S. 190 (1943), 511
National Collegiate Athletic Association v. Tarkanian, 488 U.S. 179 (1988), 38-40
National Endowment for the Arts v. Finley, 524 U.S. 569 (1998), 392
National Institute of Family and Life Advocates v. Becerra, 585 U.S. 755 (2018), 431-433, 452
National Rifle Association v. Vullo, 602 U.S. 175 (2024), 459-460
Near v. Minnesota, 283 U.S. 697 (1931), 382-383, 391
Nebbia v. New York, 291 U.S. 502 (1934), 71-72
Nebraska Press Association v. Stuart, 427 U.S. 539 (1976), 385, 506-507
Nevada Commission on Ethics v. Carrigan, 564 U.S. 117 (2011), 375
Nevada Department of Human Resources v. Hibbs, 538 U.S. 721 (2003), 56-57
New Orleans v. Dukes, 427 U.S. 297 (1976), 245
New York v. Ferber, 458 U.S. 747 (1982), 439, 440-441
New York v. Trump, 485 F. Supp. 3d 422 (S.D.N.Y. 2020), 327
New York State Board of Elections v. Lopez Torres, 552 U.S. 196 (2008), 347
New York State Rifle & Pistol Association, Inc. v. Bruen, 597 U.S. 1 (2022), 585, 586-588, 590
New York State Rifle & Pistol Association, Inc. v. Cuomo, 804 F.3d 242 (2d Cir. 2015), 583
New York Times v. Sullivan, 376 U.S. 254 (1964), 25, 372, 407-408, 410, 414, 431
New York Times v. United States (Pentagon Papers Case), 403 U.S. 713 (1971), 35, 372, 383, 407, 414, 421
Nixon v. Administrator of General Services, 433 U.S. 425 (1977), 136
Nixon v. Shrink Missouri Government PAC, 528 U.S. 377 (2000), 415
Nollan v. California Coastal Commission, 483 U.S. 825 (1987), 152, 171, 172
Nordlinger v. Hahn, 505 U.S. 1 (1992), 248
North Carolina v. Covington, 585 U.S. 969 (2018), 340
Northwest Austin Municipal Utility District No. 1 v. 557 U.S. 103 (2009), 61
Nunez v. City of San Diego, 114 F.3d 935 (9th Cir. 1997), 132
Nyquist v. Mauclet, 432 U.S. 1 (1977), 255, 289

Obergefell v. Hodges, 576 U.S. 644 (2015), 95, 106-107, 311, 315
O'Connor-Ratcliff v. Garnier, 601 U.S. 205 (2024), 37
Oil States Energy Services, LLC v. Greene's Energy Group, LLC, 584 U.S. 325 (2018), 363
Oklahoma Call for Reproductive Justice v. Drummond, 526 P.3d 1123 (Okla. 2023), 102
Oregon v. Mitchell, 400 U.S. 112 (1970), 58
Orr v. Orr, 440 U.S. 268 (1979), 296, 297
Osborne v. Ohio, 495 U.S. 103 (1990), 438
Our Lady of Guadalupe School v. Morrissey-Berru, 591 U.S. 732 (2020), 552

Overton v. Bazzetta, 539 U.S. 126 (2003), 115-116

Pacific Gas and Electric Co. v. Public Utilities Commission of California, 475 U.S. 1 (1985), 516
Packingham v. North Carolina, 582 U.S. 98 (2017), 395-396, 516-517, 518
Pakdel v. City and County of San Francisco, 594 U.S. 474 (2021), 145
Palazzolo v. Rhode Island, 533 U.S. 606 (2001), 157, 165
Palko v. Connecticut, 302 U.S. 319 (1937), 11-13
Panetti v. Quarterman, 551 U.S. 930 (2007), 139
Papachristou v. City of Jacksonville, 405 U.S. 156 (1972), 130, 388
Papasan v. Allain, 478 U.S. 265 (1986), 364-366
Parents Involved in Community Schools v. Seattle School District No. 1, 551 U.S. 701 (2007), 273, 275, 282
Parham v. J.R., 442 U.S. 584 (1979), 121
Pasadena City Board of Education v. Spangler, 427 U.S. 424 (1976), 269
Paul v. Davis, 424 U.S. 693 (1976), 91
Pavan v. Smith, 582 U.S. 563 (2017), 311
Pell v. Procunier, 417 U.S. 817 (1974), 505
Penn Central Transportation Co. v. City of New York, 438 U.S. 104 (1978), 159-160, 162-164
Pennekamp v. Florida, 328 U.S. 331 (1946), 400
Pennsylvania Coal Co. v. Mahon, 260 U.S. 393 (1922), 156
Pentagon Papers Case. See New York Times v. United States
Perry v. Sindermann, 408 U.S. 593 (1972), 205
Perry Education Association v. Perry Local Educators' Association, 460 U.S. 37 (1983), 475, 477
Personnel Administrator of Massachusetts v. Feeney, 442 U.S. 256 (1979), 232-233
Philadelphia Newspapers, Inc. v. Hepps, 475 U.S. 767 (1986), 412
Philip Morris USA v. Williams, 549 U.S. 346 (2007), 77
Phillips v. Washington Legal Foundation, 524 U.S. 156 (1998), 146, 152
Pickering v. Board of Education, 391 U.S. 563 (1968), 455-459
Pierce v. Society of Sisters, 268 U.S. 510 (1925), 83-84, 86, 110, 363-364
Planned Parenthood Arizona, Inc. v. Mayes, 545 P.3d 892 (Ariz. 2024), 102
Planned Parenthood v. Casey, 505 U.S. 833 (1992), 94-95, 97, 98-101, 103, 119, 125, 362
Planned Parenthood Association of Kansas City, Mo., Inc. v. Ashcroft, 462 U.S. 476 (1983), 96
Planned Parenthood Great Northwest v. State, 522 P.3d 1132 (Idaho 2023), 102
Planned Parenthood of Arizona, Inc. v. Mayes, 545 P.3d 892 (Ariz. 2024), 102
Planned Parenthood of Central Missouri v. Danforth, 428 U.S. 52 (1977), 96-97
Planned Parenthood of Southwest and Central Florida v. State, 384 So.3d 67 (Fla. 2024), 102
Planned Parenthood South Atlantic v. State, 892 S.E.2d 121 (S.C. 2023), 102
Pleasant Grove City, Utah v. Summum, 555 U.S. 460 (2009), 472, 487-491
Plessy v. Ferguson, 163 U.S. 537 (1896), 10, 250-251, 258
Plyler v. Doe, 457 U.S. 202 (1982), 3, 291, 364-366, 368-369
Poe v. Ullman, 367 U.S. 497 (1961), 13
Police Department of Chicago v. Mosley, 408 U.S. 92 (1972), 461
Polk County v. Dodson, 454 U.S. 312 (1981), 42
Pope v. Illinois, 481 U.S. 497 (1987), 435
Posadas de Puerto Rico Associates v. Tourism Co., 478 U.S. 328 (1986), 435
Presbyterian Church v. Hull Church, 393 U.S. 440 (1969), 551
Press-Enterprise Co. v. Superior Court, 464 U.S. 501 (1984), 506
Presser v. Illinois, 116 U.S. 252 (1886), 581
PruneYard Shopping Center v. Robins, 447 U.S.74 (1980), 154

Randall v. Sorrell, 548 U.S. 230 (2006), 416
Rankin v. McPherson, 483 U.S. 378 (1987), 456
R.A.V. v. City of St. Paul, 505 U.S. 377 (1992), 407, 447, 449, 452
Red Lion Broadcasting Co. v. FCC, 395 U.S. 367 (1969), 484, 485
Reed v. Town of Gilbert, 576 U.S. 155 (2015), 391
Regents of the University of California v. Bakke, 438 U.S. 265 (1978), 271-272, 274-275

Reitman v. Mulkey, 387 U.S. 369 (1967), 31, 35
Rendell-Baker v. Kohn, 457 U.S. 830 (1982), 20, 29-30, 31
Reno v. American Civil Liberties Union, 521 U.S. 844 (1997), 442
Republican National Committee v. Democratic National Committee, 589 U.S. 423 (2020),
Republican Party of Minnesota v. White, 536 U.S. 765 (2002), 318
Reynolds v. Sims, 377 U.S. 533 (1964), 326, 328, 330
Reynolds v. United States, 98 U.S. 145 (1879), 104
Ricci v. DeStefano, 557 U.S. 557 (2009), 278
Rice v. Cayetano, 528 U.S. 495 (2000), 229, 317, 322
Richmond Newspapers, Inc. v. Virginia, 448 U.S. 555 (1980), 89, 506
Riley v. National Federation of the Blind of North Carolina, Inc., 487 U.S. 781 (1988), 413
Roberts v. United States Jaycees, 468 U.S. 609 (1984), 115, 492, 498-499
Rodriguez v. Popular Democratic Party, 457 U.S. 1 (1982), 317
Roe v. Wade, 410 U.S. 113 (1973), 88-89, 90, 94-103, 117, 118-119, 126, 137
Rogers v. Lodge, 458 U.S. 613 (1982), 237, 332
Roman Catholic Diocese of Brooklyn v. Cuomo, 592 U.S. 14 (2020), 556-557
Romer v. Evans, 517 U.S. 620 (1996), 309-311
Roper v. Simmons, 543 U.S. 551 (2005), 139
Rosborough v. Management & Training Corp., 350 F.3d 459 (5th Cir. 2003), 21
Rosenberger v. Rector and Visitors of the University of Virginia, 515 U.S. 819 (1995), 477, 539, 550-551
Rosenblatt v. Baer, 383 U.S. 75 (1966), 410
Rosenbloom v. Metromedia, Inc., 403 U.S. 29 (1971), 412
Ross v. Moffitt, 417 U.S. 600 (1974), 359
Rostker v. Goldberg, 453 U.S. 57 (1981), 294
Roth v. United States, 354 U.S. 476 (1957), 434
Rubin v. Coors Brewing Co., 514 U.S. 476 (1995), 428-429
Rucho v. Common Cause, 588 U.S. 684 (2019), 336-337
Ruckelshaus v. Monsanto Co., 467 U.S. 986 (1984), 146
Rumsfeld v. Forum for Academic and Institutional Rights, 547 U.S. 47 (2006), 375
Runyon v. McCrary, 427 U.S. 160 (1976), 45
Rust v. Sullivan, 500 U.S. 173 (1991), 487, 490
Rutherford v. United States, 438 F. Supp. 1287 (W.D. Okla. 1977), 119

Saenz v. Roe, 526 U.S. 489 (1999), 59, 350, 351, 353, 355, 357
Saint Francis College v. Al-Khazraji, 481 U.S. 604 (1987), 46
Salyer Land Co. v. Tulare Lake Basin Water Storage District, 410 U.S. 719 (1973), 322
San Antonio Independent School District v. Rodriguez, 411 U.S. 1 (1973), 92, 365, 368
Sandin v. Conner, 515 U.S. 472 (1995), 199, 200
Santa Fe Independent School District v. Doe, 530 U.S. 290 (2000), 522, 540
Saxbe v. Washington Post Co., 417 U.S. 843 (1974), 505
Schad v. Borough of Mount Ephraim, 452 U.S. 61 (1981), 437
Schaumburg v. Citizens for a Better Environment, 444 U.S. 620 (1980), 413-414
Schenck v. Pro-Choice Network of Western New York, 519 U.S. 357 (1997), 469-470
Schenck v. United States, 249 U.S. 47 (1919), 396-399
Schlesinger v. Ballard, 419 U.S. 498 (1975), 294
Schneider v. State, 308 U.S. 147 (1939), 465
Schuette v. Coalition to Defend Affirmative Action, 572 U.S. 291 (2014), 287
School District of Abington Township v. Schempp, 393 U.S. 203 (1963), 537
Seattle Times Co. v. Rhinehart, 467 U.S. 20 (1984), 507
Secretary of State of Maryland v. Joseph H. Munson Co., 467 U.S. 947 (1984), 413
Serbian Eastern Orthodox Diocese v. Milivojevich, 426 U.S. 696 (1976), 552
Sessions v. Morales-Santana, 706 Fed. Appx. 40 (2d Cir. 2017), 301
Sessions v. Morales-Santana, 582 U.S. 47 (2017), 300
Shaare Tefila Congregation v. Cobb, 481 U.S. 615 (1987), 46
Shapiro v. Thompson, 394 U.S. 618 (1969), 351
Shaw v. Hunt, 517 U.S. 899 (1996), 255. 276, 344
Shaw v. Reno, 509 U.S. 630 (1993), 339-340

Sheetz v. County of El Dorado, 601 U.S. 267 (2024), 169, 220
Shelby County v. Holder, 570 U.S. 529 (2013), 61
Shelley v. Kraemer, 334 U.S. 1 (1948), 23, 24-25, 32, 33, 41, 251
Sherbert v. Verner, 374 U.S. 398 (1963), 569, 570-573
Shurtleff v. City of Boston, 596 U.S. 243 (2022), 392, 490
Shuttlesworth v. Birmingham, 394 U.S. 147 (1969), 463, 469
SisterSong Women of Color Reproductive Justice Collective v. Governor of Georgia, 40 F.4th 1320 (11th Cir. 2022), 103
Skinner v. Oklahoma, 316 U.S. 535 (1942), 84
Slaughter-House Cases, 83 U.S. (16 Wall.) 36 (1872), 8-10, 47, 68, 74, 250
Smith v. Allwright, 321 U.S. 649 (1944), 18, 20-21
Smith v. California, 361 U.S. 147 (1959), 421
Smith v. Daily Mail Publishing Co., 443 U.S. 97 (1979), 508
Snyder v. Phelps, 562 U.S. 443 (2011), 379-380, 393, 413
Sorrell v. IMS Health Inc., 564 U.S. 552 (2011), 421, 431
Sosna v. Iowa, 419 U.S. 393 (1975), 104, 352
Southwest Voter Registration Education Project v. Shelley, 344 F.3d 914 (9th Cir. 2003), 349
Spallone v. United States, 493 U.S. 265 (1990), 268
Spence v. State of Washington, 418 U.S. 405 (1974), 373
St. Amant v. Thompson, 390 U.S. 727 (1968), 408
Stanley v. Georgia, 394 U.S. 557 (1969), 438
Starns v. Malkerson, 326 F. Supp. 234 (D. Minn. 1970), 354
State v. Doe, 148 Idaho 919 (2010), 132
State v. J.P., 907 So. 2d 1101 (Fla. 2004), 132
State v. Misch, 256 A.3d 519 (Vt. 2021), 586
State v. Ramseur, 524 A.2d 188 (N.J. 1987), 140
State v. Santiago, 122 A.3d 1 (Conn. 2015), 140
State Farm Mutual Automobile Insurance Co. v. Campbell, 538 U.S. 408 (2003), 77, 78-79, 82
Stenberg v. Carhart, 530 U.S. 914 (2000), 97, 100, 118
Stone v. Graham, 449 U.S. 39 (1980), 523
Stone v. Mississippi, 101 U.S. 814 (1880), 191
Stop the Beach Renourishment, Inc. v. Florida Department of Environmental Protection, 560 U.S. 70 (2010), 164, 165
Strauder v. West Virginia, 100 U.S. (10 Otto) 303 (1880), 9-10, 250
Street v. Corrections Corporation of America, 102 F.3d 810 (6th Cir. 1996), 21
Students for Fair Admissions, Inc. v. President & Fellows of Harvard College, 600 U.S. 181 (2023), 251, 254, 273, 275, 278, 283-287
Students for Fair Admissions, Inc., v. United States Military Academy at West Point, 144 S. Ct. 716 2024), 273
Sturges v. Crowninshield, 17 U.S. 122 (1819), 175
Suitum v. Tahoe Regional Planning Agency, 520 U.S. 725 (1997), 165
Sunday Lake Iron Co. v. Township of Wakefield, 247 U.S. 350 (1918), 229
Sveen v. Melin, 584 U.S. 811 (2018), 184, 185, 187, 189
Swann v. Charlotte-Mecklenburg Board of Education, 402 U.S. 1 (1971), 259

Tahoe-Sierra Preservation Council, Inc. v. Tahoe Regional Planning Agency, 535 U.S. 302 (2002), 156
Tandon v. Newsom, 593 U.S. 61 (2021), 568-569
Tanzan v. Tanvir, 592 U.S. 43 (2020), 570
Tashjian v. Republican Party of Connecticut, 479 U.S. 208 (1986), 502
Tennessee v. Lane, 541 U.S. 509 (2004), 57
Tennessee Secondary School Athletic Association v. Brentwood Academy, 551 U.S. 291 (2007), 16, 211, 458-459
Terminiello v. Chicago, 337 U.S. 1 (1949), 399, 406
Terry v. Adams, 345 U.S. 461 (1953), 18
Teter v. Conners, 460 F. Supp. 3d 989 (D. Haw. 2020), 583
Texas v. Johnson, 491 U.S. 397 (1989), 373, 413
Texas Monthly, Inc. v. Bullock, 489 U.S. 1 (1989), 574-575
Thomas v. Review Board, 450 U.S. 707 (1981), 571, 573

Thompson v. Consolidated Gas Utilities Corporation, 300 U.S. 55 (1937), 146
Thompson v. Hebdon, 589 U.S. 1 (2019), 416
Thompson v. Western States Medical Center, 535 U.S. 357 (2002), 430-431
Thornburgh v. American College of Obstetricians & Gynecologists, 476 U.S. 747 (1986), 89. 97
Thornhill v. Alabama, 310 U.S. 88 (1940), 399
303 Creative LLC v. Elenis, 600 U.S. 570 (2023), 450
Timbs v. Indiana, 586 U.S. 146 (2019), 14
Time, Inc. v. Firestone, 424 U.S. 448 (1976), 411
Timmons v. Twin Cities New Party, 520 U.S. 351 (1997), 502, 503
Tinker v. Des Moines Independent Community School District, 393 U.S. 503 (1969), 482-484
Torcaso v. Watkins, 367 U.S. 488 (1961), 547-548
Tower v. Glover, 467 U.S. 914 (1984), 42
Town of Castle Rock, Colorado v. Gonzales, 545 U.S. 748 (2005), 203
Town of Greece v. Galloway, 572 U.S. 565 (2014), 522, 526, 528
Trinity Lutheran Church of Columbia, Inc. v. Comer, 582 U.S. 449 (2017), 534, 559-560, 562, 566, 576
Troxel v. Granville, 530 U.S. 57 (2000), 112-114
Trump v. Hawaii, 585 U.S. 667 (2018), 251, 530
Tucker v. Louisiana, 578 U.S. 1018 (2016), 139
Turner Broadcasting System, Inc. v. FCC, 512 U.S. 622 (1994), 395-396, 462, 514-515
Turner Broadcasting System, Inc. v. FCC, 520 U.S. 180 (1997), 515
Twining v. New Jersey, 211 U.S. 78 (1908), 11
TXO Production Corp. v. Alliance Resources Corp., 509 U.S. 443 (1993), 76
Tyler v. Hennepin County, 598 U.S. 631 (2023), 146

United States v. Alvarez, 567 U.S. 709 (2012), 392, 406
United States v. American Library Association, Inc., 539 U.S. 194 (2003), 445-446, 474
United States v. Ballard, 322 U.S. 78 (1944), 548
United States v. Burzynksi Cancer Research Institute, 819 F.2d 1301 (5th Cir. 1987), 119
United States v. Carlton, 512 U.S. 26 (1994), 176-177
United States v. Carolene Products Co., 304 U.S. 144 (1938), 73-74, 83, 252, 317
United States v. Cox, 906 F.3d 1170 (10th Cir. 2018), 583
United States v. Dennis, 183 F.2d 201 (2d Cir. 1950), 401
United States v. Fincher, 538 U.S. 868 (8th Cir. 2008), 584
United States v. Fordice, 505 U.S. 717 (1992), 266
United States v. Grace, 461 U.S. 171 (1983), 465
United States v. Kokinda, 497 U.S. 720 (1990), 473
United States v. Kras, 409 U.S. 434 (1973), 360
United States v. LeBeau, 985 F.2d 563 (7th Cir. 1993), 119
United States v. Lee, 455 U.S. 252 (1982), 564
United States v. Miller, 307 U.S. 174 (1939), 577, 579
United States v. Morrison, 529 U.S. 528 (2000), 55-56
United States v. National Treasury Employees Union, 513 U.S. 454 (1995), 455
United States v. O'Brien, 391 U.S. 367 (1968), 373-374
United States v. Playboy Entertainment Group, Inc., 529 U.S. 803 (2000), 438
United States v. Progressive, Inc., 467 F. Supp. 990 (W.D. Wis. 1979), 384
United States v. Rahimi, 144 S. Ct. 1889 (2024), 589-590
United States v. Robel, 389 U.S. 258 (1967), 493
United States v. Skrmetti, 144 S. Ct. 2679 (2023), 121
United States v. Stevens, 559 U.S. 460 (2010), 388, 439, 446
United States v. Tagg, 572 F.3d 1320 (11th Cir. 2009), 567
United States v. United Foods, Inc., 533 U.S. 405 (2001), 426
United States v. Vaello Madero, 596 U.S. 159 (2022), 247-248
United States v. Verdugo-Urquidez. 494 U.S. 259 (1990), 3

United States v. Virginia, 518 U.S. 515 (1996), 295-296, 300, 303-304
United States v. Williams, 553 U.S. 285 (2008), 386, 389, 441
United States v. Windsor, 570 U.S. 744 (2013), 106
United States Civil Service Commission v. National Association of Letter Carriers AFL-CIO, 413 U.S. 540 (1973), 455
United States Department of Agriculture v. Moreno, 413 U.S. 528 (1973), 309
United States Trust Co. v. New Jersey, 431 U.S. 1 (1977), 185, 191-193
University of Wisconsin System v. Southworth, 529 U.S. 217 (2000), 452
Usery v. Turner Elkhorn Mining Co., 428 U.S. 1 (1976), 223

Vacco v. Quill, 521 U.S. 793 (1997), 125, 127
Valentine v. Chrestensen, 316 U.S. 52 (1942), 421
Van Orden v. Perry, 545 U.S. 677 (2005), 490, 524
Vernonia School District 47J v. Acton, 515 U.S. 646 (1995), 134
Village of Arlington Heights v. Metropolitan Housing Development Corp., 429 U.S. 252 (1977), 233, 243
Village of Belle Terre v. Boraas, 416 U.S. 1 (1974), 110, 114-115
Village of Willowbrook v. Olech, 528 U.S. 562 (2000), 229, 231-232
Virginia v. Black, 538 U.S. 343 (2003), 406, 449
Virginia v. Hicks, 539 U.S. 113 (2003), 386-387
Virginia Board of Pharmacy v. Virginia Consumer Council, 425 U.S. 748 (1976), 421, 424-425
Vitek v. Jones, 445 U.S. 480 (1980), 121, 205, 219
Vlandis v. Kline, 412 U.S. 441 (1973), 222-223, 354

Walker v. Sauvinet, 92 U.S. 90 (1876), 14
Walker v. Texas Division, Sons of Confederate Veterans, 576 U.S. 200 (2015), 489
Wallace v. Jaffree, 472 U.S. 38 (1985), 522, 537
Washington v. Davis, 426 U.S. 229 (1976), 225, 232, 236-237, 240
Washington v. Glucksberg, 521 U.S. 702 (1997), 121, 123, 125-127
Washington v. Harper, 494 U.S. 210 (1990), 121-122
Washington State Grange v. Washington State Republican Party, 552 U.S. 442 (2008), 386, 504-505
Washington State Republican Party v. Logan, 377 F. Supp. 2d 907 (W.D. Wash. 2005), 504
Washington State Republican Party v. Washington State Grange, 676 F. 3d 784 (9th Cir. 2012), 505
Watchtower Bible and Tract Society of New York, Inc. v. Village of Stratton, 536 U.S. 150 (2002), 463-464, 468, 550
Webb's Fabulous Pharmacies, Inc. v. Beckwith, 449 U.S. 155 (1980), 151
Weinberger v. Salfi, 422 U.S. 749 (1975), 223
Wesberry v. Sanders, 376 U.S. 1 (1964), 325
West v. Atkins, 487 U.S. 42 (1988), 42
West Coast Hotel Co. v. Parrish, 300 U.S. 379 (1937), 72-73
West River Bridge Co. v. Dix, 47 U.S. (6 How.) 507 (1848), 191
West Virginia State Board of Education v. Barnette, 319 U.S. 624 (1943), 399, 449-450, 547, 548
Whalen v. Roe, 429 U.S. 589 (1977), 88-89. 94, 117, 118, 136
White v. Regester, 412 U.S. 755 (1973), 328, 333
Whitney v. California, 274 U.S. 357 (1927), 398-399. 403
Whole Woman's Health v. Hellerstedt, 579 U.S. 582 (2016), 100
Widmar v. Vincent, 454 U.S. 263 (1981), 475
Wilkinson v. Austin, 545 U.S. 209 (2005), 199, 200
Williams v. Philip Morris Inc., 340 Ore. 35, 127 P.3d 1165 (2006), 80
Williams v. Vermont, 472 U.S. 14 (1985), 308
Williams-Yulee v. Florida Bar, 575 U.S. 433 (2015), 419
Williamson v. Lee Optical, Inc., 348 U.S. 483 (1955), 74, 75, 244
Williamson County Regional Planning Commission v. Hamilton State Bank of Johnson City, 473 U.S. 172 (1985), 145
Willow Inn, Inc. v. Public Service Mutual Insurance Co., 399 F.3d 224 (3d Cir. 2005), 82

Wisconsin v. Yoder, 406 U.S. 205 (1972), 563-567, 569
Wisconsin Legislature v. Wisconsin Elections Commission, 595 U.S. 398 (2022), 233, 345
Wolff v. McDonnell, 418 U.S. 539 (1974), 65, 199
Woodson v. North Carolina, 428 U.S. 280 (1976), 139
Wooley v. Maynard, 430 U.S. 705 (1977), 449-450
Worman v. Healey, 922 F.3d 26 (1st Cir. 2019), 584
Wrenn v. District of Columbia, 864 F.3 650 (D.C. Cir. 2017), 585
Wrigley v. Romanik, 988 N.W.2d 231 (N.D. 2023), 102
Wygant v. Jackson Board of Education, 476 U.S. 267 (1986), 255

Yee v. City of Escondido, 503 U.S. 519 (1992), 154
Yick Wo v. Hopkins, 118 U.S. 356 (1886), 3, 10, 237-238, 239, 250, 288
Young v. American Mini Theatres, Inc., 427 U.S. 50 (1976), 439
Young v. Harper, 520 U.S. 143 (1997), 128, 199
Young v. Hawaii, 992 F.3d 765 (9th Cir. 2021), 585
Youngberg v. Romeo, 457 U.S. 307 (1982), 93, 128, 129, 133, 134
Ysursa v. Pocatello Education Association, 555 U.S. 353 (2009), 458
Zablocki v. Redhail, 434 U.S. 374 (1978), 103, 104, 107, 314
Zadvydas v. Davis, 533 U.S. 678 (2001), 124
Zauderer v. Office of Disciplinary Counsel of Supreme Court of Ohio, 471 U.S. 626 (1985), 432-433, 449, 452
Zelman v. Simmons-Harris, 536 U.S. 639 (2002), 535-536, 544, 558
Zied-Campbell v. Richman, 2007 WL 1031399 (M.D. Pa. Mar. 30, 2007), 57
Zobel v. Williams, 457 U.S. 55 (1982), 307, 356-357
Zobrest v. Catalina Foothills School District, 509 U.S. 1 (1993), 539
Zorach v. Clauson, 303 N.Y. 161, 100 N.E.2d 463 (N.Y. 1951), 575
Zorach v. Clauson, 343 U.S. 306 (1952), 575

Index

Abortion, 58, 90, 93-103, 118-119, 121, 137-138, 196, 362-363, 423, 432-433, 461-462, 469-470, 487, 491
Affirmative action, 271-287
Alienage classifications, 227, 229, 238, 253, 257, 288-289, 291-292, 293, 303, 304, 306, 361
Arms, right to keep and bear, xxi, 13, 577-590
As-applied challenges, 322, 398, 441, 446, 497, 505, 516
Association, right of, 86, 106, 110, 114-116, 128, 386, 416, 491-505
At-large election schemes, 327, 330-334

Badges and incidents of slavery.
 See Thirteenth Amendment
Ballot, access to, 18, 318, 346-348
Bear arms, right to, xxi, 13, 577-590
Bill of Rights, xxi, 1-3, 7-15, 63, 84-88, 90, 526, 587
Black Codes, 6, 250
Bona fide residency requirements, 319, 350, 357-358
 See also Durational residency requirements; Travel
Brandeis, Louis D., 70, 398-399, 401, 403

Carolene Products footnote four, 73, 82-84, 86, 252, 317
Civil Rights Acts
 42 U.S.C. §1981, 45-46
 42 U.S.C. §1982, 44, 46
 42 U.S.C. §1983, 17, 22, 40, 49, 59, 140, 145
 42 U.S.C. §1985(3), 45-46,
 Civil Rights Act of 1866, 6-8
 Civil Rights Act of 1964, Title VII, 51, 277-278, 301, 575
Compelling interest test
 Due Process Clause, 91, 93, 95, 105, 108, 125, 129, 131, 134, 140, 317, 318, 362, 364, 372
 Equal Protection Clause, 224, 254, 257, 273, 275-279, 285-287, 289, 314, 317-318, 320, 344, 351, 356, 362, 364, 366, 372, 453, 529
 Freedom of religion, 529, 540-541, 545, 554-555, 557, 560, 563, 569-571
 Freedom of speech, 105, 315, 372, 396, 400, 415-416, 419, 430, 438, 447, 452-454, 477, 493, 499, 501-503, 506, 509-510, 518
 Second Amendment, 587
 See also Narrowly tailored; Strict scrutiny
Contraceptives, 85, 92, 94-95
 See also Privacy; Substantive due process
Contracts Clause, xxi, 2, 68, 86, 175-193
 Balancing test, 184-191
 Contractual obligation, 176, 177-185, 187-193
 Federal government, applicability to, 176
 Impairment, 176, 181-184, 185-188, 190
 Implied terms, 178-179
 Reserved powers doctrine, 184-191, 192-193
 State party to contract, 191-193
 Substantiality of impairment, 176, 181-184, 185-188, 190
Courts, access to, 57, 135, 358-361

Death caused by government officials, 140-141
Death penalty, 139-140
Discrimination.
 See Equal Protection Clause
Due process.
 See Procedural due process; Substantive due process
Durational residency requirements, 319, 350-353, 354, 356
 See also Bona fide residency requirements; Travel

Economic due process, 67-69, 71, 73-75, 83
 See Substantive due process

Education, access to, 92, 315, 363-367
Elections.
See Voting rights
Enforcement power, Civil War Amendments, 4-8, 42-61
See also Fifteenth Amendment; Fourteenth Amendment; Thirteenth Amendment
Equal Protection Clause, xxi, 2-3, 8-10, 14-15, 24, 27, 34, 41, 47-48, 55, 75, 83-84, 104, 121, 125, 127, 130, 222-224, 225-369, 529
Affirmative action, 271-287, 303
Alienage classifications, 227, 229, 238, 253-254, 257, 288-293, 303, 304, 306, 361
See also Suspect classifications
As-applied challenges, equal protection.
See As-applied challenges
Bona fide residency requirement, 319, 321, 348, 350, 353, 356-358
Class-of-one theory, 231-232
Compelling interest test, equal protection.
See Compelling interest test; Narrowly tailored; Strict scrutiny
De jure discrimination, 232, 239-240, 259-260, 263, 265, 269-270, 276, 287
See also Equal Protection Clause, Intent, discriminatory
Design, 228-230, 233, 238, 255, 271, 273, 343, 345
Discriminatory application, 228-229, 237-239
Discriminatory purpose, 229-230, 232-243, 255-258, 260-262, 265, 277, 334, 339
Disproportionate impact, 48, 230, 231, 235-237, 240, 251, 256, 258, 277
Durational residency requirements, 319, 350-354, 356
Facial, 228-230, 232, 234, 237, 299, 322, 340
See also Facial challenges
Fixed-point and fixed-date residency requirements, 350, 353-355, 357
Fundamental rights, equal protection, 313-369
Ballot, access to, 318, 346-348
Courts, access to, 358-361
Education, access to, 363-367
Impingement, 104, 313, 316, 350-352, 354-355, 357, 361-363, 366
Travel, 307, 315, 319, 349-358
Unequal vote count, 328-329
Vote, right to, 229, 293, 315, 316-349
Welfare and subsistence, 361-363
Gender classifications, 227, 229-231, 233, 237-239, 241, 272, 293-304, 306, 367-369
Gerrymandering, 233, 237, 332-337, 343-344
Intent, discriminatory, 234, 236, 238, 242, 258, 260-261, 270, 277, 341, 342
Interdistrict remedies, 260-264
Intermediate scrutiny, 227-228, 241, 272, 293-295, 300, 304, 307-308, 364-369
Invidious discrimination, 225-226, 232, 234, 236, 238, 240, 328
Keyes presumption, 232, 238-242, 261, 270
Legitimacy, 227, 304-305, 306, 367, 368, 369
Mentally retarded, 308-309, 368
Mid-level scrutiny, 293-295, 299, 300, 304
Narrowly tailored, equal protection.
See Compelling interest test; Narrowly tailored; Strict scrutiny
Nondilutional race-based districting, 337-346
Nonsuspect classifications, 230, 240
Age, 306, 318-319
Mental retardation, 306, 308-309, 368
Out-of-staters, 307-308
Sexual orientation, 309-311
Wealth, 306, 362, 366
One person, one vote, 323-330, 335, 338
Out-of-state residents, 307-308
Prima facie case, 228, 230-243
Rebuttal of, 241-243
Purpose.
See Equal Protection Clause, Intent, discriminatory
Quasi-suspect classifications, 246, 293-295, 306-308, 313, 360, 362, 367, 369
Gender, 227, 229-231, 233, 237-239, 241, 272, 293-304, 306
Legitimacy, 227, 293-295, 304-305
Rejection of new, 306-307
See also Suspect classifications
Rational basis, 227-228, 230-231, 239-244, 246-249, 251, 288, 290-293, 298, 306-311
Reapportionment, 327-328, 340, 341
Residency requirements.

See Bona fide residency requirements; Durational residency requirements
Separate but equal, 251, 258, 303-304
Sexual orientation, 309-311
Sliding scale, 319-322, 367-369, 372
Standards of review, 227, 272, 292, 304
See also Compelling interest test; Intermediate scrutiny; Narrowly tailored; Rational basis; Strict scrutiny
Substantial relationship test.
See Intermediate scrutiny
Suspect classifications, 222, 243, 246, 256-257, 272, 288-289, 293, 306
Affirmative action, 271-287
Alienage classifications, 227, 229, 288-289, 291-292, 306, 361
Federal laws, 292
State and local laws, 288-292
Brown v. Board of Education, 251, 257-260,
Racial classifications in general, 249-288
Rejection of new, 306-307
Segregation in public schools and colleges, 237-238, 240, 251, 257, 258, 260-261, 263, 265, 269-270
Colleges, 265-266
Desegregation orders, 238-240, 243, 259-260, 263, 267-271, 287
Interdistrict remedies, 260-264
White flight, 262-264
Undocumented aliens, 291-292, 369
Equal protection liberties.
See Equal Protection Clause, Fundamental rights
Establishment Clause.
See Freedom of religion
Expression.
See Freedom of speech and press

Facial challenges, 112, 113, 228-230, 232, 234, 237, 299, 322, 340, 386, 390-391, 407, 420, 441, 444-445, 462-463, 481, 488, 496-497, 504-505, 511, 516, 530, 554, 558, 560, 563, 573
Family integrity, 90, 107-115
Federalist Papers, 1
Fifteenth Amendment, 42-43, 59-61, 293, 317, 322
Congressional enforcement power, 4, 42-61
First Amendment.
See Freedom of religion; Freedom of speech and press
Fourteenth Amendment, 2-28, 31-34, 38, 42-43, 47-54, 56-59, 61, 63-64, 67-68, 71, 75-76, 84, 86-88, 101, 105-107, 111, 116, 126, 130-131, 134, 137, 143-144, 195, 202, 223, 225, 229, 243, 245, 249-253, 257-258, 272, 275, 279, 285-286, 288, 292-293, 307, 309, 311, 315, 317-320, 322, 326, 346, 349-350, 519, 526, 552, 570, 578, 581, 585, 587-589
Citizenship Clause, 4
Congressional enforcement power, 4, 47-59
Due Process Clause, 3, 5, 8-15, 31, 34, 38, 47, 63-65, 67-73, 75-76, 78, 82-89, 91-93, 95, 102-105, 107-108, 111-112, 114-117, 119, 123-125, 128-134, 137-141, 176-177, 195, 197, 199-200, 206-208, 210, 212, 217, 220, 225, 247, 258, 311, 315, 318, 359, 362, 364-365, 388, 491
See also Procedural due process; Substantive due process
Equal Protection Clause, xxi, 2-3, 5, 8-10, 15, 24, 27, 34, 41, 47-48, 55, 75, 83-84, 104, 121, 125, 127, 130, 222-227, 229-232, 240, 245, 250-251, 254, 257-258, 260, 273, 275-279, 285-287, 289, 295-296, 302-303, 306-309, 311, 313-315, 317, 319-322, 326, 333, 344, 348-352, 354-359, 361, 363-367, 369, 529
History, 7, 10, 12, 31, 53, 56, 61, 89-90, 94-95, 101, 107, 109, 111, 117, 119-120, 125-126, 250
Incorporation doctrine, 2-3, 7, 9-14, 526
Privileges or Immunities Clause, 4-5, 7-9, 13-14, 47, 130, 307, 349-355, 357-358
Text, 4-6
Freedom of association.
See Association
Freedom of expression.
See Freedom of speech and press
Freedom of movement, 128-130
Freedom of religion, 11, 315, 519-576
Accommodation of religion, 573-576
Establishment Clause, 479, 490, 519, 520-544, 551, 558, 560, 562-563, 573-574, 576
Coercion test, 522, 531, 538, 541, 543

Freedom of religion (*continued*)
Discrimination between religions, 521, 526-530, 537, 575
Disfavored status, 528-531
Endorsement, 522-523, 525-526, 530, 533, 537, 540-541, 543-544, 560
Faith-based initiative, 544
History and tradition, 528, 539, 542-543
Holiday displays, 543-544
Lemon test, 523-525, 526, 531, 537-538, 540-541, 543-544, 575
Nonpreferentialism, 520, 521-522, 528-529, 532, 537, 539, 543, 574
Officially established religions, ban on, 526
Parochial schools, aid to, 521, 532-536
Prayer in public schools, 522, 531, 536-542, 543, 556
Preferred status, 527-528, 529, 531, 537, 573
Promotion of religion, 530-544
Religious organizations, aid to, 529, 536, 544, 559, 561, 571, 575
Separationism, 520-521, 522, 530, 532, 537, 543
Tuition assistance, vouchers and grants, 535-536, 544, 558, 562, 573
Wall of separation, 521, 534, 537
Free Exercise Clause, 52, 488, 519-520, 540-541, 545-573
Belief, 519-520, 527, 537, 545-546, 547-553, 555, 559-560, 564-565, 567, 570-573, 576
Conduct, 537, 540-541, 545-546, 553-554, 557, 563-565, 567, 569-570, 572-573
Incidental burdens, 53, 204, 553, 570-573
Nonpurposeful regulation, 563-570
Purposeful regulation, 553-563
Ecclesiastical disputes, 551-553
Standards of review.
See Compelling interest test; Narrowly tailored; Strict scrutiny
Freedom of speech and press, xxi, 7-8, 24, 92, 197, 371-518
Access to criminal proceedings, 506
Access to information, 497, 505-506, 518
Access to press, forced, 505, 510-511
Ad hoc balancing, 396, 447, 452-455
Association, right of, 86, 106, 110, 114-116, 128, 386, 416, 491-505
Broadcast media, 428, 431, 441-442, 476, 510, 511-518
Cable operators, 32, 513-515
Confidential sources, 509-510
Content-based restrictions, 391-460, 461, 462, 469, 471, 479, 510, 511, 513-514, 517
Ad hoc balancing, 396, 447, 452-455
Advertising
See Freedom of speech and press, Content-based restrictions, Commercial speech
Advocacy of unlawful conduct.
See Freedom of speech and press, Content-based restrictions, Clear and present danger test
Campaign advocacy and financing, 414-420, 455, 480
Initiative process, restrictions on, 414-420, 497
Judicial elections, restrictions on, 419
Censorship.
See Freedom of speech and press, Prior restraints
Child pornography, 378, 438-441, 445-447
Clear and present danger test, 378, 396-404, 406, 434
Commercial speech, 372, 378, 396, 420-433, 443, 452, 474, 481, 498
Central Hudson test, 421, 424, 425-432
Compelled speech, 449-452, 492
Cruelty, depiction of, 387-388, 446-447
Defamation, and other torts, 25, 379, 407-414, 507, 510
Actual malice, 25, 408-412, 434
Private figures, 25, 412
Public figures and officials, 25, 411-412
Punitive damages, 412
Disclosure requirements, mandatory, 420, 432-433, 449
Fighting words, 378, 389, 396, 404-407, 441, 447
Fraud, 413, 414, 464, 495
Hate speech, 404-407, 447
Indecent speech, 395, 441-446,
Internet, 395, 442-446, 474, 515-518
Internet and indecency, 442-446
Obscenity, 372, 378, 385, 396, 434, 436-439, 444-448

Political speech, 371-372, 378, 395, 412-418, 420, 422, 454-455, 457, 460-461, 464, 466, 479-480, 483-484, 498, 513
Pornography, 378, 395, 434-435, 437-441, 445-447, 468
Prior restraints, 380-385, 438, 468-469, 507, 511
Secondary effects, 395, 460, 469
Sexually explicit speech, 394, 434-446
Standards of review.
See Compelling interest test; Narrowly tailored; Strict scrutiny
True threats, 404-407
Unprotected speech, 378, 391, 396, 405-408, 420, 439-440, 447-449
Viewpoint neutrality, 394, 472, 477, 479, 480, 487
Violence, 398, 402-403, 406, 436, 446, 448
Vulgar, 394, 441-442
Content-neutral restrictions, 372, 376, 460-471, 515, 517
Alternative channels, 460, 467-468
Narrowly tailored, 396, 398, 416, 419, 426, 430, 438, 446, 452-454, 460, 463-467, 468. 470, 493-495, 497, 502-503, 506-507, 510, 518
Neutrality, 460, 462, 477, 480, 487
Prior restraints, 380-385, 392, 438, 468, 507, 511
See also Freedom of speech and press, Time, place, and manner
Copyrights, 470-471
Expressive conduct, 373-374, 376-377, 460,
Gag orders, 506-507
See also Freedom of speech and press, Prior restraints
Government speech, 487-491
Initiative process, 414-420, 497
Injunctions, 380, 469-470, 515
Internet, 395, 442-446, 474, 515-518
Nonpublic forum, 395, 471-472, 473, 476, 479-482, 487, 490, 491
Overbreadth, 385-391, 444, 447
Pentagon Papers Case, 383-384, 391
Prior restraints, 380-385, 438, 468-469, 507, 511
Private concern, speech of, 378-380, 412, 509
Public concern, speech of, 378-380, 411, 412, 455, 456, 457, 458, 459, 508, 509
Public employees, 410, 455-459
Public forum, 22, 471-479, 482, 489
Designated, 472, 475-479, 480, 482
Limited, 472, 475, 477, 491
Traditional, 471, 472, 473-475, 476, 477, 479, 480, 488, 489
Public records, 496, 507
Public school students' free speech, 482-486
Pure speech, 376, 377, 509
Right of reply, 511
Right to know, 506
Streets, sidewalks, and parks.
See Freedom of speech and press, Public forum
Student speech in public schools, 482-486
Subsequent punishments.
See Freedom of speech and press, Prior restraints
Symbolic speech, 376-377, 466
Time, place, and manner, 376, 377, 460-471, 472, 515, 518
Truthful information, 431, 507-509,
Unprotected speech, 378, 385, 391, 396, 405, 406, 407, 408, 420, 439, 440, 447, 448
Vagueness, 385-391, 463
Viewpoint neutrality, 394, 472, 477, 479, 480, 487
Free Exercise Clause.
See Freedom of religion
Fundamental rights, 5, 7, 8, 9, 10, 11, 12, 13, 481
See also Equal Protection Clause, Fundamental rights; Substantive due process

Gays and lesbians, 406-407
See also Equal Protection Clause, Sexual orientation; Substantive due process, Noneconomic due process, Sexual intimacy
Gender classifications, 293-305, 306, 367, 368, 369, 375, 407, 447, 499
Gerrymandering, 233, 237, 332-337, 343-344
Government speech, 487-491
Group vote dilution, 318, 330-337, 338, 339

Hamilton, Alexander, 1
Hearing, right to.
See Procedural due process

Holmes, Oliver Wendell, Jr., 71, 397, 398, 399, 401
Homosexuality.
See Equal Protection Clause, Sexual orientation; Substantive due process, Noneconomic due process, Sexual intimacy

Incorporation doctrine, 2-3, 7, 9-14, 526
Informational privacy, 136-137
Intermediate scrutiny, 227-228, 241, 272, 293-295, 300, 304, 307-308, 364-369
Intimate association, 106, 110, 114-117, 128, 491-505
Irrebuttable presumption doctrine, 221-224, 302

Jefferson, Thomas, 521
Just Compensation Clause.
See Takings Clause

Legitimacy, 227, 304-305, 306, 367, 368, 369
Liberty.
See Equal Protection Clause; Procedural due process; Substantive due process; *specific freedoms*
Liberty to contract, 67, 68-70, 72, 73, 82-84, 86, 90, 198
Life, 5, 8, 63, 64, 65, 85, 91, 96, 98-103, 107, 118, 119, 122-123, 133, 137-141, 166, 195, 197, 199, 200, 206, 284, 287, 361
See also Abortion
Lochner era, 67, 69, 73, 82-84, 86, 90, 121

Madison, James, 2
Marital privacy, 85-88, 94
Marriage, 85, 90, 103-110, 114, 116, 117, 183, 223-224, 251, 311, 314-315, 352, 362, 411, 450, 491
Medical treatment, 66, 118-124, 127, 205
Lifesaving hydration and nutrition, 122-125
Mentally retarded, discrimination against, 308-309, 368
Multimember districts, 333, 334, 336-337

Narrowly tailored, 233, 254, 255-257, 272, 275, 279-287, 289, 314, 317, 343-345, 364, 366-367, 396, 398, 416, 419, 426, 430, 438, 446, 452-454, 460, 463-467, 468, 470, 493-495, 497, 502, 503, 506, 507, 510, 518, 545, 555, 557, 562, 586
Equal protection, fundamental rights, 313-369
Marriage, 251, 311, 314, 315, 352, 362
Vote, 229, 233, 237, 253, 255, 268
Equal protection, suspect and quasi-suspect classes.
Alienage, 227, 229, 238, 253, 257, 288-292, 293, 303, 304, 306
Gender, 227, 229, 230, 231, 233, 237-239, 241, 272, 293-295, 296-304, 306
Race and national origin, 249-287
First Amendment.
Religion, 545, 555, 557, 562
Speech, 396, 398, 416, 419, 426, 430, 438, 446, 452, 453, 454, 460, 463-468, 470, 507, 518
Second Amendment, 586
See also Compelling interest test; Strict scrutiny
Necessary and Proper Clause, 47, 144
Ninth Amendment, 87-88
See also Substantive due process
Noneconomic due process, 67, 82-84
See also Substantive due process
Nonparental visitation, 111-114
Nonsuspect classifications, 230, 240

One person, one vote, 323-330, 331, 333, 335, 338
Out-of-staters, discrimination against, 307-308

Parental rights, 110-112
Parent-child relationship, 110-111
Penumbras and emanations, 85-87
Personal autonomy, 94-128
Privacy.
Autonomy of decision, 94-128
Informational, 136-137
Privileges and Immunities Clause, 2, 5, 7-9, 130, 307, 349, 357, 358
Privileges or Immunities Clause, 4-5, 7-9, 13-14, 47, 130, 307, 349, 350-355, 357-358
Text, 5
Procedural due process, 64-66, 75, 77, 81, 109, 128, 138, 195-224, 359-361
Custom and practice, 197, 205, 220
Deprivation, 65, 195, 197, 199, 206-207, 209, 212-221, 360

Harmless error, 211
Hearing requirement, 198, 202, 204-205, 207, 209-224
"Bitter with the sweet," 209-210
Formality, 218-220
Independent decision maker, 219
Post-deprivation, 209, 214-217, 219-220
Pre-deprivation, 204, 217
Irrebuttable presumption doctrine, 221-224
Legislative capacity action taken in, 196-197
Liberty, 9, 195-202, 205-207, 209, 212-215, 220-222, 224
Mathews v. Eldridge test, 210-216, 218
Notice, 195-199, 201-202, 204-205, 207-210, 216-219, 224
Post-deprivation remedies, 209, 214-220
Property, 8, 195, 197, 200-214, 216-221, 360
Substantive due process compared, 10, 64-65, 75, 109, 128, 195-196, 198, 206, 359-361
Protection and care, right to, 132-135
Public employees' free speech, 455-459
Public school students' free speech, 482-486
Punitive damages, 76-82, 412,

Quasi-suspect classifications, 222, 246, 293, 306, 308, 313, 360, 362, 367, 369

Race-based districting, non-dilutional, 233, 338-344, 346
See also Voting rights
Racial discrimination.
See Equal Protection Clause, Suspect classifications
Rational basis test.
Congress's lawmaking power, 570
Due Process Clause, 74, 76, 83-84, 91-94, 102-103, 105, 108, 110, 115, 118, 120, 126, 131, 148, 176, 247, 311, 360-365, 372
Equal Protection Clause, 48, 50-51, 83-84, 127, 227-228, 230-231, 239-240, 244, 249, 251, 293, 306-311, 313, 319, 321-322, 355-356, 358, 360-361, 364-369, 372, 426, 530
First Amendment, 48, 67, 83-84, 130, 372, 426-427, 458, 530
Thirteenth Amendment, 44
Reapportionment, 327-330, 340-341
Reconstruction, 6, 36, 250, 588
Regulatory takings, 156-158, 162, 165, 167-168
Religion.
See Freedom of religion
Republican Form of Government Clause, 316
Residency requirements, 298, 319, 350-358
Bona fide, 319, 350, 356, 357-358
Durational, 319, 350-353
Fixed point or fixed date, 353-355
Right to die.
See Substantive due process, Noneconomic due process, Medical treatment; Substantive due process, Noneconomic due process, Suicide
Right to vote.
See Voting rights

Same-sex marriage, 106, 117, 311, 315, 450, 496
Second Amendment, xxi, 14, 577-590
Section five enforcement power, 45-59
See also Fourteenth Amendment, Congressional enforcement power
Segregation in public schools.
See Equal Protection Clause, Suspect classifications
Selective denial of the franchise, 318-322, 337
Sexual intimacy, 117-118
Sexual orientation, 106, 309-311
Slavery.
See Thirteenth Amendment
Speech.
See Freedom of speech and press
Standards of review, 61, 66-67, 71, 84, 85, 91, 93, 118, 122, 127, 131, 176, 183, 191, 227-228, 230, 239-241, 243-244, 248, 251, 253, 271-273, 275, 289-292, 293-295, 298-299, 303-304, 307, 310-311, 319, 329, 336, 361-363, 367, 395-396, 415-418, 431-433, 449, 459, 482-483, 492-494, 501, 503, 505, 513, 517, 530, 549, 562, 585, 586-587
See also Compelling interest test; Intermediate scrutiny; Narrowly tailored; Rational basis; Strict scrutiny
State action doctrine, 4, 14-42, 43-44, 48-49, 53, 55
Categorical Approach, 17-32
Joint activity, 25-32
Judicial enforcement, 23-25
Lugar test, 32-41

State action doctrine (*continued*)
Public function, 18-22
State actor anomaly, 42
State endorsement, 31-32
Symbiotic relationship, 27-31, 39-40
Strict scrutiny.
Due Process Clause, 67, 73, 76, 83-84, 86, 91-93, 95, 103-105, 107-108, 123, 129, 131-132, 140, 206, 314-315, 317-318, 361, 364-365, 372
Abortion, 93, 95-97, 99, 363, 433
Economic liberty, 67, 73, 76, 83-84, 361
Family integrity, 107-109
Intimate association, 116
Life, 95, 96, 99, 140, 361
Lifesaving hydration and nutrition, 123
Marital privacy, 86, 103
Medical treatment, 66, 120, 123
Movement, 129, 131-132
Equal Protection Clause.
Basis of classification, 5, 48, 222, 225-226, 243-244, 248, 249-253, 288-292, 293-295, 304-305, 306-307, 308-309, 309-311
Alienage, 227, 253, 257, 288-289, 291-293, 303-304, 306, 361
Out-of-state residents, 307, 358
Race or national origin, 227, 230, 243, 251, 253-254, 256-257, 271-276, 280, 282-283, 285-289, 293, 295, 303, 306
Affirmative action, 271-272, 274, 276, 280, 285, 287, 303
Fundamental rights, 313-319, 352, 361-369
Education, 364-366, 368-369
Marriage, 104, 224, 311, 314-315, 352, 362
Travel, 131, 315, 319, 349-352, 354-357, 361
Vote, 315-320, 322, 325, 334, 339, 343-344, 346-348
Welfare and subsistence, 361-363
First Amendment.
Speech and press, 92, 372, 379, 383, 385, 392, 396, 415, 419-420, 431, 433, 438-439, 460, 492-493, 495, 497, 499, 501-503, 507, 513-514, 517
Religion, 315, 492, 529, 540, 545, 550, 554-555, 557, 559-560, 562-564, 566, 567, 572, 574
Second Amendment, 586
See also Compelling interest test; Narrowly tailored
Subsistence benefits, 105, 138-139, 219, 362
Substantive due process, 63-141
Economic due process, 67-82
Liberty to contract, 68, 69, 72-74, 76, 82-84, 177
Punitive damages, 77-82
Rational basis test, 67, 73-74, 83-84, 148, 361
Executive abuse of power, 65-66
Fundamental rights model, due process, 90-93
87-90
Lochner era, 67, 69, 73, 82-84, 86, 90, 121
Noneconomic due process, 67, 82-83
Abortion, 58, 90, 93-103, 118-119, 121, 137-138, 196, 362-363, 423, 432-433, 461-462, 469-470, 487, 491
Courts, access to, 57, 135, 352, 358-361
Death penalty, 139-141
Family integrity, 90, 107-115
Family living arrangements, 107-110
Freedom of movement, 128-130
Impingement, 313, 316, 350-352, 354-355, 357, 361-363, 366
Intimate association, 106, 110, 114-117, 128, 491-505
Life, 5, 8, 63, 64, 65, 85, 91, 96, 98-103, 107, 118, 119, 122-123, 133, 137-141, 166, 195, 197, 199, 200, 206, 284, 287, 361
Marital privacy, 85-88, 94
Marriage, 85, 90, 103-110, 114, 116, 117, 183, 223-224
Medical treatment, 66, 118-124, 127, 205
Lifesaving hydration and nutrition, 122-125
Nonparental visitation, 111-114
Parental rights, 110-112
Parent-child relationship, 110-111
Penumbras and emanations, 85-87
Personal autonomy, 94-128
Privacy, 13, 85-88, 90, 94-95, 103, 107, 117-119, 121-122, 132, 491
Procedural and substantive due process compared, 10, 64-65, 75, 109, 128, 195-196, 198, 206, 359-361
Protection and care, right to, 132-135

Same-sex marriage, 106, 117, 311, 315, 450, 496
Sexual intimacy, 117-118
Standards of review, 66-67, 84-85, 91, 93, 118, 122, 127, 131
See also Compelling interest test; Intermediate scrutiny, Narrowly tailored; Rational basis test; Strict scrutiny
Suicide, 124, 125-128
Undue burden test, 92, 98-100, 104-105
Suicide, 124, 125-128
Suspect classifications, 222, 243, 246, 256-257, 272, 288-289, 293, 306
Alienage, 227, 229, 238, 253, 257, 273-277, 288-289, 291-292, 293, 303, 304, 306, 361
Race, 227, 230, 243, 251, 253-254, 271-276, 280, 282-283, 285-289, 293, 295, 303, 306

Takings Clause, xxi, 10, 75, 143-174
Building permits.
See Takings Clause, Conditions on use permits
Condemnation, 143-146, 148, 149, 161, 163, 167
Conditions on use permits, 149-150, 168-174
Essential nexus, 171-172
Rough proportionality, 172-174
Constructive taking, 144
De facto taking, 144-145, 149
Denominator problem, 158-162
Destroying all use or value, 156-162
Eminent domain, 144-149
Inverse condemnation, 143-146, 148, 149-150, 161, 163, 167
Just compensation, 10, 143, 144-146, 149, 152-153, 155-156, 163-170, 172
Nuisance exception, 165-167
Partial deprivations, 162-165
Personal property, 145-146, 151-152, 156, 158
Physical invasion or occupation, 150-155
Public use, 143-148, 153-155, 168, 170
Regulatory takings, 155-158, 162, 165, 167-168
Remedies, temporary takings, 167-168
Seizure.
See Takings Clause, Physical invasion or occupation
Temporary takings, 158, 167-168
Thirteenth Amendment, 4, 6, 15, 42, 43-46
Congressional enforcement power, 43-46
Travel, 76, 84, 130, 131, 132, 307, 315, 319, 349-358, 361

Unconstitutional conditions, 168-169, 204, 220-221, 362-363, 570-571
Undocumented aliens, 3, 291-292, 364, 368-369
Undue burden test, 91, 92, 98, 99-100, 104-105
Unenumerated rights.
See Substantive due process

Vote dilution, 233, 318, 323-327, 330-331, 333-335, 337-339
Voting rights, 51, 53, 59-61, 233, 279, 317, 320, 322-323, 330, 344, 346, 365, 481
Absolute right, 316-318
At-large election schemes, 327, 330, 331-332, 333, 334
Ballot access, 18, 318, 346-348
Equal right to, 51, 59, 279, 317-320, 323, 330, 334, 344, 346, 365
Gerrymandering, 233, 332, 334-335, 337, 344
Group vote dilution, 318, 330-331, 333-335, 337-338
Individual vote dilution, 318, 323-330, 333, 337-338
Multimember districts, 325, 330, 333-334
Nondilutional race-based districting, 337-346
One person, one vote, 323-330, 331, 333, 335, 338
Reapportionment, 327-330, 340-341
Selective denial of the franchise, 318, 322, 337
Unequal vote count, 318, 323-330

Welfare and subsistence, 361-363